Microsoft
Certified
Professional

Visual Basic 4.0™
Exam Guide

Microsoft
Certified
Professional

Visual Basic 4.0™
Exam Guide

Written by Howard Hawhee
with Peg Toomey

Microsoft Certified Professional Visual Basic 4.0 Exam Guide
Copyright© 1996 by Que® Corporation.

Library of Congress Catalog No.: 96-69603

ISBN: 0-7897-0864-7

98 97 96   6 5 4 3 2 1

Interpretation of the printing code: the rightmost double-digit number is the year of the book's printing; the rightmost single-digit number, the number of the book's printing. For example, a printing code of 96-1 shows that the first printing of the book occurred in 1996.

All terms mentioned in this book that are known to be trademarks or service marks have been appropriately capitalized. Que cannot attest to the accuracy of this information. Use of a term in this book should not be regarded as affecting the validity of any trademark or service mark.

Screen reproductions in this book were created using Collage Plus from Inner Media, Inc., Hollis, NH.

Credits

President
Roland Elgey

Publishing Director
Brad R. Koch

Editorial Services Director
Elizabeth Keaffaber

Managing Editor
Michael Cunningham

Director of Marketing
Lynn E. Zingraf

Acquisitions Manager
Elizabeth A. South

Product Directors
Lisa Wagner
Peg Toomey

Production Editor
Thomas F. Hayes

Editors
Elizabeth Barrett
Kate Givens

Assistant Product Marketing Manager
Christy Miller

Technical Editors
Brian Blackman

Technical Specialist
Nadeem Muhammed

Acquisitions Coordinator
Tracy Williams

Editorial Assistant
Virginia Stollen

Book Designer
Ruth Harvey

Cover Designer
Ruth Harvey

Production Team
Marcia Brizendine
Jessica Ford
DiMonique Ford
Julie Geeting
Tony McDonald
Kaylene Riemen
Sossity Smith
Staci Somers

Indexer
Tim Tate

Composed in **Bembo** and *Avenir* by Que Corporation.

To our many students and clients, who've kept us on our toes.

Acknowledgements

Thanks are due to the following people and organizations for their support during this project:

Elizabeth South, Lisa Wagner, and Thomas Hayes at Que, who made this book possible.

Pam Riter, Brigid Flood, and Pam Bernard at Productivity Point International, who provided the opportunity to write this book and gave their support during the project.

About the Authors

Howard Hawhee is a Microsoft Certified Trainer and a training partner with Productivity Point, International. He has broad experience in the world of PC development and training. He has served numerous corporate clients as a developer, consultant, and instructor over the past twelve years and has never stopped having fun using and explaining Visual Basic. He can be reached on CompuServe at **72610,425**.

Peg Toomey is a Microsoft Certified Trainer, Lotus Business Partner, and a Notes Certified Developer in Chicago. She has worked with a variety of clients both in the U.S. and Europe for over eight years. Peg can be reached on Compuserve at **104712,1774**.

We'd Like to Hear from You!

As part of our continuing effort to produce books of the highest possible quality, Que would like to hear your comments. To stay competitive, we *really* want you, as a computer book reader and user, to let us know what you like or dislike most about this book or other Que products.

You can mail comments, ideas, or suggestions for improving future editions to the address below, or send us a fax at (317) 581-4663. For the online inclined, Macmillan Computer Publishing has a forum on CompuServe (type **GO QUEBOOKS** at any prompt) through which our staff and authors are available for questions and comments. The address of our Internet site is **http://www.mcp.com** (World Wide Web).

In addition to exploring our forum, please feel free to contact me personally to discuss your opinions of this book: I'm **74404,3307** on CompuServe, and I'm **lwagner@que.mcp.com** on the Internet.

Thanks in advance—your comments will help us to continue publishing the best books available on computer topics in today's market.

Lisa Wagner
Product Director
Que Corporation
201 W. 103rd Street
Indianapolis, Indiana 46290
USA

Note Although we cannot provide general technical support, we're happy to help you resolve problems you encounter related to our books, disks, or other products. If you need such assistance, please contact our Tech Support department at **800-545-5914 ext. 3833**.

To order other Que or Macmillan Computer Publishing books or products, please call our Customer Service department at 800-835-3202 ext. 666.

Contents at a Glance

VI ▪ Appendixes

Table of Contents

II ‣ The Visual Interface   211

VI Appendixes   569

A Glossary   571

B Certification Checklist   587

Introduction

This book was written by Microsoft Certified Professionals, for Microsoft Certified Professionals and MCP Candidates. It is designed, in combination with your real-world experience, to prepare you to pass the **Visual Basic 4.0 Exam (70-65)**, as well as give you a background in general knowledge of Visual Basic 4.0.

As of this writing, the exams cost $100 each. Each one consists of 50 to 100 questions and takes up to two hours to complete. Depending on the certification level, you may have to take as many as six exams covering Microsoft operating systems, application programs, networking, and software development. Each test involves preparation, study, and, for some of us, heavy doses of test anxiety. Is certification worth the trouble?

Microsoft has cosponsored research that provides some answers.

Benefits for Your Organization

At companies participating in a 1994 Dataquest survey, a majority of corporate managers stated that certification is an *important factor* to the overall success of their companies because:

◆ Certification increases customer satisfaction. Customers look for indications that their suppliers understand the industry and have the ability to respond to their technical problems. Having Microsoft Certified Professionals on staff reassures customers; it tells them that your employees have used and mastered Microsoft products.

◆ Certification maximizes training investment. The certification process specifically identifies skills that an employee is lacking or areas where additional training is needed. By so doing, it validates training and eliminates the costs and loss of productivity associated with unnecessary training. In addition, certification records enable a company to verify an employee's technical knowledge and track retention of skills over time.

Benefits Up Close and Personal

Microsoft also cites a number of benefits that accrue to the certified individual:

◆ Industry recognition of expertise, enhanced by Microsoft's promotion of the Certified Professional community to the industry and potential clients

◆ Access to technical information directly from Microsoft

◆ Dedicated CompuServe and Microsoft Network forums that enable Microsoft Certified Professionals to communicate directly with Microsoft and with one another

◆ A complimentary one-year subscription to *Microsoft Certified Professional Magazine*

◆ Microsoft Certified Professional logos and other materials to publicize MCP status to colleagues and clients

◆ An MCP newsletter to provide regular information on changes and advances in the program and exams

◆ Invitations to Microsoft conferences, technical training sessions, and special events program newsletter from the MCP program

Additional benefits, depending upon the certification, include:

◆ Microsoft TechNet or Microsoft Developer Network membership or discounts

◆ Free product support incidents with the Microsoft Support Network seven days a week, 24 hours a day

◆ One-year subscription to the Microsoft Beta Evaluation program, providing up to 12 monthly CD-ROMs containing beta software for upcoming Microsoft software products

◆ Eligibility to join the Network Professional Association, a worldwide independent association of computer professionals

Some intangible benefits of certification are:

◆ Enhanced marketability with current or potential employers and customers, along with an increase in earnings potential

◆ Methodology for objectively assessing current skills, individual strengths, and specific areas where training is required

How Does this Book Fit In?

One of the challenges that has always faced the would-be Microsoft Certified Professional is to decide how to best prepare for an examination. In doing so, there are always conflicting goals, such as how to prepare for the exam as quickly as possible, and yet, still actually learn how to do the work that passing the exam qualifies you to do.

Our goal for this book was to make your studying job easier by filtering through the reams of VB 4.0 technical material, and presenting in the chapters and lab exercises only the information that you actually need to *know* to pass the VB 4.0 Certification Exam. Other information that we think is important for you to have available while you're working has been relegated to the appendices.

How to Study with this Book

This book is designed to be used in a variety of ways. Rather than lock you into one particular method of studying, force you to read through sections you're already intimately familiar with, or tie you to your computer, we've made it possible for you to read the chapters at one time, and do the labs at another. We've also made it easy for you to decide whether you need to read a chapter or not by giving you a list of the pre-requisite topics and skills at the beginning of each chapter.

Labs are arranged topically, not chapter-by-chapter, so that you can use them to explore the areas and concepts of VB 4.0 that are new to you, or that you need reinforcement in. We've also decided not to intermix them with the text of the chapter, because nothing is more frustrating than not being able to continue reading a chapter because your child is doing his homework on the computer, and you can't use it until the weekend.

The chapters are written in a modular fashion, so that you don't necessarily have to read all the chapters preceding a certain chapter to be able to follow a particular chapter's discussion. Chapters 2-4 contain more elementary information about VB. If you are comfortable with the material in these chapters, the other chapters should be relatively easy to follow.

Don't skip the lab exercises, either. Some of the knowledge and skills you need to pass the VB 4.0 MCP exam can only be acquired by working with VB 4.0, and the lab exercises help you acquire these skills.

How this Book is Organized

The book is broken up into 16 chapters, each focusing on a particular topic that is an important piece of the overall picture.

◆ Chapter 1, "Microsoft Certified Professional Program," gives you an overview of the Microsoft Certified Professional program, what certifications are available to you, and where VB 4.0 and this book fit in.

◆ Chapter 2, "Visual Basic Data Types," covers the simple data types of VB as well as more complex data types such as object types, user-defined types, and arrays. This chapter also discusses data-conversion functions

◆ Chapter 3, "Working with Visual Basic Code," discusses the basic VB execution control structures and other elements of VB programming such as controls and event procedures.

◆ Chapter 4, "Debugging Applications," explains the use of VB's built-in debugging facilities.

◆ Chapter 5, "Handling Errors," explains the coding techniques for trapping and handling run-time errors.

◆ Chapter 6, "Common Properties of the Form Object and Control Objects," discusses the most common properties of Forms and standard VB controls.

◆ Chapter 7, "Control and Form Object Events," discusses the most common events of Forms and standard VB controls.

◆ Chapter 8, "Menus," covers the use of the Menu Editor to implement a standard Windows menu on a Form, and how to write code for menus.

◆ Chapter 9, "Using Multiple-Document Interface (MDI)," discusses the nature of an MDI-type application and explains the main considerations the programmer faces when working with MDI applications.

◆ Chapter 10, "Using OLE Automation to Integrate Applications," discusses how to use the exposed objects of OLE Server applications in a VB application.

◆ Chapter 11, "Creating OLE Servers," explains how to create an OLE Server with VB. It also discusses Class modules in VB 4.0.

◆ Chapter 12, "Using the Data Control," discusses how to set up a data control and write code for it, and includes a discussion of Recordset types.

◆ Chapter 13, "Using Data Access Objects," includes a discussion of the Data Access Libraries, multi-user programming, transactions, and basic data manipulation with Data Access Objects.

◆ Chapter 14, "Creating 16-Bit and 32-Bit Applications," examines differences in the programming and compiling of applications for 16-bit platforms (Windows 3.x) versus applications for 32-bit platforms (Windows 95 or Windows NT).

◆ Chapter 15, "Dynamic-Link Libraries (API)," explains how to make calls to Windows API routines from a VB application.

◆ Chapter 16, "Distributing an Application with SetupWizard," explains the steps to use the SetupWizard utility so that you can create distribution media for your application.

Following these chapters are the Lab Exercises. As mentioned earlier, you can do these exercises at your own pace, when you want to—you're not tied down to the computer for every chapter.

All of the VB 4.0 exam objectives are covered in the material contained in the text of the chapters and the lab exercises. Information contained in sidebars is provided to give history, or other details, but is not actual exam material.

Finally, the many appendixes in this book provide you with additional advice, resources, and information that can be helpful to you as you prepare and take the VB 4.0 Certified Professional exam, and onwards, as you work as a VB 4.0 Certified Professional:

◆ Appendix A, "Glossary," provides you with definitions of terms that you need to be familiar with as a VB 4.0 MCP.

◆ Appendix B, "Certification Checklist," provides an overview of the certification process in the form of a to-do list, with milestones you can check off on your journey to certification.

◆ Appendix C, "How do I Get There from Here?" provides step-by-step guidelines for successfully navigating the wilderness between initial interest and final certification.

◆ Appendix D, "Testing Tips," gives you tips and pointers for maximizing your performance when you take the certification exam.

◆ Appendix E, "Contacting Microsoft," lists contact information for certification exam resources at Microsoft and at Sylvan Prometric testing centers.

◆ Appendix F, "Additional Resources," presents a list of reading resources that can help you prepare for the certification exam.

◆ Appendix G, "Internet Resources for Visual Basic," is a list of places to visit on the Internet related to VB 4.0.

◆ Appendix H, "Using the CD-ROM," gives you the basics of how to install and use the CD-ROM included with this book, which includes skill self-assessment tests and simulated versions of the Microsoft exam, and the Microsoft TechNet sampler, with over 400M of Microsoft technical information, including the Microsoft Knowledge Base.

◆ Appendix I, "Lab Exercises," are a series of exercises designed to test your knowledge of Visual Basic.

◆ Appendix J, "Sample Tests."

Special Features of this Book

The following features are used in this book:

Chapter Prerequisites

Chapter prerequisites help you determine what you need to know before you read a chapter. You meet the prerequisites either by reading other chapters in this book, or through your prior work experiences.

Notes

Notes present interesting or useful information that isn't necessarily essential to the discussion. This secondary track of information enhances your understanding of Windows, but you can safely skip notes and not be in danger of missing crucial information. Notes look like this:

 Note Microsoft posts beta exam notices on the Internet (**http://www.microsoft.com**), and mails notices to certification development volunteers, past certification candidates, and product beta participants. ▦

Tips

Tips present short advice on quick or often overlooked procedures. These include shortcuts that save you time. A tip looks like this:

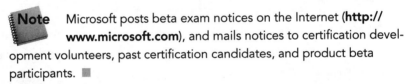

Tip
Keep your error handling code simple in order to avoid generating a runtime error within the error handler, unless you intentionally generate one with Err.Raise

In addition to these special features, there are several conventions used in this book to make it easier to read and understand. These conventions include the following.

Underlined Hot Keys, or Mnemonics

Hot keys in this book appear underlined, like they appear on-screen. In Windows, many menus, commands, buttons, and other options have these hot keys. To use a hot-key shortcut, press Alt and the key for the underlined character. For instance, to choose the Properties button, press Alt and then R. You should not study for the MCP exam by using the hot keys, however. Windows is a mouse-centric environment, and you will be expected to know how to navigate it using the mouse — clicking, right-clicking, and using drag-and-drop.

Shortcut Key Combinations

In this book, shortcut key combinations are joined with plus signs (+). For example, Ctrl+V means hold down the Ctrl key, while you press the V key.

Menu Commands

Instructions for choosing menu commands have this form:

Choose File, New.

This example means open the File menu and select New, which in this case opens a new file.

This book also has the following typeface enhancements to indicate special text, as indicated in the following table.

Typeface	Description
Italic	Italics are used to indicate terms and variables in commands or addresses.
Boldface	Bold is used to indicate text you type, and Internet addresses and other locators in the online world.
Computer type	This command is used for on-screen messages and commands (such as DOS copy or UNIX commands).
My Filename.doc	File names and folders are set in a mixture of upper and lower case characters, just as they appear in Windows 95.

Part I.

VB Programming Basics

Chapter Prerequisite

This chapter has no prerequisites. All you need is the desire to become a Microsoft Certified Professional.

1

Microsoft Certified Professional Program

As Microsoft products take an increasing share of the marketplace, the demand for trained personnel grows, and the number of certifications follows suit. Between July 1994 and July 1996, the team of Microsoft Certified Professionals increased ten-fold in number, up to 69,000 product specialists, 10,000 engineers, 5,000 trainers, and 2,000 solution developers.

This chapter covers the Microsoft Certified Professional Program. Terms and concepts covered include:

- ◆ **Microsoft Certified Professional**
- ◆ **Microsoft Certified Systems Engineer (MCSE)**
- ◆ **Microsoft Certified Product Specialist (MCPS)**
- ◆ **Microsoft Certified Solutions Developer (MCSD)**
- ◆ **Microsoft Certified Trainer (MCT)**

Exploring Available Certifications

When Microsoft started certifying people to install and support their products, there was only one certification available, the Microsoft Certified Professional (MCP). As time went on, demand by employers and prospective customers of consulting firms for more specialized certifications grew.

There are now four available certifications in the MCP program, as described in the following sections.

Microsoft Certified Product Specialists (MCPS)

Microsoft Certified Product Specialists have demonstrated in-depth knowledge of at least one Microsoft operating system or programming techniques and tools. Candidates may pass additional Microsoft certification exams to further qualify their skills with Microsoft BackOffice products, development tools, or desktop applications.

To qualify as a MCPS, the only requirement is to pass one Microsoft Operating System exam. After you receive MCPS certification, you may choose to pass other certification exams to define areas of specialization. Microsoft considers the MCPS as a stepping stone to the three other types of certification.

The Microsoft Certified Product Specialist product-specific exams are your first steps into the world of Microsoft certification. After establishing a specialty, you can work toward additional certification goals at the MCSE or MCSD level.

To become an MCPS with a specialization in VB 4.0, you need to:

1. Pass one of the following Operating System exams:

   - Exam 70-150: Microsoft Windows Operating Systems and Services Architecture I
   - Exam 70-151: Microsoft Windows Operating Systems and Services Architecture II
   - Exam 70-67: Implementing and Supporting Microsoft Windows NT Server 4.0

2. Pass Microsoft Certification Exam 70-65: Microsoft Visual Basic 4.0 for Windows

Microsoft Certified Solution Developers (MCSD)

Microsoft Certified Solution Developers are qualified to design and develop custom business solutions with Microsoft development tools, platforms, and technologies, such as Microsoft BackOffice and Microsoft Office.

In order to certify as a MCSD, you must:

1. Pass two required core technology exams:

   - Exam 70-150: Microsoft Windows Operating Systems and Services Architecture I

   - Exam 70-151: Microsoft Windows Operating Systems and Services Architecture II

2. Pass two elective exams on subjects such as Microsoft SQL Server Implementation, Microsoft SQL Server Database Design, C++ with Microsoft Foundation Class, Visual Basic 4.0, Microsoft Access, Excel with Visual Basic for Applications, or Microsoft Visual FoxPro.

To certify as a MCSD for VB 4.0, you must:

1. Pass Microsoft Certification Exam 70-150: Microsoft Windows Operating Systems and Services Architecture I

2. Pass Microsoft Certification Exam 70-151: Microsoft Windows Operating Systems and Services Architecture II

3. Pass Microsoft Certification Exam 70-65: Microsoft Visual Basic 4.0 for Windows

4. Pass the Microsoft Certification Exam for one other development product, such as Microsoft SQL Server Implementation, Microsoft SQL Server Database Design, C++ with Microsoft Foundation Class, Visual Basic 4.0, Microsoft Access, Excel with Visual Basic for Applications, or Microsoft Visual FoxPro.

Microsoft Certified Systems Engineers (MCSE)

Microsoft Certified Systems Engineers are qualified to plan, implement, maintain, and support information systems based on Microsoft Windows NT and the BackOffice family of client-server software. The MCSE is a widely-respected certification because it does not focus on a single aspect of computing, such as networking. Instead, the MCSE has demonstrated skills and abilities on the full range of software, from client operating systems to server operating systems to client-server applications.

In order to achieve the Microsoft Certified Systems Engineer certification, a candidate must pass four required ("core") exams, plus two elective exams.

The VB 4.0 Certification exam is not a required or elective exam for the MCSE program.

Microsoft Certified Trainers (MCT)

Microsoft Certified Trainers are instructionally and technically qualified to deliver Microsoft Official Curriculum through Microsoft authorized education sites.

A Microsoft Certified trainer must fulfill the following requirements:

◆ Complete the Microsoft Certified Training course for which he or she wishes to Certify, including any prerequisite courses.

◆ Pass the corresponding Microsoft Certification Exam.

◆ Demonstrate instructional abilities by taking an authorized Microsoft Train-the-Trainer course and showing a history of successful experience as an instructor.

In order to become a Microsoft Certified Trainer for VB 4.0, you would need to:

◆ Complete the Microsoft curriculum for VB, MOC-403 and MOC-404.

◆ Pass Microsoft Certification Exam 70-65: Microsoft Visual Basic 4.0 for Windows.

◆ Demonstrate instructional abilities by taking an authorized Microsoft Train-the-Trainer course or showing a history of successful experience as an instructor.

For further information on becoming a Microsoft Certified Trainer, call Microsoft at (800) 765-7768.

Understanding the Exam Requirements

The exams are computer-administered tests that measure your ability to implement and administer Microsoft products or systems, troubleshoot problems with installation, operation, or customization, and provide technical support to users. The exams do more than test your ability to define terminology and/or recite facts. Product *knowledge* is an important foundation for superior job performance, but definitions and feature lists are just the beginning. In the real world, you need hands-on skills and the ability to apply your knowledge—to understand confusing situations, solve thorny problems, and optimize solutions to minimize downtime and maximize current and future productivity.

To develop exams that test for the right competence factors, Microsoft follows an eight-phase exam development process:

◆ Analyze the tasks that make up the job being tested.

◆ Develop test objectives.

◆ Rate the objectives developed in the previous phase.

◆ Review and revise exam items.

◆ Perform alpha review for technical accuracy and clarity.

◆ The next step is the beta exam. Beta exam participants take the test to gauge its effectiveness. Microsoft performs a statistical analysis, based on the responses of the beta participants, including information about difficulty and relevance, to verify the validity of the exam items and to determine which will be used in the final certification exam. When the statistical analysis is complete, the items are distributed into multiple parallel forms, or versions, of the final certification exam.

On the Web

Microsoft posts beta exam notices on the Internet and mails notices to certification development volunteers, past certification candidates, and product beta participants. These notices can be found at

http://www.microsoft.com

Tip

If you participate in a beta exam, you may take it at a cost that is lower than the cost of the final certification exam, but it should not be taken lightly. Beta exams actually contain the entire pool of possible questions, of which, about 30 percent are dropped after the beta. The remaining questions are divided into the different forms of the final exam. If you decide to take a beta exam, you should review and study as seriously as you would for a final certification exam. Passing a beta exam counts as passing the final exam—you receive full credit for passing a beta exam.

Also, because you will be taking *all* of the questions that will be used for the exam, expect a beta to take 2-3 times longer than the final exam. For example, the final version of the Windows 95 exam has a time limit of an hour. The beta version had a time limit of over three hours, and more than three times as many questions as the final versions of the exams!

Also during this phase, a group of job function experts determines the cut, or minimum passing score for the exam. (The cut score differs from exam to exam because it is based on an item-by-item determination of the percentage of candidates who answered the item correctly.)

◆ The final phase, Exam Live!, is administered by Sylvan Prometric, an independent testing company. The exams are always available at Sylvan Prometric testing centers worldwide.

Note You can contact Sylvan Prometric to register for any Microsoft Certification Exam (including the VB 4.0 exam, number 70-65) at 1-800-745-6887. ▪

Note If you're interested in participating in any of the exam development phases (including the beta exam), contact the Microsoft Certification Development Team by sending a fax to (206) 936-1311. Include the following information about yourself: name, complete address, company, job title, phone number, fax number, e-mail or Internet address, and product areas of interest or expertise. ▪

Continuing Certification Requirements

Once you attain an MCP certification, such as the Microsoft Certified Systems Engineer certification, your work isn't over. Microsoft requires you to maintain your certification by updating your exam credits as new products are released, and old ones are withdrawn.

A Microsoft Certified Trainer is required to pass the exam for a new product within three months of the exam's release. For example, the Visual Basic 4.0 exam (70-65) was released in April, 1996. All MCTs, including the authors of this book, were required to pass exam 70-65 by July, 1996 or lose certification to teach the course.

Holders of the other MCP certifications (MCPS, MCSD, MCSE) are required to replace an exam that is giving them qualifying credit within six months of the withdrawal of that exam. For example, the Windows for Workgroups 3.10 exam was one of the original Electives for the MCSE certification. When it was withdrawn, MCSEs had six months to replace it with another Elective exam, such as the TCP/IP exam.

Chapter Prerequisite

Before reading this chapter, you should already know how to manipulate variables and how variables behave in an application.

2

Visual Basic Data Types

Variables can have a number of "personality types." We call these personality types *data types*. Data types are distinguished from each other by:

- ◆ The amount of memory a variable takes up
- ◆ The way Visual Basic accesses a variable

Concepts and skills covered in this chapter include:

- ◆ Manipulating Visual Basic's standard **data types** that hold information about single whole numbers or floating-point (decimal) numbers, strings of text, dates, and a few more specialized types.
- ◆ Using Visual Basic's complex or dimensioned data types, such as **arrays** and **collections**.

◆ Using **object variables**, which are basically references to complex structures in memory. An object variable might refer to a standard Windows object, such as a Form or a CommandButton. It also might refer to a type of object more specific to VB, such as the RecordSet object of a database.

◆ Using the **data types** for **object variables**, such as Forms and Controls.

◆ Setting up and manipulating *user-defined data types*.

Declaring Variables Before You Use Them

Visual Basic is one of the few modern programming languages that doesn't require you to declare variables before you use them.

The compiled version of a computer program should be as efficient as possible in its use of the computer's resources and memory. If you tell your language's compiler beforehand what data type you are going to associate with each variable name, the compiler is then able to allocate only as many resources as that variable will need.

Notice that we said Visual Basic doesn't *require* you to declare your variables before you use them. It does, however, *permit* you to explicitly declare them. Because this is a very good idea, any programmer with much experience will always want to declare variables before using them. There are several ways to declare a variable, depending on the scope you want the variable to have. See the section in this chapter on "Variable Scoping," for more information.

Implicit versus Explicit Variables

Because Visual Basic doesn't require the programmer to declare a variable before using it, you can just start using a variable without explicitly declaring it.

The practice of letting your variables declare themselves is known as *implicit* variable declaration.

If you have done much programming, you can probably think of several reasons why implicit variable declaration isn't such a good idea:

◆ It uses Visual Basic's Variant data type, which has drawbacks (for drawbacks of the Variant type, see "Variant Data Type").

◆ It sanctions the programmer's typographical errors in variable naming by making the errors into new variables. For example, if you were using a variable named iBudget and mistakenly typed the line

```
iBuget = 410
```

somewhere in your program, the variable iBudget would be unaffected and you would have implicitly declared a new variable, iBuget.

That is why you will always want to declare variables explicitly using a declaration statement.

Forcing Explicit Variable Declaration with Option Explicit

It's such a good idea to declare variables explicitly that you might wish that Visual Basic would simply force you to declare all variables.

Well, you can get your wish—on a file-by-file basis, anyway. Whenever you bring up a module such as a Form, a Standard module, or a Class module, you should check the its General Declarations section. One of the lines should be:

```
Option Explicit
```

If Option Explicit appears in the General Declarations section, then the Visual Basic compiler will check all variables in that module to see if they've been declared (see fig. 2.1). If the program contains an undeclared variable, Visual Basic will generate a compiler error.

This is the first thing you should always do when you inherit someone else's code to maintain: Go to the General Declarations section of all modules and make sure Option Explicit is there. If it isn't, you are probably going to uncover some interesting errors when you first compile.

There are two ways to include Option Explicit in your code:

◆ By typing it in each module's General Declarations Section, as we've just seen.

◆ By making Option Explicit an automatic option of the VB environment, as we'll see in the following section.

FIG. 2.1 ⇒

You can type Option Explicit in the General Declarations section of each Form, Class, or Standard module to ensure that Visual Basic enforces variable declarations in that module.

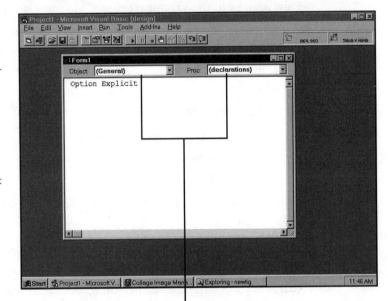

Put Option Explicit in the General Declarations
Section of each module

Setting Environment Options to Put Option Explicit in New Modules

VB can automatically insert Option Explicit at the top of every new module you add.

To make Visual Basic automatically put Option Explicit at the top of every module you initialize, execute the following steps (see fig. 2.2):

1. Choose the Tools, Options menu choices.

2. In the Options dialog box, select the Environment tab.

3. Check the Require Variable Declarations option.

4. Click the OK button of the Options dialog box.

FIG. 2.2 ⇒
Select the Require
Variable Declara-
tion option on the
Environment tab
of the Options
dialog in order to
ensure that Option
Explicit will appear
at the top the
General Declara-
tions section of
every new Form,
Class, and Standard
module.

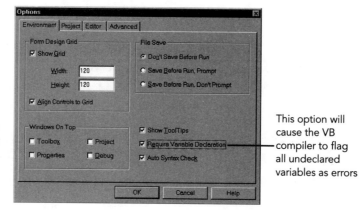

This option will
cause the VB
compiler to flag
all undeclared
variables as errors

> **Caution**
> Checking the Require Variable Declaration option in your Environmental
> Options dialog box only affects future modules you create on your
> system. It does *not* affect modules that already exist. You must still
> examine them individually and type Option Explicit in the General
> Declarations section of each Form, Class, and Standard module if it
> wasn't there already.

Understanding Visual Basic's Standard Simple Data Types

A simple data type stores just one basic type of information at one place
in your computer's memory. Other data types, which we'll discuss
shortly, aren't so easy to characterize. They usually represent more complex data divided into a number of areas with special functions.

To be able to select a data type properly, you should know:

◆ What kind of information each data type can hold

◆ How much memory each data type takes up

◆ What the range of data is in each data type

Numeric Data Types

Programmers who haven't used languages supporting multiple numeric types may wonder why we need more than one type to store numeric values. The answer is efficiency in storage and access.

There are two kinds of data type (Integer and Long) that hold whole-number information and two more types (Single and Double) that hold floating point numbers—that is, numbers that store a movable decimal point. There are two of each type to accomodate different storage needs. You would use the larger of each pair (Long for whole numbers and Double for floating point) when you had to and the smaller of each pair (Integer and Single) whenever possible. The sections in this chapter on each data type give specific information about when to use the various numeric data types.

Tip

Don't store Social Security numbers, phone numbers, or Customer ID numbers as numeric data. These are really textual information masquerading as numbers.

Integer: for Small Whole Numbers

Type of information: whole number
Amount of memory required: 2 bytes
Range of data: –32,768 to 32,767 (64K total)

Integer is a good choice for most incrementing counters (unless you plan to increment beyond the 32K limit) and for a lot of "every day" kinds of information. Examples would include things like:

◆ Age to the nearest year (for human beings, at least)

◆ Number of the day or month

◆ Number of tax-deductible dependents (let's hope it's not more than 32K).

Long: for Larger Whole Numbers
Type of information: whole number
Amount of memory required: 4 bytes
Range of data: -2,147,483,648 to +2,147,483,647

When to use: Longs are appropriate for whole-number information that is too big to fit in an integer (outside the 32K range, in other words). Examples of good Long data type candidates would be:

◆ Salary in whole dollars

◆ Population of a city

Single: for Smaller Fractional Numbers
Type of information: floating-point (fractional) number
Amount of memory required: 4 bytes
Range of data: -3.402823E38 to -1.401298E-45 and +1.401298E-45 to +3.402823E38

When to use: Just about any non-whole number can fit in a Single. After all, 10^{-45} is a pretty small number and 10^{38} is pretty big. No business application will probably ever require anything bigger than a Single.

Double: for Larger Fractional Numbers
Type of information: floating point
Amount of memory required: 8 bytes
Range of data: -1.79769313486231E308 to -4.94065645841247E-324 and 4.94065645841247E-324 to 1.79769313486232E308

When to use: When you need to store astronomically large or small values. More scientific and engineering applications might require you to use Double. Examples of values requiring double are:

◆ Number of elementary particles in the Universe

◆ Number of seconds (estimated) since the Universe began

◆ Size of a quark (a subatomic particle), in millimeters

Currency: for Financial Calculations

Type of information: number with four fixed decimal places
Amount of memory required: 8 bytes
Range of data: –922337203685477.5808 to 922337203685477.5807

> **Caution**
>
> Most applications outside of Visual Basic (such as C routines in DLL calls) don't recognize Currency, and so you must convert a Currency-type variable to Single before you pass it.

▶ **See** "Understanding Differences between C and VB Data Types," **p. 538**

When to use: Currency is best used with applications in which you need to keep track of money. Unlike the Single data type, Currency eliminates small rounding errors that can, in some situations, creep into calculations with Single and Double. Accountants will thank you for using Currency.

String: for Text

Type of information: textual information
Amount of memory required: 10 bytes plus one byte for each character.
Range of data: 0 to approximately 2 billion characters for Win95 and NT, and 0 to approximately 65,400 for earlier versions of Windows

A string can be fixed or variable length. You declare a variable-length string as you would any other variable type:

```
Dim MyString as String
```

You declare a fixed-length string by specifying the number of characters the string will hold:

```
Dim MyString as String * 20
```

If a string is variable-length, you can add or delete characters or reinitialize it at run-time as in the following three examples:

```
MyString = MyString & "."
MyString = Left(MyString,3)
MyString = ""
```

In each of these cases, the string's size can change to reflect the new number of characters in the string.

If a string is of fixed-length, you can't change its size. Any statement that appears to change the size of the string, still leaves the string with the same number of bytes. In the following example, the Debug.Print statement will always display a value of 11 for the string's length, because the string is fixed length:

```
Dim str1 As String * 11
str1 = "Hello World"
Debug.Print Len(str1)
str1 = Left(str1, 3)
Debug.Print Len(str1)
```

> **Caution**
> You can't declare a fixed-length string as a Public variable in a Form Module. If you try to do so, you'll get a compiler error.

When to use: You should, of course, store any type of data that contains variable textual information, in a string. Notice that we said *variable* textual information. If a certain piece of information can always be represented by three values ("Married," "Single," "Divorced") for instance, then perhaps that information should be stored as an integer with values from 0 through 2 or 1 through 3 (1=Married, 2=Single, 3=Divorced). If the information is always one of two values ("Male," "Female"), consider implementing such dual-valued information as a Boolean data type (call the variable blnIsFemale, give it a true value if dealing with a Female and a false value if dealing with a Male).

▶ **See** "Boolean," **p. 33**

Much information that appears to be numeric is actually better off as a string. This is because Strings are the most pliable type of data and can be manipulated in numerous ways. In the example:

```
MyString = "Hi, I'm Gumby"
NewString = Mid(MyString,9,3)
```

NewString would end up holding the value "Gum." Try doing that with a number sometime.

Tip

In general, if you don't plan to perform mathematical calculations with a number, store the number as a string.

Date: Date and Time Data

Type of information: date and time information—stored as floating point with fractional part representing time, and whole number part representing date

Amount of memory required: 8 bytes

Range of data: January 1, 100 to December 31, 9999 including fractional days (i.e. time of day)

When to use: Use it when you need to store or manipulate a date or time.

Tip

You can do arithmetic operations, such as addition and subtraction, with variables stored as dates. The DateDiff() function returns the amount of time elapsed between two date-type variables.

It's easy to determine *when* to use a Date type. Now let's discuss *how* to use a Date-type variable.

Using the Now Keyword to Get the Current System Date

You can store the current date and time in a Date-type variable using the Now system keyword.

```
datToday = Now
```

You can use the value of datToday with the Format() function to extract readable String information about the date, day of the week, or time.

Tip

You can set the computer's system date and time from a Visual Basic program with the Date and Time statements.

Using Special Date/Time Functions to Extract Information from a Date Variable

If you need to extract components of a date (year, month, day of the month, hour, minute, or second), use a separate function for each of these pieces of information.

For more information on using these functions, see the Language Reference and the Programmers Reference Guide for the following functions: Year(), Month(), Day(), Hour(), Minute(), and Second() functions. Note also the Timer() function, which returns the number of seconds elapsed since midnight.

Storing Your Own Information in a Date Variable

What if you need to store information into a Date-type variable other than the current date-time stamp of your system?

The DateSerial() function is one way to directly store date information in a Date-type variable. It takes three arguments: a year, a month, and a day (all three values must work together to produce a valid date: 95,2,29 would not be valid, for instance, because there was no February 29, 1995).

You can directly store time information in a Date-type variable with the use the TimeSerial() function.

You can add the results of the DateSerial() and TimeSerial() functions together to store date/time information in a single variable.

```
Dim MyDate as Date
Dim intYear as Integer
Dim intMonth as Integer
Dim intDay as Integer
Dim intHour as Integer
Dim inMinute as Integer
intYear = cInt(txtYear.Text)
intMonth = cInt(txtMonth.Text)
intDay = cInt(txtDay.Text)
```

```
intHour = cInt(txtHour.Text)
intMinute = cInt(txtMinute.Text)
MyDate = DateSerial(intYear,intMonth,intDay) + _
         TimeSerial(intHour,intMinute,0)
? MyDate
```

This example assumes that the user has typed desired values for year, month, day, hour, and minute into text boxes. The program converts these values to integers using the CInt function and stores them in integer variables. Then, these integer variables are used as arguments to DateSerial() and TimeSerial(). The program sums the return values of these two functions and stores the sum as a Date-type variable. Of course, a more robust application would validate the contents of the text boxes.

Byte: for Single-Byte Information

Type of information: a single byte of data

Amount of memory required: 1 byte

Range of data: 0 to 255 (positive values only)

When to use: Byte is most useful when you are exchanging information that is in some binary format, between Visual Basic and another environment, such as when your program calls a DLL routine or when it directly accesses a file with binary information.

Tip

When a C routine in a DLL file needs C's char type in an argument, pass a variable of type Byte.

Caution

When you convert a variable to type Byte, make sure that the variable you're converting represents a number between 0 and 255 (positive values only). Any other value will cause an Overflow run-time error.

Boolean: for Logical Values (True/False)

Type of information: one of two values—true or false
Amount of memory required: 2 bytes
Range of data: True or False

When to use: Whenever a piece of information will always take on two, and only two, values, and these two values are logically opposed to each other. For example you might use Boolean to show:

Part
I
Ch
2

- ◆ Whether a loan is approved or not
- ◆ Whether an employee is a 401k participant or not
- ◆ Whether an employee is married or not
- ◆ Whether data has changed or not

It is *not* a good idea to use a Boolean to represent:

- ◆ Employee type, when there are more than two types
- ◆ Marital status, if you need more than two possible choices (such as Married, Single, Divorced, and Widowed)

In such cases, you would want to use either an integer to represent the different possibilities, or perhaps a string containing a description of the particular option.

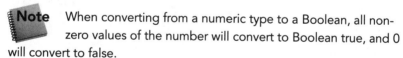 **Note** When converting from a numeric type to a Boolean, all non-zero values of the number will convert to Boolean true, and 0 will convert to false.

When converting from a Boolean to a numeric type, true will convert to -1 and false will convert to 0. ▪

> **Caution**
> To successfully convert a string to a Boolean, the string can only contain "true" or "false." Any other value in the string will cause a run-time error.

Variant: the Lonely Default

Type of information: Any type of data

Amount of memory required: The amount of memory required to implement whatever type of data has been stored in the Variant, plus another 22 bytes of overhead.

Range of data: Depends on the data type of its contents.

When to use: As little as possible. A Variant has a negative effect on memory resources and speed/performance issues; Visual Basic must perform internal conversions every time your program accesses a Variant variable.

Two times when you should use Variant are:

◆ You are writing code for a routine that can take a parameter of ambiguous type (usually declared as Variant).

◆ You want to implement a ParamArray, which is an array of Variant.

The Empty Value and the IsEmpty Function

A variable of type Variant can take on a special value that you denote in code with the keyword Empty. Although we just said that it can store an Empty value, it's probably more accurate to say that Variant variables are initialized as Empty. The Empty value only shows up in variables which have never been assigned a value. You can detect whether or not a Variant contains an Empty value either by writing

```
If MyVar = Empty Then
```

or by using the IsEmpty() function in a line such as

```
If IsEmpty(MyVar) Then
```

The Null Value and the IsNull Function

If a Variant has nothing in it, but has already seen some activity, it will not contain an Empty value. Instead, it will contain a value that you denote in code with the keyword Null.

Remember, a Variant variable that has never held anything contains an Empty value, while a Variant variable that has been initialized with a value (including nothing) but currently holds nothing has a Null value. You can detect whether or not a Variant contains a Null value either by writing

```
If MyVar = Null Then
```

or by using the IsNull() function in a line such as

```
If IsNull(MyVar) Then
```

Understanding Arrays

An array is a dimensioned version of a basic data type. That is, instead of an array variable name referring to a single integer, for instance, it can refer to many integers. You can distinguish between the array's elements with a subscript or index argument to the array.

Thus,

```
MyCounter = 7
```

would refer to a single-dimensioned or non-array variable. On the other hand,

```
MyCounter(17) = 7
```

would refer to one of the elements (possibly the 17th or 18th element, as we shall see shortly) of the MyCounter array.

An array has bounds; that is, it has a highest and a lowest position among its elements. As you might imagine, we call these the upper bound and lower bound, respectively.

Caution
Visual Basic will generate an error if you try to refer to an array element that does not exist.

Declaring an Array

An array can take the same data types as other variables, but when you declare it, you must specify that it is going to be an array. To do so, you must put two parentheses after the array's name. You also can specify the upper bound (highest-numbered index) of the array within the parentheses when you declare the array, as in the declaration

```
Dim MyNames(10) as string
```

The 10 tells Visual Basic the array's upper bound, or highest-numbered element in the array.

By default, Visual Basic starts the lower bound (lowest-numbered element) of its array elements at 0. So in the example above, MyNames has 11 elements because its lower bound is 0 (the default) and its upper bound is 10.

> **Caution**
> If there are no further specifications in your code, Visual Basic starts an array's default lower bound at 0. This means an array dimension declared with a single number will have one more element than the upper bound.

> **Caution**
> You can't declare an array variable using the Public keyword in a Form module. You'll get a compiler error.

Specify Number of Elements and Bounds of a Dynamic Array

When you specify an array's upper bound, you are committed to the specified number elements for the duration of the program. However, you can change the number of elements of a *dynamic array* at run time. You declare a dynamic array by omitting the specification of the bounds in the parentheses of the declaration. For example:

```
Dim MyNames() as String
```

will declare a one-dimensional array with no initial elements. You can dynamically resize the array in your code. Later in this chapter, the section on "Dynamically resizing an array with Redim" explains how to add and remove elements in a dynamic array.

Default Lower Bound of an Array and Option Base Statement

As mentioned in previous sections, the default lower bound of an array is 0. This means that the first element in the array will have an index of 0.

You can change the default base for an array's lower bound to be 1, on a file-by-file basis, in Visual Basic by inserting the statement:

```
Option Base 1
```

at the top of the general declarations section of the module (see fig. 2.3).

Therefore, the declaration

```
Dim MyNames(10) as String
```

would yield an array with 10 elements if the Option Base 1 statement were at the top of the General Declarations section in its module; and it will yield 11 elements if there were no Option Base statement or if the statement were Option Base 0.

Note   Only Option Base 1 and Option Base 0 are possible. Option Base 0 is the default, but many developers include it in their modules anyway to make their intentions clear. ■

Caution
It's not a good idea to change the Option Base on a module after you have declared array variables, since this may change the lower bound of each array and cause unforeseen problems.

FIG. 2.3 ⇒

You can type Option Base 1 at the top of a file's General Declarations section to make 1 the default lower bound for all arrays you declare in that module.

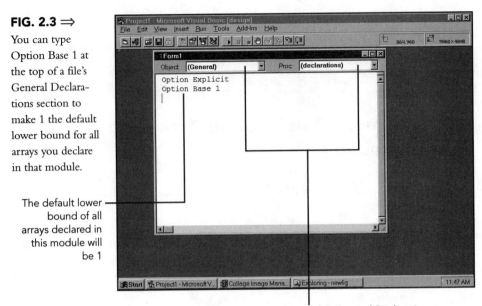

The default lower bound of all arrays declared in this module will be 1

Put this statement in a module's General Declarations

Specify Lower Bound

You may actually specify the lower bound of an array as well as the upper bound. For example:

```
Dim MyNames(5 to 10) as String
```

would tell Visual Basic to start the lower bound at 5 and put the upper bound at 10. This would yield 6 elements in the array (the array would have elements 5 through 10, inclusive).

You also may start the lower bound at a negative number. For example:

```
dim MyNames(-5 to 10) as String
```

would tell VB to start the lower bound at –5 and put the upper bound at 10. This would yield 16 elements in the array (0 would be included in the range of indices).

Note Array bounds are inclusive and you must take them into account when you reckon the number of elements an array has. See the section "Calculating Total Elements in an Array" in this chapter. ■

Dynamically Resizing an Array with Redim [Preserve]

You may resize an array if it is declared as a dynamic array. Visual Basic recognizes a dynamic array if you specify no bounds or dimensions in its Declare statement.

```
Dim MyFriends() as String
```

declares a dynamic array which you can later resize. Static arrays cannot be resized. For example,

```
Dim MyNames(10) as String
```

declares a fixed array which you cannot later resize.

You may resize your array later in a line of code with the Redim statement.

```
Redim MyFriends(17)
```

would give 18 elements to the MyFriends array we declared a few lines above (assuming the default array base has been left at 0).

There is no limit to the number of times you could resize an array with Redim. A few lines later in your array, you could make the statement

```
Redim MyFriends(19)
```

to resize the array again.

One little drawback—each time you use Redim, you reinitialize the data held in the array, thereby destroying anything you had stored there earlier.

Not to worry—you save the contents of an array when you resize it by inserting the Preserve keyword after the word Redim.

```
Redim Preserve MyFriends(22)
```

would have kept data in the first 21 elements intact.

Note Redim Preserve preserves the existing values in array elements only when you resize the last dimension of an array. Resizing other dimensions or changing the number of dimensions with Redim Preserve will destroy the contents of existing array elements. ■

Specify Dimensions

An array might also have more than one dimension. That is, each element may actually point to another "mini array" of elements. If each element of an array has one other set of elements associated with it, we say the array is "two-dimensional." We usually think of such an array as being made up of rows and columns, where the first dimension represents the rows and the second dimension represents the columns. Although it's a common way to visualize two-dimensional arrays, the row-column approach is a purely arbitrary way of looking at a two-dimensional
array.

You might declare a two-dimensional array as in the following example:

Private Values(1 To 10, 1 To 3) As Integer

The array Values would then contain 10 "rows" in the first dimension and each "row" would hold 3 "columns" (the second dimension).

If each element of an array's second dimension has another "mini array" associated with it, we say the array is "three-dimensional." For instance, the declaration:

Private Values(1 To 10, 1 To 3, 1 To 2)

would create an array with 10 "rows," 3 "columns" per row, and two values per "column."

In fact, this process of creating dimensions within dimensions can go on indefinitely in Visual Basic, so that we can have "n-dimensional" arrays. You can probably guess that the human mind has a little trouble visualizing arrays beyond three dimensions, though many applications do use such arrays.

To refer to an element of a two-dimensional array, a line of code might read:

```
MsgBox Squares(1,7)
```

to tell Visual basic that we wanted the first element of the first dimension, and then within that first element we wanted to access the seventh element.

Each dimension of an array has upper and lower bounds, just like a single-dimensional array.

If you want more than one dimension in an array, you can specify each dimension after the first with a comma-delimited list.

```
Dim MyNames(5,6,7)
```

tells Visual Basic to allocate memory for a three-dimensional array of Variant (remember, Variant is the default.) with upper bounds of 5, 6, and 7 respectively. Recall that the lower bound of each dimension will be 1 if the Option Base 1 statement has been issued. Otherwise, it will be 0.

You may specify lower and upper bounds separately for each dimension of a multi dimensional array. For example:

```
Dim MyNames(5 to 10, 21 to 40, 21 to 40)
```

specifies three dimensions, and none of them start at the default of 0 (or possibly 1, if we've set Option Base 1).

You don't need to use the same specification style for all the dimensions in an array.

```
Dim MyNames(5 to 10, 40, 21 to 40)
```

specifies both the lower bound and upper bound for the first and third dimensions, but only the upper bound for the second dimension. The lower bound of the second dimension would be either 0 or 1 (depending on the specification in the Option Base 1 statement).

Calculating Total Elements in an Array

To compute the total number of elements in an array, simply multiply the number of elements in all the array's dimensions.

That wasn't hard, was it?

But wait—how many elements are there in a given array dimension?

Remember to take into account the fact that arrays dimensions begin by default at elements 0 (unless re-specified with Option Base 1).

Also remember that if the array's lower bound is specified, you must include the lower bound element when counting number of elements in a dimension.

Remember that without Option Base 1 specified,

```
Dim MyNames(5,10) as String
```

specifies 66 elements (6 times 11) and not 50, since we must include element 0 in each of the dimensions.

Also,

```
Dim MyNames(5 to 20, 3 to 4) as String
```

specifies 32 elements (16 by 2), because we must include the lower bound when reckoning the size of a dimension.

Understanding User-Defined Data Types

Sometimes you have a collection of variables that you would like to treat as a unit, because you always seem to need to haul them around to the same places. The variables, however, are of different data types and therefore, an array would not be the best way to store them together. For instance, all the information about an employee, such as First, Last, and Middle Names, Social Security Number, Hire Date, Position, Salary, and other things, would be nice to keep in a single place where we can access the information as a unit.

A user-defined data type allows you to define a structured variable type; that is, a variable type that admits several pigeonholes of disparate type inside. You can then declare variables of this type, manipulate the variables as single entities, and access the pigeonholes for things like First Name and Social Security Number (SSN) whenever you wish. You can think of the pigeonholes as named fields within the variable.

Assume that we have a user-defined type known as EmpType, which contains fields for FirstName, LastName, and SSN. We could declare a variable (say, NewEmployee) of this type and then refer to the fields of NewEmployee with syntax like the syntax we use to refer to the property of a control.

So, if you had a form with the appropriate text boxes on it and a special type known as EmpType, which held fields with names like FirstName, LastName, and SSN, you could write code like this:

```
Dim NewEmployee as EmpType
NewEmployee.FirstName = txtFirstName.Text
NewEmployee.LastName = txtLastName.Text
NewEmployee.SSN = txtSSN.Text
```

Then you could do things with NewEmployee, like pass it as a parameter to a routine, write it as a record to a random access file, or just keep it around until you need it later.

Type...End Type Construct

Before you can use a user-defined type, you must define it. Visual Basic only enables you to define user-defined types in the General Declarations sections of modules. Like variables, they can be Public or Private.

Once you know the fields you need in a user-defined type, you can define it in the General Declarations section of a module as follows:

```
Type EmpType
    FirstName as String
    LastName as String
    SSN as String * 9
    Dependents() as String
    LastThreeJobs(1 to 3) as String
    CurrentSalary as Long
End Type
```

Other parts of your code can now use EmpType as a variable type in the same way they use Integer or String. Notice that, in the above example, an element of a user-defined type can use either a fixed or variable-length string as well as a dynamic or static array.

Common Uses of User-Defined Types

User-defined types are useful (and sometimes even necessary) whenever we need to hide complex detail kept in a group of variables or whenever we need to treat a group of variable information as a unit.

Random Access Records

You have to use user-defined types to communicate with Random-Access files. You must set up the user-defined type to have the same structure as the structure of a record in the Random Access file. You must then open the Random Access file specifying the length of the user-defined type (that is, the amount of memory it takes up) so that Visual Basic will know how big a chunk of the file to read and write when it manipulates records in the file.

Note Microsoft's Visual Basic 4.0 Certification exam doesn't cover Random Access File I/O. If you wish to know more about techniques for Random Access I/O, you can check the Visual Basic 4.0 Programmer's Guide under the "Random Access" section of the chapter entitled "Processing Files." ■

Handling a Collection of Variables as a Single Object

As in the previous example, you might want to encapsulate all of the information about an employee into a single variable unit, such as a special type you would call "EmpRec." The user-defined type gives your application a cleaner, more straightforward design. You don't have to keep referring to every single variable element of the employee information by name each time you need to manipulate an employee's data.

Database Records

You may consider emulating the field structure of a database record in a user-defined type. You could declare a variable of the user-defined type to hold information from the current record in the database. When you read or write a database record, you can make a one-to-one assignment between the data fields and the elements of that variable.

Arrays of Complex Information

If you need to track several pieces of information about each member of a group of objects, you can create an array with an element in the array for each of those objects. The type of data held in the array could be some special user-defined type whose elements store the individual pieces of information about each member. For instance,

```
Type EmpRec
    FirstName as String
    LastName as String
    SSN as String * 9
    Dependents() as String
    LastThreeJobs(1 to 3) as String
    Salary as Long
End Type
Dim Employees(10) as EmpRec
```

would enable you to keep track of 11 employees. You could refer to each employee by an index in the Employees array and then retrieve or store information about that employee. In the following example, we process the array of Employee records and accumulate each employee's salary into the variable TotalSal:

```
Employees(7).FirstName = "Bill"
Employees(7).LastName = "Smith"
```

or

```
Dim lcv as Integer
Dim TotalSal As Long
For lcv = 0 to 10
    TotalSal = TotalSal + Employees(lcv).Salary
Next lcv
```

Exploring Object Variables

Of course, you know about objects from even a casual use of Visual Basic. Controls are objects, Forms are objects, and, in addition, there are many other built-in types of objects in Visual Basic that are not necessarily visible to you on the ToolBox. Objects are basically complex memory structures that encapsulate special data locations (properties) and special functions (methods).

You can set up an object variable to point to an existing object:

```
Dim frmMyForm as Form
Set frmMyForm = frmMain
```

In the foregoing example, an object variable named "frmMyForm" was declared with type Form. The following statement establishes frmMyForm to refer to a specific Form. Notice that you must use the Set keyword when initializing an object variable. The = operator works by itself only for simple data types.

You can also set up an object variable to point to something that has just been returned or created by a function, as in these examples:

```
dim db as DataBase
dim rs as RecordSet
Set db = OpenDataBase("C:\VB\BIBLIO.MDB")
Set rs = db.OpenRecordSet("Titles",dbOpenTable)
```

In the previous example, we declared two object variables of type DataBase and type Recordset, respectively. The OpenDataBase function returned a DataBase-type object, and so we could set the db variable to refer to that object. We then set the rs variable to refer to the result of the OpenRecordset method.

▶ **See** "Database Objects and the Databases Collection," **p. 481**

▶ **See** "Recordset Objects and the Recordsets Collection," **p. 484**

You also can declare an object variable as a New instance of some object type:

```
Dim frmNewChild as New frmChild
```

This example is from the chapter, "Using Multiple Document Interface (MDI)." In this example, frmNewChild is actually a brand new child MDI form that we have created or instantiated in our code, using frmChild as a template. In the earlier example "Dim frmMyForm as Form," frmMyForm must be set to point to an existing form before we use it.

We will be seeing a lot more objects in this book.

See the chapters on "Using OLE to Integrate Applications," "Creating OLE Servers," "Using Data Access Objects," and "Using Multiple Document Interface (MDI)," for extensive treatment of object variables in different practical contexts.

Understanding Variable Scope and Lifetime

In order to effectively use and understand Visual Basic code, you must understand and master the concept of variable scope—the places a variable is known in an application—and variable lifetime—how long a variable retains its assigned value.

Variable Scope

You need to give each of your variables the right amount of scope: too much scope and your application suffers memory bloat and your variables are more vulnerable to unwanted changes; too little scope and you can't find a variable when you need it.

Public Scope

This is the widest scope you can give a variable in an application. It means the variable is known throughout the entire application.

 Note You can only declare a public variable in the General Declarations section of a Class, Standard, or Form module. ■

Like Dim, you use the Public keyword to declare a variable:

 Note There was no Public keyword in VB version 3.0 and under. ■

```
Public strMyName as String
```

You will now be able to refer to strMyName anywhere in your project's code without causing your compiler to cough.

There is a great difference, however, in how Public variables are referenced, depending on which type of module they're declared in (see fig. 2.4).

In a Standard module, the Public keyword makes its variable available by simply declaring a name throughout the entire application:

```
strMyName = "Bill"
```

In a Class or Form module, however, Public variables are considered to be properties of the Class or Form. If you had declared strMyName as a Public variable in the form frmMain, you would reference it from elsewhere in the application with the line:

```
frmMain.strMyName = "Bill"
```

You can also use the Global keyword—but only in a Standard module's General Declarations section—to make a variable public.

> **Caution**
> Visual Basic 4.0 enables the Global keyword in a Standard module for purposes of downward compatibility only. Microsoft discourages you from using it in new code.

Private Scope

Like the Public keyword, Private can only be used in the General Declarations section of a Form, Class, or Standard module. When you declare a variable Private, you are limiting its use to the module where you declared it. There is no way to access the variable from outside the module. A variable declared as

```
Private strMyName
```

would not be visible outside its module. An attempt to reference the variable somewhere else would generate a compiler error.

You can also use the Dim statement in a module's General Declarations section to make a variable private.

> **Caution**
> Visual Basic 4.0 enables the Dim keyword at the module level for purposes of downward compatibility only. Microsoft discourages you from using it in new code.

The variable blnIsTrue is only visible in this Form module

The variable blnIsOK is visible in the entire application

Form Module

Standard Module

blnModule OK is available to all modules in the application since it's Public

FIG. 2.4 ⟹

You can access a Class or Form's Public variables in another module if you use the Form's name in front of the variable name. You can access a Standard module's Public variables from elsewhere without using the module name. Private variables are unavailable outside their native module.

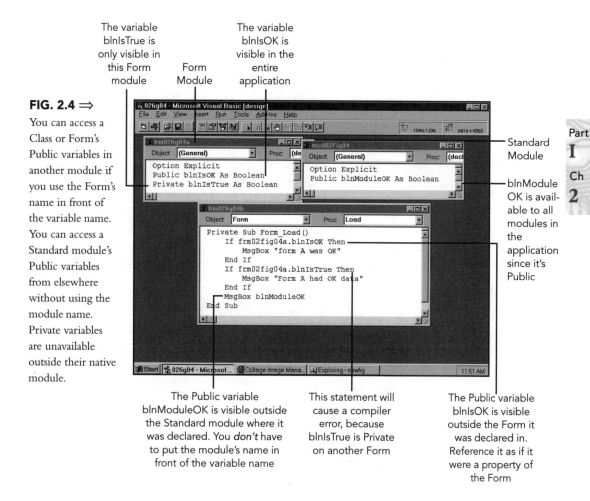

The Public variable blnModuleOK is visible outside the Standard module where it was declared. You *don't* have to put the module's name in front of the variable name

This statement will cause a compiler error, because blnIsTrue is Private on another Form

The Public variable blnIsOK is visible outside the Form it was declared in. Reference it as if it were a property of the Form

Calling Public Variables Declared in Forms

To reference a Form's public variable from elsewhere in your project, you would need to use the syntax:

```
FormName.VarName
```

so that the compiler would understand the reference to the variable. Notice that this looks a lot like the reference to a control's property. That is because Microsoft wants you to think of these Public Form variables as being user-defined properties of the Form.

This fact would enable you to define the same Public variable name in all the Forms in a given project so that you could implement a common custom property for all the Forms in that project. The variable

```
Public blnDirtyFlag as Boolean
```

for example, would tell you if changes had been made by the user to data on that Form. When you're ready to close your application, check the blnDirtyFlag property of each Form to decide if you need to take some action to save information.

Note You can define Public variables with the same name in more than one Standard module, as well. You could then use the Standard module's name in front of the variable name when you wanted to refer to that module's copy of the variable from outside the module. ■

Local Scope

We say that a variable has Local scope when we define it inside a procedure, that is, in an event procedure, a general procedure, or in a function that you write (see fig. 2.5).

FIG. 2.5 ⇒
The Public variable in this illustration is available in the entire project. The Private variable is available in all routines in the module. The variable blnLoadIsOK is a Local variable and is visible only in the routine in which it is declared.

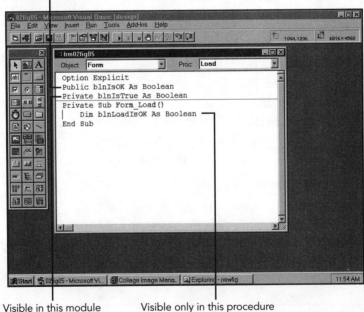

Visible in the entire application

Visible in this module   Visible only in this procedure

There are two ways to declare a variable locally. You must write

```
Dim VarName
```

or

```
Static VarName
```

inside the code of a procedure or subroutine. Both the Dim and Static keywords guarantee that the variable will only be visible inside the routine. However, as you'll see in the section on "Variable Lifetime," Dim and Static differ about the length of a variable's life.

The Visual Basic Stack and Variable Scope

The "stack" in a program's environment is a special area in the computer's memory dedicated to "scratch" results. In other words, the stack is a temporary storage area. When a routine such as an event procedure, a function, or a procedure that you have written begins to run, it gets space on the stack to do its work. When it finishes running (basically, when its End Sub or End Function statement executes) Visual Basic reclaims its part of the stack for other uses.

Because a routine implements all its local variables on its part of the stack, you can see that as soon as the routine ends these variables and their values will be lost. That is what makes a Local variable Local—the fact that it is implemented on its routine's stack space.

Deciding Between Public, Private, and Local Scope

Whenever you can, make a variable Local. If that doesn't work, then the variable should be Private. If that doesn't work, then you'll have to resign yourself to Public.

Tip

You should always make a variable's scope as narrow as possible.

There are several good reasons for keeping variable scope as narrow as possible. All experienced programmers know these reasons, and they can be reduced to two points:

◆ *Conserving memory.* a Local variable is implemented on the stack, so it's only around as long as its routine runs. Public and Private variables have considerably longer lifetimes and so must take up memory for longer. Having a lot of Public and Private variables increases the amount of memory your application needs at any given moment.

◆ *Better project organization and development.* If a variable has broader scope (application- or module-wide scope as opposed to Local scope), you are basically going to have problems knowing where it was last or where it is going to be needed in the future. So, you can't trust its contents to hold the information that you may need. You are also going to be more apprehensive about modifying its contents lest you break some other routine that was depending on it.

So when would it be a good idea to create a variable that is not Local? Well, basically, only when you have to. This would include information that has to be kept in common for more than one routine or for the entire application.

Precedence of Variables with the Same Name but Different Scope

Visual Basic enables you to use the same variable name at different levels of scope in your program. This is not a good idea, perhaps, but it can happen.

If you run into such a situation, what will Visual Basic do when it reaches a line in your code that refers to this many-headed variable? For example, let's say you have the following situation:

```
[General Declarations of Standard Module]
Public MyVar as String
[General Declarations of a Form]
Public MyVar as String
[Inside a routine belonging to the Form]
Dim MyVar as string
MyVar = "YooHoo"
```

In this case, the Local copy of MyVar, declared in the Dim statement is modified. This is because VB always accesses the most Local copy of two variables with the same name.

If we had referenced the variable in another routine of the form without declaring it locally, we would have accessed the Form's MyVar property.

If we had referenced the variable anywhere outside the Form, without using the Form's name in front of the variable name, we would have referred to the application-wide variable MyVar, declared in the Standard module.

Note A Local variable takes precedence over a module-wide or application-wide variable. A module-wide variable takes precedence over an application-wide variable. ▪

Variable Lifetime

In most cases, a Local variable's scope and its lifetime are identical. That is, when a Local variable goes out of scope, Visual Basic also takes it out of memory.

There are occasions, however, when you will need a Local variable's lifetime to outlast its scope.

Scope versus Lifetime

Scope and lifetime are usually identical at the procedure level because they are defined by the same thing: presence in memory.

Sometimes, however, you might want the code management benefits of local scope while still needing a variable's value to stick around longer than a single function call.

For instance, you might want to track the number of times a user triggers the Click() event procedure of a command button. You could track this information in a Local counter variable, but unfortunately a Local variable's contents are reinitialized every time the procedure runs. So you need a longer lifetime than your scope provides.

In such a case you would have a difference in the scope and lifetime requirements of the variable.

The Visual Basic Stack and Variable Lifetime

As we noted in the section on "The Visual Basic stack and variable scope," as soon as a routine ends its Local variables, their values will be lost because Visual Basic reallocates their stack space for other uses.

Therefore, not only do Local variables (which are always implemented on the stack) go out of scope when their routine ends, their lifetime is also over.

Static Variables

If a variable requires Local scope but a long lifetime, you should use a Static variable (see fig. 2.6).

You can only use the Static keyword locally, that is, inside a routine.

A Static variable will have Local scope but it is not stored on the stack. This enables your application to let the Static variable keep its value even after its routine has finished.

Though the variable and its value aren't visible anywhere else, the value will still be there the next time its routine runs.

A Static variable initializes to its default value (0 for numeric values, "" for Strings) only once: when the application starts. The run-time environment initializes a regular Local variable every time its routine begins again.

This is why you can hold long-term information in a Static variable, but not in a normal Local variable.

Consider the following routine:

```
Private Sub MySub()
    Dim intLocal as Integer
    Static intStatic as Integer
    intLocal = intLocal + 1
    intStatic = intStatic + 1
End Sub
```

If the application calls this routine three times, the value of intLocal will be 1, because the run-time environment will initialize intLocal to 0 on each pass through the routine. The value of intStatic, however, will be 3 because intStatic will get initialized to 0 only once—when the application loads into memory. After that, it will retain its value between calls to the routine.

FIG. 2.6 ⇒

The Static variable intStaticCounter can retain its value between calls to the procedure where it resides. IntStaticCounter, however, is only available in the procedure in which it was declared.

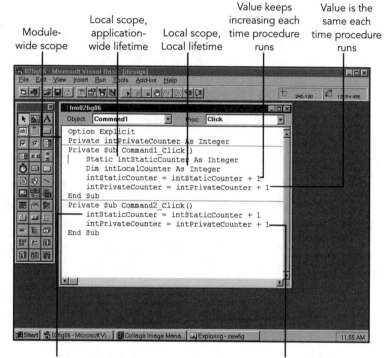

Module-wide scope

Local scope, application-wide lifetime

Local scope, Local lifetime

Value keeps increasing each time procedure runs

Value is the same each time procedure runs

This line causes an error, because intStaticCounter has local scope in a different procedure

This line causes no error, because intPrivateCounter has module-wide scope.

When to Use a Static Variable

You basically need Static variables when you want and can use Local scope with all of its management benefits, but you need to have the routine remember the previous value of the variable.

Caution

Don't go wild with Static variables, because after all they stay in memory, for the lifetime of the application. If your application has a lot of them, they will consume a greater amount of memory.

Checking the Type of a Variable

Although good programming practice encourages you to keep track of variable types, there are times when it's legitimately possible to be ignorant of a variable's type. This can happen in the following situations:

◆ You are writing code for a routine that can take a parameter of ambiguous type (usually declared as Variant).

◆ You are looking at object variables. You may know a variable is an object, but you need to know what kind of object it is. This could happen, for instance, when you are looking at a Form's Controls collection (see the section in this chapter on Collections.

IsNumeric(), IsArray(), and IsDate() Functions

The IsArray() function takes the name of a variable as its single parameter and returns a Boolean. It will Return true if the variable is an array. For example,

```
Dim MyNames() as string
If IsArray(MyNames) then...
```

IsArray will evaluate to a true value.

IsNumeric() and IsDate() can actually do more than tell us if a particular variable is one of the numeric types or if the variable is of type Date. These two functions will also accept a String and determine whether Visual Basic can interpret the contents of the String as a number or a date. For example, in the code fragment:

```
strIsIt = "897.90"
If IsNumeric(strIsIt) then...
```

IsNumeric would evaluate to a true value. We could then perhaps use the CDbl function (mentioned in the following section on the "C" functions) to convert the contents of the strIsIt variable in numeric computations.

TypeOf Statement and TypeName() Function

TypeName() provides a general way to determine the data type of a non-object variable. TypeName() returns a string giving the data type's name. In the following example, you will see the word "Integer" in the Messagebox:

```
Dim MyVar        'no explicit data type defined - so this is a
Variant
MyVar = 1
MsgBox TypeName(MyVar)
```

TypeOf will tell you the specific type of an object. It has the following special syntax:

```
If TypeOf MyControl Is TextBox then...
```

Because of its syntactic format, you can only use TypeOf in logical expressions. We shall see more examples of TypeOf in the section in this chapter on the Controls collection.

Converting a Data Type

Very often, you need to use different data types together in the same expression.

Visual Basic can often perform data type conversion automatically, and you, as the programmer, need not concern yourself with what goes on behind the scenes in these cases.

At other times, however, you will need to convert a variable to another data type before you use it. This is necessary when you want to pass a variable as an argument to a function or procedure, and the procedure is expecting a parameter of a different data type.

Note When you call a function or procedure with arguments, the data types of the arguments must match the data types in the parameter list. ■

Automatic Type Conversion

Visual Basic is very versatile in converting between data types, especially between String and other types. In many cases you can just let Visual Basic do an internal conversion for you in numeric and string expressions without having to use any special conversion functions or other precautions.

Automatic Conversion between Numeric Values

When you are dealing with different numeric data types, there is no problem because Visual Basic automatically does the necessary conversion between types, including any rounding.

```
Dim intFahrenheit as Integer
Dim dblCelsius As Double
dblCelsius = 31
intFahrenheit = (dblCelsius * 9 / 5) + 32
```

In this example, the actual result of the calculation is 87.8, but Visual Basic gracefully assigns a value of 88 to the integer variable.

Caution
You must also beware of trying to stuff a value into a container (that is, a variable type) that isn't big enough to hold it. Always check the value you are trying to convert to make sure it fits the range allowed in the target data type.

Although you can assign a larger data type, such as Double, to a smaller data type, such as Integer, you must make sure the Double variable doesn't contain a number larger than 32K, which is an Integer's upper limit. Otherwise, you are asking for a run-time Overflow error. You should be checking the value of the larger type on the following conversions:

- ◆ Double to Single
- ◆ Double to Long
- ◆ Double to Integer
- ◆ Double to Byte
- ◆ Single to Integer

- Single to Byte
- Long to Integer
- Long to Byte

Automatic Conversion of String Expressions to Numeric Values

If a String variable or control property of type String holds a string that can be evaluated to a number, it can be used as an element in a numeric expression.

```
Dim strRate as String
strRate = "11.50"
    If IsNumeric(txtHours.Text) then
        intEarnings = strRate * txtHours.text
    Else
        MsgBox "Enter a valid number in the Hours field"
    End If
```

Notice that in this example we needed to check to see if the TextBox control's Text property holds a valid number. If we had performed the calculation without checking and txtHours.Text didn't hold a valid numeric expression, Visual Basic could have generated a run-time error.

As with Numeric-to-Numeric type conversions, you must be careful that a numeric String doesn't represent a value larger than the capacity of the type you want to convert to.

Automatic Conversion of Numeric Expressions to Strings

Visual Basic will also automatically convert any other data type into a string whenever non-string variables are used in a string assignment or other expression requiring a string, as in the following example:

```
Dim dblEarnings as double
txtEarnings.Text = dblEarnings
MsgBox dblEarnings
```

The Text property of a TextBox holds String-type data and the MsgBox normally takes a string argument. In the example, VB converts a Double to a String both when assigning a Double to a TextBox Control's Text property and when passing a Double to the MsgBox statement as its Prompt argument.

Conversion of Non-String Arguments in String Concatenation

In most programming languages, including Visual Basic, the + operator can add two numbers together and it can also concatenate two string expressions, as in the following example:

```
strMine = "Mine"
strYours = "Yours"
strOurs = strMine + " and " + strYours
```

Visual Basic also uses the & symbol for string concatenation.

Note   The & operator automatically converts its operands into strings before using them. ■

Tip

Microsoft recommends that you use the & operator instead of the + for string concatenation; & is more versatile.

The expression

```
strOurs = StrMine + " and " + 0
```

is illegal, because the + operator can take only Strings as its arguments.

However, the expression

```
strOurs = StrMine & " and " & 0
```

is legal, because the & operator is more intelligent and tries to interpret all its arguments as strings, even when they are not originally strings. In this example, strOurs would end up holding the string "Mine and 0".

Val and Str Functions

The Val and Str functions are older functions.

The Val function takes a String variable or expression as its argument and converts it to any numeric type you wish to assign. In the following example, the String-type variable strEarnings is converted to a numeric type before being assigned to an Integer-type variable:

```
IntMyEarnings = Val(strEarnings)
```

The Str function does the opposite. The Str function takes a numeric variable or expression and converts it into a string. In the following example, the Integer-type variable intMyEarnings is converted to a String before being assigned to a String-type variable:

```
strEarnings = Str(intMyEarnings)
```

Asc()

The Asc() function takes a String argument and returns an Integer-type value representing the ASCII code of the String's first character. No matter how long the String argument is, Asc() only pays attention to the first character in the String.

In the following example, the MessageBox will display a 65, which is the ASCII value of the letter A, the first letter in the string:

```
Dim strName As String
strName = "Alice"
MsgBox Asc(strName)
```

AscB()

The AscB() behaves just like Asc(), except that its return value is of the Byte type. AscB() would be useful, for instance, when an external routine such as a DLL call needs a single-byte parameter referring to a character. Usually, such routines will have been written in C and will require a variable of the char data type, which is specific to C.

Chr() and ChrB()

These functions perform the reverse operations of Asc() and AscB(). They take an Integer data type as their argument and return a character corresponding to the ASCII code of the argument.

> **Caution**
> You must remember to pass only Byte values or Integers in the range 0–255 as the argument to Chr() and ChrB(). If you pass a number outside this range, Visual Basic will generate an Overflow error.

The "C" Functions

Use these functions when you want to be sure that Visual Basic will convert some variable or other expression to a specific data type. Each of the "C" functions work in the following format:

```
NewValue = CFunction(any expression)
```

where `NewValue` has the data type that CFunction converts to.

CBool

CBool will convert any non-zero numeric expression to true and will convert any expression containing 0 to false.

```
Dim blnHasProblem as Boolean
Dim intProblemCount as Integer
intProblemCount = 30
blnHasProblem = CBool(intProblemCount)
```

It will convert strings to Booleans, as long as the strings hold "true" or "false" or any alternate capitalization of those words. Otherwise, it will generate a run-time error.

CByte

CByte will convert any valid numeric string expression or any numeric type to a byte, as long as the range of the number or numeric expression is 0-255. If you supply a number outside of this range, you'll get an Overflow run-time error from Visual Basic. If you supply a string that is not numeric, you'll get a Data Type Mismatch error.

```
Dim bytWing as Byte
bytWing = CByte(200)        'OK: argument is number 1-255
bytWing = CByte("100")       'OK: string is numeric 1-255
bytWing = CByte(256)       'ERROR: number is > 255
bytWing = CByte(-200)       'ERROR: number is < 0
bytWing = CByte("ASD")        'ERROR: string doesn't evaluate to
a number
```

Numeric: CCur(), CDbl(), CInt(), CLng(), and CSng()

Each of these functions will take any other numeric type (including Date and Byte) or any numeric string expression and convert it to Currency, Double, Integer, Long, or Single, respectively.

> **Caution**
> You must be careful when doing a numeric conversion from a "larger"
> data type (one which has a larger size in memory) to a smaller one. If
> you are using CInt or CSng, be especially careful to check that the value
> you are passing to the function doesn't exceed the bounds for an
> Integer or Single variable.

CStr()

CStr() will convert any argument to a string. You don't have to worry
about something "not fitting" into the return value, because a String
can be very long.

Cvar()

Like CStr(), CVar() will take any argument and convert it to a Variant.

CVErr()

CVErr() takes a number representing any valid VB error number as its
argument. CVErr() returns a variant.

```
Dim MyVar as Variant
MyVar = CVErr(200)
```

The Format Function

The Format function is very useful for putting the finishing cosmetic
touches on an application, because it takes any expression and converts
it to a formatted string. The Format function's second argument is a
string representing a formatting template, which instructs the function
how to display the string. A few examples should make this clearer:

```
datToday = Now
dblMucho = 1000000.003
Msgbox Format(datToday,"hh:mm:ss")
MsgBox Format(dblMucho,"###,###,###.####")
MsgBox Format(dblMucho,"000,000,000.0000")
```

The first MessageBox would display a time such as 17:27:53.

The second MessageBox would display 1,000,000.003.

The third MessageBox would display 001,000,000.0030.

There are numerous other ways to use Format, including many Visual Basic constants for built-in types of formatting. Check Visual Basic's online help or the Visual Basic 4.0 Language Reference for more details.

Using Control Arrays

A control array is a special array of controls of a single type. You can create multiple elements of the control array at design time, and you can also dynamically resize the array at run-time. All elements of the control array share the same event procedures and the same initial property values.

You can use a control array in the following situations:

◆ You need to deal with several controls as a group, letting them share the same event procedure code and have the same initial properties.

◆ You want to dynamically add and delete controls on a Form as your program runs.

Three Ways to Define Control Array Elements at Design Time

Although you only need to define the first element of a control array at design time, you can go ahead and set up more elements at design time as well.

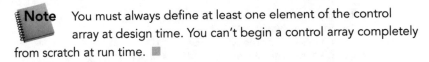

Note You must always define at least one element of the control array at design time. You can't begin a control array completely from scratch at run time. ■

There are several ways to define control array elements at design time.

Setting the Index Property

All controls in Visual Basic have an Index property. If you look at the Properties list of a control, the value of Index is normally blank.

When you set Index to some integer value, you change the nature of the control to an element of a control array (see fig. 2.7). To set a control as an element of a control array:

1. Select the control you want to make into a control array element.

2. Bring up the control's Properties window.

3. Select the Index property.

4. Type an entry in the data field of the Index property. You will probably want to choose either 0 or 1.

5. Notice that the name of the control at the top of its Properties window immediately changes. It is now followed by the Index number you typed inside a set of parentheses. For example, Command1(0).

6. You can repeat steps 1–5 as many times as you need. Always remember to increment the Index value by 1 for each new control you add.

Part
I
Ch
2

FIG. 2.7 ⇒

You can define a control as the first element of a control array by entering a value (usually a 0 or a 1) in its Index property.

This control started out as an ordinary Text Box

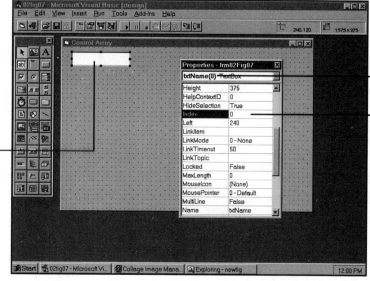

Array subscript becomes part of control name

Set Index property to create a design-time control array element

Tip

Setting a control's Index property to begin a control array is especially useful when you intend to add the other elements of the control array at run time.

Using Copy/Paste

You can also begin a control array by copying and pasting from a single existing control (see fig. 2.8). To create a control array with Copy/Paste:

1. Put the first copy of the control on the form or select an existing control.

2. Copy the control to the Windows Clipboard by choosing Edit, Copy from the Visual Basic menu or by keying Ctrl+C.

3. Paste the copy of the control from the Windows Clipboard with the Edit Paste Visual Basic menu choice or by keying Ctrl+V.

4. Visual Basic will prompt you with a message asking if you wish to create a control array.

5. Click Yes.

6. Repeat steps 2–5 as many times as necessary to get the number of elements you want in the array. You may also copy and paste more than one control at the same time by selecting multiple controls to copy.

Tip

Using Copy/Paste to create a control array is especially useful when you want to create multiple controls at design time.

FIG. 2.8 ⇒

You can define subsequent elements of a control array by copying a control and then attempting to paste it back onto its original Form.

Answer "Yes" and you'll get two design-time elements of a control array

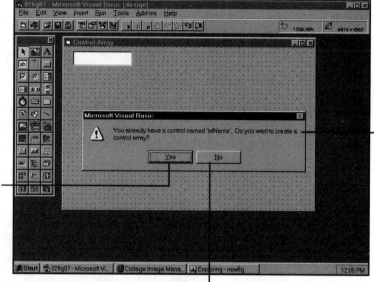

You'll see this message when you try to copy and paste a control

Answer "No" and you'll create an ordinary contol with a different name

Creating Multiple Controls with the Same Name

To create a control array by using the same control name, take the following steps (see fig. 2.9):

1. Put the first copy of the control on the Form or decide on an existing control to use.

2. Put another control of the same type on the Form, or select a second existing control of the same type as the control of step 1.

3. Bring up the second control's Properties window.

4. Select the control's Name property.

5. Change the control's name so that it's identical to the first control's name. VB will warn you before it accepts this change.

6. Notice that the name of the control at the top of its Properties window immediately changes. It now has changed to the name you typed, followed by an index number in parentheses—for example, Command1(1).

7. Repeat steps 2–6 as many times as needed to get the right number of controls into the array.

FIG. 2.9 ⇒

Giving a second control the same name as an existing control on the Form will make both controls into control array elements.

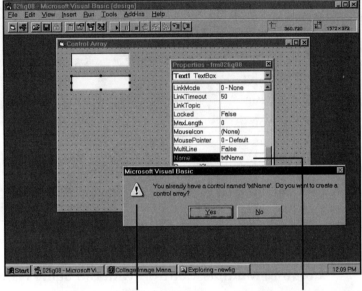

Once again (as in fig. 2.8) VB asks us if we want to create a control array

We attempt to give an existing control the same name as another existing control

Tip

Sometimes you may want to change a group of existing non-array controls into a control array. Consider giving each member of a set of controls the same name to create a control array.

Adding and Deleting Control Array Elements at Run-Time

One of the great advantages of control arrays is that you can dynamically manipulate their members at run-time. This includes adding new elements and deleting existing elements.

This means that sometimes you could have three command buttons on a Form and at other times you could have five or any other number the application needs.

Limitations of Run-Time Manipulation of Control Arrays

If you fail to follow any of the following rules, Visual Basic will generate a run-time error.

◆ You can't create control arrays entirely from scratch at run time. That is, every control array must start out with at least one design-time element.

◆ You can't delete a control at run time that was created at design-time.

◆ You can't add a control array element with the same index number as an existing control array element.

Initializing Control Array Elements with the Load Statement

You can initialize a run-time copy of a control array with the Load statement. The syntax of the Load statement for a new control array element would be

```
Load ControlName(NewIndex)
```

where *ControlName* is the name of the control array and *NewIndex* is an index value not being used by any existing element of the control array.

You are responsible for maintaining a value for *NewIndex* that is not already in use and that you can keep track of in case you want to add more elements to your array or delete them. You will want to maintain (probably by incrementing) the value of NewIndex before each Load of a new element.

Deleting Control Array Elements with the Unload Statement

UnLoad ControlName(ExistingIndex) will immediately take an existing control array element name out of memory as long as ControlName represents the name of a control array and ExistingIndex (as its name implies) represents the index of a control array element that was in memory up to this point.

Once again, you are responsible for maintaining enough information about the array so that you know the valid indexes of elements that can be unloaded. You will want to maintain (probably by decrementing) the value of ExistingIndex after each Unload of an existing element (see fig. 2.10).

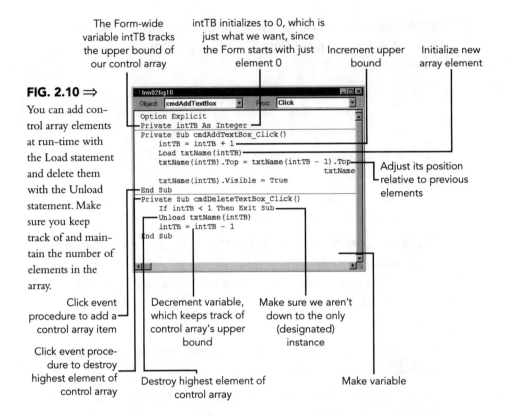

The Form-wide variable intTB tracks the upper bound of our control array

intTB initializes to 0, which is just what we want, since the Form starts with just element 0

Increment upper bound

Initialize new array element

FIG. 2.10 ⇒ You can add control array elements at run-time with the Load statement and delete them with the Unload statement. Make sure you keep track of and maintain the number of elements in the array.

Adjust its position relative to previous elements

Click event procedure to add a control array item

Click event procedure to destroy highest element of control array

Decrement variable, which keeps track of control array's upper bound

Make sure we aren't down to the only (designated) instance

Make variable

Destroy highest element of control array

Using Control Array Elements at Run-Time

The key idea here is that of the Index. You can access individual controls in the array and distinguish between them in their common event procedures by using the Index. The Index identifies an element by its position in the array.

Accessing a Specific Control Array Element's Properties and Methods

A control in a control array has the same methods and properties as its non-array cousin.

To access a property or call a method of a control in a control array, you must be able to reference its Index. For instance, if we had an array of command buttons named cmdMe and we wanted to change the caption of element 3, we could write:

```
cmdMe(3).Caption = "OK"
```

or if we wanted to move element 3 by calling its Move method, we could write

```
cmdMe(3).Move cmdMe(2).left, cmdMe(2).Top + cmdMe(2).Height
```

Notice that in this example we have moved it in relation to another element in the control array.

Note If you created your control array by changing the name of several design-time controls to the same name, the control array elements' initial properties may not be the same.

Also note that no matter how you created elements of a control array, the elements' Index and Tabindex will never be the same. ■

Using the Index Parameter in Event Procedures

Because all elements of a control array share the same event procedures, VB passes an Index parameter to a control array's event procedures. This Index parameter uniquely identifies which control received the event.

For instance, if your user clicks element 3 of an array of command buttons, you probably want something different to happen from when the user clicks element 5 of the same array.

Fortunately, event procedures for control arrays work in a slightly different way from event procedures for non-array controls. Control array event procedures automatically receive a special parameter: Index.

When you edit the event procedure of a control array, it looks like this:

```
Private Sub cmdMe_Click(Index as Integer)

End Sub
```

If you compared this with the click event procedure of a non-array command button, you'd see that the Index parameter was missing from the "normal" button's event procedure.

The Index parameter will be different depending on which of the controls in the array received the event. You can therefore put code in the event procedure in order to look at the Index parameter and then make decisions about what to do based on the value of the Index. This, in effect, enables you to distinguish which member of the array received the event (see fig. 2.11).

Event procedures of a control array always have an extra Index parameter to indicate which element of the array received the event

FIG. 2.11 ⇒
You can use the Index parameter of a control array's event procedures to distinguish which element of the array actually received the event.

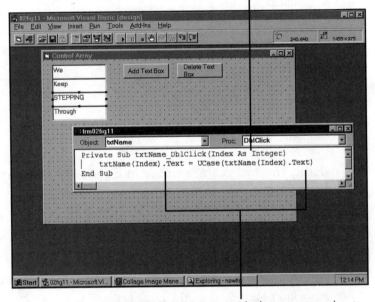

Use the Index parameter inside the event procedure to refer to the control array element receiving the event

Working with Collections

A collection is a special set of items in Visual Basic. Visual Basic itself implements some collections as a part of any program's running environment. All collections have an array of the contained items and a Count property.

Some of Visual Basic's important collections are the Controls collection, which refers to all the controls on the current form, and the Forms collection, referring to all the forms currently loaded in memory in the running application.

You can refer to an item in a collection by its array index.

```
MsgBox Controls(0).Text
```

would, for instance, display the Text property of element 0 of the Controls collection.

The array of items of a collection is zero-based.

In Visual Basic 4 you can also loop through the items of a collection with the For Each loop. See the section on the "For Each…Next loop" in the next chapter.

You will be getting a little preview of how to use the For Each…Next loop in the following sections, because that is the preferred way to traverse a collection in Visual Basic 4.

 Note   In Visual Basic 4, the programmer can also implement custom collections. ▪

▶ **See** "Storing Multiple Instances of an Object in a Collection," **p.370**

Accessing Loaded Forms with the Forms Collection

As we just mentioned, you can use the Forms collection to refer to any currently loaded form in the running application.

Notice how the example code prepares to use the For Each…Next loop by declaring a Form variable. This variable will serve as the pointer to a different form in the Forms collection on each pass through the loop. Thus we will be able to manipulate each form in turn on each pass through the loop.

```
Dim frmThisForm as Form         'declare a holder variable
For Each frmThisForm in Forms    'set each form to the var.
     frmThisForm.Show           'show current form
Next frmThisForm
```

Accessing a Form's Controls with the Controls Collection

Visual Basic also provides a Controls collection, which, by default, refers to the Controls on the current form.

We can access individual Controls on the form and traverse the Controls collection in the same way we traversed the Forms collection in the previous section.

Traversing All the Controls on a Form

Once again, notice how the example code prepares to use the For Each...Next loop by declaring a Control variable. This variable will serve as the pointer to a different control in the current form's Controls collection on each pass through the loop. Thus we will be able to manipulate each Control in turn on each pass through the loop.

```
Dim ctlThisControl As Control          'holder variable
For Each ctlThisControl in Controls    'set ea. Ctrl to var
    ctlThisControl.Font.Size = 24      'manipulate con-
trol
Next ctlThisControl
```

Notice that we blithely assume that each Control we may encounter has a font.size property—but this isn't always the case. In particular, some Controls that are not directly visible to the user at run-time (Timers and Common Dialog controls, for example) have no need of a Font object.

If our code were to hit a Control which did not support the referenced properties or methods, Visual Basic would dutifully generate a run-time error.

We need a way to figure out what kind of Control we are looking at so we can avoid problems in our code (see fig. 2.12).

Determining the Type of Each Control

As we saw in the section entitled "TypeOf Statement and TypeName() Function," the TypeOf statement can help us determine the type of an object. Because a Control is an object, we can use TypeOf to figure out if a particular control in the Controls collection is the type we want.

```
If TypeOf ctlThisControl Is TextBox Then ...
```

FIG. 2.12 ⇒
A For…Each loop can step through the Controls collection, enabling you to visit each Control on the current Form. Use TypeOf to make sure you only access Controls of the type you are interested in.

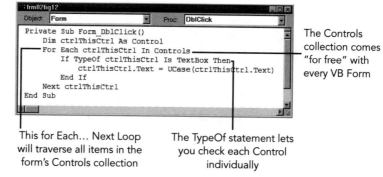

```
Private Sub Form_DblClick()
    Dim ctrlThisCtrl As Control
    For Each ctrlThisCtrl In Controls
        If TypeOf ctrlThisCtrl Is TextBox Then
            ctrlThisCtrl.Text = UCase(ctrlThisCtrl.Text)
        End If
    Next ctrlThisCtrl
End Sub
```

The Controls collection comes "for free" with every VB Form

This for Each… Next Loop will traverse all items in the form's Controls collection

The TypeOf statement lets you check each Control individually

Notice that all common and custom Controls have their own special data types. Here are examples of three data types (which are considered as VB keywords):

◆ TextBox

◆ CommandButton

◆ Label

and so on. We can check for any of these types as we loop through a Controls collection.

Using On Error Resume Next When Accessing the Controls Collection

If we only wanted to handle a certain type of Control as we loop through the Controls collection, we could use the TypeOf statement as a gatekeeper to only allow our code to process Controls whose type matched the type we were looking for.

```
Dim ctlThisControl As Control
For Each ctlThisControl in Controls
    If TypeOf ctlThisControl Is TextBox Then
    ctlThisControl.Text = Ucase(ctlThisControl.Text)
    End If
Next ctlThisControl
```

But, what if we want to access all types of Controls which, for example, support a certain method or property? For instance, there are several Controls that have a Text property. Perhaps we want to change the Text property to uppercase for all Controls that have a Text property, ignoring all others.

It would get pretty cumbersome if we had to write the following:

```
If TypeOf ctlThisControl Is TextBox Or _
    TypeOf ctlThisControl Is MaskEdit Or _
    TypeOf ctlThisCtonrol Is ComboBox Or _
        '...and so on
```

Another solution is at hand, however. We could omit the checking with TypeOf and simply allow the error to happen when we hit a Control that doesn't have the property we're talking about. We can temporarily tell Visual Basic to continue to the next line when it encounters an error by using the On Error Resume Next statement. See the section, "On Error Resume Next" in the chapter on "Handling Errors" for more details on how this statement works.

```
Dim ctlThisControl As Control
On Error Resume Next     'Just go on without causing error
For Each ctlThisControl in Controls
    ctlThisControl.Text = Ucase(ctlThisControl.Text)
Next ctlThisControl
```

This example will traverse every Control on this Form. Because the On Error Resume Next statement is in force, any error that happens will not stop our code. The routine will simply continue processing the loop. Thus, it doesn't matter if there are Controls on our Form without a Text property. The routine will ignore errors caused by attempts to access the nonexistent properties of those Controls.

Pointing to the Controls Collection of a Non-Active Form

By default the Controls collection refers to Controls on the currently active Form. What if we want to refer to groups of Controls on other loaded Forms?

No problem. All we need to do is use the Form name in front of any reference to the Controls collection. The code,

```
MsgBox "The number of controls on frmDataEntry is " &
frmDataEntry.Controls.Count
```

would then refer to the Count property of the Controls collection on the Form named frmDataEntry. We could traverse those Controls with a For...Each loop if the head of the loop read:

```
For Each ctrlThisControl in frmDataEntry.Controls...
```

Traversing All Controls on All Loaded Forms

What if we want to traverse all Controls on all loaded Forms? Well, let's see—we can point to Controls on any Form by referring to the Form in front of the Controls collection. And we can refer to all Forms by traversing the Forms collection.

So, let's put the two together in a set of nested loops. The inner loop will traverse the Controls collection of a Form and the outer loop will traverse each Form. Here's what the code would look like:

```
Dim frmThisform as Form          'holder for form
Dim ctlThisControl As Control    'holder for control
On Error Resume Next             'just go to next line
For Each frmThisForm in Forms    'traverse each form
For Each ctlThisControl in frmThisForm.Controls
     ctlThisControl.Font.Size = 24
Next ctlThisControl
Next frmThisForm
```

Variable Naming Conventions with Hungarian Notation

In this book, as well as in a lot of other places, you will see Visual Basic variable names with a little three-letter prefix in lowercase:

- ◆ blnIsOK
- ◆ strFirstName
- ◆ lngSalary

You have probably noticed that the prefix seems to correspond to the data type of the variable. So, in the previous example,

◆ bln= Boolean

◆ str= String

◆ lng= Long

and so forth. This practice of affixing a type identifier to the variable name is known as *Hungarian Notation*, so named for the nationality of its inventor, Charles Simonyi. Though there is no complete industry-wide standard for Hungarian Notation prefixes, there is a pretty strong consensus among most programmers working in any given language about what the prefixes should be for the variable types within that language.

Note Visual Basic programmers use Hungarian notation for Object variables, including controls and forms. So, for example, a typical Command Button name might be cmdOK. ■

Hungarian Notation can be learned mostly by reading examples of code written with Hungarian Notation. Because Hungarian Notation is not covered in the Visual Basic Certification exam and because just about every other book on Visual Basic gives a table of Hungarian Notation prefixes for Visual Basic, we will refrain from doing so here.

Variables versus Constants

Although Microsoft doesn't list the word "constant" in its Exam Objectives, you should probably make sure you have a basic understanding of how constants work in Visual Basic before you take the Certification Exam.

Basically, a constant, like a variable, represents a named allocation of memory space. Unlike a variable,

◆ You assign the constant's value at the same time you declare it.

◆ You can't reassign the constant's value after you declare it. Its value is fixed.

You declare a constant in your code in the following manners:

```
Const MyConstant = 1
```

or

```
Const MyConstant as Long = 1
```

In the second previous example, we've forced the type of the constant to be a Long. In the first example, the compiler would have taken its best shot at guessing the type and probably would assign it to be an Integer.

Constants can have scope just like variables. You should place the Public or Private keyword in front of the Const keyword in a Form, Class, or Standard module's General Declarations section:

```
Public Const MyConstant = 1
```

> **Caution**
> You can't declare a Public constant in a Form module. If you try to do this, you'll get a compiler error.

Taking the Disc Test

 If you have read and understood the material in the chapter, you are ready to test your knowledge. Insert the CD-ROM that comes with this book and run the self-test software as described in Appendix H, "Using the CD-ROM."

From Here...

For an in-depth look at topics touched in this chapter, take a look at the following chapters:

 ◆ We will see how to use a control array with a dynamic menu in Chapter 8, "Menus."

Part
I

Ch
2

◆ You learn about data-type agreement issues between Visual Basic and DLL routines written in the C language in Chapter 15, "Dynamic-Link Libraries."

◆ We will talk about the use of object variables more fully in Chapter 9, "Using Multiple-Document Interface (MDI)," Chapter 10, "Using OLE to Integrate Applications," Chapter 11, "Creating OLE Servers," and Chapter 13, "Using Data Access Objects."

Chapter Prerequisite

To get the most out of this chapter, you should already be familiar with the concepts of data types and variable manipulation presented in Chapter 2 and with the VB run-time environment.

3

Working with Visual Basic Code

In the previous chapter, we saw how different types of variables behave in a VB program.

In this chapter, we will explore how to put variables, controls, and elements of the VB language together in code. Concepts and skills covered in this chapter include:

- ◆ Writing VB **Sub** and **Function** procedures: how to set them up, how to call them, and how to pass arguments to them
- ◆ Using program **control structures** in VB for looping and branching
- ◆ Using **String manipulation** functions
- ◆ Understanding **events**, their relation to each other, and their relation to **event procedures** and their controls

◆ Understanding **Class Modules** (discussed briefly in this chapter and more in Chapter 11 on "OLE Servers")

◆ Using Special **VBA** constructs for writing more efficient code (With...End With and For Each...Next structures)

◆ Creating custom properties and methods for forms

◆ Using the Microsoft Windows common controls in code

The Compiler and One Line of Code

Sometimes a single line of code in VB can be quite long, making it difficult to read on-screen. VB 4.0 has a line continuation feature allowing you to split a single line of code across multiple lines for easier readability. You can split a single statement across up to ten lines of text using the line continuation character, the underscore "_". One line can be up to 1023 characters long. Simply insert a space and an underscore character "_" where you want the code line to split:

```
lblQuestion.Caption = _
        "Where would you like to eat today?"
```

You can insert the space+underscore combination anywhere in the line, with one obvious exception: You can't insert a line continuation directive right in the middle of a literal (that is, quoted) string.

If you want to split a long quoted string across multiple lines, you can do so by rewriting it as a concatenation of several smaller strings and split the line at each concatenation:

```
lblQuestion.Caption = _
        "Where would you like to eat after " & _
        "you go where you would like to go?"
```

Sometimes you have the opposite problem: Maybe you would like to logically group together several short lines that can be considered as a unit. The colon ":" character can be used to group more than one code line on a single line of text. Just insert the colon between all the lines you want to appear together. Then, you could write:

```
Me.Cls : Me.Print "Where indeed" : Me.Print "Here"
```

instead of

```
Me.Cls
Me.Print "Where indeed"
Me.Print "Here"
```

Conditional Compilation

Conditional compilation determines which blocks of Visual Basic code will be compiled based on the value of a **conditional compiler constant**. Code excluded during conditional compilation is completely omitted from the final executable file, so it has no size or performance effect.

Constants defined using #Const are called conditional compiler constants. These types of constants are used by compiler directives to determine if a Visual Basic block of code is compiled. You receive an error if a standard constant (a constant defined by Const) is used instead.

VB has defined its own conditional compilation constants with the names WIN16 and WIN32. They are Boolean values which indicate whether the currently running version of VB is 16-bit or 32-bit. Thus, Win16 is True if 16-bit VB is running and Win32 is True if 32-bit VB is running. These constants are typically used to compile the same code for different platforms. You can also create your own conditional compiler constants.

▶ **See** "Variables versus Constants," **p. 78**

See "Variables versus Constants," p. 78

You may use the #Const statement in a module to set up your own conditional compiler constants. Thus, you might set up a constant IsDebug in a form's or standard module's Declarations section:

```
#Const IsDebug = True
```

Later in your code (either in a sub or function procedure or just further on in the General Declarations section), you can test the value of the compiler constant that you had set up:

```
#If IsDebug Then
    'Do something
#Else
    'Do something else
#End If
```

Part

I

Ch

3

At first, this might seem like it's the same as the following:

```
Private Const IsDebug = true
If IsDebug Then . . . etc.
```

The difference is that the #If . . . #Else . . . #End If directives are not part of the Visual Basic language. Instead, they are compiler directives, telling the compiler whether or not to include code blocks in the compiled version of the program. If the #If condition is false when the compiler runs, the compiler will ignore everything between the #If and the #Else (or between the #If and the #End If, if there is no #Else).

All the lines of an If . . . Else . . . End If construct are part of your final compiled product. In contrast, only those lines that satisfy the condition of an #If . . . #Else . . . #End If are compiled.

The obvious advantage is that you can keep irrelevant code from bulking up the size of your finished product.

 Note Conditional compiler constants are always evaluated at module level. There is no such thing as a public conditional compiler constant. ▪

Procedures

Subroutines are the stuff of which modern computer programs are made. Long gone are the days when programmers conceived of their programs as one long sequence of instructions. Nowadays, our programs are collections of subroutines that interact with each other and, if we're Windows programmers, with the Windows operating environment.

In VB (as in many structured programming languages), we have two different types of subroutine—the sub procedure and the function procedure.

Sub Procedures

A sub procedure is a named section or block of code within the project that can be called by another part of the project to perform its instructions on demand. The sub procedure may accept parameters, and it may even act on them, but it does not itself have any defined return value, which is the main difference between a Sub and Function procedure.

All Sub procedures start with a **Sub** and end with **End Sub**:

```
Private Sub ProcedureName(list of parameters)
 'code goes here.
End Sub
```

The name of the sub procedure is followed by parentheses, even if there are no parameters.

Part

You can call a sub procedure from somewhere else in your code (providing the procedure is in scope) just as you would call a built-in VB statement. To call the sub procedure ProcName, simply type the sub procedure name at the appropriate point in your code:

I

Ch

3

```
ProcName
```

▶ **See** "Passing Arguments to General (Sub or Function) Procedures," **p. 91**

▶ **See** "Scope of Procedures," **p. 104**

Sub procedures are classified into two distinct types—event procedures and general procedures.

Event Procedures

An event procedure is different from other procedures in a couple of respects:

◆ Event procedures are triggered by an event associated with a control or form.

◆ All Event procedures are provided by VB and are associated with a particular control or form. VB uses the following syntax when naming the event procedure: *Sub ControlName_EventName*.

◆ Event procedures are stored in form modules.

An event procedure for the Click event of a command button named cmdQuit might look like this:

```
Private Sub cmdQuit_Click()
     UnLoad Me
End Sub
```

The programmer has put code (Unload Me) inside the procedure stub provided by VB.

 Note Event procedures are always sub procedures, never functions. ■

You can find an event procedure's code by following these steps:

1. While in design mode, double-click a control or Form.

2. The code window opens and displays one of the event procedures belonging to the selected control or Form.

3. To view all of the event procedures belonging to the control or form, click the drop-down arrow to the right of the Proc combo box located at the top right of the code window (see fig. 3.1).

 Tip

If you double-click a control or Form and no code exists in any of the event procedures, VB first displays the event procedure it considers the object type's most commonly used procedure (for example, Click for a Command Button and many other controls, Change for a Text Box, Load for a Form). If code exists in some of the control's event procedures, VB displays the first event procedure that contains code.

 Tip

By default, VB lists only one procedure at a time within the code window. If you prefer to look at all procedures in the code window as a single scrollable listing, select the Full Module View check box in the Options dialog box (Tools, Options, select the Editor tab).

Note Typically, Event procedures are triggered by the user (Click, KeyDown, MouseMove). Some Event procedures, however, are triggered by the system (Load, Unload, Timer).

In addition, you can force an Event procedure to trigger simply by explicitly calling it as you would a general procedure. For example, to trigger the click event for cmdQuit:

cmdQuit_Click ■

FIG. 3.1 ⇒

You can view available event procedures for a Form or control from the Code Window of any of the object's event procedures.

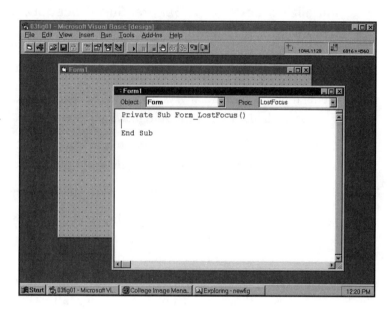

Part
I
Ch
3

General Procedures

A general procedure is designed to run only when it is explicitly called from somewhere in code. In addition, you must create a general procedure from scratch (unlike an event procedure).

If you create a sub procedure called CleanUp in a Form, Standard, or Class module, it might look like this:

```
Private Sub CleanUp(blnUnload as Boolean)
    Dim frmCurForm as Form
    If blnUnload Then
        For Each frmCurForm in Forms
            Unload frmCurForm
        Next frmCurForm
```

```
        End If
      End
End Sub
```

To call the CleanUp sub procedure, simply type the procedure name followed by any parameters:

```
CleanUp True
```

Notice that this syntax resembles a call to a built-in VB statement.

Initializing Code for a General Sub Procedure or Function from the Insert Menu

While VB can automatically supply stubs for event procedures, you must create general procedures on you own.

General procedures are always stored in the General section of the Form, Standard, or Class module in which they are created.

You can create a general procedure stub in one of two ways—a menu-accessible dialog box or simply by typing the procedure stub.

To create a general procedure using the menu:

1. Open the code window for the desired Form, Standard or Class module. (Opening the code window is required. It's not important what the code window displays when it is opened.)

2. From the VB menu, choose Insert, Procedure to access the Insert Procedure dialog box (see fig. 3.2).

3. Type the desired name in the Name text box.

4. Choose the procedure's type from the Type group—Sub, Function, or Property.

   ▶ **See** "Custom Properties for a Form with Property Let and Get Procedures," **p. 129**

5. Choose the procedure's scope from the Scope group (see a discussion of a procedure's scope later in this chapter).

   ▶ **See** "Scope of Procedures," **p. 104**

6. Click OK.

7. VB places the general procedure stub in the General Declaration section (it was not important what the code window displayed when it was opened because all general procedures will be stored in the General Declaration section).

FIG. 3.2 ⇒

The Insert Procedure dialog box lets you insert a new general procedure into your application.

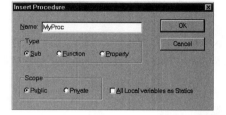

Initializing Code for a General Sub or Function Procedure by Typing in the Code Window

You also can initialize a new sub procedure or function by typing it within the code window (see fig. 3.3):

1. Open the code window of the desired Form, General, or Class module.

2. Move to the General Declaration section (or position the cursor after the End Sub or End Function of an existing procedure).

3. Type the first line of the procedure declaration. You need not include the parentheses for the parameter list because VB includes them automatically.

4. Press the Enter key and VB completes the procedure stub with End Sub or End Function.

FIG. 3.3 ⟹

You can create a new procedure in your application by typing a header for the procedure on a blank line outside of any procedure in the Code Window.

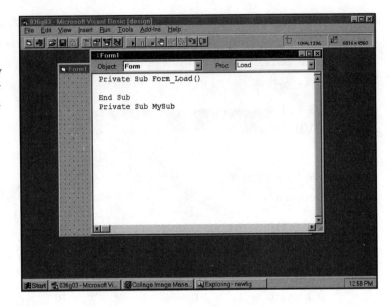

Functions

A function is a general procedure that returns a value. Unlike a general procedure of the Sub type, a function procedure includes some extra components to its procedure stub:

- ◆ A function must include a data type for its return value. You declare the return value's data type with an *As DataType* clause.

- ◆ You must specify the function's return value within the function's code block. In VB, you do this by using the function's name as if it were a variable and assigning a value to it.

In this example, the function Tomorrow( ) has a return type of Date, and the return value is assigned within the function's code block.

```
Private Function Tomorrow() As Date
    Tomorrow = Now + 1
End Function
```

To call the function named Tomorrow somewhere within code:

```
datDeadline= Tomorrow()
```

In this example, the variable datDeadline stores the return value of the function named Tomorrow.

Declaring the Data Type of a Function's Return Value

Because a function has a return value, it needs a data type just like a normal variable. To specify the data type, append:

```
As DataType
```

at the end of the function's declaration line, where *DataType* is a standard VB data type. For example,

```
Private Function Tomorrow() As Date
```

would be a valid Function declaration, specifying Date as the data type of Tomorrow's return value.

You may, when necessary, declare the return type to be Variant:

```
Private Function Tomorrow() As Variant
```

Because Variant is VB's default data type, the declaration

```
Private Function Tomorrow()
```

is legal and is equivalent to an explicit Variant declaration.

Setting the Return Value

As previously stated, you set a function's return value by assigning a value to a variable with the same name as the function. Because most functions require more than a single line to complete their task, you might consider declaring a local variable inside the function to hold the return value, finally assigning that variable's value to the function name at the end:

```
Private Function Tomorrow() As Date
    Dim datRetVal As Date
    'involved procedure which assigns a value to datRetVal
    '.
    '.
    '.
    Tomorrow = datRetVal
End Function
```

Passing Arguments to General (Sub or Function) Procedures

Arguments enable dynamic information to be passed to a procedure. A procedure declaration specifies the number and type of arguments required by the procedure within the parentheses that follow the procedure name. Typically, the complete list of arguments from the procedure point-of-view is called the parameter list. The general format for specifying a parameter list for a sub or function procedure is:

```
Private Sub ProcedureName(list of parameters)

Private Function FunctionName(list of parameters) as DataType
```

When you specify a parameter you assign it a name, by which it will be known inside the procedure, and a data type:

```
datToday As Date
```

This name is known only inside the body of the procedure. In the following example, the Function procedure, called NextDay, expects a single Date-type parameter which will be known as datToday inside the procedure:

```
Function NextDay(datToday As Date) As Date
     NextDay = datToday + 1
End Function
```

When we want to call this function procedure from elsewhere in our code, we must pass a Date-type value as an argument:

```
Dim datTomorrow As Date
Dim datStartDate As Date
datStartDate = Now
datTomorrow = NextDay(datStartDate)
```

In this example, when the NextDay function procedure is called, the value of datStartDate is passed to datToday, a date-type parameter referenced within the NextDay function.

Notice that the argument, datStartDate, has a different name from datToday, the parameter for which the value of datStartDate is passed. This is because an argument is passed to its corresponding parameter by position and data type, not by name.

Caution
Don't be misled by many examples that use the same name for a variable passed as an argument and for its corresponding parameter.

Also, don't be misled by application- or file-wide variables or local variables in a calling routine that have the same name as parameters: The parameters are local variables to the procedure and it is therefore their values that are changed and do not affect any other variables' values.

Procedure Calls and the VB Stack

Many programming languages, including VB, set aside a special area of memory known as the stack for holding temporary values. Among the temporary values stored on the stack are all local variables and the parameters of procedures, as well as the return values of function procedures.

Whenever VB calls a procedure, it initializes space on the stack for:

Part

I

Ch

3

◆ The memory address of the caller to this procedure

◆ The memory addresses of any parameters

◆ Any local variables in the procedure

◆ Return value of the routine, if it's a function procedure

Once VB encounters the End Sub or End Function in the procedure, it returns to the address of the caller, uses any return value or modified parameter as needed, and then frees that part of the stack for other uses. This is the reason local variables have their limited lifetimes: their references on the stack are destroyed once the routine is over.

▶ **See** "The Visual Basic Stack and Variable Scope," **p. 51**

You will find it useful to learn about the stack when answering some of the questions on the Certification Exam and for better understanding the reasons for the way VB passes arguments to routines.

▶ **See** "Understanding the Differences between C and Data Types," **p. 538**

By Reference and By Value Arguments

Since VB passes memory addresses on the stack from caller to subroutine, you can see that it doesn't matter that the argument names used by the caller don't match the parameter names in the procedure.

Both caller and subroutine are looking at the same memory address when the caller passes an argument that the subroutine sees as a parameter.

In the following example, the function NextWorkingDay takes as its parameter a date-type variable, which it calls datToday. Notice that in the course of executing the code block, NextWorkingDay modifies the value of datToday, incrementing it by a value of either 1 or 2.

```
Function NextWorkingDay(datToday As Date) As Date
     Dim intDayOfWeek as Integer
     'Examine the argument, and
     'if it falls on Sunday or Saturday, change it to
'the following Monday's date
     intDayOfWeek = WeekDay(datToday)
     If intDayOfWeek = vbSunday Then
          datToday = datToday + 1
        ElseIf intDayOfWeek = vbSaturday Then
          datToday = datToday + 2
     EndIf
     'If the argument is Friday, next working day is Monday
     If intDayOfWeek = vbFriday Then
     NextWorkingDay = datToday + 3
'Otherwise, it's the next day.
     Else
     NextWorkingDay = datToday + 1
EndIf
End Function
```

In the following example, we call the NextWorkingDay function, passing a Date-type variable, datStartDate, to the function. When we display the value of datStartDate after the function has run, we see that it has changed. When the function changed the value of its parameter, it changed the contents of the memory location of datStartDate.

```
Dim datTomorrow As Date
Dim datStartDate As Date
datStartDate = Now
datTomorrow = NextWorkingDay(datStartDate)
? datStartDate          'value was changed in the function
```

When VB passes the original address of an argument to a procedure as a parameter, we say that VB has passed the argument By Reference. Passing By Reference is the default method for argument passing in VB. Changes made to the parameter by the procedure will appear in the variable passed as an argument from the calling routine. This is because both the argument and the parameter point to the same memory location.

Sometimes, however, we would rather not allow changes to be made to the variables we pass as arguments to our function or procedure. In such cases, we can force VB to make a copy of the argument at another memory location and pass the copy instead of the original. Thus, the subroutine gets the same value as the original argument, but doesn't get its hands on the underlying variable. This style of argument-passing is known as passing By Value.

We can specify that a parameter always be passed By Value by putting the keyword ByVal before its name in the subroutine's declaration:

```
Function NextWorkingDay(ByVal datToday As Date) As Date
```

In the preceding example, VB always uses a copy of any variable that a caller passes to datToday, rather than passing the original memory address.

> **Note** Notice that the ByVal keyword is placed in front of the specified parameter within the procedure declaration. An alternative way to specify by value passing is to use parentheses () instead of the keyword ByVal. ■

▶ **See** "Extra Parentheses Around Each Argument Passed by Value," **p. 102**

Multiple Arguments

Our examples of procedures with parameters in this chapter have so far shown only a single parameter in the subroutine declaration. If we wish to pass more than one value at a time to a subroutine, we need only specify several parameters separated by commas in the parameter list.

In the following example, the more generalized function NextDay takes a second parameter telling the function whether to return the next working day rather than simply the next calendar date (sorry, holidays are included):

```
Function NextDay(datToday As Date, _
blnWorkingDay As Boolean) As Date
Dim intDayOfWeek as Integer
If blnWorkingDay Then
     'Examine the argument, and
     'if it falls on Sunday or Saturday, change it to
     'the following Monday's date
     intDayOfWeek = WeekDay(datToday)
     If intDayOfWeek = 1 Then
          datToday = datToday = datToday + 1
     ElseIf intDayOfWeek = 7 Then
          datToday = datToday = datToday + 2
     EndIf
     'If the argument is Friday, next working day is Monday
     If intDayOfWeek = 6 Then
          NextDay = datToday + 3
     'Otherwise, it's the next day.
     Else
          NextDay = datToday + 1
     EndIf
Else
     NextDay = datToday + 1
End If
End Function
```

Note The Weekday function seen in the example is a built-in VB function, which returns an integer indicating the day of the week (1 = Sunday, 7 = Saturday). VB 4.0 uses constants such as vbSunday, vbMonday, and so forth to test these values. ▪

When calling the NextDay function, provide two arguments (note that the second argument is a literal value rather than a variable):

```
Dim datTomorrow As Date
Dim datStartDate As Date
datStartDate = Now
datTomorrow = NextDay(datStartDate, False)
```

Optional Arguments and the IsMissing() Function

Visual Basic 4.0 provides a way to specify optional arguments. To define an optional argument, place the Optional keyword in front of the corresponding parameter. In addition, you need to define the parameter as a variant.

Of course, you'll have to write extra logic in your procedure to determine whether or not the argument was passed by the specified caller.

The procedure uses the IsMissing( ) function to determine whether the caller has passed a value to the parameter.

We have changed the example in the previous section to indicate that the second argument is optional. The IsMissing( ) function is used to check whether the caller passed a value to the Optional parameter. If not, the procedure assigns a default value for the Optional parameter.

```
Function NextDay(datToday As Date, _
Optional blnWorkingDay As Variant) As Date
If IsMissing(blnWorkingDay) Then
     blnWorkingDay = False
End If
...
```

In the previous example, if a value is not passed to bInWorkingDay, its value is set to False.

You can call the NextDay function by passing a value to the second parameter or by ignoring the second parameter entirely:

```
datTomorrow = NextDay(datStartDate, True)
datTomorrow = NextDay(datStartDate, False)
datTomorrow = NextDay(datStartDate)
```

Note All parameters listed after the first Optional keyword are optional as well, and you must use the Optional keyword before each Optional parameter. All Optional parameters must be declared as Variant. ■

Array Arguments and the ParamArray Argument

You say a specific number of optional parameters isn't good enough and you want to pass an undetermined number of optional parameters whenever you feel like it? Well, all right.

VB can do that for you with a ParamArray argument. The ParamArray argument must appear last in your parameter list in the procedure's declaration.

You must observe the following rules to implement a variable number of parameters in a procedure declaration:

◆ Specify the final parameter as an array by appending a set of parentheses to its name

- ◆ Place the keyword ParamArray before the parameter name
- ◆ Specify as Variant type

You can then put code within the procedure to check the array's upper and lower bounds and process its elements.

In this example, we write a procedure that can accept an indeterminate number of TextBox parameters and convert the contents of each TextBox control's Text property to all uppercase or all lowercase.

We first initialize two Private constants to indicate an upper- or lower-case flag:

```
[General Declarations]
Option Explicit
Private Const intUCase = 1
Private Const intLCase = 2
```

In this procedure, we take an initial parameter to indicate whether to convert to upper- or lowercase, and then we specify a ParamArray that holds the TextBox controls whose Text properties we want to convert:

```
Private Sub ConvertText(intType As Integer, _
ParamArray boxes() As Variant)
    Dim BoxCounter As Integer          'For loop counter
    Dim FirstBox As Integer            '1st array element index
    Dim LastBox As Integer             'last array element index
    FirstBox = LBound(boxes)           'get 1st element index
    LastBox = UBound(boxes)            'get last element index
    For BoxCounter = FirstBox To LastBox
        If intType = intUCase Then
           boxes(BoxCounter).Text _
          = UCase(boxes(BoxCounter).Text)
        Else
           boxes(BoxCounter).Text _
          = LCase(boxes(BoxCounter).Text)
        End If
    Next BoxCounter
End Sub
```

We can call the routine with the names of as many text boxes as we wish:

```
[Click event procedure of a command button]
Private Sub cmdConvert_Click()
    ConvertText intUCase, Text1, Text2, Text3, Text4
    ConvertText intLCase, Text2, Text3
End Sub
```

Using Exit Sub or Exit Function as an Escape Hatch

You can use Exit Sub or Exit Function to immediately cause Visual Basic to terminate the current procedure or function. No more code in this procedure or function will execute, the stack area allocated for this routine will be cleared, and control will return to the calling code.

Sticklers for good structured programming techniques try to avoid using Exit Sub/Function as much as possible. Thus, if you had a routine that needed to check some condition before running, you could put an If construct around all the code in the routine, so the routine would only do its business if some condition were true:

```
Sub MySub()
If IsBadIdea Then
     '. . . do everything the routine is supposed to do
End If
End Sub
```

A slightly less awkward way to accomplish this would be to use the Exit Sub statement if you encountered a bad condition:

```
Sub MySub()
If Not IsBadIdea Then Exit Sub
'. . . do everything the routine is supposed to do
End Sub
```

Using Exit Sub in the previous example is perhaps an aesthetic choice. Structured programming purists will argue that you shouldn't use it because it promotes unmaintainability, whereas others will argue that having the entire procedure's code wrapped in some initial evaluation is logically silly.

The following example, however, would be tedious to implement without Exit Sub/Function. In this example, something happens nested way down inside some internal logic that causes us to want to drop everything we're doing in the routine immediately. While it's possible to set up a bunch of flags and checks to avoid using an Exit, the extra effort makes the code harder to follow and easy to break. Exit Sub/Function, on the other hand, provides a quick escape hatch to escape the whole mess and forget about it:

Part
I

Ch
3

```
Sub MySub()
'. . . do everything the routine is supposed to do
'. . . and then, maybe somewhere way down nested
'. . . a couple of levels into some loops or If
'. . . constructs, we just need to GET OUT NOW:
Do While something
     If somethingelse Then
    'Try doing this without Exit Sub —
        Exit Sub 'we're outta here!
    EndIf
Loop'. . . etc. etc.
End Sub
```

Caution
Although an Exit Sub/Function can be handy, use it sparingly, because overuse can mean more difficulty at the debugging stage and code maintenance nightmares.

Calling Conventions for Procedures

Thus far, we've reviewed the basics of how sub and function procedures are called.

The following explores variations in calling sub and function procedures.

Positional versus Named Arguments

There are two ways to specify arguments—positional and named. Up to this point, we have exclusively used positional arguments.

Positional arguments are identified by their particular order in the argument list. Take, for example, the NextDay function. Assume that NextDay requires two values, datToday and bInWorkingDay:

```
Function NextDay(datToday As Date, _
blnWorkingDay As Boolean) As Date
'some code
End Function
```

When we call the NextDay function, we are obligated to pass the date variable first and the Boolean value as the second argument because this order has been defined for us in the NextDay function procedure:

```
datTomorrow = NextDay(datStartDate, false)
```

Visual Basic's own functions, procedures, statements, and methods support positional arguments. For example:

```
strResponse=MsgBox(prompt[, buttons][, title][, helpfile,
context])
```

If I call the Msgbox function, I must pass the arguments in the order specified by the Msgbox function. This requires that I maintain a placeholder for the third argument, title, if I do not pass title an explicit value.

```
iSave=Msgbox("Save current record?",vbYesNo, ,"DEMO.HLP",1000)
```

Named arguments eliminate the need to pass arguments in a predefined order. The VBA language engine, now included in VB 4.0, allows you to pass arguments without concern over the order they are passed. This new feature, however, requires some additional work to pass named arguments.

```
Function NextDay(datToday As Date, _
blnWorkingDay As Boolean) As Date
'some code
End Function
```

In the previous example, we have defined the parameter names within the NextDay function as blnWorkingDay and datToday. When calling the NextDay function, these parameter names must be used in order to pass the arguments in any desired order. For example, calling the NextDay function can take on many forms:

```
datTomorrow = NextDay(datToday := datStartDate, _
blnWorkingDay := false)
```

or

```
datTomorrow = NextDay(blnWorkingDay := false , _
 datToday := datStartDate)
```

Remember, named arguments do not eliminate the need to pass required arguments. It simply alleviates the need to pass the arguments in a particular order.

Tip

The use of named arguments also applies to some of VB 4.0's procedures, functions and statements. However, named arguments aren't supported universally in Visual Basic 4.0. If you are not sure, consult Help or the Object Browser on the specific topic. For example:

```
iSave=MsgBox Title:="SAVE", Prompt:="Save current record?",
Buttons:=vbYesNo
```

The following is a summary of the advantages of named arguments:

- Your code is easier to read and maintain
- You don't have to provide blank placeholders in your argument list for unused optional arguments
- You don't have to pass arguments in the default order

Calling Sub Procedures with the CALL Statement

There are two ways to invoke a sub procedure:

```
ConvertText intLCase, Text1, Text2, Text3
```

or

```
CALL ConvertText(intLCase, Text1, Text2, Text3)
```

When you use the keyword CALL to invoke a sub procedure, you must enclose the argument list in parentheses, whether there is one argument or multiple arguments.

Caution

If you are not passing any arguments, do not use parentheses with the CALL keyword:

```
Call MySub()     'Wrong
Call MySub       'Correct
```

Extra Parentheses Around Each Argument Passed by Value

You can always force an argument to a procedure to pass by value, regardless of whether the procedure's declaration specifies ByVal or takes the default By Reference. All you have to do is put an extra set of parentheses around each individual argument that you wish to pass by value. Even though the procedure's declaration might specify that the parameter is passed by value, the extra set of parentheses around an argument will cause the argument to be passed by value instead.

In the first call to the NextDay procedure in the following example, notice the extra set of parentheses around the first parameter, datToday. This specifies that datToday will be passed by value. The second call does not contain extra parentheses around its arguments, and so VB will pass each argument as specified by the procedure.

```
'datToday will be passed by Value:
datTomorrow = NextDay((datToday), blnWorkingDay)
'datToday will be passed by Reference:
datTomorrow = NextDay(datToday, blnWorkDay)
```

The following sub procedure calls would not normally use parentheses around its arguments (notice these examples do not include the keyword CALL, which requires an initial set of parentheses around all of its arguments). The first example indicates that the argument bInWantUnload is to be passed by value since the argument is surrounded by parentheses. Observe the sub procedure call, which passes multiple arguments. Notice that the argument list itself takes no parentheses, but the parentheses around the argument, text2, indicates that text2 will be passed by value.

```
 'blnWantUnload will be passed by Value:
CleanUp (blnWantUnload)
'Text2 will be passed by Value:
ConvertText intUCase, Text1, (Text2)
'blnWantUnload will be passed as specified by the CleanUp
procedure:
CleanUp blnWantUnload
'Text2 will be passes as specified by the ConvertText:
ConvertText intUCase, Text1, Text2
```

The final examples display sub procedure calls that use the CALL keyword to invoke a procedure. As we know, parentheses must surround argument lists when the keyword, CALL, is used. However, notice a second parenthesis around any argument that will be passed by value.

```
 'blnWantUnload will be passed by Value:
CALL CleanUp((blnWantUnload))
'Text2 will be passed by Value:
CALL ConvertText (intUCase, Text1, (Text2))
```

```
'blnWantUnload will be passed as specified by the CleanUp
procedure:
CALL CleanUp(blnWantUnload)
'Text2 will be passed as specdified by the ConvertText proce-
dure:
CALL ConvertText (intUCase, Text1, Text2)
```

Use of Parentheses When Ignoring a Function's Return Value

You can call a function without using its return value simply by omitting a variable to absorb the return value as well as omitting the parentheses around the argument list.

Assume we have a function, MyFunc, which takes two parameters. In this instance, the return value of MyFunc is assigned to a variable called RetVal:

```
RetVal = MyFunc(MyParam1, MyParam2)
```

If you don't plan to use the function's return value, however, simply call the function in the same way you would call a sub procedure, omitting a reference to the return value as well as parentheses around the argument list:

```
MyFunc MyParam1, MyParam2
```

And finally, if you don't need the return value but need to make sure an argument is passed by value, just remember to put the extra parentheses around any arguments you wish to be passed by value. In the following example, MyParam1 will be passed by value:

```
MyFunc (MyParam1), MyParam2
```

Note   This rule works with built-in VB functions as well. For example, you can call the MsgBox function with or without using its return value:

```
intChoice = MsgBox("Continue?", vbYesNo)
MsgBox "There are no customers left." ■
```

Scope of Procedures

In Chapter 2, we reviewed the different types of scope, or visibility assigned to a variable within a VB application. Recall that a variable's scope is determined, in part, by the keyword used to declare it.

Procedures follow scoping rules similar to the scoping rules for variables. You can use the keywords Private or Public to indicate the scope of a procedure.

Visual Basic offers two distinct levels of availability or scope for procedures within an application—Private(Module-level) or Public(Project level):

◆ Private(Module-level). Private procedures can only be called from other procedures within the same Form, Standard, or Class module. If you place the keyword *Private* before the procedure name, the compiler only recognizes the procedure's name from code that runs from within the same Form, Standard, or Class module.

◆ Although the keyword, Private, is not explicitly stated, the default scope for Event procedures is Private.

```
Sub Command1_Click() 'Event procedures are Private by
default.  The 'Private keyword is inplied.
Private Sub MySub(MyParam as Integer)'Sub procedure
with private scope
Private  Function MyFunc(MyParam1 as Integer) as
Long'Function procedure with private scope
```

◆ Public(Project-level). Public procedures can be called from anywhere within the project. If you place the keyword *Public* before the procedure name, the compiler recognizes the procedure's name from anywhere in your application.

```
Public Sub MySub(MyParam as Integer) 'Sub procedure
with public scope
Public  Function MyFunc(MyParam1 as Integer) as Long
'Function procedure
'with public scope
Public  Function MyFunc(MyParam1 as Integer) as Long
'Same Public scope as previous line. 'general proce-
dures are, by default, Public.
```

◆ Although the keyword, Public, does not need to be explictly stated, the default scope for general procedures is Public.

◆ Remember, however, that even if it's Public, you must call a routine in a Form from elsewhere in your application with the form name prefixed to the routine name. When you call a

Form's public routine from elsewhere in the application, in other words, you must call the routine as if it were a method of the Form:

```
frmMain.MySub intPara1
```

 Note You may call general procedures stored in Standard modules with the module name in front of the routine, but this is not required. ■

 Note In previous versions of Visual Basic, all routines stored in a Form automatically had Private scope and could not be changed to Public scope. ■

Writing Conditional Code and Control Structures

The backbone of a modern structured programming language is its implementation of the control structures of looping (or iteration) and branching (or selection). These control structures allow the programmer to efficiently and consistently enable selective and repeated execution of lines of program code. VB, of course, offers its special control structures to let you perform these basic chores.

Branching or Selection

VB offers two basic types of branching constructs:

- ◆ The If structure, used most often when you want to implement one or two alternative execution routes in your code, or when there are multiple alternatives with disparate conditions
- ◆ The Case structure, used when there are multiple alternatives for the same expression or variable value

If

You use an If statement when you want code that follows the If statement to execute conditionally. An If statement always has the keyword If followed by a logical condition (a condition that can evalute to true or false) and terminates with the keyword *Then*.

In the If construct's simplest form, all the lines that follow the If statement up through the End If statement will execute only if the condition is true. If the If condition is not met, program control is moved to the last line, End If:

```
If UCase(Left(LastName,2)) = "MC" Then
    '. . . Do some stuff
End If
```

The second simplest form of the If statement allows a second set of statements to execute when the condition is false. In such a situation, you insert the Else statement between the If and the End If. Everything between the Else and the End If will execute only if the condition is false:

```
If UCase(Left(LastName,2)) = "MC" Then
    '. . . Do some stuff
Else
    '. . . Do something different
End If
```

Finally, if you have several conditions and wish to have something different happen in each case, you can put as many instances as you need of the ElseIf statement inside the If construct. The line containing ElseIf statement must have a condition to evaluate and ends with the word Then. Everything after the ElseIf up to the next ElseIf, Else, or End If will execute provided:

◆ The condition of the ElseIf is true

◆ No previous condition in the If construct was true. In other words, no more than one of the branches of an If construct will execute each time the program runs through the If construct.

You can put a final Else condition between the last ElseIf and the End If if you need to catch any situation where none of the previous conditions were true (a "none of the above" condition):

```
If UCase(Left(LastName,2)) = "MC" Then
    '. . .
ElseIf UCase(Left(LastName,2)) = "O'" Then
    '. . .
ElseIf UCase(Left(LastName,3)) = "VAN" Then
    '. . .
ElseIf UCase(Left(LastName,2)) = "DE" Then
    '. . .
Else      'Handle all other types of last name
    '. . .
End If
```

The If Construct within One Line of Code

If there is only one line of code to run between the If and the End If,
you can put that line right after the Then and leave off the End If:

```
If IsBadIdea Then MsgBox "Bad"
```

Similarly, if there is also an Else clause with only one line of code as
well, you can include the Else clause on the same line. Similar to the
previous example, the End If is not required:

```
If IsBadIdea Then MsgBox "Bad" Else MsgBox "Good"
```

Case

The Case structure also offers conditional branching, but with more
limited use. It's only practical to use a Case structure when you want to
take different actions based on different values of the same variable or
expression.

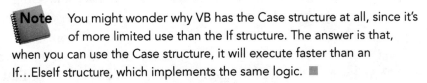

Note   You might wonder why VB has the Case structure at all, since it's
of more limited use than the If structure. The answer is that,
when you can use the Case structure, it will execute faster than an
If…ElseIf structure, which implements the same logic. ■

A Case structure begins with the words Select Case, followed on the
same line by the variable or an expression to be evaluated.

The Case structure ends with a line containing the words End Select.
Between the Select Case and End Select statements you can put any
number of Case statements. After each Case statement, place a value for
the expression or variable that is being evaluated. The lines of code following the Case and continuing until the next Case or the End Select

will execute if the Select Case statement's expression matches the value provided by the Case.

In the following example, the comparison expression is UCase(Left(ProductID,3)). Assuming that the first three characters of ProductID specify the product's color, the following example provides three possible values for UCase(Left(ProductID,3)):

```
Select Case UCase(Left(ProductID,3))
    Case "RED"
    '. . .
    Case  "BLU"
    '. . .
    Case "YLW"
    '. . .
End Select
```

> **Note** As with the If construct, no more than one of the Case construct's options will execute within a single pass through the construct. ▪

Enumerating Values in a Case

You can go beyond enumerating one or more simple values in the Case statement.

◆ You can use the keyword Is before a comparison operator (<, <=, >, >= and so on) when evaluating literals. (Even if you omit the Is when typing, VB will automatically include it for you).

◆ You can enumerate possible individual values in a comma-separated list.

◆ You can use the keyword To between two values to designate an inclusive range.

◆ You can combine any of the three previous options together.

```
Dim MyStuff As String
MyStuff = UCase(Left(Text1.Text, 1))
Select Case MyStuff
Case Is < "C" 'A or B
        MsgBox "Before C"
Case "D", "E" 'D or E
        MsgBox "D, E"
```

```
              Case Is < "K", "Z"  'evaluates the following choices: C
              F,G,H,I,J,Z
                      MsgBox "<K, Z"
              Case "K" To "M"     'evaluates the following choices: K,
              L, M
                      MsgBox "K-M"
         Case "N" To "Q", "S"   'evaluates the following choices: N, O,
         P, Q, S
                 MsgBox "N-Q, S"
         End Select
```

Case Else or "None of the Above"

Case Else is optional and is inserted as the last case statement. It represents a "None of the Above" option where none of the previous Case statements satisfied the evaluating variable or expression:

```
    '. . . other Case statements
    Case Else
            MsgBox "N/A"
          End Select
```

Looping

VB offers the programmer a veritable cornucopia of Looping constructs (at least seven at last count). Though you could get by with just one looping construct, it's nice to know that there is a looping construct for every need.

Do While...Loop for a Loop that May Never Run

The Do While Loop is useful when you want code to run only while a given condition is true.

A Do While construct begins with a line containing the Do While statement that includes a logical condition that evaluates to a true or false.

All the lines of code between the Do While and the Loop statements will execute as long as the condition in the Do While is true. The loop is terminated when the loop's condition evaluates to false. Because the condition is at the beginning of the Do Loop, it's possible that program control will never pass through the loop if the initial condition is evaluated to false. For example:

```
Do While intOptions > 0
    . . .
      intOptions = intOptions - 1
Loop
```

The loop will run if the initial value of intOptions is 12 but will never run if the initial value of intOptions is –4.

Do...Loop While for a Loop that Runs at Least Once

If VB only offered the Do While. . . construct, you would have to go through some contortions if there were a loop which always needed to run at least a single time. You might have to "prime the loop" by artificially contriving to make the Do While condition true before the loop began.

For these types of situations, you can simply include the condition within the Loop statement at the end of the loop. In this way, the condition will never be evaluated until the loop has already run once.

```
Do
    . . .
      intChoice = MsgBox("Do another one?", vbYesNo)
Loop While intChoice = vbYes
```

Do Until...Loop for a Loop on a Negative Condition

Many structured programming purists feel that having to use a negative condition in a Loop's While clause makes a loop less easy to understand. To address this concern, VB provides the Do as long as the condition specified after the word Until is *not* true. That is, the loop will terminate as soon as the condition is evaluated to true:

```
Do Until datQuestions.RecordSet.EOF
    . . .
      datQuestions.RecordSet.MoveNext
Loop
```

The same example with a negative condition in a Do While clause would read:

```
Do While NOT datQuestions.RecordSet.EOF
    . . .
      datQuestions.RecordSet.MoveNext
Loop
```

Do...Loop Until

As with the Do While loop, you can place the Until condition after the Loop keyword. This ensures that VB will always run the loop once before the Loop Until statement gets a chance to evaluate the condition for the first time.

```
Do
    . . .
    strUserResponse = Trim(txtResponse.Text)
Loop Until strUserResponse = ""
```

The For...Next Loop

In contrast to the Do...Loop, which interates based on a condition, the For...Next loop iterates through the loop a specified number of times. Thus, a For...Next loop requires a counter which tracks that number of loop iterations.

The programmer must initialize a loop counter variable (usually an integer type), which will be incremented upon each pass through the loop. The structure of the For statement looks like:

```
For lcv = StartValue To StopValue
```

The lcv variable, a common name in VB program documentation samples for the counter variable, stands for the loop counter variable. StartValue and StopValue are the starting and ending values for the loop counter variable. VB will automatically increment the loop counter variable by 1 on each successive pass through the For...Next loop.

The Next statement ends the For loop. You may put the name of the loop counter variable after the Next statement, but this is optional.

```
Dim lcv as Integer
For lcv = 1 To 10
    msgBox "Square of " & lcv & " is " _
        & lcv * lcv
Next lcv    'use of lcv name is optional here
```

The start and stop values in the For statement can be literal values typed directly into your code, as in the above example, or one or both of them can be a variable or constant:

```
For intCounter = 1 To intMaX    'where intMax=25
```

By default, the increment of the loop counter variable is 1. If you want to increment by some value other than 1, you can specify a Step quantity, using the following optional syntax:

```
For lcv = StartValue To StopValue Step Increment
```

The value of Step can represent a negative or even a fractional number:

```
For intCounter = 10 To 0 Step -1
    txtCountDown.text = Str(intCounter)
Next intCounter
```

Because VB changes the loop counter variable each time it encounters the Next statement, the lcv will increment (or decrement if Step is a negative value) one more time than there are passes through the loop. Thus, in the code

```
Dim intCounter as Integer
For intCounter = 1 To 10
    msgBox "Square of " & intCounter & " is " _
        & intCounter * intCounter
Next intCounter
MsgBox "lcv = " & intCounter
```

the value of intCounter in the final line will be 11.

The For Each...Next Statement

You can traverse all the objects in a collection without knowing either their names or the number of objects in the collection. The For Each...Next construct takes a placeholder variable, similar to the For...Next loop. In contrast to the For...Next loop, however, this placeholder does not represent a counter but rather an object of the type found in the collection. The object points to each element of the collection as we iterate through the loop. This allows us the possibility to evaluate and manipulate any of the collection's elements. The format of the For Each...statement is:

```
For Each ObjVarName in CollectionName
```

Just as you must first declare a variable to represent the counter in a For...Next loop, so you must first declare a variable of the appropriate object type to represent the For Each...Next loop's placeholder:

```
Dim ctrlCurrControl as Control
For Each ctrlCurrControl in Controls
```

```
       If TypeOf ctrlCurrControl Is TextBox Then
             ctrlCurrControl.Text = ""
       EndIf
   Next ctrlCurrControl
```

Notice that we can reference the placeholder's name after the word "Next" in the loop's final line. As is the case with the For...Next loop, this usage is optional.

▶ **See** "Working with Collections," **p. 72**

Getting Out of a Loop in a Hurry with Exit

We spoke of how to quickly exit a procedure or function in the previous section, "Using Exit Sub or Exit Function as an Escape Hatch." Similarly, you can stop the currently executing loop cold in its tracks with an Exit statement. If you're in the middle of one of the Do loops (Do While/Until...Loop, Do...Loop While/Until), the statement

```
   Exit Do
```

will cause VB to go immediately to the first line following the end of the current loop.

> **Caution**
> You can't use Exit Do in a While...Wend construct. This will generate a compiler error. See the discussion of While...Wend in the section entitled "While...Wend" later in this chapter.

If it's a For...Each or For...Next loop you need to exit in a hurry,

```
   Exit For
```

will do the trick. As with the Exit Do, VB will immediately begin processing the first line after the For...Next loop.

> **Caution**
> As when using Exit within procedures, use Exit in looping structures sparingly, because they can make your code harder to follow at maintenance time.

The With...End With Statement

Although the With...End With construct is not technically a control structure (it doesn't redirect flow of execution), it does affect all the lines of code inside it. This construct has two advantages—it saves you some typing and it helps your code to execute faster.

You can use this construct when you need to call several methods or properties belonging to the same object, such as a form, control, or other type of object (such an OLE server or a user-defined class). You begin the construct with the line

```
With ObjectName
```

and then everything between this line and the End With can refer to one of the object's properties without requiring you to type the object name. Instead of typing *ObjectName.Method/Property* you only need to type *.Method/Property* inside the With...End With construct. You could, for example, replace the code:

```
frmMain.Caption = "Hello, World"
frmMain.Top = 0
frmMain.Show
```

with:

```
With frmMain
    .Caption = "Hello, World"
    .Top = 0
    .Show
End With
```

You can nest With constructs within each other. Thus, in the following example, we can refer to a Data Control's RecordSet object using a nested With construct within the With construct for the Data Control:

```
With Data1
    .Caption = "Categories"
    .RecordSetType = dbOpenTable
    .RecordSource = "Categories"
    .Refresh
    With Data1.RecordSet
        .MoveFirst
        .Index = "ID"
    End With
End With
```

Part

I

Ch

3

Notice that, even though the RecordSet object belongs to the Data control and appears inside the Data control's With construct, we still had to make full reference to the RecordSet (including the Data Control) when we started its own With construct.

> **Caution**
> Although you can nest With constructs within each other, you must be sure to give the entire object name for each nested With.

Obsolete Techniques

There are many ways to modify flow-of-control in VB. Some of them are included for downward compatibility with earlier versions of BASIC and aren't recommended by Microsoft for new development. The two techniques discussed here are from earlier versions of the BASIC language—before VB came on the scene.

While...Wend

The While...Wend construct is similar to a Do...Loop with some limitations. First, you are limited to placing the condition at the top of the loop. Second, the While...Wend construct does not recognize any type of Exit device. That is, While...Wend constructs do not allow you to exit the loop early.

```
While intOptions > 0
        . . .
        intOptions = intOptions - 1
Wend
```

> **Caution**
> If you invoke Exit Do within a While...Wend construct, you will generate a compiler error.

GoTo (Except in Error Handling)

There was a time in the history of programming when just about the only control the programmer had over flow of execution was to evaluate a condition and then jump to another place in the program based on the result of the evaluation.

Constructs like the If construct, the Case construct, and the various flavors of While and For that we find in languages like VB arose out of the difficulty programmers had in maintaining code with lots of jumping back and forth.

As a throw back to this earlier time, VB still allows you some limited ability to jump immediately to another line in your application. You can use the GoTo statement to do this. Here are the rules for using GoTo:

◆ You can only jump to a location inside the current routine.

◆ You must jump to a named label. A named label is a line in VB that contains some unique name followed by a semicolon.

```
GoTo JumpPoint
'. . .this code gets skipped
JumpPoint:
'. . .do some stuff after the jump
```

Note   We will, however, see in Chapter 5, "Handling Errors," that we use GoTo in VB to construct error handlers. Therefore, a statement like:

On Error GoTo JumpPoint

is a standard approach to contructing VB error handlers. ▪

Common String Manipulation Functions

As we mentioned in the previous chapter on data types, the String is one of the programmer's favorite data types because it is so easy to chop, slice, dice, and splice strings.

In the following sections, we discuss some of the workhorse functions used to parse string expressions.

Left

The Left function takes two parameters—a string expression to parse, and a number representing how many of the leftmost characters we want returned from the string.

```
strMyName = "Bill M. Smith"
strFirst = Left(strMyName,4)
```

After the above code runs, the value of strFirst is "Bill."

Right

The Right function works like the Left function, but instead of giving us the leftmost characters, it returns the rightmost characters:

```
strMyName = "Bill M. Smith"
strLast = Right(strMyName,5)
```

After the above code runs, the value of strLast is "Smith."

Mid

Use the Mid function in those ticklish situations where you need to dice out something from neither the right nor the left side of a string, but from the middle. Mid takes three arguments:

◆ The string to examine

◆ The position of the starting character (1-based)

◆ The number of character to parse (starting with the character position specified in the second argument)

Suppose you know that the ProductID field in a database table represents specific information about the product. In the following example, the product color is stored in strProductID. The character position of 5-7 represents the product color. We can parse out the color code by passing three arguments to the MID function. The variable strProductColor in the example contains the string "BLU" in positions 5-7. The second argument, 5, represents the first character position of the expression you want to parse. The third argument represents the number of characters you want to parse from the starting position.

```
strProductID = "423-BLU-099"
strProductColor= Mid(strProductID, 5, 3)
```

The Mid function is even more versatile than that, however. It not only dices, it slices! And how does it accomplish this amazing feat? Simply by leaving off the third parameter. If you don't tell Mid how many characters you want after the designated position, it goes nuts and grabs all characters through the end of the string. The following example will return everything in the string from the ninth position through the end of the string:

```
strMyName="John J. Thomas"
strLast = Mid(strMyName,9)
```

strLast will return "Thomas," because the "T" in "Thomas" is the ninth character in the string and therefore Mid will return everything from the ninth character on.

Instr

The Instr function doesn't return a string as do the other string manipulation functions. Instead, it returns an integer pointing to a position in a string where a character pattern was found. You can therefore use Instr to find things out about strings and then manipulate them with this information.

Instr takes two required parameters, both strings:

- ◆ The string to examine
- ◆ The string expression to search for

In the following example, we check for a space in the string variable strName. If Instr returns a non-zero value, representing the starting character position of the string expression you are searching for, then we parse all characters to the left of the space as a first name:

```
strName="John Thomas"
intSpacePos = Instr(strName ," ") 'look for a space
If intSpacePos <> 0 Then          'There's a space
    'and everything to its left is the first name
    strFirst = Left(strName intSpacePos-1)
End If
```

Instr takes a third, optional argument. We say "third" only figuratively, because if you use this argument, you must list it first. It is an integer representing the position from which you want Instr to start scanning the target string in its quest for a match. Thus,

```
Instr(9,MyString," ")
```

will only tell you about spaces it finds from the ninth character on in MyString. The positional number it returns, however, will be with respect to the entire original string. For example, the lines

```
strMyString = "ABCDE"
intPos = Instr(3,strMyString,"D")
```

will return the value 4 to intPos.

Len

The Len function tells you how many characters a string contains.

```
If Len(Trim(txtResponse.Text)) = 0 Then
    MsgBox "You must enter a response"
    txtResponse.SetFocus
End If
```

Note You can use the Len function with variables of any data type, not just strings. When used with these other types of variables, Len will return the amount of memory the variable uses. ▪

A Parsing Example Using String Manipulation Functions

Let's see how we could use string manipulation functions to parse a string out into individual elements, placing those elements in an array for later use. We would write a function and call it "ParseOut."

ParseOut would take three arguments—the string to be parsed (strSource), the character to use as a parsing character (strParseChar), and the array to deposit the parsed results in (strTarget), one parsed element per array element.

ParseOut would return an Integer giving the number of elements parsed out.

The basic strategy of the function is to traverse the original string looking for the parsing character. Every time we find the parsing character, we take everything to its left and put it into a new array element. Then we chop the string down to just what remains after the parsing character and repeat the operation on what remains.

When nothing is left, we know we're done. See the comment on each line of code for more detail about how this works:

```
Public Function ParseOut(ByVal strSource as String, _
strParseChar as String, _
strTarget() As String) As Integer
    'Counter for number of elements parsed:
    Dim intElements as Integer
    'Holder for the currently parsed-out element:
    Dim strCurElement as String
    'Where we found the parsing character in the string:
    Dim intParsePos as Integer
    'Make sure the array is zeroed out
    Redim strTarget(0)
    'Loop until we've run out of material to parse:
    Do
        'Find position of parsing character in string:
        intParsePos = Instr(strSource, strParseChar)
        'If we found the parsing character then
        If intParsePos > 0 Then
            'current element's everything to left of
            'where we found parsing character:
            strCurElement = _
        Left(strSource,intParsePos - 1)
            'now chop element we just used off of the
            'source string:
            strSource = _
                Mid(strSource,intParsePos + 1)
        Else      'this is the last element
            'so next parsed element is everything that
            'remains:
            strCurElement = strSource
            'and so nothing else remains to parse:
            strSource = ""
        EndIf
        'So count one more element:
        intElements = intElements + 1
        'Make another array element to hold it:
        ReDim Preserve strTarget(intElements)
        'and assign it to the new array element:
        strTarget(intElements) = strCurElement
    Loop Until strSource = ""
    'When done, the number of elements is the
    'return value of this function:
    ParseOut = intElements
End Function
```

You could call the ParseOut function with the string you wanted to parse after first preparing an empty String array. You could then use the return value of ParseOut to traverse the resulting array.

```
Dim strWords() as String
Dim iWords as Integer
Dim iCount as Integer
iWords = ParseOut(strSentence," ",strWords)
For iCount = 1 To iWords
        '. . . Do something to each word
Next iCount
```

Causing an Event to Occur in Another Event's Procedure

Usually, event procedures are triggered by a user or system action. However, sometimes code can trigger an event procedure to occur. Table 3.1 is a partial listing of common methods and statements that trigger event procedures.

Table 3.1 VB Code that Triggers Specific Event Procedures		
Action	Event caused	Controls affected
Load *FormName*	Load	Form controls are currently on the form
Initialize		Form
FormName.Show	Load	Form (only if form wasn't previously loaded)
Activate		Form
		GotFocus Form (only if not active)
UnLoad *FormName*	UnLoad	Form
Set *FormName* = Nothing	Terminate	Form (must be called after Unload)
Control.value = True	Click	Command Button, Check Box, Option Button

Action	Event caused	Controls affected
Control.Text = [string]	Change	TextBox, ComboBox
Control.SetFocus	GotFocus	any control that can receive focus
Control.SetFocus	LostFocus	happens to control which had focus up to this point

 Note See Chapter 7, "Events," for further discussion of when Form and Control events can occur. ▪

The code in the following examples cause the events noted in the comments:

```
cmdOK.Value = True      'causes the click event
txtName.Text = ""       'causes the change event
txtName.SetFocus        'causes the GotFocus event
                        'for txtName and the LostFocus
                        'event on the current control
```

Synchronizing Events with DoEvents

If you do something in an event procedure's code to cause an event to happen, when will that event actually occur? Will it necessarily occur before the subsequent lines in the calling procedure? This is not a trivial question, because Windows is a multitasking, event-driven environment and because you may be depending on the relative timing of certain event procedures with respect to certain lines of code.

Let's say you have a command button whose Click event forces the focus to another control, such as a text box. Calling that control's SetFocus method triggers its GotFocus event.

In the following code, will the Text Box' GotFocus event happen before any more of the calling procedure's code executes? In particular, will we see the "Called SetFocus" Message Box before or after the Text Box' GotFocus event runs and displays its own Message Box?

Part

I

Ch

3

```
Private Sub cmdGoToTextBox_Click()
    txtTest.SetFocus      'triggers txtText's GotFocus event
    Me.Print "Called SetFocus on txtText"
End Sub

Private Sub TxtTest_GotFocus()
    Me.Print "GotFocus event on txtTest"
End Sub
```

The answer is that you'll see the command button's event procedure code finish before you see the code in the Text Box' event procedure run. This is because Windows sees the call to TxtTest_GotFocus procedure and places its code in a Windows message queue, which it processes when it has finished the current task (the command button's Click event procedure).

But what if you're counting on the Text Box's GotFocus event to happen as soon as you invoke the SetFocus method? Fortunately, you can use DoEvents immediately after you call the SetFocus method. DoEvents tells Windows to immediately process all pending events on message queues before going on to the next line of code:

```
Private Sub cmdGoToTextBox_Click()
    txtTest.SetFocus
    DoEvents      'txtTest's GotFocus event will happen
    Me.Print "Already Set Focus"
End Sub
```

Triggering an Event Procedure versus Programmatically Forcing the Code in an Event Procedure to Run

Caution

Calling an event procedure in your VB code does not cause the event itself to happen.

You can call an event procedure from your VB code just as you call any other procedure you have written. Thus,

```
cmdOK_Click
```

is a perfectly good line of code, as long as the cmdOK_Click procedure is in scope at the moment.

Because calling an event procedure is not the same as causing the event to occur, you must make sure that you are not counting on side effects of the event to happen every time the event's procedure is called. For instance, one side effect of the Click event on a command button is for the command button to receive focus. If you call the click event procedure directly from elsewhere in your code, you can't count on the button having focus after the event procedure's code has run.

You can ensure that these desired side effects will always happen by explicitly forcing them to happen in the event procedure's code. For instance, you could call a command button's SetFocus method from its Click event procedure. Although a command button will automatically get focus when its Click event happens, the extra call to SetFocus ensures that the button will also receive focus when the event procedure is called from elsewhere:

```
Private Sub cmdOK_Click()
    cmdOK.SetFocus              'ensures we  always have focus
    If MsgBox("Is data OK?",vbYesNo) = vbYes Then
        UnLoad Me
    EndIf
End Sub
```

Tip

Don't put lots of code directly inside an event procedure. Instead, write a general procedure and call the general procedure from the event procedure. This will help standardize your control's behavior and make your project more maintainable if controls have to be renamed later.

Control Names and Event Procedure Code

Visual Basic provides you with an event procedure stub based on the control's current name. If you change the name of the control, VB will provide you with a set of new event procedure stubs based on the control's new name. The code you wrote under the previous name's event procedure still exists; however, it is no longer associated with the control whose name has been changed.

For example, if you add a command button named Command1 to a form, write code in its Click event procedure, and then change Command1's name to cmdOK—the event procedure name does not change and would still be named Sub Command1_Click. Therefore, the procedure would no longer be associated with the command button (Sub cmdOK_Click would be the name of the current Click event procedure and obviously, this event procedure contains no code).

> ### Caution
> When you rename a control, its event procedures are no longer associated with the control. For example, if you rename a text box control named txtFName to txtCompanyName, the event procedures (txtFName_Change(), for example) do not get renamed and, therefore, any code you have written in the control's event procedures are no longer associated with the control.

Conversely, if you happen to write a general procedure and later rename a control in such a way that one of its event procedure names happens to match the name of the existing general procedure, then that general procedure becomes an event procedure for the control.

For example, if you write a general procedure whose declaration looks like this:

```
Private Sub Bozo_Change()
```

and then later rename a text box control as "Bozo," VB associates the Bozo_Change procedure with the text box named "Bozo."

Tip
Finalize the names of all your controls and rename them to the desired names before you put any code in their event procedures or write any other code that calls these event procedures by name.

Class Modules

In addition to Form and Standard Modules, VB 4.0 allows the programmer to implement a Class Module.

Each Class Module lets the user implement a class for a specific type of custom object in an application, including collections of objects.

Note See Chapter 11, "OLE Servers," for a full discussion of how to implement a custom class of objects with a Class Module, including a custom collection. ▪

Standard Modules versus Class Modules

In general, you can use both Standard Modules (.BAS files) and Class Modules (.CLS files) to group common functionality in your applications.

The main conceptual difference between a Standard Module and a Class Module is that you would use a Class Module to implement custom objects in your application, while a Standard Module would group common functionality whose components nevertheless did not necessarily have any relation to each other.

You might use a Standard Module to group all your customized string handling functions and procedures (such as the parser we looked at in the earlier example in this chapter) into one convenient, shareable location. These routines have a lot in common conceptually, and they might even share some underlying utility routines and data, but they don't function together as a unit.

Examples of common types of functionality you could group together in one Standard Module would be error handling, file i/o, or data access. If the programmer takes care to keep routines in a Standard Module generic, the Standard Module's file (.BAS extension) can be shared as a general library file among various projects.

On the other hand, you'd use a Class Module to group functionality together as a coherent whole, which would provide a template for customized objects. Perhaps you might provide a class to implement an object that encapsulates the various pieces of information and actions associated with an employee, or with an open text file. In other words, Class Modules usually correspond to some real conceptual object in your program or in the world your program is modeling.

A Class provides the abstract definition, or template for an object. VB is itself based on built-in classes such as Forms, the various types of controls, and other object classes not available in the Toolbox (such as Data Access Objects). You can instantiate an object from its defining class using the techniques described in Chapters 10 "Using OLE Automation to Integrate Applications" and 11 "Creating OLE Servers."

 Note Class Modules were not available in versions of VB before version 4.0. ▪

Creating Custom Methods and Properties for a Form

VB 4.0 allows the programmer to define custom properties and methods for Forms, similarly to the way you can define them for Class Modules (see this chapter's section on Class Modules and see also Chapter 11, "Creating OLE Servers").

Custom Methods for a Form Using Public Procedures

Basically, any Public procedure in a Form module is a custom method of that form. If you wrote the following procedure in a Form:

```
Public Sub ChangeColor(lngColor As Long)
    Me.BackColor = lngColor
End Sub
```

then you could call that Sub procedure from elsewhere in your project with a line such as:

```
frmPubProp.ChangeColor vbRed
```

Notice that this call resembles a call to a VB method and that's the way Microsoft would like you to see it. You could also call a function procedure in the same way. This would then be a method that provided a return value.

As the previous example shows, to turn a procedure, which is stored in a Form, into a custom method, include the keyword Public in the procedure's name.

Using Public Procedures to Create Custom Properties for a Form

It's possible to create custom properties for a Form by using a Public variable that is declared in the Form.

The last chapter discussed the possibility of declaring a Public variable in a Form by placing the declaration in the Form's General Declarations section:

```
Public strPassword As Integer
```

Remember, you must include the Form name if you plan to reference a Form's public variable from outside the Form:

```
frmMyForm.Password= "Joe"
```

Once again, this looks exactly like a reference to a VB property, and so it is—a reference to a Form's custom property that you created.

Custom Properties for a Form with Property Let and Get Procedures

An alternative way to produce custom properties for a Form is to create Property procedures—Property Get and Property Let procedures. The Property Get and Property Let procedures enable you to create a custom property that returns a standard data type. You define the property procedures in pairs—one to assign the current value of the property (Property Let) and one to return the current value of the property. You assign both procedures the same name, which represents the name of the property.

Property Let procedure takes at least one parameter, which represents the value for the property. This parameter must always be last within the parameter list. For example, you could begin writing the Let procedure for a Form property called UserName with the following sub:

```
Sub Property Let UserName (s as string)
End Sub
```

Property Get procedure is a function procedure that simply returns the current value of the property. The beginning of the Property Get procedure for the same UserName Form property would look like this:

```
Sub Property Get UserName () as string
End Sub
```

As opposed to creating public variables to implement custom properties, property procedures offer more flexibility in controlling the value of and access to a custom property. For example, you can define a custom property as read-only if you create a Property Get procedure without a corresponding Property Let procedure.

Property procedures are created within the Form as public procedures. Property Let and Get procedures typically use a Form-level Private variable to store the value of the property between calls to the Get and Let procedures.

In the following example, a Form, called frmEmpCompensation, contains confidential employee information. Not suprisingly, a user is required to type a password before frmEmpCompensation is displayed on the screen. Once the password is verified and the Form displays, the user is able to change the password using the Tools menu. Property Let and Get procedures are used to create a custom property named Password. The Password property is used to read and write the current value of the password setting.

```
[General Declarations section of the Form]
Private strPassword as string

Public Property Let Password(NewPassword as string)
'Write code to store new value of strPassword in a file
strPassword=NewPassword
End Sub

Public Property Get Password() as string
Password=strPassword    'returns the current value of the
user's password
End Sub


Sub mnuToolsSetUserPassword()
'Code to allow user to change value of their password
strNewPassword=Inputbox("Type your new password")
'Confirm user wants to save new password
If Msgbox("You will be prompted for this password each time
you request this form" + _
vbCR + vbLF _+
"Save new password permanently?", _
vbYesNo, "Password Changes")=vbYES  Then
frmEmpCompensation.Password=strNewPassword    'call Let proce-
dure
End IF
```

The previous example uses a custom property, Password, to store and to change the value of a password required to access the Form, frmEmpCompensation. Use this example to review using property procedures when creating custom Form properties:

◆ The custom property, Password, is a property of frmEmpCompensation, the Form where the custom property is created. Use the same syntax to reference custom properties as you use to reference standard VB properties. The format for the syntax would be:

```
object.property=value  'change the property value
x=object.property    'read the property value
```

◆ Password, the name of the Let and Get property procedures, is used to name the custom property.

◆ Define the Password property procedures as public if you allow the Password property of frmEmpCompensation to be read or written outside of the Form.

Note See Chapter 11, "Creating OLE Servers," for a discussion of how to use Property Let and Property Get procedures in a Class Module. ■

Visual Basic Standard Controls

The VB standard controls form a group of controls that provide common components of a Windows standard GUI (for example, Command-Button, TextBox, and OptionBox).

In addition, Microsoft provides custom controls with all three editions of VB 4.0 (Standard, Professional, and Enterprise). These custom controls provide common components of the Windows 95 standard GUI (for example, slider, progress bar, Windows 95 status bar, and toolbar). These custom controls are only available in the 32-bit version of VB 4.0. Therefore, the Microsoft Windows custom controls are not installed with a 16-bit version of VB 4.0.

▶ **See** Common Properties of the Form Object and Control Objects," p. 213

Picture Box

The PictureBox control is used for a variety of purposes. The PictureBox is often used to display graphics in common formats and to possibly allow the user to interact with the graphic by clicking, dragging, and dropping the PictureBox. Drag-and-drop events are usually associated with a task. Imagine a PictureBox that contains an image of a document. The user can drag and drop the image of the document on top of a second PictureBox containing an image of a garbage can.

Once you have placed a PictureBox on a form, you can place a graphic into the Picture Box at design time or at run time.

To place a graphic image in a PictureBox at design time, set the Picture property using the following steps (see fig. 3.4):

1. Access the property window of a PictureBox.
2. Select the Picture property.
3. Click the Browse button (three dots) to the right of the Picture property.
4. You will see a file open dialog box.
5. Select a valid graphics file (.BMP, .WMF, .ICO).
6. Click OK.
7. You should now see the graphics image in the Picture Box control.

FIG. 3.4 ⇒

You can assign a PictureBox Control's Picture property at design time from the Properties Window.

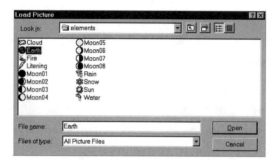

Part

I

Ch

3

You can also load a graphics image into a PictureBox control at run time with the LoadPicture function. The syntax for using LoadPicture is:

```
picBoxName.Picture = LoadPicture(FilePath)
```

where *PicBoxName* represents the name of the Picture Box control and *FilePath* represents a full path and file name to a valid graphics file.

The following code loads the image in the file "C:\Images\File.bmp" into the picFile PictureBox control:

```
picFile.Picture = LoadPicture("C:\Images\File.bmp")
```

Use the LoadPicture function, without an argument, to clear the value of the picture property:

```
picTemp = LoadPicture()
```

The previous code line would clear out the image in the picTemp PictureBox and would also free the memory used to hold the bitmap.

You can also use the picture property of another PictureBox (or Image control) to set the picture property of a PictureBox. For example, picFile.picture contains an image you want to appear in a PictureBox named picTemp:

```
picTemp.Picture = picFile.Picture
```

The three approaches to populating the picture property (assign at design time through the property window, use the LoadPicture function at run time, or assign the picture property from another PictureBox or Image at run time) produce differences in performance and efficiency.

◆ If you populate the picture property at design time, the bitmap assigned to the picture property becomes part of the executable when you compile your application. The advantage is that the bitmap is immediately available from within the application. In addition, the application doesn't need to access the disk to locate the bitmap file at run time. These advantages encourage better performance. However, the graphics data is bound to the app's exe and increases the size of the executable file.

◆ If you use the LoadPicture function to populate the picture property at run time, your application's executable will require less space. However, the application will take more time to run whenever it encounters the LoadPicture function, since the application needs to locate and load the graphics file from disk. Reading a separate file from disk requires that you make the graphics file available to each user who runs the application.

◆ This third approach to populating a picture property is widely used since it attempts to minimize some of the disadvantages mentioned in the previous two techniques.

At design time, load your graphics files into specified PictureBox or Image control. These PictureBox or Image controls will be used as containers or repositories for graphic files you will need at run time. In fact, your user will never see these PictureBox or Image controls because the visible property of these controls will be set to false.

Now, place the PictureBox controls on the form that you will be using in your application. Each time you need to display an image in this PictureBox, use the picture property from the PictureBox or Image controls that are not visible.

```
'populate picGraphics with the contents of an invisible
PictureBox named pic1
picGraphics.picture=pic1.picture
```

The AutoSize property of the PictureBox causes the boundaries of a PictureBox to snap to the actual size of the underlying graphic. Note that PictureBoxes don't have any special property or method to allow the image to stretch to fit the size and dimensions of the PictureBox (a special API function, BitBlt, allows you to do this). Image controls, however, do have a Stretch property.

Note   Like the Form, the PictureBox is considered a container object. Therefore, you can use the same graphics output methods (including the Print method) that are available to the Form object. These methods draw text or graphical elements in container objects. For more information about how these methods work, see the section "Using Significant Form Methods" in Chapter 7. ▪

▶ **See** "Image," **p. 154**

▶ **See** "Common Properties of the Form Object and Control Objects," **p. 213**

TextBox

The TextBox is one of the most handy and popular controls in a Windows application. It's a common approach to getting free-form input from the user. You can manipulate a TextBox control's contents and detect changes the user makes to the TextBox through several properties and methods:

◆ The MultiLine property is only writable at design time, though you can check its value at run-time if you wish. MultiLine is False by default, meaning that everything in the TextBox control will appear on a single line. If MultiLine is True, the TextBox will perform word-wrapping and also breaks a typed line after a hard return—perfect for populating a comment field in a database table!

◆ The ScrollBars property is only writable at design time, though its value can be checked at run-time. The default value is None, but you can also choose Horizontal, Vertical, or Both. Scrollbars enable the user to scroll through the contents of a multiple line TextBox.

◆ The SelText property is used to assign or return the contents of the currently selected text in a TextBox. If you populate the SelText property at run time, you'll replace the currently highlighted text with the contents of SelText.

◆ The SelStart property is an integer value giving you the position of the first highlighted character in the TextBox. It's zero-based. If there's no text currently selected, SelStart will represent the current position of the text cursor within the TextBox control. If you change the SelStart property at run time, you'll deselect whatever text was highlighted and move the text cursor to the indicated position.

◆ The SelLength property is an integer that indicates the number of selected characters in the TextBox. You can change SelLength at run time, for example, to change the number of selected characters. You can also deselect any highlighted characters by setting SelLength to 0.

◆ The Text property is the TextBox control's default property. You can set it at design time or run time, and you can also read it at run time. The Text property represents the current visible, editable contents of the TextBox.

◆ The Change event is the TextBox control's default event. It happens every time the Text property alters. This could be because of user input or also because your code has done something to change the Text property.

   ▶ **See** "Validating User Input with the Keystroke Events" **p. 246**

Frame

This control is considered a container because it contains other controls (see fig. 3.5). To ensure that the controls displayed on the Frame's surface are truly 'contained' in the Frame, you should click the toolbox and draw the control on the Frame instead of double-clicking the toolbox and dragging the control on top of the Frame. To test whether you have correctly placed controls on a Frame, move the Frame around the Form. The controls contained on the Frame should move along with the Frame.

Part

I

Ch

3

> **Caution**
> Don't place a control onto a Frame by just dragging it from the Form to the Frame. The control will still belong to the Form. You can test this by moving the Frame around the Form at design time. The controls, located on the Frame, should move as the Frame is being moved.

◆ The Caption property of the Frame control will set the text which appears at the upper-left of the Frame.

The Frame control also has a special relationship with OptionButton controls (also known as radio buttons). All the OptionButton controls in a Frame make a single logical unit of OptionButtons and only one of them can be selected (i.e., its value property is set to True) at any one time. If you have a set of OptionButtons on two different Frames, you will have two different mutually exclusive groups of OptionButtons.

▶ **See** "OptionButton," **p. 140**

FIG. 3.5 ⇒

A Frame control can hold other controls.

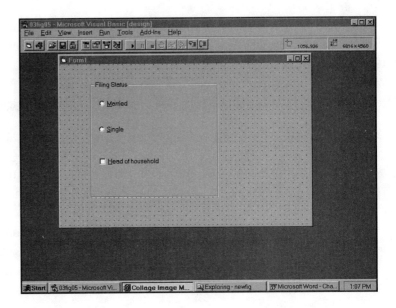

CommandButton

Along with the TextBox and Label controls, the CommandButton control is one of the most familiar sights in a Windows application.

The main function of the CommandButton control is to trigger code when the user clicks on.

◆ The Click event is the default event (i.e., the event that appears in the code window when you double-click a newly created CommandButton). Notice that the CommandButton control does not have a DoubleClick event.

◆ Caption property is the most commonly manipulated property of the CommandButton. The Caption property contains the text displayed on the CommandButton. This property can be changed at design time and run time.

◆ Cancel property is a Boolean type. It allows VB to associate the Escape key with the CommandButton's Click event procedure. Thus, if you set Cancel to true, the Click event procedure triggers when the user presses the escape key. Cancel buttons are usually associated the escape key.

Notice we did not state that the Click event itself happens. Instead, we simply say that the Click event procedure is triggered. There is a difference.

▶ **See** "Triggering an Event Procedure versus Programmatically Forcing the Code in an Event Procedure to Run," **p. 44**

◆ Default property is a Boolean type. It allows VB to associate the Enter key with the CommandButton's Click event procedure. Thus, if you set Default to true, the Click event will trigger if the user presses the enter key. Commonly, OK buttons are usually associated with the enter key.

◆ Value property is only available at run time. If you set the Value property to true within your code, the Command Button's Click event triggers and the Click event occurs. Notice that this time, we said the Click event will happen, not just that the Click event procedure will trigger.

▶ **See** "Common Properties of the Form Object and Control Objects," **p. 213**

CheckBox

Use CheckBox controls when you want to give the user a set of choices that are not mutually exclusive (see fig. 3.6). For instance, you might present a pick-list of choices for payroll deductions, including 401K, medical insurance, and dental insurance. In this case, you'd want to let the user choose more than one type of deduction if necessary.

You will typically place CheckBox controls on a Frame (though this isn't necessary).

◆ The Caption property contains the string expression located to the right of the check box. You can set this property at design time or run time.

◆ The Value property tells you the status of this CheckBox. You might be surprised to learn that there aren't just two states (vbChecked and vbUnChecked) but actually three, the third being vbGrayed. You can set this property at design time or at run time. Most importantly, however, you can read the Value property to determine whether the user has selected the CheckBox.

 Note   Setting a CheckBox control's Value property at run time will also trigger its Click event. ▓

▶ **See** "Common Properties of the Form Object and Control Objects" **p. 213**

◆ The Click event happens when the user clicks the CheckBox control. Programmers often put validation or other code in a CheckBox control's Click event procedure. Setting the Value property causes the Click event to trigger.

FIG. 3.6 ⇒
A CheckBox control's Value property can have three different settings.

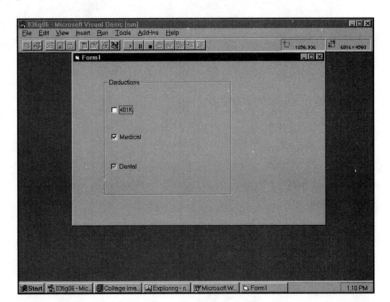

OptionButton

Use OptionButton control when you want to give the user a set of choices that are mutually exclusive (see fig. 3.7). For instance, you might present to the user a set of choices for marital status, including single, married, separated, divorced, or widowed. In this case, only one martial status is valid.

You will almost always want to put OptionButton controls on a
Frame control (see the earlier section on the Frame control). The
OptionButtons contained on a single Frame represent a set of mutually
exclusive OptionButtons where only one of the OptionButtons can be
chosen at any give time. If you have several different Frames, each with
its own set of OptionButtons, each set of OptionButtons will behave
independently of the others.

Note   In addition to OptionButtons contained on Frames, you can put
OptionButtons directly on the Form's surface. All the
OptionButtons on the Form's surface will then behave as a single group,
apart from any OptionButtons placed in Frames. ■

Part
I

Ch

3

◆ The Caption property contains the string expression located to
the right of the Checkbox. You can set it at design time or run
time.

◆ The Value property provides the status of an OptionButton,
which is either true (selected) or false (not selected). You can set
the status of an OptionButton control at run time. Only one
OptionButton in any group of OptionButtons can have its
Value set to true.

▶ **See** "Common Properties of the Form Object and Control
Objects," **p. 213**

◆ The Click event triggers when the user clicks the
OptionButton control or when the Value property is reset
within code. Programmers often put validation or other code in
an OptionButton control's Click event procedure.

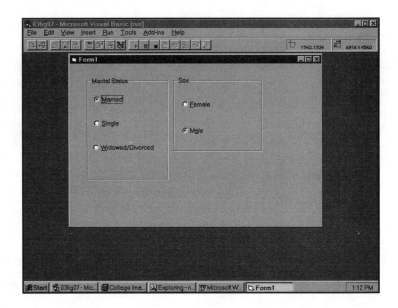

FIG. 3.7 ⇒
You can group
OptionButton
controls on differ-
ent Frames.

ComboBox

The ComboBox control (see fig. 3.8) has the following notable
properties:

◆ The IntegralHeight property is a Boolean-type value whose
default is true. When this property is set to true, you will not
see part of the last visible row of data cut off in the middle of
the row. The ComboBox height will snap to display only whole
rows.

◆ The ItemData array property can contain long integers. You can
fill it with index values to parallel the List array property.
ItemData contains an element for every run-time or design-
time element of the List array, and you can both read and set
the values of elements of ItemData by referring to the position
in the array:

```
lstNames.ItemData(lstNames.ListIndex)
```

would refer to the ItemData element of the currently selected
list element. (See the following discussion of the List array
property and the ListIndex property for further information.)

◆ The List array property contains the actual elements displayed on each of the ComboBox control's rows. At design time you can add and edit items in the list (see fig. 3.9) by selecting the List property, bringing up the drop-down list, and adding items one at a time to the list, pressing Ctrl+Enter to go to the next item. When you press Enter, you exit the list. To add, delete, or detect items at run time, see the discussions below of the AddItem, Clear, and RemoveItem methods and the ListCount and ListIndex properties.

◆ The ListCount property is read-only and only available at run time. It returns the number of items in the List array; that is, how many items are currently contained in the ComboBox control.

◆ The ListIndex property is only available at run time. It tells you the position in the List array of the ComboBox control's currently highlighted item. It is zero-based, so the first element's ListIndex is element 0 and the last element has a ListIndex value of ListCount - 1. If no item is selected then ListIndex has a value of –1. You can set the ListIndex property programmatically to force a particular item to be selected.

◆ The Sorted property is false by default, and can only be set at design time. If you set it to true, then all items will appear in alphabetical order in the ComboBox control, whether these items were added at run time or design time. If you have set the Sorted property to true, don't specify the position in the list for the AddItem method (see the following discussion of AddItem method), because this will confuse the sort order and cause subsequent additions to appear at unpredictable locations in the List.

◆ The Style property can only be set at design time. Select one of the three ComboBox styles—drop-down combo, simple combo, or drop-down list (see fig. 3.10).

◆ The Text property contains the text of the currently selected row in the ComboBox control. If no item is currently selected, the Text property contains the design-time value. If the Style of the ComboBox control is drop-down or simple combo, the user can edit the contents of the Combo's text box. Notice that this does not, however, change the corresponding highlighted item unless you write special code to do so. For instance, you would need to put code in the Change event procedure or in a keypress event procedure in order to change the highlighted item as the user types into the text box of the ComboBox.

FIG. 3.8 ⇒

A ComboBox control at run time, showing three choices available to the user in a list box and the selected choice in a text box.

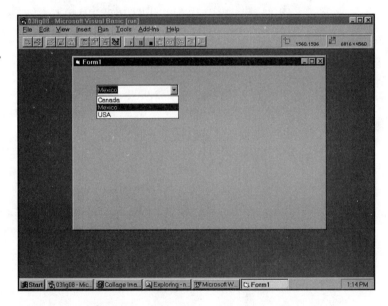

◆ The AddItem method allows you to add an item to the List at run time. It has two possible syntaxes:

```
ControlName.AddItem ItemText
```

or

```
ControlName.AddItem ItemText ListPosition
```

where *ControlName* is the name of the ComboBox control, *ItemText* is the string expression to add, and *ListPosition* is an integer representing the position in the list (zero-based) for the added item. If you don't use *ListPosition*, the newly added item shows up either at the end of the list (if the Sorted property is false) or in the proper alphabetical order within the list (if Sorted is true). It's not a good idea to use *ListPosition* if Sorted is true, because this can cause subsequent additions to be inserted at unpredictable positions in the list.

FIG. 3.9 ⟹
You can edit a ComboBox control's List property at design time.

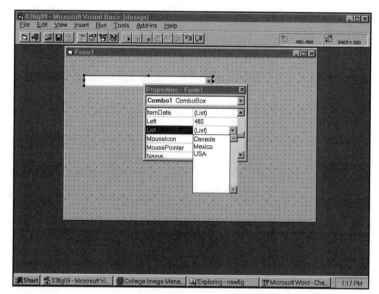

FIG. 3.10 ⟹
The ComboBox control has three styles.

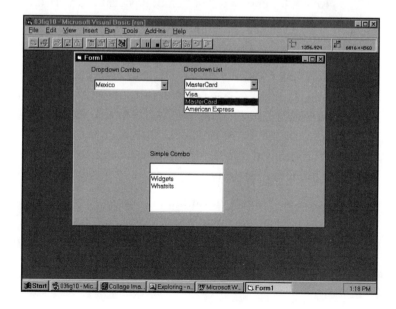

Part

I

Ch

3

◆ The Clear method removes all items from the List.

◆ The RemoveItem method removes a single item from the List. You must provide the position of the item you want to remove as its argument:

```
ControlName.RemoveItem ListPosition
```

◆ The Change event happens whenever the user or your code changes the Text property of the ComboBox control. Notice that changing the Text property does not automatically change the contents of the current item in the list. You would have to write special code to do that.

◆ The Click event happens whenever the selected item in the ComboBox changes, whether by the user clicking an item or by other means (such as changing the list index).

▶ **See** "Common Properties of the Form Object and Control Objects" **p. 213**

ListBox

The ListBox shares its special events, methods, and properties with the ComboBox. See the previous section on the ComboBox control.

 Note In contrast to the ComboBox control, the ListBox control has no Type or Text property and no Change event. ■

Horizontal and Vertical Scroll Bars

The purpose of a horizontal or vertical scroll bar is to give the user an interface to numeric or positional information. The user can see a value relative to a range of values by observing where the scroll bar's "elevator box" is sitting. The user should also be able to move the "elevator box" to change the quantity.

A scroll bar control's most important property is its Value property, which reflects the current position of the "elevator box" inside the scroll bar control (see fig. 3.11). You can read the Value property to adjust something else in your application, or you can set the Value property to display some value to the user.

Every time the Value property changes, the scroll bar's Change event happens, so you can be sure to have code that will catch any change to the value.

The following are the distinctive properties of a scroll bar control:

- ◆ The LargeChange property determines how many units the elevator box will move when the user clicks the shaft of the scroll bar. The default is 1.

- ◆ The SmallChange property determines how many units the elevator box will move when the user clicks one of the arrow buttons located at either end of the scroll bar. The default is 1.

- ◆ The Max property defines the upper limit of the Value property. The default is 32K.

- ◆ The Min property defines the lower limit of the Value property. The default is 0.

- ◆ The Value property is read/write at design time and run time. You can check the Value property in the Change event to see where the user has just placed the scroll bar elevator box. You can also set the scroll bar's Value property from elsewhere in the application to provide the user with information on those changes.

- ◆ The Change event happens whenever the Value property changes; that is, when code changes the Value property or when the user manipulates the scroll bar's elevator box. The scroll bar's Change event is where you would put code to react to any change on the scrollbar.

The horizontal scroll bar and vertical scroll bar work the same way. The only difference is their orientation on the form.

Part

I

Ch

3

FIG. 3.11 ⇒
A horizontal
scrollbar control.

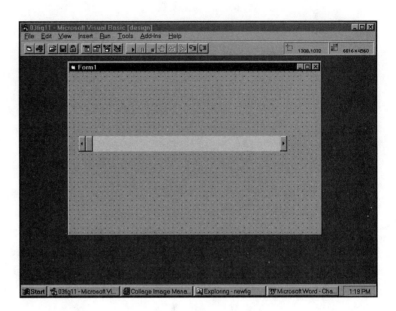

Timer

The Timer control lets your application asynchronously execute instructions at periodic intervals. For example, trigger the application to beep every two seconds, regardless of what other tasks are occurring. A slightly more practical example might be to query a database at periodic intervals for changes.

The Timer control is one of the simpler controls containing few properties:

- ◆ The Enabled property is true by default. When it's set to false, the Timer is disabled and will not run.

- ◆ The Interval property determines how often the Timer event will happen. It's an integer between 0 and 64K representing the number of milliseconds between occurrences of the Timer event. Thus, a value of 1000 means one second. Since the maximum value of the Interval is 64K, then you can make the Timer event fire in intervals of up to about 64 seconds.

◆ The Timer has only one Event procedure—the Timer event. This event is triggered whenever the amount of time determined by the Interval property rolls around (provided the Enabled property is True).

▶ **See** "Common Properties of the Form Object and Control Objects" **p. 213**

DriveListBox, DirectoryListBox, and FileListBox Controls

When you need to develop your own file dialog box and the Common Dialog control doesn't give you enough control, you can create a file dialog box using the Drive, Directory, and FileList controls.

When you put a DriveListBox, DirectoryListBox, and FileListBox control on a form, you're about 75 percent of the way to having a working file dialog. If you run a form with these three controls, you will see that they already contain "live" information from the system (see fig. 3.12). However, these three controls are not aware of each other. For example, when you change the drive on the Drive control, the Directory control does not change to indicate the directory stucture for the current drive.

Part

I

Ch

3

FIG. 3.12 ⇒

You can use the DriveListBox, DirListBox, and FileListBox controls to create your own file dialog.

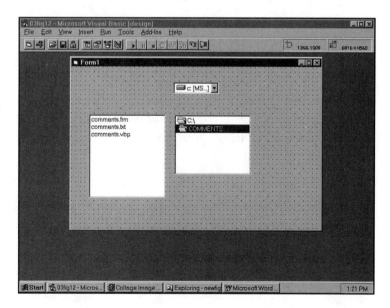

Through code, you will coordinate the three controls so that:

◆ The directory structure will change when the current drive changes

and

◆ The list of files will change when the directory structure changes

Luckily, these three controls have events and properties which you can link together to produce a coherent file dialog box.

The Drive control has a Drive property that indicates the currently selected drive. The Directory control has a Path property that shows the currently selected Path. You can programmatically synchronize these two controls by setting the Drive Property equal to the Path property:

```
Private Sub drvTest_Change()
    dirTest.Path = drvTest.Drive
End Sub
```

Notice that the previous code line is placed in the Drive's Change event. Each time the user selects a drive in the Drive control, the directory control will update the path property to indicate the directory structure for the current drive.

You can update the list of files in the file list box by linking the Path property of the Directory control to the FileList control.

```
Private Sub dirTest_Change()
    filTest.Path = dirTest.Path
End Sub
```

Just the two lines of code mentioned so far will sufficiently tie together the three File Dialog controls so that you will have a functioning dialog box.

You can then check the FileList control's FileName property to find the name of the exact file chosen:

```
Private Sub cmdOK_Click()
    MsgBox "You chose: " & filTest.filename
End Sub
```

You can also specify the file types displayed in the FileListBox control by manipulating its Pattern property. A common way to allow the user to determine the file types displayed in the FileListBox control is to use a ComboBox control.

Place a ComboBox on the form. Add items to the ComboBox that represent common file patterns, such as *.txt, *.doc, *.*. In the Click event of the ComboBox control, write code to change the files specified in the FileList box based on the selected item in the ComboBox:

```
Private Sub cmbPattern_Click()
    filTest.Pattern = cmbPattern.Text
End Sub
```

You can include multiple files within the same pattern by placing them on a single line and by separating each pattern with a semicolon. For instance, if you wanted to locate any Class, Standard, and Form modules, you could provide an entry in the ComboBox control that looked like:

```
*.bas;*.cls;*.frm
```

You may also choose the Common Dialog custom control for a very easy, but less flexible (it's modal!) file dialog box. See Chapter 11 on "Dialogs" in the *VB 4.0 Programmer's Guide* for more information on this control, or check the on-line help for the Common Dialog control.

The Lightweight Controls

These controls aren't recognized outside of a Visual Basic application. They don't have the hWnd property and so have no "legal" identity in the rest of the system. The upside of this is that they don't require as much of the system's resources to run.

Graphics Levels on the Form and the ZOrder Method

You need to know about the special techniques and restrictions for placing controls on top of and underneath each other on a form. Normally, you can think of the design surface and the user interface as a two-dimensional surface with an X-axis (horizontal dimension) and a Y-axis (vertical dimension).

Occasionally, you need to think of a third dimension, the dimension which extends outward from the plane of the screen and inward beyond the plane of the screen. This dimension belongs to a Form and would be the Z-axis in Cartesian coordinates.

A VB Form's Z-axis really has three levels or layers. Each type of control or other visible object belongs in one of the three layers. You can shuffle around controls that belong on the same level with respect to each other, but an object on a lower layer can never appear above an object on a layer above it.

The highest layer contains all controls that can receive focus.

The middle layer holds the lightweight controls (see the following sections).

The bottom layer holds information output directly to the Form during program execution. This includes the output of calls to the Print method and the Graphics methods (see the following sections).

At design time, you can manipulate controls along the Z-axis with respect to controls on the same graphics level with the Edit menu's Bring to Front and Send to Back options, or with the Ctrl+J and Ctrl+K key combinations (see fig. 3.13).

At run time, you can shuffle controls to the front or back of a pile of controls on the same graphics level with the ZOrder method. You can make one of the following two calls, depending on where you want a control to appear within its own graphics level:

```
ControlName.ZOrder vbBringToFront
ControlName.ZOrder vbSendToBack
```

You can also call the ZOrder method on a Form to send the Form to the front or back of a group of Forms. This method works on normal Forms as well as MDI Child Forms (see Chapter 9, "Using Multiple-Document Interface (MDI)").

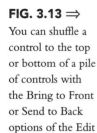

FIG. 3.13 ⇒
You can shuffle a control to the top or bottom of a pile of controls with the Bring to Front or Send to Back options of the Edit menu.

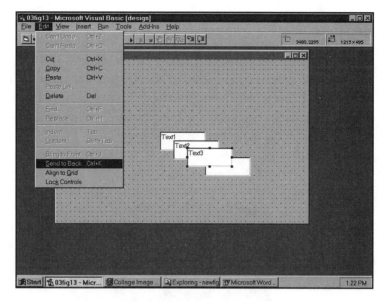

Label

The Label control's main function is to passively show the user information in its Caption property. Although you can change its Caption property programmatically, the user can't edit its contents directly.

◆ The Caption property of the Label control really is the most important. It simply contains whatever it is you want the user to see. Customarily, you will set the Caption property at design time. The Label control is also good for showing changing status at run time by changing its value programmatically. You will also often use it in applications with data to show the value of a read-only field.

◆ The Click and DblClick events are available with a Label control, even though the Label control can't get focus. In other words, the user still might click or double-click over the label control, even though the focus would stay with another control.

▶ **See** "Providing an Access Key for the TextBox," **p. 232**

Part

I

Ch

3

Image

The Image control works in a similar fashion to the PictureBox control. All that we have said regarding the PictureBox control is true of the Image, with the exception of the PictureBox control's AutoResize property, which the Image control doesn't have. Instead, the Image control has a Stretch property (which the PictureBox doesn't). If you set the Stretch property to true, the graphic in the control will stretch (with possible distortion and loss of resolution, of course) to fit the boundaries of the Image control itself (see fig. 3.14).

FIG. 3.14 ⇒

Setting an Image control's Stretch property to True allows its image to fit the control's boundaries.

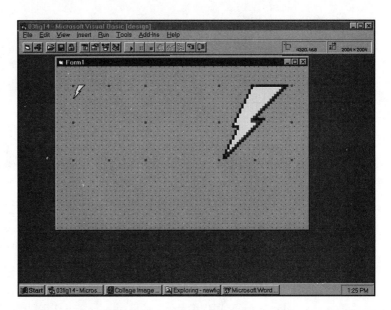

Other than this, what is the difference between the PictureBox and Image controls? In a word, the Image is a lightweight control. This means that it isn't a Microsoft Windows common control. In particular, it takes up less memory than a common control but doesn't have the ability to be identified outside the current VB application because it doesn't have an hWnd property.

▶ **See** "Common Properties of the Form Object and Control Objects"
p. 214

Shape

You can display and programmatically manipulate simple geometrical shapes—rectangles, circles, and ovals—with the Shape control (see fig. 3.15).

◆ The BackColor property determines the color of the background that will show through behind whatever pattern has been chosen for FillStyle. If BackStyle is Transparent, you won't see this color.

◆ The BackStyle property can be Opaque or Transparent. If BackStyle is Transparent, the color of the background as specified in BackColor won't show up and you'll be able to see through the FillStyle pattern to anything underneath the Shape control.

◆ The FillColor property determines the color of the pattern specified in FillStyle.

◆ The FillStyle property specifies the type of pattern to put inside the shape's borders, such as diagonal or horizontal lines, cross-hatching, or a solid color (Solid style).

◆ The Shape property determines just what shape the control will have—sharp-cornered or rounded-corner rectangle or square, circle, or oval. The control always appears on the design surface as a rectangle. If the Shape property is circle or square, the largest possible true circle or square that can fit in the control's rectangular boundaries (specified by Height and Width properties) will appear. If the Shape property is oval, the four extremes of the oval will touch each of the control's sides.

FIG. 3.15 ⇒
Use the Shape control to manipulate shapes.

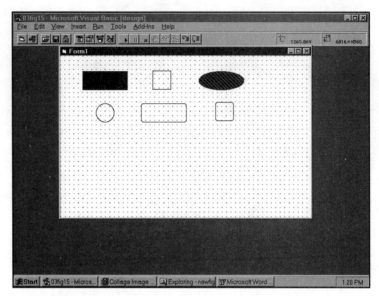

Line

The Line control (see fig. 3.16) has the following useful properties:

◆ The BorderColor property determines the line's color.

◆ The BorderStyle property determines what type of line (solid, dashed, and so on) the user will see.

◆ The BorderWidth property determines the thickness of the line in Twips.

◆ The DrawMode property determines how the line's appearance will interact with the form's background.

◆ The X1, X2, Y1, and Y2 properties determine the coordinates of the line's two endpoints.

▶ **See** "Common Properties of the Form Object and Control Objects" **p. 213**

FIG. 3.16 ⇒

You can manipulate the properties of the Line control to change its appearance.

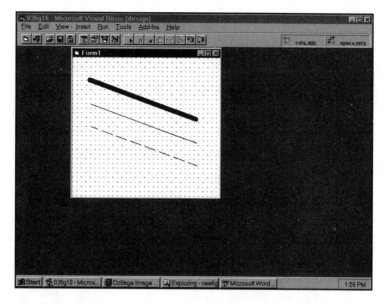

Taking the Disc Test

If you have read and understood the material in this chapter, you are ready to test your knowledge. Insert the CD-ROM that comes with this book and run the self-test software as described in Appendix H, "Using the CD-ROM."

From Here...

This chapter and Chapter 2, "Visual Basic Data Types," are really the backbone of an elementary knowledge of VB. If you feel comfortable with the material in these two chapters, you're well on your way to being able to pass the Certification exam. Many of the questions you'll encounter in the exam that are about more advanced topics still require a knowledge of elementary coding techniques and variable manipulation in order for you to understand and answer them properly. This is especially true of items such as:

◆ Scope of data and code

◆ Argument passing, including By Reference and By Value arguments

◆ Special features (events, methods, and properties) of each type of Microsoft common control.

If you are mainly interested in some of the more advanced topics in this book, such as data manipulation, OLE, 32-bit/16-bit issues, or DLLs, you could skip many of the chapters between this chapter and those topics. However, you should be comfortable with the topics in at least two of the other less advanced chapters: Object Properties (Chapter 6) and Object Events (Chapter 7).

Chapter Prerequisite

Because code debugging is a fundamental and necessary component of application development, the prerequisites for this chapter are minimal. Specifically, you should have basic knowledge of the Visual Basic language discussed in Chapters 2 and 3.

4

Debugging Applications

Visual Basic provides interactive debugging tools for locating run-time errors and program-logic errors. Perhaps the term "debugging" is too limiting to indicate the extensive debugging tools provided by Visual Basic. These debugging tools are also great for proactively testing your code to see how it operates and checking that everything is behaving as you would expect.

In this chapter you learn about:

- ◆ Debugging Logical Errors
- ◆ Break Mode
- ◆ The Debug Window
- ◆ Watch Expressions and Instant Watch Command
- ◆ Step Mode
- ◆ Other Debugging Tools
- ◆ Choosing the Correct Debugging Tool for the Job

This chapter begins by reviewing the various types of programming errors that can occur when an application runs. Programming errors generally fall into three distinct types:

◆ *Syntax errors.* You have used an element of the VB programming language incorrectly such as typing an unknown keyword, or missing required arguments. Visual Basic will sometimes catch the syntax error when you move off the line if you have the Auto Syntax Check turned on (Tool, Options, Environment tab). If the syntax error is not detected when you leave the line, it catches the error just before the code runs and notifies you with a description of the problems.

◆ *Run-time errors.* Your code can't carry out an operation because the operation makes assumptions that may not be true such as a missing file that your program tries to open, a nonexistent drive, or a data record that can't be deleted by the system when you request it. You will create an error handler for these error types. (For more information, see Chapter 5, "Handling Errors.")

◆ *Logical errors.* The program runs, but the logic does not do what you thought it would. For example, you intend to return an average of the quarterly sales but instead, the app returns the sum. You need to test the code to verify that the results are what you had intended. Some logical errors also produce run-time errors.

Logical errors can be the most difficult to debug because your application may run without generating an error. To assist you in locating and fixing these error types, Visual Basic offers debugging tools.

Debugging Logical Errors

There are many debugging tools that assist in locating logical errors within your code. Some of the more common debugging features are located on the toolbar and the Run menu:

◆ *Toggle Breakpoint.* Defines or removes a breakpoint. A breakpoint is a code line that designates where your application will suspend execution. You can set a breakpoint at design time or run time while in break mode.

◆ *Instant Watch.* Displays the current values of a variable, property, or other expression. Available only in break mode.

◆ *Calls.* Displays a list of currently active procedures calls. Available only in break mode.

◆ *Step Into.* Executes the code line-by-line. If the code calls another procedure, Step Into mode will continue executing line-by-line in the called procedure before returning to the first procedure.

◆ *Step Over.* Executes the code line-by-line. If the code calls another procedure, Step Over mode will run the called procedure completely before stepping through the next line of the first procedure. Aside from the Step Into and Step Over, VB offers a Step to Cursor mode that is only available from the Run menu.

Using Break Mode

Shifting your application from Run mode to Break mode is the first step to accessing most of the debugging tools. Break mode suspends the execution of your code so that you can search for such errors as incorrect data types, missing variable declarations, problems in logical comparisons, endless loops, unreadable output, problems with user-defined data types, array bounds, and so on. You can also suspend code to monitor code flow or examine information in the current state.

When Visual Basic encounters one of the conditions that sets it into Break mode, code execution is suspended. The following will cause Visual Basic to enter Break mode (remember, most debugging tools require that you switch to Break mode before you begin using the debugging tool):

Part

I

Ch

4

◆ Step Into or Step Over

◆ Breakpoints

◆ Stop statement

◆ Watch expression

◆ Keyboard interaction

◆ Run-time errors

Step Into or Step Over

Discussed previously, these Step modes run code one line at a time.

Breakpoints

A breakpoint is a marked line in your code that indicates where execution is suspended when the code runs. All code lines will run normally until a breakpoint is encountered that halts the execution of the code. You usually set a breakpoint on the line(s) where you suspect a problem. A *breakpoint* marks the code line in a different color. You can change color settings in the VB environment through Tools, Options, Editor tab.

To set or clear a breakpoint:

1. Position your cursor within the line that you want to set a breakpoint.

2. Do one of the following:

    • Select the Run, Toggle Breakpoint menu option (as shown in fig. 4.1)

    • Press the F9 key

    • Click the Toggle Breakpoint button on the toolbar

    • Right-click the line and select the Toggle Breakpoint option from the pop-up menu

FIG. 4.1 ⇒

The Toggle Breakpoint option in the Run menu toggles the breakpoint. It's usually handier to use its shortcut key, F9.

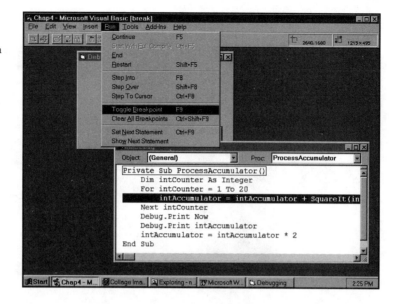

Remember, the methods listed above are toggles. They will set or clear breakpoints.

You can also remove all current Breakpoints at the same time. You could, of course, simply save the project and exit, then retrieve the project. This is one way to clear out all breakpoints, because breakpoints don't get saved. An easier way to clear all breakpoints is to access Run, Clear All Breakpoints menu option (see fig. 4.2) or the Ctrl+Shift+F9 shortcut key.

> **Note** Compiler directives, variable declarations, Const statements, Type…End Type statements, comments, and blank lines are not considered executable lines, so VB won't enable you to mark these lines with breakpoints. However, you can mark procedure declarations with breakpoints as well as End Sub or End Function statements, because these are executable code. ■

FIG. 4.2 ⇒
The Clear <u>A</u>ll
Breakpoints option
in the <u>R</u>un menu
clears all currently
set breakpoints.

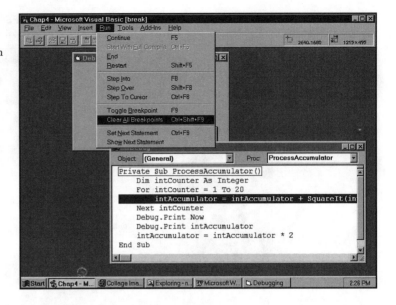

Caution

Remember, Visual Basic enables you to fit multiple code statements on a single line by separating each statement by a colon. If you set a breakpoint on a line that contains multiple code statements, the break always occurs at the first statement within the line.

Caution

Breakpoints are only good for the current session of VB. VB doesn't save Breakpoints with your file, so you will need to set up your Breakpoints every time you open the project.

Stop Statement

Placing the keyword *Stop* anywhere in your code indicates a switch to Break mode when you run the application. The Stop statement, unlike the Breakpoint, is included in the app as a code line and therefore, it can be saved with the file.

> **Caution**
> You must remember to take the Stop statements out of your application before you compile it for distribution. When an executable file encounters the Stop statement, the application ends.

Watch Expression

Depending on the settings you choose, Watch expressions can cause the application to enter Break mode.

Keyboard/Mouse Interaction

Aside from preplanning when the application will switch to Break mode (by setting a breakpoint, a watch expression, or by inserting the keyword Stop within your code), you can also switch to Break mode manually during run time. The following approaches cause the application to enter Break mode during run time:

◆ Pressing the Ctrl+Break keys

◆ Clicking the Break button on the toolbar

Part

I

Ch

4

Run-Time Errors

If Visual Basic encounters an untrapped run-time error, the code enters Break mode while in the design environment.

Using the Debug Window

The Debug Window monitors the value of variables, properties, and other expressions while stepping through the program code. You can also use the Debug Window to setup 'What If' scenarios by changing the values of expressions and observing how these values affect the code.

The Debug window is always displayed when an application runs in the VB design environment. It is composed of two panes—the Watch Pane and the Immediate Pane.

The Watch Pane

The Watch Pane displays the current Watch Expressions—values of variables, properties, and other expressions that you have chosen to monitor while the code runs.

The context column in the Watch Pane indicates the context in which the expression is evaluated (procedure, module, or modules). The Watch Pane can only display a value for the Watch Expression within the specified context.

Tip

You may have to expand the Debug Window to show the Watch Pane.

The Immediate Pane

While the Watch Pane displays only those expressions that have been added as Watch Expressions, the Immediate Pane provides an interactive means to query expressions simply by typing the expression into the Immediate Pane at run-time. Further, the Immediate Pane is more flexible because you can interrogate, experiment with, and display information about the currently running environment. In general, it's safe to say that you can type anything in the Immediate Pane that you could type as a line of VB code.

There are three ways to display information in the Immediate Pane, as discussed in the following sections.

Print

The Print method is used to query the current value of an expression. At run-time, simply type Print followed by the expression you want to evaluate. For example:

```
      Print lngSalary
            42000
      Print lngSalary * .05
            2100
      Print Ucase(txtCity.text)
            CHICAGO
```

Question Mark (?)

The question mark (?) is useful shorthand for the Print method.

```
      ?lngSalary
            42000
      ?lngSalary * .05
            2100
      ?Ucase(txtCity.text)
            CHICAGO
```

Debug.Print

Debug.Print can be placed within code to enable you to send output
to the Immediate Pane. Unlike the print method or ?, Debug.Print
writes output to the Immediate Pane without entering Break mode. In
addition, Debug.Print is a code statement that enables you to save this
query to the Immediate Pane within the file. For example:

```
      Private Sub GetCityField()
            For lcv = 0 To UBound(strCity)
               Debug.Print strCity(lcv)
                  .
                  .
                  .
               Next lcv
      End Sub
```

This example might print the following to the Immediate Pane:

```
      New York
      Houston
      Atlanta
      Chicago
```

While you can insert Debug.Print into your code, it has no effect when
the compiled executable file runs. This means that you can permanently
leave Debug.Print statements in your production code without any
problems for your executable file.

The contents of the Immediate Pane accumulate over an entire VB
session (see fig. 4.3). In other words, it does not clear itself every time
you start to run your design-time app. It only clears itself when you exit
the VB session.

FIG. 4.3 ⇒

You can use the Immediate Pane to view the results of Debug.Print statements, interrogate and set the values of variables that are currently in scope in your code, and even make calls to functions or procedures.

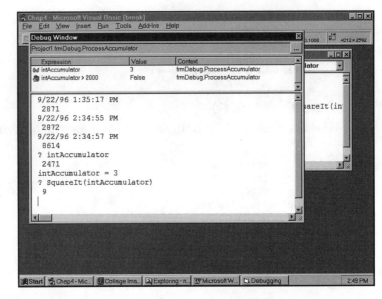

Using Watch Expressions and Instant Watch Commands

There are two ways to monitor the value of a variable or expression at run time: a Watch Expression and the Instant Watch command. Watch Expressions enable you to determine the expressions you want to monitor at run time. You need to determine Watch Expressions at design time through the Tools menu. Many times when you run an application, you'll want to spontaneously query an expression that you did not define as a Watch Expression. The Instant Watch command enables you to check the current value of a variable or expression for which you have not defined a Watch Expression.

Watch Expression

As the previous section mentions, Watch Expressions are expressions (variables, properties, and other expressions) you decide to monitor as the code runs.

The value of a Watch Expression is displayed in the Watch Pane of the Debug Window when the application enters Break mode as shown in figure 4.4.

FIG. 4.4 ⇒

The Debug Window will display the values of Watched variables in its Watch Pane. The Debug Window will appear on the screen if you've specified Break When Value is True or Break When Value Changes when setting up the watch.

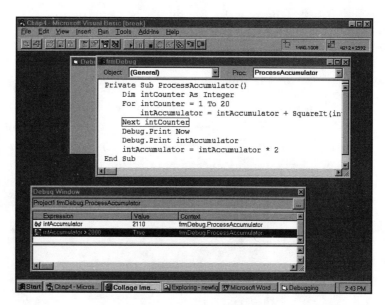

Part

I

Ch

4

The following section outlines how to add a Watch Expression. Note that Visual Basic offers three Watch types. You choose the Watch type when you add the Watch Expression.

To add a Watch Expression through the Add Watch command:

1. Choose Tools, Add Watch.

2. In the Expression box, type the expression you want to evaluate. (If the expression appears in your code, highlight the expression within the code window before accessing the Tools menu. This will automatically populate the Expression box with the selected expression.)

3. Within the Context frame, select the Procedure and Module name to set the scope of the Watch Expression.

4. Select an option within the Watch Type frame. This determines how you want VB to respond to the Watch Expression. The three Watch types are described later.

Modifying or Deleting an Existing Watch Expression

If you want to edit the expression or its setting, you can access the Edit Watch dialog box (see fig. 4.5) by any one of the following steps:

◆ Choosing Tools, Edit Watch menu option

◆ Ctrl+W shortcut key

◆ Double-clicking the Watch Expression on its corresponding row in the Watch Pane of the Debug Window

Notice that you can delete the Watch Expression by clicking the delete button within the Edit Watch dialog box. You can also delete a Watch Expression, at design or run-time, by selecting its row in the Debug Window's Watch Pane and pressing the Delete key.

FIG. 4.5 ⇒

The Edit Watch dialog box lets you change the settings on an existing Watch or delete it.

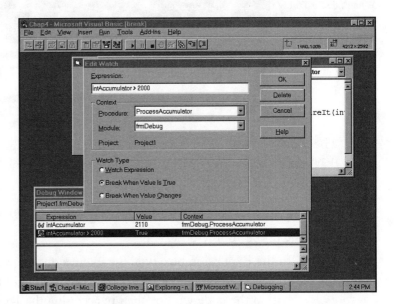

Visual Basic offers three Watch types. Remember, you choose the Watch type when you Add/Edit a Watch Expression:

Watch Type: Watch Expression

The default Watch Type is Watch Expression. This Watch Type will simply list the variable's name and value (when in scope) in the Debug Window's Watch Pane (see fig. 4.6). Whenever you want to know an expression's current value, you can access the Debug Window with either View, Debug Window or Ctrl+G.

FIG. 4.6 ⇒

The Watch Expression option is the default setting for the Watch Type. When you accept the default, check the Debug Window's Watch Pane whenever you need to know the expression's current value.

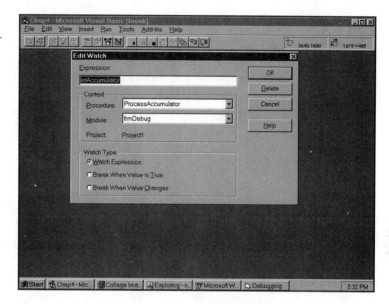

Watch Type: Break When Value is True

This Watch Type causes Visual Basic to enter Break mode when the value of the expression becomes True during execution. This type is handy when you're uncertain about the exact behavior of the expression and there is complicated code involved.

Unless the variable you're monitoring is of Boolean type, you typically won't stipulate a variable's name in the Expression field of the Add Watch dialog box (see fig. 4.7). Instead, you'll put some type of comparison expression involving the variable, because what you're trying to do here is refine how often VB will break to the Debug Window.

For example, your code includes a variable which gets changed inside a loop. You are not, however, interested in all cases where the variable is changed, but only in cases where it takes on a certain range of values, say values greater than 100. Then, you might specify the following expression:

variablename > 100

Now, instead of being interrupted on every pass through the loop, VB notifies you only when the expression evaluates to true.

Of course, observing the expression's current value (which will be either True or False) in the Debug Window's Watch Pane doesn't give you much information about the variable's precise value. Therefore, you will typically use this type of Watch in tandem with a simple non-breaking Watch, that is a Watch Type of Watch Expression.

As an example, imagine a loop with the line:

intAccumulator = _
intAccumulator + SquareInt(intCounter)

You want to make sure that intAccumulator never approaches a value which could max out the carrying capacity of the Integer type, that is 32K. To test this, you could create two watch expressions:

- The first watch expression's type would be Watch Expression and the Expression would be just the name of the variable, intAccumulator.

- The second watch expression would be of the type Break When Expression Has Changed, and the Expression would be something like intAccumulator >=30000 (if we waited for exactly 32K, it would be too late!)

So, when you run your application from the VB design environment with these two watches set, you'll see nothing unless intAccumulator gets to or above 30,000. If that ever happens, VB will go into break mode, the Debug Window will come up, and you'll see the exact value on the first Watch Expression's line in the Watch Pane.

Watch Type: Break When Value Changes

If you select the Break When Value Changes Watch Type in the Add Watch dialog box (see fig. 4.8), Visual Basic will enter Break mode when the initial value of the expression changes during execution.

FIG. 4.7 ⇒

You can put a logical expression in the Expression field of the Edit Watch dialog box and check the Break When Value is True option so that the program will go into break mode only when some specified condition applies.

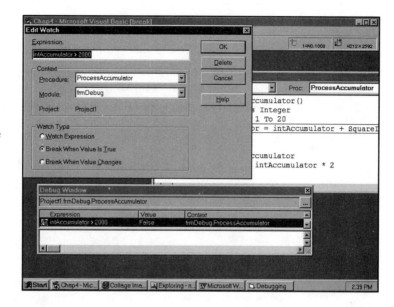

A Watch Type of Break When Value Changes automates the process of monitoring the variable. When you set up a Watch of this type, the Debug Window (with a row in the Watch Pane listing the variable's current value in the top pane) will come up automatically every time the variable's value changes.

Part

I

Ch

4

FIG. 4.8 ⇒

By checking the Break When Value Changes option in the Add Watch dialog box, you can get your design-time copy of the application to stop each time a variable or expression has changed.

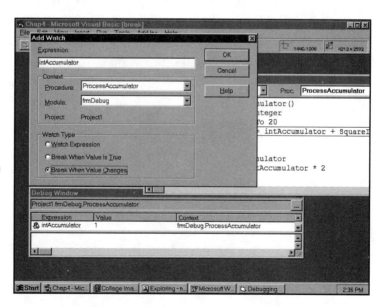

Instant Watch

The Instant Watch dialog box enables you, during run time, to check the values of specified expressions for which you did not set a Watch Expression. The Instant Watch command enables you to spontaneously check the value of any expression during run time. Therefore, you are not required to specify all of the expressions you want to observe prior to running an application. In contrast to a Watch Expression, the values of an Instant Watch do not appear in the Watch Pane of the Debug Window. Instead, they appear in an Instant Watch dialog box that displays when you access the Tools, Instant Watch menu option at run time (see fig. 4.9).

To display an Instant Watch:

◆ While in Break mode, select the expression within the code window that you want to check. Use any of the following methods to display the current value of the expression:

- Choose Tools, Instant Watch.
- Use the Shift+F9 shortcut key.
- Click the Instant Watch button on the toolbar.
- Right-click the selected expression in the code window. Select the Instant Watch menu option from the popup menu.

You can add a Watch Expression to the Watch Pane based on the expression in the Instant Watch dialog box. Follow these steps:

1. While in the Instant Watch dialog box,
2. Choose the Add button if you want to add the expression as a Watch Expression to the Watch Pane on the Debug Window.

FIG. 4.9 ⇒

During debugging activities you can quickly check on any variable's value with the Instant Watch screen.

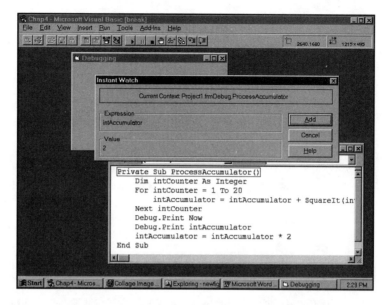

Using Step Mode

While in Break mode, the Step mode enables you to determine where to suspend and start program execution. There are three types of step mode: Step Into, Step Over, Step to Cursor.

Step Into Mode

As we stated at the beginning of this chapter, Step Into executes the code line by line. If the code calls another procedure, Step Into mode will continue executing line by line in the called procedure before returning to the first procedure.

You can enter Step Into mode through one of the following methods:

◆ Choosing Run, Step Into

◆ Use the F8 shortcut key

◆ Clicking the Step Into icon on the VB ToolBar

Your application will behave differently depending on when you invoke Step Into mode:

◆ If the application is not already running, invoking Step Into mode starts the application.

◆ If your application is already running but no code is currently executing, nothing will happen when you invoke Step Into mode. However, the next time code begins to run, for example, when the user clicks a command button, code runs in Step Into mode.

◆ If your application is running and code is executing, that code will begin to execute Step Into when you invoke Step Into mode.

Tip

If you are currently running in step mode and wish to resume normal execution at any time, invoke run mode by choosing Run, Continue from the menu, clicking the Run icon on the toolbar, or pressing F5 (see fig. 4.10).

Caution

When you have run out of code to single-step, you won't necessarily see your application's user interface. You may have to use your mouse to find the current form.

Step Over Mode

Remember, Step Over is similar to Step Into in that it executes code line by line. If the code calls another procedure, however, Step Over will run the called procedure entirely before returning to the original procedure.

FIG. 4.10 ⇒

You can begin an application with F8 (Step Into mode) or the Step Into icon instead of F5 (or the Run button) to see its code run from the top of the application.

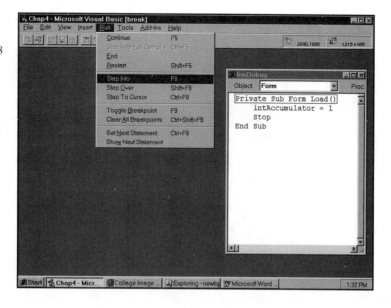

You can use Step Over mode instead of Step Into if you want to skip viewing each line of code in a procedure called from the currently executing procedure. You invoke Step Over mode in one of the following ways:

◆ Choosing Run, Step Over (see fig. 4.11)

◆ Using the Shift+F8 shortcut key

◆ Clicking the Step Over icon on the VB ToolBar

Note If you have inserted a breakpoint in a called procedure, VB will still break, even though you have requested that VB Step Over this procedure. ■

Step To Cursor Mode

When in break mode, use Step To Cursor to select a line further down in your code where you want to suspend execution. By invoking Step to Cursor, you have told Visual Basic to run continuously from the current point of execution to the line where you've placed the cursor.

FIG. 4.11 ⇒

You can step through lines of code with Step Over mode to avoid viewing a called procedure line by line.

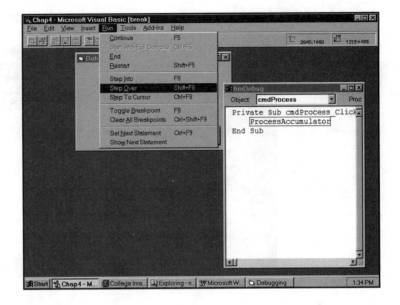

To use the Step to Cursor feature:

1. You must be running the application and currently be in break mode.
2. Place your cursor on the line where you wish to suspend execution.
3. Choose the Run, Step to Cursor menu option (see fig. 4.12) or the Ctrl+F8 shortcut key.
4. Your application will run normally until it hits the line you chose, where it will break.

 Note The code line you use for Step to Cursor does not need to be in the same procedure as the currently executing line. ■

Set Next Statement

Sometimes when you are debugging code, you'd like to see the effect of running a statement which isn't next in the logical flow of a procedure or which has already run once. You might also decide you want to skip one or more statements to see the effect of leaving them out.

FIG. 4.12 ⟹

The Run menu's Step To Cursor option (shortcut key is Ctrl+F8) lets you stay in Step Into mode, but lets the program run normally up to another line in the same procedure.

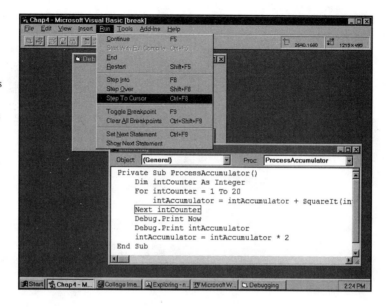

The Set Next Statement option allows you to do just that when you're already stepping through the code. To use Set Next:

1. Place the cursor on the line where you wish execution to begin.

2. Access the <u>R</u>un, Set <u>N</u>ext Statement menu option (see fig. 4.13) or press the Ctrl+F9 shortcut key.

3. VB will highlight the line you chose.

If you resume normal execution with F5 or choose the Step Into or Step Over mode, execution will resume again starting at that line.

> **Caution**
> You can only use the Set Next Statement option within the currently executing procedure.

Part

I

Ch

4

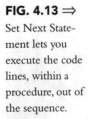

FIG. 4.13 ⇒
Set Next State-
ment lets you
execute the code
lines, within a
procedure, out of
the sequence.

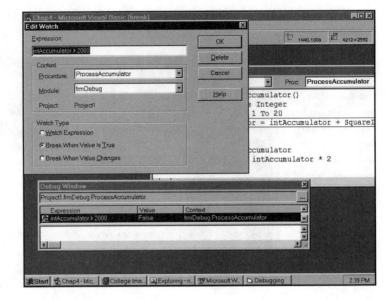

Show Next Statement

Sometimes you break in a procedure or single step to a particular line
and then begin to examine other lines in your code until you may have
lost track of the line where VB has currently paused.

If you want to return to the line where execution has paused, select the
Run, Show Next Statement menu option (see fig. 4.14).

Tracing Program Flow with the Call Dialog Box

The Call stack is a list of currently running procedures created while an
application is running. The Call stack traces execution flow through
multiple procedures. Use this tool to verify that the code follows the
correct sequence of procedures in situations. Multiple nested procedures
make it difficult to follow the execution flow.

FIG. 4.14 ⇒

The Run menu's
Show Next State-
ment takes you to
the line where
execution has
paused when you
are in Single Step
mode.

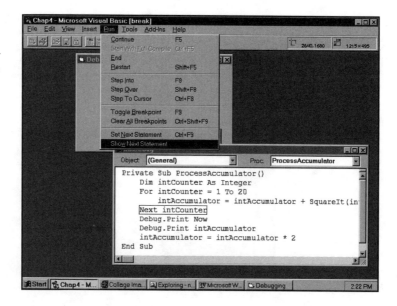

For example, cmdOK_Click calls a procedure known as ProcessIt and
ProcessIt calls a function named SquareIt. The Calls dialog box will
display:

◆ SquareIt

◆ ProcessIt

◆ cmdOK_Click

To view the call stack at any point in the program:

1. Make sure the application is in break mode.

2. Choose Tools, Calls to access the Calls dialog box (see fig. 4.15)
   or use the Ctrl+L shortcut key.

   The Calls dialog box lists each element of the call stack on a
   separate line.

Part

I

Ch

4

FIG. 4.15 ⇒

You can display the Calls dialog box by selecting the Tools, Calls menu option or Ctrl+L when your application is paused on a line of code.

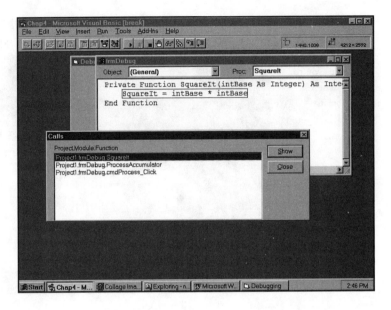

Choosing the Correct Debugging Tool for the Job

Visual Basic offers so many Debugging tools, it's sometimes difficult to determine which tool to use for different bug problems. Below is a list of common debugging tasks, along with suggestions for specific debugging techniques to accomplish these things:

◆ To trace a complicated flow of programming logic within the same procedure: Set a Breakpoint.

◆ Within a single procedure, you want to observe the effect of running the code lines out of the written sequence: Use a Breakpoint together with the Set Next statement feature.

◆ To check the value of a variable whenever the value changes: Use the Break When Value Changes type of Watch.

◆ To observe the value of a variable at different times during execution: Use a Watch Expression for the variable.

◆ If you were planning on how you might test the value of a variable at run time (specifically, you wanted to test when a variable is assigned a particular range of values at run time) add two Watches. The first should be a Watch Expression for the variable itself, and the second should be a Break When Value is True whose expression tests for the values or ranges of that variable.

◆ A variable is assigned a different value on each pass through a loop. You want VB to provide you with all of the values that were assigned to the variable but you don't want to enter break mode—Use the Debug.Print statement in code.

◆ You want to observe the effect of assigning different values to a single variable: Put a breakpoint at the point in code where you wish to test the variable value. When the break occurs, go to the Debug Window's Immediate Pane and reassign the variable's value. You might also (depending on your debugging needs) consider repeating key statements over again several times with the Set Next Statement feature.

Taking the Disc Test

If you have read and understood the material in the chapter, you are ready to test your knowledge. Insert the CD-ROM that comes with this book and run the self-test software as described in Appendix H, "Using the CD-ROM."

From Here...

It is not necessary to know about debugging to use any of the other features in VB. Debugging is a practical technique which you can apply when you write programs in the real world.

The next chapter, Handling Errors, is perhaps closest to the subject of debugging. A developer can use the debugging techniques discussed in this chapter to locate logical problems in code and decide how to handle them.

Chapter Prerequisite

You should be familiar with the fundamentals of the Visual Basic language discussed in Chapters 2 and 3. It also would be helpful to know the basics of code debugging found in Chapter 4.

Handling Errors

This chapter deals with Visual Basic's special facilities for handling run-time errors. Run-time errors are the only type of errors that you can't completely prevent after you've distributed your application, and therefore, you must make provisions in your code for the possibility that a run-time error might occur. For example, if the VB application tries to access a floppy disk from a floppy disk drive, you must anticipate problems that arise if a user forgets to insert the floppy disk.

In this chapter you learn

◆ How to set up an error trap within a procedure

◆ How to recover from errors through setting up an error handler

◆ How to standardize and centralize error handling in your application

◆ How to handle an error immediately after it occurs through Inline Error handling

Using Error Handling in an Application

Developers distinguish three types of errors in an application:

- *Syntax errors.* You have used an element of the VB programming language incorrectly, say, by typing a command that doesn't exist in the language, or by passing the wrong number or type of parameters to a built-in routine.

- *Logic errors.* The program runs, but the logical flow you have given it doesn't necessarily do what you thought it would (maybe you if'ed when you should have while'ed).

- *Run-time errors.* The syntax and logic may be just fine, but your code may make an assumption about the rest of the system that doesn't fit reality: a missing file that your program tries to open, a nonexistent drive, a data record that can't be deleted by the system when you request it.

The compiler will catch syntax errors and, if you're good at what you do, you'll catch logic errors at design time. If you're not so lucky, your user will find logic errors at a not-so-good time.

The simplest form of run-time error handling is to let VB take care of it. VB has its own default run-time error handling procedure, which is to display an error message to the user and then immediately terminate the application.

Run-time errors can occur both in design mode and when the compiled application runs. The default run-time error dialogs box looks different when the error occurs in design mode versus when it occurs within a compiled application.

The design-time error dialog box displays four buttons to choose from (see fig. 5.1):

- *Continue.* If this error is a fatal error, the button will be disabled. If it is enabled, click and your code will continue running. However, results after this point may be unpredictable.

- *End.* Stops the program from running and returns to design mode.

◆ *Debug.* The application continues to run, but it breaks at the line that caused the error and changes the mode to single-step.

◆ *Help.* A help screen is displayed with description on the error.

The compiled version of the default error dialog box provides the user with an OK button to end the application (see fig. 5.2).

FIG. 5.1 ⇒

If you don't make provisions for run-time error handling, this is what VB will do whenever it encounters a problem. This message box is what you see if a run-time error occurs while running your application in design mode.

FIG. 5.2 ⇒

This is the same error as in figure 5.1, but this is the message the user will see when running the compiled version of your application.

You will need to write your own error handling code if you want to avoid VB's default error dialog box, as well as attempt to handle the error and resume normal processing (see fig. 5.3). In order to create your own error handlers, first identify the places in your code where run-time errors could occur (files access or database manipulation, for example). Then, write error handling and a recovery routine for each possible run-time error that could arise within the specified spot in your code.

In general, VB run-time errors are handled locally (at procedure level). First, let's examine techniques for writing error handlers (error handling routines within a Sub or Function, and Inline error handling). Then we'll discuss how to centralize your error handling within the limitations of VB's run-time error system.

FIG. 5.3 ⇒

You can, however, write your own error handlers to take corrective actions when there's a run-time error. You may wish to display your own error messages. Notice that both the error number and its description are available to you.

Error Handling Routines Within a Procedure

To handle an error which occurs within a procedure, set up a special area (usually at the end of the procedure) for handling any errors. Handling the error might include any of the following:

- ◆ Determine which error occurred
- ◆ Notify the user of the error
- ◆ Notify the user of the error and request that they take corrective action
- ◆ Programmatically take corrective action
- ◆ In an attempt to recover, ignore the task that caused the error or retry the task (after corrective action has been taken and therefore, the error will hopefully not occur again)

Let's imagine a routine that could cause a run-time error: An OLE server, for instance, may not be available when we try to set a reference to it (see Chapters 10 and 11 on using and creating OLE servers for a more detailed discussion of this topic). Therefore, the following code

```
[General Declarations section of form]
Private xl As Object

[event procedure for a command button]
Private Sub cmdXL_Click()
    OpenXL
End Sub

[general procedure belonging to the form]
Private Sub OpenXL()
    Set xl = GetObject(,"Excel.Application")
End Sub
```

might fail on the line containing the GetObject function, because GetObject requires an already running instance of Excel. A run-time error occurs, in this example, if there is no current instance of Excel running while the code in the OpenXL procedure is executed.

The following five sections outline the basic steps in creating an error handling routine within a procedure.

Defining the Error-Handler with a Label

Before you can create a local error handler, you must define the handler with a labeled line.

A labeled line in VB is a line containing a unique name followed by a colon (:). The labeled line marks the beginning of where you plan to write the error handler:

```
Private Sub OpenXL()
    Set xl = GetObject(,"Excel.Application")
OpenXL_Error:
End Sub
```

We need to perform the steps in the next sections before the error handler will be ready.

Creating a Detour Around the Error Handler with Exit

When the subroutine runs without errors, we don't want to run the code in the error handler. Therefore, we put an Exit Sub statement (or an Exit Function statement) on the line before the error handler's label. That way, when the routine runs normally, it will exit before it encounters the error handler.

```
Private Sub OpenXL()
    Set xl = GetObject(,"Excel.Application")
    Exit Sub
OpenXL_Error:
End Sub
```

We're now ready to create the error handler.

Writing Code to Handle the Error

The error handler is where you write code to determine which error occurred and then attempt to rectify the problem. VB provides an Err object that contains information about the current error. Each time an error occurs, the system modifies the properties of the Err object (see the section in this chapter on the Err object). The Err.Number property receives a standard VB error number that identifies the current error. Err.Description contains a VB standard description of the current error. You can use Err.Number to detect which error has occurred and you can use Err.Description to display a description of the current error. Search for the "Trappable Errors" topic in Visual Basic Help to see a list(s) of err.numbers and their corresponding err.description.

In the following example, we check for error 429 ("OLE Automation Server Can't Create Object") and react to it accordingly. If any other error occurs, we simply inform the user of the error using both the Err.Number and Err.Description properties.

```
Private Sub OpenXL()
    Set xl = GetObject(,"Excel.Application")
    Exit Sub
OpenXL_Error:
    If Err.Number = 429 Then
        Set xl = CreateObject("Excel.Application")
    Else
```

```
                MsgBox "Error #" & Err.Number & _
                "(" & Err.Description & ")" & _
                "while attempting to open Excel"
        End If
End Sub
```

Our error-handling code still lacks one thing: it doesn't give any instructions about where to resume execution after the error has been handled. The next section discusses how to do this.

Using the Resume Statement to Recover

The Resume statement tells VB how to recover from an error once steps are taken to rectify or react to the error condition. As its name implies, Resume is going to tell VB where to branch or start executing code again. The Resume statement has three forms:

◆ *Resume.* Return to the same line that originally caused the error. This means that the line that caused the error will run again. Use Resume in situations where you've attempted to correct the problem and you want to try the error line again. Be careful—if the problem hasn't been rectified, the error will reoccur.

◆ *Resume Next.* Return to the line immediately following the line that originally caused the error. This means that that application will not rerun the error line again. Use Resume Next when either you have written code in the error handler that substitutes for the task performed in the error line or when you don't care whether the error line had a chance to run properly or not.

◆ *Resume label.* Continue execution on the line that contains the label. Use Resume *label* when you want to branch to a line other than the error line. This is often used when it's necessary to rerun other lines before re-executing the error line.

For example, a procedure prompts the user for a file name and then attempts to open that file. The line that attempts to open the file might cause a run-time error (for example, file not

Part

I

Ch

5

found). If the user wants to try to open a file again, we would need to rerun the error line but only after we have prompted the user for another file name. Accomplish this by placing a labeled line preceding the first line of code you would need to rerun. Then, branch to the labeled line when returning from the handler.

```
Sub OpenFile()
    On Error Go To Err_FileOpen
TryDifferent_File:
    'prompt user for the name of the file to open
    'open the file
    Exit Sub
Err_FileOpen:
    If err.number=53 then   'file not found
            If MsgBox("File Not Found. Try Again?", vbYesNo,
"Error")=vbYes then
                Resume TryDifferent_File:
        Else
            End
        End If
    Else
            MsgBox "Error # " & Err.Number & _
                "(" & Err.Description & ")" & _
                "while attempting to open the file"
            End
        End IF
End Sub
```

In the previous code, notice that the first time VB moves to the labeled line called TryDifferent_File:, VB ignores the line and passes over it. If the err.number of 53 occurs, the user is asked within the error handler if they want to try to open another file. If the user selects Yes, the resume statement, Resume TryDifferent_File:, returns to the labeled line, and the user is once again prompted for a file name, and an attempt is made to open the file. Lastly, notice the line On Error Go To Err_FileOpen. The program needs a directive on what line to go to if an error occurs. The purpose of the On Error statement is to provide this directive. In this example, the program will go to a labeled line called Err_FileOpen if an error occurs. The On Error statement is a required component of error handling, and it's discussed further in the next section.

Let's return to the GetObject function example we discussed earlier. The following code illustrates how we use a Resume Next after calling the CreateObject function within the handler. If the error 429 occurs, the Resume Next statement returns to the line proceeding the line that caused the error. In this case, the program would resume at the Exit Sub line. Remember, the CreateObject function creates a new instance of Excel, so we don't need to try calling GetObject again. Note also that we've decided we want to terminate the application with the End statement if we don't get the error we expected.

```
Private Sub OpenXL()
    Set xl = GetObject(,"Excel.Application")
    Exit Sub
OpenXL_Error:
    If Err.Number = 429 Then
        Set xl = CreateObject("Excel.Application")
        Resume Next
    Else
        MsgBox "Error #" & Err.Number & _
        "(" & Err.Description & ")" & _
        " attempting to open Excel"
        End
    End If
End Sub
```

 Note   The Err object's Number and Description properties are cleared whenever any type of Resume statement is executed. ▪

Our error handler is just about ready to go: all the code for the error handling has been written, and the only thing left to do is to activate it.

The On Error Statement

The purpose of the On Error statement is to enable error handling and to specify what line to branch to if a run-time error occurs. On Error can also be used to disable an error handler.

Using On Error to Enable/Disable the Error Handler

The next example demonstrates how to use On Error to enable and disable error handling.

```
Private Sub OpenXL()
    On Error GoTo OpenXL_Error:
    Set xl = GetObject(,"Excel.Application")
```

```
        On Error GoTo 0
        Exit Sub
OpenXL_Error:
    If Err.Number = 429 Then
        Set xl = CreateObject("Excel.Application")
        Resume Next
    Else
        MsgBox "Error #" & Err.Number & _
        "(" & Err.Description & ")" & _
        " attempting to open Excel"
        End
    End If
End Sub
```

The first On Error statement, On Error GoTo OpenXL_Error:, enables error handling and provides a directive on where to go if an error occurs. In the above example, the program will branch to the OpenXL_Error if an error does occur. Of course, it's a good strategy to place the On Error statement at the top of the procedure so error-handling is enabled at the start of the procedure. Remember, the error-handling is not activated until the On Error statement runs.

The second On Error statement in the above example includes a different form of On Error: On Error Go To 0. This disables any error-handling within the procedure. Any errors that occur after this On Error statement will need not be handled by the designated error handler. Instead, VB's default run-time error handler will kick in. In this example, if error 429 occurs in second line: Set xl = SetObject(,"Excel.Application"). The program would first branch to the labeled line OpenXL_Error:. Next, the error handler instructs the program to resume to On Error GoTo 0. This line disables any error-handling within the procedure. Lastly, the program would execute the last line: Exit Sub.

 Note The label you use after On Error GoTo represents a labeled line that must reside in the current procedure. ▪

Using On Error Statement with Resume

The On Error statement can also take the form:

```
On Error Resume Next
```

which means VB will immediately begin processing on the line after the error occurred. The On Error Resume Next is used for "Inline error handling" discussed in the next section.

Inline Error Handling

Another form of On Error is On Error Resume Next. This alternative is used to address an error immediately after the error line rather than branching to a specified error handler.

In this next example, we assume that the GetObject function will cause a run-time error. Notice this code attempts to handle the error on the following line by first evaluating the current value of Err.Number:

```
Private Sub XLInLine()
    Dim errTemp As Long
    On Error Resume Next
    Set xl = GetObject(, "Excel.Application")
    Select Case Err.Number
        Case 0
            MsgBox "Successfully Opened Excel"
        Case 429
            Set xl = CreateObject("Excel.Application")
        Case Else
            MsgBox "Fatal error #" & Err.Number _
                & " (" & Err.Description & ")" & _
                ": Passing the buck"
        End
    End Select
    Err.Clear
End Sub
```

The example also checks if the value of Err.Number is 0, which indicates that no error has occurred.

Notice that we call the Err object's Clear method after the Select Case structure that handles the error. This is because this style of error handling doesn't use the Resume statement, and Resume is what we normally rely on to reset the Err object. If an error did occur in the previous example and Err.Clear wasn't used, the Error object would continue to store information about this error. This could mislead a called procedure, which may have its own error handlers and depends on the value of Err.Number to function properly.

Part

I

Ch

5

Generally, you'll want to be careful about using Inline error handling. Your procedures can get quite long and more difficult to construct and maintain since an error handler must proceed each line that could cause an error.

As we mentioned previously, the On Error Resume Next statement is used within Inline error handling. There are other times, however, when the On Error Resume Next statements comes in handy.

You can use On Error Resume Next to:

◆ Ignore errors and keep on processing. This is useful when you might expect an error to occur occasionally but the error does not affect the remaining code. For example, the following code will process all the controls on the current form:

```
On Error Resume Next
For each ctrlCurr In Controls
  ctrlCurr.Text = UCase(ctrlCurr.Text)
Next ctrlCurr
```

Whenever the loop hits a control without a Text property, VB generates a run-time error. In this example, the error is not relevant and does not require handling since we want VB to simply ignore any control that does not apply (controls without a text property). The On Error Resume Next tells the system to ignore the error and to keep going.

◆ Process errors immediately after they occur. This is possible because VB still sets the values of Err.Number and Err.Description when an error occurs, even if On Error Resume Next is in effect. This allows you a second style of local error trapping, as discussed in the next section.

Centralized Error Handling Techniques

Whenever possible, it's a good idea to centralize your error handling code into a procedure whose single purpose is to handle errors. Then, simply call the error handling procedure from anywhere an error occurs within the application.

This is possible with some limitations. As we stated at the beginning of this chapter, some error recovery code must always be placed in the local procedure where the error occurred. You can, however, use a pair of techniques that standardize and centralize error handling to a great extent.

Write Generic Code for Frequently Used Functionality

Since just a few functions or statements in most applications can cause run-time errors, you should check to see whether the same error-prone function or statement is liable to be used often in one or more applications. Once you identify such statements, you should write wrapper functions for them. These wrapper functions would contain full error handling code and could return a flag indicating whether they ran with problems.

The next time you needed to use the functionality contained in the wrapper, you would call the wrapper function without having to think about the internal mechanics of handling an error. This provides an alternative to calling the naked underlying function or statement every time you needed it and repeating the error handling code in every routine you called it from.

In the following example, we see two wrapper functions.

The first wrapper function, OpenOLEServer, provides a wrapper for GetObject. For more background on how GetObject and CreateObject work, see Chapters 10 and 11 on OLE objects. The function takes a presumably blank object-type variable and a string variable as parameters. The string variable contains the name of an OLE server's application and class as found in the Windows Registry. The job of the function is to set the object parameter to the object class indicated in the string parameter. The function will return a true or false depending on whether it was successful or not.

The second wrapper function, NewObject, provides a wrapper for CreateObject. It functions similarly to OpenOLEServer. Notice that we call NewObject from within the error handler of CreateObject.

```
[Public Functions in a Standard Module]
Public Function OpenOLEServer(objServer As Object, strName As
➥String) As Boolean
    Dim blnResult As Boolean
    blnResult = True
    On Error GoTo OpenOLEServer_Error
    Set objServer = GetObject(, strName)
    OpenOLEServer = blnResult
    Exit Function
OpenOLEServer_Error:
    Select Case Err.Number
    Case 429
        blnResult = NewObject(objServer, strName)
        Resume Next
    Case Else
        blnResult = False
        Resume Next
    End Select
End Function
Public Function NewObject(objServer As Object, strName As
➥String) As Boolean
    Dim blnResult As Boolean
    blnResult = True
    On Error GoTo NewObject_Error
    Set objServer = CreateObject(strName)
    NewObject = blnResult
    Exit Function
NewObject_Error:
    blnResult = False
    Resume Next
End Function
```

One of the main reasons for having a couple of wrapper functions like OpenOLEServer and NewObject is that we can call them from anywhere else in our code whenever we need their functionality. We don't have to rewrite the error checking routine each time we want to initialize an OLE object because it's all done in one place.

The following example shows a Command Button's click event, which is able to initialize one of three objects based on which of the three option buttons the user has selected. Notice that we only need one line of code to call OpenOLEServer and store its return value. All the nasty details of error handling have been taken care of once and for all inside OpenOLEServer.

```
[General Declarations Section of Form]
Option Explicit
Private xl As Object
Private wd As Object
Private bg As Object
[Event procedure for a command button]
Private Sub cmdGenericServer_Click()
    Dim blnOpenResult As Boolean
    Dim strAppName As String
    If optExcel Then
        strAppName = "Excel"
        blnOpenResult = OpenOLEServer(xl, "Excel.Application")
    ElseIf optWord Then
        strAppName = "Word"
        blnOpenResult = OpenOLEServer(wd, "Word.Basic")
    ElseIf optBogus Then
        strAppName = "Bogus application"
        blnOpenResult = OpenOLEServer(bg, "Bogus.Application")
    Else
        MsgBox "select an application to open first"
    End If
    If Not blnOpenResult Then MsgBox "Couldn't open " &
➥strAppName
End Sub
```

Pass Error Codes to a Centralized Error-Handling Function

For common types of errors with very standard resolutions, you can set up a single function to handle errors. You can then call this function from routines where you wish to perform error handling. The function can take the error number as a parameter, decide what to do about the error based on its number, and return an integer code that tells the calling routine how to resume.

Note that this technique doesn't save you from having to write error handling code in each routine, but it does let you simplify the error handling code that you have to write, perhaps even to the point where all you have to do is paste the same error handling code into most routines that require error handling.

In order for the function to be able to communicate with other routines about types of Resume statements, you should set up some constants to stand for the various types of Resume statements:

Part

I

Ch

5

```
[General Declarations Section of Standard Module]
Option Explicit
Public Const errEND = 0
Public Const errRESUME = 1
Public Const errRESUMENEXT = 2
```

The function itself will take a required parameter representing the error number it's supposed to handle. In this example, we've also supplied an optional parameter about whether the function is to show any message to the user. If the parameter isn't supplied, we assume that the function is to show a message to the user.

You would then use a Case Select structure to determine which error or range of errors you were dealing with. In this example, we don't show any realistic error handling, but simply give various messages based on the range the error number falls in. Notice that we set the return value of the function to one of the three Resume types. The calling routine will then behave according to the way we set the function's return value:

```
[Function in Standard Module]
Public Function HandleError(ErrNumber As Long, Optional
➥ShowMessage As Variant)
    If IsMissing(ShowMessage) Then
        ShowMessage = True
    End If
    Select Case ErrNumber
        Case Is > 500
            MsgBox "Fatal Error# " & ErrNumber
            HandleError = errEND
        Case Is > 200
            MsgBox "Ignoring Error# " & ErrNumber
            HandleError = errRESUMENEXT
        Case Else
            MsgBox "Recovering from Error# " & ErrNumber
            HandleError = errRESUME
    End Select
End Function
```

The following example shows how you would use the error handling function from another routine. Note that the routine still needs its own error handler, but the error handler is now an entirely standard affair and its only job is to call the error handler with the number of the current error, and then act based on the return value of the error handler:

```
Private Sub cmdMakeError_Click()
    Dim intResumeCode As Integer
    On Error GoTo cmdMakeError_Error
    MakeError
    Exit Sub
cmdMakeError_Error:
    MsgBox "Handling error in calling routine"
    intResumeCode = HandleError(Err.Number)
    If intResumeCode = errRESUME Then
        Resume
    ElseIf intResumeCode = errRESUMENEXT Then
        Resume Next
    Else
        End
    End If
End Sub
```

Using the Err Object to Get Information About an Error

VB's Err object is a built-in object available to every running application.

The Err object's properties reflect information about any pending runtime error condition. The object's most important properties are:

- ◆ Number: The standard VB error number, or the error number belonging to the Source application, if the error was generated in a Server app. Number is the default or value property for the Err object. Remember, the default property represents a property that can be implied when you make reference to it. For example, the following two code lines both set the value of Err.Number to 429:

    ```
    Err.Number=429    'Number property set to 429

    Err=429    'Number property set to 429
    ```

- ◆ Description: A string containing a standard one-line error description that corresponds to the Number property. You can change the Description property in code.

◆ Source: A string providing the name of an object application (such as an OLE server) that generated the error. The value of the Source property will be blank if the error comes from the current VB app. You can change the Source property in code.

In previous examples in this chapter, we've seen how you can use the Number and Description properties in such lines as:

```
If Err.Number = 74 Then . . .
```

or

```
MsgBox "Error #" & Err.Number & ": " & Err.Description
```

The Err object also has two methods:

◆ *Clear.* This method clears the Err object's properties. After you call the Clear method, there is no pending error condition. Any type of Resume statement also clears the Err object's properties.

◆ *Raise.* This method causes an error. The syntax is:

```
Err.Raise number
```

where *number* represents the error number you want to generate. See the following sections for discussion of why and how to use the Raise method.

Note Note: the Err object has several other properties not listed here. See VB's online documentation on the Err object for more information. ■

Generating an Error with the Err Object's Raise Method

The Raise method enables you to generate a run-time error. You might use Err.Raise for two basic reasons:

◆ You want to test your error handling to see how it reacts to a certain error. Err.Raise can cause whatever error you want to observe in your VB application.

◆ You want to control exactly how and when errors are handled in your application. See the section later in this chapter entitled "Using Err.Raise to Pass an Error up the Call Stack"

◆ You want to generate and trap your own programmer-defined errors. Visual Basic doesn't use all of the available numbers for its own errors. If you want to generate your own errors, begin with the number 32767 and work you way down. For example:

```
Public Sub ValidateAllFields()
    On Error Go To Err_ValidateFields
    If sngHourlyRate>85 then
            Err.Raise 32700 'force your own error to
occur
    End If
    .
    .
    .

    Exit Sub
err_ValidateFields:
    If Err.Number=32700 then
            Err.Description="Hourly Rate must not exceed
$80.00"
            Msgbox Err.Description
            End If
    .
    .

    .
End Sub
```

Using Err.Raise as a Debugging Technique

Placing a temporary Err.Raise line in your code will help in debugging your app's error handling. For instance, let's say you want to see how the application reacts if the selected network device is unavailable. First, find the Err.Number associated with this error problem. You can use VB's help to look up Trappable Errors. Specifically, check the Miscellaneous Errors category. Note that the "Device Unavailable" is the Err.Number of 68. So, you could write the following code to force the error to happen:

```
Err.Raise 68
```

You'll soon find out whether your error handling code traps the error. You can use the debugger's single-step mode to observe what happens when this error occurs.

Another debugging tool uses the code line listed below. While running the app in design mode, you could prompt yourself to indicate the number of the error you'd like to cause and observe how your error handling treats the error:

```
Err.Raise cLng(InputBox("Error Number:"))
```

Using Err.Raise to Pass an Error Up the Call Stack

In the following sections on "Passing an Error up the Call Stack" and "Generating Another Error in an Error Handler," we discuss what happens when you generate an error inside an error handler and why you might even want to do this.

As you would expect, an error generated in an error handler causes a run-time error. However, the current procedure can't treat the error in the handler, and control automatically passes up to the calling procedure. If there is no calling procedure, VB displays the default error dialog box and ends the application.

In the following example, we explicitly handle Error 54 in the current error handler. If other errors occur, we pass the error number back to the procedure that called the current procedure by raising the error again:

```
Private Sub MySub()
    On Error GoTo MySub_Err
    . . . Code which might cause an error
    Exit Sub
MySub_Err:
    If Err.Number = 54 Then
        . . . handle this error
        Resume Next
    Else
        . . . let caller procedure handle other errors
        Err.Raise Err.Number 'pass the current error
(Err.Number) to the calling procedure
    EndIf
End Sub
```

In the preceding example, if the current procedure had no error handler enabled, the error automatically gets passed up the call stack to the calling procedure. That is, you would not need to use Err.Raise, since the error is passed up to the calling procedure automatically.

Anytime that an error is passed up to the calling procedure (whether automatically or by force using Err.Raise), the error continues getting passed up the call stack until either:

◆ VB encounters a routine with an error handler. The error is then considered to have happened in the routine with the error handler. That is, if the error handler includes a Resume statement, the apps resume at the level of the error handler (not necessarily the level at which the error occurred).

In the following example, the cmdOK_Click event procedure calls MySub. If an error other than error 54 happens in MySub, the Err.Raise statement will trigger the error to happen again in MySub's error handler. Since an error handler can't handle its own errors, VB passes the error back to cmdOK_Click (the calling routine). The error handler in cmdOK_Click's treats the error, and the Resume Next statement resumes locally within the cmdOK_Click event (specifically, the code resumes at the Exit Sub statement in cmdOK_Click). This is because, once the error gets passed up the call stack, VB considers the error to have occurred on the line that invoked the subroutine:

```
Private cmdOK_Click()
    On Error GoTo OK_Click
    MySub    'call to MySub procedure
    Exit Sub    'code resumes here if MySub generates an
error other than 54 OK_Click:
    . . . Handle any errors
    Resume Next
End Sub

Private Sub MySub()
    On Error GoTo MySub_Err
    . . . Code which might cause an error
    Exit Sub
MySub_Err:
    If Err.Number = 54 Then
```

```
                . . . handle this error
              Resume
          Else
                . . . let caller handle other errors
              Err.Raise Err.Number   'pass the current error
      ➥(Err.Number) up to cmdOK_Click
          EndIf
      End Sub
```

◆ VB reaches the top of the call stack without encountering an error handler. In this case, VB's default error dialog box displays and the application terminates.

Error-Handling Routines and the Call Stack

In VB, a routine without an error handler will not necessarily signify an ungraceful end to the application if an error occurs in that routine.

If an unhandled error happens in a routine, VB immediately exits that routine. If the routine where the error occurred is not the first routine on the call stack—that is, if another routine has called it—then VB will act as if the calling routine had the error. VB will consider the error to have happened on the line in the caller that invoked the routine where the error actually occurred. Similarly, if that calling routine has no error handler either, then VB exits the calling routine, and if *it* has a caller above it in the call stack, then *that* calling routine gets a shot at handling the error, and so on.

Put more succinctly, an error keeps getting passed up the call stack until either:

◆ VB encounters a routine with an error handler. The error is then considered to have happened in the routine with the error handler.

◆ VB gets all the way to the top of the call stack without encountering an error handler. In this case, VB's run-time error handler comes up and the application terminates.

As discussed in the previous section, you may want to and can pass errors "up the call stack"—that is, you can purposely let a calling routine handle the error.

Passing an Error Up the Call Stack

You might want to pass an error up the call stack when you have a main routine calling many specialized subroutines. Each specialized subroutine can handle errors peculiar just to the things that subroutine does. If an error of a more general type occurs in a subroutine, however, we might defer that error to the calling routine, which could have an error handler for these types of errors.

Remember, you can pass an error up the call stack by:

- ◆ Having no error handler in the current procedure.
- ◆ Using Err.Raise in the current procedure's error handler.

No Error Handler in Current Procedure

If the current procedure has no error handler, you must remember that all run-time errors that occur here will get passed up the call stack to be handled in the calling routine.

If the current procedure is the first procedure in the call stack, then VB's default run-time error handler will show the user an error message and terminate the application.

Part

I

Ch

5

Generating Another Error in an Error Handler

This can happen in two ways: on purpose and by accident. If you generate an error with Err.Raise, say, inside an error handler, it means you want to pass the error up the call stack. If you generate an error by accident in an error handler, it means you messed up.

TIP

Keep your error handling code simple in order to avoid generating a run-time error within the error handler, unless you intentionally generate one with Err.Raise.

Resume Statement Always Points to the Current Routine

If an error is passed up the call stack and an error handler in some calling routine finally takes over the handling of the error, then VB considers the error to have occurred in the routine where the handler runs.

This also means that the Resume or Resume Next statements will act as if the error had really occurred in the calling routine. The error is considered to have happened in the line which ultimately called the subroutine where the error actually occurred, and Resume or Resume Next will function with respect to this calling line.

In the following example, the cmdOK_Click event procedure calls MySub. If an error other than error 54 happens in MySub, the Err.Raise statement will trigger the error to happen again in MySub's error handler. Since an error handler can't handle its own errors, VB passes the error back to cmdOK_Click (the calling routine). CmdOK_Click's error handler does whatever it has to do with the error, and the Resume Next statement will resume at the Exit Sub in cmdOK_Click, not on any line in MySub. This is because, once the error has passed up the call stack, VB considers it to have happened on the line that invoked the subroutine:

```
Private cmdOK_Click()
    On Error GoTo OK_Click
    MySub
    Exit Sub
OK_Click:
    . . . Handle any errors
    Resume Next
End Sub
Private Sub MySub()
    On Error GoTo MySub_Err
    . . . Code which might cause an error
    Exit Sub
MySub_Err:
    If Err.Number = 54 Then
        . . . handle this error
        Resume Next
    Else
        . . . let caller handle other errors
        Err.Raise Err.Number
    EndIf
End Sub
```

Taking the Disc Test

 If you have read and understood the material in the chapter, you are ready to test your knowledge. Insert the CD-ROM that comes with this book and run the self-test software as described in Appendix H, "Using the CD-ROM."

From Here...

It's especially important to know about run-time error handling when you require that VB go beyond its own resources. You should keep this chapter in mind when you look at Chapters 10 and 11 on OLE and Chapters 12 and 13 on data access.

Part

I

Ch

5

Part II.

The Visual Interface

Chapter Prerequisite

You should be familiar with the fundamentals of the VB language discussed in Chapters 2 and 3.

6

Common Properties of the Form Object and Control Objects

Every form and control has a predefined set of properties. These properties define the form or control's appearance as well as some of its behaviors. For example, properties determine whether a user can click inside of a text box to type text, press the Enter key to trigger a command button, use the tab key to move through controls on a form, or use the mouse to resize a form. Many Visual Basic form and control objects share a set of common properties.

In this chapter we discuss only those properties that are important to the Visual Basic 4.0 Certification Exam and that are important to several objects. See the sections under specific control names in Chapter 3, "Working With Visual Basic Code," for discussions of properties specific to just one control.

The topics covered in this chapter will include a general discussion on properties, as well as identifying properties common to the form object and control object:

◆ Ways to change a Property Value

◆ How to reference a property in code

◆ How to reference an object's default property, known as its value

◆ How to change an object's color

◆ How to change an object's visibility and availability

◆ How to enable users to navigate the controls on a form

◆ How to change the appearance of the mouse pointer icon

◆ How to reference an object's position and size

◆ How to manipulate the contents and appearance of text appearing in/on an object

◆ How to create access keys for controls

Referencing a Property Within Code

If you need to read or write to a property within code, you need to reference the object's name in front of the property name using this general syntax:

```
ControlName.PropertyName
```

For example, if you want to evaluate a CommandButton's Enabled property within an If condition, you can do it in one of two ways. Both ways are illustrated in the following examples:

```
If cmdAdd.Enabled=True Then. . .
```

or

```
If cmdAdd.Enabled Then . . .
```

Notice that the Enabled property is a Boolean type and therefore, you can imply a true value, as in the second example.

You can also assign a value to the property as long as you assign the correct data type for the property:

```
cmdAdd.Enabled = True
```

Each form and control object has one default property known as the control's value. This property is often considered the most commonly used property of that control.

Whenever you reference a default property within code, you can imply the property name. Simply indicate the object name, and VB will understand that you're making reference to the object's default property.

For instance, since the Text property is the default property for a TextBox, we can imply the Text property:

```
txtName = "Priscilla"
```

Table 6.1   Default Properties for the Form and Common Controls

Object Type	Default Property
CheckBox	Value
ComboBox	Text
CommandButton	Value
Data Control	Caption
DirListBox	Path
DriveListBox	Drive
FileListBox	FileName
Form	Caption
Frame	Caption
Horizontal ScrollBar	Value
Image	Picture
Label	Caption
Line	Visible
ListBox	Text

Part

II

Ch

6

continues

Table 6.1   Continued

Object Type	Default Property
Menu	Enabled
OptionButton	Value
PictureBox	Picture
Shape	Shape
TextBox	Text
Timer	Enabled
Vertical ScrollBar	Value

Note   For more information on how to use these properties, see the individual sections for each control in Chapter 3, "Working with Visual Basic Code." ■

Some VB programmers prefer not to implicitly reference a control's value property within code. Obviously, the meaning of the code line is less apparent without specific reference to the control's property. Even more seriously, someone reading the code line might altogether miss the fact that you are referring to a control property.

Setting Properties Common to the Form Object and Control Object

The following sections do not represent an exhaustive list of all properties. Rather, the properties discussed here belong to a majority of VB objects (we use the term *object* within this chapter to refer exclusively to the form object and control objects).

Note   To get information about properties that are unique to just one or a few controls, see the sections for each of the standard Windows controls in Chapter 3, "Working with Visual Basic Code." ■

The Name Property

The Name property contains the identifier that you'll use to refer to a control in your program's code. A control's Name must be unique within the form. Rules for creating a property name are the same as rules for forming a variable's or constant's name:

◆ Up to 40 characters

◆ Can only contain letters, digits, and underscores

◆ Must begin with a letter

In addition, Microsoft recommends that you use Hungarian notation conventions when you name your controls. Notice the proceeding examples illustrate that the first three characters of the name property indicate the object type and are always displayed in lower case:

cmdOK	for a CommandButton
txtName	for a TextBox
lblName	for a Label
optSingle	for an Option Button
frmMain	for a form

You can't change a form or control's name property at run time. Although you use the name in code whenever you reference the form or control, the name property can't be referenced directly. For example, if you have a control whose name property is txtCity, you can't use the expression txtCity.name in your code.

Occasionally your code will need to check an unknown control's name. This can happen when the control has been passed as a parameter into a function or procedure. It can also happen when you're traversing a Form's Controls collection. In such cases, you'll need to use the Is operator, as in the following example:

```
Sub MySub (txtThisBox as TextBox)
    Dim ctrlCurr as Control
    If txtThisBox Is txtCity Then
        . . . Do something only if the
                parameter passed was txtCity
    EndIf
```

Part
II

Ch

6

```
      For Each ctrlCurr in Controls
            If ctrlCurr Is cmdOK Then
                    . . . Do something only if the
                    control is cmdOK
      Next ctrlCurr
End Sub
```

▶ **See** "Accessing a Form's Controls with the Controls Collection," **p. 74**

The Visible Property

The Visible property stores a Boolean-type value indicating whether or not the form or control is displayed on the screen. A control's Visible property is True (visible) by default.

When you make a form or control invisible, you also disable it. In other words, the user can't access an invisible form or control. However, an invisible form or control can still be referenced within the program code.

The Enabled Property

The Enabled property is a Boolean-type value that indicates whether a control is able to receive focus. Most controls appear grayed out when the Enabled property is False (see fig. 6.1).

When the Enabled property is False, the user can't access the object.

FIG. 6.1 ⇒

This form contains both enabled and disabled controls.

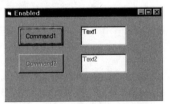

This would mean that the user is unable to trigger events that depend on user actions, such as Click, KeyPress, or GotFocus.

Note The Timer control's Enabled property has a different meaning from the meaning of the Enabled property of other objects. See the section on the Timer control in Chapter 3, "Working with Visual Basic Code," for more information. ■

The hWnd property

The hWnd property represents the unique Windows handle assigned to the object. This handle identifies the form or control outside the VB application. You will need to use the hWnd property with Dynamic Link Library (DLL) calls that require you to pass a reference to a form or control as an argument. Remember, form and controls are identified by their name property only within Visual Basic. You will need to use the hWnd property to identify a form or control outside of Visual Basic.

▶ **See** "Dynamic Link Libraries," **p. 527**

The Windows operating environment assigns the value of a control's or form's hWnd property at run time. Because Windows arbitrarily assigns its value, you can't expect the value of the hWnd property to ever be the same between any two sessions of your application. In fact, Windows has the right to change this property's value at any time during a session—so you can't even count on the value remaining the same during a single run of your program.

Because this property is only available at run time, it is not listed in the Properties window at design time.

> **Caution**
> Because Windows can actually change a control's or form's hWnd during a single session, it's not a good idea to store the hWnd property in a temporary variable.

> **Note** See the entry for the hWnd property in the *Visual Basic 4.0 Programmer's Reference* for a list of controls that support this property. ■

The Tag Property

You, the programmer, define the function of the Tag property. In other words, VB doesn't use the Tag property for any internal purpose. You can decide the type of information you want to store in this open-ended property, at either run time or design time.

The Tag property can contain String information. By default, the Tag is a blank string.

The Tag property is used for various purposes. For example, the Tag property can be used to store documentation about the object. It can also be used to store a value that needs to be passed from one form to another. MDI child forms often use the Tag property. You can place a unique identifying string in each new child's Tag property so that your code can identify the form later.

▶ **See** "Referencing MDI Children," **p. 308**

The Index Property

If a control's Index property contains a value, it indicates that the control is a member of a control array. The exact value of the control's Index property indicates the control's position in the control array.

The Index property can contain an integer value of 0 or greater and is blank by default.

▶ **See** "Using Control Arrays," **p. 64**

The Font Property

This property determines the appearance of text in a control's Text or Caption property (see fig. 6.2). Although Font is listed in the Property Window, it is actually an object rather than a property. The Font object has several properties such as Font, Style, and Size.

You can set properties of the Font object at design time with the following steps:

1. Select the control whose Font you want to change.
2. Access the Property Window.
3. Select Font.
4. Click the drop-down arrow located to the right of the Font property.
5. The Font Dialog box displays the properties of the Font Object.

The syntax for referencing the properties of the Font object at run time:

```
ControlName.Font.PropertyName
```

Notice that the Font object is unique since it is a dependent object, an object that needs to be referenced by another object.

For instance, if you wish to change the Size Property of the Font object for cmdOK, you can type the statement:

```
cmdOK.Font.Size = 12
```

The Font object has four Boolean properties that toggle aspects of the Text, or the Caption property of a form or control:

◆ Bold

◆ Italic

◆ StrikeThrough

◆ UnderLine

The Font object also has three additional properties:

◆ Name: the name of an available Font on the user's system.

◆ Size: a number corresponding to a valid font size for the specified Font Name.

◆ Weight: not available at design time. It is automatically set to 700 if Bold is true or 400 if Bold is false. You may, however, manipulate Weight at run time to obtain text with different shades of boldness.

Note There could be some confusion about the Font property for those familiar with earlier versions of Visual Basic. In earlier versions, controls had no Font object. Instead, the controls directly implemented the various Font properties, which were known as FontSize, FontBold, and so on.

You still must use these individual Font properties with the CommonDialog control. It's also still possible to reference the individual Font properties with other controls in code, but Microsoft recommends against using this obsolete technique. ▪

FIG. 6.2 ⟹

Some properties of this control's Font object have been changed.

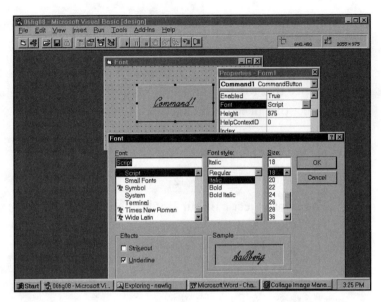

The BackColor Property, RGB, and Color Constants

The BackColor property represents an object's background color over which text and graphics are displayed.

> **Note** See the entry for the BackColor property in the *Visual Basic 4.0 Language Reference* for a list of controls that support this property and for a discussion of controls that require special consideration when using this property. ▨

To set the BackColor property at design time, you can follow these steps:

1. Select the control whose BackColor you wish to set.
2. Access the Property window.
3. Select the BackColor property.
4. Click on the drop-down arrow located to the right of the BackColor property (see fig. 6.3).
5. Select the desired color from the palette.

FIG. 6.3 ⟹

A color palette will appear when you double-click an object's BackColor or ForeColor property at design time.

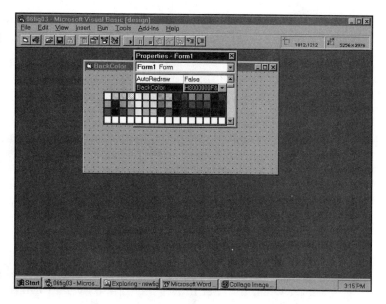

A color value represents a Long integer in hexadecimal format. You can either learn the rules for how to format the hex number or use other ways to indicate a color. To set the Backcolor property at run time, use:

◆ One of the 16 VB color constants, which all have obvious names like vbRed, vbYellow, and vbMagenta. You can read more about them in VB's help facility under the topic "color constants." An example of the use of a VB color constant looks like:

```
Me.BackColor = vbRed
```

or

◆ One of the VB constants for Windows system colors, which you can also read about in VB's help facility under the topic "color constants."

◆ The RGB (Red–Green–Blue) function, which requires three parameters. The first parameter represents the red component of the color, the last two arguments represent the Green and Blue components, respectively. The range of each parameter is an integer from 0 to 255. The RGB function will mix the three

Part

II

Ch

6

color components into a single color and will return a single Long number that you can use to set the BackColor property. Here are a few examples that use the RGB function:

```
'pure black:
Me.BackColor = RGB(0,0,0)
'pure white:
Me.BackColor = RGB(255,255,255)
'pure red:
Me.BackColor = RGB(255,0,255)
'purple, blue predominating:
Me.BackColor = RGB(100,0,255)
'yellow:
Me.BackColor = RGB(255,255,0)
```

The MousePointer Property

The MousePointer property specifies the appearance of the mouse pointer when the user moves the mouse over a form or control (see fig. 6.4). There are 16 standard mouse pointer images available in the MousePointer property's drop-down ListBox.

You can also specify 99–Custom as the MousePointer. This property value enables the mouse pointer to represent the image specified in the MouseIcon property. If no image is specified in the MouseIcon property, then the image of the mouse pointer will revert to the default of the MousePointer property.

 Note See the entry for the MouseIcon property in the *Visual Basic 4.0 Language Reference* for more information on that property. ▪

FIG. 6.4 ⇒
The MousePointer changes when the user moves the mouse over this CommandButton control, because the CommandButton's MousePointer property points to the hourglass icon.

The Top, Left, Width, and Height Properties, and the Move Method

These properties and method determine the position and size of an object.

Specifically, the Top and Left properties refer to the left and top position of an object relative to its container object. Recall that all VB objects that display on the screen have an object that contains or holds the object. A control's container object is the form in most cases. However, the form is not the only container object. A control can reside in a frame or picturebox control, both of which are examples of other container objects. A form's container object is the screen object. For example, if a textbox resides on a form at the following coordinates (left=0, top=0), then the textbox is positioned at the very top left side of the form.

The Height and Width properties determine the actual size of the object within its contain object.

Tip

At design time, the Toolbar indicates the coordinates of the Top and Left properties and the coordinates of Height and Width properties for the currently selected form or control. These coordinates are displayed on the right side of the VB Toolbar (see fig. 6.5).

You can change a form or control's left, top, width, and height directly, or you can use the Move method to change these properties all at once.

These four lines:

```
TxtCity.Top = 200
TxtCity.Left = 100
TxtCity.Width = 600
TxtCity.Height = 400
```

have the same effect as this line:

```
TxtCity.Move 200,100,600,400
```

Notice that the Move method takes four parameters representing the position and size properties. Only the first parameter (representing the

Part

II

Ch

6

Left property) is required. This could be useful for left–aligning several controls on a form.

FIG. 6.5 ⇒

At design time, the current object's position (Top and Left) and size (Height and Width) properties are displayed in the two rightmost panes of the VB Toolbar.

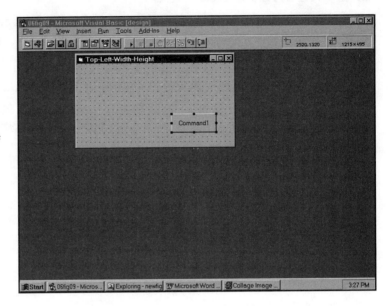

Note The Timer, as well as a few other controls, has no Width or Height property because it cannot be resized and is invisible at run time. Its Top and Left properties are only available at design time. ∎

The ScaleMode, ScaleTop, ScaleLeft, ScaleHeight, and ScaleWidth Properties

Even though these properties belong to only two objects, we include them in this summary of common control properties because they affect all the controls that can be contained in a Form or PictureBox.

The ScaleMode property determines the unit of measurement for a Form or PictureBox. You can place other controls in a Form or PictureBox, so when you specify those controls' Top or Left properties, you will specify Top and Left in the unit of measurement given by the containing form's or PictureBox control's ScaleMode. By default, ScaleMode is 1–Twip.

Note A Twip is the default unit of screen measurement in VB and is equal to 1/20th of a point. Since a point is 1/72nd of an inch, a Twip represents 1/1440th of an inch. Unlike Pixels, Twips are screen-independent so that your application will look the same regardless of the display system or resolution. ■

If ScaleMode is any value other than 0-User, then the ScaleTop and ScaleLeft automatically are set to 0, while ScaleHeight and ScaleWidth represent the form's or PictureBox control's internal size (that is, the size of the area inside the object's borders) in the specified units (see fig. 6.6).

FIG. 6.6 ⇒

The ScaleHeight and ScaleWidth properties of a form or PictureBox control represent the internal area of the object.

If you set ScaleMode to 0-User, then you may set ScaleHeight, ScaleTop, ScaleLeft, and ScaleWidth to reflect some custom coordinate system for the form or PictureBox control (see fig. 6.7).

FIG. 6.7 ⇒

The form's ScaleMode is 0-User, so the Left and Top properties of this command button are expressed in the form's custom units, rather than in twips.

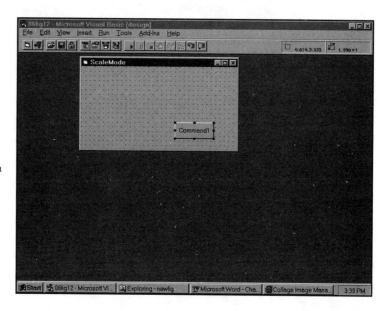

Part

II

Ch

6

Setting the Tab Order

As a user of Windows programs, you've probably noticed that you can use the Tab key to navigate through the controls in a dialog box (for example, a Print dialog box).

Your user can also use the Tab key to navigate among controls on a form in VB programs. Two properties determine the way a user tabs through controls on a form:

◆ The TabStop property specifies whether a control can be accessed with the Tab key.

◆ The TabIndex property determines the order in which controls receive focus as the user presses the Tab key.

The TabStop Property

The TabStop property is a Boolean property that determines whether or not the user can set focus to a control with the Tab key. A control's TabStop property is true by default.

Tip

Even if a control's TabStop property is false, the user can still give focus to the control by other means (like selecting the control with the mouse or programmatically giving focus to the control with the SetFocus method). If you don't want the user to be able to set focus to the control at all, you should set the control's Enabled property to false.

Those controls that have a TabIndex property also have the TabStop property (see the list of controls in the previous section).

Note The Label control doesn't have a TabStop property, even though it has a TabIndex property. (See "Providing Access keys for TextBox Control" earlier in this chapter.) ■

The TabIndex Property

A control's TabIndex property specifies the relative order on the form in which a control will receive focus when the user presses the Tab key. The TabIndex can be read and written at both run time and design time.

VB automatically assigns a value to the TabIndex property when you place a control on the form. VB assigns the TabIndex in ascending order as each control is added. The TabIndex property, therefore, indicates the order in which you placed the controls on a form.

You may reassign controls' TabIndex properties to create a different tab order from the default tab order. Whenever you change the value of a TabIndex property or delete an existing control from a form, VB automatically adjusts the value of the TabIndex properties for the other controls—to ensure that no two controls have the same TabIndex and that there are no gaps in the tab order.

Tip

When you change the value of a control's TabIndex properties, it's best to begin with the highest-numbered control in the new order and work backwards. This technique is helpful because otherwise VB shuffles tab orders around in a confusing manner if you reassign lower TabIndexes first.

The tab order is zero-based, so the first control in the tab order has a TabIndex property of 0. This control is the first to get focus once the form has loaded.

Note For a list of controls which support the TabIndex property, see the entry for this property in the *Visual Basic 4.0 Language Reference*. ▪

The Caption Property

Objects that have a Caption property will display the Caption as a run-time title on or beside the object. A CommandButton, for example, displays its caption on top of the button while the caption of an OptionButton resides to the right of this button type.

You can use the Caption property to implement an access key for a control.

Note See the following section on "Providing an Access Key for Controls with a Caption Property" for more information. ■

 Note See the entry for the Caption property in the *Visual Basic 4.0 Language Reference* for a list of controls which support this property. ■

Providing an Access Key for Controls with a Caption Property

Thus far, we know of two ways for a user to access a control. They are:

◆ Clicking the control with the mouse

◆ Moving to the control using the Tab key

These are both common ways for a user to move from one control to another. In some situations, however, these methods are not practical. Imagine that your user is navigating through a large data-entry screen that consists of 30 controls where most of the data entry requires typing. Shifting their hands from keyboard to mouse (and then back to the keyboard) each time they want to move to another control is annoying. The Tab key, on the other hand, is not always the best alternative if the user wants to jump over several controls to reach a control on the other side of the form. For example, the user must press the Tab key eight times to move from controlA with a TabIndex=1 to controlB with a TabIndex=9.

Many controls offer the ability to create an access key (ALT + underlined letter) to quickly move to a control using the keyboard. Access keys can be created for any control that has a Caption property (see fig. 6.8).

To create an access key for a control, include an ampersand (&), within the Caption property, in front of the letter that you desire as the access key; for example,

cmdOK.Caption="&OK"

FIG. 6.8 ⇒

The CommandButton's caption contains an ampersand in front of the letter "x" in Exit, displaying the letter as underlined. The user can access the CommandButton by pressing ALT + x.

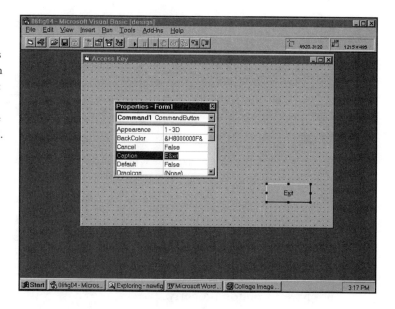

The placement of the ampersand causes the "O" to appear underlined within the Caption(<u>O</u>K). The user can access cmdOK by pressing Alt+O. In the case of a CommandButton control, the access key will also trigger the CommandButton's Click event.

Note The control must be both Enabled and Visible before its access key will work (see page 218 of this chapter for a discussion of the Enabled property and page 218 for a discussion of the Visible property). ▤

Note Remember, that some controls can never receive focus. Even if you include the "&" within a label's Caption property, for example, you will still not be able to access the label control. The "&" will result in an underlined character within the Caption but VB simply ignores the association with the access key. ▤

When the user presses the access key for different controls, these controls will behave differently depending on the type of control. You should check the online and printed documentation for VB 4.0 to verify the specific behavior of each control with an access key.

Part

II

Ch

6

Note Even though it doesn't have a Caption property, you can indirectly provide an access key for a TextBox control. See the following section "Providing an Access Key for the TextBox Control." ■

Providing an Access Key for the TextBox Control

Just as with other controls, you will often want your user to be able to use an access key to navigate to a TextBox. This is handy, for example, when you're creating a large data entry form with many textboxes. You want your user to be able to jump from the first textbox to the fifteenth textbox without picking up the mouse to select the textbox or pressing the tab key many times to reach the text box (see fig. 6.9). However, a TextBox control can't receive focus using an access key because it does not have a Caption property.

FIG. 6.9 ⇒

Each Label on this form provides an access key for the TextBox to the right of the Label.

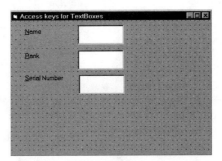

Note See the section entitled "Providing an Access Key for Controls with a Caption Property" of this chapter for a review on how to create access key for a control. ■

Recall that the Label control can't receive focus, but it does have a Caption property and a TabIndex property. The fact that the Label has a TabIndex property means that the Label has a position in the tabbing order of controls on a form.

Since the Label can't receive focus, however, VB simply skips over the Label when the user presses the Tab key or when the user attempts to access the label through its access keys. And where does VB set focus when it can't set focus to the Label? Focus goes to the next control in the tab order.

This means that if you have a Label that comes just before a TextBox in the tab order, using the label's access keys will actually set the focus to the TextBox.

In order to implement an access key for a TextBox control, you should take the following steps:

1. Place a Label on the form to the left of the TextBox.
2. Assign the Label an access key by placing an ampersand (&) in front of the desired letter within the Caption property.
3. Make sure that the Label's TabIndex property is one less than the TextBox's TabIndex property.

Taking the Disc Test

If you have read and understood the material in the chapter, you are ready to test your knowledge. Insert the CD-ROM that comes with this book and run the self-test software as described in Appendix H, "Using the CD-ROM."

From Here...

You might want to review Chapter 3, "Working with Visual Basic Code," in order to get a feel for how these properties fit within the framework of a VB application. Chapter 3 sections on each of the standard control types also help to provide a full picture of the properties available to a particular control.

Part
II

Ch
6

Chapter Prerequisite

You should be comfortable with the VB design-time environment, especially adding new Forms to a project and navigating through the Code Window.

You should also be familiar with user actions that occur in a Windows-based environment (drag and drop with the mouse, pressing a key on the keyboard, and so on).

7

Control and Form Object Events

This chapter covers common events of the Form and control objects, as well as VB's system objects. Terms and concepts covered include:

- ◆ **Mouse events**
- ◆ **Keystroke events**
- ◆ **Dragging and dropping with the mouse**
- ◆ **Form events and methods**
- ◆ **Implicit loading of a Form**
- ◆ **The active Form**
- ◆ **Modal and modeless Forms**
- ◆ **Refreshing graphics at run time**
- ◆ **VB System objects**

Programming with Mouse-Related Events

You will discover that programming mouse-related events is a common task within most applications. This is because the mouse is the most common device for user interaction within a Windows-based user interface.

In particular, the Click event is possibly the most commonly programmed event in a VB application. All the mouse events except MouseMove are directly related to the click action of one of the mouse buttons. For controls that support mouse events, the click-related events take place in the following order:

◆ MouseDown

◆ MouseUp

◆ Click

◆ DblClick

◆ MouseUp (after DblClick only)

Click

The Click event happens on a control when the control is enabled and the user both presses and releases a mouse button while the mouse pointer is over the control. If the mouse pointer is over a disabled control or if the mouse cursor is over a blank area of the Form, then the Form receives the Click event.

The Click event is easy to understand intuitively, because it represents a common user action that occurs dozens of times over a single session in any Windows-based application.

Notice that in our definition of the Click event in the first paragraph, we say that the user must *both* press and release the mouse button over the same control. The Click event won't occur if the user presses the mouse button over one control and then moves the mouse pointer off the control to release it. The same goes for a Form's Click event: The user must press and release the mouse button over an exposed area of the form or over a disabled control in order for the form to receive the Click event.

The Click event also can be triggered through a control's access key.

▶ **See** "Providing an Access Key for Controls with a Caption Property," **p. 230**

▶ **See** "Providing an Access Key for the TextBox," **p. 232**

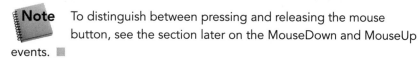 **Note** To distinguish between pressing and releasing the mouse button, see the section later on the MouseDown and MouseUp events. ▪

The following controls support the Click event as noted:

- ◆ *CheckBox* Only the left mouse button triggers a Click event for this control. You can also trigger a CheckBox control's Click event by changing its Value property to any of the three valid values (vbChecked, vbUnchecked, or vbGrayed).

- ◆ *ComboBox* In addition to triggering the Click event using the mouse, the user can also trigger the Click event by selecting an item in the list with the arrow keys.

- ◆ *CommandButton* The right mouse button will not trigger a Click event for this control, but the left button will. Pressing Enter or SpaceBar when a CommandButton has focus will trigger the Click event. Programmatically setting its Value property to True will also trigger the Click event.

- ◆ *Data-aware custom controls (DBCombo, DBGrid, DBList)* Left or right mouse button will trigger the Click event. The DBCombo and DBList behave like the ComboBox control.

- ◆ *DirListBox* Same as the ComboBox control

- ◆ *FileListBox* Same as the ComboBox control

- ◆ *Frame* Left or right mouse button

- ◆ *Form* Left or right mouse button

Part
II

Ch
7

- *Image* Left or right mouse button
- *Label* Left or right mouse button
- *ListBox* Same as the ComboBox control
- *Menu control* Right mouse button will not trigger the click event, but the left button will. If the menu control has a defined access key or shortcut key, the Click event triggers with either an access key or shortcut key.
- *OptionButton* Right mouse button will not trigger the click event, but the left button will. The SpaceBar triggers the Click event when the OptionButton control has focus. Programmatically setting the OptionButton control's Value property to True will also trigger its Click event.
- *PictureBox* Left or right mouse button
- *TextBox* Left or right mouse button

> **Caution**
> Setting Default or Cancel to true will only cause the CommandButton's Click *event procedure* to run. The Click *event* itself will not occur.

DblClick

The Double-Click event occurs on a Form or a control when it's an enabled object, the mouse pointer is directly over the Form or control, and the user clicks the mouse twice in rapid succession over the Form or control. Windows determines whether the user's two clicks represent a double-click or two single clicks. The user can access the Windows Control Panel to set the maximum time interval between two clicks for these two clicks to count toward a double-click.

Double-Click events are defined for the following objects:

- ComboBox
- CommandButton
- Data-aware custom controls (DBCombo, DBGrid, DBList)

- ◆ DirListBox
- ◆ FileListBox
- ◆ Form
- ◆ Frame
- ◆ Image
- ◆ Label
- ◆ ListBox
- ◆ Menu control
- ◆ OptionButton
- ◆ PictureBox
- ◆ TextBox

 Note Only with the left mouse button will the DblClick event trigger. ▮

When the user double-clicks a Form or a control that supports the DblClick event, Windows generates a Click event followed by a DblClick event for that control. When the user double-clicks a control such as a CommandButton that doesn't support the DblClick event but does support the Click event, Windows will generate two Click events for the control.

MouseDown and MouseUp

The MouseDown event triggers when the user presses a mouse button over a control or Form. Similarly, the MouseUp event occurs when the user releases the mouse button over a control or Form. Because the user can move the mouse between pressing and releasing the button, one object may receive the MouseDown event while a different object may receive the MouseUp event.

A MouseDown and a MouseUp event always occurs just before the Click event of a Form or control.

A MouseUp event also occurs just after a DblClick event.

Part
II

Ch
7

The MouseDown and MouseUp events have the same parameter list that can be used to detect whether the left or right mouse button is pressed, whether or not one of the auxiliary keys (Shift, Alt, or Ctrl) also is depressed during the mouse event, and the mouse pointer position within the Form or control.

All this information is available in parameters that the MouseUp or MouseDown event procedure receives from the system. The four parameters are:

- *Button As Integer.* A value representing which mouse button triggered the event. The value of this parameter is either vbLeftButton, vbRightButton, or vbMiddleButton.

- *Shift As Integer.* This parameter represents an integer that indicates whether an auxiliary key is pressed during the mouse event. It contains a value of 0 (none), 1 (Shift), 2 (Ctrl), 4 (Alt) or the sum of any combination of those keys. For example, if both the Ctrl and Alt key were pressed, the value of the Shift parameter is 6. You can check for the state of any one of the auxiliary keys with one of the VB constants vbAltMask, vbCtrlMask, or vbShiftMask. The following code illustrates how you could store the state of each auxiliary key in a Boolean variable within the MouseDown or MouseUp event procedure. The bit-wise representation of 1, 2, or 4 in the Shift parameter is 000000001, 000000010, 00000100. By doing a logical AND between the Shift parameter and one of the VB shift-key constants, you can pick out whether each of the three shift keys is currently pressed:

```
Dim blnIsAlt As Boolean
Dim blnIsCtrl As Boolean
Dim blnIsShift As Boolean
blnIsAlt = Shift And vbAltMask
blnIsCtrl = Shift And vbCtrlMask
blnIsShift = Shift And vbShiftMask
```

- *X As Single.* Horizontal position of the mouse pointer from the internal left edge of the control or Form receiving the event.

- *Y As Single.* Vertical position of the mouse pointer from the internal top edge of the control or Form receiving the event.

MouseMove

The MouseMove triggers every time the mouse is moved over a Form or control. The MouseMove event could therefore trigger dozens of times as the user quickly and casually moves the mouse. Remember, a user can trigger several contiguous MouseMove events just by being bored enough to move the mouse around while waiting for relatively long processes to complete (for example, data access, OLE Automation).

The MouseMove event has the same parameters as the MouseUp and MouseDown events.

You might use the MouseMove event to react to the user moving the MousePointer onto a control.

Implementing Drag-and-Drop

The process of dragging includes dragging a particular control with the mouse while dropping means moving the control onto another control or the Form. The drag-and-drop process does not happen automatically. The programmer must enable drag-and-drop for a specified control.

Drag-and-drop takes on different forms depending on what control the user is acting on. For instance, you might enable the user to physically move a control such as a PictureBox to another place within the Form. You might also use drag-and-drop to enable the user to drag a component of a particular control to another control. The user, for example, drags a file name from a FileListBox control and drops the file name on top of a PictureBox containing an image of a garbage can. Obviously, this action communicates that the user wants to delete this file. The FileListBox control is not dragged and dropped, but rather a property or some other attribute of the control.

Depending on your objectives, enabling drag-and-drop capabilities for a specific control usually includes two main steps:

Part

II

Ch

7

1. Make the control dragable using either the:

    DragMode property

or

    Drag method

2. Physically move the control by using the Move method.

The following sections in this chapter discuss how to write code for the drag-and-drop operation.

DragMode Property

You can use the DragMode property to determine whether a control is dragable. If the value of DragMode is Automatic, the user is able to drag the control without writing any code to implement the dragging.

DragMode's default value is Manual, which means that the user can't drag the control without some code supplied by the programmer.

Setting DragMode property to Automatic may save you from writing one or two lines of code. However, the control's mouse events respond in unexpected ways when the DragMode property is set to Automatic.

Drag Method

If you decide to make a control dragable through code and not the DragMode property, you need to use the Drag method. The Drag method is used to start, end, or cancel the drag operation of any control except the Line, Menu, Shape, Timer, or CommonDialog. The Dragging operation automatically ends as soon as the user releases the mouse button.

The most typical place to invoke the control's Drag method is in the control's MouseDown event procedure:

```
Private Sub picPretty_MouseDown(Button As Integer, _
Shift As Integer, _
X As Single, _
Y As Single)
    picPretty.Drag
End Sub
```

You might think that this could cause problems, because it would happen whenever the user just wanted to click or double-click the control (recall that a MouseDown event happens before every Click and DblClick).

However, the dragging operation ends as soon as the user releases the mouse button. Thus, when the user clicks this control, the dragging operation stops as soon as the user releases the mouse button during the click and no harm will be done.

DragDrop Event

The DragDrop event procedure triggers when the user drops the control being dragged. Use the DragDrop event to specify what happens when the user drops the control being dragged. You must place code in the DragDrop event of the receiving or destination control. That is, the DragDrop event is triggered for the control or form that receives the dropped control.

The DragDrop event procedure takes three parameters:

◆ *Source As Control*. This parameter indicates the name of the control being dragged.

◆ *X As Single*. The horizontal position of the mouse pointer within the destination control or Form.

◆ *Y As Single*. The vertical position of the mouse pointer within the destination control or Form.

Typically, you reference the Source parameter within the code to indicate what control you want to manipulate. A common reaction to a user dragging the *Source* (the control being dragged) is to move the *Source* to the current mouse pointer coordinates. In the following example, the code triggers when the user drops the source onto Myform:

```
Private Sub MyForm_DragDrop(Source As Control, _
X As Single, _
Y As Single)
    Source.Move X, Y
End Sub
```

Part

II

Ch

7

Tip

If you tested the previous code, notice the code line Source. Move X, Y always positions the control so that its upper left corner is aligned with the tip of the mouse pointer. If you want the control to drop so that it stays in the same relation to the mouse pointer as it did during the drag, you'll have to write a bit more code. See Chapter 12 of the VB *Programmer's Reference* for an example.

You've already seen that the code in the DragDrop event often contains the Move method to move the control being dragged. The next example uses the Additem method to move one item from a ListBox to another ListBox. Notice that the code is written in the DragDrop event for lstNewList, the destination control.

```
Private Sub lstNewList_DragDrop(Source As Control, _
        X As Single, _
        Y As Single)
        lstNewList.AddItem Source.List(Source.ListIndex)
End Sub
```

DragIcon Property

The DragIcon property is any bitmap image used to represent the Source while it's being dragged. You can set the DragIcon property at design time or run time in the same way that you set a PictureBox control's Picture property.

You may change the DragIcon property in your code during the dragging operation by using the DragOver event procedure discussed in the next section.

▶ **See** "PictureBox," **p. 132**

DragOver Event

The DragOver event, like the DragDrop event, doesn't happen to the control being dragged. Instead, it happens to the destination control, the control on which the *Source* (the control being dragged) is dropped. Like the DragDrop event, DragOver also receives parameters indicating which control is being dragged and the current position of the dragged image in the current control:

◆ *Source As Control.* The control being dragged.

◆ *X As Single.* The horizontal coordinate of the mouse pointer in the control or Form receiving the DragDrop event.

◆ *Y As Single.* The vertical coordinate of the mouse pointer in the control or Form receiving the DragDrop event.

DragOver also receives a fourth parameter indicating whether the event was triggered as the dragged control was dragged into the current control, as it left the current control, or as it moved from one location to another on the current control.

◆ *State as Integer.* This parameter can have three possible values corresponding to the value of one of the VB internal constants vbEnter, vbLeave, or vbOver. The value of this parameter indicates whether the dragged Source control has just exited the boundary of the current control, just entered it, or is moving over the current control.

You can use the DragOver event procedure to change the Source control's DragIcon when it enters and leaves the "air space" over the current control.

Imagine the user dragging an item from one ListBox and dropping it in another ListBox. For example, the first ListBox (lstCityEast) contains a list of city names which define the company's Eastern marketing territory. Within this application, your user wants the ability to redefine the Eastern marketing territory by adding to or deleting from the city names in lstCityEast. To provide the user an interface to add/delete items from lstCityEast, include a second ListBox (lstCityAll) that lists the city names for all the marketing territories. To delete a city from the Eastern marketing territory, the user would drag a city item from lstCityEast and drop the item into lstCityAll. Use the lstCityEast's DragIcon property to provide the user with a visual roadmap as to where they should drop the city item in order to delete it from lstCityEast.

In the following example, when the user drags the city item within lstCityEast or lstCityAll, the lstCityEast's DragIcon changes to a bitmap image of the Eastern portion of the U.S. When the user drags the city item outside of either of the ListBoxes, the lstCityEast's DragIcon changes to a NO symbol (a circle with a line drawn through it):

```
Private Sub lstCityAll_DragOver(Source As Control, _
X As Single, _
Y As Single, _
State As Integer)
    If State = vbEnter Then
        Source.DragIcon = picEastmap.Picture
    ElseIf State = vbLeave Then
        Source.DragIcon = picNoSymbol.Picture
    EndIf
End Sub
```

Validating User Input with the Keystroke Events

You will often want to validate keyboard input from the user. In the following sections, we discuss how to use three keystroke events to intercept, interpret, and modify each keystroke.

You can validate keystrokes on two different levels in VB:

◆ Control-level: You write validation code in the keystroke events of each separate control. The validation code in a control's keystroke event runs when that control has focus and the user sends keyboard activity.

◆ Form-level: The Form also has keystroke events that can intercept all keyboard input while that Form is the active Form. When Form-level key handling is active, the Form's keystroke events receive the key before the currently active control's key events receive it.

By default, Form-level key handling is not active.

▶ **See** "The Form's KeyPreview Property," **p. 247**

The Form's KeyPreview Property

The KeyPreview property is a True/False property belonging to the Form. KeyPreview determines whether or not the Form's keystroke events (KeyDown, KeyUp, and KeyPress) will be active.

If KeyPreview is set to its default value of False, user keyboard input will not trigger the Form's keystroke events and all keystroke handling will happen at the level of the individual control.

If KeyPreview is True, the Form's keystroke events will receive user keyboard input first, and then the active control's keystroke events will receive the keyboard input.

KeyPress

The KeyPress event happens after the KeyDown event, but before the KeyUp event. It detects the ASCII value of the character representing the pressed key. The KeyPress event only triggers if the key that is pressed represents an ASCII character.

The KeyPress event's single parameter is KeyASCII. KeyASCII, an integer, represents the ASCII value of the character generated by the user's KeyPress.

For instance, if the user keys an uppercase A, the KeyPress event triggers, and KeyASCII will have a value of 65 (65 is the ASCII code for uppercase A). You can use the Chr function to convert KeyASCII to a character value. You can also use the Asc function to convert a character back to its corresponding ASCII integer value.

▶ See "Asc," **p. 61**

▶ See "Chr and ChrB," **p. 61**

If you write code in the KeyPress event to change the value of KeyASCII, the system will then see the newly assigned character as the character which the user has just keyed. If you change the value of KeyASCII to 0, then the system will see no keystroke, and you have in effect thrown away the keystroke.

In the following example, we make sure that all characters keyed in by the user are converted to lowercase. The KeyPress event procedure converts KeyASCII to its character equivalent with the Chr function, then converts that character to lower case, converts the result back to an ASCII value with the Asc function, and finally reassigns the lowercase ASCII value back to KeyASCII:

```
Private Sub txtPassword_KeyPress(KeyASCII as Integer)
    Dim KeyChar As String
    KeyChar = Chr(KeyASCII)
    KeyChar = LCase(KeyASCII)
    KeyASCII = Asc(KeyChar)
End Sub
```

In the following example, the KeyPress event procedure checks to see whether the user has keyed a vowel. If so, it discards the character by changing the value of KeyASCII to 0:

```
Private Sub txtPassword_KeyPress(KeyASCII as Integer)
    Dim KeyChar As String
    KeyChar = UCase(Chr(KeyASCII))
    If Instr("AEIOU",KeyChar) <> 0 then
        KeyASCII = 0
    EndIf
End Sub
```

KeyDown and KeyUp

The KeyDown and KeyUp events happen when the user respectively presses and releases a key on the keyboard. Their event procedures take two parameters:

- KeyCode As Long: Contains a code for the physical key that the user pressed. You can check for a particular key by comparing KeyCode with one of the VB internal Key constants.

- Shift: Indicates if any of the three shift keys (Alt, Ctrl, or Shift) is pressed at the moment. You can use the KeyUp and KeyDown event procedures' Shift parameter in the same way you use the Shift parameter for the MouseDown and MouseUp event procedures.

KeyDown and KeyUp don't detect exactly the same information as
KeyPress. While KeyPress detects a character in its KeyASCII parameter,
KeyDown and KeyUp detect a physical keystroke in their KeyCode
parameter. KeyUp and KeyDown can therefore detect any keystroke
not recognized by KeyPress, such as function, editing, and navigation
keys.

In the following example, we use the KeyDown event procedure to
detect when the user keys Shift+F10. Note the use of the internal VB
constant to detect the keystroke:

```
Private Sub Form_KeyDown(KeyCode As Long, Shift As Integer)
Dim blnIsShift As Boolean
blnIsShift = Shift And vbShiftMask
If blnIsShift And (KeyCode = vbKeyF10) Then
        If MsgBox("Are you sure you want to delete the
current record?", vbYesNo)= vbYes then
            .
            .
            .
        EndIf
End Sub
```

Tip

When in design mode, you can see the names of the internal VB keystroke constants by invoking the Object Browser with the F2 key, choosing
VB from the Libraries/Projects List, and then choosing KeyCodeConstants
from the Classes/Modules list.

How do you decide whether to use KeyDown and KeyUp as opposed
to KeyPress?

You use KeyDown and KeyUp when you need to detect keystrokes
that don't necessarily have an ASCII representation, such as the function
keys or the arrow keys, or when you are more interested in the physical
keystroke as such, rather than in the actual character which the keystroke generated.

Part
II

Ch

7

For instance, when the user presses the letter on the keyboard, the KeyCode parameter of KeyDown and KeyUp has the same value, regardless of whether the user has keyed a capital or lowercase letter. The KeyPress event would distinguish between the upper and lowercase versions of this letter.

Though you'll get the same value for KeyCode whether or not the user is holding the Shift key, you can evaluate the Shift parameter to tell whether Ctrl, Alt, or Shift is being held. The Caps Lock key generates its own KeyDown and KeyUp events.

▶ **See** "MouseDown and MouseUp," **p. 239**

Programming with GotFocus and LostFocus Events

A control receives a GotFocus event when the control receives focus and the control receives a LostFocus event when the control loses focus.

When focus moves from one control to another control, the first control's LostFocus event triggers, and then the GotFocus event of the second control.

> **Caution**
> Although Forms have LostFocus and GotFocus events, these Form events aren't triggered very often. This is because a Form can only receive focus when there is no control on the Form capable of receiving focus for itself. This means that the Form either has no controls at all or that all controls are disabled or invisible.

▶ **See** "Activate/Deactivate versus GotFocus/LostFocus," **p. 258**

Redrawing Graphics on Forms and PictureBoxes

Both Forms and PictureBox controls can contain graphical or textual information which is the result of graphics methods such as Print, Circle, Line, or Pset.

▶ **See** "Graphics Methods," **p. 264**

Forms and PictureBox controls can be temporarily covered by an overlying object when a VB application runs (see fig. 7.1). Forms and PictureBox controls also can be resized while the application is running.

When a Form or PictureBox gets resized or uncovered, its underlying graphics need to be redrawn. You can either redraw these graphics programmatically in the Form's or PictureBox control's Paint event, or you can enable automatic redrawing by setting the object's AutoRedraw property to True.

FIG. 7.1 ⇒

Forms and PictureBox controls can be temporarily covered by objects within the VB application or by other applications.

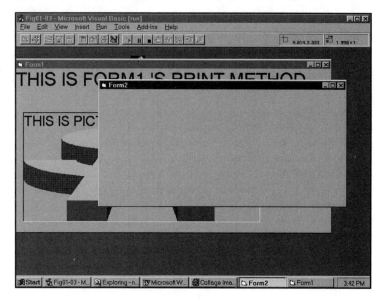

The AutoRedraw Property

AutoRedraw is a True/False property whose default value is False.

The AutoRedraw property influences a Form or PictureBox control's behavior when that object is resized or is uncovered by another object. AutoRedraw will determine whether or not the PictureBox or Form's graphics will be automatically refreshed.

Windows can maintain an image buffer, or "canvas," for every existing Form or PictureBox. This canvas contains an image the size of the entire screen.

Setting a PictureBox control's or Form's AutoRedraw property to True enables this canvas and causes Windows to refresh the PictureBox control or Form every time the object is resized or uncovered (see fig. 7.2).

When AutoRedraw is False, Windows doesn't maintain a canvas for the object and so doesn't refresh the object's graphics (see fig. 7.3). Instead, the object's Paint event is enabled.

The advantage to setting AutoRedraw to True is, of course, that the Form or PictureBox refreshes automatically. The disadvantage is that Windows will use up more memory maintaining the "canvas" image of the object. To conserve memory, you can leave AutoRedraw False and program the Paint event as discussed in the next section.

FIG. 7.2 ⇒

Form and
PictureBox control
with AutoRedraw
set to True after
being uncovered
by another object.

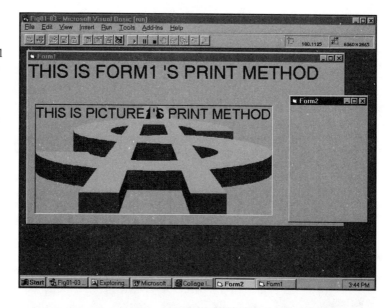

FIG. 7.3 ⇒

Form and
PictureBox control
with AutoRedraw
set to False after
being uncovered
by another object.

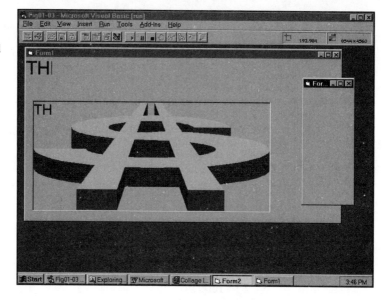

The Paint Event

You can use the Paint event to programmatically refresh graphics in a Form or PictureBox control. A Paint event occurs whenever something happens in the system that may cause the object's graphics to need redrawing.

A Form or PictureBox control's Paint event can happen only when the object's AutoRedraw property is set to False. This is because an AutoRedraw property with a True value will cause graphics to redraw automatically, thus making the Paint event unnecessary.

Examples of activities that cause the Paint event to occur are:

◆ An overlying window moves to uncover part of a previously obscured Form or PictureBox control.

◆ A Form or PictureBox control is manually or programmatically resized at run-time.

The Paint event is most effective when there are a few simple, permanent graphics to redraw on the Form or PictureBox.

Programming with Form Events

A VB Form supports many events to help you efficiently manage the phases of a Form lifetime within the application.

These events can become quite important for tying together parts of your application, for startup and cleanup operations, and for validating user changes to controls on a Form.

Relative Timing of the Various Form Events

You might wish to refer to this section as you read the following sections on individual Form events.

The following events will occur in the order listed when a Form first loads into memory:

- ◆ Initialize
- ◆ Load
- ◆ Activate
- ◆ GotFocus (triggered only if there are no enabled or visible controls on the Form)

The following events will occur in the order listed when a Form becomes the active Form:

- ◆ Activate
- ◆ GotFocus (triggered only if there are no enabled or visible controls on the Form)

The following events happen to an active Form when another form becomes active:

- ◆ LostFocus (triggered only if there are no enabled or visible controls on the Form)
- ◆ DeActivate

The following events will occur in the order listed when a Form is unloaded from memory:

- ◆ QueryUnload
- ◆ UnLoad
- ◆ Terminate (triggered only if you set the Form to Nothing in or after the UnLoad event)

Initialize and Terminate

The Initialize and Terminate events are the first and last events, respectively, to trigger for a Form.

The Initialize event happens when an instance of the Form is created in your application. For Forms, Initialize always happens just before Load.

Part

II

Ch

7

The Terminate event happens when all the Form's variables have been set to Nothing. The Terminate event happens only when you explicitly set the Form to Nothing in your code during or after the Unload event procedure. For example, you could use the statement:

```
Set Form1 = Nothing
```

after calling the UnLoad statement for Form1.

Load, Unload, and QueryUnload

The Load event happens when the Form loads into memory. This event's procedure is the customary place for programmers to insert code that sets Form-level variables and properties and performs other startup processes.

The QueryUnload and Unload events happen when a Form unloads from memory. The Unload event procedure is where programmers usually put cleanup code. QueryUnload happens just before Unload. Its main purpose is to let you detect why the Form is being unloaded and to programmatically halt unloading.

The QueryUnload event procedure takes two parameters:

- ◆ *Cancel.* This is a True/False value which is False by default. When Cancel is False, it means that the unload won't be stopped. You can set it to true to stop the Form from unloading.

- ◆ *UnLoadMode.* This parameter can take several values, corresponding to how QueryUnload event was triggered. You can compare UnLoadMode's value with one of the following VB internal constants:

- ◆ *VbFormControlMenu.* The form's QueryUnload event was triggered because the user is closing the Form.

- ◆ *VbFormCode.* The form's QueryUnload event was triggered by code which programmatically closes the Form.

- ◆ *VbAppWindows.* The QueryUnload event was triggered because the Windows session is ending.

◆ *VbAppTaskManager.* The QueryUnload event was triggered because the Windows Task Manager is closing your application

◆ *VbFormMDIForm.* The Form is an MDI Child, and the MDI Parent is closing.

A common use of the QueryUnload event is to prompt the user to save changes (see fig. 7.4). One of the options you give the user is to cancel the unload. If the user chooses to cancel, you can set the Cancel parameter to true, as in the following code:

```
Private Sub frmData_QueryUnload(Cancel as Integer, _
        UnLoadMode As Integer)
    Dim intUserChoice As Integer
    intUserChoice = MsgBox("Save Changes?" , _
        vbYesNoCancel)
    If intUserChoice = vbYes Then
        Call SaveData
    ElseIf intUserChoice = vbCancel Then
        Cancel = True
    EndIf
End Sub
```

The Unload event procedure takes a single parameter, the Cancel parameter. Unload's Cancel has the same function as QueryUnload's Cancel.

It is possible to stop the Form from unloading in the Unload event procedure, but since the Unload event doesn't receive the UnLoadMode parameter, your code has less information about why the Form is being unloaded.

For non-MDI Child Forms, QueryUnload always happens just before Unload.

Note In an MDI application, MDI Child Forms have a slightly different timing for QueryUnload and Unload events. See Chapter 9, "Multiple-Document Interface (MDI)," for more information. ■

Part

II

Ch

7

FIG. 7.4 ⇒

A typical use of the QueryUnload event is to prompt the user to save changes.

MessageBox displayed in Form's QueryUnload event procedure

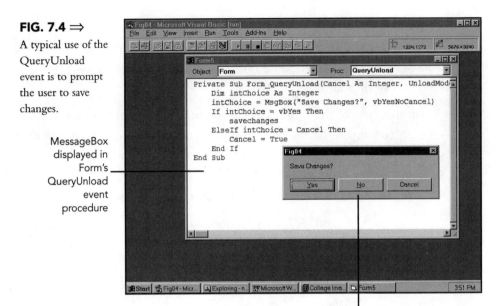

Cancel parameter is set to True based on user response to MessageBox. This will cancel the unloading process and the Form will stay in memory

Activate/Deactivate versus GotFocus/ LostFocus

A Form is the *active* Form in an application when the focus in the application is within that Form (see fig. 7.5). This could mean that either the Form has the focus or that a control on the Form has focus. The user can tell what Form is active because the title bar appears highlighted and the Form appears in the foreground.

A Form receives an Activate event when it becomes the active Form and a DeActivate event when it loses its active status to another Form in the same application. The Activate and DeActivate event procedures are ideal places to put code that deals with the user's navigation between Forms.

For instance, you might put some type of Form-level validation code in a DeActivate event.

Tip

When a Form first loads into memory, the Activate event happens after the Load event. The Activate event procedure is a better place than the Load event procedure to put startup code that affects the Form's appearance (such as calls to the graphics methods), or code that manipulates Data-Bound controls (see Chapter 12, "The Data Control"). This is because the Load event happens a bit too early for these operations to have their proper effect. In fact, putting some types of code in the Load event can cause a run-time error if the code tries to manipulate run-time properties of controls that aren't fully initialized.

Forms also support GotFocus and LostFocus events, as do controls. However, GotFocus and LostFocus do not usually occur for a Form. You might think that GotFocus and LostFocus event procedures would be good places to put code that reacts to a user entering and leaving a Form in a multi-Form application. However, an active Form can only receive focus if it contains no enabled or visible controls. Because most Forms have at least one enabled or visible control, GotFocus and LostFocus don't normally occur on Forms when the user moves between Forms in an application.

Note Activate, DeActivate, GotFocus, and LostFocus only occur with respect to Forms within the current application. When the user changes to or returns from another application, none of these events occur. ∎

FIG. 7.5 ⇒

The active Form has a highlighted caption, while inactive Forms have unhighlighted captions.

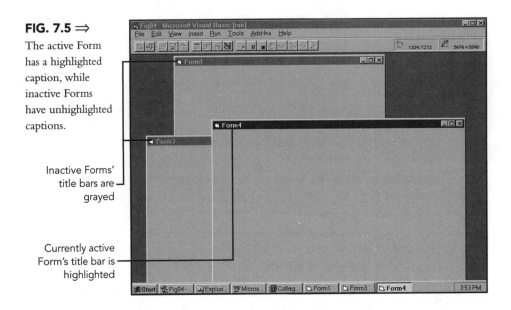

Inactive Forms' title bars are grayed

Currently active Form's title bar is highlighted

Show/Hide Methods versus Load/Unload Statements

The Load and Unload statements cause a Form to be loaded into memory or to be unloaded from memory, respectively. Both statements take a Form's name as their parameter. For example, the statement

```
Load frmMain
```

would cause frmMain to load into memory, and the statement

```
Unload frmMain
```

would take it out of memory.

Although the Load statement brings a Form into memory, it doesn't make the Form visible. You must call the Form's Show method or set its Visible property to True in order to make it visible to the user.

You might ask, since calling the Show method or setting the Visible property will load the Form anyway, why bother ever using the Load statement?

You might also ask, since calling the Unload statement would make the Form invisible anyway, why bother with ever using the Hide method?

VB provides programmers with both Load and UnLoad statements and Show and Hide methods because there are two different strategies for Form management in an application. Which strategy you choose depends on how your application needs to balance speed of operation with efficient use of memory. The two strategies are:

- *Faster.* Load all the Forms you'll need in your application when your application begins to run. While the application is running, use only the Show and Hide methods of forms. Only use the Unload statement when your application is ending.
- *Memory Efficiency.* Only load a Form (either with the Show method or a combination of the Load statement and Show method) when you need to use it. Immediately unload a Form as soon as you don't need it in the application.

When you look at the Faster strategy, it might appear that there would be a big delay at the beginning of the program as your application loaded all the Forms it was going to use. While this is objectively true, programmers usually cover up for the fact by supplying a "splash" screen to show the user flashy graphics as the application loads the forms. This is such a common technique in Windows programming (see fig. 7.6) that users have come to expect a delay of several seconds when a program begins to run. Then, once the Forms are loaded, there will be no further delays at all as the application runs, because no Forms need to be loaded after that.

In truth, you'll find yourself using a combination of both the speed and memory strategies. Not all VB applications, for example, will be able to load and maintain all of its Forms in memory throughout the entire session of the application.

▶ **See** "Implicitly Loading a Form," **p. 263**

FIG. 7.6 ⇒
VB uses the splash screen technique to distract its user (the programmer) from the amount of time that it takes to initialize.

VB's own splash screen

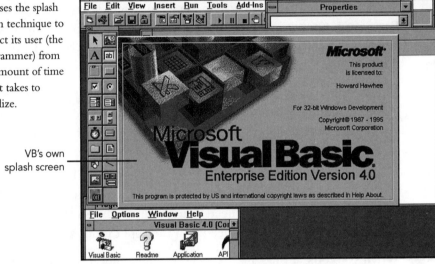

Using Significant Form Methods

The following sections discuss a Form's Show and Hide methods and the graphics methods that Forms share with the Printer object and the PictureBox control.

Default References to the Active Form

It is possible to omit the reference to a Form's name in code when you are using a property or method, as in these examples:

```
Caption = "Hello"
Hide
```

VB assumes that that you are referring to the currently active Form. Though this technique is sometimes useful for writing generic, Form-independent code, it also can be confusing because it doesn't make your intentions clear to someone reading your code.

Be aware of this technique because you may see it used in documentation and in the VB Certification Exam.

Implicitly Loading a Form

A Form which is not yet in memory will load into memory automatically whenever you refer to any of its methods or properties in code, or to any of the methods of properties of a control on the Form. Thus, statements such as

```
Form1.Caption = "Hello"
Form1.txtCity.Text = "Chicago"
Form1.Show
```

would cause Form1 to load if it had not already been loaded.

Causing a Form to load in this way is known as *implicit loading*.

Show and Hide

These methods toggle a Form's visibility. As a result of a call to a Form's Show method, the Form's Visible property is set to True, and the Form is now the application's active Form. After a call to a Form's Hide method, the Form's Visible property will be False and the Form will no longer be the application's active Form.

The Show method does more than simply toggle a Form's Visible property: it also can accept a parameter that indicates the Form's modal state.

◆ A *modeless* Form is the default way of managing a Form in an application. When a Form displays modalessly, the rest of the VB application continues any execution it needs to finish and the user is able to freely navigate between this *modaless* Form and any other Forms in the application. Since modaless is the default state, modaless is implied when there is no reference to the parameter.

```
Form1.Show
MsgBox "Form1 visible" 'this line runs immediately
```

If you wish to provide more clarity in your code, you can use the vbModeless parameter:

```
Form1.Show vbModeless
```

◆ A *modal* Form demands more attention from the user. If the Form is displayed modally, the user cannot navigate to other Forms in the application. The Form remains active until the Form is closed. In addition, the code procedure that contains *Form1.Show vbModal*, the procedure which originally shows the modal Form, will not resume until the Form has been unloaded or hidden by either user action or code. You can display a Form modally by calling the Show method with the vbModal constant as a parameter:

```
Form1.Show vbModal
MsgBox "Finished Form1"   'won't run till after
                          'Form1 is dismissed
```

▶ **See** "Show/Hide Methods versus Load/Unload Statements"
p. 263

Graphics Methods

These methods are supported by Forms, PictureBox controls, and the Printer system object. Figure 7.7 illustrates the output of these methods.

FIG. 7.7 ⇒

The output of Graphics methods on a Form and a PictureBox.

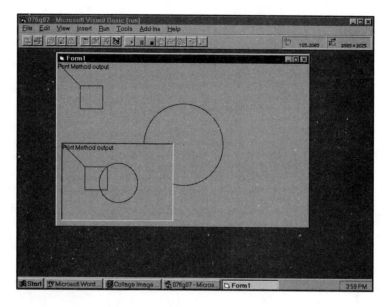

CurrentX and CurrentY Properties

A Form's CurrentX and CurrentY properties give the horizontal and vertical coordinates, respectively, for the output of the next graphics method. For example, a value for CurrentX of 0 and CurrentY of 0 would position the output of the next Print method at the upper left corner of its object.

You can programmatically change CurrentX and CurrentY to position the output of such methods as Print.

The Graphics methods discussed in the following sections will affect CurrentX and CurrentY.

Part

II

Ch

7

Print Method

The Print method takes a string as its argument and outputs that string at the CurrentX, CurrentY position in the containing object.

After a call to the Print method, CurrentX and CurrentY will advance in the object. Normally, CurrentY will augment by the height of one line, and CurrentX will change to 0. The effect of this is therefore like a carriage return/line feed combination. However, if you place a semicolon (;) after the output of the Print method, CurrentY will not advance to the next line and CurrentX will advance further to the right. The following lines illustrate both ways of using the Print method:

```
Form1.Print "Where will the Next line be?  " ;
Form1.Print "Right Here."
Form1.Print "And now here."
```

Figure 7.8 illustrates how the output of these statements would appear to the user.

FIG. 7.8 ⟹

The effect of using a semicolon with the Print method.

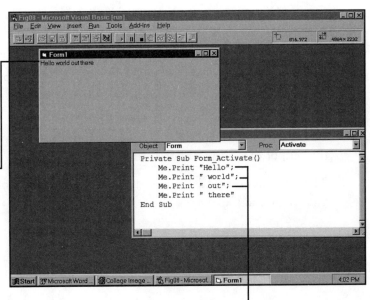

Outputs of
different Print
methods are
concatenated
on one line

Semicolon after each call to the Print method

Circle Method

As its name implies, this method allows you to draw circles on a Form, PictureBox control, or Printer object. You must specify the position and radius of the circle. You can also optionally specify a color, whether the circle will be a full circle or an arc, and whether it will be a perfect circle or an ellipse.

The Circle method leaves CurrentX and CurrentY at the coordinates of the Circle's center.

See Microsoft's printed or online documentation for more information.

Line Method

The Line method allows you to draw a line from one pair of coordinates to another. You can also optionally specify a color for the line, and whether or not you want the two pair of coordinates to specify a rectangular box instead of a line.

See Microsoft's printed or online documentation for more information.

PSet

PSet draws a single point on the Form, PictureBox or Printer. You must specify the coordinates for the point. You also can optionally specify a color and whether the coordinates are relative to the containing object's upper left corner or relative to the previous value of CurrentX and CurrentY.

The simplest format for PSet would be:

```
PSet (x,y)
```

where x and y are horizontal and vertical coordinates for the point, respectively. Notice the use of parentheses, which are required here.

To specify a color you simply add a third parameter, which can be Long value representing a system color. To obtain a useful color value, you can use either the RGB function or one of the VB internal color constants. The following lines would both place a red dot at different positions on a Form:

Part

II

Ch

7

```
Me.PSet (100,100) , RGB(255,0,0)
Me.PSet (200,200) , vbRed
```

If you want the point to be placed relative to the last graphics output, recall that CurrentX and CurrentY are reset by each graphics output statement. You can then include the keyword Step directly before the coordinate specification.

```
Me.PSet Step (200,200), vbRed
```

would place a red dot 200 units below and to the right of the output of the last graphics output statement.

PSet resets CurrentX and CurrentY to the coordinates of the point it draws.

Cls

Cls clears the results of all previous graphics output to the Form or PictureBox control.

Cls resets both CurrentX and CurrentY to 0 (upper left corner).

TextHeight and TextWidth

You can use TextHeight and TextWidth to calculate how much space will be needed inside an object to display a given string of text.

TextHeight and TextWidth act as functions. They each take as their argument a string and they return a number corresponding to the amount of space (height and width, respectively) it would take to display the string on the current Form or PictureBox object. The units of measure of these methods' return value is given by the ScaleMode of the object using the method. Recall that by default, this is in Twips.

Calling System Objects in a VB Application

Several ready-made *system objects* are available when your application runs. The programmer doesn't create or initialize these objects and they aren't available at design time. Instead, VB initializes the objects when your application begins to run.

Printer

The Printer object represents the current printer that the Windows system will write to.

The Printer object supports the graphics methods and properties listed in the section "Graphics Methods" with the exception of the Cls method, which it doesn't support. Calling one of these methods on the Printer object will cause the appropriate output to appear at the printer.

In addition, the Printer object supports the following significant methods:

- ◆ *EndDoc.* Releases the current print job to the printer.
- ◆ *KillDoc.* Terminates the current print job without releasing it to the printer.
- ◆ *NewPage.* Causes the printer to physically go to the next page.

Note The Printer object supports several other methods besides those previously listed, as well as several dozen specialized properties, which are beyond the scope of this exam. ■

App

This object contains general information about the current VB application as it runs. It has no methods, and most of its properties give information to help identify the application and its executable. Three useful properties are:

- ◆ *EXEName.* The name (with no extension or path) of the compiled executable file which is currently running. When you run your application in design mode, this will be the name of the current VB Project.
- ◆ *Path.* The path without file name to the compiled executable file which is currently running. When you run your application in design mode, this will be the path where the project has been saved. If the project hasn't been saved yet, this will be the name of the directory where VB resides.

Part
II

Ch
7

◆ *PrevInstance.* This True/False property lets you know whether another copy of this application is already running. If you don't want two copies of your application running at the same time, you can test this property when your application starts and call the End statement if you find that PrevInstance is True. With just a little more work (it would require an API call) you could instead locate the other instance of the application and switch to it before ending this new instance.

 Note The App Object has numerous other specialized properties which are beyond the scope of the Certification Exam. ▦

Debug

The Debug object has just one task, which is to print information in the Immediate Pane of the Debug Window when your application is running in design mode. It has a single method: Print.

▶ **See** Chapter 5, "Handling Errors," **p. 185**

Clipboard

The Clipboard object represents the Windows system Clipboard in your application. You can both store text and graphics to the Clipboard and retrieve text and graphics from the Clipboard with its half-dozen methods.

Because the Clipboard can hold various types of data (text data and various other formats), VB 4.0 provides several internal constants for identifying Clipboard data types.

◆ *Clear.* Clears the contents of the Clipboard.

◆ *GetData.* Lets you retrieve non-text data from the Clipboard.

```
PicWorking.Picture = Clipboard.GetData vbCFBitMap
```

◆ *GetFormat.* Lets you query the Clipboard about the type of data it currently holds. You use GetFormat by passing it the Clipboard data type constant you're looking for. GetFormat returns a True or False depending on whether the data is of that type or not. The following example checks to see if the Clipboard currently holds text data:

```
If Clipboard.GetFormat(vbCFText) Then . . .
```

◆ *GetText.* Lets you retrieve text data from the Clipboard.

```
txtName.SelText = ClipBoard.GetText vbCFText
```

◆ *SetData.* Lets you store non-text data to the Clipboard.

```
Clipboard.SetData picWorking.Picture, vbCFBitMap
```

◆ *SetText.* Lets you store text data to the Clipboard. You don't have to specify the second parameter when storing text. If you don't, however, subsequent calls to GetFormat won't recognize that the type of the Clipboard's data is vbCFText:

```
Clipboard.SetText picWorking.Picture, vbCFText
```

Screen

The Screen object contains visual information about the current Windows desktop where your application is running. It has no methods and the following properties:

◆ *ActiveControl.* Provides a pointer to the control in your application which currently has focus. This comes in handy when there is code which you only want to execute when a particular control or type of control has focus, as in the following examples:

```
If Screen.ActiveControl Is txtName Then
    '. . . Do something
EndIf
If TypeOf Screen.ActiveControl Is OptionButton Then
    '. . . Do something
EndIf
```

Part

II

Ch

7

♦ *ActiveForm.* Provides a pointer to the Form which is currently active.

♦ *Height.* Height of the screen in Twips.

♦ *MousePointer.* This affects the appearance of the MousePointer only while it is over objects in your application. The settings for the Screen's MousePointer work like the settings for the MousePointer of controls and Forms (see Chapter 6). If you set the Screen object's MousePointer, this setting will override the settings for MousePointer in any Form or control in the application.

♦ *Width.* Width of the screen in Twips.

Err

The Err Object contains information about the current pending run-time error condition. Its most important properties are:

♦ *Description.* A string giving the standard system description of the error which has occurred.

♦ *Number.* The error number of the error which has occurred.

♦ *Source.* The application or object which originated the error.

Note The Err Object has a number of other specialized properties. You can read about those properties in Microsoft's on-line and paper documentation. ■

The Err Object has two methods:

♦ *Clear.* Clears out the pending run-time error condition and sets the Err Object's properties to blank values.

♦ *Raise.* Generates the run-time error condition corresponding to the error number you supply as a parameter.

▶ **See** Chapter 5, "Handling Errors," **p. 185**

Taking the Disc Test

 If you have read and understood the material in this chapter, you are ready to test your knowledge. Insert the CD-ROM that comes with this book, and run the self-test software as described in Appendix H, "Using the CD-ROM."

From Here...

This chapter, together with the previous chapters in this book and the following chapter on Menus, provides the core information on VB. You should consider the information on events in this chapter together with the information on writing VB code in Chapter 3.

Part

II

Ch

7

Chapter Prerequisite

You should be comfortable with VB's fundamental techniques and concepts as discussed in Chapters 2 through 7.

8

Menus

A menu is one of the most familiar sights to a Windows user, and anyone who has ever used a Windows application will be able to navigate through your application's options if you present them to the user in the form of a menu. Terms and concepts covered include:

◆ Adding a menu interface to a form using VB's built-in Menu Editor utility

◆ Manipulating the menu's appearance at design-time and at run-time

◆ Implementing access keys and shortcut keys for menu items

◆ Running code when the user clicks on a menu item

◆ Dynamically adding and deleting menu items at run-time with a menu array

Adding a Menu Interface to a Form

There are two main steps to implement a menu in an application (see fig. 8.1):

1. Use the Menu Editor to create menu items and set their behavior and appearance.
2. Make each menu item execute an action when the user clicks them by putting code in their click event procedures.

FIG. 8.1 ⇒
You can implement a standard menu bar with all standard features on any VB form.

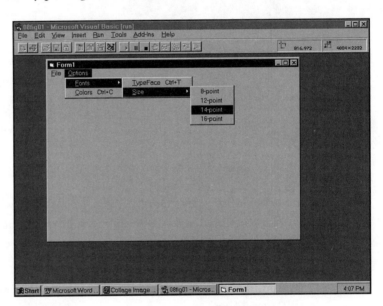

> **Note** A menu, like any other control, belongs to a form. Therefore, you can have different menus on different forms, and you must specify each form's menu system separately. If you want the same menu on many forms, you should consider an MDI interface. For more information, see Chapter 9, "Using Multiple-Document Interface (MDI)." ■

The Menu Editor

Each item on a menu is a separate control with its own methods, properties, and one event procedure—Click.

You won't find a menu control in the Visual Basic ToolBox, however, and you can't bring up the familiar-looking Properties Window for a menu item as you can for other types of controls.

Instead, you invoke the Menu Editor utility to manipulate menus and menu items at design-time. You can invoke the Menu Editor in one of three ways:

- ◆ Choose Tools, Menu Editor from the VB menu.
- ◆ Key Ctrl+E.
- ◆ Click the Menu icon in the VB ToolBar.

 Note The access key for the Menu Editor has changed in Visual Basic 4.0 to Ctrl+E. ▨

The Menu Editor plays the same role at design time as the Properties Window does for other controls. The Menu Editor also lets you see a scrolling list of all menu items on the current form.

The top half of the Menu Editor dialog box gives information for a single menu item (see fig. 8.2).

The bottom half of the Menu Editor dialog gives a scrolling list of all existing menu items for the current form. The top half will show the properties of the currently selected item from the bottom half of the list.

A finished list of menu items will look like an outline, with items appearing at different levels of indentation. Each indentation level appears with four dashes ("——") in front of it. What you are viewing is the hierarchy of menu items. In other words, a menu item which is indented one more level than the item above it belongs to that previous item's submenu.

▶ **See** "Menu Level," **p. 286**

FIG. 8.2 ⇒

The Menu Editor allows you to add and delete menu items and set each item's properties.

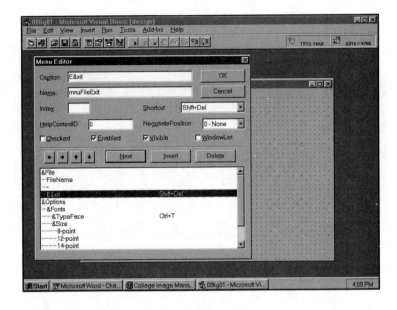

To edit a new or existing menu on a form:

1. Make sure you're in design mode on an open form (not in a code window).

2. Press Ctrl+E to invoke the menu editor.

3. To enter a new menu item, select the first blank row of the list of menu items.

4. Select an existing menu item to edit that item. You can use the Next button to move forward in the list or to move to a new blank menu item.

5. You must enter the item's name and a caption. Other properties are optional.

6. Adjust the item's level in the menu hierarchy with the right arrow to move the item down a level or the left arrow button to move the item up a level. See the section on "Menu Level" in this chapter for more information.

7. Repeat steps 3-6 as many times as you need for individual menu items.

Name Property

Just like any other type of control, each menu item must have a name that is unique on its form. The Name property is the second item from the top of the Menu Editor dialog.

Tip

The standard Hungarian notation prefix for menu items is "mnu."

▶ **See** "Variable Naming Conventions with Hungarian Notation," **p. 77**

Note Although VB provides a default name for every other type of control, you must make an original name from scratch for each menu item. If you forget to do so, VB won't allow you to exit the Menu Editor. ■

Caption Property

A menu item's Caption is what the user sees on the menu. Just as with many other controls, you can use the ampersand ("&") to define an access key.

Tip

Remember that an access key by definition only functions when the user can see a menu item. A shortcut key will work even when the user can't see the menu item on its pulldown menu. (See the sections in this chapter titled "Shortcut Keys," and "Access Keys versus Shortcut Keys.")

Navigating, Adding, and Deleting Menu Items in the Menu Editor

To move through existing menu items, you can:

◆ Use the mouse or the keyboard's arrow keys.

To add a new item at the end of the list, you can either:

◆ Select the last existing item, and click the <u>N</u>ext button. The new item will automatically take on the same menu level as the item before it.

Or:

◆ Click below the last item on the list. The new item will automatically take on the highest menu level.

To insert a new item somewhere else in the list, you can:

1. Select the existing item which will follow the new item.

2. Click the <u>I</u>nsert button.

To change an item's order in the list:

1. Select the item whose order you wish to change.

2. Click the up or down arrow in the middle of the Menu Editor dialog box to move the item up or down one row at a time.

Separator Bars

A separator bar allows you to visually group menu items within the same submenu.

A separator bar is considered to be a distinct menu item. You can insert it just like you would any other menu item in the Menu Editor. If you put just a hyphen ("-") in the Ca<u>p</u>tion (see fig. 8.3), then the menu item will become a separator bar when the menu displays (see fig. 8.4).

Tip

Though they may all look alike, each separator bar menu item needs its own distinct name.

FIG. 8.3 ⟹

You can add a
separator bar to
any submenu by
inserting an item
whose caption is a
single hyphen ("–")
character.

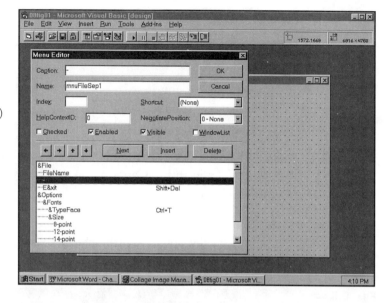

FIG. 8.4 ⟹

The separator bar
will help you set
off logical group-
ings within the
same submenu.

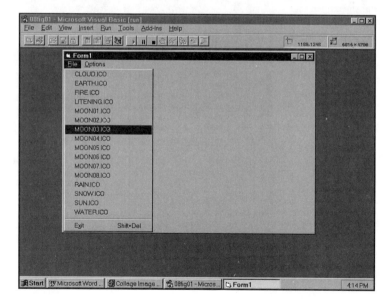

Access Keys

An access key works the same for a menu item as it does for other controls:

◆ It appears in the menu item's caption as an underlined letter

◆ If the user keys the Alt+*access key* letter combination, the item's click event will happen

◆ To give a menu item an access key, put an ampersand ("&") in front of the letter in the Caption that will be the access key (see figs. 8.5 and 8.6).

> **Note** The user doesn't need to press the Alt key to make a submenu item's access key work. The user only has to key the letter by itself. This is true of no other type of control. ∎

FIG. 8.5 ⟹

Put the ampersand ("&") character in front of the desired access key in the item's Caption.

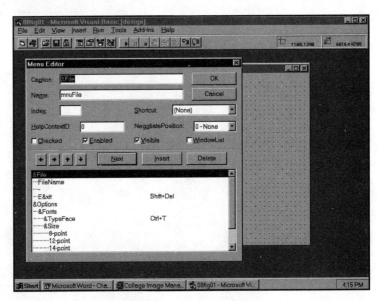

FIG. 8.6 ⇒

The menu item's caption will then show up with the corresponding letter underlined. The user can use the Alt- key with that letter to trigger that menu item's click event.

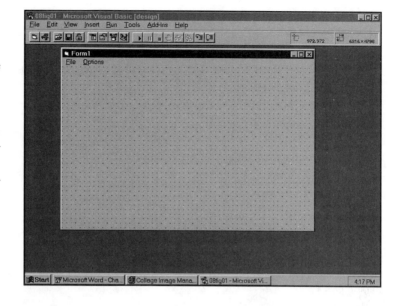

Shortcut Keys

A menu item's shortcut key combination will work from anywhere on the form, whether or not the user can see the menu item. You can therefore only use a particular shortcut key combination on a form once.

In the Menu Editor you will notice a Shortcut property for the current menu item. This property actually contains a list box that gives you a list of possible shortcut key combinations (see figs. 8.7 and 8.8).

You can assign a shortcut key combination to a menu item as follows:

1. From the design view of the form, press Ctrl+E to invoke the Menu Editor.
2. Select and click the desired menu item.
3. Click the List Box arrow beside the Shortcut property to see a scrolling list of possible Shortcut key combinations.
4. Select the shortcut key combination you wish to assign to this menu item.

Caution

The shortcut key list in the Menu Editor doesn't indicate the shortcut keys already in use. Be careful not to pick the same Shortcut combination for two different menu items.

Caution

You can't give a menu control a shortcut key if the menu control has submenu items.

FIG. 8.7 ⇒

When you're editing a menu item's properties, you can pick a shortcut key for that item off the shortcut drop-down list.

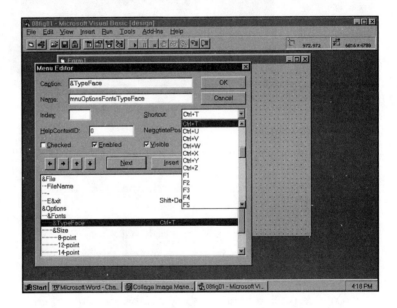

FIG. 8.8 ⟹

The shortcut key notation automatically appears to the right of the item's Caption when the menu runs. A shortcut key will work even when the menu item isn't visible.

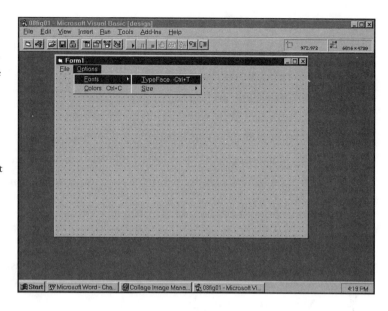

Access Keys versus Shortcut Keys

What's the difference between an access key and a shortcut key?

An access key:

◆ Appears as an underlined letter in a control's caption

◆ Works in combination with the Alt key. The Alt key is unnecessary for submenu items

◆ Only works when the user can see the caption

◆ Only needs to be unique within its own submenu

A shortcut key:

◆ Works even when the user can't see the control it belongs to

◆ Must be unique among all menu items on the form

◆ Can be represented by a function key as well as by an alphabetic key

Menu Level

Just like chickens in a pecking order, every menu item has an exact and definite position in the menu hierarchy:

◆ *Menu titles* are at the top level, or level 0. These are the items the user sees displayed across the form's menu bar before clicking a menu choice.

◆ *Menu items* are at level 1, one level below a menu title.

◆ Lower level menu controls are known as *submenu items*.

 Note Visual Basic permits a maximum of five menu levels below the menu titles of the top level. ■

You can change a menu item's level by selecting the desired menu item on the list and using the left and right arrow buttons in the middle of the Menu Editor dialog.

If a menu item contains submenu items, the user will see a right-pointing arrow to the right of that item. This lets the user know that there is a sub-menu attached to the item (see figs. 8.9 and 8.10).

> **Caution**
> You can't skip menu levels. The first item in the entire menu list must be at the top level. Any other menu item must be at the same level or one level lower than the item preceding it.

FIG. 8.9 ⇒
The level of indentation in the menu editor determines an item's menu level. You can promote and demote an item through menu levels by using the left- and right-pointing arrows just above the list of items to change its indentation.

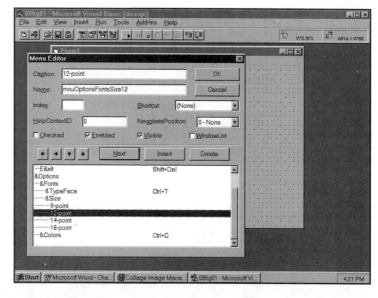

FIG. 8.10 ⇒
The menu editor levels in the previous figure would yield the visual interface shown in this figure.

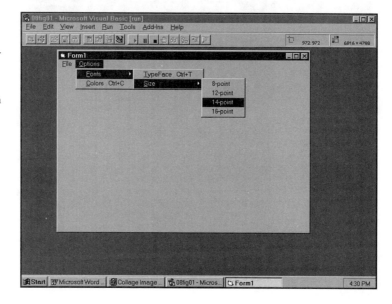

Attaching Code to a Click Event Procedure

A menu control has a single event procedure: the Click event procedure.

You can access a menu control's Click event procedure by single-clicking the menu item from the design-time copy of the menu.

Tip
The only way you can edit a menu title item's event procedure is to navigate to it in the VB Code Window (see fig. 8.11).

FIG. 8.11 ⇒
You can view and edit the Click event procedure of a main menu item by finding the item in the Objects list of a VB Code Window.

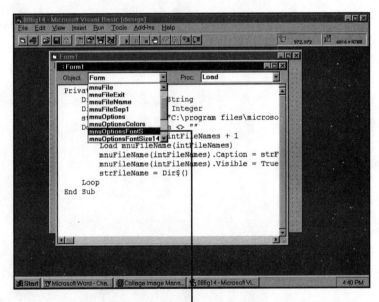

Menu title item listed in Objects list of VB Code Window.

Modifying Menu Appearance Dynamically

Most of the properties that you can see in the Menu Editor, such as Enabled, Checked, and Visible, are also available at run-time.

FIG. 8.12 ⟹

All items on this submenu are visible, available, and unchecked.

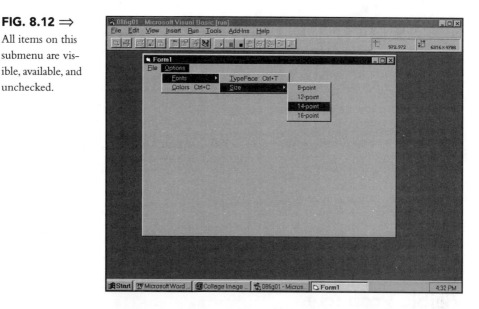

FIG. 8.13 ⟹

This is the same submenu from figure 8.11 seen at a different point in the running of the application. Some menu items' properties have changed.

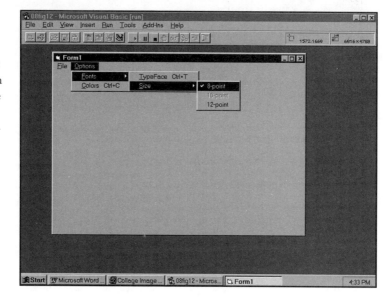

Checked Property

You might use the checked property as a user-definable flag. A menu item's Click event procedure could toggle the checked property to its opposite value (refer to fig. 8.12). Later, your code could use the value of this menu item's Checked property to make a logical decision:

```
Private Sub mnuMyChoice_Click()
    mnuMyChoice.Checked = NOT mnuMyChoice.Checked
End Sub
[Somewhere else in your code]
...
If mnuMyChoice.Checked Then
...
```

Of course, we could have put code in the Click event procedure in the example to cause other things to happen as well.

Visible Property

This is a no-brainer:

mnuMyItem.Visible = False

if you don't want to display the menu item at this time. If you want to display it:

mnuMyItem.Visible = True

The menu item will disappear from the level it was on, and any of its submenus will, of course, be unavailable as well.

An invisible menu item won't leave a gap behind if it appeared between two other items on the same level. Instead, the remaining visible items will close in around it (refer to figs. 8.12 and 8.13).

Enabled Property

The Enabled property works the same way as it does with other VB controls:

It's true by default, meaning a menu item is accessible to the user and appears normally highlighted. When you set the Enabled property to false, the item turns gray and the user can't select it (refer to fig. 8.12).

WindowList Property

The WindowList property allows a menu topic to display a standard interface for handling MDI child documents. The WindowList property is only meaningful in an MDI application.

▶ **See** "The WindowList Property," **p. 315**

NegotiatePosition Property

This property is useful when you are going to include an embeddable or linkable OLE object in an OLE Container control. If the form has its NegotiateMenus property set to True, then the OLE object's menus will show up in the form's menu bar when the object is active.

If you want your form's menus to disappear when the OLE object becomes active, just make sure all top-level menu items have their NegotiatePosition property set to None.

If you set a menu's NegotiatePosition property to any value besides None, the menus in question will show up on the menu bar with the active OLE object's menu in the relative position specified by the property's value.

You can set a menu's NegotiatePosition property by selecting the desired position from the property's drop-down list.

▶ **See** "Using the OLE 2.0 Container Control," **p. 336**
▶ **See** "Using OLE Automation to Integrate Applications," **p. 323**

HelpContextID Property

You can associate a topic in your application's help file (extension .hlp) with a menu item by setting the menu item's HelpContext ID property in the Menu Editor.

 Note The use of Help Files in your project is beyond the scope of the Certification Exam. ■

Adding and Deleting Menu Items Dynamically

There are really two ways to dynamically add or delete menu items at run-time.

The first way, the "not-so-dynamic" way, really doesn't add or delete menu items at run time—it only toggles their visible properties. In other words, you:

1. Create all the items you would ever need at design time
2. Set each item's respective visible property to true or false as the application runs

Then there is the "really dynamic" way: control arrays. This is the same technique we introduced in Chapter 2, "Visual Basic Data Types."

Menu Control Arrays

A menu control array has the following features in common with a regular control array:

◆ A menu control array must have at least one design-time element.

◆ You can create the first element of a menu control array at design-time by setting the Index property of a menu item.

◆ You can use the Load and Unload statements to initialize and destroy run-time elements of a menu control array.

◆ You can't Load or Unload a design-time element of a menu control array.

A menu control array lacks the following feature of regular control arrays:

◆ You can't copy and paste a menu item to create a control array at design time.

The following snippet of code adds elements to a menu control array, and it compares very closely with the examples in Chapter 2 where we initialized a control array of text boxes:

```
[Global Declarations section of form]
Private IntMenuCount As Integer
...
[Somewhere in the form's code]
intMenuCount = intMenuCount + 1
Load mnuItem(intMenuCount)
mnuItem(intMenuCount).Caption _
= "Item #" & intMenuCount
mnuItem(intMenuCount).Visible = true
```

Notice that the biggest difference is what's missing in this code: We don't have to worry about positioning each element of the menu control array, since that's taken care of for us automatically by Visual Basic and Windows.

As with all control arrays, you can't attempt to Load an element that already exists.

To delete a menu item from a menu control array, you use the Unload statement in the same way as you would with other types of control arrays:

```
[somewhere in the form's code]
UnLoad mnuItem(intMenuCount)
intMenuCount = intMenuCount - 1
```

Note that this example always unloads the last item in the menu control array. You must be sure, as with any control array, that you don't try to unload an element that does not exist or an element that was created at design time.

Index Property

The difference between a regular menu item and the design-time instance of a menu control array is whether or not the Index property contains a value. Normally, you'll want to set the Index property to 0 or 1 to begin a menu control array.

If you want the menu control array to have more than one design-time instance, then simply give a second item the same name as the first item, making sure to give it a distinct Index value.

> **Caution**
> The menus in the control array must be at the same submenu level.

Example with Dynamic Lists of Files

We will create an example which presents a dynamic list of all the Microsoft Access files (extension MDB) in a directory.

When the user clicks one of the files under the file menu, something will happen to that specific file. In a real-life application, we might print or delete the file. In this application, we'll just show the file's name in a message box. We'll also grey that file's name in the menu, so that the user can't click it a second time.

Here are the steps to creating this example (see fig. 8.14):

1. Select the startup Form in a VB project.
2. Press Ctrl+E to invoke the menu editor.
3. Enter the menu structure shown in figure 8.13. Press the Next button each time you're ready to move to a new menu item.
4. Make sure you change the Index property of the mnuFileNames item to 0 as shown in figure 8.13.
5. Click OK.
6. Make the coding changes shown in the code listing. Be sure to use the name of a directory available to your application at run time in place of the directory name in the sample Form_Load event procedure.
7. Run the application to test it.
8. Click the File menu. You should see something like the screen shown in figure 8.15.
9. When you click one of the file names in the menu, you should see the file's name echoed back to you in a MessageBox.

```
[Global Declarations section of form]
Private IntFileCount As Integer
...
[In the Form_Load event]
Dim strFileName As String
strFileName = Dir$("C:\MyData\*.MDB")
Do While strFileName <> ""
    intFileCount = intFileCount + 1
    Load mnuFileName(intFileCount)
    mnuFileName(intFileCount).Caption = strFileName
    mnuFileName(intFileCount).Visible = true
    strFileName = Dir$()
Loop
[in the Click event procedure for the menu item]
Private Sub mnuFileName(Index As Integer)
    Dim intCount as Integer
    MsgBox mnuFileName(Index).Caption
    For intCount = 1 To intFileCount
        If intCount <> Index Then
            mnuFileName(intCount).Checked = False
        Else
            mnuFileName(intCount).Checked = True
        EndIf
    Next intCount
End Sub
```

FIG. 8.14 ⇒

Create this menu structure for the example. Notice that the Index property on the mnuFileNames menu item is now 0. Setting the Index property automatically creates a control array from that menu item.

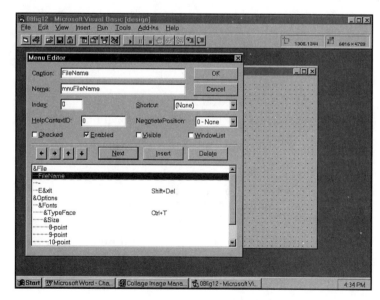

FIG. 8.15 ⟹

The application dynamically added the file names on this menu in the Form's Load event procedure.

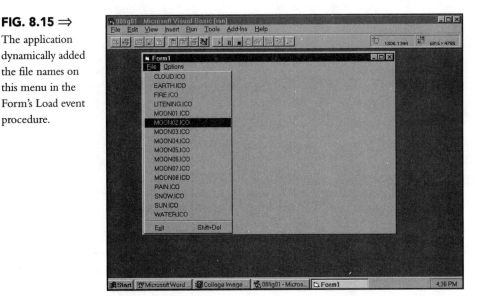

Adding Pop-Up Menus

You have probably seen commercial end-user applications where the user can right-click the mouse button somewhere on the application's visible surface and see a floating popup menu, that is, a menu not attached to the form's menu bar.

Such behavior is extremely easy to cause: it can require as little as one line of code to call the form's PopupMenu method (see fig. 8.16).

In the MouseDown event of a Form or control you might put the following code:

```
If Button = vbRightButton Then
    frmThisForm.PopupMenu mnuMyMenu
End If
```

Note that "Button" is from the Button parameter passed to the MouseDown event and corresponds to the value for the mouse button the user actually pressed. The value vbRightButton is of course a VB 4.0 predefined constant.

In the example, mnuMyMenu must be the name of a valid menu belonging to the form.

Tip

You don't have to make a menu visible to be able to pop it up. This means, of course, that you can design menus which never appear except as popups.

Note A menu item with no submenu items of its own can't be used as a popup. ▦

FIG. 8.16 ⇒

You can call the form's PopUpMenu method to cause any menu with subitems to appear on the form wherever you click without the submenu having to be attached to the menu bar.

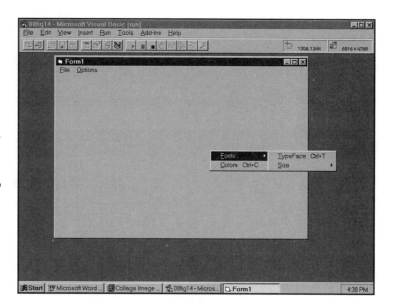

Taking the Disc Test

If you have read and understood the material in this chapter, you are ready to test your knowledge. Insert the CD-ROM that comes with this book and run the self-test software as described in Appendix H, "Using the CD-ROM."

From Here...

You can study this chapter together with the following chapter on Multiple Document Interface because MDI applications depend heavily on menus. A menu control's WindowList property, for example, only has meaning in an MDI application.

You should also note the use of menus in applications which use OLE embedded controls. A menu control's NegotiatePosition property is useful here. See the section, "Using the OLE 2.0 Container Control," in Chapter 10, "Using OLE Automation to Integrate Applications."

Chapter Prerequisite

You should be familiar with the Form events and methods discussed in Chapter 7 as well as with the use of menus as discussed in Chapter 8.

You also should be comfortable with managing multiple open documents in an MDI-type application.

9

Using Multiple-Document Interface (MDI)

This chapter covers the basic information you need to create Multiple Document Interface (MDI) applications in VB. *Multiple Document Interface* refers to the fact that the application contains an MDI form that acts as a container for other forms known as MDI children. Terms and concepts covered include:

- ◆ **MDI Form or MDI Parent Form**
- ◆ **MDI Child Form**
- ◆ **Instantiation of a Child Form**
- ◆ **MDI menu management**
- ◆ **MDI toolbars**
- ◆ **The Windows menu in MDI applications**
- ◆ **Unload and QueryUnload Form events on MDI children**

Understanding MDI Applications

The main feature of an MDI application is its ability to produce and manage an indefinite number of identical Forms at run time known as *child forms*. Child Forms, of course, may become different from each other once they've been created.

Every MDI application must have a special parent form to act as the container for the Child Forms. This container form is called an *MDI Form* or *MDI Parent*. MDI Children cannot exist outside of the application's MDI Form. The user can't drag an MDI Child outside of the boundaries of the MDI Form, and when an MDI Child is minimized, its icon shows up on the MDI Form's surface rather than on the Windows taskbar (see fig. 9.1).

Examples of MDI applications include Microsoft Excel or Microsoft Word for Windows. In these applications, the main program is represented by a container MDI Parent window. The user can open as many word processing or spreadsheet documents as the computer's memory will allow. Each spreadsheet or word processing document is a Child window. When the application runs, the first Child opens as a blank document and is identical to all other blank documents. It has the same menu, the same options, and the same features. As the user puts information into the spreadsheet or the Word document, the document becomes unique.

FIG. 9.1 ⟹

A screen running Microsoft Excel illustrates some of the features an end user sees when running an MDI application.

All documents are contained in the MDI Parent

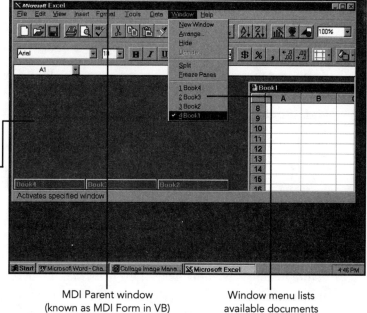

MDI Parent window
(known as MDI Form in VB)

Window menu lists
available documents

Setting Up an MDI Form

In order for a VB application to contain MDI Child Forms, it must possess an MDI Form, or Parent Form. An MDI Form is a special object distinct from regular VB Forms. You must set it up with the following steps:

1. From VB's main menu, choose Insert, MDI Form (see fig. 9.2).

2. You will see a new form with the default caption and name MDIForm1. Its default background color will be different from the background color of ordinary Forms (see fig. 9.3).

Notice that, once you've set up an MDI Form in your VB project, the MDI Form option under the Insert menu is disabled. This is because VB allows for only one MDI Form per application.

If you want your application to begin with an MDI Form and no children, you will want to make the MDI Form be your project's Startup Form. To do so,

1. From the VB menu, choose Tools, Options.

2. Choose the Project tab from the Options dialog.

3. From the Startup Form list box, choose the MDI Form (see fig. 9.4).

4. Click the Option dialog's OK button.

If an application attempts to load an MDI Child Form into memory before loading the container MDI Form, then the MDI Form will load automatically with the MDI Child visible inside it. You also will get the same effect if you let an MDI Child be the application's Startup Form. The application starts with the MDI Parent containing the MDI Child.

FIG. 9.2 ⇒

Inserting an MDI Form in your application at design-time.

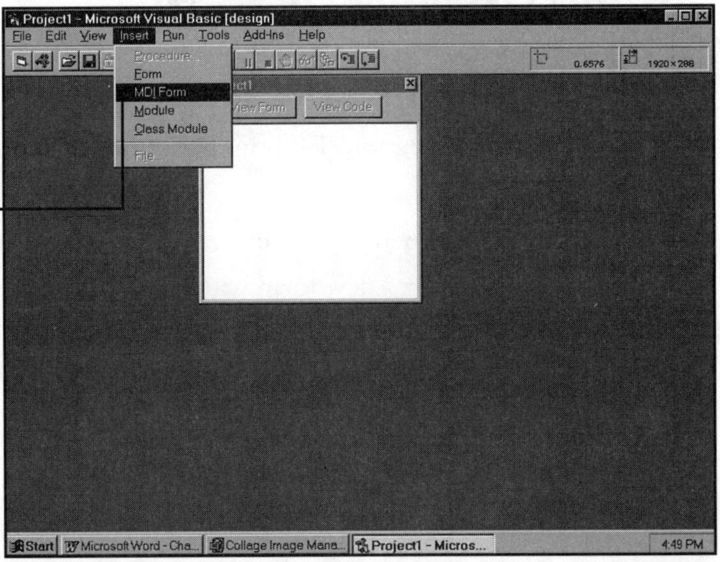

MDI Form option of Insert menu

FIG. 9.3 ⇒

What a newly inserted MDI Form looks like at design-time.

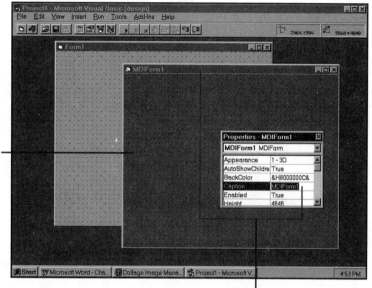

Default background color is different from default background color of regular VB Forms

Default Caption and Name are MDIForm1

FIG. 9.4 ⇒

Changing the project's Startup Form to the MDI Form on the Project tab of the Tools Options menu choice.

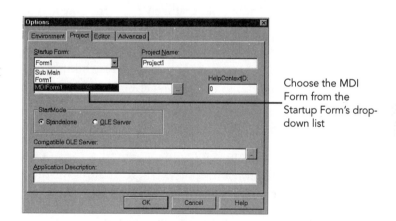

Choose the MDI Form from the Startup Form's drop-down list

Setting Up MDI Child Classes

An MDI Child Form is an ordinary VB Form with its MDIChild property set to true. If you create an MDI Child Form by simply setting its MDIChild property to true, this Form is no longer independent. It can't exist without the Parent or MDI Form. In order to make a VB Form into an MDI Child Form at design-time, you must take the following steps:

1. Click the Form's blank surface to make sure it's the currently selected object.
2. Access the Property Window for the Form.
3. Select the MDIChild property.
4. Set the MDIChild property to True by double-clicking the property, typing True as the property's value, or selecting True from the property's ListBox (see fig. 9.5).

When you make an ordinary Form into an MDI Child Form, you are no longer just designing a single VB Form. Instead, you're creating a whole class of Forms. The Child Form you created at design-time is now a model, a template, or an abstract description for a Form class. You'll be able to write code that uses this child template form at run-time as the model to create new copies or *instances* of the *ancestor class* represented by the Child Form.

▶ **See** "Initializing MDI Children with AsNew," **p. 306**

At design-time, you can manipulate the Form's properties, place controls on its surface, and code event procedures for the MDI Child form, just as you would for an ordinary VB form.

However, the application can use the Child Form as a template by creating copies or instances of the Child Form at run-time. Each instance of the Child Form that is created will have the same controls, properties, and event procedures as the original design-time instance.

An MDI application can have more than one type of Child Form or template. For instance, a spreadsheet application such as Microsoft Excel might have spreadsheet and chart-type Child Forms. You must create a design-time Child Form/template for each type of Child Form you want to create at run-time.

An MDI application may still have Forms that are neither an MDI Form (Parent) nor MDI Children. These Forms can stand alone from the MDI Parent and will behave as any standard VB Form. An example would be an About Form that is accessed when the user clicks the Help menu and selects About.

FIG. 9.5 ⇒
Changing the MDIChild property of a regular Form to True to make it into an MDI Child Form.

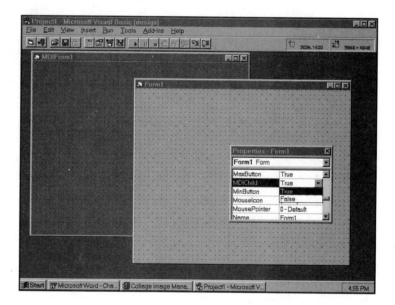

Placing Code in an MDI Application

In comparison with non-MDI applications, you generally will put more code for general procedures in Standard (BAS) Modules and less code in Form modules with MDI applications. Because MDI Parent and Child Forms may often need to share the same functionality, it's a good idea to place common-use functions in a more easily accessible and central location like a Standard Module.

For example, both the MDI Parent Form and Child Forms will usually have menu options to create a new document (a File, New option in most applications). Instead of putting the code to create an instance of a new child directly into the menu's Click events, you'll want to put the code in a general procedure within a Standard Module. You can then call the general procedure from the various event procedures that need to initialize a new Child.

Initializing MDI Children with As New

You will use the design-time Child Form as a template or class description for creating new instances of the Child Form. You can create a general procedure to initialize a new Child instance in a Standard Module:

```
Public Sub NewChild
    Dim frmNew As New frmChild
    frmNew.Visible = True
End Sub
```

Notice that one line of code creates a new child instance (Dim frmNew as New frmChild). We declare an object variable, frmChild, to reference the new instance of the child. Notice that the type of the newly created Form is not simply a generic Form; its type is actually frmChild, the name of the design-time Child! In other words, the Child you worked on at design-time is now an actual object class type and can be used to create new objects. In fact, the line

```
Dim frmNew As New frmChild
```

actually creates the new instance. The second chore we need to do here is make sure the newly created child is visible. We set its Visible property to true. Or, we could have used the Show method to display the newly created Child Form.

Because we declare frmNew in this procedure, the variable frmNew has no scope outside the procedure and the newly created Child is essentially nameless once you reach the end of this procedure. Notice that the newly created Child Form will exist beyond the procedure but its reference, frmNew, will not.

▶ **See** "Referencing MDI Children," **p. 308**

You'll typically let the user create a new Child Form instance from a menu option such as File, New. Create a menu item on the MDI Parent Form with the following steps (see fig. 9.6).

1. Select MDI Parent Form.

2. Access the Menu Editor window.

3. Enter the information for the first menu item. Type **mnuFile** for the name property and **&File** for the caption.

4. Click the Next button in the menu editor to move to the next blank line in the list of menu items.

3. Enter the information for the second menu item. Type **mnuFileNew** for the name property and **&New** for the caption.

6. Click the right arrow in the middle of the menu editor to indent the mnuFileNew item.

7. Click the Menu Editor's OK button to confirm your changes.

In mnuFileNew's Click event, call the general procedure we showed you previously to create a new Child:

```
Private mnuFileNew_Click()
     NewChild      'name of general procedure to create a new
➥child
End Sub
```

Note Review how to place code in a Standard Module and in a menu control's Click event procedure in Chapters 3 and 8, respectively. ▧

FIG. 9.6 ⇒

Using the Menu
Editor to create a
File New menu
option for an MDI
Form.

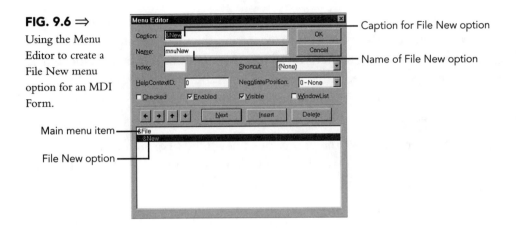

Main menu item

File New option

Referencing MDI Children

As noted in the previous section on "Initializing MDI Children with As New," an MDI Child instance in a running application has essentially no reference name to distinguish it from other instances of the same MDI Child class.

You can't provide a unique reference to each MDI Child instance by assigning a distinct value to their name property since this property is changeable only at run-time. There exists, however, at least two other ways to give it an MDI Child instance a unique identity:

◆ Populate each Form's Caption property with a unique string. This string displayed in the title bar enables the user to distinctly reference each form instance.

◆ You'll also want to be able to mark the Child instance in some special way so that your code can tell two instances apart. The Tag property can hold such distinguishing information.

The following code example expands the rudimentary subroutine from the previous section for creating a new Child instance to include an incrementing Static counter *ChildCount*, which keeps track of the number of children we've created. Place that counter in the new instance's Caption and in its Tag property to provide identification both for the user and in code.

```
[in a Standard Module]
Public Sub NewChild
    Static ChildCount As Integer
    Dim frmNew As New frmChild
    ChildCount = ChildCount + 1
    frmNew.Caption = "DOC #" & ChildCount
    frmNew.Tag = cStr(ChildCount)
    frmNew.Visible = True
End Sub
```

Tip

Consider making the Static variable *ChildCount* into a Public variable if you need to know information about the Child Forms throughout the application—for example, the total number of Child Form instances that have been created.

Using the Original MDI Child Instance

The original design-time copy of the MDI Child Form provides a template for all future instances of MDI children. It also is the first copy of the Child Form in the application. Remember, frmChild is the value of the name property for the design-time copy of the MDI Child Form. In the lines of code

```
Dim frmNew As New frmChild
frmNew.Visible = True
```

we are basically using frmChild, the original Child Form, as a template for new forms, but we are not using frmChild for anything else. It always remains invisible and is available to us when we want to instantiate new Children.

If you wanted to be more efficient with memory, you could use frmChild as the first form to show up the first time you wanted to instantiate a new Child Form. Instead of always using As New to instantiate a new form, we initialize a reference (or object variable) to the form object with *Dim frmNew As Form*. Then, we check to see if this is the first time we're trying to create a new Child. If it is the first, we set the reference to the existing original copy of the Child without creating a new instance of the Child. If it's not the first time, we create a new instance of the Child with the Dim As New syntax and then set frmNew to point to this new instance.

```
Public Sub NewChild
      Static ChildCount As Integer
      Dim frmNew As Form
      ChildCount = ChildCount + 1
      If ChildCount = 1 Then
            Set frmNew = frmChild
      Else
            Dim frmNewChild as New frmChild
            Set frmNew = frmNewChild
      EndIf
      frmNew.Caption = "DOC #" & ChildCount
      frmNew.Tag = cStr(ChildCount)
      frmNew.Visible = True
End Sub
```

Determining Parent or Child Menu Visibility

When you create menus on an MDI Form and on MDI Children, you must beware that both sets of menus will never be visible at the same time (see figs. 9.7 and 9.8).

If an MDI Child has a menu, its menu appears in place of the Parent's menu at the top of the Parent. Therefore, an MDI Parent Form's menu will only show up if:

- ◆ No Child instance is active on the Parent Form, or
- ◆ The active Child has no menu

If you need to duplicate functionality on both Parent and Child menus, call identical code from both the Parent and Child's menus. Write code for such duplicate menu items in a separate standard module, and then call the code from each of the menu items' event procedures. This will save you the headache of writing the same code in two separate places and having to maintain two separate pieces of identical code.

FIG. 9.7 ⇒
An MDI Form's menu is visible only when no Children are active or when none of the active Children has a menu.

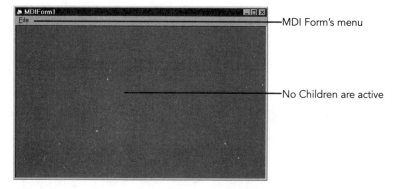

—MDI Form's menu

—No Children are active

FIG. 9.8 ⇒
When an MDI Child with a menu becomes active, MDI Child menus override an MDI Form's menus.

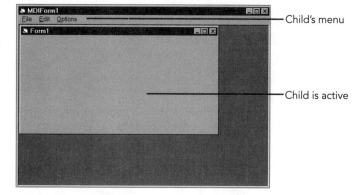

—Child's menu

—Child is active

Creating Toolbars

A toolbar contains icons the user can click to perform common actions. These actions are usually the same as actions performed by selected menu items. The toolbar usually resides at the top of the MDI Parent Form's design surface, and MDI Children will never cover the toolbar (see fig. 9.9).

An MDI Form can only contain controls that support the Align property, and the PictureBox control is the only standard VB control that has an Align property. This means that you can create a simple toolbar for your application by using the PictureBox control. The PictureBox control is a container control, which means, among other things, it can contain other controls. The basic way to implement a toolbar is to place a PictureBox on the MDI Form and then place other controls such as Image controls, PictureBox, or Command buttons within the original PictureBox control.

You can then put code inside the Click events of the controls that reside on the toolbar. This code can then perform the desired actions when the user clicks the "icons" of the toolbar. If you follow the advice of the previous section on "Determining Parent or Child Menu Visibility," you'll have the code for each menu item in its own general procedure in a Standard Module. You can then simply call the same general procedure corresponding to a menu item from the toolbar item's Click events. For example, you can create a new MDI Child instance from either the menu or the toolbar. In both cases, the menu item and the icon on the toolbar call the same code from a general procedure.

Note You can use the custom toolbar control along with the custom ImageList control to implement a toolbar with all the bells and whistles, such as group push buttons and a central repository (the ImageList control) for all the icons used in the toolbar. ■

FIG. 9.9 ⇒
A design-time view of a toolbar implemented with a PictureBox.

PictureBox control placed inside the toolbar as an icon

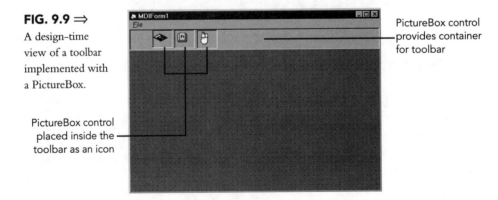

PictureBox control provides container for toolbar

Creating a Windows Menu

The Windows menu is a standard sight to users of MDI applications. When users pull down the Windows menu in the application, they'll always see a list of the MDI Child Forms that are currently open. Clicking any one of these forms listed in the Window menu will make that form the active form. Windows menus may contain other options as well. Some of the most common options affect how to arrange Child documents within the MDI Parent Form (see fig. 9.10).

The following sections discuss how to implement a Windows menu containing the names of all available Child Forms and common ways to arrange Child Forms within the Parent MDI Form.

To prepare a menu to be a Windows Menu, follow these steps (see fig. 9.11):

1. Select the Parent MDI Form.
2. Access the Menu Editor Window.
3. Navigate through the list of menu items to highlight the spot in the list where you want the Windows menu to appear.
4. Use the Menu Editor's Insert button, if necessary, to clear a space in the menu list for the new item.
5. Click the left arrow button in the middle of the Menu Editor, if necessary, to unindent the Windows menu.
6. Enter the information for the Window menu using the Name *mnuWindow* and the Caption *&Window*.
7. Click Next in the menu editor to move to the next line in the list of menu items.
8. Use the Menu Editor's Insert button if necessary to clear a space in the list for the next menu item.

9. Enter the information for the first submenu item under Windows using the Name *mnuArrangeAll* and the Caption *&ArrangeAll*.

10. Click the right arrow in the middle of the menu editor to indent mnuArrangeAll menu item.

11. Repeat steps 7 through 9 to enter three more menu items—*mnuTileVertical* with the Caption Tile &Vertical, *mnuTileHorizontal* with the Caption Tile &Horizontal, and *mnuCascade* with the Caption &Cascade. (Step 10 doesn't need repeating, because the new items will stay at the same level as mnuArrangeAll.)

12. Click the Menu Editor's OK button to confirm your changes.

FIG. 9.10 ⇒
A Windows menu in a running MDI application.

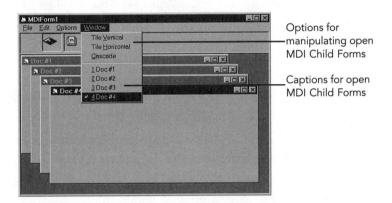

Options for manipulating open MDI Child Forms

Captions for open MDI Child Forms

FIG. 9.11 ⇒
Menu Editor view of menu items for a typical Windows menu in an MDI application.

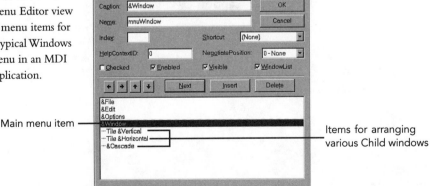

Main menu item

Items for arranging various Child windows

The WindowList Property

In order to enable the Windows main menu to display the captions of the available MDI children, set the menu item's *WindowList* property to True. To set the WindowList property, follow these steps:

1. Select the Parent MDI Form.
2. Access the Menu Editor Window.
3. Select the Windows menu item within the list.
4. Click the check box entitled <u>W</u>indowList. You have just enabled the menu's WindowList property.
5. Click the Menu Editor's OK button to confirm your change.

When you run the application and add several MDI Child Forms, you'll see their captions listed when you access the Windows menu. If you select one of the form's captions, you will activate that Child Form within the Parent MDI form.

The Arrange Method

The Arrange Method belongs to an MDI Form. You can call the Arrange Method with a parameter whose value indicates the physical arrangement of the MDI children forms. The various possible values for the Arrange method's parameter are provided by internal VB constants. They are:

◆ *vbArrangeAll*. All Child Forms that have been minimized to icons will arrange in neat rows on the MDI Form's surface (see fig. 9.12).

◆ *vbCascade*. Open and non-minimized Child Forms will arrange in a cascading pattern on the MDI Form's surface (see fig. 9.13).

◆ *vbTileHorizontal*. Open and non-minimized Child Forms will arrange in a horizontally tiled pattern on the MDI Form's surface (see fig. 9.14).

◆ *vbTileVertical*. Open and non-minimized Child Forms will arrange in a vertically tiled pattern on the MDI Form's surface (see fig. 9.15).

All you need to do to use the Arrange method is to call it in a single line of code from the Click event of a menu item such as those we added in the example in the section, "Creating a Windows Menu." You would call the Arrange method with the following syntax:

```
MDIFormName.Arrange ArrangeType
```

where *MDIFormName* is the name of the application's MDI Form and *ArrangeType* is one of the four values vbArrangeAll, vbCascade, vbTileHorizontal, or vbTileVertical. The Click event procedures for the menu items created in the example in the previous section look like this:

```
Private Sub mnuArrangeAll_Click()
    MDIForm1.Arrange vbArrangeAll
End Sub
Private Sub mnuCascade_Click()
    MDIForm1.Arrange vbCascade
End Sub
Private Sub mnuTileHorizontal_Click()
    MDIForm1.Arrange vbTileHorizontal
End Sub
Private Sub mnuTileVertical_Click()
    MDIForm1.Arrange vbTileVertical
End Sub
```

FIG. 9.12 ⇒

Minimized Child Forms' icons have been arrayed on the MDI Form's surface with the Arrange All option of the Windows menu.

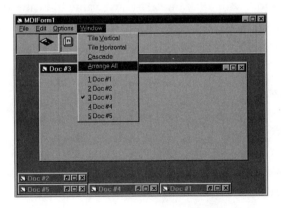

FIG. 9.13 ⇒
Child Forms arranged on the Parent with the Cascade option of the Windows menu.

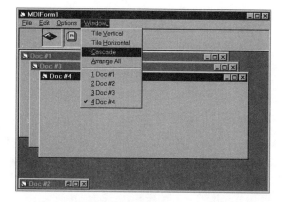

FIG. 9.14 ⇒
Child Forms arranged on the Parent with the Tile Horizontal option of the Windows menu.

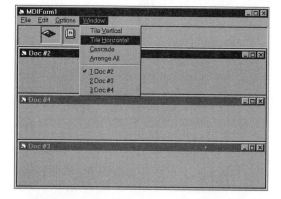

FIG. 9.15 ⇒
Child Forms arranged on the Parent with the Tile Vertical option of the Windows menu.

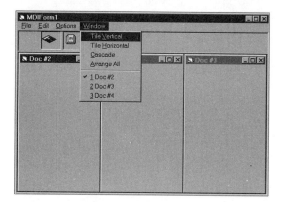

Using Unload and QueryUnload

In Chapter 7, we noted that a Form's QueryUnload event happens before its Unload event. Both QueryUnload and Unload event procedures receive a Cancel parameter that you can programmatically set to True to stop the Form from unloading.

When you attempt to unload the main MDI form in an MDI application, VB unloads all the open Child Forms first. This means that the various Unload and QueryUnload events have a special timing relationship in an MDI application. When there is an attempt to unload the main MDI Form, the order of the Unload and QueryUnload events is as follows:

1. The MDI Form's QueryUnload event
2. The QueryUnload event of each open Child Form
3. The Unload event of each Child Form
4. The Unload event of the MDI Form

If Cancel is set to true within any of these event procedures, the entire unloading process stops. If unloading is halted during any of the QueryUnload event procedures, then none of the Unload events is triggered and no Form is unloaded. If unloading is halted during any of the Unload event procedures, then only the Forms whose Unload events happened before the one where the Cancel occurred will unload.

▶ **See** "Load, Unload, and QueryUnload," **p. 256**

Taking the Disc Test

If you have read and understood the material in the chapter, you are ready to test your knowledge. Insert the CD-ROM that comes with this book and run the self-test software as described in Appendix H, "Using the CD-ROM."

From Here...

After finishing this chapter, you might find it useful to review Chapter 8 on Menus and Chapter 7 on Events (especially the section on Unload and QueryUnload). The topics covered in this chapter may give you a broader perspective on the use of menus and Form events.

The concept of the design-time MDI Child Form as a class is also a good preparation for the class concepts that we develop at greater length in the chapters on OLE Automation and OLE Servers.

Part II Ch 9

Part III

Using OLE to Tie Applications Together

You should be familiar with the
general syntax and techniques
in Visual Basic for manipulating
objects such as controls and
Forms discussed throughout
Chapter 2 "Visual Basic Data
Types," Chapter 3 "Working
with Visual Basic Code," Chapter 6 "Common Properties of
the Form Object and Control
Objects," and Chapter 7 "Control and Form Object Events."

Using OLE Automation to Integrate Applications

The acronym OLE stands for *Object Linking and Embedding.* Although
OLE still allows the programmer to visually link or embed objects in a
program, Microsoft has now expanded OLE into a general standard for
interapplication communication under Windows.

As of this writing, Microsoft has rolled out a new standard for reusable
components and interapplication communications known as ActiveX.
Although the VB Certification exam will probably continue to use the
term OLE, you will begin to see discussions of ActiveX (as opposed to
OLE) in journal articles and Microsoft and third-party documentation.

One of the most exciting things you can do with OLE as a programmer is OLE Automation, that is the ability to declare an object within
your application which makes available to you the functionality of a

different application (an OLE server). This chapter focuses on how to use OLE automation within your VB application to exploit the functionality of existing OLE server application.

Terms and concepts covered include:

◆ **OLE 1.0 and 2.0 standards**

◆ **Linking and Embedding**

◆ **OLE Container Control**

◆ **OLE Automation**

◆ **OLE Server and OLE Controller**

◆ **Exposed Objects**

◆ **References to external objects in VB**

◆ **Object library**

◆ **Instantiating objects**

◆ **Early and late binding**

◆ **Object hierarchy in an OLE Server**

Understanding OLE Automation

OLE Automation is the process of using functionality from one application inside another application by means of objects.

The application that requests or uses the objects is known as an *OLE controller*, and the application that provides the objects to the OLE controller is known as the *OLE Server*. A programmer might write an application specifically to be an OLE Server, but some available commercial end-user applications also can expose objects and become OLE Servers.

Some examples of important end-user applications that also are OLE Servers would be Microsoft Excel and Microsoft Word for Windows. In fact, every component of Microsoft's Windows 95 Office Suite is supposed to be an OLE server.

Note   Microsoft Access 7 is an OLE server, but earlier versions of
Access are not. ◼

An OLE Server contains an object structure that is visible to OLE
Controller applications. Objects that are available outside the OLE
Server are known as *exposed objects*. In order for an object to be an
exposed object, it must be listed in the Windows Registry.

Exposed objects have their own methods and properties, which an OLE
controller such as a VB application can manipulate with standard object
syntax.

OLE is a standard for interapplication communication. The OLE standard currently has two levels:

Part

III

Ch

10

◆ Level 1.0 provides a simple, relatively inflexible standard for
   Object Linking and Embedding. Although Linking and Embedding are not the main thrust of this chapter, the Certification Exam may contain a few questions.

◆ Level 2.0 is the specification for OLE Automation through
   exposed objects of OLE Servers and is the main focus of this
   chapter and the next chapter. In order for your VB application
   to access an OLE server's exposed objects you must set up the
   application to recognize the OLE server and then declare
   instances of objects you want to use in your code.

Using OLE Automation to Control an OLE Server

OLE Server's class objects have characteristics similar to VB objects. You
can manipulate their properties and methods as you would the properties and methods of VB controls and other objects.

To use an OLE Server's exposed objects in your VB application:

1. Set a reference to the server in your application.
2. Be familiar with the declared objects' methods and properties.

3. Declare an instance of the server's object or objects that you want to use.

4. Manipulate the declared objects in your code through their methods and properties.

The following sections detail the steps to use an OLE Server's exposed objects.

Setting a Reference to an OLE Server

In order to use an OLE server's exposed objects, you have to make the server available to your application by setting a reference to the server's *object library*. An object library is a collection of information about another application's objects. You can find this information in a .TLB (Type Library) file, an .OLB (Object Library) file, or in an OLE server's EXE or DLL file. Check with the OLE Server application to see which file it uses to store its object library.

Your application must contain a reference to a server's object library before it can use the server's object classes.

In order to make an OLE sever available to your application, you should execute the following steps:

1. Choose Tools, References from the main VB menu.

2. Scroll through the Available References list until you find the name of the OLE server you want (see fig. 10.1). Recall that the object library list you see here is not a VB-specific feature. Rather, it's generated from the Windows Registry.

3. If the server you need isn't in the list, click Browse to find and select the TLB, OLB, EXE, OCX, or DLL file containing the server's object library (see fig. 10.2).

4. Select the desired OLE server by clicking the check box to the left of the server name.

5. Click OK on the References dialog.

FIG. 10.1⇒
Use the References dialog box to set a reference in your project to an OLE server.

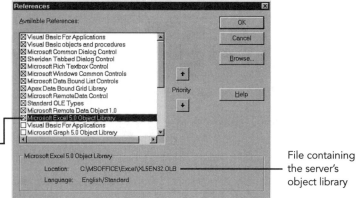

Server name is checked to include a reference in the project

File containing the server's object library

FIG. 10.2⇒
You can browse for the file containing a server's object library if the server isn't listed in the Available References list of the References dialog box.

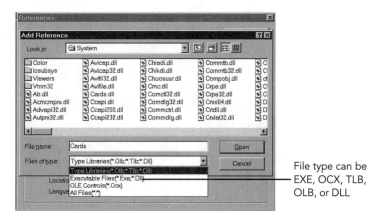

File type can be EXE, OCX, TLB, OLB, or DLL

Using the Object Browser to Find Out About an OLE Server

You can find out about an OLE Server's exposed objects by using the Object Browser, just as you would find out about the native objects provided by VB. To see the OLE Server's information in the Object Browser, you must first have set a reference to the Server, as described in the previous section, "Setting a Reference to an OLE Server."

In order to use the Object Browser with a server, you must execute the following steps (see fig. 10.3):

1. Access the Object Browser within VB.

2. Select the OLE server from the list of references in the Projects/Servers list.

3. Select a class from the Classes/Modules list.

4. Select a property or method from the Methods/Properties list.

5. Notice the brief description of the method or property at the bottom of the Object Browser dialog, just to the right of the ? icon.

6. If the server's object library has a help file, you can click the ? icon to get more information about the selected method or property (see fig. 10.4).

▶ **See** "Using Your OLE Server and the Object Browser," **p. 383**

Classes in the object library   Object library to browse

FIG. 10.3 ⟹

The Object Browser can give you detailed information about an OLE server's objects and their methods and properties.

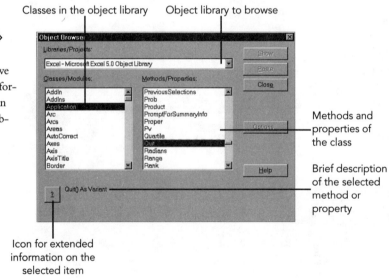

Methods and properties of the class

Brief description of the selected method or property

Icon for extended information on the selected item

Extended help screen on the
selected item

FIG. 10.4⟹
Clicking the ? icon
in the Object
Browser brings up
an extended help
screen for the
selected item when
you're browsing
information about
an OLE Server.

Selected item in
the Object
Browser

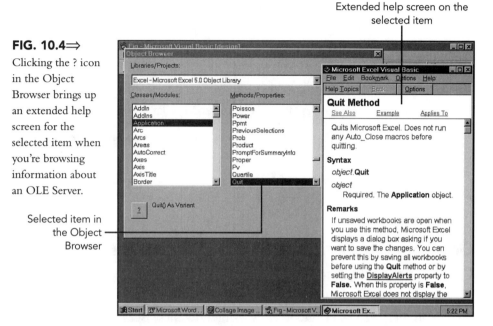

Using As New to Declare and Instantiate an OLE Server Class

Once you've set a reference to an OLE server in your application, you
can decide what object Classes of the server you want to use in your
application.

You may declare an object variable for the Server Classes you want to
use. You can then use this object variable to point to an instance of the
corresponding Class. The *As New* keyword is Microsoft's preferred technique for instantiating object variables from server classes.

> **Caution**
> Many OLE servers do not yet support the *As New* keyword. Refer to
> each server's documentation to see whether or not it supports *As New*.

If the server whose Class you wish to instantiate supports *As New*, all you need to do is declare a variable of appropriate scope (usually Private or Public) and the object is ready to use in your application. For example, if you wish to use a Class called MyClass from a server application called MyServer, your variable declaration would look like this:

Dim objMyObj As New MyServer.MyClass

You could then manipulate the object's methods and properties through your VB code.

Servers created in VB 4.0 always support the *As New* keyword.

▶ **See** "Creating OLE Servers," **p. 349**

Declaring a Variable to Hold an Instance of an OLE Server Class

Because many OLE Servers do not yet support the *As New* keyword, you will need to create object variables for these Server Classes with the CreateObject or GetObject functions.

▶ **See** "CreateObject Function versus GetObject," **p. 332**

You'll typically want to declare these object variables with Module-level or Public scope, because your application will use them in more than one procedure.

You can declare object variables to implement Class objects either as generic Object-type variables or as variables of the specific type provided in the Server's Class library. For example,

```
Dim objExcel As Excel.Application
```

and

```
Dim objExcel As Object
```

would both be valid declarations for an object that will later point to an instance of the Excel Server's Application Class.

The first declaration is preferable, however, as it provides *early binding* of the Server's class in our application while the second, more generic declaration is an example of *late binding*.

Binding refers to the point when a system recognizes references to external objects. For instance, you might reference a declared object's Visible property in your code. If Visible is an invalid property, when will the system let us know that there is an error? If you've declared the object with early binding, your system's compiler can check the Server's class library and catch any syntax errors before the application runs. If, however, you use the As Object declaration to provide late binding, the compiler won't be able to check the Server's Class library and so the compiler won't detect any syntax errors in the use of the object. Instead, syntax errors with respect to objects from OLE servers will cause run-time errors in your application.

> **Note**   You don't need to set a reference to a server if you're going to use late binding. For some servers (those without an available object library, such as the versions of Microsoft Word through version 7.0), late binding is the only option, because the application provides no object library to set a reference to. ∎

For instance, the Excel server's most important object is the Application object. Application has a Visible property which, as you might expect, sets the object's visibility to a user. Suppose you have the following declaration in your code:

```
Dim objExcel As Excel.Application
```

and later on you have the following line:

```
objExcel.Visable = True
```

The compiler catches the misspelling of the Visible property's name as soon as you try to run the application during design mode or when you try to make an executable file.

If, however, you'd declared the object with the line

```
Dim objExcel As Object
```

the compiler wouldn't be able to check the syntax of

```
objExcel.Visable = True
```

against Excel's Class library. The error (Visible is misspelled) goes undetected until such time as VB attempts to execute this line, at which point the application would generate a run-time error.

If you don't have a Server's Class library available to you, you must use late binding. For instance, Microsoft Word for Windows doesn't provide a Class library for its object Classes. You must, therefore, always use the As Object syntax to declare a Word object.

> **Caution**
> Early binding only works with versions 7.0 and later of Excel. If your Excel server is a version earlier than 7.0, you must use late binding.

CreateObject Function versus GetObject

The CreateObject and GetObject functions return a reference to a Server Class object. Use them both with the Set keyword to assign their return values to a previously declared Class object variable:

```
Set objExcel = GetObject(,"Excel.Application")
```

or

```
Set objExcel = CreateObject("Excel.Application")
```

The CreateObject function takes a single parameter, which is the name of the Class you're instantiating. It always instantiates a new object in your application.

You can use GetObject to refer to an object that already exists.

> **Caution**
> The following discussion of GetObject applies to many Microsoft products and other OLE servers. However, the use of GetObject is application-specific. In fact, some OLE Server applications don't support GetObject at all. You should refer to the application's documentation to find out whether GetObject is supported and, if so, what the proper syntax for using GetObject would be. If GetObject isn't available, you must always use CreateObject.

GetObject takes two possible parameters. You must always specify at least one of the two parameters:

- ◆ GetObject's first parameter gives the path and file name of a data file associated with the server application and its Class.

- ◆ GetObject's second parameter is the same as CreateObject's single parameter: the name of the Class you're instantiating.

There are several rules to keep in mind when using GetObject's parameters:

- ◆ If you leave the first parameter completely blank (that is, a single comma before the second argument), GetObject will always reference an existing object. If there is no existing object, a run-time error occurs.

- ◆ If you specify a valid file name in the first parameter and the file is of the type that is associated with the Server application, you may leave the second parameter blank. GetObject will open the file with the associated Server application. GetObject will use an existing reference to the object if it exists, or it will open a new copy of the object if none existed before in the application.

- ◆ If you specify a blank file name ("") in GetObject's first parameter, then you must specify the second parameter. GetObject will then always open a new copy of the object, regardless of whether one already exists in the application.

Using the Server's Object Hierarchy

An object Class in an OLE server may contain other Classes or Class collections. Subclasses or collection elements might repeat this nesting structure and could in turn contain other object Classes and collections.

Only objects in the topmost level of the Server's hierarchy can be created directly with CreateObject( ). The subordinate objects in the hierarchy either already exist as subobjects of the higher objects or must be created with methods of the higher objects.

For instance, one of the Excel Server hierarchy's topmost objects is the Application object. An Application object can contain (among other objects) a collection of WorkBook objects. Each WorkBook object of the collection can in turn contain a collection of WorkSheet objects, and each WorkSheet object can contain a Range object.

You would initialize the Application object as we've seen in the previous two sections:

```
Dim objExcel As Excel.Application
Set objExcel = CreateObject("Excel.Application")
```

You must always reference the WorkBooks collection directly through the Application object, adding a new WorkBook to the WorkBooks collection with the Add method:

```
objExcel.Workbooks.Add
```

As an alternative, you can declare another variable to point to the newly added element of the Workbook collection. The Excel Server contains a Workbook Class. You can declare a variable of this Class and use the Set keyword to assign the declared object variable to the results of the Add method:

```
Dim wb As Excel.Workbook
Set wb = objExcel.Workbooks.Add
```

You could add a Worksheet object to the Workbook object's Worksheet collection. A full example might look like this:

```
[General declarations section]
Option Explicit
Private objExcel As Excel.Application
Private wb As Excel.Workbook
Private ws As Excel.Worksheet
[Form Load event procedure]
Private Sub Form_Load()
    Set objExcel = CreateObject("Excel.Application")
    Set wb = objExcel.Workbooks.Add
    Set ws = wb.Worksheets.Add
End Sub
```

You should refer to each Server application's documentation to find out about its object hierarchy.

Manipulating the Server's Methods and Properties

Once you have instantiated an exposed object from an OLE Server Class in your application, you can programmatically manipulate it just as you would any other object in VB such as a control or a Form.

You must, of course, know how to use the object's methods and properties. If the server application has a class/type library, the Object Browser gives you a list and a brief description of each method or property. You will probably also want to refer to any documentation on the Server's Classes as published by the Server application's vendor.

The Excel Server's various classes, for example, have methods and properties that allow you to manipulate an Excel application and every aspect of an Excel Spreadsheet or Chart. Assuming that objExcel is an instance of Excel.Application (see the previous three sections in this chapter), the following lines of code would terminate the running instance of Excel without prompting the user to save any changes:

```
Dim wb As Excel.Workbook
For Each wb In objExcel.Workbooks
    wb.Saved = True 'consider workbook as saved-don't
  ➥prompt
Next wb
objExcel.Quit objExcel.Quit      'End Excel application
```

The Excel Server's Worksheet Class contains a subclass known as the Range object. The Range object takes a string argument that defines the range of cells to manipulate. Range in turn has a Value property that you can either read or write. The effect of setting or getting the Range object's Value property is to read or set the cell value specified in the argument to the Range object. The following line of code assumes that the current VB form contains a TextBox control named *txtCellValue* and that there's a Worksheet object variable named *ws*:

```
txtCellValue.Text = ws.Range("A1").Value
```

This line of code would assign the contents of cell A1 to the TextBox control.

The following line of code would reverse the process, setting the contents of cell A1 to be the same as the contents of the TextBox control:

```
ws.Range("A1").Value = txtCellValue.Text
```

Using the OLE 2.0 Container Control

The OLE 2.0 Container Control provides the visual interface for an OLE Server object's visual interface. These objects can be either embedded or linked to your application. In the original version (1.0) of OLE, linking and embedding were the main features of the OLE standard. See the following sections on Linking and Embedding for a description of the differences between linked and embedded objects.

You would use the OLE Container instead of the OLE Automation techniques discussed earlier in this chapter when the user needs to view and manipulate an OLE Server's data using the Server's own visual interface.

The user or the programmer can activate the interface of the Server contained in the OLE Container, in effect invoking the OLE Server application. Some OLE servers support *in-place activation*, which means that the server interface will appear completely within the OLE Container control. OLE servers that don't support in-place activation will display their interface in a separate window.

The OLE server's menus can also appear on the containing Form's menu area and can either override the Form's own menu or coexist with the Form's menu (see fig. 10.5). In order to display the Container object's menu on the Form at run-time, you must be sure that:

◆ The Form's NegotiateMenus property is set to True (the default is True)

◆ The Form has at least one menu item of its own. If you don't plan a menu for the Form, you can add a "dummy" menu item and set its Visible property to False. If you do wish any of your

Form's menus to appear alongside the OLE server's menus, then you must set the NegotiatePosition property of the top-level menu item to some value other than its default of None (see fig. 10.6). The other possible values for NegotiatePosition are 1-Left, 2-Middle, and 3-Right. Choosing one of these values will cause the Form menu item to appear respectively to the left of the Server's menu, in the midst of the server's menu items, or to the right of all of the server's menu items but Help.

▶ **See** "Programming the OLE Container Control" **p. 342**

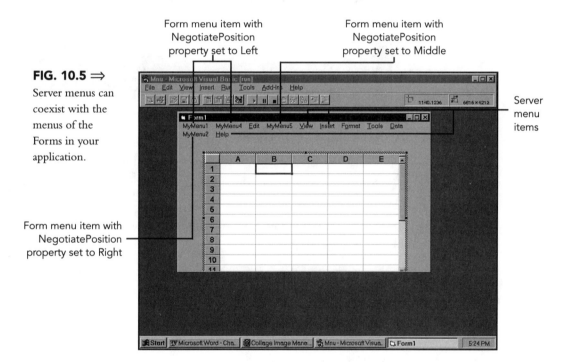

Form menu item with NegotiatePosition property set to Left

Form menu item with NegotiatePosition property set to Middle

FIG. 10.5 ⇒
Server menus can coexist with the menus of the Forms in your application.

Server menu items

Form menu item with NegotiatePosition property set to Right

Linking

When you link an object to your VB application using the OLE 2.0 Container Control, the data for the object resides separately from your application and is stored in the native data format of the OLE Server application.

FIG. 10.6 ⇒

You can set a menu item's NegotiatePosition value in the Menu Editor.

Choices for NegotiatePosition

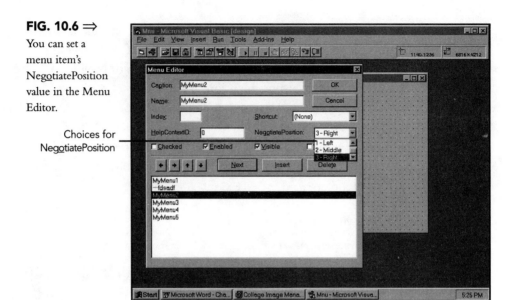

For example, if you wanted to link Excel spreadsheet data to your application, the data would reside in its own XLS file (Excel spreadsheet format). Other applications, such as Excel or other OLE controllers that link to the spreadsheet, could read and write this linked data.

In order to include a linked object in your application at design time, you should follow these steps:

1. Double-click the OLE 2.0 Container control on the toolbox.

2. You will see the Insert Object dialog box (see fig. 10.7).

3. Choose the Create from File option.

4. The appearance of the Insert Object dialog changes to look like figure 10.8.

5. Use the mouse to check the Link checkbox.

6. Click Browse to bring up the Browse file dialog (see fig. 10.9).

7. Choose a data file from the Browse dialog and click OK.

8. You will see the Insert Object dialog with the data file you chose in the File Textbox and the file's corresponding Server object listed just above the Textbox.

9. Click OK on the Insert Object dialog.

10. After a few seconds, the data file appears in the OLE Container control on the Form.

11. You may resize and move the Container as desired.

▶ **See** "Programming the OLE Container Control," **p. 342**

FIG. 10.7 ⇒

The Insert Object dialog box appears whenever you add an OLE Container control to a form.

This option will create a blank embedded object

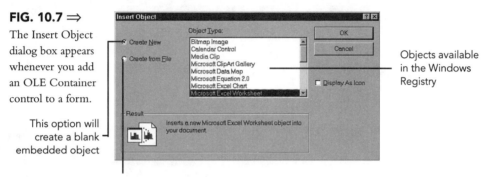

Objects available in the Windows Registry

This option allows you to use an existing data file to create a linked or embedded object

FIG. 10.8 ⇒

When you choose the Create From File option, the Insert Object dialog box changes its appearance.

This button allows you to find a data file

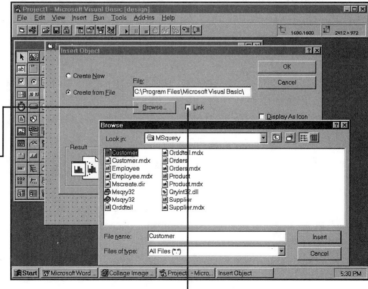

This option creates a linked object when checked and an embedded object when unchecked

FIG. 10.9 ⇒

The Browse dialog box allows you to choose a data file when inserting an OLE object into an OLE container control.

Choosing this Excel data file will cause the object to become an Excel Worksheet object

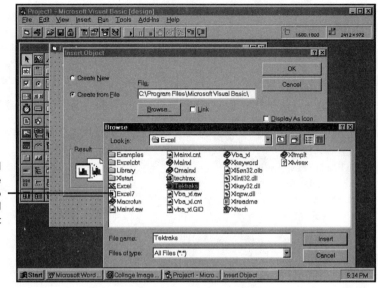

Embedding

When you embed an object in your VB application using the OLE 2.0 Container Control, the data for the object is stored with your application and isn't saved anywhere in the Server application's native data format.

For example, if you wanted to embed Excel spreadsheet data in your application, then the data would reside with your application's executable file and would load into and disappear from memory along with the executable. Other applications, such as Excel or other OLE controllers, would have no access to the embedded object.

Note It is possible to store an embedded object's data separately from the executable in a special OLE format. See the section "Programming the OLE Container Control" for more information. ▪

You have two options for initially displaying an embedded object to the user:

◆ The user can see a blank editing surface with no data.

◆ The user can see data in the embedded object. You can base this data on an existing data file of the server application. Once you use the data from the file, however, there is no further connection between the data in the object and the data in the file. The user can't save changes to the data file.

In order to include a blank embedded object, follow these steps:

1. Double-click the OLE 2.0 Container control on the toolbox.

2. You will see the Insert Object dialog box (see fig. 10.10).

FIG. 10.10 ⇒

Creating a blank embedded object with the Insert Object dialog box.

Create <u>N</u>ew option guarantees a blank embedded object

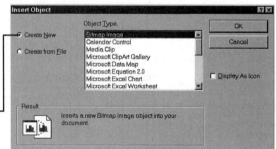

3. Choose the object type to insert from the Object <u>T</u>ype listbox.

4. Click OK on the Insert Object dialog box.

5. You may resize and move the Container as desired.

In order to include an embedded object based on an existing data file in your application at design time, you should execute the following steps:

6. Follow steps 1–11 of the previous section on Linking. Omit step 5, making sure that the Link check box stays unselected.

▶ **See** "Programming the OLE Container Control" **p. 342**

Objects in the Toolbox

If you use a particular type of OLE Server object in OLE Containers a lot, such as Excel spreadsheets or Word documents, you can include the object as an icon in the VB Toolbox along with other controls. You can then add the object to a Form just as you would any other control.

In order to add an object to the VB Toolbox, you need to follow these steps:

1. From the VB menu choose Tools, Custom Controls or key Ctrl+T to invoke the Custom Controls dialog.
2. In the Available Controls list box, scroll to the OLE Server you want to include in the Toolbox.
3. Use the mouse to make sure the box to the left of the entry for the OLE Server is checked.
4. Click OK.
5. In the VB Toolbox you should now see an icon for the OLE Server you chose in the Custom Controls dialog box.

You can add the object from the VB Toolbox just as you would any other control from the Toolbox.

Programming the OLE Container Control

You can manipulate the OLE Container Control through its properties and methods. Specifically, you can

◆ Change the object's appearance within its container
◆ Change the type of object in the container at run-time
◆ Control the object's behavior
◆ Control the object's behavior with OLE automation

Controlling the Object's Appearance

The OLE Container's DisplayType property determines whether the contained object displays as an icon or will show the data contents.

When you set up an OLE Container at design time, the Display As Icon check box in the Insert Object dialog box determines the value of the DisplayType property:

```
0 - vbOLEDisplayContent
1 - vbOLEDisplayIcon
```

You can't change DisplayType once the OLE Container has a control in it. You would need to delete the embedded or linked object before changing DisplayType.

The OLE Container's SizeMode property will determine the relation between the object's data or icon and its control.

- ◆ vbOLESizeClip-0: The OLE data maintains its original size and may or may not fit within the container (default).

- ◆ vbOLESizeStretch-1: The OLE data resizes to fit the container exactly. The data may appear distorted because it doesn't keep its original proportions.

- ◆ vbOLESizeAutoSize-2: The OLE Container control resizes to fit the data.

- ◆ VbOLESizeZoom-3: The OLE data resizes to fit the container as closely as possible while still maintaining its original proportions.

Linking and Embedding at Runtime

You can display data from an existing file as a linked object in an OLE Container by calling the OLE Container control's CreateLink method with the full path and file name as its argument. The file's extension must be recognizable by the user's Windows system as belonging to a particular OLE Server.

For example,

```
OLE1.CreateLink "C:\MyFiles\BUDGET.XLS"
```

would create a linked Excel spreadsheet object in the OLE Container, linking to the file specified in the argument.

You can create an embedded object just as easily from data in an existing file by using the CreateEmbed method. For example,

```
OLE1.CreateEmbed "C:\MyFiles\BUDGET.XLS"
```

You can display data from an existing file as either embedded or linked data in an object in an OLE Container by setting the Container control's SourceDoc property to hold the full path and file name of the file you wish to use.

You can use the InsertObjDlg methods to give the user a dialog box at run-time that will allow the choice of OLE objects which you normally get at design time. You can also use the PasteSpecialDlg method to give the user a chance to paste from the Windows system Clipboard into the OLE Container.

An OLE Server's Verbs

The *verbs* of an OLE Container are actions, such as *edit*, *play*, or *open*, which the user can execute against the currently contained object. The verbs will vary depending on the type of object and on the object's current state. The user can see a pop-up menu of available verbs by right-clicking the object with the mouse (see fig. 10.11). The OLE Container's AutoVerbMenu property must be set to its default value of True for the pop-up menu of verbs to be displayed.

> **Caution**
> If its AutoVerbMenu property is True, the OLE Container won't recognize Click or MouseDown events for the right mouse button.

The OLE Container's DoVerb method allows you to activate one of the contained object's verbs. The seven standard verbs, with their VB constant values are (note the use of negative integer values):

- ❖ *0 vbOLEPrimary*   The default action for the object. This will vary depending on the server you're using.
- ❖ *1 vbOLEShow*   Activates the object for editing.
- ❖ *2 vbOLEOpen*   Opens the object in a separate application window.

- ◆ *3 vbOLEHide* Hides the server application.
- ◆ *4 vbOLEUIActivate* Prepares the object for in-place activation and shows any user interface tools. Be sure the object supports in-place activation, or this will generate a run-time error.
- ◆ *5 vbOLEInPlaceActivate* Prepares the object to be edited when the user clicks the mouse over it. Warning: Some objects don't support a click for activation. Calling this verb on these objects will generate a run-time error.
- ◆ *6 vbOLEDiscardUndoState* Disables the Undo feature when editing the object.

You could call one of the standard verbs by passing its VB constant as an argument to the DoVerb method as in the following example:

```
OLE1.DoVerb vbOLEShow
```

Part

III

Ch

10

The contained object also may support other verbs besides the standard ones. These verbs are contained in a run-time array property of the OLE container known as *OLEVerbs*. The OLEVerbs array will change as the application runs, depending on the current state of the contained object. You can use the FetchVerbs method to refresh the OLEVerbs array, and you can find out how many verbs are in the array with the OLEVerbsCount property. OLEVerbs is a zero-based array, so the first item in the array will be at position 0 and the last item will be at position OLEVerbsCount - 1.

In the following example, a CommandButton control's click event procedure refreshes a ListBox with the current contents of the OLEVerbs array:

```
Private Sub cmdRefreshVerbs_Click()
    Dim lcv As Integer
    OLE1.FetchVerbs
    lstVerbs.Clear
    For lcv = 0 To OLE1.ObjectVerbsCount - 1
        lstVerbs.AddItem OLE1.ObjectVerbs(lcv)
    Next lcv
End Sub
```

You can invoke nonstandard verbs by passing the position of the verb in the OLEVerbs array as the argument to the DoVerbs method.

In the following example, the DblClick event procedure of a ListBox containing the contents of OLEVerbs invokes the corresponding verb:

```
Private Sub lstVerbs_DblClick()
    Dim Index As Integer
    Index = lstVerbs.ListIndex
    OLE1.DoVerb Index
End Sub
```

FIG. 10.11 ⇒

If the OLE Container's AutoVerbMenu property is True, the user can right-click over the OLE Container to see a list of available verbs.

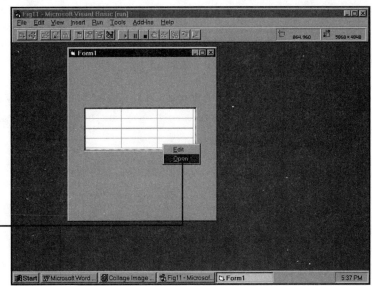

This list of verbs may be different at another point in the program

OLE Automation with the Object Property

The only difference between manipulating the OLE Container and manipulating a declared OLE object is the Object property of the Container control. Object is a run-time property that holds all the contained object's methods, properties, and sub-classes. Whenever you want to refer to the object's properties, methods, collections, or sub-classes in your code, you put the OLE Container's name and the object property in front of them. For example, if an OLE Container named OLE1 held an Excel Worksheet object, you could manipulate its contents programmatically with lines such as:

```
OLE1.Object.Range("A1").Value = txtCellValue.Text
```

Compare the preceding line of code with

```
ws.Range("A1").Value = txtCellValue.Text
```

where *ws* is an object variable pointing to an instance of an OLE object.

You also may set an object variable to point to an OLE Container control. Subsequently, when you manipulate the object variable, you will be manipulating the object contained in the OLE Container. This only works when the Container control and the object variable hold the same type of object. In the following example, the OLE Container control (named OLE1) holds an Excel.Worksheet object:

```
Dim ws As Excel.Worksheet
Set ws = OLE1.object
ws.Range("A1").Value = txtValue.Text
```

▶ **See** "Manipulating the Server's Methods and Properties," **p. 335**

Taking the Disc Test

If you have read and understood the material in the chapter, you are ready to test your knowledge. Insert the CD-ROM that comes with this book and run the self-test software as described in Appendix H, "Using the CD-ROM."

From Here...

Many of the concepts of this chapter provide a good introduction to Chapter 11, "Creating OLE Servers." These introductory concepts include:

- ◆ **OLE Automation**
- ◆ **OLE Server and OLE Controller**
- ◆ **Exposed Objects**
- ◆ **References to external objects in VB**
- ◆ **Object library**
- ◆ **Object Browser**
- ◆ **Instantiating objects**
- ◆ **Early and late binding**
- ◆ **Object hierarchy in an OLE Server**

Chapter Prerequisite

You should be familiar with
fundamental VB programming
concepts as presented in Chapter 2, "Visual Basic Data Types,"
Chapter 3, "Working with Visual
Basic Code," Chapter 6, "Common Properties of the Form
Object and Control Objects,"
and Chapter 7, "Control and
Form Object Events." You
should also know the material
in Chapter 10.

Creating OLE Servers

If you took the Visual Basic 3.0 Certification Exam, one of the biggest
differences you'll notice when you take the Visual Basic 4.0 Exam is its
increased emphasis on OLE. In particular, your score sheet will have a
new category, "Creating OLE Servers." Visual Basic 4.0 is the first
release of Visual Basic that enables you to create an OLE server. The
ability to create OLE servers as exposed object classes gives the VB
programmer the main advantage of Object-Oriented Programming –
reusable system components.

In Chapter 10, you saw how to make your Visual Basic 4.0 application
act as an OLE automation controller. In this chapter, we'll turn the
tables and see how you can create an OLE server. Your application can
now offer its services to other applications acting as controllers. A controller application can use the software drivers of the OLE Automation
Layer to invoke the OLE server application you write. The controller
can then instantiate objects from classes belonging to your server.

Terms and concepts covered include:

- ◆ Creating a simple OLE server from scratch
- ◆ Implementing custom object Classes
- ◆ Testing an OLE server at design time with a test controller application
- ◆ Determining whether a server should be in-process (DLL) or out-of-process (EXE)
- ◆ Registering your OLE server
- ◆ Controlling version compatibility of your OLE server

Exploring the Basic Steps

The main secret behind an OLE server is a custom object class. While you can create custom object Classes for other purposes, Microsoft's published documentation and courseware mostly shows examples of Classes used to implement OLE servers.

Recall the syntax we saw in the last chapter for instantiating OLE objects in a controller application:

```
Dim xl as Excel.Application
```

and

```
set xl = CreateObject("Excel.Application")
```

or

```
set xl = GetObject(,"Excel.Application")
```

Some servers (including all those you create with VB) support Microsoft's recommended standard, Dim…As New. Assuming you had created a server MyServer with a Class MyClass, you could set up an object variable reference to the server Class with the line:

```
Dim objSvr As New MyServer.MyClass
```

This is the only line of code you'd need, because the As New keyword declares and instantiates the object variable in a single line of code.

The common thread in each of these sample lines is the *appname.objecttype* syntax we use when referring to our server Class.

The statements above that reference the system name of the server and its Class (Excel.Application or MyServer.MyClass) assume that you have already set a *reference* to the server in the controller project.

In this chapter, you see how to create, test, and maintain object Classes that can behave as Excel.Application did in the examples from Chapter 10.

To implement object Classes in VB 4.0, you must first create a server application. Then, in your server application, you can define Classes that will become the server's exposed objects.

In this section, you learn the basic steps for creating a server and implementing Classes in the server. Later in this chapter, you also see how to test, fine-tune, and maintain your server.

To create a server application, you should follow these basic steps:

1. Start a new project for the server Class.
2. Change the project's name to match the desired *appname* for the server you want.
3. If the server is to be in-process (an OLE DLL), you must change the startup form to be Sub Main().
4. If you are going to test the server at design time, set its StartMode to OLE Server.

For each exposed object Class that you want to implement in the server, follow these steps:

1. Add at least one Class Module to the project.
2. Set the Class Module's *Name* property to the desired *objecttype* name for the server.
3. Set the Class Module's *Public* property to True and its *Instancing* property to Creatable SingleUse or Creatable MultiUse.
4. Implement properties of the server object with Public variables or Property Get/Set/Let functions.
5. Implement methods of the server with Public Sub or Function procedures.

Understanding Out-of-Process versus In-Process Servers

In the 32-bit version of Visual Basic, you have the option of either creating an EXE file that can act as an OLE server or an OLE DLL. In the 16-bit version of Visual Basic, you can create only an EXE file.

The OLE EXE runs as an *out-of-process server* while the OLE DLL will run as an *in-process server*. The difference between these server types is with respect to the controller application.

When a server runs out-of-process with respect to its controller, it has the following characteristics:

◆ It can run as a stand-alone application.

◆ It does not share the same processing environment under the operating system.

◆ It can be instantiated either as Creatable SingleUse or Creatable MultiUse.

When a server runs in-process with its controller, it has these important features:

◆ The server and controller share the same executable space under the operating system.

◆ The server and controller share some of the same memory, such as public variables.

◆ An in-process server can be instantiated only as Creatable MultiUse.

As you might imagine, there are pros and cons to both in-process and out-of-process servers (otherwise, why would Microsoft have provided both?).

Performance: In-Process Servers Win

Because an in-process server shares the same process space with its controller at run time, communication between the in-process server and its controller can avoid the OLE interface. The controller can therefore call the in-process server very efficiently.

To compile your project as an in-process server:

1. Choose File, Make OLE DLL.
2. Click the OK button in the Make OLE DLL dialog box.

Flexibility and Availability: Out-Of-Process Servers Win

Here is a list of things only an out-of-process server can do:

◆ Run in a 16-bit environment

◆ Provide Classes which are Creatable SingleUse

◆ Display modeless Forms (not recommended)

◆ Use the End statement (not recommended)

To compile a project as an out-of-process server:

1. Choose File, Make EXE.
2. Click OK in the Make EXE dialog box.

Creating an Externally Creatable Object

An object is *externally creatable* when an application that can serve as an OLE controller is able to declare an instance of that object as a variable and then manipulate the methods and properties of that object.

 Note Developers of potential controller applications can find out about your server by looking at the Windows Registry. ■

You can register your server in the Windows Registry in one of several ways, which we will discuss further in the section "Registering Your OLE Server."

A Visual Basic 4.0 project provides an externally creatable object through certain project settings and by possessing a Class Module whose properties you have set appropriately.

Setting Project Options to Create an OLE Server

When you create a project to be an OLE server, the first thing you should do is set its Project options. To do this:

◆ Choose Tools, Options.

◆ From the Options dialog box, click the Project tab (see fig. 11.1).

Startup Form will be Sub
Main for an OLE server

Project name will become the
name of your server in the
Windows Registry

FIG. 11.1 ⟹

You will set the
Project Name,
Help File, Startup
Form, Start Mode,
and Compatible
OLE Server
options on the
Project Options
dialog box.

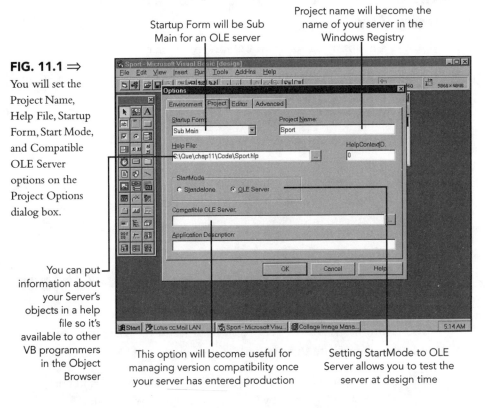

You can put
information about
your Server's
objects in a help
file so it's
available to other
VB programmers
in the Object
Browser

This option will become useful for
managing version compatibility once
your server has entered production

Setting StartMode to OLE
Server allows you to test the
server at design time

Six of the eight Project options you need when working with an OLE server are on this screen.

Name

An OLE server is known to the system by a name of the form *appname.classname*. Your OLE server project's Name will become the *appname* part of the object name when controller applications refer to it.

The project Name will also be the name other programmers see in the Tools, References dialog box when they need to include your server in one of their projects and they will see your project listed under Projects/Libraries in the Object Browser.

Appname and *classname* cannot be the same, so make sure that your project's Name doesn't conflict with any Class Module's Name property.

Startup Form

If you have decided to make your server into an in-process server, then you *must* set the Startup Form of your server's Class project to be **Sub Main()**.

If you create an out-of-process server, you may, of course, wish to consider changing the Startup Form to be Sub Main() or some form besides the default startup.

> **Caution**
> When you choose Sub Main() as the Startup Form, then don't forget to supply it in a standard (.BAS) module!

Start Mode

You will set this property to OLE Server when you are ready to test your server in the design-time environment. Such a property is handy, because the easiest way to test an OLE server is for the programmer to run it in design mode, switch to another instance of Visual Basic, and run a test controller application in design mode. If you ran your server in design mode as a normal application, VB would start the application by running its Sub Main(), encounter no code, and terminate the application immediately! The application would then, of course, be unavailable to test against a controller application. By changing StartMode to OLE Server, your application will stay resident in memory when you run it in design mode, enabling you to run a controller application to test it.

Setting your server project's Start Mode to OLE Server will:

◆ Let Visual Basic make a temporary entry in the Windows Registry for the server.

◆ Keep it resident in memory.

Your controlling application will then find the server in the Windows Registry and can to point to its running copy in design mode.

Compatible OLE Server

Visual Basic uses this property to check future changes to your server for compatibility against the currently compiled version.

You will set this property once you have compiled and distributed a copy of your server. It will point to the compiled DLL (in-process server) or EXE (out-of-process server) file. To set the name of the compiled OLE server:

◆ Click the triple-dotted browse button to the right of the Compatible OLE Server field.

◆ Choose the compiled file from the resulting file dialog box.

For more information about the importance of this option and more detailed information on how to use it, see the section in this chapter on "Managing Compatibility of Versions of Your Server."

Help File

To make a project point to a help file:

1. Choose Tools, Options from the Visual Basic menu.

2. Choose the Project tab on the Options dialog box.

3. Click the browse icon (the three dots) by the Help File item.

4. Use the file dialog box to select the help file for this project.

5. Click OK in the help file dialog box.

6. Click OK on the Options dialog box.

You can use the topics in this help file to provide detailed documentation for the methods and properties you implement in your server.

This help will be available to programmers using the Object Browser to examine your class.

 Note The creation of help files is beyond the scope of this book and is not covered on the Certification Exam. ▪

Advanced Options: Error Trapping

When you are testing your server against a controller application running in another Visual Basic session, you would probably want server-generated errors to cause execution to return to the server. This option should do the trick. It is not on the same tab of the Options dialog box as the other options. To set it:

1. Choose Tools, Options from Visual Basic's main menu.
2. Choose the Advanced tab.
3. Find the Error Trapping group.
4. If you want all errors handled in the server, click the Break in Class Module option button.
5. If you want the server to be able to pass errors to the controller, click Break on Unhandled Errors.

   ▶ **See** "Testing and Debugging at Design Time," **p. 387**

Advanced Options: OLE DLL

If you're planning an in-process server, your design environment unfortunately won't be able to run it as in-process. To more closely simulate the limitations of an in-process server, you should set the OLE DLL Advanced option as follows:

1. Choose Tools, Options from Visual Basic's main menu.
2. Choose the Advanced tab (see fig. 11.2).
3. Find the OLE DLL item.
4. Use your mouse to check on the box labeled Use OLE DLL Restrictions.

VB will break in the server at design time when an error happens there, no matter how your code handles errors

VB will let the server pass errors to the controller at design time if your code is written that way

FIG. 11.2 ⇒
You will need to choose an Error Trapping option on the dialog box. If your application will be in-process, you'll want to test it with the OLE DLL option turned on as well.

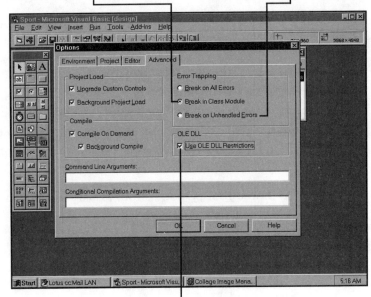

Checking this option helps your server's design time instance to behave like an in-process server

Adding a Class Module to Implement the Object

Once you've created a project for your OLE server and set the project's properties, you must add at least one Class Module to your project. Though your server may have more than one Class, there will always be at least one Class that can be initialized by a controlling application. This Class will represent the *objecttype* component of an *appname.objecttype* invocation of your server in the controlling application.

Your server may have more than one object type. All Classes that can be initialized directly from a controlling application will have their built-in instancing properties set to Creatable SingleUse or Creatable MultiUse.

To add a Class Module to your project, choose Insert, Class Module
from the Visual Basic menu (see fig. 11.3).

FIG. 11.3 ⟹

Use the Insert,
Class Module
command to
begin work on
your OLE server's
Class object.

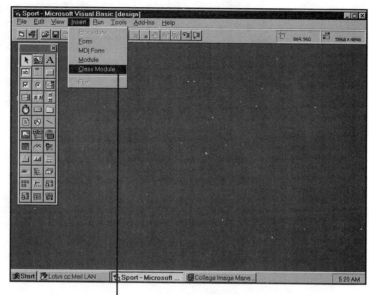

Creates a new Class Module in the current project

Built-In Class Module Properties for an OLE Server

Besides implementing properties and methods that you design for the
Class, a Class Module also has three built-in properties that you must set
to allow the Class to be called from a controller.

To see your Class Module's built-in properties while the Class Module's
code window is open, you can:

- ◆ Right-click your mouse
- ◆ Click the properties icon
- ◆ Choose View, Properties

After taking one of these actions, you should see the Class Module's
properties window displayed as in figure 11.4.

FIG 11.4 ⇒

You can change the three built-in properties for a Class Module in the module's Properties list.

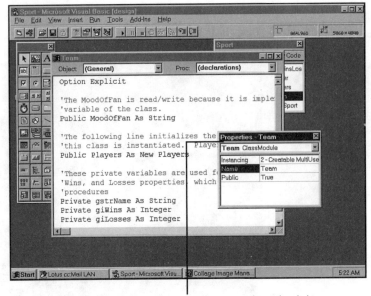

View the Class Module's three built-in properties by right-clicking your mouse in a Code Window of the Class Module

Name

This will be the external identifier for your class. It will provide the objecttype component of the appname.classtype instantiation of your class in the controlling application.

> ### Caution
> Because the VB Project Name (as set in the Tools, Options dialog) provides the *appname* component, and because *appname* and *classtype* can't be the same, make sure your Class Name property is different from your Project Name.

Public

This property determines whether or not your Class can be seen from outside this application. In other words, if you want controller applications to be able to instantiate objects of this Class, then you should set Public to True and also set the Instancing property to an appropriate value (Creatable SingleUse or Creatable MultiUse).

Instancing

This property determines whether and how controlling applications can create instances of this Class object. Instancing may either be Not Creatable, Creatable Single Use, or Creatable MultiUse.

◆ If Instancing is *Not Creatable*, controlling applications cannot instantiate this Class. If Public is True, other applications may be able to see instances of the Class.

◆ A *SingleUse* instance of a server Class will allow exactly one instance of a public Class. If two controllers want to instantiate copies of the *same* SingleUse Class from your server at the same time, OLE creates a second instance of the server each time an instance of a Class is created. For example, if a controller app requests several instances of ClassA, a separate server is started for each instance of ClassA. However, if two controllers want to instantiate copies of two *different* Classes in your server at the same time, OLE will allow both of them to use the same copy of your server, as long as that is the first requested instance for each Class.

◆ A *MultiUse* instance of a server will allow multiple instances of any one of its Classes without having to create a second instance of the server. One OLE server can create multiple instances of a Class. The first request for a Class instance starts the OLE server exe. All subsequent requests are serviced by the already running server. For example, if a controller app requests several instances of a ClassA, one server executable creates all instances of ClassA.

Whenever you create an in-process OLE server (that contains three Classes, for example), the Instancing property of each Class must be set to Creatable MultiUse. Remember, in-process servers always run within the same memory space as the controller and the controller has no way of using a second copy of the server.

If your OLE server is going to be compiled as an out-of-process server, it can be either Creatable Single Use or Creatable MultiUse.

Part

III

Ch

11

Tip

When you test your server in design mode, you should always set the Instancing property to Creatable MultiUse before you run a test controller application against your server. If you intend the distributed copy of the server to be Creatable SingleUse, remember to set Instancing back to Creatable SingleUse after testing and before recompiling.

Note If the built-in Public property has been set to False, Visual Basic ignores the value of the Instancing property (see fig. 11.5). Instancing is always considered to be Not Creatable unless Public is True. ■

FIG 11.5 ⟹

You can choose the setting you want for the Instancing property.

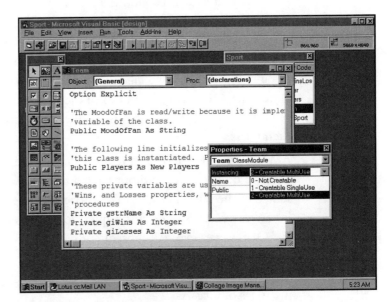

SingleUse versus MultiUse Servers

The main advantage of a MultiUse server is that it uses less system resources because the OLE Manager needs to run fewer copies of it.

The main advantage of a SingleUse server is to reduce "blocking" of one controller's use of a method by another controller. Recall that in-process (OLE DLL) servers can only be Creatable MultiUse.

Note Blocking can happen when a server is MultiUse and more than one controller is trying to call the same code at the same time. The single copy of the server will attempt to satisfy requests for the same service from more than one controller at a time. Since all the instances of a MultiUse server run in a single thread, one controller's requests for a service from the server will effectively block all other requests for that service until the request is completed. ▨

Tip

If you have time-intensive code in your server and expect several instances of the server to be active at the same time, you can avoid end-user frustration by making the server SingleUse so that controllers don't experience delays while they queue up for their turn to use a MultiUse server.

Class Initialize Event Procedure

Every Class Module contains an Initialize and Terminate Event.

The Class initialize event is triggered the first time a controller's code references an object variable of your Class but after the controller has instantiated the object. In the example:

```
Dim MyObj as New MyProject.MyClass   'declare object variable
to create class instance


MyObj.Compute      'reference it for 1st time
```

The Initialize event is triggered on the second line of code, because this is the first reference to the object once it has been declared.

 Tip

You might use the Initialize event procedure to set up the object's default environment. For instance, you could set the default values of Class properties, open files, make database connections, and do other tasks to prepare the object for a useful life.

To view and modify the Class Initialize event:

◆ Click the Object drop-down list box from anywhere in your Class Module's code.

◆ Choose the Class object.

◆ Click the Proc drop-down list box (see fig. 11.6).

◆ Choose the Initialize or Terminate procedure from the Proc drop-down list box.

Class object is built into   Class object has built-in Initialize
Class Modules   and Terminate events

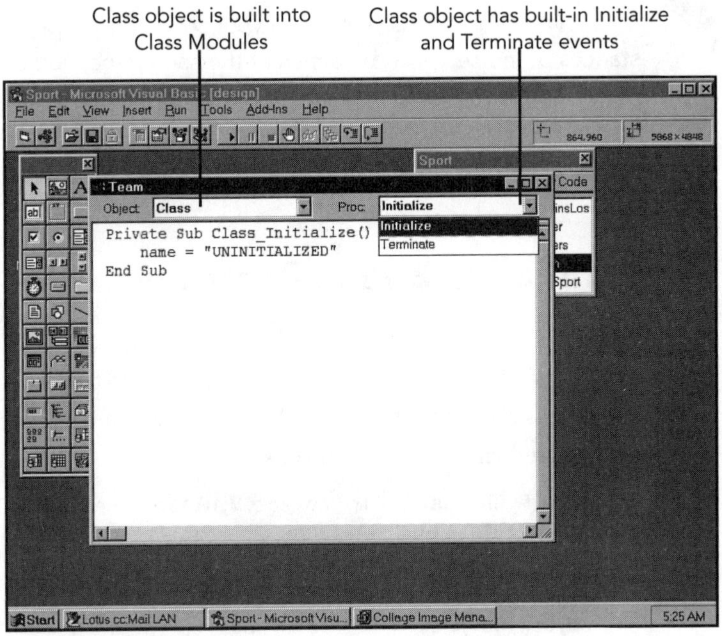

FIG. 11.6

You can view and customize the built-in procedures for the Initialize or Terminate event of the Class.

```
Private Sub Class_Initialize()
    name = "UNINITIALIZED"
End Sub
```

Class Terminate Event Procedure

Visual Basic provides this event procedure for you automatically inside every new class module.

The Class Terminate event is triggered when the system closes down your server. This will happen when OLE shuts down your server.

Tip

The terminate event procedure is good for cleanup, such as closing files.

To view and manipulate the Class Terminate event procedure, you can follow the same steps as for the Initialize event procedure.

Sub Main() as an Entry Point

When your server starts, you want it to unobtrusively become resident. The controller can initiate any server actions by calling the server's methods and manipulating properties. You, therefore, typically don't want the server to have a Startup Form, because, of course, this would immediately display the Form whenever the controller initiated a copy of the server.

The way to prevent any Visual Basic application from immediately displaying a form at startup is to set the Startup Form of the Project to Sub Main() as we discussed previously.

You *may want* to set Startup Form to Sub Main() if your server is going to be an out-of-process server (an EXE).

You *must* set Startup Form to Sub Main() if your server is going to be an in-process server (a DLL).

Once you have set this project option, you must, of course, provide your project with a Sub Main(). Since a Sub Main() startup routine can exist only in a Standard (.BAS) Module, you will need to include a Standard Module in your server project and then put a Sub Main() routine in it. The Sub Main() does not need to have any code in it. It simply provides an entry point for your application.

A standalone application would end immediately if there was nothing in its Sub Main(). An in-process server, however, will stay resident when its compiled version runs.

Part

III

Ch

11

Tip

If you are running your in-process server in design mode, it will terminate immediately if the Startup Form is Sub Main() and Sub Main() is empty. You can fix this problem by setting the project's Start Mode option to OLE Server as discussed previously.

Using Custom Methods with Public Subs And Functions

To provide methods for your Class, simply create Public procedures in the Class Module. A controller application can then call these procedures directly as methods of the server Class. In the example, a controller application could cause a nifty spirit-raising message box to appear on the user's desktop by calling the RahRah method of the Team Class:

[General section of the Team Class Module]

```
Public Sub RahRah(TeamName as String)
    MsgBox "Go " & TeamName
    End Sub
```

[code in the controller application]

```
Dim MyTeam as New Sport.Team
MyTeam.RahRah "HippoPhants"
```

Note Just like any other procedure, methods can take parameters. If we had wanted the method in this example to provide a return value to the controller application, we would have declared it as Public Function, specified a return type in the header, and assigned a return value somewhere in the body of the function.

Using Custom Properties

While the Class Module's "built-in" properties (those which VB provides automatically) help to determine the behavior and availability of your class (see the section "Built-In Class Module Properties for an OLE Server"), you create *custom* properties as part of the functionality that the server object provides to controller applications.. You can implement custom properties either as Public variables of the Class or by using special Property Let and Property Get procedures.

Implementing Properties as Public Variables

A Public variable in a Class Module is handled as a property of the object Class. You can declare Public variables in a Class Module in the same way you declare Public variables for Form and Standard (.BAS) Modules.

▶ **See** "Public Scope," **p. 47**

To add a property called "Name" to our Team class, we would write the following code:

[General Declarations section of Class Module]

```
Public Name as String
```

This is, of course, similar to the way Forms use Public variables as well. Thus, when a controller uses your server, the controller can manipulate the properties of the object it declares:

[Code in the controlling application]

```
Dim HomeTeam as New Sport.Team
HomeTeam.Name = "Hippophants"
```

and later...

```
MsgBox HomeTeam.Name
```

The advantage of implementing an object property with a Public variable is that it is very easy to do. The downside is that:

◆ You can't create a read-only property, because Public variables are always writable.

◆ You have no way of triggering an automatic action when the property is manipulated (such as hiding an object when a Visible property is set to False).

◆ Different simultaneous instances of a Class share the same Public variables, thus causing all sorts of interesting confusion among different controllers trying to use your server at the same time.

Part
III

Ch
11

Implementing Properties with Get Property and Let/Set Property Procedures

With just a little more work, you can overcome the disadvantages of properties implemented in Public variables.

You can use the special Property procedures instead. In order to implement our Team Class' Name property with Get and Let procedures, we would put the following code in the server Class Module:

[General Declarations section of Class Module]

```
Private gstrName as string
```

[General Section of Class Module]

```
Public Property Get Name() as string
  Name = gstrName
End Property

Public Property Let Name(strName as String)
  gstrName = strName
End Property
```

The Property Let is a Sub procedure that will run whenever the controller attempts to assign the value of the property as when, say, it runs code such as:

[code in the controller application]

```
HomeTeam.Name = "Hippophants"
```

Notice that the Property Let procedure sets no return value and takes a parameter. That is because its job is to receive the value that the controller wanted to assign to the property. If our controller ran the above line of code, then the value of the paraName parameter in the Property Let would be "Hippophants."

 Note   The choice of parameter name is arbitrary and can be anything you like. ▪

The Property Get procedure is a Function procedure that will run whenever the controller attempts to read the value of the property, as in either of the following two lines:

[code in the controller application]

```
ThisName = Team.Name
MsgBox "Go " & Team.Name & "!"
```

Notice that the Property Get takes no parameters but has a return type and sets a return value like a function does. This is because its job is to pass a value back when the controller requests it. Again, in this example, the ThisName variable would end up holding "Hippophants" and the Message Box would display "Go Hippophants!"

Using a Global Private Variable to Store a Property

Notice that we used a Private variable whose scope is the Class Module file. Notice further that the Property Let and Get procedures write and read this variable. In short, we are using the Private variable to store the value of the property between calls to the Property Let and Property Get procedures.

> ### Caution
> Don't create Public variables for storing Property Let/Get's intermediate values, because then controller apps can read and write them directly, which will confuse the issue of how we access the property. Make them Private instead.

Implementing a Read-Only Property

If you would like a property to be read-only to the controller application, all you have to do is leave out the Property Let procedure. That way, the controller has no way of writing the property. You can still store the value of the property in a Private variable of the Class Module. Other parts of your server Class can manipulate the property by changing the Private variable, but the controller app can't change it directly.

In the following example, we have implemented an integer-type property called Wins, which is stored in a filewide Private called giWins. Wins would be updated indirectly through giWins every time the WinOneGame method was called by a controller, but because we have no Property Let for Wins, there is no way for the controller to change it directly.

[General Declarations of Class Modules]

```
Private giWins as Integer
```

[General Section of Code Module]

```
Property Get Wins() as Integer
   Wins = giWins
End Property

Public Sub WinOneGame()
  giWins = giWins + 1
End Sub
```

Storing Multiple Instances of an Object in a Collection

Depending on the specific needs of the project, you might implement a second object as a fully creatable object, meaning that a controller application could directly declare an instance of this object. To do this, you would set the second Class' Public property to True and its Instancing property to Creatable SingleUse or MultiUse.

 Note Your project can contain more than one Class and therefore could implement more than one type of custom object. ▪

You might also, however, decide that the additional custom object cannot be directly created by a controller, but only through methods of the first custom object. In this case, you would set the additional Class' Public property to True and Instancing to None. For example, a Sport server with a Team Class might also have a Player Class. A Player could be accessed only through a Team because a Player object would have to belong to a Team object.

We would then call Player a *dependent class* because it could be implemented only through the Team Class.

You might also decide that this internally implemented object could have an indeterminate number of instances. To continue our example, we don't know exactly how many Players can belong to a Team, but it would certainly be more than one. We have already seen a concept in Visual Basic that would allow us to implement something like this— the *collection*.

To implement your own collection in an OLE server, you need to add two Classes to your project:

◆ A *dependent class*, which implements a single object of the collection

◆ A *dependent collection class*, which implements the collection of dependent Class objects

The existing creatable Class is then known as a *parent class* to the dependent Class.

Setting Up the Dependent Class

To start a dependent class in your server project:

1. Choose Insert, Class Module from the Visual Basic main menu.

2. On the resulting Class Module window, enter the class properties by right-clicking; pressing F4; or choosing the Properties icon from the toolbar (see fig. 11.7).

3. Change the Name property to a singular noun describing the class you want to implement.

4. Make sure the Instancing property is 0–Not Creatable.

5. Change the Public property to True.

Tip

Once you've determined the behavior you want the dependent object to have, you can add properties and methods to the Class to implement that behavior.

You will do this exactly as you would for any other class.

▶ **See** "Using Custom Properties," **p. 366**

▶ **See** "Using Custom Methods with Public Subs and Functions," **p. 366**

FIG. 11.7 ⇒

Set the properties of a dependent class, which will model the behavior of the member of a collection. The Name property should be a singular noun, Instancing should be None, and Public should be True.

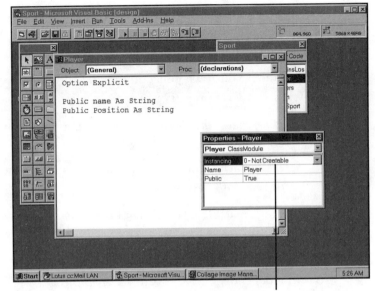

A dependent class is not directly creatable by other applications

Setting Up the Dependent Collection Class

The dependent class as described in the previous section will implement a single item in the collection. To implement the entire collection and manage individual items in the dependent class, you must create another Class known as a *dependent collection class*.

To set up the dependent collection class:

1. Choose Insert, Class Module from the Visual Basic main menu.

2. On the resulting Class Module window, enter the Class properties by right-clicking; pressing F4; or choosing the Properties icon from the toolbar.

3. Change the Name property to be a plural noun describing the class you want to implement.

4. Make sure the Instancing property is 0–Not Creatable.

5. Change the Public property to True.

6. In the General Declarations section of the Class, declare a Private collection variable, for example:

```
Private colPlayers As New Collection
```

This last step automatically initializes a collection the first time this class is referenced in code (see fig. 11.8). By making it Private, you guarantee that all code that tries to access the Class will have to come through methods provided here in the collection class. You want to do it this way because this gives you more centralized control over how a controller can manipulate the collection and its individual items.

The dependent collection class implements its collection internally, as a Private object variable

FIG. 11.8 ⟹
Set the properties of a dependent collection class, which will hold the collection members implemented by the dependent class. The Name property should be the plural of the dependent class Name, Instancing should be None, and Public should be True.

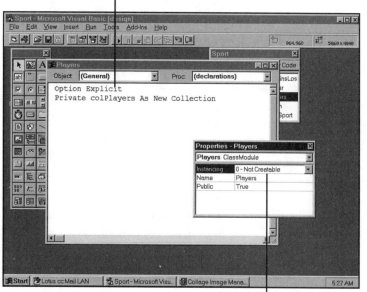

A dependent collection class is also not directly creatable by other applications

Implementing the Dependent Collection Class' Built-In Methods and Properties

Collection objects have three built-in methods and one built-in property:

◆ The Count property, which returns the number of items in the collection

◆ The Add method, which adds a new item to the collection and returns a pointer to the new item

Part
III

Ch
11

◆ The Remove method, which removes an item, given its index

◆ The Item method, which returns a pointer to an existing item, given its index

If you declare the Collection variable in the General Declarations section as Private, code outside the Class won't be able to call these methods or check the Count property directly. Instead, you should write public wrapper functions (i.e., methods of this Class), which will mediate between controller calls to the collection and the collection itself.

The Add method wrapper will return an object variable pointing to the newly added item.

Tip

You can set up the wrapper for the Add method to take any parameters you deem useful. Usually, these parameters would represent initial values for some of the properties of the new item.

Note that when we actually call the built-in add method of the collection, we pass it the initialized pointer to the new item in the dependent class. As a second parameter, we pass an identifying string. The Item() method can use this string to look up the item in the Class later. Because the string will be used as a lookup key, it should be unique to this item.

```
Public Function Add(ByVal name As String, ByVal Position As
➥String) As Player
Dim plrNew As New Player 'set pointer to new instance of  dep.
class
With plrNew
      .name = name  'use parameters to initialize properties
      .position = position
      colPlayers.add plrNew, .name 'invoke built-in add method
➥of collection
    'note second parameter can be used in
    'future to reference this item
  End With
  Set add = plrNew  'return new item we've just added
End Function
```

The Class' Count method simply wraps itself around the count method of the private collection and returns its value.

```
Public Function Count() As Long
    count = colPlayers.count
End Function
```

The Class' Delete or Remove method also wraps itself around the Remove method of the private collection. Notice the Index parameter that it takes and passes on to the collection's built-in Remove method.

Note You might expect the index in these methods to be an Integer, but instead it is a Variant. This is because the reference to an item in a collection can take as its index either a positional Integer value or a String key value that was specified in the add method. ■

```
Public Sub delete(ByVal index As Variant)
    colPlayers.Remove index
End Sub
```

Finally, the Item method wraps around the collection's built-in Item method. It will return a pointer to a particular item in the collection. To do so, it must take an Index parameter, which can be either an Integer array index or a unique key of type String. As with the remove method, this parameter must then be declared as a Variant to accommodate both these possibilities.

```
Public Function Item(ByVal index As Variant) As Player
    Set Item = colPlayers.Item(index)
End Function
```

Initializing the Collection in the Parent Class

The Parent Class shows us just the tip of the collection's iceberg. It doesn't have to do much to implement this custom object Class collection, but it does need to refer to the collection, because it provides the gateway to the collection by being the only externally creatable Class. You need to put a statement in the Parent Class' General Declarations which initializes a pointer to the dependent collection Class. For example,

```
Public Players As New Players
```

> **Note** Declaring a New Public instance of the collection Class in the Parent Class guarantees that the Parent Class will create a pointer to the collection as soon as OLE initializes the Parent Class. ■

Managing Dialog Boxes (Forms)

Depending on its function, your OLE server may or may not have any user interface. If it does, then, of course, that interface will have to be based on one or more Forms included in the server project. You must be aware of the way each Form affects the lifetime of the server application. When the server is in-process, you must also be aware of the effect your form has on the controller application.

It is important to keep in mind that the Forms and other elements of the user interface, such as message boxes, belong to your OLE server, and not to the controller application. While this is an obvious fact, its consequences might not be so obvious. For instance, when your server displays its interface, that interface may not be on top of other windows that the controller is displaying.

Remember that the controller application and the computer's end-user will determine how long your server actually runs.

Tip

Don't use *formname.hide* in your server's code when it is completely done with a Form. Instead, the server application should load the Form when it needs it and unload it whenever it does not need to be visible. If you have copies of the Form in memory, your server may continue to run even after it's not needed.

Managing Forms in an Out-Of-Process Server

In an out-of-process server, a Form may be the Startup Form for the server application's project. If you unload this Form and any other forms, the server application will stop as long as there are no controllers using the server. If there are controllers using the server application, Visual Basic will maintain an instance of the server in memory.

Tip

Your out-of-process server will continue to run if it has any Forms still loaded, even if no controllers are requesting it. An in-process server will unload if no controller is requesting it and any loaded Forms are hidden.

Managing Forms in an In-Process Server

A Form is never the entry point into an in-process server, because the server runs in the same process space as the controller and the controller itself initiates and terminates the server. Recall that an in-process server project's Startup Form must be set to Sub Main().

Because of this tighter degree of control, a DLL must always display forms modally and should unload a Form whenever it is finished using it.

Tip

Forms in DLL servers should always hide themselves as soon as possible.

The reason for these rules is that Visual Basic cannot terminate a server with visible Forms loaded. However, Visual Basic can terminate an in-process server even though it has Forms loaded, if none of those Forms is visible. Recall that Visual Basic can't terminate an out-of-process server with any Forms loaded, even though they are not visible.

[Wrong]

[In the General Declarations of the Class]

```
        Public MoodOfFan as integer  'As a Public of the class,
    ➡this is a property
```

[in a method of the Class]

```
    Public Sub ShowWinLoss()
    Dim frmWL  As New frmWinsLosses
      frmWL.show vbModeless  'it's wrong to show the form
    ➡modelessly
            'Now the method has lost control of
            'when to expect results back from the form
        'Whoa!  So we never get to unload the form - bad!
    End Sub
```

[In the Form's General Declarations]

```
Public FanMood as Integer
```

[In the Form's OK button's click event]

```
'do something to set the value of FanMood
'...
Me.Hide
```

[Right]

[In the General Declarations of the Class]

```
Public MoodOfFan as integer 'As a Public of the class, this
➡is a property
```

[in a method of the Class]

```
Public Sub ShowWinLoss()
Dim frmWL  As New frmWinsLosses
  frmWL.show vbModal 'form is shown modally
      ' so next line doesn't run till it's hidden or unloaded
     'so we can use the form's global variables
  MoodOfFan = frmWL.FanMood
  Unload frmWL  'and we unload it when finished with it
  End Sub
```

[form's General Declarations]

```
Public FanMood as String
```

[In the Form's OK button's click event]

```
'code to determine value of FanMood
'...
Me.Hide
```

Closing Your OLE Server

A normal Visual Basic application's life is over when it has unloaded all its Forms and is no longer executing any code, or when the *End* statement executes somewhere in the application's code.

Your server's lifetime, however, depends on the controller application and the computer's end-user as well as its own design. An OLE server ends when it meets all three of the following conditions:

◆ No controller is requesting or using an instance of your server.

◆ None of your server's code is executing.

◆ None of your server's Forms are loaded.

If you want to remember a few basic rules and save yourself the trouble of reading the next two sections, just keep in mind that:

◆ You should never let an OLE server terminate itself.

◆ You should not keep Forms loaded for any longer than they are absolutely necessary.

Closing an Out-Of-Process Server—Shouldn't Use End

You *shouldn't* close an out-of-process server with the End statement, though you *may*. Recall from our discussion of form management that the End statement is the last statement to execute in any application. Therefore, no Unload or QueryUnload Events will happen, so any code you put in those events' procedures will not run.

> **Caution**
> In an OLE server, the Terminate events of any classes will not happen after the End statement is executed and, of course, any cleanup code you have inserted in their event procedures will not have a chance to run either.

Closing an In-Process Server—Can't Use End

You absolutely cannot close an in-process server with the End statement. To do so would probably cause the controller to terminate, because an in-process server runs in the same process space as the controller. At any rate, you'd never get that far because the compiler itself considers the End statement to be a syntax error when it attempts to compile a project as an OLE DLL.

Of course, if you really have your heart set on seeing weird results, you could run an End statement in your in-process server at design time, because Visual Basic's runtime interpreter doesn't know yet whether this is going to be an OLE DLL or an EXE server and so it won't know that the End statement is illegal here.

Handling Errors in the Server and the Controller

Two applications will be running when the system invokes an OLE server: the controlling application and the server. When an error happens in your server, you want to make sure the error is handled adequately. The general philosophy of OLE server process management is to make sure that as much control as possible is out of the hands of the server application and in the hands of the controller application.

This doesn't mean, however, that you can just sit back and let errors happen in your server. If an unhandled error happens in the server without some provision for letting the controller deal with it, the server will, of course, be unable to respond intelligently to the problem.

There are two methods for letting your controlling application know that an error has occurred:

◆ Let the server's methods return a result code showing success or failure to the controller.

◆ Raise an error code in the server that the system can pass back to the controller.

Passing a Result Code to the Controller

This "soft" method of error handling will not generate an error condition in the controller. It will let the controlling application decide whether it is worth checking for an error after calling a method of your server. If the controlling application does check your server method's return value, it can determine whether an error occurred and decide what to do next.

To implement this technique, you must, of course, write your server methods as functions with an integer return type. The return type will be, say, 0 or some other encouraging-sounding number if no error happens in the function. You need to write and enable an error-trapping routine in the function that returns a negative integer or some other equally dire value when an error does occur.

Tip

A popular error return code would be the error number of the error that occurred.

The controller can then check the return value of the server's method to see whether all has gone well. If it gets an error code back from the method, it can then decide what to do.

[Method in the server class]

```
Public Function MaybeWeGottaProblem () as Integer
 MaybeWeGottaProblem = 0  'Initialize return value to OK
 On Error Goto MaybeWeGottaProblem_Error
     .
     . 'do stuff that could possibly cause an error
     .
 Exit Function
MaybeWeGottaProblem_Error:
 MaybeWeGottaProblem = Err.Number    'Set return value to
➥error code
 Resume Next
 End Function
```

[Code in the controller application]

```
Dim iResult as Integer

'Following lines check method's result code to see if an
error happened
 iResult = HomeTeam.MaybeWeGottaProblem()
 If iResult <> 0 then
  ' do something to handle the error
 EndIf

'Or - Following line ignores the method's result code - maybe
we don't care!
 HomeTeam.MaybeWeGottaProblem
```

Raising an Error to Pass Back to the Controller

This method has a more "in-your-face" attitude toward the controller. It generates a hard error condition in the controller and forces the controller to do its own error handling to deal with the server's error.

Part

III

Ch

11

As you can see in the example, the method in the server does not have to be a function, because we're not using its return code to signal a success-or-failure status. The method still uses an error handler as it did in the previous technique, but now instead of setting a return value, it uses Err.Raise to cause another error to happen in the error handler.

We append the Visual Basic predefined constant *vbObjectError* to the error code we are raising. This will tell the system to pass the error through to the controller. When the controller receives the error, the value of *vbObjectError* will be stripped off the error code it sees, and the controller will see only the error code's original value.

Tip

With this type of error handler, you might consider implementing your own system of error codes. You must use integer values above 512, as lower values can conflict with existing OLE error codes.

Because an error now occurs in the controller, the controller must have its own error-handling routine in place.

Note that Visual Basic's default error-handling strategy is to always break in the Class of the server application. To use this strategy, you must set the Advanced Option known as Error Trapping to Break on Unhandled Errors. See "Advanced Options: Error Trapping."

[Method in the server class]

```
Public Sub MaybeUGottaProblem ()
 On Error Goto MaybeUGottaProblem_Error
 .
 . 'do stuff that could possibly cause an error
 .
 Exit Sub
MaybeWeGottaProblem_Error:
 Err.Raise 1000 + vbObjectError   'controller will see
Err.Number as 1000
 End Sub
```

[Code in the controller application]

```
On Error GoTo MaybeIGottaProblem_Error
HomeTeam.MaybeUGottaProblem
Exit Sub
```

```
MaybeIGottaProblem_Error:
   ' do something to handle the error
```

> **Caution**
> Error codes at or below 512 will not pass through properly because they conflict with OLE error messages.

Using Your OLE Server and the Object Browser

Once your OLE server has been registered with the system, you can now include the server in other projects with the Tools References... command (see the sections on "Testing and Debugging an OLE Server at Design Time" and "Registering Your Compiled OLE Server").

To get help on an available OLE server while you are writing a controlling application:

Part
III

Ch
11

1. Press the F2 key for the Object Browser.
2. Find your server listed under the Projects/Libraries combo box.
3. Select your server.
4. You will see your server's classes and modules listed in the Classes/Modules list box.
5. Choose a class by single-clicking with the mouse.
6. You will see the Methods and Properties of the class listed in the Methods/Properties box.
7. Choose an item from the Methods/Properties list by single-clicking with the mouse.
8. You can see a brief description of the item to the right of the "?" button.
9. If a help file has been attached to your server, you can also click the "?" button to get extended help for the selected item.

You may use this information just as you would use any other information in the object browser. You can paste it into your code if you want to make sure you are using the proper spelling. You can also get help on a particular item — that is, of course, if the person designing the server was thoughtful enough to include help for the item.

FIG. 11.9 ⇒

See a brief description of a server component to the right of the "?" key in the Object Browser. Pressing the "?" will give you extended help.

Your server's Project name   A class's properties and methods

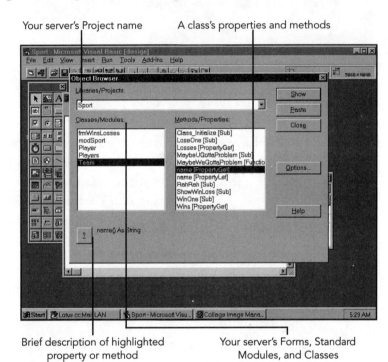

Brief description of highlighted   Your server's Forms, Standard
property or method   Modules, and Classes

Creating Brief References

As you move through the items in the Object Browser, you will see a brief description at the bottom of the Browser dialog box just to the right of the "?" icon. This description will be either blank or will change for each item you select.

In order to attach a description to an item in your project:

1. Press F2 to make sure you are in the Object Browser (see fig. 11.10).

2. Select your project from the Projects/Libraries combo box at the top of the dialog box.

3. Select the appropriate module or class from the Classes/Modules list at the left.

4. Select the appropriate item from the Methods/Properties list at the right.

5. Click the Options button.

6. You will see the Member Options dialog box.

7. Fill in the Description field for the item.

8. Click OK to accept the description.

Note You can't create your own help items for properties of your server that you have implemented as Public variables. Only properties you implement with Property Let/Get procedures can take custom help. ■

FIG. 11.10 ⇒
You can easily create brief Object Browser descriptions for items in your server by selecting an item, clicking the Options... button, and then filling in the Description field in the Member Options dialog box.

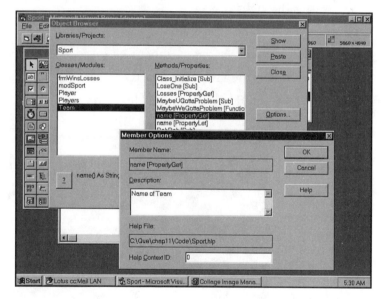

Part
III

Ch
11

Creating Extended Help

For extended help with full help screens for your server's items, you will need to first possess a help file with help topics for each item you want to document and valid context ID numbers to point to each topic.

Once you have a help file for the project, you can then point to it from your project. See the discussion about setting the Help File option for your project.

In order to attach a help file topic to an item in your project:

1. First make sure you know the Help Context ID number of the topic in the help file.

2. Press F2 to make sure you are in the Object Browser.

3. Select your project from the Projects/Libraries combo box at the top of the dialog box.

4. Select the appropriate module or class from the Classes/Modules list at the left.

5. Select the appropriate item from the Methods/Properties list at the right.

6. Click the Options button.

7. You will see the Member Options dialog box (see fig. 11.11).

8. Fill in the Help Context ID field.

9. Click OK to accept the Help Context ID.

FIG 11.11 ⇒

You can also attach an item in the Object Browser to a topic in an existing help file by selecting the item, clicking the Options... button, and then filling in the Help Context ID field in the Member Options dialog box.

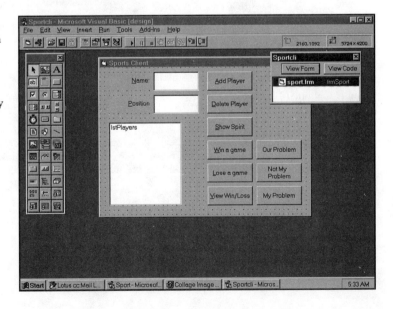

Testing and Debugging at Design Time

When you are ready to test your OLE server, a couple of problems arise that you don't have to worry about with other types of applications:

◆ In order to test your app as an OLE server, it must be registered in the Windows Registry.

◆ Your server can only be fully tested by running a controller application against it.

Here is how Visual Basic solves these problems for you:

◆ Visual Basic will register your server temporarily when you run it at design time.

◆ You can run a test Visual Basic controller application in a second instance of Visual Basic.

Tip

When you test your out-of-process server in design mode, you should temporarily set the Instancing properties of the server's Class Modules to Creatable MultiUse, even if you intend them to be SingleUse in the distributed product. Otherwise, your test controllers will attempt to start a new instance of Visual Basic itself every time they want a new instance of the object!

Temporarily Registering Your Server at Design Time

When you first set your OLE server project up, you went to Tools, Options and changed the Start Mode property to be OLE Server.

The purposes of this setting are

◆ To allow your project to run continuously in design mode.

◆ To let Visual Basic temporarily list your project in the Windows Registry as it runs in design mode.

If Start Mode was not set to OLE Server and your server was an in-process server, its Sub Main() would execute and the application would immediately terminate thereafter. With Start Mode set to OLE Server, your application will stay running, waiting for requests from controllers.

Once you are ready to test your server, all you have to do is Press Ctrl+F5 for a full compile and your server will begin to run in design mode. The Start toolbar icon should remain disabled, meaning your server is running (see fig. 11.12).

Start button grayed ⌐ ⌐ Stop button highlighted

FIG 11.12 ⟹
You can run your server in design mode when the Startup Mode option has been set to OLE Server. The Start button should be grayed, the Stop button should be enabled, and the Debug Window should become visible.

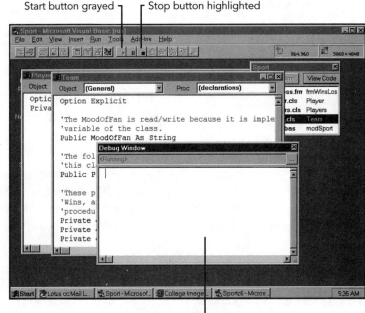

Debug window visible

Using a Second Instance of Visual Basic 4.0 as a Test Controller

Once your server is running in design mode, you can

1. Minimize the running copy of Visual Basic that is running your server.

2. Start another copy of Visual Basic.

Setting the Reference in the Controller

Just as we had to make our project refer to the Excel Object Library when writing an OLE Automation controller, so we must have our test controller refer to the custom server we have written. Since the server's Start Mode property is set to OLE Server and Visual Basic still has it running in design mode, we will see a reference to it when we look at available references.

Make sure you are still in the Visual Basic project for the test controller, and then do the following to create a reference to your server's object library:

1. Choose Tools, References from Visual Basic's main menu (see fig. 11.13).
2. In the References dialog box, you will find the name of your server's project on the list of items.
3. Click its check box to make sure it is selected.
4. Click the References dialog box's OK button.
5. Your test controller application now references the temporary registry of your server.

FIG. 11.13 ⇒
When you work with the test controller in a second instance of Visual Basic, you can locate and point to the temporarily registered object library for your server in the Tools References dialog box.

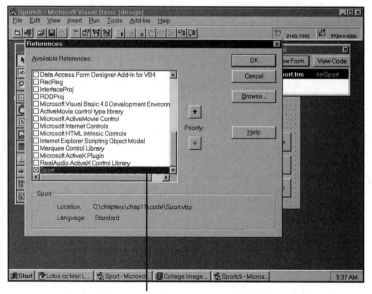

Temporary Windows Registry entry for running
design-time instance of your server

Declaring and Using Your Server in the Test Controller

Once you have set the reference to your server in the test Visual Basic controller, you can refer to it in code as you would to any other available OLE Server. You may use early binding (see Chapter 10) because your server is listed in this project's references. For example,

[somewhere in the controller application]

```
Dim HomeTeam as Sport.Team  'set up an object variable
Set HomeTeam = CreateObject("Sport.Team") 'initialize the
➥variable
```

In order to complete a test cycle with your controller and server applications, you should follow these steps:

1. Make sure you're still in Visual Basic's design mode for the controller application.

2. Write code to initialize and manipulate your server.

3. Repeatedly run the controller code in design mode, making changes as needed.

When you need to make changes to the test server:

1. Choose the Tools References menu option from the Visual Basic main menu.

2. Find the reference to your test server and uncheck its box.

3. Click the OK button in the References dialog box.

4. Minimize the controller's copy of Visual Basic.

5. Restore the server's copy of Visual Basic to normal size.

6. Stop the design time instance of the server.

7. Make your changes to the server.

8. Run the server with Ctrl+F5.

9. Minimize the server's instance of Visual Basic.

10. Return to the controller's instance of Visual Basic.

11. Choose the Tools Reference menu option from the Visual Basic main menu.

12. Find the reference to the server and check its box back on.

13. Click OK on the References dialog box.

14. Repeat these steps as needed.

What to Do About a Missing Reference

Sometimes the server may have problems as Visual Basic runs it, or you may forget to de-reference it (as in steps 6-8 in the previous section) before making changes to it.

When you return to Visual Basic's design-time copy of the controller and try to run the controller's code, you may receive error messages that the server is unavailable. If you check the Tools, References list, you will probably see the word MISSING in front of the reference to the server. This means that the old reference is pointing to something that no longer exists. To reset the reference to point to the currently running copy of the server:

1. Choose Tools, References from the Visual Basic main menu.

2. Find the MISSING reference to the server and uncheck its box.

3. Click OK on the References dialog box.

4. Choose Tools, References from the Visual Basic main menu.

5. Find the reference to the server (no MISSING should appear now) and check its box on.

6. Click OK on the References dialog box.

FIG. 11.14 ⟹
Your server's object library may turn up missing! Just uncheck the reference to it, make sure the server is running in the first instance of Visual Basic, then return to Tools, References and check it back on.

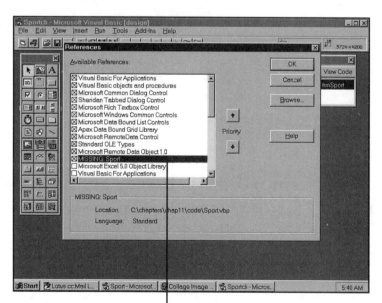

Server has stopped running

Registering/Unregistering Your Compiled OLE Server

When your OLE server has been compiled and is ready for distribution, you will want it to be permanently listed in the Windows Registry on your development workstation. You will also want the server to be registered on the workstations belonging to users to whom you will distribute the server.

Registering/Unregistering an Out-Of-Process Server

You can register an OLE executable in several ways (some of them inadvertent!):

◆ Compile it as a normal EXE application (obviously works only on the developer's workstation)

◆ Run it standalone—keeps on running after registering itself

◆ Run it standalone with the /REGSERVER argument— terminates as soon as it registers itself

◆ Install it with a Setup routine created by Setup Wizard (Setup Wizard creates code to register it)

You can remove your OLE executable from the registry by

◆ Running it standalone with the /UNREGSERVER argument

◆ Editing the Windows Registry (believe me, this is *not* a real option)

Registering/Unregistering an In-Process Server

One way to permanently register an in-process server on the developer's workstation is by compiling it. You will also want Visual Basic to track compatibility problems for future compiled versions of the server. You should take the following steps:

1. Choose File, Make OLE DLL File from Visual Basic's main menu.

2. Click OK on the Make OLE DLL File dialog box.

3. The file will compile, registering itself for the first time.

To register an in-process server from outside the development environment, you may run a utility called Regsvr32.exe against the DLL file. Regsvr32.exe is not part of the Visual Basic installation, but you can find it on the Visual Basic installation CD under the directory \TOOLS\PSS\. To use it with a server called, say, SPORT.DLL, you would run it from a command line as follows:

```
Regsvr32 sport.dll
```

Once again, you may also let Setup Wizard create a setup routine for your server that will automatically register the server when someone runs the setup routine on their system.

To unregister your in-process server, you may run Regsvr32.exe against it with the /u option in the command line, as in the following example:

```
Regsvr32 /u sport.dll
```

Managing Version Compatibility

Once your server has been distributed to users and controller applications are using it, you may need to make maintenance changes to the server.

If you give it half a chance, Visual Basic will automatically keep track of compatibility between current compiled versions of your server and some earlier version taken as a reference point. This earlier reference point is known as the *Compatible OLE Server*. You can set a Compatible OLE Server for your project by following these steps:

1. Choose Tools, Options.

2. Choose the Project tab of the Options dialog box.

3. Click the Browse icon (the three dots) to the right of the Compatible OLE Server field.

4. Use the resulting File dialog box to locate and select the DLL file you just compiled.

5. Click OK on the File dialog box.

6. Click the OK button on the Options dialog box.

7. Make sure you resave the server's project after this.

FIG 11.15 ⇒

Once you have a production compilation of your server, you can set the Compatible OLE Server option to point to the compiled version of your server through the Project option dialog box's File Dialog.

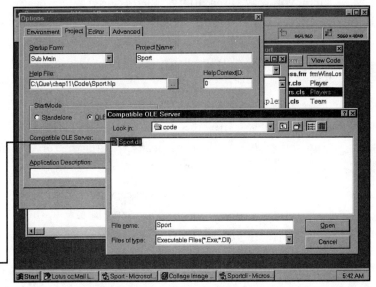

Compiled version of your server

Visual Basic recognizes three levels of compatibility:

Version Identical means that there are no new elements (methods or properties) in the newer version and that all those elements still have the same interface. That is, all methods' parameters are the same in number and data type and all properties and methods with a return value have the same data types as before. In other words, the server looks the same to all controllers that have been using it in the past. The only changes must be in the internal implementation of the methods or properties.

Version Compatible means that there may be new elements such as methods or properties, but that there have been no changes to the interface of previously existing elements. Controllers that used the server in the past can continue to use it without having to make any changes.

Version Incompatible means that there have been changes to the interface of previously existing elements.

Either the data types of properties or methods with return values have changed, or the number or data type or parameters to methods has changed, or previously existing properties or methods have been removed. Controllers that used the server in the past may have problems when they try to use the new version.

Note When there is version incompatibility between the current version of the project and the Compatible OLE Server, Visual Basic will give you warnings when you try to run the project and when you try to compile it. ■

You can do several things to avoid version incompatibility:

◆ Store the Compatible OLE Server's file in a separate place from where you do test compiles. This will prevent every temporary change you make during testing from being checked for compatibility.

◆ Make sure you keep the Compatible OLE Server in the project's Options up-to-date with the latest production release of your server. This will guarantee that Visual Basic compares the proper version of the distributed project with your working version.

◆ When you can't avoid version incompatibility, rename both your project and your compiled file. This will allow the Windows Registry to maintain entries for both. Future controllers that want to use the new and enhanced (and hopefully, improved) version of your server can point to the newer version, and controllers that have to still use the older version can point to it in the Registry.

Taking the Disc Test

 If you have read and understood the material in the chapter, you are ready to test your knowledge. Insert the CD-ROM that comes with this book and run the self-test software as described in Appendix H, "Using the CD-ROM."

From Here...

In this chapter, you have reached the pinnacle of the Microsoft Certification Exam topics. In other words, many other topics point here, but this topic itself has no other items beyond it that are on the Certification Exam.

There are, of course, other aspects of Visual Basic not on the exam that you may want to explore after assimilating the contents of this chapter:

- ◆ Visual Basic Add-Ins
- ◆ OLE Messaging
- ◆ Help File Creation

Part IV.

Handling Data

Chapter Prerequisite

You should be comfortable
with VB's fundamental techniques and concepts as discussed in Chapters 2 through
7. Some familiarity and experience with relational databases
would also be helpful.

Using the Data Control

A Data Control is a visible representation in your application of a connection to an external database. The Data Control provides a *Recordset*,
that is a specific group of records from specific fields in the database you
are connected to. You can bind certain types of controls (such as
Textboxes and Checkboxes) to specific data fields in the recordset's current record. Certain custom controls (such as the Data-Bound Grid and
the Data-Bound Combo Box or Data-Bound List Box) also provide
your user with other ways to view and browse data.

You don't necessarily have to write any code to navigate through the
data, because the Data Control itself provides the user an interface for
navigating through the data.

You may also manipulate these records and their fields programmatically.

Terms and concepts covered in this chapter include:

◆ Creating a simple application with the Data Control by manipulating its properties and the bound controls.

◆ The nature of the recordset and its three types: Dynaset-type Recordset, Snapshot-type Recordset and Table-type Recordset.

◆ Writing code to manipulate the recordset by finding, deleting, adding, and updating records.

◆ Coding the event procedures of the Data Control's special events.

◆ Using some of the custom data controls, such as the Data-Bound Grid and the Data-Bound Combo Box or Data-Bound List Box.

◆ Connecting a Data Control to various types of external databases.

Creating an Application with the Data Control

The basic steps you need to take to create an application using the Data Control are:

1. Insert a Data Control on the current form

2. Adjust the Data Control's properties to point to the data and return a recordset.

3. Place bound controls on the current form and adjust their properties to point to fields in the Data Control's recordset.

4. (optional) Write code to customize the recordset's behavior—adding, finding, deleting, and updating records.

Data Control Properties

The Data Control's properties determine:

◆ What type of data source the control will connect to

◆ The specific location of the data

◆ The actual subset of the data (the recordset) that the Data Control will access

◆ Other ways the data control will behave when the user connects to it and traverses the data (EOFAction, BOFAction, Exclusive, and ReadOnly)

Connect

This property determines the type of database the data control is going to connect to. By default, the Connect Property indicates a Microsoft Access database (see fig. 12.1).

▶ **See** "Accessing a Particular Type of Database," **p. 469**

FIG. 12.1 ⇒

The Data Control's Connect property gives you a drop-down list to choose Installable ISAM drivers. The default is Microsoft Access' Jet Engine.

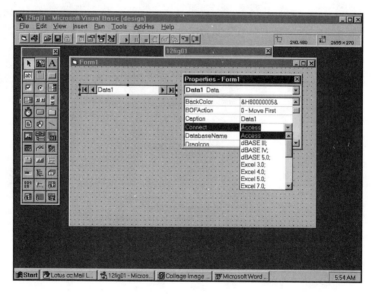

Part

IV

Ch

12

DatabaseName

This property determines the physical location of the database (see fig. 12.2). For a Microsoft Access database, this will be the name of the MDB file where all the database's information is stored. To connect to the sample Access database supplied with VB, you might set the DatabaseName property to:

C:\VB\Biblio.MDB

For most other types of database formats, a "Database" is considered to be a collection of files, and the files are considered to be "Tables" within the database. For instance, a Dbase table would be one of the individual DBF files. In such cases, the DatabaseName will not be a file but a directory where the files (representing tables) exist. For instance, if the C:\VB directory contained various DBF's we could group them together conceptually as tables of a single database and in the Data Control's DatabaseName property you could put the string:

C:\VB

FIG. 12.2 ⇒

The Data Control's DatabaseName property.

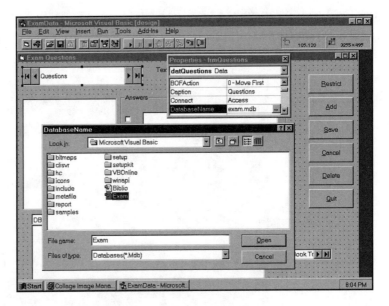

Exclusive

This property determines whether you will let anyone else look at the data you are opening with this Data Control. By default, Exclusive is false. If you set it to true, you'll only be able to use the data if no other user on the system is looking at the data. If you do get the Data Control to connect, no one else can look at it.

ReadOnly

This property determines whether the user will be able to make any changes to the data in the Recordset. It is false by default.

RecordSource

The RecordSource is a string representing the actual data that will be included in the Recordset. The RecordSource can be either:

◆ A single table name, or

◆ any valid SQL Select query

When the Data Control connects to the data specified in the DatabaseName property, it uses the RecordSource to create and run a query against that database. The rows returned by the query become the Recordset (see fig. 12.3).

> **Caution**
> Don't confuse the RecordSource, a string property of the Data Control, and the Recordset, which is a run-time object of the Data Control and contains the records indicated by the RecordSource.

▶ **See** "The Recordset," **p. 411**

FIG. 12.3 ⇒

The Data Control's RecordSource property.

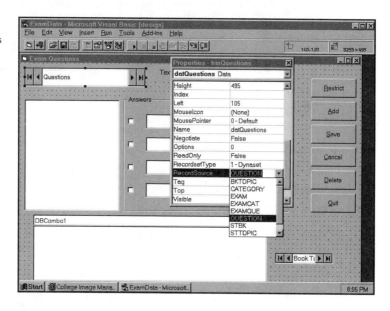

Part

IV

Ch

12

RecordsetType

This determines whether the Recordset will be of Dynaset, Snapshot, or Table type.

The default type for the Recordset is Dynaset (see fig. 12.4).

> ## Caution
> If the RecordSource is not a table name, but rather a SQL Select statement, the RecordsetType cannot be a Table, but only a Snapshot or a Dynaset.

FIG. 12.4 ⟹

The Data Control's RecordsetType properties.

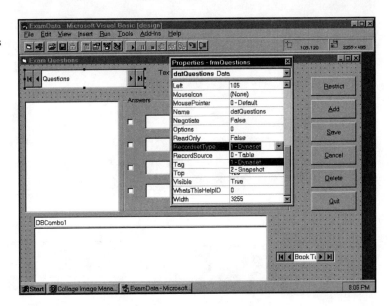

EOFAction and BOFAction

As we'll see shortly, the user can manipulate the Data Control to navigate the Recordset. When the user attempts to move forward through the Recordset onto the End-of-file buffer, Visual Basic must take some action to ensure that there won't be a problem the next time the user tries to move forward.

The EOFAction property tells Visual Basic what to do when the user has moved the Data Control's record pointer onto the End-of-File buffer. The three values of EOFAction are:

    0 Move Last (default): The record pointer repositions itself to the last true record in the Recordset, thus avoiding any future problems.

    1 EOF: The record pointer stays on the End-of-File buffer. If you choose this option, you must programmatically provide for the record pointer hitting End-of-File.

2 Add New: The AddNew method of the recordset will execute, adding a new record to the Recordset.

▶ **See** "Adding Records," **p. 417**

Tip

Set the Data Control's EOFAction property (see fig. 12.5) to EOF when you want to directly program the Recordset's behavior. You will then need to put code in the Data Control's Reposition event to handle this possibility.

FIG. 12.5 ⟹

The Data Control's EOFAction property.

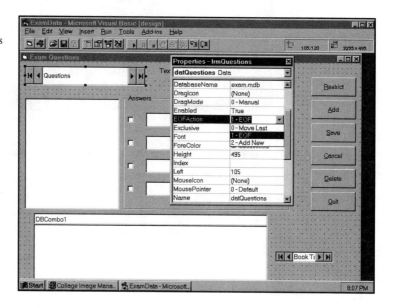

BOFAction has two possible values:

0 Move First (default): The record pointer repositions itself to the first true record in the Recordset, thus avoiding any future problems.

1 BOF: The record pointer stays on the Beginning-of-File buffer. If you choose this option, you must programmatically provide for the record pointer hitting Beginning-of-File.

Tip

Set the Data Control's BOFAction property (see fig. 12.6) to BOF when you want to directly program the Recordset's behavior. You will then need to put code in the Data Control's Reposition event to handle this possibility.

FIG. 12.6 ⇒

The Data Control's BOFAction property.

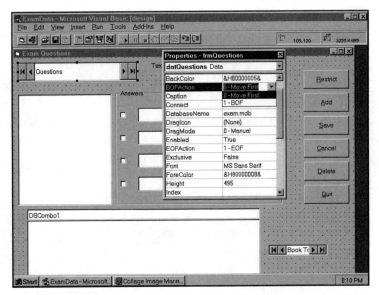

Binding Other Controls to the Data Control

A bound control is a control that automatically gives the user an interface to the data underlying the current record of a recordset. Each control is bound to a specific column, or field, of the recordset. The control will reflect the data in that field for the current record. Changes the user makes to the control's data can be written back to the underlying data.

For example, a text box, which is one of the most commonly bound controls, will show the contents of a particular field in the current record in the recordset. If the user changes the contents of the text box, the changes can be written back to the field in that record.

You can accomplish all this with no actual programming. If you want more control, you can of course write code to oversee the transfer of data between the bound control and the underlying data.

You can make an ordinary control such as a text box into a bound control by setting two special properties: the DataSource and the DataField properties.

The DataSource Property

Each bound control in VB must be bound to a specific recordset, and that means that the bound control can be set up at design time or at run-time to point to a Data Control (see fig. 12.7).

The DataSource property must contain the name of a data control on the current form for a control to be able to function as a bound control.

> ## Caution
> The DataSource property is only available at design time.

FIG. 12.7 ⇒

A Text Box Control's DataSource property.

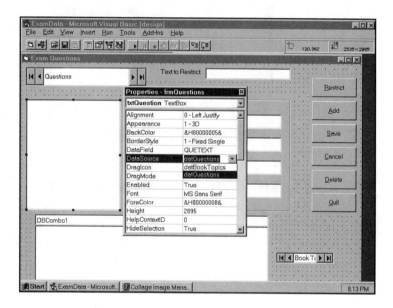

The DataField Property

The DataSource property doesn't give the control quite enough information about where to get its data. You must also tell the control which specific field in the recordset to bind to. It's the job of the DataField property to determine this. The DataField property (see fig. 12.8) will contain a valid fieldname from the DataSource's recordset.

> ## Tip
> You can redefine a control's DataField property at run-time.

Part
IV

Ch
12

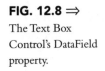

FIG. 12.8 ⇒

The Text Box Control's DataField property.

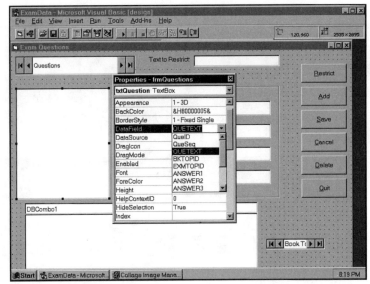

Example: Binding Text Boxes to a Data Control

In this example, we will write a simple browse screen for data held in a Microsoft Access database by manipulating properties of the Data Control and two Text Boxes. You won't have to write any code!

First, we must set up the Data Control. You should take the following steps to do so:

1. Place a Data Control on the form.
2. Select the Data Control and view its Properties Window.
3. Make sure that the Connect property is Access.
4. Select the Name property to make it the current property.
5. Type "datAuthors" and then press Enter to change the Name.
6. Click the browse button to the right of the DatabaseName property to bring up a File Open dialog screen.
7. Use the File Open dialog to find the main directory for Visual Basic on your system.
8. You should see the BIBLIO.MDB Access database file listed in the File Name list box.
9. Select the BIBLIO.MDB file and click OK.
10. You should now see the path and file name for BIBLIO.MDB in the DatabaseName property of the Data Control.
11. Select the RecordSource property.

12. Click the drop-down arrow to bring up a list of tables in the BIBLIO database.

13. Select the Authors table.

14. The Recordsource property now indicates the Authors table.

You now have a usable Data Control. When the form containing the data control loads into memory, the Data Control will connect to the database listed in the DatabaseName property and run a query for records fitting the specification of RecordSource property. The Data Control will then contain a recordset object pointing to these records.

In order to be able to see any of the information in a record, you will also have to put other controls on the form and bind them to specific fields in the Data Control's recordset.

Let's bind two text boxes to the Data Control:

1. Place a Text Box from the ToolBox onto the form.

2. In the Text Box's Properties Window select the Name property as the current property.

3. Type "txtAuthor" as the new Name.

4. Select the DataSource property as the current property.

5. Click the drop-down arrow to the right of the DataSource property to see a list of the available Data Sources. You will probably only see the single Data Control we just added.

6. Click datAuthors to choose datAuthors as the DataSource for this Text Box.

7. Click the DataField property just above the DataSource property.

8. Click the drop-down arrow list to the right of the DataField property to see a list of the available fields from this DataSource. You should see a list of available fields in the Authors table, because that was the table you specified in the Data Control's RecordSource property.

9. Click the Author field to choose it.

10. The txtAuthor Text Box is now bound to the Author field of the recordset returned by the datAuthors Data Control.

11. Repeat steps 1-6 for a second text box. In step 3 you will name the second text box "txtYearBorn" and in step 6 you will choose the "Year Born" field.

Tip

If you want to bind several controls to the same Data Control at the same time, you can select all the controls at the same time, enter their common Properties Window, and set the DataSource property just once.

Now you can test your browser applet:

1. Run the application.

2. Once the application has begun, note the contents of the Text Boxes. You should see an author's name in the txtAuthor box and a year of birth in the txtYearBorn box.

3. Click the Data Control's inner right-pointing arrow to advance the record pointer by one record. Notice that the contents of the Text Boxes change.

4. Click the Data Control's outer right-pointing arrow to advance the record pointer to the last record in the recordset. Notice that subsequent clicks of this arrow don't change the record.

5. Click the Data Control's inner left-pointing arrow to back the record pointer up by one record. Note that the contents of the Text Boxes change.

6. Click the Data Control's outer left-pointing arrow to advance the record pointer to the first record in the recordset. Notice that subsequent clicks of this arrow don't change the record.

7. Make a typing change to the contents of one of the text boxes.

8. Move off the record.

9. Move back onto the record. Notice that the typing change you made before is permanent (see fig. 12.9). If you closed the application and re-ran it, you would still see your change.

10. Stop the application from running.

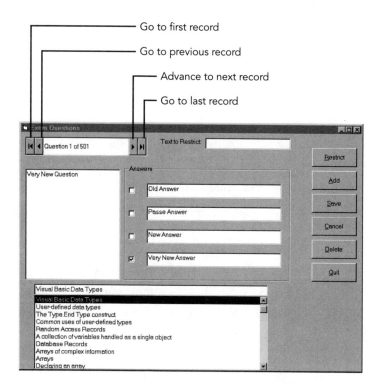

Go to first record

Go to previous record

Advance to next record

Go to last record

FIG. 12.9 ⇒
What the form
looks like at run-
time.

The Recordset

We've made liberal reference to the Recordset object up to this point in this chapter. Now it's time to get precise about the nature of the Recordset and some of the options open to you when you use a Recordset.

A Recordset represents the collection of rows, or records returned by the select statement, table name, or query specified in the Data Control's RecordSource property and runs when your Data Control connects to its database.

A Recordset is an object that belongs to the Data Control as one of the Data Control's run-time only properties.

Because it's an object, the Recordset has its own methods and properties that you can manipulate programmatically. Because the Recordset

Part
IV

Ch
12

belongs to the Data Control, the syntax for manipulating a method or property of the Recordset will always be:

DataControlName.Recordset.MethodName

and

DataControlName.Recordset.PropertyName = value

or

value = DataControlName.Recordset.PropertyName

The Recordset can exist as one of three special Recordset types.

You can distinguish among the three Recordset types by:

- The way they write from and to the copy buffer.
- The way they use resources on the user's workstation.
  ▶ **See** "The Copy Buffer and the Underlying Data," **p. 419**

Dynaset-Type Recordsets

The Dynaset-type Recordset is the Default RecordsetType and is the most flexible of the three types of Recordset.

A Dynaset-type Recordset is a set of record keys stored on the user's local system. These record keys point back to the data underlying the dynaset. The Dynaset-type Recordset maintains a *record pointer* to one of the keys. A copy of the underlying data behind this key appears in the Recordset's edit/copy buffer and in the Data Control's bound controls.

When the user or the program moves through the records, the record pointer moves through the set of keys in the Dynaset-type Recordset. Changing the record pointer also updates the information in the edit/copy buffer and the bound controls.

Information exchange between the underlying data and the copy buffer: A Recordset implemented as a Dynaset-type Recordset is essentially a collection of pointers to actual data and of key fields. Whenever you move the record pointer in the Recordset, you are essentially moving a pointer to the collection of pointers. This causes the system to retrieve the underlying data pointed to by the twice-removed pointer into the copy buffer.

Use of local resources: The Dynaset-type Recordset takes up local memory for the storage of the collection of pointers and keys. It therefore requires less memory than the Snapshot-type Recordset, but more than the Table-type Recordset.

Advantages:

◆ You have more flexibility in your specification of Recordset contents than you do with the Table-type Recordset.

◆ You can use the Find- family of methods, which is more flexible than the Table-type's Seek method.

◆ You have a more direct connection to data than you do with the Snapshot-type Recordset. A Dynaset-type Recordset lets the user see editing changes made by other users without having to run the underlying query to re-create the Recordset.

Disadvantages:

◆ You can't make changes to a Recordset of type Dynaset if the Select statement creating its RecordSource uses more than one table. For example,

> Select [last name], [order id] from _ &
>
> employees, orders where
>
> employees.[employee id] = orders.[employee id]

will produce a read-only Dynaset-type Recordset, because it draws on more than one table for its data.

◆ They take up more local resources than Table-type Recordsets.

◆ You can't use the faster Seek method of the Table-type to locate records. Only Table-type Dynasets have a Seek method. This is because the Seek method only works with indexed recordsets, and only Tables have indexes.

◆ Record additions and deletions by other users are not automatically reflected in a Dynaset-type Recordset, as they are in a Table-type Recordset. In order to be certain of seeing all record additions and deletions by other users in a Dynaset-type Recordset, you must call the Data Control's Refresh method, which, in effect, re-runs the original query and could take a long time.

When to Use:

◆ Whenever you need a connection to data with a lot of flexibility in the specification and can afford not to immediately see changes to existing records made by other users.

Table

A Table represents the most direct connection to data. It is thus the fastest way to do many things and also takes up the least local resources. However, it has some limitations to what it can do.

Information exchange between the underlying data and the copy buffer: Whenever you move the record pointer in the Recordset, you are moving a pointer which looks directly at the table in the underlying data. This causes the system to retrieve the data directly from the table into the editing buffer.

Use of local resources: A Table-type Recordset is the most thrifty of local resources, since none of it is implemented locally, except for a single pointer and a single editing buffer.

Advantages:

◆ The Seek method, which can only be used on a Table-type Recordset, is much faster than the Find methods (FindFirst, FindNext, FindLast, FindPrevious).

◆ Because a Table-type Recordset represents the most direct connection, manipulation of records runs a little faster.

◆ Also, the user can see editing changes other users have made to existing records without the potentially time-consuming task of having to re-run a query to create the recordset.

Disadvantages:

◆ You can't use a Table-type Recordset with ODBC databases.

◆ You can't use the Find methods (FindFirst, FindLast, FindNext, FindPrevious), but must use the more restrictive Seek method with a Table-type Recordset—and then only for fields with indexes.

When to Use:

◆ When you need to do fast searches and there is an indexed field available.

◆ When it's important that the user see other users' editing changes as they happen.

> **Note** A Dynaset-type Recordset will also allow you to see other user's editing changes to existing records. However, records which were deleted by other users after the dynaset was created, will cause a run-time error if you attempt to navigate to them. Records which were added by other users after the dynaset was created will not necessarily be immediately visible. ■

Snapshot

The Snapshot is a copy of the data specified in the RecordSource. There is no connection whatsoever between the Snapshot, and the original data when the user navigates and edits the data.

Information exchange between the underlying data and the copy buffer: When the Recordset type is Snapshot, the system retrieves all data specified in the RecordSource into the Recordset. There is no further direct connection with the actual data because the Snapshot is a local copy of everything. Whenever you move the record pointer in the Recordset, you are moving a pointer that looks at the local Snapshot copy of the data. The system exchanges all data between the copy buffer and this local copy.

Use of local resources: The Snapshot-type Recordset can be very re-source-intensive because, unlike the Dynaset-type Recordset, it maintains a copy of everything from the underlying data on the local system.

Advantages:

◆ A Snapshot-type Recordset provides very good performance (as long as it doesn't include so much data that it exhausts memory on the local workstation) because it is all implemented locally.

◆ You can use the Find- family of methods, which is more flexible than the Table-type's Seek method.

◆ Once a Snapshot-type Recordset is created, there is no network traffic to worry about.

Disadvantages:

◆ A Snapshot has no direct connection to the actual data once it's been created.

◆ You can't use the faster Seek method of the Table-type to locate records.

◆ It can swamp the user's workstation with its memory requirements.

When to Use:

◆ For reporting functions.

◆ When it's important to temporarily "freeze" any changes to underlying data.

◆ To view read-only data residing on a server. Using a snapshot will not cause any network traffic once it's been created, because all viewing activity will happen locally.

◆ You can also use a Snapshot for a kind of "offline" batch processing of records by a user. This would be helpful when heavy network traffic is an issue. Of course, you'd have to write code to explicitly put back the changes a Snapshot had made, since there is no direct connection to the data.

Viewing Records

To view records in the Recordset of the Data Control, all you must do is bind some control that supports the DataSource and DataField properties to a field of the Data Control. Visual Basic and the Jet Engine will take care of the rest for you.

The user only needs to click the various arrows of the Data Control to navigate the data and see the contents of different records displayed in the bound controls (see fig. 12.10).

FIG. 12.10 ⇒
How the user can
navigate data with
the Data Control.

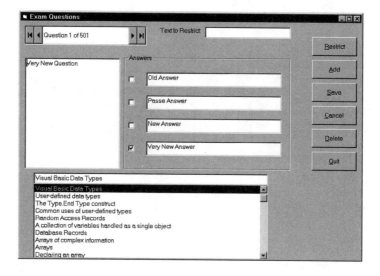

Adding Records

The user can view records and even write changes back to the data by simply moving the record pointer.

In order to enable the user to add new records, you can:

◆ Set the Data Control's EOFAction property to 2- Add New. You can set this at design time in the Properties Window or in code using the internal constant vbEOFActionAddNew. The user will see and be able to edit a temporary blank record when there is an attempt to move past the last record in the Recordset.

◆ Call the Recordset's Add New method programmatically to add a record. Add New blanks out the fields in the copy buffer and points the bound controls to the copy buffer. The user sees the blank controls and can edit the fields of the potential new record (see fig. 12.11).

After the user has edited the originally blank copy buffer in either of these scenarios, the record must be saved in one of two ways:

◆ The user must move the record pointer.

Part

IV

Ch

12

◆ You can programmatically call the Update method. For more information, see the section "Saving Editing Changes with the Update Method."

FIG. 12.11 ⟹

What the user will see at the End-Of-File with the Data Control's EOFAction property set to AddNew.

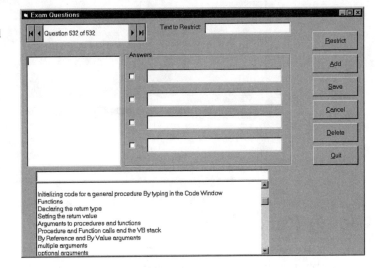

Editing Existing Records and Saving Changes

Any time the user edits controls that are bound to the Data Control, the user has changed information in the copy buffer. This is because the copy buffer is updated every time the Recordset's record pointer changes.

Changes to records will save automatically when a user or the programmer moves the Data Control Recordset's record pointer away from the current record by any means, including:

◆ Using any of the Find- methods on a Recordset whose type is Dynaset or Snapshot

◆ Using the Seek method on a Recordset of type Table

◆ Re-setting the Recordset's bookmark—even if it's only to set the bookmark back to the current record

◆ Using any of the Move- methods on the Recordset

◆ Adding another record

◆ Clicking one of the four arrow buttons on the Data Control

Moving the record pointer basically writes the contents of the copy buffer out to the underlying data.

You also can save changes programmatically by calling the Update method of the Recordset or the UpdateRecord method of the Data Control.

▶ **See** "Saving Editing Changes with the Update Method," **P. 421**

▶ **See** "The Data Control's UpdateRecord and UpdateControls Methods," **p. 438**

 Note   You can take more control of whether or not changes are saved by writing code in the Validate event. ▪

The Copy Buffer and the Underlying Data

Data must move in two directions in most applications that perform data access:

◆ Data must move from the underlying database to the user interface whenever the user moves the record pointer to a different record.

◆ Data must move from the user interface to the underlying database whenever we want to permanently save changes in the bound controls.

The copy buffer is the mediator between the user interface (bound controls) and the underlying data. The underlying data is the original physical data in the case of Dynaset- and Table-type recordsets, and the local copy of the data in the case of Snapshot-type recordsets.

◆ When the application moves the Recordset's record pointer, the underlying data refreshes the copy buffer. Bound controls refresh automatically. You can also call the UpdateControls method of the Data Control to refresh copy buffer an bound controls programmatically.

◆ When the user edits the contents of bound controls, the copy buffer changes. When the user moves from the record, these changes are automatically written from the buffer to the underlying data. The programmer can also call the Recordset's

Part
IV
Ch
12

Update method programmatically or the UpdateRecord method of the Data Control.

The Edit Method and the EditMode Property

The Edit method fills the copy buffer with values from the current record. In certain environments, it also locks a page around the current record.

▶ **See** "Page Locking," **p. 508**

You must call the Recordset's Edit method before you make programmatic changes to data or attempt to programmatically save changes or cancel changes to the current record's data.

You must have called either the Edit or AddNew method since the last time the record pointer moved and before you call code to do any of the following:

◆ Invoke the Update method of the Recordset

◆ Invoke the CancelUpdate method of the Recordset

◆ Programmatically assign values to any of the fields in the copy buffer

Canceling an Update

You can cancel a pending edit so that the changes just made won't be written to the underlying data. You can use one of two methods to do so, depending on the situation:

◆ The CancelUpdate method of the Recordset basically cancels a pending edit defined by the AddNew or Edit methods. If there is no pending edit, CancelUpdate causes a run-time error. After you call CancelUpdate successfully, the Recordset's EditMode property is always dbEditNone. The CancelUpdate method doesn't move the record pointer. The following code would enable you to call CancelUpdate without risking an error:

```
If Data1.Recordset.EditMode <> dbEditNone Then
    Data1.RecordSet.CancelUpdate
End If
```

◆ The UpdateControls method of the Data Control cancels editing changes but does not cancel the edit mode (see fig. 12.12). It refreshes the copy buffer (and so the bound controls) from the underlying data. You can call UpdateControls even without a pending edit. UpdateControls doesn't try to change the current value of the Recordset's DBEditMode property. So if there was a pending edit, UpdateControls leaves the edit pending rather than canceling it.

FIG. 12.12 ⇒
You'll want to give your user a Cancel button to cancel any pending typing changes on the screen.

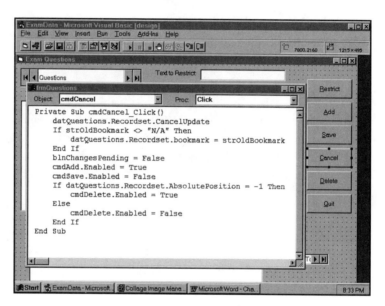

Saving Editing Changes with the Update Method

Although editing changes are automatically saved whenever the record pointer changes, you cannot depend on your user to move the record pointer in order to save changes.

The Update method will programmatically save your changes instead of waiting for the user to move. Typically, you will provide your user with a command button captioned "Save" or "Update." The command button's Click event procedure will call the Recordset's Update method.

In this way, the user takes a conscious and obvious action to save the data rather than having to understand that a save is contingent on moving the record pointer.

Part
IV

Ch

12

You cannot call the Update method unless you have called the Edit or AddNew method since the last time the record pointer moved. This is another way of saying that the Recordset's EditMode property can't be dbEditNone.

Tip

Just before you call the Update method, check the Recordset's EditMode property to make sure it's not dbEditNone.

The Update method triggers the Data Control's Validate event. See the section "Validate" later in this chapter.

> **Caution**
> Don't call the Update method from within the Data Control's Validate event procedure. Because Update triggers the Validate event, you will get an infinitely cascading set of calls to Update and Validate, and your program will crash. In this situation, you should use the Data Control's UpdateRecord method.

Tip

The Update method also usually changes the record pointer. In order to keep the record pointer on the same record, you should consider setting the current BookMark property to the LastModified property right after you call the Update method.

```
Private Sub cmdSave_Click()
    datAuthors.Recordset.Update
    datAuthors.Recordset.Bookmark = _
        datAuthors.Recordset.LastModified
End Sub
```

▶ **See** "The Recordset's Bookmark Property," **p. 428**

Deleting Records

The Recordset has a Delete method. To delete the current record, you could just call the method:

Data1.Recordset.Delete

However, a good developer would never call the Delete method by itself.

This is because:

◆ There may not be any records left to delete. You can resolve this problem by checking the RecordCount property of the Recordset to make sure it's greater than 0. You could also check the RecordCount's AbsolutePosition property to make sure it's greater than –1. Perhaps a better solution would be to check these values after every deletion and also when you first load the form. You could set the Delete command button's enabled property to false if there were no records, and set it to true after a successful add (see fig. 12.13).

◆ You don't want to keep the user sitting on top of a deleted record as the current record. Therefore, you want to move the record pointer with, say, the MoveNext method after a delete—but wait, maybe you just deleted the record at the end of the Recordset. So, you need to put in more logic to handle that possibility. Also, you may have just deleted the only record in the Recordset. Trying to call MoveLast after that would generate a run-time error. So yet more logic:

```
Private Sub cmdDelete_Click()
    If Data1.Recordset.RecordCount > 0 Then
        Data1.Recordset.Delete
        If Data1.Recordset.RecordCount > 0 Then
            Data1.Recordset.MoveNext
            If Data1.Recordset.EOF Then
                Data1.Recordset.MoveLast
            EndIf
        Else
            cmdDelete.Enabled = false
        End If
    Else
        cmdDelete.Enabled = false
    End If
End Sub
```

Part
IV

Ch
12

> **Caution**
> Don't rely on the RecordCount property's accuracy until you've moved
> the record pointer to the end of the data set once. In your form's
> Activate event procedure you might consider putting code to invoke
> the MoveLast and the MoveFirst events of the Recordset, just to set the
> RecordCount property.

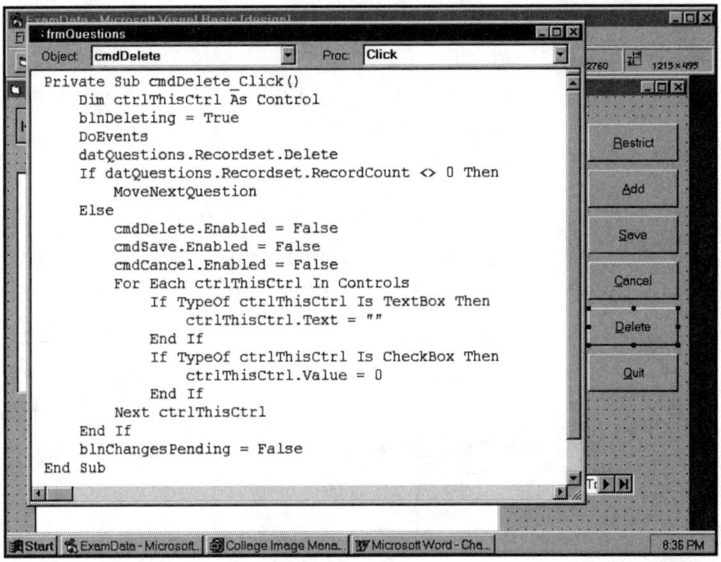

FIG. 12.13 ⇒
You'll want to give
your user a Delete
button to delete
the currently
visible record.

Locating Specific Records

The user can use the Data Control's built-in interface to move sequentially through the Recordset.

However, the user also needs to be able to look up a record according to information in the record. For instance, we might want to look up an author's record by typing in the author's name.

Because of the way the different Recordset types are implemented, there are different methods for Table-type Recordsets as opposed to Dynaset- and Snapshot-type Recordsets.

The Seek method belongs only to the Table-type Recordset. It is very fast, but it requires an index and is not very flexible.

The Find- methods (FindFirst, FindLast, FindNext, FindPrevious) belong to Dynaset- and Snapshot-type Recordsets. These methods are more flexible in what they enable you to search for, but they are extremely slow compared with the Seek method.

Find Methods (Dynaset- and Snapshot-Type Recordsets Only)

Each of the Find methods takes a string argument that specifies the record or records we are trying to locate. The String argument must fit the rules for the syntax of a SQL Where clause, without the "Where." Some examples of valid calls to the Find methods with arguments would be:

datAuthors.Recordset.FindFirst "Author = 'Adams, Pat'"

datAuthors.Recordset.FindNext "[Year Born] = 1944"

datAuthors.Recordset.FindLast "Author Like 'B★'"

You might be surprised to learn there are four Find- methods. Many other programming environments get along just fine with one such statement or method, so one might ask why VB has four.

Four Find- methods, however, give us more flexibility in exactly where and what we can search for. The Find- methods work sequentially through the Recordset. That is, the search engine looks sequentially at all records, applying the condition supplied in the parameter to each record in turn. When the search engine finds a match, it stops.

The difference in the four Find- methods have to do with where the search engine starts to look and in which direction it traverses the records:

◆ *FindFirst.* Starts at the beginning of the Recordset and moves forward.

◆ *FindLast.* Starts at the end of the Recordset and moves backward.

◆ *FindNext.* Starts at the current record location and moves forward.

◆ *FindPrevious.* Starts at the current record location and moves backward.

Notice that with FindFirst and FindLast, you will always find the same record given the same search criteria. This is because these two methods always start over at the same point. Thus, if you call

FindLast "Author Like 'B★'"

several times in a row, you'll always find the last author name in the data which begins with "B."

With FindNext and FindPrevious, however, subsequent calls to the same method with the same search criteria will yield different results; the search engine does not reset the record pointer each time. So if you call

FindFirst "Author Like 'Smith★'"

you will always go to the same "Smith" in the data, that is, the first one. If, however, after that you then make subsequent multiple calls to

FindNext "Author Like 'Smith★'"

you'll keep moving forward through the different records for 'Smith.'

 Note The Find methods are not case sensitive, so you don't have to worry about getting the capitalization right. ■

Caution

Don't assume your Recordset's records are in any specific order. Even though alphabetical order by Author might make sense in these examples, there is no reason to assume the system was smart enough to order them that way. If you want records to appear in a specific order, use the Order By clause in the SQL statement of the Data Control's RecordSource property.

> **Caution**
> You can't use the Find methods on a forward-only scrolling snapshot-type Recordset.

The Recordset's NoMatch Property

And what if you don't find the record of your dreams? If the Find methods are unsuccessful in their search, of course the record pointer won't move to the desired record. It will instead move to the beginning or end of the data, or perhaps to just a different record.

Of course, you could just pretend like nothing was wrong, because the record pointer will end up somewhere in the Recordset and after all there is no error. Your user might be somewhat puzzled, however, especially if the user really thinks the record is there.

You will probably want to detect the problem and give the user a message or take some other corrective action.

The NoMatch property is a Boolean value that is reset every time a Seek or one of the Find- methods runs. Because the term "No Match" is already a negative, the property's values, while obvious on a moment's reflection, can be a bit confusing. Because sometimes we don't have a moment to reflect:

◆ NoMatch is *true* after an *unsuccessful* search
◆ NoMatch is *false* after a *successful* search

So, remember, a negative result is "good," and a positive result is "bad" in this case. You could use the NoMatch property after a Find to decide whether or not to give the user a "Not Found" message, as in the following example:

```
Data1.Recordset.FindFirst "Author Like 'Smith*'
If Data1.Recordset.NoMatch Then
    MsgBox "Smith Not Found"
End If
```

Part
IV

Ch
12

The Recordset's Bookmark Property

If your search was unsuccessful—which you can detect by checking the NoMatch property—you're going to need to recover somehow, because, of course, the record pointer will not be anywhere pretty. It will probably end up at the very first or very last record of the file. As we noted in the previous section, this won't cause an error.

Even if you programmatically check the NoMatch property and display some sort of error message in a message box, your user may still be inconvenienced. This is because the user would probably like to just forget the whole unfortunate episode with the nonexistent record. The user would probably just want to carry on with the record that was current before this notion of a wild goose chase entered into the user's head.

Why not put the record pointer back to the record it was on before the unsuccessful search began?

Luckily, the Recordset object supports a BookMark property, which allows you to store and, if necessary, reset the position of the record pointer. Therefore, the strategy for using the Find- methods would be to:

1. Store the bookmark to a string variable

2. Perform the Find

3. If the Find was unsuccessful, restore the stored value of the bookmark and show an error message

Caution
You shouldn't try to display the BookMark's contents directly to the user, as it represents internal system data and would just look like garbage. The user would probably appreciate your efforts more if you used the AbsolutePosition property to display record position.

▶ **See** "The Recordset's AbsolutePosition Property," **p. 441**

Note You might think that the AbsolutePosition property of the Recordset would work for storing and resetting the record pointer's position. However, a record's AbsolutePosition can change as other records are added or deleted. A BookMark is more stable because it always points to the same physical location for the record. ■

The Seek Method (Tables Only)

There is good news and bad news if your Recordset is of type Table.

The bad news is that you won't be able to use the Find- family of methods that you could use with the Dynaset- and Snapshot-type Recordset. You won't have the flexibility of being able to locate records that fit any valid condition you can think of. To locate records with the Seek method you can only look for values that fit the keys of valid indexes on the underlying data's Table.

The good news is that the Seek method, which you now have to work with, is much faster than the Find- family of methods. This can be very important if you have a large amount of data and need to do many and frequent searches.

Index Property of a Table-Type Recordset

In order for the Seek method to work on a Recordset of type Table, the Index property of the Recordset must be set to the name of an index on the underlying data's table. Of course, the key of this index must make sense in terms of what it is you want to seek. For instance, if you plan to seek by last name, the current index should be keyed on a last name field and not on a field representing, say, date of birth. You must know the name of the index ahead of time, of course. For efficiency's sake, you probably want to set the Index property of the Recordset early in your session. The form's Activate event could serve as a place to set the index property, as in the following example:

```
Private Sub Form_Activate()
    DatAuthors.Recordset.Index = "Name"
'**Note: there IS NO Name index on the Authors table in the
'sample BIBLIO.MDB database supplied with Visual Basic.
'This example will only work if you create a Name index.
'based on the Author field.
End Sub
```

Caution

If you try to set the Index property in the Form's Load event procedure, you will receive a run-time error. This is because the Data Control has not yet connected to the underlying data, and so information about the Recordset can't be accessed yet. The Activate event procedure will work, because the Activate event only happens after the form has loaded into memory and the Data Control is fully connected.

Caution

The Index property is only available to Recordsets of type Table. If you try to set it for the other two types of Recordset, you will receive a run-time error.

Comparison Type Parameter

Although the Seek method is only one method, its first parameter enables you to specify different behaviors when it runs.

The [Comparison Type] parameter is a string containing one of the valid comparison operators:

- >
- <
- =
- >=
- <=

Search String Parameter

The Seek method's syntax is actually more involved than the syntax of the Find- family of methods, since it takes two parameters as opposed to one parameter for the Find- methods. The form of the Seek method is:

DCName.Recordset.Seek [Comparison Type], [Search String]

(where *DCName* is the name of the Data Control that owns the Recordset)

The [Search String] parameter contains data you are going to try to match to the current index's key field in the Recordset. For example, if the current index property is set to an index called "Name" whose key field is the "Author" field, then the search string would hold names you are expecting to find in the "Author" field. As opposed to the parameter of the Find- family of methods, the Seek method's search string is a single value rather than a logical expression.

"Adams, Pat"

would be a reasonable search string for the Seek method, but

"Author = 'Adams,Pat'"

would not.

Example: Using the Seek Method

 Note The Seek method, like the Find methods, is not case-sensitive. ▪

The Seek method's [Comparison Type] parameter tells the Seek method how to search the index key field for the information in the [Search String] parameter.

"=" tells the Seek Method to set NoMatch to false only if it finds an *exact* (but case-insensitive) match. If the Seek is successful, the record pointer is on the record containing the exact match in the key field.

"<" tells the Seek Method to set NoMatch to false only if it finds a record whose key field comes *before* the [Search String] in the sorting order. If the Seek is successful, the record pointer is on the first record in the index order that fits this criterion.

">" tells the Seek Method to set NoMatch to false only if it finds a record whose key field comes *after* the [Search String] in the sorting order. If the Seek is successful, the record pointer is on the first record in the index order that fits this criterion.

">=" tells the Seek Method to set NoMatch to false if it finds either an *exact* (but case-insensitive) match *or* a record whose key field comes *after* the [Search String] in the sorting order. If the Seek is successful, the record pointer is on the first record in the index order that fits this criterion.

"<=" tells the Seek Method to set NoMatch to false if it finds either an *exact* (but case-insensitive) match *or* a record whose key field comes *before* the [Search String] in the sorting order. If the Seek is successful, the record pointer is on the first record in the index order that fits this criterion.

If we had a current index whose key field was the Author Field and the Author fields of all the records contained:

> Adams
>
> Anderson
>
> Baker
>
> Jones
>
> Menendez
>
> Smith

then we'd get the following results with various flavors of Seek:

> datAuthors.Recordset.Seek "=" , "A"

would be unsuccessful (NoMatch would be true) because there is no key field in the Recordset with an exact value of "A."

> datAuthors.Recordset.Seek "<", "A"

would be unsuccessful (NoMatch would be true) because there is no record before "Adams," and "Adams is already after "A" in the sorting order.

> datAuthors.Recordset.Seek ">", "A"

would be successful (NoMatch would be false). The Record Pointer would be resting on "Adams," because "Adams" is the first record in the sorting order to come after "A."

Notice that

> datAuthors.Recordset.Seek ">", "Smith"

would be unsuccessful (NoMatch = true) because there are no records with key fields after "Smith" in the sorting order.

> datAuthors.Recordset.Seek ">=", "A"

would be successful (NoMatch would be false). Once again, the Record Pointer would be resting on "Adams," because, while "Adams" is not equal to "A," it is the first record in the sorting order to come after "A."

> datAuthors.Recordset.Seek "<=", "A"

would be unsuccessful (NoMatch would be true) because there is no record with an exact value of "A," nor is there a record before "Adams," and "Adams is already after "A" in the sorting order.

You might think that you could perform an inexact match (say, look for "Ba" to find a record whose key field began with those two letters) simply by using the ">=" criterion. The reality of the situation is a bit more complex, however. For instance,

> datAuthors.Recordset.Seek ">=", "Ja"

would be successful (NoMatch = false) even though there were no records beginning with "Ja," because there are records after "Ja" in the sorting order, such as "Jones."

Clearly, we must use some extra logic if we want to do partial matches. The following example shows how to do that. Its logic differs from the logic of the example we saw under the Find- section of this chapter in that we must do some extra checking to make sure our partial match is still a match:

```
Save the current bookmark
Get the value of the search string
Run the Seek with ">=" as the comparison criterion
If NoMatch was false (Seek was successful)
        n = length of search string
        f = leftmost n letters of the found record's key field
        Compare search string and f
        If the comparison works, our seek was successful
```

Here is the actual code to implement such logic:

```
Sub cmdSeek()
'NOTE: This example assumes we've previously set the
'current table-type Recordset's Index property to
'an index with an appropriate key for the type of
'search we want to do
      Dim strOldPosition As String
      Dim strNameToFind As String
      Dim blnFound as Boolean
      Dim strNameFound as String
      Dim intLength as Integer
      'Make it upper case - this will make comparison easier
later
      strNameToFind = Ucase(Trim(txtFindName.Text))
      intLength = Len(strNameToFind)
      strOldPosition = datAuthors.Recordset.BookMark
      datAuthors.Recordset.Seek ">=", strNameToFind
      If datAuthors.Recordset.NoMatch Then 'we found nothing
for sure
            blnWasFound = false
      Else                                     'did we
really find anything?
            'put current record's field into a variable and
            'change to upper case so we can compare
            strNameFound = UCase(Trim(txtFindName.Text))
            'Reduce it to the same length as our search string
   strNameFound = Left(strNameFound,intLength)
   'If two strings match, we've REALLY found something
   blnWasFound = (strNameFound = strNameToFind)
     End If
     If Not blnWasFound Then
            datAuthors.Recordset.BookMark = strOldPosition
            MsgBox "Couldn't Find " & strNameToFind
     End If
End Sub
```

Understanding the Data Control's Special Events

If you haven't used the Data Control before, you may be thinking "This isn't a very serious tool for user interface. Every time the user moves the record pointer, any changes to the previous record are automatically written out to the data. I can't live like this! I need to be able to prevent the user from automatically (often unconsciously) making unauthorized, invalidated changes."

Well, relax.

The Data Control's Validate event and its corresponding event procedure will allow you to catch (and undo, if necessary) unwanted changes to the data.

In addition, the Reposition event procedure will allow you to specify behavior whenever the user moves onto a new record.

Finally, the Error event allows you to trap errors that aren't even your fault. What a deal! You get to do error trapping for Microsoft's own code!

Validate

The Validate event happens whenever there is an attempt to move the record pointer off the current record. Remember that this is not a trivial time for data integrity, because when the record pointer moves, any changes to the copy buffer are written to the data.

Luckily, the Validate event happens before the pointer actually moves. It is therefore possible to check the state of the copy buffer's data and either stop the record pointer from moving or stop the copy buffer from being written out to the data.

You can accomplish these things with the help of the Validate Event's two parameters.

Save Parameter

The Save parameter is a true-false Integer.

> **Note** The Save parameter shows up as Integer rather than Boolean in the Validate event procedure's declaration. This is because earlier versions of Visual Basic didn't have a Boolean data type, so the Integer type is there for downward compatibility. ▪

The Save parameter will come into the event procedure as false if the user has made no changes to the copy buffer since moving onto the current record, and true if there have been changes.

Besides reading the Save parameter, you can reset it to prevent the copy buffer from being written out to the data.

If you set the Save parameter to false, changes won't be written from the copy buffer to the data.

So, your code in the Validate event procedure could look like:

```
Private Sub datAuthors_Validate(Action as Integer, Save as
Integer)
     If Save Then
           If MsgBox("Save changes?",vbYesNo) = vbNo Then
                 Save = false
           EndIf
     EndIf
End Sub
```

Of course, this is better than letting the user unconsciously save changes just by moving between records, but this example still leaves things in the user's hands.

Of course, you could change the situation by putting some other logic inside the outer If...End If construct which didn't depend on a user decision. For example:

```
Private Sub datAuthors_Validate(Action as Integer, Save as
Integer)
     If Save Then
           If txtAuthor.Text = "" Then
                 MsgBox "Can't Save:  Must type Author name"
                 Save = false
           End If
     EndIf
End Sub
```

In this example, you're not *asking* the users if it's OK to save, you're *telling* them what you're doing!

Action Parameter

The Validate event happens when the record pointer is about to change. In the previous section, we saw how you can use the Save parameter to cancel an update from the copy buffer to the underlying data.

However, the record pointer still moves away from the current record if you only manipulate the Save parameter.

You can change the Action parameter to a value of 0 (also represented by the internal constant vbActionCancel) to prevent the record pointer from moving. You can also check the Action parameter to see what has caused the Validate event to occur.

Because the Action parameter can have many initial values depending on why the record pointer wants to move, it is implemented as a many-valued integer rather than a logical.

The Action parameter can have 11 initial values. Each value has a corresponding VB internal constant. In the following list, these constants correspond to the number 1 through 11.

> VbDataActionMoveFirst: MoveFirst event has executed.
>
> vbDataActionMovePrevious: MovePrevious event has executed.
>
> vbDataActionMoveNext: MoveNext event has executed.
>
> vbDataActionMoveLast: MoveLast event has executed.
>
> vbDataActionAddNew: The AddNew method has just executed. Record will move to the new blank temporary record.
>
> VbDataActionUpdate: The Update method has just executed. Note that this doesn't refer to the UpdateRecord method of the Data Control. UpdateRecord doesn't cause a Validate event.
>
> VbDataActionDelete: The Delete method has just executed.
>
> vbDataActionFind: Any of the Find- family of methods has executed.
>
> vbDataActionBookMark: There is some VB code which is trying to change the BookMark.
>
> vbDataActionClose: The Recordset has just closed.
>
> VbDataActionUnload: The form containing the Data Control has just Unloaded.

In addition, there are other values not supported by constants, such as 27 (Seek) and 16 (Load).

Part

IV

Ch

12

You can check the Action parameter because you might want to have your system behave differently depending on why the record pointer is moving.

```
Private Sub datAuthors_Validate(Action as Integer, Save as
Integer)
      If Save and (Action <> vbDataActionUpdate) Then
            'Do stuff
      End If
End Sub
```

You can also set the Action parameter to 0. If you set it to 0, or vbDataActionCancel, the record pointer will not move. This is obviously useful if you detect an error in the user's data entry and don't want the user to move off the record until responding to the problem.

```
Private Sub datAuthors_Validate(Action as Integer, Save as
Integer)
      If Save Then
            If txtAuthor.Text = "" Then
                  MsgBox "Can't Save:  Must type Author name"
                  'Changes won't save:
                  Save = false
                  'Record pointer won't move:
                  Action = 0 ' or vbDataActionCancel
            End If
      EndIf
End Sub
```

The Data Control's UpdateRecord and UpdateControls Methods

Whenever you call the Update method (which resets the record pointer) or reset a Bookmark property (even to its current value), you will trigger the Validate event. Other events can happen as well.

Tip

The Update and AddNew methods will change the record pointer.

If you want the record pointer to stay on the record just updated or added, use the code

```
Data1.Recordset.Bookmark _ = Data1.Recordset.LastModified
```

to position the record pointer back to the record just written to.

Sometimes you need to perform actions without calling the Validate event.

The Data Control's UpdateRecord method will write from the copy buffer to the underlying data, just like the Update method, but it won't trigger the Validate event or any other event.

The Data Control's UpdateControls method will refresh the copy buffer from the underlying data and so, will also refresh the bound controls without triggering any other events.

Reposition Event

Like the Validate event, we can also say that the Reposition event happens when the record pointer changes. The Reposition event happens on the other end of the change, however.

If the Validate event happens just before the record pointer changes (so that the current record is still the old record), the Reposition event happens just after the record pointer has moved. Thus, the current record during the Reposition event is the new record just moved to.

Because of its timing, the Reposition event will be useless to you for validating changes. However, it can still come in handy any time you need to check things, or take specific actions upon moving to a different record.

For instance, when you first come into a new record, you might want the button labeled "Save" or "Update" to be unavailable to the user. After all, it doesn't make sense to allow the user to save changes if they haven't made any changes.

```
Private Sub datAuthors_Reposition()
        cmdSave.Enabled = false
End Sub
```

The following sections (on the AbsolutePosition, PercentPosition, and RecordCount properties) tell you about other nifty information you can use in the Reposition Event procedure.

Part

IV

Ch

12

Tip

At some point, you could enable the Save or Update button during the KeyPress event procedure of the various bound controls or just once in the Form's KeyPress event procedure. (Remember to set the Form's KeyPreview property to true if you go with the second way!)

The Recordset's RecordCount Property

This dynamic little property will tell you the number of undeleted rows in the current Recordset. You can display it every time the Reposition event procedure runs in a special label on the form, on the form's background, or even in the caption of the Data Control:

```
Private Sub datAuthors_Reposition()
      Me.Cls
      Me.Print datAuthors.Recordset.RecordCount
      'or
      lblStatistics.Caption = _
CStr(datAuthors.Recordset.RecordCount)
      'or
      datAuthors.Caption = datAuthors.Recordset.RecordCount
End Sub
```

Tip

You might not want to read the value of Recordset.RecordCount every time the Reposition event occurs, because the system must run an internal routine to check the RecordCount property every time it's called. It would be more efficient to store the RecordCount in a form-wide (i.e., Private) variable and use this variable in the Reposition event. You could reset the variable whenever there was an add or a delete to the Recordset.

Caution

The RecordCount property of Dynaset and Snapshot-type Recordsets doesn't get properly set during a data session until after you have visited the last record in the Recordset. You should use the MoveLast method immediately after opening your Recordset to properly set RecordCount.

The Recordset's AbsolutePosition Property

AbsolutePosition tells you the position the current record in the recordset occupies with respect to the other records (whether you will encounter it first, second, and so on in the logical order of the record set). You could use AbsolutePosition to update visible information about the current record every time the Reposition Event runs.

```
Private Sub datAuthors_Reposition()
    Dim strStats as String
    With datAuthors.Recordset
        strStats = AbsolutePosition + 1 & " of " & _
RecordCount & " Records"
    End With
    Me.Cls
Me.Print strStats
    'or
    lblStatistics.Caption = strStats
    'or
datAuthors.Caption = strStats
End Sub
```

Note that AbsolutePosition doesn't give the position of the current record in the underlying data file, but rather in the Recordset. Recall that a query creates the Recordset, and this query is based on the Data Control's RecordSource property. The query runs when the Data Control first connects. The Data Control connects to its data when the form containing it loads into memory.

The same row's information may have a different AbsolutePosition if you create it with the query

Select ★ from Authors Order By Author

than if you use the query

Select ★ from Authors Order By [Year Born]

Tip

AbsolutePosition is 0-based, so you may want to add 1 to its value before you display it. (See the accompanying example.) Otherwise, the last record will seem to have a position of 1 less than the number of records (as found in the RecordCount property) and the first record will have a position of 0 instead of 1.

Part

IV

Ch

12

Besides reading the value of AbsolutePosition, you can also set its value (see fig. 12.14). This would have the effect of repositioning the record pointer.

FIG. 12.14 ⇒

You might use the RecordCount and AbsolutePosition properties to display current record position in the Recordset.

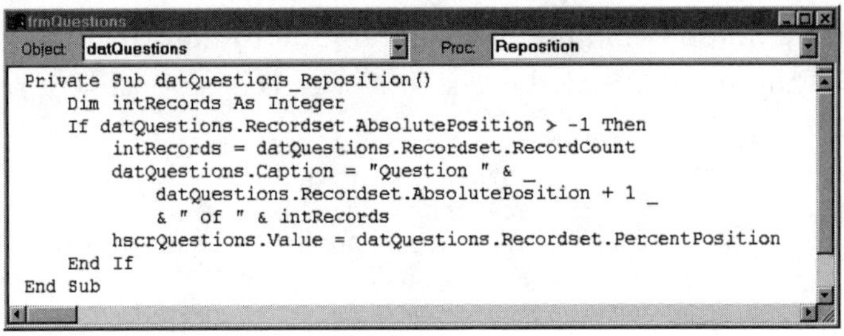

```
: frmQuestions                                                         _ □ ×
Object: datQuestions              ▼    Proc:  Reposition                ▼
Private Sub datQuestions_Reposition()
    Dim intRecords As Integer
    If datQuestions.Recordset.AbsolutePosition > -1 Then
        intRecords = datQuestions.Recordset.RecordCount
        datQuestions.Caption = "Question " & _
            datQuestions.Recordset.AbsolutePosition + 1 _
            & " of " & intRecords
        hscrQuestions.Value = datQuestions.Recordset.PercentPosition
    End If
End Sub
```

The Recordset's PercentPosition Properties

The PercentPosition property is a Single-precision number which can have a value between 0 and 100. Like the AbsolutePosition property, it gives information about the current record's position relative to other records in the Recordset.

You could use PercentPosition to display information as in the example under the section on the AbsolutePosition property. You could also use PercentPosition to update a ScrollBar, Slider, ProgressBar, or Gauge control.

You could put the following line of code in the Data Control's Reposition event procedure to update a ScrollBar:

vscrPercent.Value = datAuthors.Recordset.PercentPosition

Tip

If you want to try this example, don't forget to change the ScrollBar control's Max property to 100 and make sure its Min property is at the default value of 0.

If you have considerably fewer than 100 records in your Recordset, the user may not see the ScrollBar hit bottom when on the last record.

Because the PercentPosition property is also writable, you could let the user use the ScrollBar or Slider control to move the record pointer graphically through the data. This will only give approximate results and Microsoft recommends against using PercentPosition to reset the record pointer.

In your Data Control's Reposition event, you could put code, such as the following line, to tie a Horizontal scrollbar into your Data Control's Recordset's PercentPosition property:

hscrQuestions.Value = datQuestions.Recordset.PercentPosition

This example will work as expected, provided you've set the ScrollBar control's MaxPosition property to 100 and its MinPosition to 0.

> **Caution**
> If you are accessing a Jet database with version 2.5 of the Data Access Objects Library and you're using a Table-type Recordset, you must set the Index property of the Recordset to be able to use the PercentPosition with that Recordset (see fig. 12.15).

▶ **See** "Visual Basic, the Jet Engine, and the Data Access Libraries," **p. 477**

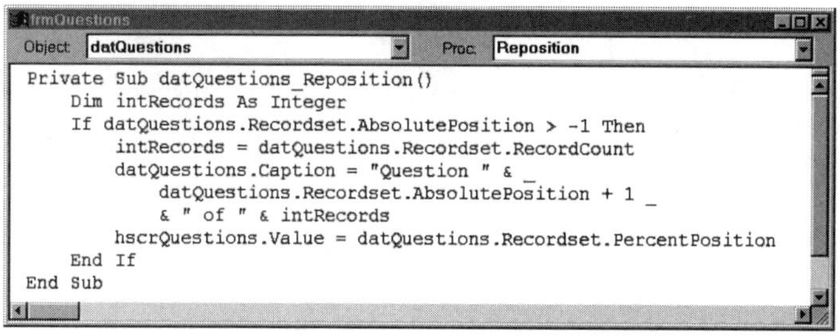

FIG. 12.15 ⇒
You could use PercentPosition to update a scrollbar or other type of indicator control such as the custom ProgressBar control. You could also use a scrollbar to set the PercentPosition and so move the record pointer, though this isn't recommended.

```
Private Sub datQuestions_Reposition()
    Dim intRecords As Integer
    If datQuestions.Recordset.AbsolutePosition > -1 Then
        intRecords = datQuestions.Recordset.RecordCount
        datQuestions.Caption = "Question " & _
            datQuestions.Recordset.AbsolutePosition + 1 _
            & " of " & intRecords
        hscrQuestions.Value = datQuestions.Recordset.PercentPosition
    End If
End Sub
```

> **Caution**
>
> The PercentPosition property isn't available on a forward-only scrolling snapshot-type Recordset, or on a Recordset opened from a pass-through query against a remote database.

Error Event

This event happens when the Data Control's own internal data navigation routines encounter a run-time error, or when a custom data control tries to manipulate your Recordset.

For instance, if the user clicks one of the data control's movement buttons and Visual Basic attempts to move to a record that has already been deleted, a run-time error could happen.

Because none of your code will be running when the user clicks the Data Control, you must put error handling code for such eventualities in the Data Control's error event.

> **Caution**
>
> The Data Control's Error event does not free you from writing error handlers in your own data manipulation code!
>
> For a more detailed comparison of the handling of errors in the Error event versus error handler in your own code, see the section "The Error Event versus Error Handlers Written by the Programmer" later in this chapter.

Error Event Procedure's DataErr Parameter

This parameter of the Error event procedure contains the error code itself. You can use this parameter as you would use the Err.Number property in your own error handler.

Response Parameter

The Response parameter is a true/false integer. If Response is left at its default value of true, the system will display its own error message. You can disable the system error message by setting Response to false at some point in the Error event procedure.

The Error Event versus Error Handlers Written by the Programmer

The Data Control's Error event will often handle the same errors as those which occur in your code when you do things like move the record pointer.

You must write error handling routines in both places. In order to avoid lots of duplicate code, this is a good place to practice the techniques suggested in the section "Centralized Error Handling Techniques" in Chapter 8.

Here is imaginary code that has to handle the same error both in the Error event procedure and in a Command Button's Click event procedure. Notice how we call the same error handling routine from both the Error event and the Click event procedure's error handler.

```
Private Sub Data1_Error(DataErr As Integer, Response As Inte-
ger)
HandleDataError DataErr
Response = false       'suppress default error message
End Sub

'We have decided to give the user a command button to move
'to the next record as well as letting the Data Control
'move there
'Notice we still need skeletal error handling in here,
'but we turn the details over to the centralized
'error handling procedure we've written
Private Sub cmdMoveNext()
      On Error GoTo MoveNext_Error
      Data1.Recordset.MoveNext
      If Data1.Recordset.EOF then
            Data1.Recordset.MoveLast
      EndIf
ExitMoveNext:
      Exit Sub
```

```
MoveNext_Error:
        HandleDataError Err.Number
        Resume ExitMoveNext
End Sub
'This centralized error handling procedure be more
'thorough because we can invest more time in writing the
'handling routine for each type of error.
'Our example only shows how we'd handle error 3167 =
'Record already deleted by another user.
Private Sub HandleDataError(ErrNumber as Integer)
If ErrNumber = 3167 Then
            Data1.Recordset.Delete
            Data1.Recordset.MoveNext
            If Data1.Recordset.EOF then
                    If Data1.RecordCount > 0 then
                            Data1.Recordset.MoveLast
                    End If
            End If
        End If
End Sub
```

Understanding Data-Bound List Box and Data-Bound Combo Box

Although they aren't part of VB's standard control set, Microsoft distributes these data-aware controls with Visual Basic 4.0's Professional and Enterprise editions.

The Data-bound list box and Data-bound combo box control functions very similarly to each other (like the similarity between the list box and combo box controls). The following discussion of properties and techniques will apply to both.

Because List Boxes and Combo Boxes generally show us multiple elements of data, you would expect a data-bound version of these controls to let you see more than one record of a Recordset at once; and that is just what these controls will do for you.

There are two levels of sophistication for the Data-Bound List/Combo control.

On the first level, you can use the control as a simple, unattached look up. The user can use it for reference purposes.

On the second level, you can use the control to directly link a main recordset to a set of lookup records. The Data-Bound List/Combo control will then provide the user the choices from a lookup table for entering information into a field in another table. You use this Data-Bound control to tie the lookup table to the field in such a way that the user can *only* use the information from the lookup table to populate the field in the main table. This makes it easier for the user to enter error-free data and cuts down on the validation code you have to write.

Fields to Create a Lookup into a Recordset

To create a simple, non-binding lookup table, you will need a Data Control that can furnish the appropriate Recordset at run-time, and your Data-Bound List or Combo Box will need to have two properties set.

- ◆ The RowSource property will point to the Data Control.
- ◆ The ListField property will tell the Data-Bound control which field to display.

RowSource Property

The RowSource property works like the DataSource property of simpler bound controls like the Text Box: it points to a Data Control that will provide us with a source for the data that this control will look at.

The RowSource property gets its name from the fact that it points to the Data Control which will supply the information for the Combo or List Box rows.

You can follow these steps to set a RowSource:

1. Make sure you have a fully-prepared Data Control on your form.

2. Locate the DataBound Combo Box icon in the VB ToolBox.

3. Click the icon with the mouse to select it.

4. Use your mouse to draw a rectangular area on the form; this will place a Data-Bound Combo Box on the form.

5. Press F4 to view this control's Properties Window. You may also click the Properties Icon on the VB ToolBar or choose View Properties from the VB main menu.

6. In the Properties Window, scroll to the RowSource property.

7. Click the RowSource property to make it the current property.

8. Click the List-Box icon (down arrow) to the right of the RowSource property to bring up a list of available Data Controls (see fig. 12.16).

9. Choose the Data Control you want to connect this Combo Box to.

   ▶ **See** "Data Control Properties," **p. 401**

FIG. 12.16 ⟹

A Data-Bound Combo or List Box control's RowSource property.

ListField Property

You can set the ListField property once you've selected a RowSource. The ListField is the Field in the Recordset of the RowSource's Data Control whose values will appear on separate rows of the Combo or List Box. To set up a list field for a Data-Bound Combo Box or List Box:

1. Make sure you have already assigned a RowSource property to this control (see the previous section).

2. In the Properties Window for this control, select the ListField property as the current property.

3. Click the drop-down arrow to the right of the ListField property to bring up a list of available fields in the Recordset of the Data Control specified by the RowSource.

4. Choose the field you want to display in this Combo Box.

5. Press F5 to run your application and test the Data-Bound Combo Box.

6. When the application has loaded, click the Data-Bound Combo Box' down arrow icon.

7. You should see a scrollable list of records in the Data Control's Recordset, with the value of the ListField displayed for each record.

Note Changing the contents of the Combo Box's text box has no effect on the data (see fig. 12.17). If you wanted to implement field changes based on the user typing into the text box, you would have to write your own code. ▓

FIG. 12.17 ⇒
A Data-Bound
Combo or List
Box control's
ListField property.

Additional Fields to Implement a Validated Lookup for Data Entry into Another Recordset

The RowSource and ListField properties of the Data-Bound Combo or List Box let you create an independent lookup into a table.

The DataSource, DataField, and BoundColumn properties let you take this a step further by connecting the DBCombo or List's underlying data to a second Recordset which will use the DBCombo/List's underlying Recordset as a lookup.

For example, let's imagine that we have a Data-Bound Combo for a Recordset of Authors. The RowSource will point to the Data Control whose Recordset holds the information about the Authors and its ListField will hold, say the Author field (representing the name).

Now let's say we want to use the data in this DBCombo as a lookup for a browse of Titles. In other words, as the user looks at the information on the individual title, we want the book's author's name to appear in the DBCombo. If the user wants to assign an author to the book, the user should be able to pick another author from the DBCombo. The act of clicking the author's name in the DBCombo should be enough to assign a different author to the book.

Let's see how you can use the DataSource, DataField, and BoundColumn properties to let a second Recordset use your DB Combo or List as a lookup.

DataSource Property

The DataSource property will point to the second Recordset's Data Control, that is, the Recordset that will look up data in the Recordset of the RowSource. In order to set up this field, you should take the following steps:

1. Make sure you have a fully-prepared Data Control on your form for the main Recordset (that is, the Recordset that will be looking up data in the Recordset of the RowSource—see earlier sections in this chapter).

2. Select the DataBound Combo or List Box control and view its Properties Window.

3. In the Properties Window, select the DataSource property as the current property.

4. Click the drop-down arrow to the right of the DataSource property to bring up a list of available Data Controls (see fig. 12.18).

5. Choose the other Data Control which you want to connect to this control's RowSource.

FIG. 12.18 ⇒

A Data-Bound Combo or List Box control's DataSource property.

DataField Property

The main RecordSource (the DataSource, or the Titles data in our running example) must have a foreign key field that contains a unique identifying value from a primary key field in the lookup RecordSource (the RowSource, or the Authors data in the example). The DBCombo or DBList will then use this foreign key from the main RecordSource to look up the appropriate record in the RowSource.

The DataField property holds the name of the foreign key field in the DataSource's RecordSource. In our example, the Titles RecordSource will hold an Author ID field that corresponds to a unique Author ID in the Authors RecordSource. It would be the Title RecordSource's Author ID field that we would set as the DBCombo's DataField property.

In order to set up the DataField property, you should take the following steps:

1. Make sure you have already assigned a DataSource property to this control (see the previous section).

Part

IV

Ch

12

2. Select this control and view its Properties Windows.

3. In the Properties Window, select the DataField property as the current property.

4. Click the drop-down arrow to the right of the DataField property to bring up a list of available fields in the Recordset of the Data Control specified by the DataSource (see fig. 12.19).

5. Choose the field you want the RecordSource belonging to the DataSource to use as a foreign key for finding a record in the RecordSource of the RowSource.

FIG. 12.19 ⟹

A Data-Bound Combo or List Box control's DataField property.

BoundColumn Property

As we have just seen, you need the DataField property to specify the foreign key field in the main RecordSource in order to tie the two RecordSources together.

To complete the knot, you also need to set the BoundColumn property; this will specify the name of the primary key field in the lookup RecordSource (the RowSource). The DBCombo will then use the field of the BoundColumn property to tie the current record in the main RecordSource (belonging to the DataSource's Data Control) to a record in the lookup RecordSource (which belongs to the RowSource's Data Control).

In our example, the Authors RecordSource holds a unique Author ID field that the Titles RecordSource can use to look up an author corresponding to its own Author ID foreign key. So, we would set up the Authors RecordSource's Author ID field as the DBCombo's BoundColumn property.

In order to set up a DBCombo or DBList Box's BoundColumn property, you should take the following steps:

1. Make sure you have already assigned a DataSource and a RowSource property to this control.
   - ▶ **See** "The DataSource Property," **p. 406**
   - ▶ **See** "RowSource Property," **p. 447**

2. Select the control and view its Properties Windows.

3. In the Properties Window, select the BoundColumn property as the current property.

4. Click the drop-down arrow to the right of the BoundColumn property to bring up a list of available fields in the Recordset of the Data Control specified by the RowSource.

5. Choose the field you want the RecordSource belonging to the RowSource to use as a primary key so the DBCombo/List can find a record given by the key of the RecordSource of the DataSource.

6. In order to fully test this application, you should add some controls, such as text boxes, to your form and bind them to the Data Control for the RecordSource of the DataSource (the main RecordSource).
   - ▶ **See** "Binding Other Controls to the Data Control," **p. 406**

7. Press the F5 key to run your application and test the browse with the Data–Bound Combo Box as a lookup.

8. When the application has loaded, click the arrows in the Data Control of the DataSource.

Part

IV

Ch

12

9. When the record pointer in the DataSource changes, you should see the highlighted record in the Data-Bound Combo or List Box change.

10. If you use the mouse to choose a different item in the Data-Bound Combo of List Box, the change will be permanent for this record in the DataSource (see fig. 12.20).

> ### Caution
> Don't be thrown off by the fact that the BoundColumn and DataField will often have the same name in many databases. They represent two distinct fields in two different Recordsets.

FIG. 12.20 ⟹

A Data-Bound Combo or List Box control's BoundColumn property.

Using the BoundText Property to Keep Track of Key Values

> ### Caution
> The record pointer to the RowSource's Recordset doesn't move when the user changes the selection in a DB Combo or DB List Box. The BoundText control's value, however will change to reflect a key field's changing value as the user changes the selection in a DB Combo or List Box.

The BoundText property at run-time will reflect the contents of the BoundColumn field in the current record. For example, if BoundColumn is, say QueID (the unique identifier of a Question record in our example), then BoundColumn might contain values like 234, 12, 137—that is, whatever the current record's QueID field contains.

If you'd like a way to check the key field's contents in the RowSource Recordset as the user moves around the DB Combo or DB List Box, then you must get creative with the BoundText property.

```
'If it's a DB List, put it in the Click event
Private Sub DBcmbCategories_Change()
   Dim strCriterion As String
    strCriterion = DBcmbCategories.BoundText
    datStudyTopics.RecordSource = _
"Select * from STTopic Where CatID = " & strCriterion
    datStudyTopics.Refresh
End Sub
```

Note We don't need this property when linking two Recordsets together with a DB Combo or List Box, so we don't mention it in the following example. To see this example in action, see the form called frmCategories in the complete EXAM example. ▪

Example of Browsing and Adding Data

We will set up an example in two stages.

The first stage will let us look at a list of the 16 Categories in Microsoft's VB 4.0 Certification Exam in a DB List box.

In the second stage, we will set up a browse of the Exam Study Topics as published by Microsoft. We will then connect the current record on this browse to its corresponding category in the categories shown on the DB List box. The user can browse through the topics and see each topic's category highlighted in the list box.

Setting Up a Simple Lookup of Exam Categories

> **Note** If you have worked through some of the examples in this chapter, you may already have a form for browsing Study Topics. You can use that existing form for the following steps. ▪

In this first step, we'll simply set up a DBList Box to provide information about Exam Categories as contained in a Data Control's Recordset. You'll need to take the following steps to do so:

Make sure you have the right Form:

1. If you don't have a Form for the Study Topic browse (see the note above), then click the Form icon or choose Insert Form from VB's Main Menu. If you already have such a Form, make it the current Form in design mode.

Add a Data Control to point to Exam Categories:

1. Add a Control to the Form.

2. View the Data Control's Properties Window.

3. Select the Name property to make it the current property.

4. Type "**datCategories**" to change this Data Control's name.

5. Select the DatabaseName property as the current property.

6. Click the browse button to the right of the DatabaseName property to bring up a File Open dialog screen.

7. Use the File Open dialog to find the example data files for this book on your system.

8. You should see the EXAM.MDB Access database file listed in the File Name list box.

9. Choose the EXAM.MDB file from the file dialog.

10. You should now see the full path and file name in the DatabaseName property of the Data Control.

11. Select the RecordSource property as the current property.

12. Click the drop-down arrow to the right of the RecordSource property to bring up a list of tables in the EXAM database.

13. Click the Category table.

14. You will see the Category table now listed in the RecordSource property.

Add a DataBound List Box and point it to the Exam Categories Data Control and the CatName field:

1. Place a DataBound List Box on the Form.

2. In the DataBound ListBox control's Properties Window, select the RowSource property.

3. Click the drop-down arrow to bring up a list of available Data Controls.

4. Choose the control named datCategories.

5. Select the ListField property.

6. Click the drop-down arrow to bring up a list of fields available in the Recordset of the datCategories Data Control.

7. Choose the CatName field to display in the List Box.

Test the DBList Box:

1. Press the F5 key to run your application and test the Data-Bound List Box.

2. When the application has loaded, click the Data-Bound Combo Box' down arrow icon (see fig. 12.21).

3. You should see a scrollable list of records in the Data Control's Recordset, with the value of the ListField displayed for each record.

FIG. 12.21 ⇒

A Data-Bound
Combo Box to
provide a simple
lookup to the Data
Control that points
to Categories.

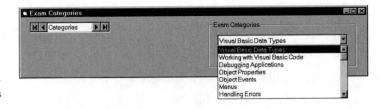

Tying the Study Topic Browse to the Exam Categories

Now that we've set up an independent lookup of the Exam Categories,
let's make it a bit more dependent on the Exam Study Topics. That is, as
the user browses through the Exam Study Topics we'd like the user to
see each Topic's Category in the DBList box.

To do so, you should take the following steps:

Tie the DB List Box control to the Study Topics Data Control:

1. If you don't have a browse of Study Topics set up on this form,
   you should set one up now. See the example in the section
   "Example: Binding Text Boxes to a Data Control" in this
   chapter.

2. Select the DataBound List Box control as the current control
   on your design surface.

3. In the Properties Window of the DataBound List Box, select
   the DataSource property.

4. Click the DataSource property's drop-down arrow to bring up
   a list of available Data Controls.

5. Choose the datStudyTopics Data Control as the RowSource.

Specify the foreign key for Study Topics with the DataField property:

1. Select the Data-Bound List Box as the current control on your
   design surface.

2. In the Properties Window, select the DataField property.

3. Click the DataField property's drop-down arrow to bring up a list of available fields in the Recordset of the Data Control specified by the DataSource.

4. Choose the QueID field as the foreign key for datStudyTopics to use when it looks up a record in datCategories.

Tie the two Recordsets together by using the BoundColumn property to specify the primary key in datCategories to use in a lookup:

1. In the Properties Window, scroll to the BoundColumn property.

2. Click the BoundColumn property to make it the current property.

3. Click the BoundColumn property's drop-down arrow to bring up a list of available fields in datCategories.

4. Choose the QueID field.

Test the browse:

1. Press F5 to run your application.

2. When the application has loaded, click the arrows in the datStudyTopics Data Control.

3. When the record pointer in datStudyTopics changes, you should see the highlighted record in the Data-Bound List Box change (see fig. 12.22).

4. If you use the mouse to choose a different category in the Data-Bound List Box, the change will be permanent for this study topic.

Part
IV
Ch
12

FIG. 12.22 ⇒

Use the Data-Bound Combo Box to provide a validated lookup from Exam Topics into Categories.

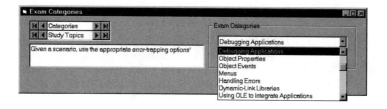

Using Data-Bound Grid

The DB List and DB Combo boxes can provide the user with multiple-record information for single fields.

If you want a browse with more teeth in it—"teeth" being things like multiple, editable fields/columns with scrolling between columns, direct connection to the underlying data, and a more customizable look, then you need something like the DBGrid control.

Note Microsoft arranged with a third-party vendor to supply the DBGrid control with Visual Basic. For more extensive and up-to-date information on this control, you should refer to the vendor by double-clicking the DBGrid's About property in the control's Properties Window. ▪

Initializing a Data-Bound Grid

The Data–Bound Grid, as its name implies, needs to be bound to a Data Control's Recordset before it can do its magic.

You need to set only one property of the DBGrid to do this—the DataSource property. This property will, of course, contain the name of the Data Control to bind to.

The DBGrid doesn't have a single DataField property like the Text Box and other bindable controls. This is because the DBGrid can have multiple columns, each column corresponding to a field in the DataSource.

We will see, in the next section, how you can bind columns of the DBGrid to fields in the DataSource.

Setting Up the Columns of a Data-Bound Grid at Design Time

Once you have a DBGrid control on your Form with a valid DataSource, you may use the fields from the DataSource as–is in the you must tell the DBGrid to initialize its columns with the fields from the DataSource.

The DBGrid control uses a Columns() collection which will be available at run-time. Each object in the Columns() collection is called, strangely enough, a Column.

To do this, follow these steps:

1. Right-click the mouse on the DBGrid control. You will see a custom menu for the DBGrid control.

2. Choose Retrieve Fields from the custom menu. This puts default information into the Columns() collection.

3. The DBGrid should change appearance, displaying field names as columns across the top.

4. Right-click the mouse on the DBGrid control to bring up the custom menu a second time.

5. Choose Properties from the custom menu.

6. You will see the Apex Data Bound Grid Control Properties tabbed dialog box.

7. Click the Columns tab to see Column information.

8. The topmost list, labeled Column, gives you a scrolling list of the Columns that are now members of this DBGrid's Columns collection. The other elements on the Dialog box refer to the selected Column in the Column list.

9. Change a Column's heading as it appears in the DBGrid at run-time by typing the desired heading into the Caption field of the dialog.

10. Change the field to which the Column is bound by picking a field from the Data Field drop-down List.

11. Keep a Column from showing up in the DBGrid by un-checking its Visible property.

12. As you finish with each Column, you may click the Apply button. This lets you change properties without having to Click the OK button and exit the dialog each time you finish with a column.

Part

IV

Ch

12

13. Repeat steps 9–12 for all the Columns in the DBGrid (see fig. 12.23).

14. When you're done with the Columns, click the OK button to close the dialog box.

15. You can press F5 to test your application with the newly customized DBGrid (see fig. 12.24).

FIG. 12.23 ⟹

Call up the custom editing box for a DBGrid control. Note the Retrieve Fields and Properties… choices.

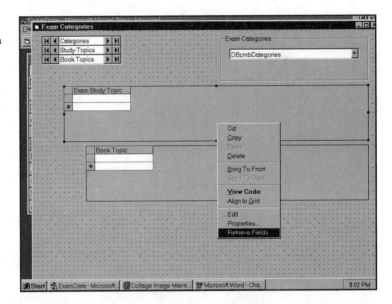

FIG. 12.24 ⟹

Editing a DBGrid's Column information.

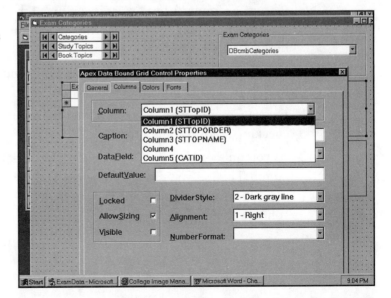

Manipulating the Properties of the DBGrid's Columns at Run-Time

You can manipulate a Column member of the DBGrid's Columns collection at run-time by setting or reading its properties and calling its methods.

```
Private Sub Form_Activate()
Me.WindowState = vbMaximized
DBgStTopics.Columns("STTOPNAME").Width = DBgBkTopics.Width
DBgBkTopics.Columns("BKTOPNAME").Width = DBgStTopics.Width
DBgQuestions.Columns("QUETEXT").Width = DBgQuestions.Width
End Sub
```

In the example, we access a particular Column by using the name of the underlying data field as an argument.

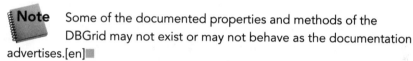 **Note** Some of the documented properties and methods of the DBGrid may not exist or may not behave as the documentation advertises.[en]■

Retrieving and Setting Information in the Data-Bound Grid at Run-Time

You can let the DBGrid change and retrieve information automatically without writing any code. In this respect, the DBGrid functions like controls such as Text Boxes that you have bound to a Data Control:

◆ When the user visually moves onto a row of the DBGrid, the Grid's row contents at that point update from the corresponding row in the Recordset's underlying data.

◆ When the user moves off the current record in the DBGrid, any changes the user has made to cells in the current row are written automatically to the underlying data.

We can define several points in the process of user interaction with information in the row of a DBGrids. We list the various events and their event procedures that will happen at these points in the editing process:

1. User changes the Grid's row-pointer with the mouse. This will populate the Recordset's copy buffer with the corresponding underlying data.

   - RowColChange(LastRow As Variant, ByVal LastCol As Integer)

2. User makes changes to contents of a Column, moving to another Column in the same row. This will move data from the Grid's Column to the copy buffer for that Column.

   - BeforeColUpdate (ByVal ColIndex As Integer, OldValue As Variant, Cancel As Integer)
   - AfterColUpdate (ByVal ColIndex As Integer)

3. User moves to a different row of the Grid. This will trigger a write from the Recordset's copy buffer to the underlying data.

   - BeforeUpdate (Cancel As Integer): occurs when user attempts to move off changed record.
   - AfterUpdate: occurs after changes have been saved to underlying data.

4. User attempts to delete a row by selecting the entire row with the mouse and pressing the DEL key. Remember that you must set the DBGrid's AllowDelete property to true before the user will be able to delete records.

   - BeforeDelete (Cancel As Integer): occurs when user presses DEL key
   - AfterDelete: occurs after record has been removed from the Recordset.

5. User attempts to add a new row by positioning mouse in a Column on the blank record at the bottom of the grid and beginning to type. Remember that you must set the DBGrid's AllowAddNew property to true before the user will be able to delete records.

- BeforeInsert (Cancel As Integer): occurs when user attempts to type first letter in new record.
- AfterInsert: occurs when user attempts to move off newly edited data.

Note the use of a Cancel parameter in all of the "Before-" event procedures listed earlier. This Integer parameter can have a true or false value. Obviously, it will allow you to programmatically do some validation before letting the change go through. If you set the value of Cancel to true, the change will not get written to the copy buffer, in the case of BeforeColUpdate, or to the underlying data, in the case of BeforeUpdate, BeforeDelete, and BeforeAdd.

The DBGrid recognizes a number of other special events. You might wish to investigate their respective event procedures:

◆ ColResize(ByVal ColIndex As Integer, Cancel As Integer)

◆ HeadClick(ByVal ColIndex As Integer)

◆ RowResize(Cancel As Integer)

◆ SelChange(Cancel As Integer)

Note The DBGrid control was still under development as Visual Basic hit the market. Some of the documented events may not exist or may not behave as the documentation advertises.[en]■

Part
IV

Ch
12

Example: Using a Data-Bound Grid to Show On-the-Fly Results

Although we've warned you several times that the DBGrid control is still in development, here's a slick trick you can do with it that will work for sure.

This particular technique lets you do a "child" browse of multiple records related to a single record in another table. For instance, every time the user selects a different Exam Category, we would like to see a list of all the Study Topics which fall under that Exam Category.

Here is what you should do to make the user's browse of the Categories DBCombo update a DBGrid of Exam Topics:

Verify that the DBCombo for Categories is set up properly:

1. Make sure that frmCategories is the current form in VB's Design environment.

2. Click the dbcmbCategories DBCombo control.

3. Press F4 or choose View Properties from the menu or click the Properties icon to bring up the Properties Window.

4. Find its BoundColumn property and make sure it's set to CatID.

    Add another Data Control for the DBGrid to point to.

5. Add a Data Control to your form.

6. Make sure it's the selected control.

7. Press F4 or choose View Properties from the menu or click the Properties icon to bring up the Properties Window.

8. Set its Name property to datStudyTopics.

9. Set its Visible property to false (since the user won't interact with it directly).

10. Set its DatabaseName property to be the Exam.MDB database.

11. Set its RecordSource property to be the STTOPICS table.

Add the DBGrid control to do the browse:

1. Add a DBGrid control to your form.

2. Press F4 or choose View Properties from the menu or click the Properties icon to bring up the Properties Window.

3. Find the DBGrid's Name property and change it to dbgStudyTopics.

4. Find the DataSource property and set it to datStudyTopics.

5. Close the Properties Window.

Customize the DBGrid's columns:

1. Right-click the DBGrid control to bring up its custom menu.

2. Choose the Retrieve Fields option to populate the DBGrid's design-time Columns.

3. Right-click the DBGrid control to bring up its custom menu again.

4. You will see the Apex Data Bound Grid Control Properties tabbed dialog box.

5. Click the Columns tab to see Column information.

6. The topmost list, labeled <u>C</u>olumn, gives you a scrolling list of the Columns that are now members of this DBGrid's Columns collection. The other elements on the Dialog box refer to the selected Column in the <u>C</u>olumn list.

7. Find the Column whose data field is the STTOPICNAME field. Change Column's heading as it will appear in the DBGrid at run-time by typing the desired heading into the Caption field of the dialog.

8. Change to all the other Columns and keep them from showing up in the Grid at run time by un-checking their Visible properties.

9. When you're done with the Columns, click the OK button to close the dialog box.

Code the Change event of the DBCombo to re-filter the records which the DBGrid points to:

1. Double-click the DBCombo control to bring up its event procedures.

2. Go to the Procs list arrow and click to see a list of event procedures for this control. Scroll to the Change event procedure and click it to choose it.

3. In the Change event procedure's code window type:

```
Dim strSQL as String
StrSQL = "Select * from STTopic WHERE " & _
      "CatID = " & dbcmbCategories.BoundText
datStTopics.RecordSource = strSQL
datStTopics.Refresh
```

Now you can test the DBCombo/DBGrid combination:

1. Press F5 to run your project in Design mode.

2. Click the DBCombo control and choose a category name.

3. You should see the contents of the DBGrid control change each time you click a different category name in the DBCombo control (see fig. 12.25).

We can actually extend this to a cascading set of browses! Every time the user selects a Study Topic, the user can see a list of the Book Topics that belong to that Study Topic.

User chooses this Exam Category in DataBound ComboBox

FIG. 12.25 ⇒

The first DBGrid updates each time we change to a different item in the DBCombo Box. The second DBGrid changes each time we change the selection in the first DBGrid.

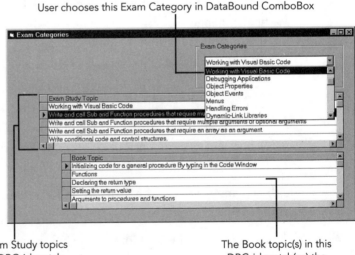

The Exam Study topics in this DBGrid match chosen Exam Category

The Book topic(s) in this DBGrid match(es) the chosen Exam Study topic

Accessing a Particular Type of Database

Visual Basic itself is not a DBMS. However, Visual Basic is set up to use the Microsoft Jet Engine for database access. The Jet Engine is the same collection of objects that Microsoft Access uses to interface with databases.

▶ **See** "Visual Basic, the Jet Engine, and Data Access Libraries," **p. 477**

Though the Jet Engine's default database format is, of course Microsoft Access, it can also provide a connection to a staggeringly large number of database formats through two systems of drivers: Installable ISAM drivers and ODBC.

The difference in a program for database access is very minimal, as long as you stick to "vanilla" types of data access. The main thing you, as a developer, would have to do differently would be to change the Data Control's Connect property.

Microsoft Access with the Jet Engine

This is the preferred data connection for Visual Basic. With a Microsoft Access connection through the Jet Engine, you have the full capability of everything we have discussed in this chapter.

To set your Data Control to a Microsoft Access connection, you need to do—nothing. The Data Control's Connect property is

```
Access
```

by default.

Your Visual Basic program will then make calls to the Jet Engine, which will, in turn, talk to the data in the Access database.

Installable ISAM Drivers

The Jet Engine also recognizes Installable ISAM drivers. These are typically non-client-server database systems. In other words, they perform their operations on the local workstation. Data may reside in a remote location (a non-local server), but all processing, including underlying data retrieval and storage operations, happens locally.

Part
IV

Ch
12

VB automatically recognizes Installable ISAM drivers available on your system and gives you a list of these drivers at design-time.

All you have to do to connect to data with one of these drivers is to change the Data Control's Connect property. You would perform the following steps:

1. Click the Data Control on your Form to make sure that it's the currently selected control.

2. Press F4 to see the Data Control's properties.

3. Scroll to the Connect property and click it to make it the current property.

4. Click the List Box icon (down arrow) to the right of the Connect property. You will see a scrolling list of available Installable ISAM drivers.

5. Pick out one of the Installable ISAM drivers.

Your Visual Basic program will then make calls to the Jet Engine, which will use the Installable ISAM driver which will, in turn, talk to the data in the underlying database.

Tip

The Data Control's DatabaseName property for many types of databases will not be a file name as it is for Microsoft Access databases, but rather a directory.

The reason for the difference is that Access stores all of a database's tables in a single file with an MDB extension. Therefore, the entire database is in a single file. Many other DBMS's (such as Dbase, Paradox, and many SQL databases) store each table's information in a separate file. Therefore, the entire database for these DBMS's is the directory where the individual table files reside.

When you set the DatabaseName property for such DBMS's, you should still select an individual file, but you need to make sure the file name isn't included in the resulting string as it appears in the Properties Window.

The available installable ISAM drivers that you will see in the Connect property include:

- ◆ Access
- ◆ Various versions of Dbase
- ◆ Various versions of Excel
- ◆ Various versions of FoxPro
- ◆ Various versions of Lotus 1-2-3
- ◆ Various versions of Paradox
- ◆ A read-only text file driver

 Note   Refer to figure 12.1 for a view of the Connect property's list of available ISAM drivers. ▪

ODBC

ODBC, or Open DataBase Connectivity, is a protocol for data driver interfaces. In other words, these are the rules a DBMS vendor can follow to write drivers to connect data in their DBMS to other vendors' software.

Microsoft provides you with an ODBC manager, which is a layer of software that knows how to negotiate between the vendor-supplied ODBC drivers and a Microsoft data interface, such as the Jet Engine.

To use ODBC as a Visual Basic programmer, you only have to know about a Data Source Name. The Data Source Name, or DSN, is a named entity that you or a database administrator have previously set up for the user. The Data Source Name represents information about the type of ODBC driver you are going to use for a particular application and possibly also about the actual name and location of the underlying data.

 Note   You can set up a DSN manually on an individual system using the ODBC icon in the Control Panel. ▪

A Data Control application that uses ODBC will look just like an application that uses Access or Installable ISAMs, except for its Connect property. A typical, simple Connect property for an ODBC connection would look like this:

ODBC;DSN=Company;

You might also want to specify other connection information, such as logins for remote data as in this example:

ODBC;DSN=Company;UID=EMP05;PWD=rutabaga;

(UID, in case you hadn't figured it out, is "User ID" and PWD is "Password.")

Notice that the ODBC connect string holds multiple fields, and each field terminates in a semicolon. The first element of an ODBC connect string must always be:

ODBC;

To enable a Data Control in your application for an ODBC DSN, you would perform the following steps:

1. Check the ODBC or ODBC32 icon in the Windows Control Panel to make sure of the Data Source Name you want to use.

2. Click Data Control on your Form to make sure that it's the currently selected control.

3. Press F4 to see the Data Control's properties.

4. Scroll to the Connect property and click it to make it the current property.

5. Type the appropriate ODBC connect string, as we discussed earlier in this section.

Your Visual Basic program will then make calls to the Jet Engine, which will call the ODBC manager, which will use the specific ODBC driver, which will, in turn, talk to the data in the underlying database.

Tip

If an ODBC DSN contains specific information about where your data base is located, you don't need to fill in the DatabaseName property of a Data Control which uses that DSN.

Taking the Disc Test

If you have read and understood the material in the chapter, you are ready to test your knowledge. Insert the CD-ROM that comes with this book and run the self-test software as described in Appendix H, "Using the CD-ROM."

From Here...

Many, if not most, of the Data Control's methods and properties apply directly to the Recordset of the Data Access Object, which we will cover in the next chapter.

Part
IV

Ch
12

13

Using Data Access Objects

Data Access Objects (DAO) provide you with more direct access to data than the Data Control does. Because both the DAO and the Data Control use the same data access engine, you can leverage your knowledge and experience with the Data Control to provide a basis for learning about the DAO.

Terms and concepts covered in this chapter include:

- ◆ **Comparing Data Access Objects with the Data Control**
- ◆ **The Jet Data Access Engine**
- ◆ **Data Access Libraries**
- ◆ **The DAO Object Hierarchy**
- ◆ **The DBEngine Object and Workspaces Collection**
- ◆ **The Database Object**

- ◆ **The Recordset Object**
- ◆ **Dynaset-type Recordsets**
- ◆ **Table-type Recordsets**
- ◆ **Snapshot-type Recordsets**
- ◆ **Manipulating and Navigating a Recordset**
- ◆ **Transactions**
- ◆ **SQL (Structured Query Language)**
- ◆ **SQL JOIN Statements**
- ◆ **SQL Pass-through**
- ◆ **Record Locking with Multi-User Databases**

Comparing Data Access Objects with the Data Control

The *Data Control* provides a visible, easy-to-program interface to the Jet Engine.

Data Access Objects (DAO) provide a more direct connection to the Jet Engine for the programmer. The advantages of the DAO over the Data Control are:

- ◆ Greater efficiency and speed in accessing data
- ◆ Greater data access flexibility and versatility

The disadvantages of the DAO compared with the Data Control are:

- ◆ More detailed and involved to program
- ◆ The code can be too DBMS-specific (especially when using SQL pass-through) and therefore won't be as portable if your application needs to be converted to a different data access method in the future.

Visual Basic, the Jet Engine, and the Data Access Libraries

Visual Basic uses the same Microsoft Jet Engine that Microsoft Access uses to interface with databases. The data access objects that provide a programming interface to the Jet Engine are found in the DAO Object Libraries, a collection of Dynamic-Link Library (DLL) files. These libraries are listed in the following section.

The Data Control itself is simply a programmer-friendly wrapper for the DAO. When you use the Data Control, the details of which DAO Object Library you will use and how you will connect to those libraries are taken care of automatically by VB.

When you use the DAO, you must be more aware as a programmer of which library you are using and of the presence of these objects in your application. The following section details some of the added concerns you will have when using the DAO.

Setting a Reference to a Type Library

If you want to use the DAO in your application, you must choose one of the following DAO object libraries:

◆ *DAO 2.5 Object Library.* Used by 16-bit VB and by earlier versions of VB. Use this library if you're maintaining an application which you need to compile as both a 16- and a 32-bit application, because the 32-bit version of VB can use the 16-bit library.

◆ *DAO 3.0 Object Library.* Used by 32-bit VB. Use this library if you're maintaining an application only for 32-bit platforms. It will provide more efficiency, stability, and forward compatibility than the 2.5 Object Library. In addition, the 3.0 library is multithreaded.

Part

IV

Ch

13

◆ *DAO 2.5/3.0 Compatibility Layer.* Used by 32-bit VB to provide an interface with older versions of the DAO (2.5 and below). Use this library if you're converting data access applications written in earlier versions of VB to a 32-bit platform.

In order to choose a DAO Object Library, you should execute the following steps in the VB design environment (see fig. 13.1):

1. From the main menu choose Tools, References.

2. In the Available References list, locate the desired DAO object library.

3. Select the object library by checking the box to the left of the library name.

4. Click OK.

Caution

Only use the Compatibility layer when absolutely necessary. You should use the 3.0 Library whenever possible, because future versions of VB may not support the older features of the Compatibility Layer.

You can avoid using the Compatibility Layer in older applications converted to exclusively 32-bit applications by re-writing 2.5-specific code when you convert (see the accompanying Note in this section).

Tip

Programmers who are new to the DAO in VB 4.0 may encounter the compiler error message "Unknown type" when they try to use the DAO object variable declarations in their code. This message occurs because the programmer hasn't set a reference to one of the DAO object libraries (to learn how to set a reference to a DAO object library, see the previous instructions).

FIG. 13.1 ⇒
Choose a DAO
Object Library
from the Refer-
ences dialog box
accessed from the
Tools menu.

Available DAO
Object Libraries

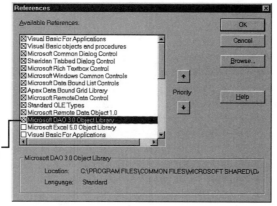

The DBEngine Object

Whenever you set a reference to one of the DAO Object libraries in
your application, the application automatically contains a DBEngine
object. DBEngine represents the programming interface to the entire
DAO Object library and contains within itself all other Data Access
objects.

Understanding the Database Object Hierarchy

The following schematic diagram illustrates the hierarchy of objects
underneath the DBEngine object. The use of "…" after the name of an
object type indicates that more than one of these objects can exist (note
that all such multiple objects belong to collections).

DBEngine

Workspaces collection

Workspace object …

Users collection

User object ...

Groups collection

Group object ...

Database collection

Database Object ...

QueryDefs Collection

TableDefs Collection

Recordsets Collection

Recordset Object ...

Fields Collection

Field Object ...

Indexes Collection

Index Object ...

The Default Workspace and the Workspaces Collection

A Workspace object represents a set of security permissions and a transaction space. The Workspaces collection belongs directly to the DBEngine object. By default the Workspaces collection always contains a single Workspace object element known as Workspaces(0).

You normally won't need more than one Workspace object in a single application, so you may not need to add a Workspace object to the Workspaces collection (recall that you already have one element by default). If you need to have more than one Workspace object in an application, you can refer to the various objects by their position in the Workspaces collection. The index of the Workspaces collection is zero-based, so the default first Workspace object can be referred to by its name of Workspaces(0).

If you only plan to use one Workspace object in your application, you need not reference it explicitly in code. For example, to open a database, the full syntax is:

```
Set db = DBEngine.Workspaces(0).OpenDataBase("Nwind.MDB")
```

You may omit the reference to DBEngine and Workspaces(0) throughout your application. The above statement would then read:

```
Set db = OpenDataBase("Nwind.MDB")
```

A Workspace object contains three types of collection:

- ◆ A Users collection, each of whose User elements contains information about the permissions of an individual user defined for the Workspace.

- ◆ A Groups collection, each of whose Group elements contains information about a user group defined for the Workspace.

- ◆ A Databases collection, each of whose Database objects encapsulates all the information and functionality of a single open database.

Database Objects and the Databases Collection

The role of a Database object in the DAO may be compared with the function of a Data Control. Like the Data Control, a Database object has a Connect property (the Connect property can be left blank if the default Access connection is in force). The Database object also has a Name property which, like the Data Control's DatabaseName property, contains the name of the physical database to which it is connected. Most likely, you'll be setting these properties through the OpenDatabase method discussed below.

Unlike the DAO's DBEngine object and Workspaces(0), there is no default Database object in an application using the DAO. You must declare a Database object variable and you must use the Workspace object's OpenDatabase method. The OpenDatabase method sets a reference to a specified database object and also opens the database.

Note the following syntax:

```
'declare a Database object variable
Public ObjVarName as Database

'set a reference to the Database object variable
Set ObjVarName = DbEngine.Workspace(0).OpenDatabase(
dbname[,Exclusive[,ReadOnly[, Source]]])
```

The syntax for the OpenDatabase method includes four parameters that correspond to various properties of the Data Control:

◆ *dbname* is a string expression that represents the location and name of a database file or registered ODBC data source name. If the filename includes an extension, it is required. You can also specify a network path if your network supports it. For example:

   "\\SERVERNAME\HRSHARE\EMPDIR\
   EMPLOYEES.MDB"

   If dbname refers to a database that is already open for exclusive access by another user, an error occurs. If it does not refer to an existing database or valid ODBC data source name, an error occurs.

◆ *Exclusive* is a Boolean indicating whether the Database is being opened for Exclusive access. The default is False.

◆ *ReadOnly* is a Boolean indicating whether the Database is being opened for read-only access. The default is False.

◆ *Source* corresponds to the Connect property of the Data Control. It is required for non-Access data connections. It should contain the name of an installable ISAM driver or of an ODBC data source name.

Examples:

The first example opens an Access database with read-only access. Note the last parameter, Source, is not required for an Access-type database:

```
Public db as Database
Set db =
DBEngine.Workspaces(0).OpenDatabase("C:\EmpInfo\Employees.MDB",,
True)
'-OR-
Set db = OpenDatabase("C:\EmpInfo\Employees.MDB",, True)
```

The second example opens a dBase III database. Because dBase stores
the tables of a database in separate (.DBF) files, the directory where all
table files reside is referenced for the dbname parameter and not a single
database file:

```
Public db as Database
Set db = DBEngine.Workspaces(0).OpenDatabase("C:\EmpInfo\", ,
, "dBase III;")
'-OR-
Set db = OpenDatabase("C:\EmpInfo\", , , "dBase III;")
```

Because DBEngine is always present in a DAO application, and because
Workspaces(0) is the default Workspace, you don't need to refer to
DBEngine Workspaces(0) in code. They are implicitly referenced.

You can access all the open databases in a Workspace with the
Workspace's Databases collection. The following example fills a Listbox
control with the names of the open databases in Workspace(0) (the default Workspace):

```
Dim db as Database
lstDB.Clear
For Each db in Workspaces(0).Databases
    lstDB.AddItem db.Name
Next db
```

Note We will not explicitly refer to DBEngine Workspaces(0) in the
rest of the examples in this chapter. However, if you're planning on database activities that require or encourage the use of multiple
Workspaces, like adding multiple security levels or asynchronous transactions, it might be a good idea to refer explicitly to Workspaces(0) in your
code. Then there would be no ambiguity or confusion when you later add
other Workspaces to the application. ■

Unlike the Data Control, a Database object can reference multiple
Recordset objects.

These Recordset objects are members of the Database object's Recordsets collection. You can open a new Recordset in the Database object's Recordsets collection with the Database object's OpenRecordset method, which we discuss in the next section.

Recordset Objects and the Recordsets Collection

A Recordset is the most important object of the Data Access Objects. A Recordset represents the collection of records in a specific table or SQL query result set from the database. The Recordset's properties and methods are the primary vehicle a programmer uses to manipulate and interrogate data.

There are three Recordset types—Dynaset, Table, and Snapshot. Each of the Recordset types provides its own type of functionality and behavior, which you can select among depending on your specific needs.

▶ **See** "The Recordset," **p. 411**

To open a Recordset, you must decide the type of Recordset you want and you must declare a Recordset variable that will hold the Recordset. Because a Recordset is contained by a database, you open a Recordset with the Database object's OpenRecordset method. The syntax for the OpenRecordset method is:

```
Set RecordsetName = DatabaseName.OpenRecordset(expr,type,
➥options)
```

where *expr* is a string representing either a table name of the Database or a valid SQL Select statement for the Database.

▶ **See** "Using SQL Queries," **p. 500**

The *type* argument specifies whether the Recordset is a Dynaset, Snapshot, or Table, and the *options* argument can combine one or more internal VB constants to affect the behavior of the Recordset. The *type* and *options* arguments are optional. If you don't specify *type*, then the Recordset's type will be:

◆ Table if *expr* is a single table name

◆ Dynaset if *expr* is a SQL Select statement

If you wish to specify the type of Recordset to open in the *type* argument, the internal VB constants are:

◆ vbOpenTable

◆ vbOpenDynaset

◆ vbOpenSnapshot

For Table, Dynaset, and Snapshot-type Recordsets, respectively.

▶ **See** "Choosing the Right Options on the Recordset," **p. 487**

To illustrate the use of the OpenRecordset method, we might open the Nwind Database's Employees table in a Recordset with the following statement:

```
[in General Declarations section of a Form or Standard Module]
Public db as Database
Public rsEmployees as Recordset
[somewhere in code]
Set db = db.OpenDatabase("C:\VB40\NWIND.MDB")
Set rsEmployees = db.OpenRecordset("Employees")
```

If you want rsEmployees to be a Dynaset-type Recordset, replace the last line in the previous example with:

```
Set rsEmployees = db.OpenRecordset("Employees", dbOpenDynaset)
```

Note Visual Basic 4.0 still supports the obsolete DAO 2.5 objects Dynaset and Snapshot as well as the corresponding CreateDynaset and CreateSnapshot methods on Database objects, as well as the obsolete OpenTable method (the TableDef object is not considered obsolete). However, Microsoft recommends that you not use these features in new VB 4.0 programs and that you convert these older features to the DAO 3.0 features discussed in this section when you convert VB 3.0 programs to VB 4.0. Future version of VB may not support these obsolete features. ■

The Recordset object behaves like the Recordset of the Data Control. In general, the methods and properties of the Recordset Object in the DAO are the same as those of the Data Control's Recordset. You can assign a Recordset object variable to a Data Control's Recordset. For example, the Dynaset-type Recordset variable rsEmployees could be assigned to the Recordset of the Data1 data control with the following lines of code:

```
Set datEmployees.Recordset = rsEmployees
datEmployees.Refresh
```

Notice the use of the Refresh method, so that the Data Control can properly display the data. You also can assign a Data Control's Recordset to a Recordset variable which has already been declared. For example, assigning the Recordset of the Data Control named datEmployees to the rsEmployees Recordset would require the following line of code:

```
Set rsEmployees = datEmployees.Recordset
```

Each Recordset object contains a Fields collection. Each Field object in the Fields collection has Name, Value, Type, and Size properties as well as numerous other properties mentioned in Microsoft's online and printed documentation. The Fields object in the Fields collection contains information about a specific field of the Recordset. You could loop through the Fields collection for a Recordset with code similar to that in the following example:

```
Dim fldTemp As Field
For Each fldTemp in rsEMployees.Fields
    Me.Print fldTemp.Name
    Me.Print "  " & fldTemp.Value 'value in current record
    Me.Print "  " & fldTemp.Type
    Me.Print "  " & fldTemp.Size
Next fldTemp
```

Because the Recordsets of a Database are contained in a Recordsets collection, it's possible to write nested loops to traverse each Recordset in a Database and in turn traverse each Field in the Fields collection of each Recordset. Both a Recordset and a Field object have a Name property, which is useful in displaying general information. A nested looping example for the Recordsets collection of a Database might look like this:

```
Dim rsTemp As Recordset
Dim fldTemp As Field
For Each rsTemp in db.Recordsets
    Me.Print rsTemp.Name
    For Each fldTemp in rsTemp.Fields
            Me.Print "   " & fldTemp.Name
    Next fldTemp
Next rsTemp
```

Choosing the Right Options on the Recordset

You can specify one or more options in the optional third argument of the database object's OpenRecordset method. These options modify the behavior of the Recordset, typically restricting the use of the Recordset in some way. Some of the more commonly used options are:

◆ *dbAppendOnly*. Use with a Dynaset-type Recordset if you only need to append new records without traversing existing records. This enables the local system to use less resources in tracking existing records.

◆ *dbForwardOnly*. You can use this option on a Snapshot-type Recordset to restrict movement through the Recordset to a forward direction only. The advantage of such an option is that the local system doesn't have to spend as much resources tracking all records and can discard each record once it's been traversed. A good use of this feature would be in a client/server environment. The drawbacks are severe, however, because you can only move forward in the data, and then only with the MoveNext method. You can use this option when you need to perform a one-time-only pass through the data.

◆ *dbDenyRead*. Open a Table-type Recordset without enabling other users to view it.

◆ *dbDenyWrite*. Open a Recordset and deny other users the ability to write.

◆ *dbReadOnly*. Open a Recordset without the ability to change data (other users may have write privileges, however).

◆ *dbSqlPassThrough*. When opening a Dynaset-Type Recordset on an ODBC data source, you can bypass VB's query compiler and pass the query directly to the underlying DBMS.

Part
IV

Ch

13

▶ **See** "When to Use SQL Pass-Through," **p. 507**

If you wish to have more than one of these options on a Recordset, you may concatenate them. For instance, a Recordset with DenyWrite privileges both to other users and the current user might read as follows:

```
Set rsEmployees = dbOpenRecordset("Employees", _
    dbOpenTable, dbDenyRead + dbReadOnly)
```

Note   See Microsoft's online and printed help on the OpenRecordset method for a discussion of other options. ■

Recordset Properties Showing Record Count and Position

You can use the RecordCount property to indicate the number of records in a Recordset. Because it actually indicates number of records *accessed* during this session, it won't accurately reflect the number of records in a Dynaset or Snapshot until you call the MoveLast method. It's always accurate for a Table-type Recordset.

AbsolutePosition represents how many records the record pointer is beyond the first record (record 0) of a Recordset. PercentPosition is a number between 0 and 100 representing the proportional distance of the record pointer from the beginning of the Recordset.

▶ **See** "The Recordset's RecordCount Property," **p. 440**

▶ **See** "The Recordset's AbsolutePosition Property," **p. 441**

▶ **See** "The Recordset's PercentPosition Property," **p. 442**

Navigating Through a Recordset

The Recordset's five most common methods that enable you to programmatically position the record pointer are:

◆ *Move.* This method takes a positive or negative Long value as a required parameter. The parameter specifies the number of records to move away from the current record pointer position. Positive values indicate forward movement, while negative values indicate backwards movement. An optional second parameter enables you to specify the Bookmark of a different record. Specifying this second parameter causes the movement to happen relative to the record of the Bookmark.

▶ **See** "The Recordset's Bookmark Property," **p. 428**

◆ *MoveFirst.* Moves the record pointer to the first row of the Recordset's data.

◆ *MoveLast.* Moves the record pointer to the last row of the Recordset's data.

◆ *MoveNext.* Moves the record pointer one row beyond its current position in the Recordset.

◆ *MovePrevious.* Moves the record pointer one row before its current position in the Recordset.

You might call these methods to programmatically process records, or you might call them in response to some user action, such as clicking buttons labeled Next, Previous, First, or Last.

It's posssible to move the record pointer too far (that is, past the beginning or end of the Recordset) with the MoveNext and MovePrevious methods. In order to help you avoid this problem, every Recordset has "buffer records" just before its first row and just after its last row. When you move the record pointer onto one of the beginning or ending buffer records, no error happened but the Recordset's Boolean property BOF (Beginning-of-file) or EOF (End-of-file) becomes True.

You should always test for BOF immediately after calling the MovePrevious method and for EOF after every call to MoveNext. The following two examples present code that you might put in the Click event procedures for Next and Previous CommandButtons (notice the call to ReadFromData, a procedure the programmer has written to populate controls with field data from the Recordset's copy buffer):

```
Private Sub cmdNext_Click()
    rsEmployees.MoveNext
    If rsEmployees.EOF Then
            rsEmployees.MoveLast
    EndIf
    ReadFromData
End Sub
```

Part

IV

Ch

13

```
Private Sub cmdPrevious_Click()
    rsEmployees.MovePrevious
    If rsEmployees.BOF Then
            rsEmployees.MoveFirst
    EndIf
    ReadFromData
End Sub
```

If you programmatically loop through a Recordset, you must also check for the EOF property. You can perform this type of navigation by writing a loop which keeps advancing the record pointer with MoveNext until EOF is True. An example of a Record-processing loop might look like the following code:

```
rsEmployees.MoveFirst
Do Until rsEmployees.EOF
    '...some code to process a record
    rsEmployees.MoveNext
Loop
```

Using Other Recordset Methods

The most direct manipulation of data with Data Access Objects takes place through the Recordset. The methods for the DAO's Recordset Object are basically the same as the methods for the Data Control's Recordset Object. You may therefore read the sections on the specific Recordset Methods as applying to both the Recordset of the Data Access Objects and the Data Control's Recordset. Notice that the technique for adding a record is significantly different between the DAO and the Data Control.

There is no explicit binding of controls to the data as there is with the Data Control. Because Data Access objects lack this automatic binding of controls to data, the programmer must refresh controls in code whenever any action happens which would move the record pointer or otherwise change the contents of the fields.

▶ **See** "Binding Other Controls to the Data Control," **p. 406**

Similarly, the programmer must explicitly move data from controls to the copy buffer whenever data should be saved.

Because a data access program must perform these two tasks so often, it is most efficient for the programmer to provide one routine to read data from the copy buffer into controls and another routine to write data from controls into the copy buffer. The program can then call these routines whenever it needs to perform these tasks.

The following two sections, "Programmatically Reading a Record into VB Controls" and "Programmatically Writing VB Controls to a Record," describe how you can write routines to manually refresh data in both directions (reading and writing) when you use the DAO.

Programmatically Reading a Record into VB Controls

As mentioned in the previous section, there is no automatic binding of controls between the underlying data and controls when using the DAO. This means that you must programmatically "bind" data to controls. In this section, we discuss how to programmatically populate controls with underlying data from the current record, and in the following section we discuss how to write data back from controls to the underlying data.

You can assign data to controls on a field-by-field basis, assigning one field's contents to a control. There are several ways to refer to a field's contents in a Recordset:

syntax:	RecordsetName![FieldName]
example:	rs![First Name]

The previous syntax provides quick and explicit data access (the field name is actually compiled into your code) but it is also the least flexible method, because there would be no way to change the field name at run time. Notice that the square brackets are required if the field name contains a space(s).

syntax:	*RecordsetName(FieldNameString)*
example:	rs("First Name")

This syntax provides greater flexibility than the previous method, because you could use a variable name for the field name string at run time and thus change the contents of the variable. However, the run-time engine must do more interpreting, so this method is also slower.

syntax: *RecordsetName*.Fields(*FieldIndex*).Value

example: rs.Fields(0).Value

The previous syntax uses FieldIndex, an integer representing one of the fields in the Recordset's Fields collection. A great advantage here is that you don't have to know a field's name to access its contents in a particular row. On the other hand, you must know the position of the field you want in the Fields collection. This method is most useful when you're traversing all the fields in a record.

Unless there is a need for flexibility at run time, the first method is probably the best to use, because it's fast and explicitly identifies the field you want to access. For example, if you wish to read the contents of the current record's Last Name field into the text property of txtLastName, the line would look like:

txtLastName.Text = rsEmployees![Last Name] & ""

Remember, the Text property of a TextBox control does not accept null data. The use of the final characters & "" at the end of the line ensures that, even if the underlying field contains null data, an error will not occur. The & "" makes sure that at least a blank string is contained in the data being written to the TextBox.

Typically, you'll write a procedure to populate controls with field contents from a Recordset. You'll call such a routine from every place in your application which potentially updates the record pointer.

```
Sub PlaceDataInControls()
    txtFirstName.Text = rsEmployees![First Name] & ""
    txtLastName.Text = rsEmployees![Last Name] & ""
    txtDepartment.Text = rsEmployees!Department & ""
    txtPhoneExt.Text = rsEmployees!PhoneExt & ""
    chkFullTime.Value = rsEmployees![Full Time]
End Sub
```

Programmatically Writing VB Controls to a Record
When the user makes changes to controls you want to save to the underlying data, you must programmatically write the contents a control back to the underlying data in two steps:

1. Write the contents of each control to its corresponding field in the copy buffer.

2. Save the contents of the copy buffer to the underlying data of the Recordset.

To update a field in the copy buffer with a control's contents, you might code:

> *RecordsetName![FieldName]* = *ControlContents*

For example, if we wished to write the Last Name field of rsEmployees which we read in the last section, we could write:

> rsEmployees![Last Name] = txtLastName.Text

You would typically write a procedure to write controls to their corresponding fields, with one line of code similar to the previous example for each control-field assignment. You could call this procedure as the first step in saving data from controls in the Recordset's underlying data.

The second phase of writing to a record requires the use of the Recordset's Update method in tandem with the Edit or AddNew method. This phase is discussed in the following section "Updating a Record."

Updating a Record

In order to write the contents of a DAO Recordset Object's copy buffer to its underlying data, you must follow three steps:

1. Have previously called the Edit (or AddNew) method of the Recordset.

2. Write to each field in the copy buffer.

3. Call the Recordset's Update method. After calling the Update method, the record pointer usually moves off the record just written. To keep the record pointer on the row just written, you should set the Recordset's Bookmark property to its LastModified property.

Part

IV

Ch

13

The following example illustrates using the three steps in updating a record. To review the purpose of the WriteEmployeeRecord procedure, refer to the section "Programmatically Writing VB Controls to a Record."

```
Sub UpdateRecord
    rsEmployees.Edit        'step 1: call the Edit method
    WriteEmployeeRecord     'step 2: write controls to buffer
    rsEmployees.Update      'step 3: call the Update method
    rsEmployees.Bookmark = rsEmployees.LastModified
End Sub

Sub WriteEmployeeRecord()
    rsEmployees![First Name] = txtFirstName.Text
    rsEmployees![Last Name] = txtLastName.Text
    rsEmployees!Department = txtDepartment.Text
    rsEmployees!PhoneExt = txtPhoneExt.Text
    rsEmployee![Full Time]= chkFullTime.Value
End Sub
```

Notice that you might decide to call the Edit method in a separate procedure, long before you actually write the record.

Using the Update method will produce a run-time error if:

Another user has the record locked. You can check the Updatable property of the Recordset to determine this.

The value of the Recordset's EditMode property is dbEditNone. The other values of EditMode are dbEditAdd and dbEditInProgress which are set by calling the Recordset's AddNew and Edit methods, respecitvely.

▶ **See** "Adding a Record," **p. 495**

▶ **See** "The Edit Method and Pessimistic Locking," **p. 510**

You can protect against these possible errors when calling the Update method by writing code as in the following example:

```
Sub UpdateRecord()
    If rsEmployee.Updatable Then            'Record available?
        If rsEmployees.dbEditNone Then      'Edit/Addnew called?
        rsEmployees.Edit                    'if not, call Edit
        End If
        WriteEmployeeRecord   'call procedure that writes
        ➥controls to buffer
        rsEmployees.Update
```

```
            rsEmployees.Bookmark = rsEmployees.LastModified
        Else
            MsgBox "Record unavailable for update"
        End If
    End Sub
```

In a fully developed application, you also need to trap for possible run-time errors caused by the calls to the Edit and Update methods.

▶ **See** "Locking Example," **p. 511**

Canceling User Changes Before They're Saved

To enable the user or your code to cancel pending changes that the user has made to controls and that haven't been written yet to the underlying data, you can call the CancelUpdate method and then simply call whatever procedure you've written to programmatically refresh controls with the data from the current record. This will cause the controls to reflect the existing state of the field in the record buffer and will therefore overwrite any changes the user has made to controls.

You should only call CancelUpdate if the Edit or AddNew method has previously been called. You can check to see if Edit or AddNew has been called by checking the Recordset's EditMode property. If it's value is dbEditNone, no Edit or Add is pending and you should not call the CancelUpdate method.

The code in a Cancel button's click event procedure might look like this:

```
    Private Sub cmdCancel_Click()
       If rsEmployees.EditMode <> dbEditNone Then
        rsEmployees.CancelUpdate
       End If
       PlaceDataInControls    'General procedure to populate
       ➥controls from current record
    End Sub
```

Adding a Record

You must perform four steps to add a new record to a DAO Recordset object:

1. Set the controls to blank or default values. Now, allow the user to add new data to the controls.

2. When the user is ready to save the new data, invoke the Recordset's AddNew method, which will append a blank record to the Recordset and position the record pointer at this blank record.

3. Write the data from the controls to the Recordset's copy buffer.

4. Invoke the Update method to move the new data from the copy buffer to the underlying data.

Notice that the last two steps are the same steps discussed for saving data in general in the sections "Programmatically Writing VB Controls to a Record" and "Updating a Record."

The code to implement these four steps might be contained in the click event procedures for buttons with captions such a as Add and Save New. The following code provides an example of how to add a new record:

```
Private Sub cmdAdd_Click()
    cmdSaveNew.Enabled = True
    txtLastName = ""
    txtSalary = "0"
    txtFirstName = ""
End Sub

Private Sub cmdSaveNew_Click()
    rsEmployees.AddNew
    WriteControlsToData 'our routine to update copy buffer
    rsEmployees.Update
    rsEmployees.BookMark = rsEmployees.LastModified
    cmdSaveNew.Enabled = False
End Sub
```

Caution
The timing of your calls to the DAO Recordset's AddNew method might differ from the timing of your call to a Data Control Recordset's AddNew method. Whereas you might call the Data Control Recordset's AddNew method as soon as the user decides to add a record, you probably don't want to call the DAO Recordset's AddNew method until it's time to save the edited data for the new record. It just doesn't make sense to allocate resources or force locking before you need to.

In order to enable the user to cancel adding a record while the user is editing fields, all you need to do is call the routine that refreshes controls from the copy buffer fields.

Deleting a Record

The Recordset's Delete method will delete a record from the underlying data. Typically, you'll want to take the record pointer to a different record after calling the Delete method. Before moving the record pointer you should check the RecordCount property to make sure that at least one record is left in the Recordset.

After moving the record pointer, of course you'll need to check the Recordset's EOF property to make sure you haven't moved beyond the end of the data. If you have, you'll want to call the MoveLast method. The code for these operations might look like the following example:

```
Private Sub cmdDelete_Click()
    rsEmployees.Delete
    If rsEmployees.RecordCount > 0 Then
            rsEmployees.MoveNext
            If rsEmployees.EOF Then
                    rs.Employees.MoveLast
            EndIf
    Else
            cmdDelete.Enabled = False
    EndIf
End Sub
```

Other Objects in the Database Object Hierarchy

Although the Recordset object is the most important object in the DAO 3.0 object hierarchy, there are several other object class types and collections that belong to the DAO's database object hierarchy:

◆ *The TableDef object and the TableDefs collection.* A TableDef object contains information about physical tables in the underlying database upon which the Database object is based. The TableDefs colleciton is the collection of all the TableDef objects contained in a particular database. TalbeDefs objects in turn contain Fields and Indexes collections. The individual Field and Index objects in each of these collections has a Name property and other properties that can be used for informational purposes.

◆ *The QueryDef object and the QueryDefs collection.* Only Microsoft Access databases support the QueryDefs object. A QueryDef object can point to a named query in the underlying Access database or can represent an on-the-fly query constructed at runtime in your code.

◆ *The Relation object and the Relations collection.* Each Relation object describes a relation defined between two tables in the underlying database. Relations can be defined on-the-fly in your code, but they can only be stored in Microsoft Access databases.

◆ *The Container object and the Containers collection.* The Containers collection holds information about all objects in a Database object's hierarchy.

Using Transactions

A transaction is a set of actions performed on your data that you wish to consider as a logical group. You need the concept of a transaction so that all the changes made by a group of actions can stand or fall together. This promotes better data integrity of your system.

A transaction is necessary when a given change (say, the deletion of a customer) doesn't make sense without another change (the deletion of all the orders belonging to that customer). If for any reason one of the changes doesn't takes place (the server goes down in the midst of writing the changes or the user changes his or her mind), then the entire set of changes should be canceled.

In VB, transactions are methods that belong to the Workspace object. The BeginTrans method signals that a transaction has begun and it is issued before any changes to the data. You end a transaction either by writing all changes with the CommitTrans method or canceling all changes with the Rollback method. The three transaction methods are described as follows:

◆ The BeginTrans method defines the start of a transaction. All actions performed on data in the Workspace will be buffered until the transaction is closed by one of the other two transaction methods.

◆ The CommitTrans method on the Workspace writes all buffered changes because the most recent BeginTrans method was called and terminates the transaction begun with the most recent BeginTrans method.

◆ The Rollback method cancels the transaction begun with the most recent BeginTrans method and discards all actions stored in the transaction's buffer.

▶ **See** "Programming Multi-User Applications," **p. 508**

Because the transaction methods belong to the Workspace object, you don't need to specify the Workspace object when calling the transaction methods if you're calling the transaction methods for the default Workspace. You therefore type either

Workspaces(0).BeginTrans

or

BeginTrans

to initiate a transaction on the default Workspace.

In the following example, the Sub procedure FundsTransfer manipulates data in order to transfer funds between two accounts. We begin a transaction before manipulating any data. If there is an error anywhere in the data manipulation process, we call Rollback to cancel all changes. Otherwise, we call CommitTrans to save all changes:

```
Public Sub FundsTransfer
On Error GoTo Transfer_Error
BeginTrans
'Code to debit first account
```

Part

IV

Ch

13

```
'Code to credit second account
CommitTrans
Exit_Transfer:
Exit Sub
Transfer_Error:
    Rollback
    Resume Exit_Transfer
End Sub
```

You can have more than one transaction pending at the same time on a Workspace. This will work as long as you are careful to pair BeginTrans-CommitTrans/Rollback sequences together. These nested transactions will work because a CommitTrans or Rollback method only undoes the actions because the most recent pending BeginTrans method was called.

In the following example, the programmer has defined three nested transactions. Transaction A is the outer transaction, as its BeginTrans and CommitTrans methods contains the others. Transaction B contains Transaction C for the same reason. Notice which of the transactions each action belongs to:

```
BeginTrans'start of Transaction A
'...actions here are part of Transaction A
        BeginTrans'start of Transaction B
        '...actions here as part of  Transaction B
              BeginTrans'start of Transaction C
              '...actions here are part of Transaction C
              CommitTrans'end of Transaction C
      '...actions here are part of Transaction B
      CommitTrans'end of Transaction B
'...actions here are part of Transaction A
CommitTrans'end of Transaction A
```

You may nest transactions in this way up to five levels deep.

If you need to implement multiple transactions that aren't nested, you will need to open more than one Workspace in your application and define the un-nested transactions on different Workspaces.

Using SQL Queries

Structured Query Language (usually referred to as SQL) is the language you use to specify the data included in a Recordset. It can also provide you the vehicle for specifying changes to data through the Database object's Execute method.

You can use a SQL Select statement in the form of a string as the first argument to the Database object's OpenRecordset method when you wish to open either a Dynaset or Snapshot-type Recordset.

You also can use a SQL statement to update data and even modify database structure (such as table definitions and fields) when you pass such a statement in a string to the Database object's Execute method.

The following sections under this heading detail some of the more important features of a SQL Select statements.

In addition, the section "SQL Statements for Modifying Data and Data Structure" briefly details other types of SQL statements, which you would use with the Execute method of the Database object.

Writing Basic SQL Queries

A SQL Select statement provides a query that can be interpreted by a particular DBMS to retrieve particular data from its tables. The VB Jet Engine provides a common interface to all the DBMS's supported with installable ISAM drivers or ODBC so that you can use the same syntax for all SQL Select statements, regardless of the type of DBMS you are working with.

The most basic form of the SQL statement specifies columns (fields) to retrieve from one or more tables in the rows (records) of its result set. In VB terms, the result set will be the records of a Recordset object. The syntax for this most elementary SQL Select statement is:

Select *FieldList* From *TableName*

where *FieldList* is a comma-delimited list of field names existing in the specified table denoted by *TableName*. For example, you might specify a Recordset containing rows, each of whose contents represented the Last Name and First Name fields from the Employees table of the current database:

Select [First Name], [Last Name] From Employees

Part

IV

Ch

13

The square brackets [] around the field names are only necessary because the field names in the example contain spaces. You can also specify all fields from the table by using the ★ character instead of writing out all their names:

Select ★ From Employees

You would use a SQL statement such as this as the argument to the OpenRecordset method of a Database object, as in the following example:

Set rsEmployees = _

db.OpenRecordset("Select ★ From Employees")

Because the argument is a SQL Select statement rather than a simple table name, VB defaults the type of Recordset to be a Dynaset-type Recordset. You could also assign the text of the SQL Select statement to a string variable and then pass the variable as the first argument to the OpenRecordset method, as in the following example:

Dim strSQL As String

strSQL = _

"Select [First Name],[Last Name],Salary From Employees"

Set rsEmployees = db.OpenRecordset(strSQL, vbOpenSnapshot)

The advantage of this method is that it makes the line with the OpenRecordset method more readable and, more importantly, it enables you to possibly build the DQL statement in several steps in your code, thus permitting more complex logic to be used in your program to query data.

In addition to the basic SQL structure which specifies fields and a table, you may add a number of different types of clauses to the statement. Only the Where, Order By, and Join clauses are discussed here. You should be aware that other types of clause exist for SQL Select Queries.

Using the Where Clause to Filter Rows

You can use a Where clause in a SQL statement to filter which records are returned in the query's result set. The syntax of a SQL statement containing a Where clause would be:

Select FieldList From TableName Where Condition

The *Condition* of the Where clause can be one or more comparison statements using the usual comparison operators such as =, >, <, >=, <= as well as other operators more specific to the SQL language such as LIKE (for text comparisons) and BETWEEN...AND (for specifying a range of values).

A Where clause that only returns records with a field matching a particular value would use the = operator, as in the following example:

Select ★ From Employees Where Dependents = 0

A Where clause to return values above a certain value would use the > operator, as in the following example:

Select ★ From Employees Where Salary > 40,000

You would use similar rules for the <, =, <=, and >= operators.

Note that when quoting literal strings for comparison in a SQL Where clause, you use the single quote character, as in the following example:

Select ★ From Employees Where [Last Name] = 'Smith'

When using a literal date value in a Where clause comparison, you must use the U.S. date format (mm/dd/yy)—even when you're not looking at data with a U.S. date format. You must then set the date off with the # character. The following example illustrates the use of a date value in a SQL Where clause:

Select ★ from Employees Where [Hire Date] < #1/1/89#

You can use BETWEEN...AND to specify a range of values to allow in the result set, as in the following example, which would allow all employee records into the result set with salaries between 40,000 and 80,000 inclusive:

Select ★ From Employees Where Salary BETWEEN 40,000 AND 80,000

To obtain a text match with a field that contains a certain string combination (but does not exactly match the string), you may use the LIKE operator and specify "wild card" characters similar to Unix, DOS, or Windows operating system "wild card" characters as used in file specifications. Use the * character to specify any number of characters and the ? character to specify a single character. In the following example, we query for all records with a Last Name field beginning with the letter S:

Select * From Employees Where [Last Name] Like 'S*'

Note   The version of SQL in VB (known as "Jet SQL") uses different wildcard characters from the wildcard characters of standard SQL ("ANSI SQL"). In ANSI SQL, the single-character wildcard is the underscore _ and the multi-character wildcard is the % symbol. ■

String comparisons in Where clauses are not case-sensitive.

Using the Order By Clause to Logically Sort Rows

The Order By clause in a SQL Select statement will put the rows of the result set in a specified order. The Order By clause contains one field name, or several field names separated by commas. If there are several field names, then the major sort order starts with the first field name and works on down through the list of field names. The default sorting order for field names of any data type is Ascending (lowest to highest in numeric order and case-insensitive alphabetical order for strings). You can specify Descending order for any field in the Order By clause with the keyword DESC after the field name. In the following example, we order the employees by hire date (in descending order) and then by last name:

Select * From Employees Order By [Hire Date] DESC, [Last Name]

Although the default sorting order is Ascending order, you may specify Ascending order for clarity with the ASC keyword.

Using the Where Clause to Connect Tables

You can use the Where clause to bring data from more than one table into the result set of a query.

You may specify more than one table's data in the result set of a query by simply specifying the field names from each table and the table names in the basic syntax of the Select statement. However, you will always want to explicitly specify the relation between the tables with either a Where clause or a JOIN clause in order for the combination of the data from the two tables to be meaningful.

Let's say you'd like to see a list of ever order's date from an Orders table in our database along with the customer name for each order. Customer names are held in a Customers table and the Orders table contains a Customer ID field that keys to the Customer ID field in the Customers table. An example of a Select clause that would properly return the information we're seeking would read as follows:

Select [Order Date], [Company Name] From Orders, Customers

Where Orders.[Customer ID] = Customers.[Customer ID]

If it didn't include the Where clause, the Select statement would return a Cartesian product of the two tables—that is, it would match every record in Orders with every Customer and return a huge, meaningless result set! Note that we don't have to specify which table a field comes from as long as that field's name is unique within the tables we've specified in the From clause. If a field's name isn't unique within the tables used in the query, we specify its originating table with the tablename.fieldname syntax.

Dynaset-type Recordsets that are populated by a Where clause joining two or more tables are not updatable. If you want to be able to update a Dynaset-type Recordset that is based on more than one table, you will need to use one of the JOIN clauses as discussed in the next section.

Using JOIN Clauses to Connect Tables

If you wish to update records in a Dynaset-type Recordset based on information from more than one table, you will need to create the Recordset with a query using one of the JOIN clauses. There are two types of JOIN, and these two JOIN types are implemented by three different possible JOIN clause types. These types of JOIN and the clauses which implement them are:

◆ An *equi-join* or *inner join*. This type of join creates records in a result set only when there are matching records from both tables. You can use an INNER JOIN clause to create an equi-join.

◆ An *outer join*. Result sets create using this type of join contain all the records from a specified master table and only those records from a related lookup table which match the records in the master table. You can implement an outer join with either the LEFT JOIN or RIGHT JOIN clause. The difference between these two types of join is the order in which you specify the master and lookup tables.

To specify an equi-join between the Customers table and the Orders table, you write a query as in the following example:

Select [Company Name], [Order Date] From Customers
INNER JOIN Orders ON Customers.[Customer ID] =
Orders.[Customer ID]

The result set would contain only matching information from the Customers and Orders tables.

If you wished to display a list of Customers and the dates of their orders, but you wished to include even customers without any orders, you could specify this result set with a LEFT JOIN as in the following example:

Select [Company Name], [Order Date] From Customers LEFT
JOIN Orders ON Customers.[Customer ID] = Orders.[Customer
ID]

You could achieve the same effect with a RIGHT JOIN clause as follows:

Select [Company Name], [Order Date] From Orders RIGHT
JOIN Customers ON Orders.[Customer ID] =
Customers.[Customer ID]

When to Use SQL Pass-Through

Normally, VB uses the Jet Engine to compile an SQL query and then sends the compiled query to the underlying DBMS. A *pass-through query*, however, is not compiled by VB. Instead, VB sends the query directly to the server DBMS and lets the server compile and run the query.

There are various reasons for which you might want to use pass-through queries. These reasons break down into two main categories:

◆ You can get functionality not available in Jet SQL. Because VB doesn't compile the query, it doesn't require you to use syntax specific to Jet SQL. You can use non-standard SQL features recognized by the server, and you can execute stored procedures on the server.

◆ You can obtain better performance for action queries.

You use the dbSQLPassThrough constant as an option to specify a pass-through query when you call a Database object's OpenRecordset method or when you run a query with the Execute method.

When you use a pass-through query to open a Recordset, the Recordset must be a Snapshot. An example of a pass-through query in the OpenRecordset method might look like the following example:

Set rs = db.OpenRecordset _

(strSQL, dbOpenSnapshot, dbSqlPassThrough)

The variable strSQL in this case would contain the text of some SQL statement recognizable to the server or the proper server-specific syntax for invoking a stored procedure.

If the pass-through query you wish to execute is an action query and therefore doesn't return any results that you can store in a Recordset, then you'll use the Database object's Execute method, as in the following example:

db.Execute strActionSQL, dbSQLPassThrough

Part
IV

Ch
13

strActionSQL is in this case a string containing the SQL syntax for the action query on the server or the proper server-specific syntax for invoking a stored procedure.

Programming Multi-User Applications

Most data-aware business applications are multi-user applications. That is, they allow more than one user to access the same data at the same time. The two main issues you'll confront when programming a multi-user application are:

◆ *Where will the common data reside and be processed?* Often, you as developer have no direct control over decisions on questions of this type. For better or worse, administrators or earlier developers may have decided these issues long before anyone had even conceived of the application you're working on. This question breaks down into a couple of more specific issues:

Type of database management system (Oracle, Access, DBase, SQL Server, or other).

Type of hardware platform (mainframe, other type of network server). Specific hardware issues are usually transparent to the developer. You will meet these issues only indirectly, in the consequences they've had for client/server decisions and DBMS choices.

◆ *How will the application handle data access conflicts between users?* This is the issue of *concurrency*—more than one user trying to write the same records at the same time. The usual solution to concurrency problems is some sort of record-locking scheme.

▶ **See** "Adding a Record," **p. 495**

Page Locking

In order to avoid conflicts between two database users trying to write the same information at the same time, the Jet Engine supports a 2K *page-locking* scheme. This means that your application can lock, or temporarily deny write privileges to others, for the physical area surrounding the data you are writing. In particular, 2K of data is locked by the Jet Engine whenever you attempt an Update on multi-user data from your application.

The remaining sections of this chapter discuss how to implement page locking with the DAO.

> **Caution**
>
> Page locking only applies to non-ODBC databases. ODBC DBMS systems implement their own internal record-locking schemes.

> **Note** Many DBMS systems employ a record-locking scheme to secure data during a write rather than the page-locking scheme favored by the Jet Engine. In a record-locking scheme, only the data of the actual records being written is locked.
>
> It is not easy to predict exactly which other records will be locked in a Jet page lock for a particular record you are writing, because previous record deletions, logical sort order, and other factors will cause a great deal of variation. ∎

LockEdits Property and Pessimistic versus Optimistic Locking

A developer can use two types of locking strategy in a multi-user data access system:

♦ *Optimistic locking.* This is just-in-time locking, where the record is only locked for the brief amount of time that it takes to write from the copy buffer to the underlying data.

♦ *Pessimistic Locking.* This strategy locks the record for a longer period, usually the entire time that the user is editing it.

The Recordset's LockEdits property is a True/False property controlling whether your locking strategy is optimistic or pessimistic. When LockEdits is True (its default value), locking can be pessimistic, and when LockEdits is False, locking is optimistic.

◆ To implement pessimistic locking, you must call the Edit method when the user starts editing data (typically a Form's KeyPress event could call the Edit method of the Recordset) and you must make sure that the Recordset's LockEdits property is True (its default value).

◆ To implement optimistic locking you must set the Recordset's LockEdits property to False. Any Edit methods on the Recordset have no effect in setting locks. Calling the Recordset's Update method will lock 2K pages of data in the underlying database automatically.

> **Caution**
> Even though you plan to use optimistic locking, you still must call the Edit method before issuing an Update.

Locks are automatically removed after:

The Recordset's Update method runs

The Recordset's CancelUpdate method runs

The Recordset is closed

The Recordset's record pointer moves

The Edit Method and Pessimistic Locking

When LockEdits is True (pessimistic locking is in force), the Recordset's Edit method determines when the lock is initiated. Between the time you call the Edit method and the time the lock is removed, other users will not be able to lock or update the 2K page where your data resides.

It's possible that another user has already locked your data when you call the Edit method to lock the page. If this is the case, you'll receive a run-time error in your application.

Calling the Edit method also sets the Recordset's EditMode property to dbEditInProgress. You can check the EditMode property if you need to check whether the Edit method has been called. See the section "Updating a Record" for an example of the use of the EditMode property.

Locking Example

In the following example, we show code that implements pessimistic locking. In the Form's Keypress event we call the Edit method and trap for error 3260 (another user has locked the record), error 3197 (underlying data has changed since this Recordset last refreshed its copy buffer); and error 3167 (another user has already deleted the record) can happen if you're using a dynaset.

Note that re-setting the Bookmark property (even if we only set it to its own value) will refresh the copy buffer:

```
Private Sub Form_KeyPress()
        Dim strMsg
        On Error GoTo Form_KeyPress_Err
        rsEmployees.Edit
        Exit Sub
Form_KeyPress_Err:
        If Err.Number = 3260 Then 'Someone else already has locked
            strMsg = "Record currently locked by another user."
            MsgBox strMsg
            Resume Next
        ElseIf Err.Number = 3197 Then
                rsEmployees.Bookmark = _
            rsEmployees.Bookmark 'refresh copy buffer
                ReadFromData 'our routine to populate controls
        Else If Err.Number = 3167 Then 'someone deleted record already
                MsgBox "Record was deleted by another user"
                cmdDelete_Click 'call event proc to delete from
                ➡this Recordset too
                Resume Next
        Else
                strMsg = "Can't Edit.  Error: " & Error.Description
                strMsg = strMsg & " (#" & Error.Number & ")"
                MsgBox strMsg
                Resume Next
        End If
End Sub
```

In the Click event procedure for the Update button, we write the data from the controls the user has just edited to the fields of the copy buffer and then call the Update method. If we are using pessimistic locking and have called the Edit method before, there should be no possible locking errors. We include error trapping code in case LockEdits has been set to false (causing optimistic locking to be in effect). We trap for errors 3186 (record locked when attempting Update) and 3197

Part
IV

Ch
13

(underlying data changed since last refresh of copy buffer). Notice that calling Update a second time (after error 3197 occurs) overrides the error condition and writes the changes to the data:

```
Private Sub cmdUpdate_Click()
    Dim strMsg
    WriteControlsToData 'our routine to update copy buffer
    On Error GoTo Update_Err
    rsEmployees.Update
    Exit Sub
Update_Err:
    If Err.Number = 3186 Then 'record locked by someone else
            MsgBox "Record locked by another user"
    ElseIf Err.Number = 3197 Then 'data changed since last
    ➥refresh
            strMsg = "Data changed by another user.  Save
            ➥anyway?"
            If MsgBox(strMsg, vbYesNo) = vbYes Then
                    Resume 'calling Update 2nd time overrides
                    ➥changes
            Else
                    rsEmployees.CancelUpdate
                    Resume Next
            EndIf
    Else    'Some other error
            strMsg = "Can't Save.  Error: " & Err.Description
            strMsg = strMsg & " (#" & Err.Number & ")"
            MsgBox strMsg
            Resume Next
    End If
End Sub
```

Taking the Disc Test

 If you have read and understood the material in the chapter, you are ready to test your knowledge. Insert the CD-ROM that comes with this book and run the self-test software as described in Appendix H, "Using the CD-ROM."

From Here...

If you're comfortable with the concepts in this chapter, it would be a useful exercise to review Chapter 12, "Using the Data Control" and compare concepts. You will find that the Data Control's Recordset is almost identical to the Recordset of a Data Access Object. Such a comparison should help you consolidate your knowledge of data access in VB.

Chapter 16, "Distributing an Application with Setup Wizard," also deals with setup issues related to data access.

Part V.

Managing Your VB Application's Running Environment

Chapter Prerequisite

In order to get the most out of
this chapter, you should already
know how to use the Windows
API (see Chapter 15). You also
will want to be familiar with the
Setup Wizard (see Chapter 16).

14

Creating 16-Bit and 32-Bit Applications

Before VB 4.0, all versions of Visual Basic compiled 16-bit executable
files. Because the 32-bit operating systems such as Windows 95 and
Windows NT are downwardly compatible with application software,
16-bit applications created with earlier versions of VB can run in the
32-bit environment.

Of course, 16-bit applications can't take advantage of the performance
improvements and new features of the 32-bit environment. VB 4.0's
ability to produce 32-bit applications is therefore a welcome enhance-
ment over earlier versions of VB.

At this time in the evolution of the PC desktop, developers find themselves caught in the transition between the earlier 16-bit operating environments (Win 3.X) and the 32-bit environments of Windows 95 and
Windows NT. Although any 16-bit VB application can run in a 32-bit

environment, developers often need to convert existing 16-bit applications to 32-bit for performance considerations. Further, developers who support users running on both 16- and 32-bit platforms maintain both a 16- and 32-bit version of the same application.

This chapter discusses the main issues in converting applications from 16- to 32-bit and in maintaining an application that can compile as either a 16- or 32-bit application. Terms and concepts covered include:

◆ **Differences between 16- and 32-bit applications**

◆ **Conditional compilation**

◆ **Conditional compiler constants**

◆ **Differences between 16- and 32-bit Windows API**

◆ **VBX custom controls**

◆ **OCX (OLE) custom controls**

◆ **Converting VB 3.0 applications to VB 4.0**

Understanding 16-Bit and 32-Bit Application Differences

Programmers see differences between 16- and 32-bit VB applications in four areas:

◆ *Performance.* A 16-bit application will generally not perform as well in a 32-bit environment as the same application compiled in a 32-bit application.

◆ *API calls.* The 32-bit Windows API uses DLLs with different names than the 16-bit API. The functions and procedures contained in the DLLs are named differently, and sometimes their functionality varies between 16- and 32-bit APIs. New API calls have been added in the 32-bit API, and some 16-bit API calls have been discontinued.

◆ *Custom Controls.* 32-bit and 16-bit VB 4.0 applications use OLE Custom Controls (files with OCX extension) while 16-bit applications written in earlier versions of VB use Visual Basic Extension (VBX) files.

◆ *String manipulation.* You will seldom notice or have to do anything about this. We mention a few considerations about string manipulation in the section "Understanding Differences in String Manipulation," later in this chapter.

> **Note** The general "look and feel" of applications running under different operating systems depends on the operating system you use, not on the way the application was compiled. For instance, the same Form in an application running under 16-bit Windows or versions of NT below 4.x will show its Caption centered, while in Windows 95 or NT 4.x and higher, the caption will be left-aligned. ■

Maintaining One Project for Both 16- and 32-Bit Operating Systems

You can use the same source code for both 16- and 32-bit versions of an application. All you need to do is make sure you have both the 16- and the 32-bit versions of VB installed on your development machine. When you install VB from its distribution media (CD or floppies), the setup routine will automatically sense whether you're installing to a 32- or 16-bit platform. Setup will offer you a choice of installing the 16- or 32-bit version of Visual Basic, but the default version it offers you will be the correct version for the platform it detects.

If you have the 32-bit VB on your system, you can add the 16-bit version by re-running the setup routine on the distribution media and specifying a 16-bit install when the setup routine prompts you.

> **Note** The Enterprise version handles 32- versus 16-bit distribution differently. You're presented with a master setup screen with several buttons of which two are for VB 16 and VB 32. However, if you are installing to Win3.x the 32-bit button will be grayed out. ■

When both 16- and 32-bit versions of VB are installed on your system, you'll see a separate icon for each version. The two different versions of VB are represented by separate copies of the main VB executable file,

Part
V
Ch
14

typically VB.EXE for the 16–bit version and VB32.EXE for the 32–bit version. These copies will install to the same directory by default.

Note   You can't install 32-bit VB under a 16-bit version of Windows, so you must be running Windows 95 or Windows NT to be able to install both the 16- and 32-bit VB 4.0 compilers.

The Standard Edition of VB 4.0 does not have a 16-bit compiler.   ■

To compile your application for both a 16- and 32–bit environment, you need to take the following steps:

1. Make sure you have both 16- and 32– bit versions of VB installed on your system as described in the previous paragraphs.

2. Run one of the versions of VB.

3. Use VB's File, Open command to open the application you want to compile.

4. Compile the application with VB's File, Make Exe menu option.

5. Close VB.

6. Repeat steps 1–3 with the other version of VB, making sure to give the executable file a different name and/or path.

7. When you're ready to distribute your application, create separate sets of installation disks for each executable file with the Setup Wizard.

   ▶ **See** "Distributing an Application with SetupWizard," **p. 551**

Using Conditional Compilation with the API

In the previous section, we pointed out that it is possible to create a 16–bit and a 32-bit executable file from the same source code. You simply need to compile the application using both VB's 16–bit and 32-bit compilers. For the most part, a VB application compiles and runs equally well in 16- or 32-bit environments. However, there will be times when you need different API declarations or different string manipulation code depending on which platform you're compiling for (see the following two sections in this chapter). Conditional compilation is a tool typically used to compile the same program for different platforms by conditionally compiling blocks of code.

Conditional compilation allows the compiler to leave selected code out of your application's compiled EXE file based on conditional tests it performs at compile time.

To allow you to detect what compiler is running against your project, VB provides two built-in conditional compiler constants, Win16 and Win32.

♦ If you're running the 16-bit version of VB, Win16 is True, and Win32 is False.

♦ If you're running the 32-bit version of VB, Win32 is True, and Win16 is False.

You can use these two conditional compiler constants inside an *#If…#Else…#End If* compiler construct anywhere in your source code. The following example illustrates the use of a compiler constant within the conditional construct:

```
#If Win32 Then
      ' do things specific to 32-bit platform
#Else
      ' do things specific to other platforms
#End If
```

The syntax of an *#If..#Else..#End If* construct is the same as the syntax for *If..Else..End If* (including the optional use of #ElseIf). However, *#If..#Else..#End If* is not a part of your application's code and never compiles to anything in the finished executable file. Instead, the compiler reads the logical condition of this construct to determine whether or not it should compile the lines of code within the construct. In the example, the compiler only compiles the lines before the #Else if the current running version of VB 4.0 is the 32-bit version. Otherwise, it compiles the lines of code between the #Else and the #End If.

> **Note** You may put the *#If..#Else..#End If* construct in a module's Declarations section as well as inside the code of procedures and functions. ■

Using Conditional Compilation with API Declarations

As mentioned earlier, 16-bit Windows (Windows 3.x or Windows for WorkGroups) has a different set of DLLs and different API function and procedure names from the DLLs and function names in the 32-bit Windows API.

You can use a conditional compiler construct in a module's Declarations section to determine which API declaration will be compiled into your executable file. If you use the Alias clause, you can make sure that the API function will always have the same name in your application regardless of its original source or underlying name.

In the following example, the conditional compiler construct has the compiler first check to see if we're compiling under the 32-bit version of VB 4.0. If so, then we declare the *GetWindowsDirectoryA* function in the *kernel32* DLL library, using the name *GetWindowsDirectory*. If we are not compiling under the 32-bit version, then we declare the *GetWindowsDirectory* function in the *kernel* library, keeping the original name *GetWindowsDirectory*. The end result is that our application can now refer to the GetWindowsDirectory function elsewhere in code with a uniform name, no matter what platform we're compiling for.

```
#If Win32 Then
    Declare Function GetWindowsDirectory _
    Lib "kernel32" Alias "GetWindowsDirectoryA" _
    (ByVal lpBuffer As String, ByVal nSize As Long) _
As Long
#Else
    Declare Function GetWindowsDirectory _
    Lib "kernel" _
    (ByVal lpBuffer As String, ByVal nSize As Long) _
As Long
#End If
```

Note If you use Declare statements in a Form or Class module, you must prefix the Private keyword before the Declare keyword. ■

▶ **See** "Dynamic-Link Libraries (API)," **p. 527**
▶ **See** "Alias Clause," **p. 532**

Converting a VB 3.0 Application to VB 4.0

Often, converting a VB 3.0 Application to 4.0 is as transparent as opening the original 3.0 project in 4.0 and simply recompiling. However, to take advantage of the better performance and functionality in VB 4.0, you should convert custom controls from VBX (Visual Basic Extension) to OCX (OLE Custom Control) files and you should change API declarations to take advantage of 32-bit DLLs.

 Note The project file extension for a VB 3.0 project is MAK, and VBP for a VB 4.0 project. ■

Converting VBX to OLE Controls

You can simply do nothing and continue to use your VB 3.0 application's VBX controls with your application when you move it into VB 4.0. However, you'll be missing performance enhancements by not converting the VBX's to OCX's, and you'll also have to worry about maintaining and distributing an application with obsolete VBX files in the future.

VB will replace the VBX file(s) in an older application with the appropriate OCX file(s) whenever you load a project, provided you've enabled the Upgrade Custom Controls option in the Advanced Options dialog. To enable VB to replace VBX controls with OCX controls, take the following steps (see fig. 14.1):

1. Choose Tools, Options from the VB menu.
2. Choose the Advanced tab in the Options dialog.

3. Make sure the CheckBox entitled Upgrade Custom Controls is checked.

4. Click OK.

The next time you open a project containing VBX controls which have OCX replacements, VB will prompt you with a dialog box giving the names of the VBX files to be upgraded (see fig. 14.2). If you respond to the dialog box by clicking its Yes button, VBX files will be replaced by OCX files in the current project.

Advanced tab

FIG. 14.1⇒

Checking the Upgrade Custom Controls option in the Tools Options dialog box's Advanced tab lets VB replace VBX controls with OCX controls in older projects.

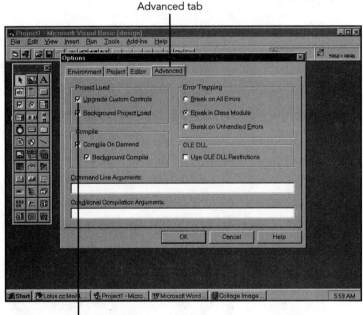

Make sure you've checked the
Upgrade Custom Controls option

The VB.INI file (which typically resides in your system's main Windows directory) contains VBX-to-OCX conversion information under the section [VBX Conversions32]. You should not try to edit this section yourself. Microsoft and third-party vendor's custom control setup routines will modify this section as needed.

FIG. 14.2⇒

If you've checked the Upgrade Custom Controls option, then VB will prompt you with this dialog box whenever you load a project containing VBX files that can be upgraded to OCX files.

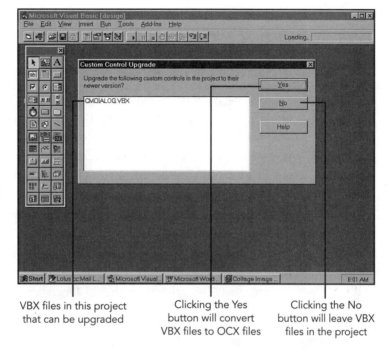

VBX files in this project that can be upgraded

Clicking the Yes button will convert VBX files to OCX files

Clicking the No button will leave VBX files in the project

Note Many custom controls come from third-party (non-Microsoft) vendors. Microsoft automatically distributes the OCX upgrades of most (though not all) of its custom controls along with VB 4.0. If you have a third-party vendor's VBX, you'll have to make arrangements with that vendor to get the OCX upgrades for the controls that the vendor distributes. ■

Converting API Calls

If your VB 3.0 project uses API calls and you want to convert to a VB 4.0 application, then you may have to rework some of your code. You will find two areas of concern about API calls when you convert a project from VB 3.0 to VB 4.0:

◆ *Obsolete API calls.* Some API calls are no longer appropriate in the newer operating systems, and Microsoft has discontinued them from the API. This obsolescence can cause big conversion problems because you may need to rethink how some of your

Part

V

Ch

14

code operates in order to adapt to new (or obsolete) API calls. A common problem which VB 3.0 programmers have experienced is the GetModuleUsage function, which no longer exists in the 32-bit API. See Chapter 15 for more details.

◆ *Different names in the 32-bit API.* The same functions in the 32-bit API may have different names than in the 16-bit API and will reside in differently-named DLL files. If you plan to convert your application to be only a 32-bit application, you'll need to learn these new names and change your API declarations accordingly. You can use the Alias clause in the API declaration (see Chapter 15 for more details) to allow your code to continue using the same name as before. If you plan to maintain an application that can be 16- or 32-bit, you'll need to use conditional compilation as described in the section "Using Conditional Compilation with API Declarations" earlier in this chapter.

Note See Chapter 15, "Dynamic-Link Libraries (API)," for more information on specific DLL files and API calls that may need conversion or may need special consideration because they handle Strings. ▨

Taking the Disc Test

If you have read and understood the material in the chapter, you are ready to test your knowledge. Insert the CD-ROM that comes with this book and run the self-test software as described in Appendix H, "Using the CD-ROM."

From Here...

The information in this chapter provides background information for topics discussed in Chapter 15, "Dynamic-Link Libraries (API)," and Chapter 16, "Distributing an Application with SetUpWizard."

Chapter Prerequisite

You should be familiar with the fundamentals of the VB language discussed in Chapters 2, 3, and 4. You should pay special attention to the sections in Chapter 2 on each data type, the section "The Visual Basic Stack and Variable Scope" in Chapter 2, and the section "Arguments to Procedures and Functions" in Chapter 3.

15

Dynamic-Link Libraries (API)

The Windows API (Applications Programming Interface) is a collection of functions and procedures stored in Dynamic-Link Libraries; that is, files with a DLL extension (you also can find API functions and procedures in files with an EXE extension). You can interface your VB application with the API so that you can use individual API calls in your VB application. The capability of calling outside functions and procedures at run-time greatly extends the functionality and versatility of a VB application.

Terms and concepts covered in this chapter include:

◆ **Declaring API functions and procedures**

◆ **Passing arguments to API functions and procedures**

◆ **Using online documentation**

◆ **Differences between C and VB data types in API calls**

◆ **Handling strings in API calls**

◆ **16- and 32-bit issues and conditional compilation**

◆ **The Alias clause in an API declaration**

◆ **Special Windows data types**

Declaring and Calling a DLL Routine

Before you can use an API call, your application must *declare* the API procedure or function in the General Declarations section of a Form, standard, or Class module.

The Declare statement, which we discuss in the following sections, is VB's vehicle for using an API call in an application.

Once you've declared an API call in your code, you can use the declared procedure or function in your code just as you would any procedure or function.

API subroutines and functions are found in dynamic-link libraries. These libraries can be located either in EXE or DLL extension files, though it's most typical to find them in DLL files. The Windows operating environment possesses a number of dynamic-link libraries. The three most basic libraries are known in 16-bit Windows as "User," "Kernel," and "GDI." In the 32-bit environment their names are "User32," "Kernel32," and "GDI32." These files are actually EXE files in 16-bit Windows and DLL files in 32-bit Windows. There are also other, less-used system libraries.

In addition to the operating environment's libraries, there are libraries available from other sources, such as third-party vendors. Since you can't count on these libraries being available to all users, you should distribute them with your application (see Chapter 16 on "Distributing an Application with SetupWizard"). You must make sure that you have distribution rights to these files before distributing them to users.

Declare Statement

A declaration statement has the format:

```
[Private¦Public] Declare Sub¦Function RoutineName Lib
⮕LibFileName _
[Alias RealName] [(ArgumentList)] [As ReturnType]
```

The various parts of the declaration statement tell your VB compiler:

- ◆ Where the API call can be used in this application. The Private keyword indicates the API call is only available in the current Form, Class, or Standard module. The Public keyword indicates that it is available throughout the entire application.

- ◆ Whether the API call is a function or a sub: the word Sub or Function immediately after the Declare keyword in the above model

- ◆ The name of the API call to use in your code: *RoutineName* in the above model

- ◆ The library to find the call in: *LibFileName* in the above model

- ◆ (optional) The actual name of the routine as found in the dynamic-link library file. You only need this if *RoutineName* is not the original name of the API call: Alias *RealName* in the above model gives the real name of the routine as found in the library file

- ◆ Arguments to pass to the API call: *ArgumentList* in the above model. This is a comma-separated list listing argument names and types, with an optional ByVal keyword in front of each argument name

- ◆ The API call's return type (functions only): *ReturnType* in the above model

The components of the Declare statement are discussed in more detail in the following sections.

The Declare Keyword

The Declare keyword can appear in the Declarations section of a Form, standard, or Class module. It indicates that you want VB to use an external procedure in the current application.

If you declare a routine in a Form or Class module, you must insert the keyword *Private* in front of the Declare keyword. If not, you'll get a compiler error:

```
[General declarations section of a standard module]
Declare Function CharUpper Lib "user32" Alias _
  "CharUpperA" (ByVal lpsz As String) As String

[General declarations section of a Class or Form module]
Private Declare Function CharUpper Lib "user32" Alias _
  "CharUpperA" (ByVal lpsz As String) As String
```

Function or Sub Clause

The vast majority of API calls are functions, but there are also API calls without a return value, which are, therefore, subroutines instead.

In order to distinguish between these two types of API calls, the Declare statement is immediately followed by the keyword Sub or Function to indicate which type of routine you are declaring.

The `GetSystemTime` API declaration in the following example declares a Sub procedure, while the `GetTempPath` declaration declares a Function. Notice that `GetSystemTime` has no return type specified in its declaration, while `GetTempPath`'s return type is specified to be As Long:

```
Declare Sub GetSystemTime Lib "kernel32"  _
    Alias "GetSystemTime" (lpSystemTime As SYSTEMTIME)

Declare Function GetTempPath Lib "kernel32" _
    Alias "GetTempPathA" _
    (ByVal nBufferLength As Long, _
    ByVal lpBuffer As String) As Long
```

Name of API

The name you specify here (immediately after Declare Function|Sub) will be the name that the rest of your VB application uses to recognize this routine. If you don't use an Alias clause, this name is also the actual name of the routine appearing in the dynamic-link library.

Thus, the declaration

```
Declare Sub "MySub" Lib "MyLib"
```

enables a Sub procedure `MySub` from the library file `MyLib` available to your application. Because there is no Alias clause in this declaration,

MySub is also the actual name of the routine found in the MyLib dynamic-link library.

▶ **See** "Alias Clause," **p. 532**

Note   The name of the API routine is case sensitive in 32-bit versions of Windows (Windows 95 and Windows NT) but not in 16-bit versions. This means that you must use the exact capitalization of the routine name as you find it in the API documentation when using 32-bit versions of Windows. ■

▶ **See** "Pasting Declarations from Online Documentation," **p. 535**

Library Name

The Lib clause in the API declaration tells VB where to find the API routine. The string specified in the Lib clause will typically be the name of a DLL or EXE file. You may specify a path for non–system libraries, as well as the file name. If you don't specify the path for a library file, VB will search for the file in the following places, in the order listed:

◆ Directory where executable file resides (VB directory when in design mode)

◆ Current directory (directory from which executable was called—VB directory when in design mode)

◆ Windows system directory

◆ Windows directory

◆ Directories in PATH variable

The following two declarations declare an API Sub without arguments. This declaration would cause the compiler to look for the routine MySub in a specific file, named MyLib, found in a specific directory:

```
Declare Sub "MySub" Lib "C:\MyDir\MyLib.dll"
```

This declaration would cause the compiler to search the locations described in the above list until it found the first occurrence of the file MyLib:

```
Declare Sub "MySub" Lib "MyLib"
```

Alias Clause

The Alias clause allows you to use a different name for the API call in your code from the actual name used in the dynamic-link library.

The syntax for the use of the Alias clause is:

```
Declare Sub¦Function NewName Lib LibName Alias OrigName. . .
```

Notice that you put the actual name of the routine after the Alias keyword, while the new name you wish to use comes after the keyword Sub or Function. Therefore, in the following example, the original name of the routine is FindWindowA, but the programmer is going to use the name FindWindow to call the routine in the current VB application:

```
Declare Function FindWindow Lib "user32" _
Alias "FindWindowA" _
(ByVal lpClassName As String, _
ByVal lpWindowName As String) As Long
```

▶ **See** "Alias Clause," **p. 532**

16-Bit versus 32-Bit Compilation of the Same Source Code

Another reason for the use of the Alias clause is to assist in easily maintaining the same application for both 16- and 32-bit operating systems, even though API calls across the two systems have different names.

Because 16- and 32-bit operating systems use different versions of the Windows API, you can use conditional compilation to compile differing API calls into your code depending on whether you're compiling with the 16- or the 32-bit version of VB.

The 16- and 32-bit operating systems use different names for their dynamic-link library files and different names for the corresponding API routines in each file. Even if you need to maintain a project for both 16- and 32-bit systems, however, you can still use a single name to call an API routine in your code. The trick is to use a conditional compiler directive with the Declare statements for your API calls.

Use the Alias clause in the Declare statements so that both 16- and 32-bit versions of the calls will have the same name in your VB code. By using the same API names for both 16- and 32-bit versions, you only have to be concerned about conditional compilation in the Declarations of your modules and not in the rest of your code.

In the following example, we declare a function that exists in the 16-
and 32-bit versions of VB under slightly different names. The conditional compiler directive checks to see which version of VB we're
compiling for, and the Alias clause in the 32-bit declaration ensures that
our VB application will see the same name no matter which of the two
versions we compile for:

```
#If Win16 Then
    Declare Function GetTempPath Lib "kernel" _
        (ByVal nBufferLength As Long, _
        ByVal lpBuffer As String) As Long
#ElseIf Win32 Then
    Declare Function GetTempPath Lib "kernel32" _
    Alias "GetTempPathA" _
    (ByVal nBufferLength As Long, _
    ByVal lpBuffer As String) As Long
#End If
```

▶ **See** "Creating 16-Bit and 32-Bit Applications," **p. 517**

Using the Same Name for Unicode and ANSI Versions

You can use the Alias clause to use the same name for Unicode and
ANSI versions of 32-bit string handling API routines.

The 32-bit Windows operating systems (NT and 95) use the Unicode
standard for encoding character information, while the older, 16-bit
versions use the ANSI standard. The ANSI standard uses a single byte to
hold character information, and thus allows a total of 256 different values for a character (the familiar 0-255 values for the ASCII character
set). The Unicode standard uses two bytes for each character, thus allowing a total of over 64,000 different characters.

Although VB uses the Unicode standard internally, it converts all strings
to ANSI for any use visible to the programmer, including API calls.

The Windows 95 API still uses the ANSI standard in its string manipulation. The 32-bit API therefore supports dual ANSI- and Unicode-
compatible versions of API calls that handle strings. The routines have
the same name, except for the last letter, which is "A" for the ANSI
version and "W" ("wide") for the Unicode version.

For example, the API function that places information about the
system's current TEMP directory in a string argument is known as
GetTempPathA (ANSI) or GetTempPathW (Unicode).

In the API Text Viewer declaration of this API function, it's named `GetTempPath`, without an A or W at the end. If you examine the declaration, you'll see that it's Aliasing the ANSI version:

```
Declare Function GetTempPath Lib "kernel32" _
    Alias "GetTempPathA" _
    (ByVal nBufferLength As Long, _
    ByVal lpBuffer As String) As Long
```

Currently, the API Text Viewer for VB allows you to copy and paste the ANSI versions of API calls. With a view to future developments, it would be wise to go along with the practice of the API Text Viewer and allow the ANSI names to be Aliased to more generic names. Then, if some future version of VB supports Unicode and your application is distributed entirely on Unicode-compatible platforms, all you'll have to do is change the name of the API call in its Declaration. The rest of your code can continue to use the same Aliased API names.

APIs with Names that are Incompatible with VB

You can use the Alias clause whenever an API call's name is an invalid procedure name in VB. Because DLLs are typically written in some version of the C language, there can be situations when the naming conventions for C routines conflict with the naming conventions for VB Sub and Function procedures. There are basically two situations when this might happen:

- ◆ API procedure has the same name as a VB keyword. Because the C language and VB don't have the same keywords, an API procedure could have a name that is legal in C (it's not a keyword of the C language) but that is a keyword in VB.

- ◆ An API procedure name begins with an underscore. This is the one place where C and VB naming conventions conflict. In VB, a variable or procedure name must begin with an alpha character. In C a variable or function name can begin with an alpha character or an underscore.

The following two declaration lines give examples of how to fix both types of problem with the Alias clause:

```
Declare Sub Beeep Lib "MyLib.Dll" Alias "Beep"
Declare Sub MySub Lib "MyLib.Dll" Alias "_MySub"
```

Argument List

The argument list follows the same syntactic rules as the argument list for a Function or Sub procedure you'd write in VB. You list each argument in the list, separated by commas. Each argument item contains an argument name and a type of the format *ArgName* As *TypeName*. You should always explicitly list the type of an argument to a DLL, or else the compiler will understand the type to be Variant.

The argument list in the following example should look familiar to you from your previous knowledge of VB:

```
Declare Function GetPrinterDriverDirectory _
Lib "winspool.drv" Alias "GetPrinterDriverDirectoryA" _
(ByVal pName As String, ByVal pEnvironment As String, _
ByVal Level As Long, pDriverDirectory As Byte, _
ByVal cdBuf As Long, pcbNeeded As Long) As Long
```

▶ **See** "Understanding Differences between C and VB Data Types," **p. 538**

As <data type> Clause (Functions Only)

You specify the return type of an API Function in the same way you specify the return type of VB Functions you write yourself—with As *DataType* following the function's argument list. In the following example, we can see that GetTempPath returns a Long Integer:

```
Declare Function GetTempPath Lib "kernel32" _
    Alias "GetTempPathA" _
    (ByVal nBufferLength As Long, _
    ByVal lpBuffer As String) As Long
```

Pasting Declarations from Online Documentation

Because 32-bit API declarations are case-sensitive and because API declarations can become very involved, it's important that you type a Sub or Function declaration accurately.

VB has an API Text Viewer utility that allows you to copy API declarations to the Windows Clipboard (see figs. 15.1, 15.2, and 15.3). You can then paste these declarations directly into your VB application's code.

To view and copy information from the API documentation, you should execute the following steps:

1. Start the API Text Viewer utility from the Windows VB Program Group.

2. From the API Text Viewer's File menu, choose the desired API Text file or MDB file—typically WIN32API (see fig. 15.1).

Convert a currently loaded text file to
Access Database format

FIG. 15.1⇒

You can load various API documentation files into the API Viewer.

Text and Access Database files

3. If you chose a text file in the previous step, VB may prompt you to convert it to an MDB (see fig. 15.2). If you choose to convert, you may experience a delay of several seconds. The MDB file will load faster in the future.

4. Choose whether you wish to view Constants, Types, or Declarations—typically declarations (see fig. 15.3).

5. Scroll through the list of Available items until you've selected the one you need. You can also type the first letters of an item's name to locate it (see fig. 15.3).

6. Double-click the item or click the Add button to add it to the list of Selected items at the bottom of the dialog box (see fig. 15.3).

FIG. 15.2⇒
The API Viewer
will prompt you to
convert a Text file
to Access format
whenever you
load it.

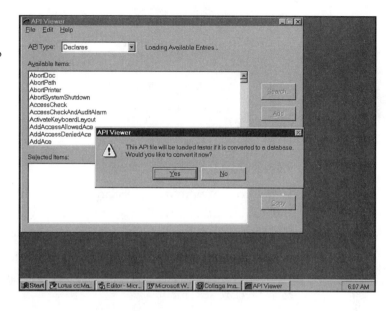

Choose among lists of Windows Constants,
API Declarations, and Windows Data Types

FIG. 15.3⇒
The API Viewer
allows you to copy
Declarations to the
Windows Clip-
board for use in
your VB applica-
tion.

Scroll to the item
you wish to copy

Copy Selected
Items to the
Windows
Clipboard

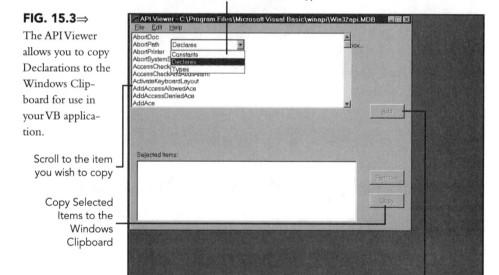

Add the item's name to
the list of Selected Items

7. If you change your mind or mistakenly Add an item to the Selected Items list, you can select the item in the Selected Items list and click the Remove button to delete it from the list.

8. Repeat steps 5, 6, and 7 for each item you need to copy.

9. Select all of the items you want to copy in the Selected Items list.

10. Click the Copy button to copy all Selected Items to the Windows Clipboard.

11. Switch to the appropriate Declarations section in your VB application and choose Edit, Paste from the VB menu or key Ctrl+V to paste the declarations into your application.

12. If you're pasting into the Declarations section of a Form or Class module, be sure to type the keyword Private in front of each Declare statement.

When you install VB on your system, the API documentation files are all in Text format. The Text Viewer will prompt you to convert these files to MDB (Microsoft Access) format whenever you load them (refer to fig. 15.2). If you choose not to convert them at that time, you can still convert them in the future with the Convert Text to Database option of the File menu (refer to fig. 15.1). The MDB format allows you to load the information into the API Text Viewer faster and also would allow you greater flexibility in the future if you wanted to browse or modify the information outside of the API Text Viewer.

Understanding Differences between C and VB Data Types

The API routines in most Dynamic-Link Libraries are written in the C or C++ language. Since your VB program must pass arguments to API routines, and since VB data types and C data types are not the same, there are a number of problems you can run into when you try to pass arguments to an API call. Furthermore, some C and VB data types (such as Strings) that appear similar are actually implemented differently by each language, causing further complications. The most important of these issues is discussed in the following sections.

Many of the issues in these sections are handled automatically when you copy and paste API declarations from the API Text Viewer. However, you may find yourself declaring API routines in your application based on written documentation from other sources. Much of the documentation for Windows programming (including API documentation) is oriented toward the C language. It is therefore important to understand the differences and possible conflicts between C and VB data types when declaring and calling API routines.

Visual Basic Strings and C DLL Routines

Surely one of the thorniest issues when calling the Windows API from VB is the use of the String data type. The problems with String variables between VB and the API arise from the different ways in which VB and C/C++ implement Strings internally.

There are three basic rules you should observe when passing Strings from VB to API routines written in C:

- ◆ Always pass String arguments to API routines by Value, even when you intend the String to be passed by Reference.
- ◆ If you expect the API routine to modify a String argument, pad it with extra characters so that it's at least 255 characters long.
- ◆ If you need to use the modified value of a String argument in your VB code after the API call, then be sure to strip off any ASCII null character (ASCII 0) that might be visible in the String after the API call.

We discuss the problems which give rise to the need for these rules in the following three sections.

Pass String Arguments to API Calls by Value

The actual information C stores in a String variable is the memory address of the first character in the String. (Such a memory address is also called a *pointer* by C programmers.) This is known as the LPSTR format (Long Pointer to STRing).

The actual information VB stores in a String variable is the address of an address. In other words, a VB String contains a memory address, but the information stored in that memory address is just a second memory address. The second memory address indicates the location of the String's first character. This is known as the BSTR format (Basic STRing).

> **Note** The reason for VB's dual-address system for Strings is beyond the scope of the exam. Essentially, VB stores special header information about the String in the 10 bytes of memory preceding the first character. The BSTR dual addressing system helps VB find the header information. ■

An API routine written in C can therefore have problems interpreting a String parameter passed to it from VB. The solution is actually simple to state—*always pass Strings to API routines By Value.*

The reason this works is that the By Value reference passes only the second memory address of the BSTR format, ignoring the first address. Since C's LPSTR format expects a single memory address, the C-based API routine will correctly interpret the single address as referring to the first character of the String.

You should note that, even though we always pass a String argument By Value to an API routine, *the VB application always sees changes* made to the String by the API routine.

Stuff String Arguments with Extra Characters

You should prepare any String that will be passed as an argument to an API routine by padding that String so that it holds at least 255 characters.

When a C-based API routine makes changes to a String it is possible that it might add characters to the end of the String. This simple fact could have disastrous and unpredictable results, because VB has no way of informing the API routine about any important data that might be in memory just beyond the end of the original String. The API routine could therefore corrupt other data in memory by simply adding to a String.

There are two ways to pad a blank String before passing it to an API routine:

Populate the String with 255 null characters (ASCII 0)

Declare the String as fixed length with 255 characters

Tip

A variable-length String will be easier to change later with functions like Left, Right, Mid, and String concatenation.

Strip String Argument's Null Terminator after API Call

Once an API routine written in C has manipulated a String argument, the argument will then have a null terminator character (ASCII 0) on its end. This null terminator will be visible to VB and can cause problems if you need to do anything further to the String that will resize it. This would include such operations as String concatenation, reassigning the String's value, or examining it with functions such as Left, Right, or Mid.

After calling an API routine with a String argument, you must look for and eliminate any null terminator character at the end of the String. There are several ways to do this:

◆ If you're lucky, the API call you've made may return a value indicating the length of the modified String. You could then use this value with the Left function to get the new String (see the following section entitled "Common Features of Many String-Handling API Calls").

◆ For a more general solution, you could write a function that searches for and strips off the null terminator from any String (see the following section).

Utility Function to Strip Off Null Terminator

Here we give an example of a function that a programmer could use in an application that calls API functions that modify strings. Since the strings may end up with an unwanted null terminator visible to the VB application, this function will examine a String for the null terminator and return a version of the String with the null terminator stripped off:

```
Private Function StripNulls(Source As String) As String
    Dim Target As String
    Dim NullPosition As Integer
    NullPosition = InStr(Source, Chr(0))
    If NullPosition > 0 Then
        Target = Left(Source, NullPosition - 1)
    Else
        Target = Source
    End If
    StripNulls = Target
End Function
```

Common Features of Many String-Handling API Calls

Many common API routines that handle and modify Strings share a couple of common features:

In addition to the String argument itself, such routines will take an additional argument that must specify the original size, in characters, of the String being passed.

If the routine is a function, the function's return value will be a number representing the adjusted length of the String argument.

In the following example, the GetTempPath API Function takes two parameters. The second parameter is a String parameter that the function will fill with the name of the system's Temp directory. The first parameter is a number giving the initial size of the String argument as passed to the function.

The GetTempPath API Function's return value is a number indicating the number of characters in the modified String.

Note how we prepare the String parameter by padding it with 255 null characters. 255 is therefore the value of the first parameter because that number represents the String's original length. After we make the function call to `GetTempPath`, we use the function's return value inside the Left function to strip off any trailing characters such as the null terminator character:

```
[In declarations section of a module]
Declare Function GetTempPath Lib "kernel32" _
    Alias "GetTempPathA" _
    (ByVal nBufferLength As Long, _
    ByVal lpBuffer As String) As Long

[In the application's code]
Dim strTempPath As String
Dim lLength As Long
strTempPath = String(255,0) '255 ASCII 0 characters
lLength = GetTempPath(lLength, strTempPath)
strTempPath = Left(strTempPath,lLength)
```

Passing a Null Pointer to a DLL Routine

If C-oriented documentation asks you to pass a "null pointer" (that is, a blank memory address) to an API call, then you should:

1. Declare the argument As String in the Declare statement.
2. Pass the vbNull constant as the argument when you call the API routine.

> **Note** Earlier versions of VB didn't support the vbNull constant. The proper way to pass a Null pointer in those versions of VB was to pass ByVal &0. You may still see this usage in older code. ∎

C "int" Data Type as a DLL Argument

If C-oriented documentation specifies C's int data type for an API argument:

◆ When working with a 16-bit VB environment, declare the argument as type Integer.

◆ When working with a 32-bit VB environment, declare the argument as type Long.

C "char" Data Type as a DLL Argument

The char data type in C typically represents an ASCII value. It is actually a very short integer, with a legal range of 0–255. The VB type that most closely approximates C's char type is the Byte type. When C-oriented API documentation specifies that an argument should be of type char, your VB application should declare the argument with ByVal Byte.

Passing an hWnd Property as an Argument

When an API call manipulates a Form or a standard Windows control such as one of the standard controls in the VB Toolbox, it typically requires the object's hWnd property as a ByVal argument. Recall that the hWnd property provides a handle for the Windows operating system to track an object. The argument is usually named "hwnd" in the API documentation.

In the following example, the FlashWindow API Function will flash a Form's title bar. It requires the Form's hWnd property as a first parameter. The second parameter, bInvert, will cause the Form's title bar to:

◆ switch to the reverse of its current color if bInvert is passed as a value of 1

◆ take on the highlighted color, regardless of its current state if bInvert is passed as a value of 0

The declaration for FlashWindow (which we can paste from the API Text Viewer) looks like this:

```
Declare Function FlashWindow Lib "user32" _
    (ByVal hwnd As Long, _
    ByVal bInvert As Long) As Long
```

We can cause the Form's title bar to reverse its present color with the following code elsewhere in the application:

```
Dim rc As Long
rc = FlashWindow(Form1.hwnd, 1)
```

Since we have no need for FlashWindow's return value, we could also leave the parentheses off the argument list and call FlashWindow like this:

```
FlashWindow Form1.hwnd, 1
```

▶ **See** "The hWnd Property," **p. 219**

The VB Variant Data Type

Unless the API function you're calling is an OLE function that recognizes the Variant Data Type, you can't pass a Variant-type variable by Value as the API function won't be able to handle it.

You may pass a Variant variable by Reference, but passing a Variant by Reference simply passes a variable of the type that the Variant is holding. You must of course make sure that the Variant holds data of the type expected in the argument.

Currency

The Currency data type is a special VB data type and so API routines written in C won't recognize Currency-type arguments properly.

You should convert Currency-type variables to Long before passing them.

Passing Control Properties

Always pass Control Properties by Value.

Passing Array Arguments

You can pass arrays of numeric information by passing the first element of the array. The API routine will then be able to find the other elements of the array based on the memory address of the first element.

Special Data Types as Argument Types

Windows supports numerous special structured data types that can hold information having to do with many aspects of the system. You can find these data types in the API Text viewer and paste VB-compatible user-defined type declarations into the Declarations of Form, Class, or standard modules. You can then declare variables of these types and pass these variables to the API calls that require them.

Typically, you'll find arguments of these special data types being passed By Reference to an API call that will fill up the components of the structure with some special type of information. For instance, the declaration for the GetSystemTime API call looks like this:

```
Declare Sub GetSystemTime Lib "kernel32" _
    Alias "GetSystemTime" (lpSystemTime As SYSTEMTIME)
```

As you can see, its only parameter, lpSystemTime, is of type SYSTEMTIME. SYSTEMTIME is a structured type, and you can find a VB-compatible Type...End Type declaration for this type in the API Text Viewer. To paste the Type declaration for a special data type, you can use the API Text Viewer similar to the way in which you use it to paste API Declarations. You should execute the following steps to paste a Type declaration from the API Text View into your code:

1. Start the API Text Viewer utility from the Windows VB Program Group.

2. From the API Text Viewer's File menu, choose the desired API Text file or MDB file—typically WIN32API (refer to fig. 15.1).

3. From the API Type list, choose to view Types.

4. Scroll through the list of Available items until you've selected the type you need. You can also type the first letters of an item's name to locate it.

5. Double-click the item or click Add to add it to the list of Selected Items at the bottom of the dialog box.

8. Select all the type you want to copy in the Selected Items list.

9. Click Copy to copy the selected item to the Windows Clipboard.

10. Switch to the appropriate Declarations section in your VB application and choose <u>E</u>dit, <u>P</u>aste from the VB menu or key Ctrl+V to paste the type declaration into your application.

11. If you're pasting into the Declarations section of a Form or Class module, be sure to type the keyword **Private** in front of the Type statement.

> **Caution**
> Make sure you paste the Type declaration before the declaration of any API that uses arguments of that type.

If you execute these steps for the SYSTEMTIME type and paste it above the GetSystemTime API declaration, your module's Declarations section will contain the following lines:

```
[Declarations section of a module]
Type SYSTEMTIME
        wYear As Integer
        wMonth As Integer
        wDayOfWeek As Integer
        wDay As Integer
        wHour As Integer
        wMinute As Integer
        wSecond As Integer
        wMilliseconds As Integer
End Type
Declare Sub GetSystemTime Lib "kernel32" _
        Alias "GetSystemTime" (lpSystemTime As SYSTEMTIME)
```

Somewhere else in your application, you might want to print out system time information with the following code:

```
Dim Mysystime as SYSTEMTIME
GetSystemTime Mysystime
Me.Cls
Me.Print Mysystime.wMonth & "/";
Me.Print Mysystime.wDay & "/";
Me.Print Format(Mysystime.wYear, "####")
Me.Print Format(Mysystime.wHour, "0#") & ":";
Me.Print Format(Mysystime.wMinute, "0#") & ":";
Me.Print Format(Mysystime.wSecond, "0#")
```

GetWindowsDirectory in 16-Bit and 32-Bit Versions

Microsoft's VB 4.0 Exam Guidelines specifically mention the GetWindowsDirectory API call as something that you should be familiar with. This is because the GetWindowsDirectory API call is useful, simple to understand, and illustrates String-handling and cross-platform issues in API calls.

We give a full example of the use of GetWindowsDirectory in this section and then illustrate some points about the use of the API. Notice that the example declares the API function and then uses the function in a CommandButton control's Click event procedure to retrieve and display the name of the system's Windows directory:

```
[In the Declarations section of a Standard Module]
#If Win32 Then
    Declare Function GetWindowsDirectory Lib "kernel32" _
            Alias "GetWindowsDirectoryA" _
            (ByVal lpBuffer As String, _
            ByVal nSize As Long) As Long
#Else If Win16 Then
    Declare Function GetWindowsDirectory Lib "kernel" _
            (ByVal lpBuffer As String, _
            ByVal nSize As Long) As Long
#End If

[In the Click event procedure of a Command Button]
Private Sub Cmdwindir_Click()
    Dim iWinDirLength As Integer
    Dim strWinDir As String
    strWinDir = String(255, 0)
    iWinDirLength = GetWindowsDirectory(strWinDir, 255)
    strWinDir = Left(strWinDir, iWinDirLength)
    Me.Cls
    Me.Print Trim(strWinDir) & " is the Windows Directory"
End Sub
```

Let's look at each of the issues raised by this example:

Conditional compile for 16- and 32-bit versions: The 16- and 32-bit API Text Viewers will reveal that GetWindowsDirectory resides in the "kernel" library for a 16-bit platform and that its 32-bit ANSI and

Unicode versions reside in the "kernel32" library. We therefore use the
Win32 and Win16 compiler constants to conditionally compile from a
different library, depending on which compiler we're using at the moment.

Alias clause to give same name to 16- and 32-bit versions: We
use the Alias clause in the 32-bit branch of the conditional compile so
that both the 32-bit and 16-bit version of `GetWindowsDirectory` can be
known by the same name in our application. Putting a conditional
compile in the Declarations section is preferable to putting a conditional compile everywhere else that we expect to use this function in
our code.

Ansi or Unicode for the 32-bit version? This is really a non-issue at
the moment, because VB supports ANSI externally and so does Window 95, while Windows NT can support either, depending on the API
call. Notice that the original name of the Aliased 32-bit version is
`GetWindowsDirectoryA`. Recall that the final A means that this is the
ANSI version.

Preparing the String argument: Recall that Strings to be passed to
an API routine must be padded to hold at least 255 characters. The
statement:

```
strWinDir = String(255, 0)
```

will fill the variable with 255 ASCII null characters.

Passing the String argument: String arguments must always be
passed to API routines By Value. Notice that the Text Viewer has taken
care of this for us by putting ByVal in front of the argument's name in
both versions of the Declare statement. Notice that the second parameter to GetWindowsDirectory is a Long integer that takes the size of
the original String—255 in this case.

Using the return value to determine the length of the String:
`GetWindowsDirectory` returns a Long integer indicating the length of the
String that was written. We can use this return value to shorten the
String to its meaningful length, as we do in the line:

```
strWinDir = Left(strWinDir, iWinDirLength)
```

If we omitted this line, then the line

```
Me.Print Trim(strWinDir) & " is the Windows Directory"
```

would not display the words "is the Windows Directory" on the Form because the Trim statement would be hampered by the null terminator on the end of the String and would not be able to reduce the size of `strWinDir`.

Taking the Disc Test

If you have read and understood the material in this chapter, you are ready to test your knowledge. Insert the CD-ROM that comes with this book and run the self-test software as described in Appendix H, "Using the CD-ROM."

From Here...

Many of the issues in Chapter 14, "Creating 16-Bit and 32-Bit Applications," have to do with the use of the Windows API. If you found Chapter 14 somewhat puzzling, you might want to review it again once you're comfortable with the concepts of this chapter.

Similarly, some of the issues in Chapter 16, "Distributing an Application with SetupWizard," will be clearer once you have become comfortable with the material in this chapter.

Chapter Prerequisite

Before reading this chapter, you should have a basic familiarity with OLE automation (Chapter 10) and OLE servers (Chapter 11). You should pay special attention to the role of class libraries in an application that uses OLE.

16

Distributing an Application with SetupWizard

Visual Basic's SetupWizard utility saves you a great deal of work and frustration by allowing you to automatically create a distributable copy of your application, complete with setup disks and a professional-looking setup program. SetupWizard also produces customizable VB source code for those situations when you need to fine-tune SetupWizard's generic product.

Terms and concepts covered in this chapter include:

◆ **The SetupWizard utility**

◆ **Setting up OLE applications**

◆ **Customizable VB setup routines**

◆ **Standard Microsoft setup files**

Running SetupWizard

The SetupWizard utility is a separate application that you can find in your Windows operating system with the Visual Basic 4.0 utilities.

You run SetupWizard when you've finished your application and are ready to create a distribution vehicle for the application. Such a distribution vehicle might be either distribution disks or a special directory on a network. The distribution vehicle would contain compressed versions of all files necessary to install and run the application.

Preparing to Run SetupWizard

Before you run SetupWizard you should take the following steps:

◆ Use the Tools, References option on the VB menu to remove any unneeded references to Data Access Objects or class libraries.

◆ Use the Tools, Custom Controls option on the VB menu to remove references to any unused custom controls.

◆ Save your application's project and close it.

◆ If you're planning to create distribution files in a special directory, make sure the directory exists.

◆ If you're planning to create distribution disks, have five to ten blank, formatted disks on hand.

Screen for Step 1: Designating the Project to Set Up

The first SetupWizard screen allows you to designate the project to set up (see fig. 16.1). You can access this screen by running the SetupWizard application from its icon in Windows' Visual Basic program group.

If you want to use an existing SetupWizard template as the basis for this setup, you can click the Open Template button to choose an existing

Setup Template file (VBZ extension). You can then follow the setup steps of the selected template by simply clicking the Next button on all subsequent steps—or you can modify a particular step while running the template.

If you don't have an existing Setup template, you will need to designate the project being set up. You can either type the project (VBP) file's path and file name in the Project File field or use the browse button to find the file on your system. If the project's EXE or DLL file doesn't already exist, VB will compile it. If you wish to force a recompile regardless of whether the compiled file exists, you can check the box labeled Rebuild the Project's EXE File.

Part
V
Ch
16

Once you've chosen a Setup template or a project, you can continue to the next screen by clicking the Next button.

You may browse to find the
file of the project to be set up

FIG. 16.1⇒

SetupWizard's first screen allows you to specify the project to be set up. You may also specify an existing Setup template to use.

You may open an existing setup template

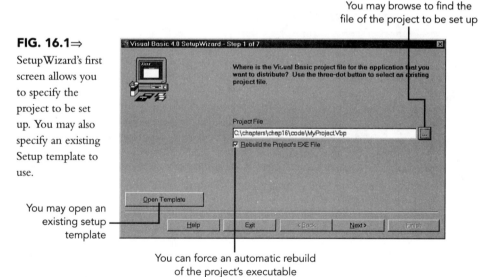

You can force an automatic rebuild
of the project's executable

Screen for Step 2: Data Access Engine

The Screen for this step, as shown in figure 16.2, only appears if SetupWizard detects that the project is using the Data Control or a Data Access Object library.

If you are only using Microsoft Access to connect to data, you need do nothing, as the Access driver is included automatically with your project.

If you are using installable ISAM drivers, you should pick the ones you need from the list, checking each driver to be included in your project.

If you are using ODBC, then you must include an ODBC setup disk along with your application. You can find the image of this disk on your VB CD or among your VB disks.

When you're done designating drivers to distribute, you may click the Next button to move to the next step.

▶ **See** "Accessing a Particular Type of Database," **p. 469**

▶ **See** "Visual Basic, the Jet Engine, and the Data Access Libraries," **p. 477**

Tip

If you aren't using any kind of data access in your application but this screen appears anyway, it means that your project has an unnecessary reference to a data access object library. Before continuing with SetupWizard, you should edit your application's project and use the Tools References VB menu option to remove the reference.

Screen for Step 3: Target for Setup Files

This screen (see fig. 16.3) allows you to specify where SetupWizard will write your application's setup files.

You can select either a disk drive or a directory as the target for setup files:

◆ If you select the Disk Drive option, you can select the Drive letter and the type of medium from the Drive and Type lists. If you select this option, you must have blank formatted disks on hand.

◆ If you select the Directory option, you must then select the target drive and directory from the scrolling lists.

Once you've selected the target, you may click the Next button to go to the next step.

Check installable ISAM
drivers your application uses

FIG. 16.2⇒

This screen only
appears if you have
used data access in
your application.

Reminder to
distribute ODBC
setup disks

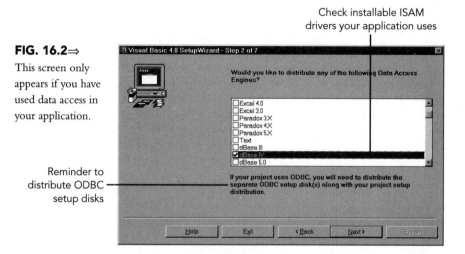

Specify disk drive or directory

FIG. 16.3⇒

You can specify
either a directory
or disk media as
the target to hold
your application's
distribution files.

Type of disk media

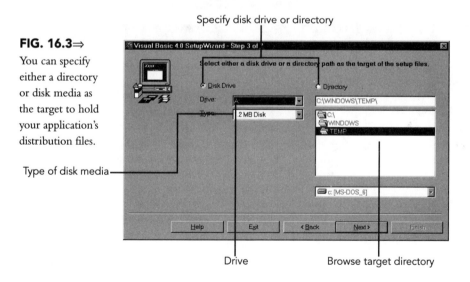

Drive   Browse target directory

Screen for Step 4: OLE Servers

This screen (see fig. 16.4) allows you to confirm or modify, if necessary, the list of OLE Servers referenced by your project.

You can uncheck any unneeded server on the list if you are sure your project doesn't need it or if you don't have distribution rights for it.

If your project needs servers that aren't on the list, you can click the Add OLE Servers button to browse for the OLE servers' EXE or DLL files. Only EXE or DLL files that have self-registration capability can be added as OLE Servers on this screen.

The File Details screen will give you detailed information about the highlighted OLE Server file (see fig. 16.5).

 Note OLE Servers created with VB are automatically created as self-registering files. ■

Uncheck OLE server's name to avoid distributing

FIG. 16.4⇒
Step 4 of the SetupWizard allows you to modify the list of OLE Servers to be distributed with your project.

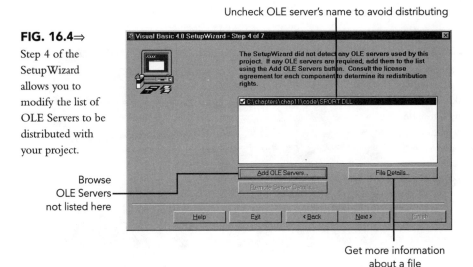

Browse OLE Servers not listed here

Get more information about a file

FIG. 16.5⇒
Clicking the File
Details button on
Step 4's screen
(refer to fig. 16.4)
will show you
detailed informa-
tion about an OLE
Server file.

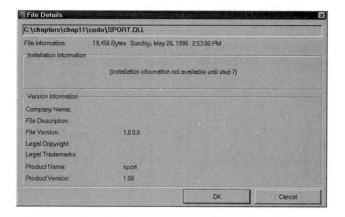

Screen for Step 5: Custom Control and Object References

This screen (see fig. 16.6) allows you to modify the list of custom control and custom object references. You may uncheck any file that you
know your project doesn't use, that are already on the user's system, or
to which you don't have distribution rights.

FIG. 16.6⇒
Step 5's screen
allows you to edit
custom control and
object references.

Uncheck reference
to exclude it from
setup files

Get more
information
about a file

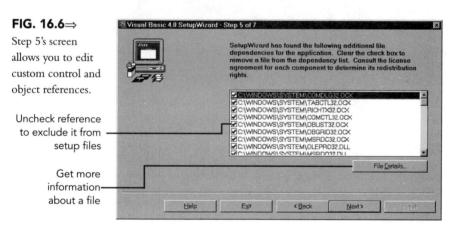

When done editing this list, you can click the <u>N</u>ext button to proceed
to SetupWizard's next step.

Tip

Before running SetupWizard, you should remove all unneeded custom controls and other references in your project with VB's Tools, Custom Controls, and Tools References menu options.

Screen for Step 6: OLE Automation

Depending on the Deployment Model you choose on this screen (see fig. 16.7), you can have your application installed in its own directory or in the OLESVR directory. If installed in the OLESVR directory, your application will be considered a shared OLE component and other applications can use it as an OLE server.

After making your choice on this screen, click the Next button to go to Step 7 of the SetupWizard.

This option allows your application
to have its own directory

FIG. 16.7⇒

Step 6 allows you to install your application in the OLESVR directory as a shared OLE automation component, or in its own directory as a stand-alone application.

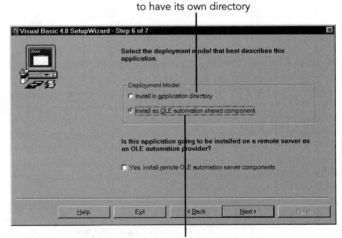

This option will install your application
in the OLESVR directory

Screen for Step 7: Additional Files

Besides custom controls, objects, and OLE Servers, a VB application needs other files to run properly. This screen lists all additional files needed by your application (see fig. 16.8). Such files include:

◆ Files needed by all VB applications, such as the VB run-time libraries.

◆ Files required by special features of your application. For instance, if you use the Data Control you will see the appropriate Type Library file for your environment.

You can uncheck files on this list if you know that your users already have them, or if you don't possess distribution rights to these files.

Part
V

Ch
16

Add Files button   VB run-time library file

FIG. 16.8⇒
SetupWizard's final step lets you manage other files that your project may need to run properly.

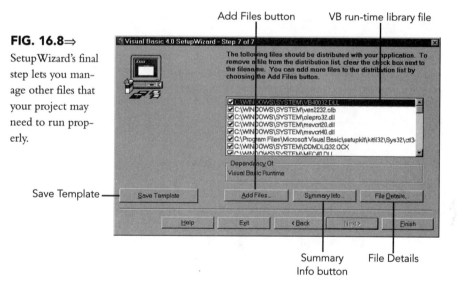

Save Template

Summary
Info button   File Details

You can browse for files to add with the Add Files button, as well. Such files might include a special local database file, a text file, or an INI file, which your application will need to run properly.

The File Details button will give detailed information on the high-lighted file (refer to fig. 16.5).

The Summary Info button will display a screen telling you the total number and uncompressed size of files to be distributed (see fig. 16.9).

If you click the Save Template button, you can then save the Setup information collected in the SetupWizard's seven steps to a setup template file with a VBZ extension (see fig. 16.10). Setup templates are useful when you want to run SetupWizard a second time to create duplicate setup disks, or when you want to create a setup routine that is only slightly different from a previous setup.

When you're done with the activities for this step, you can click the Finish button to create your application's distribution files.

Number of files

FIG. 16.9⇒

The File Summary screen gives you information on the total number and size of files to be distributed with your application.

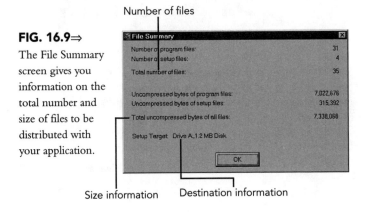

Size information   Destination information

FIG. 16.10⇒
Clicking the Save Template button displays this screen. The Save Template As file dialog allows you to save the current Setup parameters to a Setup Template file with a VBZ extension.

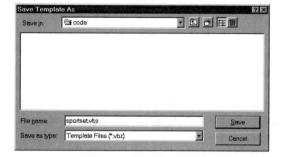

Final Screens

Once you've clicked the Finish button in step 7, SetupWizard compresses the distribution files. You'll see a screen similar to that shown in figure 16.11, giving you progress information on the file compression.

Uncompressed source file

FIG. 16.11⇒
SetupWizard informs you of its progress as it compresses distribution files.

Compressed file

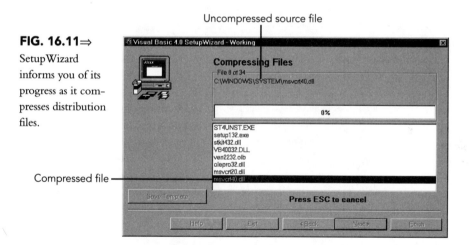

When SetupWizard finishes file compression, it will begin copying files to the distribution target you specified in Step 3. You will see a progress screen similar to that shown in figure 16.12. SetupWizard will prompt you for disks if you chose to distribute to disks in Step 3.

After the distribution files have been copied to the target, you will see a final screen confirming SetupWizard's success in creating your distribution files (see fig. 16.13). SetupWizard gives you another chance to save this Setup in a template file.

Your setup is now complete and you may exit the SetupWizard utility by clicking the Exit button.

FIG. 16.12⇒

The Copying Files screen lets you know the progress that SetupWizard is making as it copies compressed files to the distribution media. If you're distributing on disk, you'll get a prompt for the next disk as each disk is filled.

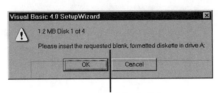

Prompt to insert blank diskette

FIG. 16.13⇒

SetupWizard's final screen.

Save Setup template file

A Customized Setup Program

You can modify the setup routine for your application by locating and editing its VB source code. The SetupWizard creates a customized setup program (Setup1.exe) for your application. This application is a VB application, and its VB project exists under your VB directory in the path SETUPKIT\SETUP1\SETUP1.VBP.

 Note For an explanation of the relationship between Microsoft's Setup.exe and your customized setup routine, see the section "Setup.Exe and SetupWizard's Custom Setup." ■

You can customize this project and save it in a separate directory so that future runs of SetupWizard won't overwrite it. The SETUP1 project contains many files, but the main focus of your customization efforts will probably be the Load event of the projects main form, frmSetup (see fig. 16.14).

Though the details of setup customization are beyond the scope of the Microsoft Certification exam, you may read the section "Creating a Custom Setup Program" in Chapter 30 of the VB Programmer's Guide to get information about customized setup using the Setup Toolkit.

FIG. 16.14⇒
You can customize an application's setup routine by opening and modifying SETUP1.VBP.

Customize the code in frmSetup's Load event procedure

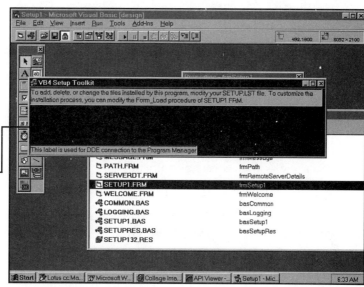

Understanding the Files for a Standard Microsoft Setup

A standard Microsoft setup routine requires the user to invoke Setup.exe. Setup.exe is, however, not the file customized by you or the SetupWizard. The customized setup executable is normally named Setup132.exe on 32-bit systems and Setup1.exe on 16-bit systems, though this is not a required name. Setup.exe runs this customized setup routine.

Setup.exe uses a special text file named Setup.lst to determine the name of the customized routine and the names of files needed by the setup routine to run on the user's system. Setup.lst also contains the name of other files to be installed on the user's system. SetupWizard also writes to Setup.lst

The following sections explain the relation between Setup.exe, the custom setup routine, and Setup.lst.

Setup.Lst and Other Files

SetupWizard creates a special text file named Setup.lst for each application that you set up. Setup.lst looks somewhat like an INI file (see the accompanying example). It has named sections with headers surrounded by brackets. Each section contains entries of the form:

```
ItemName=value
```

Many of the entries in this file are the names of files to be copied to the user's system. The contents of *value* for these entries is a long comma-delimited list detailing the compressed and uncompressed names of each file as well as version information.

Setup.lst's BootStrap section contains the names of files that must exist on the user's system before the customized setup routine can run. For instance, if the customized setup routine is a VB program, then the setup routine itself, along with the VB run-time libraries, must be copied to the user's system before it can run. The first file listed under the

BootStrap is the customized setup routine itself.

The Files section lists other files to be copied to the user's system during setup.

The Setup section contains non-file information needed during setup, such as screen captions and install directories.

The developer may insert other file sections as part of the customization process.

Further detail on the Setup.lst file is beyond the scope of the Certification Exam.

Part
V

Ch
16

Note For more detailed information on the meaning of the entries in Setup.lst and ways to customize this file, see the section "Creating the SETUP.LST File" in Chapter 30 of the *VB Programmer's Guide*. ▪

```
[BootStrap]
File1=1,,setup132.ex_,setup132.exe,$(WinPath),$(EXESelfRegister),,8/
➡15/1995,171520,4.0.0.2422
File2=1,,stkit432.dl_,stkit432.dll,$(WinSysPath),,$(Shared),8/
➡15/1995,24576,4.0.2422.0
File3=1,,VB40032.DL_,VB40032.DLL,$(WinSysPath),,$(Shared),8/
➡15/1995,721168,4.0.24.22
File4=1,,ven2232.ol_,ven2232.olb,$(WinSysPathSysFile),,,,9/29/
➡1995,37376,2.0.0.5524
File5=1,,olepro32.dl_,olepro32.dll,$(WinSysPath),$(DLLSelfRegister),
➡$(Shared),9/29/1995,72976,4.0.0.5254
File6=1,,msvcrt20.dl_,msvcrt20.dll,$(WinSysPathSysFile),,,9/
➡29/1995,253952,2.11.0.0
File7=1,,msvcrt40.dl_,msvcrt40.dll,$(WinSysPath),,$(Shared),9/
➡29/1995,312832,4.0.0.5254
File8=1,,ctl3d32.dl_,ctl3d32.dll,$(WinSysPathSysFile),,,8/15/
➡1995,27136,2.29.0.0
[Files]
File1=1,,sport.dl_,sport.dll,$(CommonFiles)\OleSvr,$(DllSelfRegister),
➡$(Shared),5/26/1996,19456,1.0.0.0
File2=1,,excel.EX_,excel.EXE,$(AppPath),$(EXESelfRegister),,8/
➡8/1996,16384,1.0.0.0
[Setup]
Title=excel
DefaultDir=$(ProgramFiles)\excel
Setup=setup132.exe
AppExe=excel.EXE
AppPath=
```

```
; The following lines may be deleted in order to obtain extra
; space for customizing this file on a full installation
➥diskette.
;
; XXXXXXXXXXXXXXXXXXXXXXXXXXXXXXXXXXXXXXXXXXXXXXXXXXXXXXXX
; XXXXXXXXXXXXXXXXXXXXXXXXXXXXXXXXXXXXXXXXXXXXXXXXXXXXXXXX
```

Setup.Exe and SetupWizard's Custom Setup

Microsoft's Setup.exe utility is the file the end user will run to install your application. Setup.exe itself contains no customized information about a specific application, however. Rather, its job is to prepare the environment for the customized setup routine and start the customized setup routine running.

Setup.exe's main tasks are:

1. Read the text file Setup.lst (see the previous section).
2. Copy all the files in Setup.lst's BootStrap section to the user's system.
3. Run the first file listed in the BootStrap section—this is assumed to be the custom setup routine.

At this point, the customized setup routine (with a default name of Setup132.exe for 32-bit systems and setup1.exe for 16-bit systems) takes over and finishes the installation of your application, copying the other files listed in Setup.lst, and performing any other customized tasks.

Taking the Disc Test

If you have read and understood the material in the chapter, you are ready to test your knowledge. Insert the CD-ROM that comes with this book and run the self-test software as described in Appendix H, "Using the CD-ROM."

From Here...

Upon completion of this chapter, you should be in good shape to pass the Microsoft Certification Exam for Visual Basic 4.0.

Part VI.

Appendixes

Glossary

16-bit An operating environment, operating system, or application which uses a two-byte (16-bit) scheme for memory addresses and data manipulation. Windows 3.x is a 16-bit operating environment. You can install a 16-bit version of VB 4.0 on either 16- or 32-bit operating systems in order to create 16-bit applications.

32-bit An operating environment, operating system, or application which uses a four-byte (32-bit) scheme for memory addresses and data manipulation. Windows 95 and Windows NT are 32-bit operating systems. You can install a 32-bit version of VB 4.0 on 32-bit operating systems in order to create 32-bit applications.

A

active window   The window that appears in front of any other window and has a highlighted title bar to distinguish it from other visible windows.

American National Standards Institute   See *ANSI character set.*

American Standard Code for Information Interchange   See *ASCII character set.*

ANSI character set   Represents the American National Standards Institute (ANSI), an 8-bit character set used by Microsoft Windows. This set allows you to represent up to 256 characters (0-255) using your keyboard. The first 128 characters (0-127) correspond to the letters and symbols on a standard U.S. keyboard. The second 128 characters (128-255) represent special characters, such as letters in international alphabets, accents, currency symbols, and fractions.

API   See *Application Programming Interface.*

application   A collection of code and graphical elements that are combined as a single program. Developers build and run VB applications within the VB development environment, while users run applications as executable files outside the development environment.

Application Programming Interface (API)   An API is a list of supported functions. Windows 95 supports the MS-DOS API, Windows API, and Win32 API. If a function is a member of the API, it is said to be a supported, or documented function. Functions that make up Windows, but are not part of the API, are referred to as *undocumented* functions.

application window   A general term which defines the first window that an application displays. It usually contains general information about the application; for example, the application name, version number, release date/year, and license and copyright information.

argument   A variable or value that is passed to a parameter in a procedure when the procedure is called. By default, VB passes the address of the argument variable and not its value.

ASCII   See *ASCII Character Set.*

ASCII character set   Represents the American Standarl Code for Information Interchange (ASCII), a 7-bit character set widely used to represent letters and symbols found on a standard U.S. keyboard. The ASCII character set is the same as the first 128 characters (0-127) in the ANSI character set.

B

BAS file (.BAS)   A standard module file.

Basic String (BSTR)   The OLE data type that Visual Basic uses to reference strings. Since C and the Windows API use a different memory model (LPSTR), the VB programmer must make special consideration when passing string arguments to Windows API routines.

beginning of file (BOF)   When working with data access, BOF is the location before the first record. In Visual Basic file I/O, it is the location of the first record in a file.

bitmap   An image file which usually has a BMP file extension. The image is represented by pixels and stored as a set of bits where each bit corresponds to one pixel. On color systems, more than one bit corresponds to each pixel.

BMP   The extension used for Windows bitmap files.

BOF   See *beginning of file (BOF).*

Bookmark   A string property of a recordset object that contains an identifier to the current record.

Boolean Expression   An expression that evaluates to either True or

False.

BSTR See *Basic String (BSTR)*.

Buffer A temporary holding area in memory where information can be stored.

C

Cartesian product Usually results from executing an SQL Select statement which references two or more tables in the FROM clause and does not include a WHERE or JOIN clause that indicates how the tables are to be joined. The Cartesian product will contain all rows from the first table matched with all rows from the second table, which is normally an enormous and meaningless set of data.

class The formal definition or template used to create an object. The class acts as the template from which an instance of an object is created at run time. The class defines the properties of the object and the methods used to control the object's behavior.

Clipboard A temporary storage area used by Microsoft Windows to contain and move text, graphics, and other types of information.

CLS file (.CLS) A class module file.

collection An object that contains an array of similar objects. The position of any specific object in the collection is not fixed and may vary.

compile error An error that occurs during compile time because of incorrectly assembled code.

compile time The action of translating source code into executable code.

compiler A program or utility which compiles (translates) a program's source code (written by a programmer) into executable code. The VB compiler creates an EXE file directly from your design-time application with the File, Make EXE menu option. You can also compile your application to memory when you run it at design time.

copy buffer   A location created by the Microsoft Jet database engine used to hold the contents of a record that is open for editing. When the current record pointer is moved or reset, the contents of the copy buffer is discarded.

custom control   A Visual Basic file with a VBX or OCX file extension. Custom controls can be added or deleted from the toolbox and are not part of a Visual Basic EXE file. In addition, custom controls also represent insertable objects that can extend the toolbox.

custom dialog box   A dialog box you create using a form that contains controls which allow the user to supply information to the application.

D

DAO   See *Data Access Objects (DAO)*.

Data Access Objects (DAO)   An object library which represents the functionality of the Microsoft Jet database engine. These objects are used to create, organize, and manipulate data within the program code.

Data Control   A standard control used to connect a selected data source with a VB application.

data types   Defines what kind of data a variable can store including Boolean, Integer, Date, String, and so on.

database management system (DBMS)   Software used to create, examine, organize, and modify information stored in a database.

DBMS   See *database management system (DBMS)*.

Debug   The process of determining and fixing both logic and syntax errors within an application.

design time   The time during which an application is built in the VB development environment. In comparison, run time defines the time during which you run the application within the development environment.

dialog box   A form/window used to get or provide information to the user (Print dialog box, Save As dialog box, and so on.)

DLL   See *Dynamic-Link Library (DLL)*.

Dynamic-Link Library (DLL)   A library containing functions and/or procedures that are accessible to and called from a VB application.

E

Empty   A value that specifies that no initial value has been assigned to a Variant variable. Empty variables are equal to 0 when working with numbers or zero-length when working with strings.

End of File (EOF)   In Visual Basic file I/O, the location of the last record in a file. In data access, the location after the last record.

EOF   See *End of File*.

Error handling   Code created to specifically deal with some types of errors at run time.

error number   A number from 0 to 65,535 that indicates which error occurred. In VB, you can find the current error number through the Err object's number property (Err.number).

event   An action, such as clicking with the mouse or pressing a key on the keyboard, which is associated with an object. These actions can be triggered by the user, the system, or through code.

event procedure   A procedure triggered by an event initiated by the user, program code, or system. A programmer places code in the event procedure that executes when the procedure gets triggered.

executable file (EXE)   An application that can run outside the development environment and has an EXE file extension.

explicit declaration   The process of explicitly declaring a variable with a name and data type before you reference it. VB does not require explicit declaration within a module unless the module includes the Option Explicit statement. See *Option Explicit.*

expression   Contains a combination of VB keywords, operators, variables, and constants that results in a action. For example, an expression can perform a calculation, manipulate strings, or test data.

F

fatal error   a type of run-time error that generates an error message, stops execution and closes the program.

flag   A variable used to track a condition in your application (e.g., Has the user changed the contents of a textbox control? Has the system deleted the specified file?).

focus   Defines the form or control that would receive any current mouse clicks or keyboard input. The object with focus is often visually distinguished by a blinking cursor or a highlighted title bar, for example.

form   A window or dialog box that functions as a container for controls.

FRM file (.FRM)   A form file.

function   A procedure that returns a value.

G

general procedure A procedure, created by the programmer, that must be explicitly called in order to run.

graphical user interface (GUI) An interface that consists of graphical objects that the user operates in order to get information from or provide information to the application.

GUI See *graphical user interface (GUI)*.

H

handle A unique integer defined by the system to identify an object, such as a form or control. A form and some controls have a run-time property, called hW

nd, which stores the value of the handle.

Hexadecimal (or Hex) A numerical notation system based on the number 16 and used often when specifying numeric values (such as color values or other constants) belonging to the operating system. This notation system uses the digits 0-9 to represent their usual values and the letters A–F to represent the numbers 10 through 15. In VB you can specify that a literal number is to be interpreted as a Hex number by prefixing &H to the number (for example: &H0010 would represent the decimal number 16).

hWnd See *handle*.

I

implicit declaration Describes the use of a variable without previously declaring its name and type. See *explicit declaration*.

INI file A Windows initialization file, which is a text file with the extension INI. An INI file has a special format consisting of section headers and keywords which define parameters to be read by an application at run time.

initialize   1) to cause an object such as a Form or an OLE server class to be instantiated in an application's memory space. 2) to assign a value to a variable for the first time.

installable ISAM driver   A driver that enables a VB application to access external database formats such as dBase and Paradox. ISAM is an acronym for Indexed Sequential Access Method.

instance   Refers to an object created from a specified class. For example, the txtEdit control object is an instance of the TextBox class.

instantiate   Create an instance of a class at run time (create an object).

ISAM drivers   See *installable ISAM driver.*

J

Jet Engine   The database engine used by Microsoft Access and VB. It consists of a set of routines contained in DLL files which allow an application to manipulate information stored in databases.

L

line-continuation character   Used to extend a single code statement onto multiple lines. The line-continuation character in Visual Basic is the combination of a space followed by an underscore (_).

line-continuation symbol   See *line-continuation character.*

LPSTR   Long Pointer to String; the memory model which C and the Windows API recognize for referencing strings. Since VB uses a different memory model (BSTR), the VB programmer must make special considerations when passing string arguments to Windows API routines.

M

MDI   See *multiple-document interface (MDI)*.

metafile   A file that stores an image as graphical objects rather than as pixels. It usually has a WMF file extension.

method   A procedure that belongs to an object and that operates on the object.

Microsoft Jet database Engine   A database management system that is built into both Microsoft Access and Visual Basic.

modal   An attribute of a window or dialog box that requires the user to take some action before the focus can switch to another form or dialog box.

modaless   Describes a window or dialog box that does not require user action before the focus can be switched to another form or dialog box.

module   A Visual Basic file that contains code. VB has several module file types including form, standard, and class module files.

multiple-document interface (MDI)   An interface that has a special form (an MDI form) whose principle role is as a container for other forms. An application can include only one MDI form. Microsoft Excel and Word for Windows are examples MDI applications.

N

Null   A Variant subtype; it specifies that a variable intentionally contains no valid data.

O

Object Browser   A dialog box that provides a list of available object libraries and information about the objects for a specified library.

Object library   An OLB file that provides information about objects available to OLE Automation controllers (like Visual Basic). Use the Object Browser to examine the contents of the object library which includes a list of objects and their properties and methods.

object variable   A variable type that references an object.

object   A particular instance of a class. Most of the internal data structures in Windows 95 are objects.

OCX file   A VB 4.0 custom control file supplied by Microsoft or a third-party developer. See *custom control*.

ODBC   See *Open Database Connectivity (ODBC)*.

OLB file   See *Object library*.

OLE (Object Linking and Embedding)   A standard that gives rules for defining interfaces between applications. An OLE Server application's interface uses *exposed objects* which provide properties and methods visible to other applications, known as OLE controllers or OLE clients.

OLE Automation   The part of the OLE standard that specifies the rules for manipulating an OLE server through its exposed objects.

OLE server   An application that uses the rules of the OLE standard to expose objects for the use of other programming tools.

Open Database Connectivity (ODBC)   A standard protocol that enables applications to connect to a variety of external database servers or files.

Option Explicit   A statement that indicates all variables must be explicitly declared within the module where the statement resides.

P

parameter   A variable that receives an argument passed to a procedure. In VB, the programmer specifies the number, relative position, and types of parameters in the header or declaration of a procedure.

pixel   Short for *picture element*; a dot that represents the smallest graphic unit of measurement on a screen. The actual size of a pixel is screen-dependent, and varies according to the size of the screen and the resolution being used.

pop-up menu   A menu that appears over a form usually when the right mouse button is clicked. Different pop-up menus can be associated with each control within a form so that a unique menu appears as the user clicks each control.

procedure   A named block of code that is executed as a unit. Function, Property, and Sub are types of procedures in Visual Basic.

project   In VB, a project is defined as a group of files that comprise an application.

project file   A VBP file that tracks the components and settings of a project: files, objects, project options, environment options, EXE options, and references associated with a project.

properties   Define the characteristics or behaviors of an object.

R

record   A set of related data about one item (e.g., person, product, invoice). A database table stores data in record or row format.

routine   A generic term that refers to a block of code that can be called and executed within a program.

run time   The period of time when code is running either as an executable file or within the design environment.

S

scope   Defined as the accessibility of a variable, procedure, or object. For example, a variable declared within a local procedure is available only within the procedure and therefore, has procedural-level or local scope.

shortcut key   A key or combination of keys that performs an operation. VB enables you to create shortcut keys for your own menu items within the Menu Editor.

splash screen   See *application window.*

SQL   An acronym for Structured Query Language. SQL is a script language that is used to manage the structure of a relational database as well as the data stored within the relational database. For example, SQL can be used to add, delete, query, and update data as well as create table structures.

stack   The fixed amount memory that Visual Basic uses to store local variables and arguments during procedure calls.

standard control   A control that is always included in the Toolbox and contained within a Visual Basic EXE file. Standard controls in VB include the commandbutton, textbox, and the label. See *custom control.*

startup form   The form designated in a VB project as the first form displayed in the application. By default, the first form created when you start a new project is the startup form. However, you can change the startup form using the Project Options dialog box.

sub main   A procedure that provides an alternative to starting an application with a startup form (see *startup form*). You can specify, in the Option dialog box, that you prefer to start the application with a sub main procedure rather than a form. If you choose this option, you must create a procedure called sub main within a standard module.

subroutine   See *routine*.

suspend   To temporarily stop a process.

syntax   The defined order and punctuation of components that comprise a programming language statement.

T

toolbar   An area of a form/window that contains buttons used as shortcuts to commonly used menu items.

toolbox   Displays the VB controls that are currently available within the design environment.

trappable error   An error that can be trapped and handled by an error-handling procedure while an application is running.

twip   The default standard of measurement for the Windows and VB visual interface. A twip represents $1/1440^{th}$ of an inch, since a twip is one twentieth of a point (a point is $1/72^{nd}$ of an inch). By default, the size and position of a visible object is measured in twips.

U

Unicode   A character-encoding scheme that uses 2 bytes for every character regardless of whether or not it is an ASCII character. This scheme is supported by the Microsoft Windows NT platform.

V

variable scope   See *scope*.

VBA   See *Visual Basic for Applications*.

VBP file (.VBP)   A project file. In previous versions of Visual Basic, a project file has a MAK extension.

VBX file   A VB 3.0 custom control file supplied by Microsoft or a third-party developer. See *custom control*.

VBZ file   The three–letter extension of a SetUpWizard template file used to save customized setup information. The developer can use this template as the basis for future setups of the same application.

Visual Basic for Applications (VBA)   The scripting/macro language currently used in many Microsoft Office Suite products such as Excel and Access. VB 4.0 uses the VBA language engine.

W

Win32 API   The 32-bit application programming interface used to write 32-bit Windows based applications. It provides access to the operating system and other functions.

Windows clipboard   See *clipboard*.

Windows Registry   A database maintained by Windows in the file REG.DAT. In 16-bit Windows, the registry contains information about OLE servers and in 32-bit Windows it contains other information as well (Microsoft intends that the Windows registry will eventually make the use of INI files obsolete). You can view and edit the Windows Registry's contents with the REGEDIT application.

B

Certification Checklist

In addition to a resource like this book, this list of tasks tells you what you need to know to continue the certification process.

Get Started

Once you have decided to start the certification process, you should use the following list as a guideline for getting started:

1. Get the Microsoft Roadmap to Education and Certification. (See "The Certification Roadmap" sidebar at the end of this appendix.)

2. Use the Roadmap Planning Wizard to determine *your* certification path.

3. Take the Visual Basic 4.0 Assessment Exams located on the CD-ROM that accompanies this book to determine *your* competency level. For Microsoft products other than VB 4.0, you can use the Assessment Exams located on the Roadmap to get a feel for the type of questions that appear on the exam. (See "Assessment Exams" in Appendix C.)

Get Prepared

Getting started is one thing, but getting prepared to take the certification exam is a rather difficult process. The following guidelines will help you prepare for the exam:

1. Use the training materials listed in the Planning Wizard:

   - Microsoft Online Institute (MOLI). (See "The Microsoft Online Training Institute," in Appendix C.)

   - Self-Paced Training. (See "Self-Paced Training," in Appendix C.)

   - Authorized Technical Education Center (ATEC). (See "Training Resources," in Appendix C.)

   - Additional study materials listed in the roadmap.

2. Review the Exam Study Guide in Appendix C.

3. Review the Exam Prep Guide on the roadmap.

4. Gain experience with VB 4.0.

Get Certified

Call Sylvan Prometric at 1-800-755-EXAM to schedule your exam at a location near you. (See "How Do I Register for the Exam?" in Appendix C; and Appendix D, "Testing Tips.")

Get Benefits

Microsoft will send your certification kit approximately 2–4 weeks after passing the exam. This kit qualifies you to become a Microsoft Certified Professional. (See "Benefits Up Close and Personal," in the Introduction to this book.)

The Certification Roadmap

The Microsoft Roadmap to Education and Certification is an easy-to-use Windows-based application that includes all of the information you need to plan a successful training and certification strategy. The roadmap:

- Provides comprehensive information on the requirements for Microsoft Certified Professional certifications, with detailed exam topic outlines and preparation guidelines.

- Includes detailed outlines and prerequisites for Microsoft courses that are related to specific certification exams, helping you determine which courses teach the skills you need to meet your certification goals.

- Includes information on related Microsoft products and services.

- Helps you create a personal training and certification plan and print a to-do list of required certification activities.

You can request the Roadmap from Microsoft. In the U.S. and Canada, call 1-800-636-7544. Outside the U.S. and Canada, contact your local Microsoft office.

Or you can download it at the following online addresses:

- The Internet: **ftp://ftp.microsoft.com/Services/MSEdCert/E&CMAP.ZIP**

- The Microsoft Network (MSN): Go To MOLI, Advising Building, E&C Roadmap.

- Microsoft TechNet: Search for "Roadmap" and install from the built-in setup link.

How do I Get There from Here?

Becoming certified requires a certain level of commitment. The information in this appendix will answer some of the questions you may have about the certification process.

What Will I be Tested On?

You should be able to apply your knowledge and experience with Visual Basic 4.0 to perform the following tasks:

- ◆ Determining user requirements
- ◆ Developing and recommending technology-based solutions to solve business problems

◆ Designing and coding software applications

◆ Performing software testing and quality assurance

To successfully complete the VB 4.0 certification exam, you need, according to Microsoft, "[the] ability to apply a comprehensive set of skills to the tasks necessary to design, build, and implement business solutions by using Visual Basic 4.0."

Analysis is Good, but Synthesis is Harder

Microsoft Certified Professional exams test for specific cognitive skills needed for the job functions being tested. Educational theorists postulate a hierarchy of cognitive levels, ranging from the most basic (knowledge) up to the most difficult (evaluation) and a set of skills associated with each level.

◆ *Knowledge* is the lowest cognitive level at which you can identify, define, locate, recall, state, match, arrange, label, outline, and recognize items, situations, and concepts. Questions that ask for definitions or recitation of lists of characteristics test at this level.

◆ *Comprehension*, the level built immediately upon knowledge, requires that you translate, distinguish, give examples, discuss, draw conclusions, estimate, explain, indicate, and paraphrase, rather than simply play back answers learned by rote.

◆ *Application* is the level at which hands-on activities come into play. Questions at this level ask you to apply, calculate, solve, plot, choose, demonstrate, design, change, interpret, or operate.

◆ *Analysis*, one of the top three levels, requires a thorough grounding in the skills required at lower levels. You operate at this level when you analyze, state conclusions, detect logic errors, compare and contrast, break down, make an inference, map one situation or problem to another, diagnose, diagram, or discriminate.

◆ *Synthesis* (which is harder than analysis) requires some creativity and the ability to rebuild and reintegrate what may have been disassembled during analysis. This level requires you to construct a table or graph, design, formulate, integrate, generalize, predict, arrange, propose, tell in your own words, or show a relationship.

◆ *Evaluation*, the highest cognitive level, is based on all the skills accumulated at lower levels. At this level, you assess, apply standards, decide, indicate fallacies, weigh, show the relationship, summarize, decide, look at a situation and tell what is likely to occur, or make a judgment.

Exam Objectives

The following list of objectives defines the specific skills Microsoft wants the exam to measure. As you review the list, you can see the level at which the Visual Basic 4.0 exam tests your knowledge and ability to implement, maintain, and troubleshoot the operating system. When an objective or item on the exam includes a verb or verb phrase associated with a given cognitive level (see the previous section, "Analysis is Good, but Synthesis is Harder"), it is asking you to perform at that cognitive level.

For example, the exam objective "Differentiate between an OLE server compiled as an executable file and an OLE server compiled as an OLE DLL" asks you to perform at the Analysis level because it asks you to "discriminate" (differentiate) between items. It's a good idea to be prepared to be tested at the Analysis level or higher for each objective.

You should review the following objectives and be able to apply the listed skills to the tasks described earlier in "What will I be Tested On?"

Visual Basic Data Types

◆ Use a user-defined data type to meet specified needs.

◆ Given an array declaration, identify how many elements the array contains.

◆ Given a scenario, identify the appropriate data type to use.

◆ Given a scenario, choose whether to use public or private scope.

◆ Given a scenario, decide whether to declare a variable **Static**.

◆ Use conversion functions to convert between given data types.

◆ Create an application that adds and deletes controls at run time.

◆ Use the **Forms** collection and the **Controls** collection.

Working with Visual Basic Code

◆ Write and call **Sub** and **Function** procedures that require multiple arguments or optional arguments.

◆ Write and call **Sub** and **Function** procedures that require an array as an argument.

◆ Write conditional code and control structures.

◆ Use the string manipulation functions **Left**, **Right**, **Mid**, **Instr**, **Len**.

◆ Describe the effects of causing an event to occur in another event.

◆ Describe the relationship between the name of a control and the code that is attached to that control.

◆ Create and use a class module in a Visual Basic 4.0 application.

◆ Given a scenario, choose whether to use a standard module or a class module.

◆ Use the **With** statement to perform multiple actions on a given object.

◆ Use the **For Each...Next** statement to iterate through a collection.

◆ Use **Public** procedures and **Property** procedures to communicate between forms.

◆ Use the Microsoft Windows 95 common controls.

Debugging Applications

◆ Set breakpoints to stop program execution.

◆ Set watch expressions during program execution.

◆ Use the Immediate pane to check or change values.

◆ Given a scenario, use the appropriate error-trapping options.

Object Properties

◆ Set the tab order of controls on a form.

◆ Set the value of a control property.

Object Events

◆ Describe when the Paint event occurs, and describe the effect of the **AutoRedraw** property on the Paint event.

◆ Use the **DoEvents** statement, and describe its purpose.

◆ Use the KeyPress, KeyDown, and KeyUp events to trap and validate data entry.

◆ Implement drag-and-drop operations in an application.

◆ Given a scenario, add code to the appropriate form event, such as Initialize, Terminate, Load, Unload, QueryUnload, Activate, and Deactivate.

◆ Use the Printer, Application, Debug, Clipboard, Screen, and Err objects.

Menus

◆ Add a menu interface to an application.

◆ Dynamically modify menu appearance.

◆ Dynamically add and delete menu items.

◆ Add a pop-up menu to an application.

Handling Errors

◆ Create an application that contains an error-handling routine.

◆ Create an application that uses the **Err** object to get information about an error and uses the **Err** object to generate an error.

◆ Given a scenario that involves nested procedures, ascertain which error-handling routine will be invoked.

Dynamic-Link Libraries

◆ Declare and call a DLL routine.

◆ Pass a null pointer to a DLL routine.

◆ Given a scenario, pass an argument by value and by reference.

◆ Create an application that uses both the 16-bit and the 32-bit versions of the Microsoft Windows API function **GetWindowsDirectory**.

◆ Given a scenario, identify when it is necessary to use the **Alias** clause.

Using OLE to Integrate Applications

◆ Create an application that uses OLE to link or embed an embeddable object in a Visual Basic form.

◆ Describe the purpose of references, and add a reference to an object library.

◆ Use the Object Browser to display objects, properties, and methods provided by an OLE server.

◆ Given a scenario, choose whether to use the **CreateObject** function or the **GetObject** function.

◆ Create an application that controls an OLE server in specific ways.

◆ Describe the difference between early binding and late binding.

Creating OLE Servers

◆ Create an OLE server to meet specific requirements.

◆ Make an object into an externally creatable object by setting project options and class module properties.

◆ Debug an OLE server in the design-time environment by using a second instance of Visual Basic 4.0.

◆ Use **Property** procedures and public variables to create custom properties.

◆ Use public **Sub** and **Function** procedures to create methods.

◆ Differentiate between an OLE server compiled as an executable file and an OLE server compiled as an OLE DLL.

◆ Use a collection to store multiple instances of an object.

◆ Given a scenario, choose the appropriate setting for the **Instancing** property of a class module.

Part

VI

App

C

Using the Data Control

◆ Create an application that uses the **Data** control to view, add, update, and delete data in a Microsoft Access database.

◆ Use the **Find** or **Seek** methods to search a **Recordset**.

◆ Given a scenario, describe which of the **Data** control specific events will occur.

◆ Use the data-bound list box control or the data-bound combo box control to add data to a table.

◆ Use the data-bound grid control to display information.

◆ Given a scenario, ascertain whether you can access a particular type of database.

Using Data Access Objects

◆ Given a scenario, decide which type of **Recordset** to use: dynaset, snapshot, or table.

◆ Add, modify, and delete records in a **Recordset**.

- Loop through a **Recordset**.
- Find a record in a **Recordset**.
- Navigate through a **Recordset**.
- Given a scenario, open the appropriate type of **Recordset** with the appropriate options.
- Use transactions.
- Create an application that uses a SQL pass-through query.
- Use a SQL statement to retrieve particular records from a database.
- Create an application that handles multiple users and resolves locking conflicts.

Distributing an Application

- Use the SetupWizard to create an effective setup program.
- Create a Setup program that installs an OLE server on a user's computer.

Using Multiple-Document Interface (MDI)

- Create an application that uses the MDI.

Creating 16-Bit and 32-Bit Applications

- Create an application that can be set up and installed under both 16-bit and 32-bit operating systems.
- Use conditional compilation to maintain one project for both 16-bit and 32-bit operating systems.
- Given a scenario, determine if your application can use either a VBX custom control or an OLE custom control.
- Convert a Visual Basic 3.0 application that uses VBX custom controls to a Visual Basic 4.0 application that uses OLE controls.

What Kinds of Questions Can I Expect?

The Visual Basic 4.0 Certification exam includes two types of multiple choice items: single-answer and double-answer.

Single-Answer Multiple-Choice Item

A single-answer multiple-choice item presents a problem and a list of possible answers. You must select the best answer to the given question from a list. Each answer will be preceded by an OptionButton control.

Example:

Which of the following Visual Basic object types supports the Change event?

A CommandButton

B Label

C TextBox

D Form

Your response to a single-answer multiple-choice item is scored as either correct (1 point) or incorrect (0 points).

The answer to the above question is TextBox.

Part
VI
App
C

Double-Answer Multiple-Choice Item

A double-answer multiple-choice item presents a problem and a list of possible answers. You must select the best answer to the given question from a list. The question will be followed by a phrase (pick two). Each answer will be preceded by a CheckBox control.

Example:

You can access the Menu Editor at design time by: (pick two)

A Keying Ctrl+M

B Keying Ctrl+E

C Choosing the Tools, Menu Editor option from the VB menu

D Choosing the View, Menu Editor option from the VB menu

Your response to a double-answer multiple-choice item is also scored as either correct (1 point) or incorrect (0 points). Your response is scored as being correct only if both the correct answers are selected. No partial credit is given for a response that does not include both correct answers.

The answer to the above question is (B) Keying Ctrl+E and (C)

<u>T</u>ools, <u>M</u>enu Editor.

How Should I Prepare for the Exam?

It's simple. The best way to prepare for the Visual Basic 4.0 Certified exam is to study, learn, and master Visual Basic 4.0. If you'd like a little more guidance, Microsoft recommends these specific steps:

1. Identify the objectives you'll be tested on. (See "Exam Objectives" earlier in this appendix.)
2. Assess your current mastery of those objectives.
3. Practice tasks and study the areas that you haven't mastered.

Following are some tools and techniques, in addition to this book, that may offer a little more help.

Assessment Exams

Microsoft provides self-paced practice, or assessment exams, that you can take at your own computer. Assessment exams let you answer questions that are very much like the items in the actual certification exams. Your assessment exam score doesn't necessarily predict what your score will be on the actual exam, but its immediate feedback lets you determine the areas requiring extra study. And the assessment exams offer an additional advantage; they use the same computer-based testing tool as the certification exams, so you don't have to learn to use the tool on exam day.

An assessment exam exists for almost every certification exam. You can find a complete list of available assessment exams in the Certification Roadmap.

Microsoft Resources

A number of useful resources available from Microsoft are listed as follows:

1. Visual Basic 4.0. A key component of your exam preparation is your actual use of the product. Gain as much "real world" experience with VB 4.0 as possible. As you work with the product, study the online and printed documentation, focusing on areas relating to the exam objectives.

2. Microsoft TechNet, an information service for support professionals and system administrators. If you're a TechNet member, you receive a monthly CD full of technical information.

 Note To join TechNet, refer to the TechNet section in the Microsoft Education and Certification Roadmap (see "The Certification Roadmap" sidebar in Appendix B.) ▪

3. The Microsoft Developer Network, a technical resource for Microsoft developers. If you're a member of the Developer Network, you can receive information on a regular basis through the Microsoft Developer Network CD, *Microsoft Developer Network News*, or the Developer Network Forum on CompuServe.

Note To join the Microsoft Developer Network, refer to the Microsoft Developer Network section in the Roadmap. ▪

4. The Visual Basic 4.0 Exam Preparation Guide, a Microsoft publication that provides important specifics about the Visual Basic 4.0 test. The Exam Preparation Guide is updated regularly to reflect changes and is the source for the most up-to-date information about Exam 70-65.

Part

VI

App

C

Note The exam preparation guide can change at any time without prior notice, solely at Microsoft's discretion. Before you register for an exam, make sure that you have the current exam preparation guide by contacting one of the following sources:

- Microsoft Sales Fax Service. Call 800-727-3351 in the United States and Canada. Outside the U.S. and Canada, contact your local Microsoft office.
- CompuServe. GO MSEDCERT, Library Number 5.
- Internet. Anonymous ftp to **ftp.microsoft.com. /Services/ MSEdCert/Certification/ExamPreps.**
- Sylvan Prometric. Call 800-755-EXAM in the U.S. and Canada. Outside the U.S. and Canada, contact your local Sylvan office.

Microsoft Online Training Institute (MOLI)

The Microsoft Online Training Institute (MOLI) on MSN, the Microsoft Network, is an interactive learning and information resource where Learning Advisors (instructors) pair their expert knowledge, guidance, and motivation with electronic self-study materials.

You may access MOLI at its main Classroom Building site on the Internet at **http://moli.microsoft.com**.

You enroll in a class, pay a small tuition fee (to cover the cost of materials and the Learning Advisor's time and expertise), and then receive a shortcut to the classroom. As a student, you can participate in class by interacting with a Learning Advisor and fellow students online via Exchange (e-mail), bulletin boards, forums, or other online communication services available through MSN. You control your own time by studying when and where you choose, working at your own speed, and attending the virtual "class" as often or as little as you wish.

Only students enrolled in a class can participate in its online chat sessions and view the contents of the classroom, such as courseware and other materials provided by the Learning Advisor. In addition to MOLI campus resources, you have access to several other resources:

♦ The Assignments BBS give you access to courseware assignments, test questions that measure subject-matter comprehension, chapter review guides, lab assignments, and information
about certification exam topics. You can take advantage of these
resources anytime.

♦ One or more chat sessions per week allow you to supplement
class courseware, interact with other classmates to solve "real
life" situations, and get expert advice.

♦ The Notes BBS lets students download and play files, tips and
tools, and resources available through Microsoft.

Part
VI
App
C

Self-Paced Training

If you prefer to learn on your own, you can obtain Microsoft Official
Curriculum training (as well as non-Microsoft Official Curriculum
courses) in self-paced formats. Self-paced training kits are available
through courses offered on the Microsoft Online Training Institute,
with materials available in book, computer-based training (CBT), and
mixed-media (book and video) formats.

Microsoft Approved Study Guides, such as this book, are self-paced
training materials developed by Independent Courseware Vendors
(ICVs) to help you prepare for Microsoft Certified Professional exams.
The Study Guides include both single self-paced training courses and a
series of training courses that map to one or more MCP exams.

Self-training kits and study guides are often available through Microsoft
authorized training centers; or you can purchase them where books
from Microsoft Press are sold.

Other Online Resources

Both the Microsoft Network (MSN) and CompuServe (GO
MECFORUM) provide access to technical forums for open discussions
and questions about Microsoft products. Microsoft's World Wide Web
site (**http://www.microsoft.com**) also allows you to access information about certification and education programs.

Training Resources

Microsoft product groups have designed training courses to support the certification process. The Microsoft Official Curriculum is developed by Microsoft course designers, product developers, and support engineers to include courses that help you prepare for MCP exams.

Authorized Technical Education Centers (ATECs) are approved by Microsoft to provide training on Microsoft products and related technologies. By enrolling in a course taught by a Microsoft Solution Provider ATEC, you will get high-end technical training on the design, development, implementation, and support of enterprise-wide solutions using Microsoft operating systems, tools, and technologies.

You also may take MOC courses via face-to-face training offered by Microsoft Authorized Academic Training Program (AATP) institutions. AATP schools use authorized materials and curriculum designed for the Microsoft Certified Professional program and deliver Microsoft authorized materials, including the Microsoft Official Curriculum, over an academic term.

Fundamentals of Microsoft Visual Basic 4.0, Course 403, and *Programming with Microsoft Visual Basic 4.0*, Course 404, available from Microsoft authorized training institutions, may help you prepare for the exam. Course 403 lasts three days and Course 404 is five days long.

For a referral to an AATP or ATEC in your area, call 800-SOLPROV.

Suggested Reading and Internet Sites

When you're looking for additional study aids, check out the books and online sites listed in Appendix F.

How do I Register for the Exam?

Registering for the Visual Basic 4.0 certification exam is simple:

1. Contact Sylvan Prometric at (800) 755-EXAM, with the examination number (70-65), your Social Security number, and credit card at the ready.

2. Complete the registration procedure by phone. (Your SSN becomes the ID attached to your private file; the credit card takes care of the $100 test fee.) Request contact information for the testing center closest to you.

3. After you receive the registration and payment confirmation letter from Sylvan Prometric, call the testing center to schedule your exam. When you call to schedule, you'll be provided with instructions regarding the appointment, cancellation procedures, and ID requirements, and information about the testing center location.

You can verify the number of questions and time allotted for your exam at the time of registration. You can schedule exams up to six weeks in advance, or as late as one working day ahead, but you must take the exam within one year of your payment. To cancel or reschedule your exam, contact Sylvan Prometric at least two working days before your scheduled exam date.

 Note   At some locations, same-day registration (at least two hours before test time) is available, subject to space availability. ▪

Part

VI

App

C

Testing Tips

You've mastered the required tasks to take the exam. After reviewing and re-reviewing the exam objectives, you're confident that you have the skills specified in the exam objectives. You're ready to perform at the highest cognitive level, and it's time to head for the testing center. This appendix covers some tips and tricks to remember.

Before the Test

- Wear comfortable clothing. You want to focus on the exam, not on a tight shirt collar or a pinching pair of shoes.
- Allow plenty of travel time. Get to the testing center 10 or 15 minutes early; nothing's worse than rushing in at the last minute. Give yourself time to relax.

◆ If you've never been to the testing center before, make a trial run a few days before to make sure that you know the route to the center.

◆ Carry with you at least two forms of identification, including one photo ID (such as a driver's license or company security ID). You will have to show them before you can take the exam.

Remember that the exams are closed-book. The use of laptop computers, notes, or other printed materials is not permitted during the exam session.

At the test center, you'll be asked to sign in. The test administrator will give you a Testing Center Regulations form that explains the rules that govern the examination. You will be asked to sign the form to indicate that you understand and will comply with its stipulations.

When the administrator shows you to your test computer, make sure that:

◆ The testing tool starts up and displays the correct exam. If a tutorial for using the instrument is available, you should be allowed time to take it.

Note   If you have any special needs, such as reconfiguring the mouse buttons for a left-handed user, you should inquire about them when you register for the exam with Sylvan Prometric. Special configurations are not possible at all sites, so you should not assume that you will be permitted to make any modifications to the equipment setup and configuration. Site administrators are *not* permitted to make modifications without prior instructions from Sylvan. ■

◆ You have a supply of scratch paper for use during the exam. (The administrator collects all scratch paper and notes made during the exam before your leave the center.) Some centers are now providing you with a wipe-off board and magic marker to use instead of paper. You are not permitted to make any kind of notes to take with you, due to exam security.

◆ Some exams may include additional materials, or exhibits. If any exhibits are required for your exam, the test administrator will provide you with them before you begin the exam and collect them from you at the end of the exam.

◆ The administrator tells you what to do when you complete the exam.

◆ You get answers to any and all of your questions or concerns before the exam begins.

As a Microsoft Certification examination candidate, you are entitled to the best support and environment possible for your exam. If you experience any problems on the day of the exam, inform the Sylvan Prometric test administrator immediately.

During the Test

The testing software lets you move forward and backward through the items, so you can implement a strategic approach to the test.

1. Go through all the items, answering the easy questions first. Then go back and spend time on the harder ones. Microsoft guarantees that there are no trick questions. The correct answer is always among the list of choices.

2. Eliminate the obviously incorrect answer first to clear away the clutter and simplify your choices.

3. Answer all the questions. You aren't penalized for guessing, so it can't hurt.

4. Don't rush. Haste makes waste (or substitute the cliché of your choice).

After the Test

When you have completed an exam:

- ◆ The testing tool gives you immediate, online notification of your pass or fail status, except for beta exams. Because of the beta process, your results for a beta exam are mailed to you approximately six to eight weeks after the exam.

- ◆ The administrator gives you a printed Examination Score Report indicating your pass or fail status and your exam results by section.

- ◆ Test scores are automatically forwarded to Microsoft within five working days after you take the test. If you pass the exam, you receive confirmation from Microsoft within two to four weeks.

If you don't pass a certification exam:

- ◆ Review your individual section scores, noting areas where your score must be improved. The section titles in your exam report generally correspond to specific groups of exam objectives.

- ◆ Review the exam information in this book; then get the latest Exam Preparation Guide and focus on the topic areas that need strengthening.

- ◆ Intensify your effort to get your real-world, hands-on experience and practice with Visual Basic 4.0.

- ◆ Try taking one or more of the approved training courses.

- ◆ Review the suggested readings listed at the end of this appendix or in the Exam Preparation Guide.

- ◆ Take (or retake) the VB 4.0 Assessment Exam.

- ◆ Call Sylvan Prometric to register, pay, and schedule the exam again.

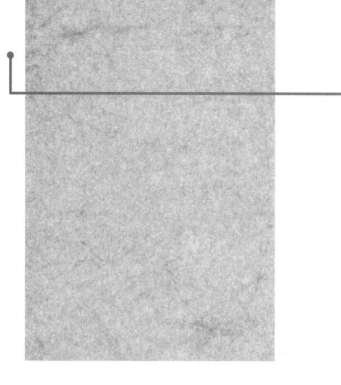

Contacting Microsoft

Microsoft encourages feedback from exam candidates—especially suggestions for improving any of the exams or preparation materials.

To provide program feedback, to find out more about Microsoft Education and Certification materials and programs, to register with Sylvan Prometric, or to get other useful information, check the following resources.

 Note Outside the United States or Canada, contact your local Microsoft office or Sylvan Prometric testing center. ▪

Microsoft Certified Professional Program

(800) 636-7544

For information about the Microsoft Certified Professional program and exams, and to order the Microsoft Roadmap to Education and Certification.

Sylvan Prometric Testing Centers

(800) 755-EXAM

To register to take a Microsoft Certified Professional exam at any of more than 700 Sylvan Prometric testing centers around the world.

Microsoft Sales Fax Service

(800) 727-3351

For Microsoft Certified Professional Exam Preparation Guides and Microsoft Official Curriculum course descriptions and schedules.

Education Program and Course Information

(800) SOLPROV

For information about Microsoft Official Curriculum courses, Microsoft education products, and the Microsoft Solution Provider Authorized Technical Education Center (ATEC) program, where you can attend a Microsoft Official Curriculum course.

Microsoft Certification Development Team

Fax: (206) 936-1311

To volunteer for participation in one or more exam development phases or to report a problem with an exam. Address written correspondence to:

> Certification Development Team
> Microsoft Education and Certification
> One Microsoft Way
> Redmond, WA 98052

Microsoft TechNet Technical Information Network

(800) 344-2121

For support professionals and system administrators. (Outside the U.S. and Canada, call your local Microsoft subsidiary for information.)

Microsoft Developer Network (MSDN)

(800) 759-5474

The official source for software development kits, device driver kits, operating systems, and information about developing applications for Microsoft Windows and Windows NT.

Part
VI

App
E

Microsoft Technical Support Options

(800) 936-3500

For information about the technical support options available for Microsoft products, including technical support telephone numbers and Premier Support options. (Outside the U.S. and Canada, call your local Microsoft subsidiary for information.)

Microsoft Online Institute (MOLI)

(800) 449-9333

For information about Microsoft's new online training program.

F

Suggested Reading

Titles from Que

Que Corporation offers a wide variety of technical books for all levels
of users. Following are some recommended titles, in alphabetical order
by author, that can provide you with additional information on many of
the exam topics and objectives.

Tip

To order any books from Que Corporation or other imprints of Macmillan
Computer Publishing (SAMS, New Riders Publishing, Ziff-Davis Press, and
others), call 800-428-5331, visit Macmillan's Information SuperLibrary on
the World Wide Web (**http://www.mcp.com**), or check your local book-
seller.

Visual Basic 4 Tutor

Author: Clint Hicks

ISBN: 0-7897-0733-0

This complete kit with its accompanying CD-ROM helps readers learn at their own pace from hundreds of hands-on video presentation segments with voice narration.

Optimizing Visual Basic 4

Author: Ward R. Hitt

ISBN: 0-7897-0206-1

This book unveils the professional secrets to speeding up all types of VB applications. Includes valuable programs for optimizing code and expert tips on optimizing graphics, data access, functions, procedures, and more.

Using Visual Basic 4

Author: Mike McKelvey

ISBN: 0-7897-0266-5

This is an easy-to-use tutorial for beginning programmers. It covers the fundamentals that a beginner needs to know to begin programming with VB.

- ◆ Relates sample programs to real tasks the new programmer might need to program
- ◆ Find-the-Bug exercises and review questions and answers in each chapter to aid in learning
- ◆ Tips, Note, Cautions, and Troubleshooting sections

Visual Basic 4 By Example

Author: Jacobs & Potts, et al.

ISBN: 0-7897-0000-X

A book for novice programmers and for experienced programmers of other languages who are learning VB Features multi-level code examples to help illustrate tutorials. Learning is reinforced at the end of each chapter with review questions and exercises.

Special Edition Using Visual Basic 4

Author: Jeff Webb, Mike McKelvey, et al.

ISBN: 0-56529-998-1

A comprehensive guide to successful VB programming providing extensive coverage of every topic and technique for creating optimized, customized applications with VB.

- ◆ In-depth coverage of OLE and data access
- ◆ Coverage of VB and Microsoft Office
- ◆ Disk with source code, interface modules, and project files
- ◆ Tutorials and practical examples

The Official Guide to Visual Basic 4

Author: Visual Basic Programmer's Journal

ISBN: 0-7897-9465-X

This is a comprehensive collection of independent chapters exploring each of the key features of Visual Basic. It covers all of the important topics, including Windows 95 development, distributed OLE, optimization, database access, using the Win32 API, communications, and more.

Building Windows 95 Applications With Visual Basic 4

Author: Clayton Walnum

ISBN: 0-7897-0209-6

With this award-winning book (Visual Basic Programmers' Journal 1996 Readers Choice Award), you will learn how to build powerful applications that demonstrate all of the new features in Windows 95.

Other Titles

PC Magazine Visual Basic Programmer's Guide to the Win 32 API, by Daniel Appleman (Ziff-Davis; ISBN 1-56276-287-7)

Visual Basic 4 Developer's Guide, by Charlesworth Boyle, et al. (SAMS; ISBN 0-672-30783-9)

Tricks of the Visual Basic 4 Gurus, by James Bettone, et al. (SAMS; ISBN 0-672-30929-7)

Microsoft Visual Basic Developer's Workshop, 3rd Edition, by John Clark Craig (Microsoft Press; ISBN 1-55615-664-2)

Object Programming with Visual Basic 4, by Joel R. Dehlen and Matthew J. Curland (Microsoft Press; ISBN 1-55615-899-8)

Teach Yourself Visual Basic 4 in 21 Days, 3rd Edition, by Nathan Gurewich & Ori Gurewich (SAMS; ISBN 0-672-30620-4)

Learn Microsoft Visual Basic Now, by Michael Halvorson (Microsoft Press; ISBN 1-55615-905-6)

Database Developer's Guide with Visual Basic 4, 2nd Edition, by Roger Jennings (SAMS; ISBN 0-672-30652)

Visual Basic API How-To, by Noel Jerke and Eric Brierley (Waite Group Press; ISBN 1-57169-072-7)

Doing Objects in Visual Basic 4.0, by Deborah Kurata (Ziff-Davis; ISBN 1-56276-337-7)

Hardcore Visual Basic, by Bruce McKinney (Microsoft Press; ISBN 1-55615-667-7)

Peter Norton's Guide to Visual Basic 4 for Windows 95, by Peter Norton and Harold & Phyllis Davis (SAMS; ISBN 0-672-30615-8)

Visual Basic 4 Unleashed, by Conrad Scott, Brad Shannon, Frank Font, Bill Hatfield, et al. (SAMS; ISBN 0-672-30837-1)

Client/Server Programming with Microsoft Visual Basic, by Kenneth L. Spencer and Ken Miller (Microsoft Press; ISBN 1-57231-232-7)

Part
VI

App
F

Internet Resources for Visual Basic

This appendix points you to some of the best resources on the Internet for Visual Basic 4.0 information and programs. Keep in mind that there are hundreds of Internet sites for each Visual Basic site mentioned in this appendix. You really only need to know a few VB sites, because the best sites contain links to all the others.

This chapter teaches you about

- ◆ *FTP Servers*. It's usually easier to find shareware programs on the World Wide Web, but this sample of FTP sites collects so many programs in a few areas that they're worth checking out.

- ◆ *Mailing lists*. Sometimes it's easier to let the information you want come to you, instead of going out onto the Internet to look for it. Mailing lists deliver information directly to your mail box.

- ◆ *UseNet newsgroups*. Newsgroups are the place to look for quickly changing information. If you need help, you can find what you need here.
- ◆ *World Wide Web*. There's little doubt that the Web is the hottest resource on the Internet. You can find a variety of Web pages dedicated to Windows 95, including personal and corporate Web pages.

 On the Web

You can find shortcuts to the Internet address described here at Que's Web site at

http://www.mcp.com

FTP Servers

The FTP servers in this section contain large collections of shareware programs. They are all well organized, so you can quickly find the program you're looking for. Note that most of these sites are indexed by **Shareware.com**. See "Shareware.com," later in this appendix, for more information.

 Tip

If you don't have an FTP client, you can use your Web browser to access FTP servers. Type **ftp://** followed by the FTP address in your Web browser's address bar.

Microsoft

FTP address: **ftp://ftp.microsoft.com**

This is the place to look for updated drivers, new files for Visual Basic, and sometimes free programs. My favorite part of this FTP site is the Knowledge Base articles that answer common questions about most of Microsoft's programs. If you're having trouble finding your way around, look for a file called DIR.MAP.TXT, which tells you what the different folders have in them. Here are some of the folders you can find on this site with a brief description of what you can find in them.

- ◆ **/BUSSYS.** Files for business systems, including networking, mail, SQL Server, and Windows NT.

- ◆ **/DESKAPPS.** Files for all of Microsoft's desktop applications, including Access, Excel, PowerPoint, Project, and Word. You can also find information for the Home series, including games and Works.

- ◆ **/DEVELOPR.** The place to look if you're a developer. There are folders for Visual C++, Visual Basic, various utilities, the Microsoft Developer Network, and more. If you subscribe to the *Microsoft Systems Journal*, check here to find the source code for articles.

- ◆ **/KBHELP.** Microsoft's Knowledge Base folder. A *knowledge base*, in this context, is a help file that contains common questions and answers about Microsoft products. This folder contains one self-extracting, compressed file for each Microsoft product. The Windows 95 Knowledge Base files are under yet another folder, called **WIN95**. If you're having difficulty with a Microsoft product, download the appropriate file, decompress it, and double-click it to load it in Help.

- ◆ **/SOFTLIB.** The folder to check out if you're looking for updated drivers, patches, or bug fixes. This folder contains more than 1,500 files, though, so you need to check out INDEX.TXT to locate what you want.

- ◆ **/PEROPSYS**. For personal operating systems.

- ◆ **/SERVICES**. Contains information about TechNet, Microsoft educational services, sales information, and so on.

 Note Many of the folders on the Microsoft FTP site have two files that you should read: README.TXT and INDEX.TXT.

Part
VI

App
G

continues

continued

README.TXT describes the types of files you find in the current folder and any subfolders. It also may describe recent additions and files that have been removed.

INDEX.TXT describes each file in the folder. It's a good idea to search for the file you want in INDEX.TXT before trying to pick it out of the listing. Note that Microsoft's site is constantly changing, so you'll want to check back here often. ▪

Caution
These Internet sites, and the description of their contents, are always subject to change without notice.

WinSite (Formerly Known as CICA)

FTP address: **ftp://ftp.winsite.com**

This archive used to be managed by the Center for Innovative Computing Applications (CICA). They've created a new group called *WinSite* to manage the archive.

This could be the only FTP site that you need. It has the largest collection of freeware and shareware programs on the Internet. It's the Internet equivalent of CompuServe's WinShare forum (a forum on CompuServe that contains shareware Windows programs).

Troubleshooting
I've tried over and over to log onto the WinSite FTP server. A very large number of Internet users look for files at this FTP site. So, you'll find it's very crowded most of the time. Keep trying. If you still can't get onto it, look at the log file that your FTP client program displays to find a *mirror site* (FTP servers containing the exact same files) near you.

Mailing Lists

VB-related mailing lists keep your mailbox full of messages. There's a lot of noise generated by these lists, but you can find a lot of gems, too. This section describes two of the most popular ones: **DevWire** and **WinNews**.

Microsoft DevWire

This is for Windows programmers. You'll find news and product information, such as seminar schedules and visual tool release schedules. To subscribe, send an e-mail to **DevWire@microsoft.nwnet.com** with **subscribe DevWire** in the body of your message.

Microsoft WinNews

This weekly newsletter keeps you up-to-date on the latest happenings at Microsoft. You also find product tips and press releases. To subscribe, send an e-mail to **enews99@microsoft.nwnet.com** and type **subscribe winnews** in the body of your message.

UseNet Newsgroups

Microsoft maintains almost two dozen VB-related newsgroups. We list them here for your convenience.

Newsgroups Under microsoft.public.vb

addins	database.odbc
bugs	database.rdo
controls	installation
controls.databound	ole
controls.internet	ole.automation
crystal	ole.cdk
database	ole.servers

continues

Part
VI

App
G

continued

Newsgroups Under microsoft.public.vb

setupwiz	winapi
syntax	winapi.graphics
3rdparty	winapi.networks

World Wide Web

If you search for the keyword **Visual Basic** using Yahoo, WebCrawler, Excite, or Lycos, you can find hundreds of Web pages dedicated to some aspect of VB, some from the corporate community such as Microsoft or Symantec. Many more exist from individuals who want to make their mark on the world by sharing what they know about VB.

The Web pages in this section are only a start. Each one contains links to other VB sites. Before you know it, your VB hot list will grow by leaps and bounds.

Microsoft Corporation

URL address: **http://www.microsoft.com**

Microsoft's Web site contains an amazing amount of information about its products, services, plans, job opportunities, and more. You can find the two most useful VB Web pages by clicking the Products link or the Support link.

Here's what you find on each:

◆ *Products link.* This Web page contains links for most Microsoft products, including Visual Basic. The bulletin board on this page also contains the latest information about Microsoft products.

◆ *Support link.* The Support Desktop Web page provides access to the Microsoft Knowledge Base, which you can use to search for articles based on keywords that you specify. It also contains links to the Microsoft Software Library and Frequently Asked Questions (FAQ) Web pages.

On the Web

This site is best viewed with Microsoft's Internet Explorer. You can get your own copy of Internet Explorer at

http://www.microsoft.com/windows/ie/ie.htm.

And it's free, too.

Carl's and Gary's Visual Basic Web Page

URL address: **http://www.apexsc.com:80/vb**

This award-winning Web site is really the only Internet site address you need to know for VB. It has updated drivers, software, hints, and links to numerous other VB-related sites, including Microsoft's VB-related Web pages.

Windows Exchange (Fawcette Technical Publications)

URL address: **http://www.windx.com**

This site is maintained by *Visual Basic Programmer's Journal.* It has the source code from each issue of VBPJ as well as lots of information and files on topics ranging from elementary VB to more advanced subjects such as OCX controls and DLLs.

Shareware.com

URL address: **http://www.shareware.com**

Shareware.com is a hot, new Web site that indexes shareware and freeware products on the Internet. You can search for products by platform, category, and so on. You can also look up the top products based on the number of downloads or recent submissions. If you're looking for a shareware product, you don't need to log onto the online service anymore; you can find it here.

Part

VI

App

G

Using the CD-ROM

Using the Self-Test Software

The tests on this CD-ROM consist of performance-based questions. This means that rather than asking you what function an item would fulfill (knowledge-based question), you will be presented with a situation and asked for an answer that shows your capability of solving the problem.

The program consists of three main test structures:

◆ *Self-Assessment Test.* This would typically be the test you take first. This test is meant to give you a sense of where your strengths and weaknesses are on Visual Basic 4.0. You will get immediate feedback on your answer. It will either be correct and you will be able to go to the next question, or it will be incorrect and the system will recommend what part of the study guide to research and you will be prompted to try again.

◆ *Chapter-End Test.* After reading a chapter from the study guide you will have the option to take a mini-test consisting of questions relevant only to the given chapter. You will get immediate feedback on your answer as well as an indication of what subsection in which you can find the answer in case your response is incorrect.

◆ *Mastery Test.* This is the big one. This test is different from the two others in the sense that feedback is not given on a question-by-question basis. It simulates the exam situation, so you will give answers to all questions and then get your overall score. In addition to the score, for all wrong answers, you will get pointers as to where in the study guide you need to study further. You will also be able to print a report card featuring your test results.

All test questions are of multiple choice type offering four possible answers. The answers are labeled A, B, C, and D. There will always be either one or two alternatives representing the right answer; thus, a right answer might be "A & D" or any other combination.

Equipment Requirements

To run the self-test software, you must have *at least* the following equipment:

◆ IBM compatible PC I386
◆ Microsoft DOS 5.0

◆ Microsoft Windows 3.x

◆ 4M of RAM

◆ 256-color display adapter

◆ Double-speed CD-ROM drive

To take full advantage of the software and run it at a more acceptable speed, however, the following equipment is recommended:

◆ IBM Compatible I486 DX

◆ Microsoft Windows 3.1 or better

◆ 8M of RAM

◆ 256-color display adapter or better

◆ Quad speed CD-ROM drive

Running the Self-Test Software

The self-test software runs directly from the CD-ROM, and does not require you to install any files to your hard drive. After you have followed these simple startup steps, you will find the software very in-tuitive and self-explanatory.

If you are using Windows 3.x, Windows NT, or Windows for Workgroups:

1. Insert the disk in your CD drive.
2. Select Run from the File menu of your Windows Program Manager, click Browse, and select the letter of your CD drive (typically D). Double-click the file name Dtique95.exe and the self-test program will be activated.

If you are using VB 4.0:

1. Insert the disk in your CD drive.
2. Click the Start button on VB 4.0 taskbar, select Run, and click Browse. Select My Computer and double-click Dtique95.exe.

As soon as Dtique95 executes, you will be in the program and will just have to follow the instructions or click your selections.

Lab Exercises

The lab exercises are an important part of your preparation for the Visual Basic Certification exam. They provide a starting point for the necessary real-world experience required to pass the exam.

You can choose to perform all of the labs, or just the ones that cover areas of VB that you're unfamiliar with.

We recommend that you perform all of the labs, however, because reading all of the chapters and performing all of the labs is the only way to be sure that you've been exposed to all of the required material.

You can do all the labs at once after reading the book, or you can do them as you go along. It's up to you.

Installation Requirements

You should have a computer running Microsoft Windows 95 or Microsoft Windows NT 3.5 or later and with Visual Basic 4.0 installed. Minimally, you should have the 32-bit version. If possible, you should install both 16- and 32-bit versions of VB.

It is possible to do most of the exercises with 16-bit Visual Basic running under an earlier version of Windows, but we do not recommend this.

These exercises have been designed with no interdependency between them. Because of this, the labs can be done in any order you desire.

Each lab begins with a list of its objectives and any special requirement needed to complete it.

The files for completing the lab exercises will be installed on the directory and drive you choose, with a subdirectory for each lab. The subdirectories are named lab01, lab02, and so on. Each lab corresponds to the material contained in one of the book's chapters, with the exception of Lab 11, which corresponds to Chapters 12 and 13, and lab 12, which corresponds to Chapters 14 and 15.

Under each lab directory, you will find further subdirectories named Answer and Exercise.

The Exercise directory contains a VB project (two VB projects for Lab 10). Each VB project contains an incomplete VB application. Each place where you must complete the code is marked as a comment beginning with the word ***Task*. The Tasks are numbered and correspond to the Tasks listed under each lab in this chapter. You can follow the instructions listed with each task to complete the exercise. After most Task descriptions, you'll find one or more commented lines which look like this:

```
'?????
```

Each line represents a point where you're expected to type a line of code to complete the Task.

In addition, you'll find that some of the Forms contain labels with additional ★★★*Task comments*. Typically, these are other tasks besides coding which you must perform in the design-time environment.

Some of the Tasks simply ask you to answer a question. The answers to these Tasks can be found in this chapter at the end of the section for each lab. Other Tasks may suggest that you experiment with running the code in different ways.

The Answer subdirectory under each Lab directory contains a completed lab exercise as it might look after you follow the exercise instructions. The ★★★*Task* comments are still in the Answer subdirectory's project, so you can see how each Task should be properly completed.

Lab 1: Data Types

Note   The material in this lab corresponds most closely to the topics of Chapter 2, "Visual Basic Data Types." To begin the lab, you should open the file lab01\exercise\lab01.vbp under the directory where you installed the lab exercises on your PC. ∎

Standard Module Module1 in File LAB01.BAS

Task 1: Make 1 be the default lower bound of all arrays declared in Module1.

Task 2: Declare a Public Boolean-type variable named blnFirstFontChange.

Task 3: Create a Public user-defined type called EmpType and let it contain four fields: firstname, lastname, salary, and hiredate. Give the fields appropriate data types.

Task 4: How many elements are in the arrays declared in this Module's General Declarations section (answer in the Answers section of this Lab)?

Task 5: Make this Module's Sub Main procedure be the point where the application begins running.

Form frmControlArrays in File CTRLARRY.FRM

This Form (see fig. I.1) contains a TextBox control named txtDynamic. You will implement these features in the Form:

◆ Make txtDynamic be element 0 of a control array.

◆ Allow the user to create and destroy control array elements by clicking the CommandButtons.

Task 6: At design time, make the txtDynamic TextBox control into a control array element.

Task 7: In the Click event procedure for cmdAddTB, add an element to the textbox control array using the following steps:

7A: Increment intTBCount by one.

7B: Load the new array element into memory.

7C: Change the new element's TOP property so it's below the previous element's TOP by the HEIGHT of the previous element.

7D: Make the new control array element Visible.

FIG. I.1⇒

This Form implements an array of TextBox controls.

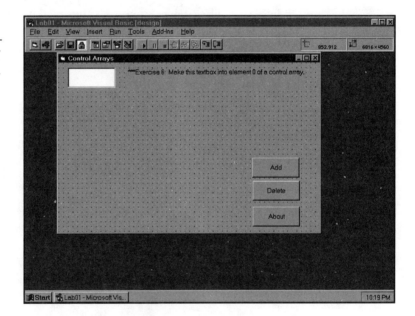

Task 8: Create a Private Integer constant in the Form's General Declarations called MAXTB with a value of 5. This places an upper limit on the number of elements we can have in the control array.

Task 9: How many elements are in each of the arrays declared in the Form's General Declarations section (answer in the Answers section of this lab)?

Task 10: Put code in the Click event procedure of cmdDelete to destroy a run-time element of the txtDynamic control array with the following steps:

10A: Take the highest-numbered element out of memory (the highest-numbered element in the array is given by the value of intTBCount).

10B: Decrement intTBCount by one.

Form frmConversions in File CONVERT.FRM

This Form (see fig. I.2) contains a TextBox named txtSource and a Label named lblTarget. The user can enter a value into txtSource, click one of the data conversion CommandButtons, and see the converted value appear in lblTarget. It is possible to generate run-time errors if the user tries an inappropriate conversion.

FIG. I.2⇒
This Form contains CommandButton controls for data conversion.

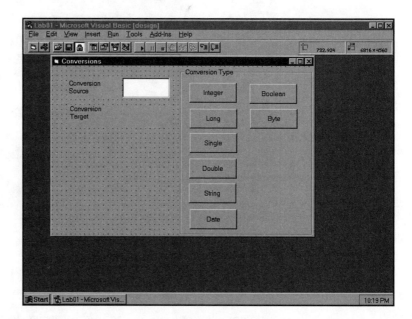

Task 11: In the click events of the appropriate CommandButtons, perform the following conversions:

11A: Convert txtSource.Text to a Boolean and assign the result to lblTarget.Caption.

11B: Convert txtSource.Text to a Byte and assign the result to lblTarget.Caption.

11C: Convert txtSource.Text to a Date and assign the result to lblTarget.Caption.

11D: Convert txtSource.Text to a Double and assign the result to lblTarget.Caption.

11E: Convert txtSource.Text to an Integer and assign the result to lblTarget.Caption.

11F: Convert txtSource.Text to a Long and assign the result to lblTarget.Caption.

11G: Convert txtSource.Text to a Single and assign the result to lblTarget.Caption.

11H: Convert txtSource.Text to a String and assign the result to lblTarget.Caption.

Form frmMain in File MAIN.FRM

This Form is the Main interface for this sample application (see fig. I.3).

FIG. I.3⇒

The main interface for the error-handling sample application.

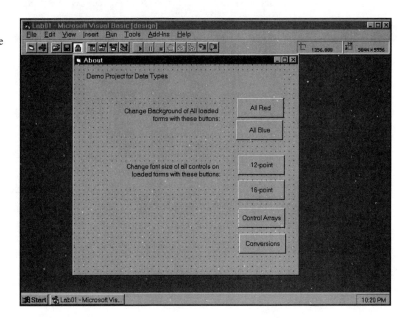

Task 12A: Use On Error Resume Next to avoid a run-time error when the code encounters a control without a Font object.

Task 12B: Loop through all loaded Forms, changing each Form's BackColor property to vbRed.

Task 13: Make frmControlArrays the active Form.

Task 14: Rename cmdSecond to cmdConversions so that this procedure becomes the Click event procedure for that command button.

Task 15: Make frmConversions the active Form.

Task 16: Loop through all Forms. In each Form, loop through all controls, changing the control's Font size.

Answers to Tasks with Questions

Task 4: How many elements are in the following arrays declared in Lab01.Bas? Note that Option Base has not been declared in this Module, so the default lower bound of an array is 0:

Public employees(1 to 10) As EmpType: 10 elements (lower bound is specified to be 1)

Public AnnualReviewDate(10) As Date: 11 elements (lower bound is 0 by default)

Public QuarterlyReview(10, 4) As Date: 55 elements (11 X 5 elements)

Task 9: How many elements are in each of the arrays declared in the Form frmControlArrays? Note that Option Base has not been declared in this Form, so the default lower bound of an array is 0:

Private Names(10) As String - 11 elements

Private QuarterlyDates(10, 4) As String - 55 elements (11 X 5)

Lab 2: Code

> **Note** The material in this lab corresponds most closely to the topics of Chapter 3, "Working with Visual Basic Code." To begin the lab, you should open the file lab02\exercise\lab02.vbp under the directory where you installed the lab exercises on your PC. ■

Standard Module Module1 in file LAB02.BAS

Task 1: Modify the function MyProcedure. The function will take birthdate and legal age parameters and will return a true/false (Boolean) value indicating whether the birthdate represents a legal age, given today's date. Modify the existing function in the following ways:

1A: The first parameter will be a String for the name. Call it strName.

1B: The second parameter, named LegalAge, will be optional. If it exists, it will indicate how many years old the individual must be to be of legal age. If it doesn't exist, legal age will default to 21.

1C: Declare a Date variable called datYoungestLegal. It will hold the latest birthdate that a person could have been born and still be of legal age.

1D: Check to see if the LegalAge parameter is missing. If it is, set the value of LegalAge to 21.

1E: Convert the strName parameter to uppercase.

1F: Create an If..Else..End If structure to test whether the datBirthDate parameter is before the date computed in datYoungestLegal. If it is, set the return value of this function to True. Otherwise, set the return value of this function to False.

Form frmPersonal in file PERSONAL.FRM

This Form gathers personal information from the user and allows the user to set personal preferences for the appearance of the application (see fig. I.4).

FIG. I.4⇒

This Form gathers personal information from the user and lets the user set preferences.

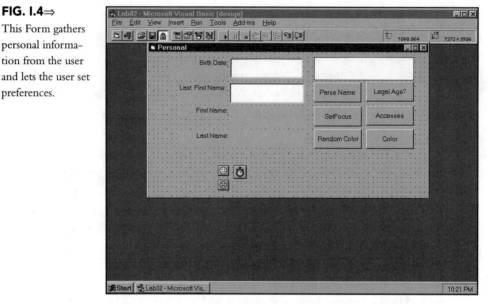

Task 2: In the Click event procedure of the CommandButton cmdName, check the entry in txtFullName and separate it into first and last name components if it contains a comma. Put the first name and last name in separate Label controls named lblFirstName and lblLastName. Use the Instr function to identify the position of the comma. You can break this task down into the following sub-tasks:

   2A: lblLastName should hold everything to the left of the comma.

   2B: Warn user to enter a comma-separated name if no comma is found.

   2C: If there's a problem, set the focus to txtFullName so user can try again.

Task 3: In the Click event procedure of cmcColor, set the backcolor of frmPersonal to vbRed and change the CommandButton's caption to "Blue."

Task 4: In the Click event of cmdLegal, set the picture property of picFeeling to imgSad and output "Not of Age" to the surface of picFeeling with the Print method.

Task 5: In the Click event of cmdLegal, warn the user to enter a valid date and set focus to the txtBirthDate textbox control so the user can try again.

Task 6: In the Click event of cmdRandom, toggle the value of Timer1's Enabled property to its opposite state.

★★★★★★★★★★★★★★★★★★★★★★★★★★★★★★

Form frmFiles in File FILES.FRM

On this Form, the user can browse through the file structure to search for valid bitmap files. The user can choose to add any files found to a list for use in a slide show (see fig. I.5). When the user holds down the mouse over the button cmdHoldShow, a slide show of the listed bitmaps begins. The slide show stops as soon as the user lets up on the mouse button. The slide show is driven by code in the Timer event of the Timer1 control.

FIG. I.5⇒

The user can choose bitmap files from the file list control and can run a slide show by holding down the mouse over the CommandButton.

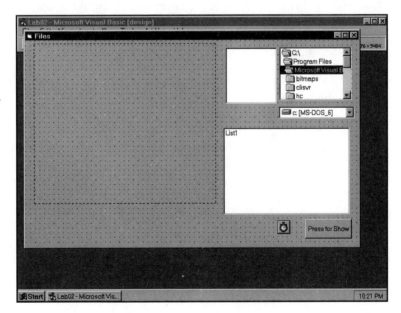

Task 7: Create a read-only property for this Form with a Property Get procedure and no Property Let procedure. Call the property Accesses. Its Property Get procedure will return an Integer value which it will get from the Private variable intAccesses. The variable intAccesses will be incremented each time the Form is accessed in the Form_Activate event procedure.

Task 8: In the MouseDown event procedure of cmdHoldShow, enable Timer1 when the user holds the mouse button down.

Task 9: In the MouseUp event procedure of cmdHoldShow, disable Timer1 when the user releases the mouse button.

Task 10: In the File1 control's Click event, load the currently selected bitmap file's contents into Image1's Picture property with the LoadFile function.

Task 11: In the click event of the File1 control, add the currently selected item in the File1 control to the listbox control List1.

Task 12: In the Form's Activate event, Increment the Public variable intAccesses by 1.

Task 13: In the Timer event of the Timer1 control, set up a Static variable intPictureCount with a type of Integer. It will be used to cycle through the files listed in the List1 control.

Task 14: In the Timer event of the Time1 control, increment intPictureCount by 1.

Lab 3: Debugging

Note The material in this lab corresponds most closely to the topics of Chapter 4, "Debugging Applications." To begin the lab, you should open the file lab03\exercise\lab03.vbp under the directory where you installed the lab exercises on your PC.

Form frmDebug in File DEBUG.FRM

This form provides a command button whose Click event procedure calls the Sub Procedure ProcessAccumulator (see fig. I.6). We use ProcessAccumulator to illustrate various debugging techniques in the Tasks of this Exercise.

FIG. I.6⇒

The Command Button on this Form calls a procedure that we use to illustrate debugging techniques.

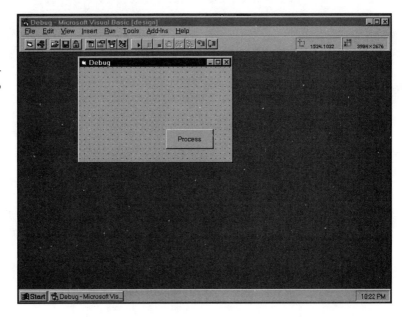

Task 1: In the Sub Procedure Process Accumulator, set a Watch for the expression:

intAccumulator > 2000

Make the Watch type be Break When Expression is True.

Task 2: In the Sub Procedure ProcessAccumulator, set a breakpoint on the line

    For intCounter = 1 To 20

and single-step through the code when execution stops at this line.

Task 3: Check the Call stack as you are single-stepping through the code in Task 2.

Task 4: Resume normal execution after viewing the For Loop in operation several times in Tasks 2 and 3.

Task 5: At the end of the Sub Procedure ProcessAccumulator, write two statements to print the current date and time to the Debug Windows' Immediate Pane and to print the value of intAccumulator.

Lab 4: Handling Errors

Note The material in this lab corresponds most closely to the topics of Chapter 5, "Handling Errors." To begin the lab, you should open the file lab04\exercise\lab04.vbp under the directory where you installed the lab exercises on your PC. ▪

Form frmError in File ERROR.FRM

This Form (see fig. I.7) provides a textbox for the user to enter a file name to open. The single CommandButton control calls a routine, MakeError, which causes an error in opening the file. We allow the user to choose which error-handling technique to use with the two OptionButton controls.

FIG. I.7⇒
The Command-
Button on this
Form calls a rou-
tine that we use to
illustrate various
error-handling
techniques.

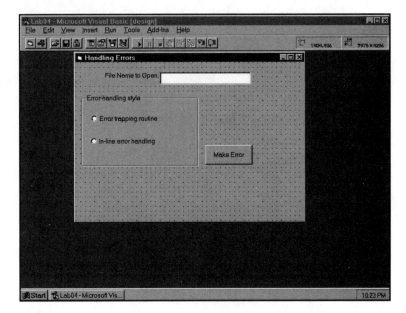

The FileOpenInLine Sub procedure will use the in-line error handling technique to trap possible run-time errors on opening a file.

Task 1: At the beginning of the FileOpenInLine Sub Procedure, Insert the correct statement to allow execution to continue after a run-time error occurs.

Task 2: In the FileOpenInLine Sub Procedure, begin the Select Case statement correctly with the appropriate expression for checking the current error condition.

Task 3: If none of the expected errors occur in the Select Case in the FileOpenInLine Sub Procedure, "the error handler" can show a MessageBox telling the user the error number and error description.

Task 4: At the end of the Select Case in the FileOpenInLine Sub Procedure, disable error trapping with the appropriate statement.

Task 5: In the Click event procedure for cmdMakeError, write a simple error handler to handle any errors which MakeError might pass back to this procedure. The error handler can simply show a MessageBox with the error number and description.

Task 6: In the OpenFile Sub Procedure, write the appropriate statement to enable the error handler which begins at the label OpenFile_Error.

Task 7: In the OpenFile Sub Procedure, write the appropriate statement to quit the subroutine before we enter the error handler.

Task 8: In the error-handling section of the OpenFile Sub Procedure, write a statement to resume processing on the line after the line which caused the error.

Lab 5: Common Properties

Note The material in this lab corresponds most closely to the topics of Chapter 6, "Common Properties of the Form Object and Control Objects." To begin the lab, you should open the file lab05\exercise\lab05.vbp under the directory where you installed the lab exercises on your PC. ▪

Form frmProperties in File PROPERTY.FRM

This Form contains four TextBox controls for the user to fill in (see fig. I.8). By manipulating the properties of these TextBox controls and their accompanying labels, you can help the user to navigate the Form.

FIG. I.8⇒

You can define access keys and set tabbing order on this Form to help the user navigate the controls.

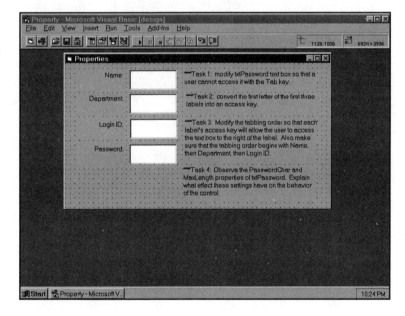

Task 1: Modify the txtPassword text box so that a user cannot access it with the Tab key.

Task 2: Convert the first letter of the first three labels into an access key.

Task 3: Modify the tabbing order so that each label's access key will allow the user to access the text box to the right of the label. Also, make sure that the tabbing order begins with Name, then Department, then Login ID.

Task 4: Observe the PasswordChar and MaxLength properties of txtPassword. Explain what effect these settings have on the behavior of the control.

Lab 6: Events

Note The material in this lab corresponds most closely to the topics of Chapter 7, "Control and Form Object Events." To begin the lab, you should open the file lab06\exercise\lab06.vbp under the directory where you installed the lab exercises on your PC. ∎

This application displays two forms (Events and Events2). Events receives the output of graphics methods and also contains a PictureBox control which receives similar output. MessageBoxes and Print methods help you to observe the timing of various event procedures.

Standard Module Module1 in File LAB06.BAS

This Module's Sub Main provides the application's startup routine, which calls the Show method of both forms.

Task 1: In the Sub Main routine, check to see whether another copy of this application is already running. If another copy of this application is running, give the user a warning message and terminate this copy of the application.

Form frmEvents in File EVENTS.FRM

This Form has messages in a number of its events so we can monitor their occurrences. It also allows the user to drag the button labeled Graphic Output, or to put the output of several graphics methods on the Form's surface when the button is clicked (see fig. I.9).

A couple of Private variables, intDragXOffset and intDragYOffset, will keep track of the offset of the mouse pointer inside a control while the control is being dragged by the user.

In the Sub Procedure GraphicOutput, we cause some graphics output on the Form's surface. First, we clear the Form's surface and reposition the graphics cursor to the upper left corner. Then, we output text to the Form surface and draw a circle on the Form's surface.

FIG. I.9⇒

Clicking the button labeled Graphic Output will produce various figures on the Form and the PictureBox. The user can also drag and drop the Graphic Output command button.

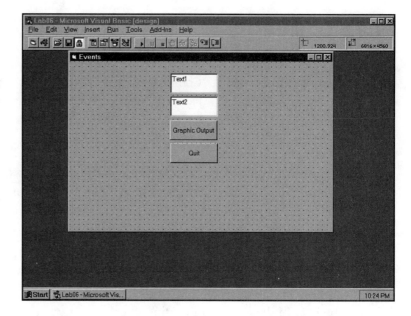

Task 2: In the MouseDown event procedure of the cmdGraphic Output CommandButton, allow the user to drag this control when pressing the mouse button down. Execute the following sub-tasks to help implement dragging:

> **2A:** Store the current X,Y position of the mouse cursor inside the control to the private variables intDragXOffset and intDragYOffset.
>
> **2B:** Enable dragging of this control.

Task 3: In the Form's DragDrop event procedure, call the Source control's Move method to move the control being dragged to the X,Y coordinates on the Form where the user has released the mouse button. Use the X and Y parameters to determine the new position on the form for the Source control. Use the offset amounts stored in the Private variables intDragXOffset and intDragYOffset to keep the mouse pointer at the same position inside the control.

Task 4: In the Click event procedure of the cmdQuit Command Button, unload both of the Forms in this application, 'frmEvents and frmEvents2, and set each of them to Nothing. Setting the Forms to Nothing will trigger the Terminate event of each Form.

Task 5: Observe when the Activate event is triggered by running the application and switching back and forth between the two Forms with the mouse.

Task 6: Observe when the Deactivate event is triggered by running the application and switching back and forth between the two Forms with the mouse.

Task 7: Observe that the Gotfocus event of the Events Form is never triggered when switching back and forth between the two Forms with the mouse. Why is this so?

Task 8: Observe that the Lostfocus event of the Events Form is never triggered when switching back and forth between the two Forms with the mouse.

Task 9: Enable the Event Form's Keypress event by setting the Form's KeyPreview property to True.

Task 10: In the Event Form's Keypress event, change the value of KeyAscii so that all characters entered at the keyboard are converted to uppercase.

Task 11: When the Event Form's AutoRedraw property is False (its default value), the Paint event will trigger. Put a call to the GraphicOutput Sub procedure in the Form's Paint event procedure so that the Form's graphic output will be redrawn when the Form is uncovered.

Task 12: In the KeyUp event procedure of the Text1 control, Put conditional logic (IF...EndIf) around the MessageBox code so that it will occur only when the user has pressed the F1 key. (The VB constant for the F1 key is vbKeyF1.)

Task 13: Comment the DoEvents statement out of Text1's LostFocus event procedure and the Text2 GotFocus event procedure. Observe the difference in the sequencing of the events without DoEvents.

Form frmEvents2 in File EVENTS2.FRM

Since this Form contains only Label controls (which are incapable of receiving focus), the Form itself can receive GotFocus and LostFocus events (see fig. I.10).

FIG. I.10⇒

This Form contains no controls capable of receiving focus. Therefore, the Form itself may receive and lose focus.

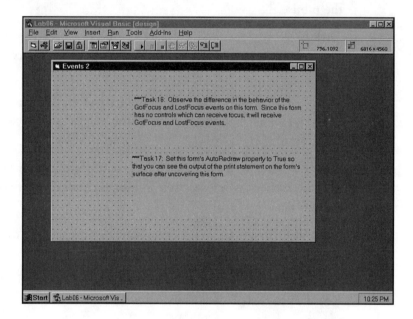

Task 14: In the QueryUnload event procedure of the Events2 Form, when will the condition *UnloadMode = vbFormControlMenu* be true?

Task 15: In the QueryUnload event procedure of the Events2 Form, insert code to ask users in a MessageBox whether they really want to unload this Form. If they don't want to unload, then cancel the unloading.

Task 16: Observe the difference in the behavior of the GotFocus and LostFocus events on this Form. Because this Form has no controls which can receive focus, it will receive GotFocus and LostFocus events.

Task 17: Set this Form's AutoRedraw property to True so that you can see the output of the print statement on the Form's surface after uncovering this Form.

Answers to Tasks with Questions

Tasks 7 and 8: The Events Form never receives GotFocus or LostFocus events because it contains controls which can receive the focus.

Task 14: vbUnLoadMode will be the value of the QueryUnload's UnloadMode parameter when the user tries to close the Form by clicking the Close button.

Lab 7: Menus

Note The material in this lab corresponds most closely to the topics of Chapter 8, "Menus." To begin the lab, you should open the file lab07\exercise\lab07.vbp under the directory where you installed the lab exercises on your PC. ■

This application allows the user to pick a directory holding bitmap files. It keeps a list of up to ten of those files in a dynamic menu control array under the File menu of the Menus Form. When the user clicks one of the files listed in the dynamic menu array, the bitmap contents of the file displays in an image control on the Form's surface.

The menu also contains other unimplemented items illustrating various features of a VB Menu.

Task 1: Implement the following menu structure in the Form file Menu.frm:

    mnuFile Caption = "&File"

        mnuFileName Caption = "XXX" Index = 0 (control array!)

        mnuFileSep1 Caption = "-"

        mnuFileGet   Caption = "&Get File Names"

        mnuFileClear Caption = "&Clear File Names"

        mnuFilePrint Caption = "&Print"

        mnuFileExit Caption = "&Exit"

    mnuOptions Caption = "&Options"

        mnuOptionsColor Caption = "&Colors" Checked = True

        mnuOptionsFonts Caption = "&Fonts"

        mnuOptionsFontsUnderlined Caption = "&Underlined"

        mnuOptionsFontsBold Caption = "&Bold"

        mnuOptionsSpecial Caption = "&Special"

        mnuOptionsLong Caption = "&Short Menus"

mnuColors Caption = "&Colors"

    mnuColorsRed Caption = "&Red"

    mnuColorsGreen Caption = "&Green"

    mnuColorsBlue Caption = "&Blue"

Standard module modMenus in File MENUS.BAS

This Module holds a Public variable indicating the number of files listed under the Files menu in the Menus Form and a Public variable to hold directory path to files listed under the Files menu.

Form frmStart in file START.FRM

This Form is displayed modally from the Load event procedure of the MENUS Form. It is also displayed modally from the Click event of the mnuFileGet menu item on the MENU Form. It shows File dialog controls allowing the user to choose a directory with bitmap files (see fig. I.11). When the user clicks the <u>O</u>K button, the code resets the dynamic menu control array under the MENU Form's File menu.

FIG. I.11⇒

Using this form as a modal dialog, the user can choose a directory containing bitmap files.

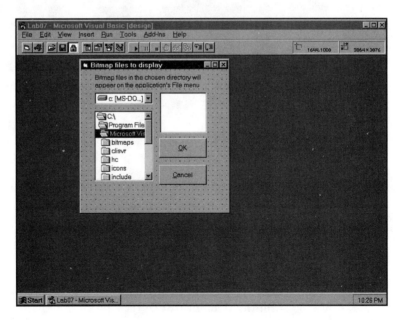

Task 2: In the Click Event procedure of cmdOK, Load up to 10 file names from the chosen directory into the dynamic menu control array mnuFileName on the MENU Form. Execute the following sub-tasks to help accomplish this task:

2A: Use Load statement to initialize next element in the frmMenus.mnuFileName dynamic array (index of new element will be intNumFiles).

2B: Make the caption of the new element be the corresponding element from the List object of the filBitmaps control.

2C: Set the Visible property of the new element to True.

Form frmMenu in File MENU.FRM

This Form implements a menu with many common features (See fig. I.12).

FIG. I.12⇒

This Form implements a menu.

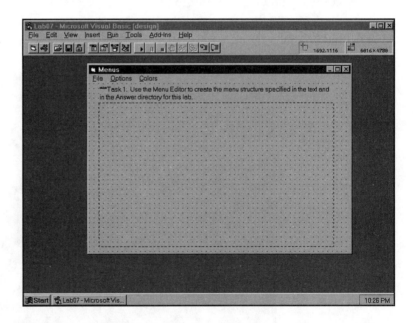

The mnuFileGet Click event procedure shows the Start Form modally, thus allowing the dynamic list of files under the File menu to be reset.

The mnuFileClear Click event procedure unloads all items in the menu array mnuFileName.

The ShowExtraMenus Sub Procedure takes a Boolean parameter indicating whether certain menu controls in the menu system are to be displayed or not. It sets the Visible properties of these controls to be the same as the value of the Boolean parameter.

Task 3: In the ShowExtraMenus Sub Procedure, make the Visible properties of mnuFilePrint and mnuOptionsSpecial take on the value of the parameter blnLong.

Task 4: In the mnuFileGet Click event procedure, disable the Get Files option and enable the Clear Files option on the File menu.

Task 5: In the Click event procedure for the menu control array item mnuFileName, Form strFileName as a concatenation of

strBitmapDir & "\"

and the Caption property of the currently selected element of mnuFileName (which can be determined from the Index parameter passed to this event procedure).

Task 6: In the Click event procedure of the mnuOptionsColor menu item, toggle the Checked property of this menu item to its opposite value (use the Not operator).

Task 7: At the end of the Click event procedure of the mnuOptionsColor menu item, if this menu item is now checked, then enable the mnuColors menu. If not, disable mnuColors.

Task 8: In the Click event procedure of mnuOptionsFontsUnderlined, toggle this menu item's checked property to its opposite value.

Task 9: In the Click event procedure of mnuOptionsLong, if this menu item's caption is "Long Menus," then call ShowExtraMenus with a True argument and change the caption to "Short Menus." Otherwise, call ShowExtraMenus with a False argument and change the caption to "Long Menus."

Lab 8: MDI

Note The material in this lab corresponds most closely to the topics of Chapter 9, "Using Multiple-Document Interface (MDI)." To begin the lab, you should open the file lab08\exercise\lab08.vbp under the directory where you installed the lab exercises on your PC. ■

Form frmchild in File CHILD.FRM

This is the Child Form for the MDI application (see fig. I.13)

FIG. I.13⇒
An MDI Child
Form.

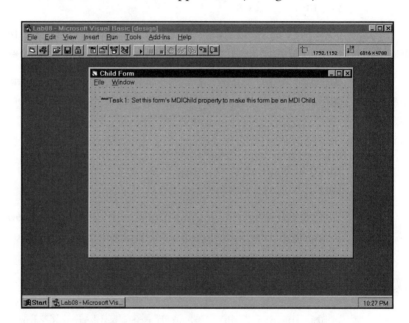

Task 1: Set this Form's MDIChild property to make this Form be an MDI Child.

Task 2: Use frmParent's Arrange method to Cascade open Child Forms.

Task 3: Use frmParent's Arrange method to Tile open Child Forms Vertically.

Standard Module Module1 in File LAB08.BAS

This file contains code for the MakeNewchild Sub Procedure and also holds the Public variable intNumChildren to keep track of the number of MDI Children which have been instantiated during this session.

The MakeNewChild routine creates a new MDI Child Form instance by making a copy of the Form frmChild.

Task 4: Use the New keyword to create a new instance named frmNewChild, of the frmChild Form.

Task 5: Create a string for the caption of the newly instantiated frmNewChild which using the value of intNumChildren to make the caption unique.

Task 6: Make frmNewChild visible.

MDI Parent Form frmParent in File PARENT.FRM

This is the MDI Parent for this application (see fig. I.14).

FIG. I.14⇒

An application's MDI Parent Form.

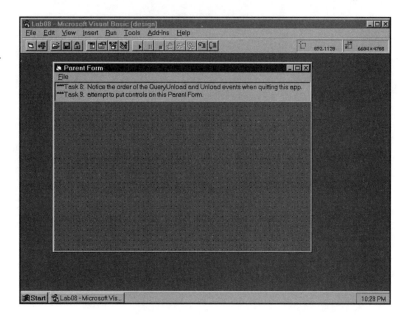

Task 7: From the Click event procedure of the mnuFileNew menu control, call the MakeNewChild procedure.

Part

VI

App

I

Task 8: Notice the order of the QueryUnload and Unload events when quitting this application.

Task 9: Attempt to place controls directly on the surface of this Parent Form.

Lab 9: OLE Automation

Note The material in this lab corresponds most closely to the topics of Chapter 10, "Using OLE Automation to Integrate Applications." To begin the lab, you should open the file lab09\exercise\lab09. vbp under the directory where you installed the lab exercises on your PC. ■

Form frmOLEAuto in file OLEAUTO.FRM

This Form provides and OLE Automation interface to Excel (see fig. I.15).

FIG. I.15⇒

OLE Automation interface for Excel.

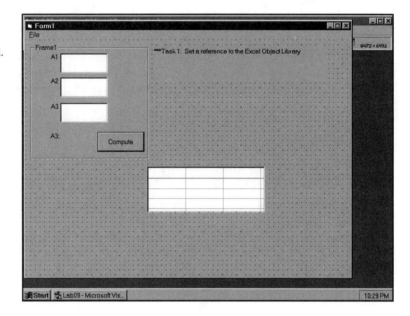

Task 1: Set a Reference to the OLE Object library for Excel.

Task 2: Declare a Private object variable objExcel with early binding. It should be an instance of Excel.Application (Excel is the server, Application is the class).

Task 3: In the Form_Load event procedure, use the GetObject function to set the Private variable objExcel to point to the return value of the GetObject function. The first argument to the function should be blank and the second argument should be a string representing the server.class combination.

Task 4: In the error-trapping section of Form_Load event procedure (means GetObject failed), use the CreateObject function to set the Private variable objExcel to point to the return value of the CreateObject function. The single argument to the function should be a string representing the server.class combination.

Task 5: Set the Visible property of objExcel to False. Suggestion: Experiment with both True and False values of Visible to observe the effects.

Task 6: Set the OLE1 container control's Object property to point to the newly instantiated objExcel.

Task 7: In the Click event procedure for cmdCompute, set the worksheet's A2 cell to hold the value of txtA2.Text.

Task 8: Make lblResult.Caption hold the contents of cell A3 from the worksheet.

Task 9: In the Form_Unload event procdeure, set the Saved property of wb to True. (This will cause Excel to ignore any changes to data when the workbook is closed and so the user will not see any prompts to save work.)

Task 10: In the Form_Unload event procedure, call the Quit method of objExcel.

Lab 10: OLE Server

Note The material in this lab corresponds most closely to the topics of Chapter 11, "Creating OLE Servers." To begin the lab, you should open the file lab10\exercise\lab10.vbp under the directory where you installed the lab exercises on your PC. ■

Standard Module modSport in File SPORT.BAS

Task 1: Add an empty Sub Main procedure to this module. Then, choose Tools Options Project from the VB menu and set the Startup Form option to point to this Sub Main routine.

Class Module Players in File PLAYERS.CLS

This Class implements the Players collection. It contains

◆ add and delete methods (public procedures) for adding a new player to the collection

◆ a Count function for implementing the collection's Count property

◆ an Item function for returning a reference to a specific member of the collection

A Collection object has built-in Add, Remove, Count, and Item procedures. We provide wrapper procedures so that the controller must go through this Players class to use these procedures.

Task 2: Right-click the mouse anywhere in a code window for this Class to adjust this Class Module's built-in properties:

Instancing = Not Creatable

Name=Players

Public=True

Task 3: Declare a private variable colPlayers As New Collection. By making it private, we guarantee that the controller can't access it directly, but must always go through this Class.

Task 4: In the Add function, set the return value of this function to point to the newly initialized object plrNew.

Task 5: In the count function, make the return value of this function be the count property of the colPlayers collection.

Task 6: Why is the Index parameter a Variant in the Delete and Item procedures?

Class Module Team in File TEAM.CLS

Task 7: Implement a Class property MoodOf Fan as a Public String variable.

Task 8: Use Property let/get procedures to implement a string-type property called Name. It will store and retrieve its value in the Private variable gstrName. The Wins property is read-only because it has only a Property Get procedure and no Property Let procedure. It uses the Private variable giWins to retrieve its value.

Task 9: Implement a read-only Losses property of type Integer with a Property Let procedure. It will use the giLosses Private variable to retrieve its value.

Task 10: Create a method WinOne which will increment the variable giWins by 1, thus indirectly updating the Wins property.

Task 11: Show frmWinsLosses modally. The Form merely hides itself when done so we can check its FanMood Public variable and adjust this object's MoodOfFan property accordingly.

Task 12: When running the test controller, create a greater number of losses than wins and call this routine to observe the system's behavior.

Task 13: When running the test controller, create a greater number of losses than wins and call this routine to observe the system's behavior.

Task 14: Right-click the mouse anywhere in a code window of this module to adjust this Class Module's built-in properties:

Instancing = Not Creatable
Name=Player
Public=True

Task 15: Implement two string-type properties of the Player object as Public variables. Their names will be respectively Name and Position.

Form frmWinsLosses in File WINLOSS.FRM

This Form provides some user interface from the OLE Server (see fig. I.16).

Part

VI

App

I

FIG. I.16⇒

This Form belongs to the OLE Server and is invoked modally from a method of the Team Class.

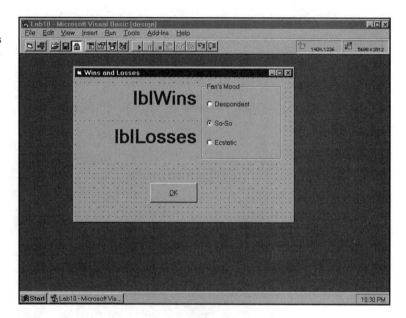

Task 16: In the cmdOK button's Click Event, Hide this Form rather than unloading it. This will keep it available for reference by the ShowWinLoss method which called it. *Tip: Don't refer to the Form by name. Use the Me keyword instead.*

Task 17: Prepare to test this server and its Classes by setting the appropriate Project options from the Tools Options menu:

Startup Form = Sub Main

StartMode = OLE Server

Task 18: Even if you intend this server Class to be Single Use, you must temporarily set its built-in Instancing property to Creatable MultiUse when testing at design time.

Task 19: Test this server by running it at design time, minimizing this copy of VB, and starting or switching to another copy of VB to run a test-controller application.

Project SportCli in File Sportcli.VBP

Form frmSport in File SPORT.FRM

This Form provides the user interface for the OLE test-controller application (see fig. I.17).

FIG. I.17⇒

A test-controller
application for our
OLE server.

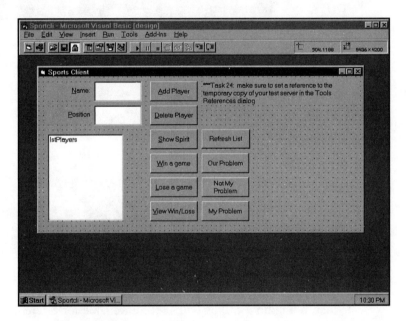

Task 20: Make sure to set a reference to the temporary copy of your test server in the Tools References dialog.

Task 21: Declare a Public object variable of the Sport.Team server.class combination. Use the As New syntax and name the variable Home Team.

Task 22: Call the HomeTeam object's rahrah method with the string parameter, giving a team name such as "Hippophants" or "Algolids" or your favorite sports team's name.

Task 23: Call the hometeam object's LoseOne method.

Task 24: Notice use of lstPlayers.list (listindex) as argument to the Item method. This is a string which should match an item's key in the Players collection.

Answers to Tasks with Questions

Task 6: Because we might refer to or delete and item either by using the item's numeric index or its name.

Part

VI

App

I

Lab 11: Data Control and Data Access Objects

Note The material in this lab corresponds most closely to the topics of Chapter 12, "Using the Data Control" and Chapter 13, "Using Data Access Objects." To begin the lab, you should open the file lab11\exercise\lab11.vbp under the directory where you installed the lab exercises on your PC.

To be able to run this demo, you will need the sample Microsoft Access database file BIBLIO.MDB which is distributed with Visual Basic and can usually be found in the main VB directory. This application will automatically make a backup of the file.

Standard Module modBiblio in File BIBLIO.BAS

This module provides the startup routine Sub Main and determines the name of the database file and its backup, calling the Form frmGetfile if necessary. It loads the main Forms frmPublishers and frmTitles.

Form frmFindTitle in File FINDTTL.FRM

This auxiliary Form furnishes a one-field dialog to the user with an OK button (see fig. I.18). It's used to ask the user for a title string to find. It contains Public variables which can be examined after the Form has run to find out whether or not the user pressed OK (variable is blnOK) and what string the user typed in the text box (variable is strFind).

Form frmGetFile in File GETFILE.FRM

This auxiliary Form contains a Common Dialog control (see fig. I.19). It can be called from other places in the application.

Form frmTitles in File TITLES.FRM

The Data Control datTitles and associated bound controls on this Form allow the user to browse book titles held in the Titles table of the database (see fig. I.20). Add, Save, Delete, and Cancel buttons provide standard editing capabilities to the user.

A Find button allows the user to find titles containing any specified string of characters. A button labeled PUBLISHERS allows the user to see detail inFormation on publishers.

The Databound ListBox control dblstPublishers provides a dynamic lookup from the current title into the Publishers table.

FIG. I.18⇒

A simple dialog to get a title string from the user.

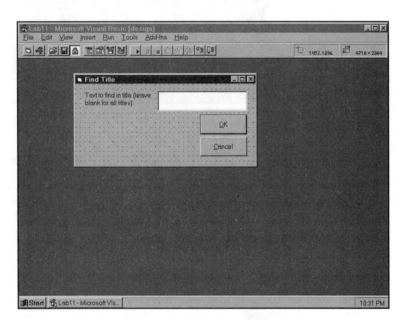

FIG. I.19⇒

This Form may be displayed modally when the application starts to determine the location of the Biblio database file.

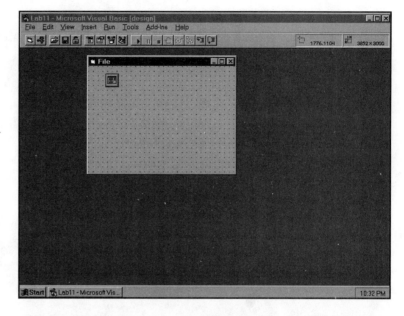

FIG. I.20⇒

The user can browse book titles from the Biblio database on this Form.

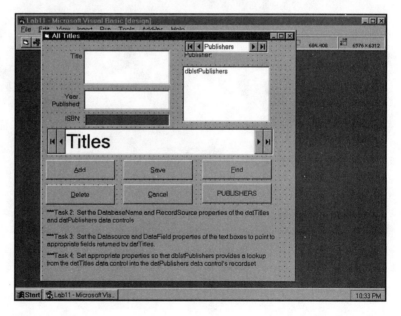

Task 1: Make the DatabaseName property of the datPublishers data control be the file-wide string variable DBNAME.

Task 2: Set the DatabaseName and RecordSource properties of the datTitles and datPublishers data controls.

Task 3: Set the Datasource and DataField properties of the text boxes to point to appropriate fields returned by datTitles.

Task 4: Set appropriate properties of dblstPublishers so that dblstPublishers provides a lookup from the datTitles data control into the datPublishers data control's recordset.

Task 5: In the Form's Keypress event, lock the current page for the recordset of datTitles whenever the user begins typing.

Task 6: In the Reposition event procedure of datTitles, store current record's position in filewide variable strOldBookmark.

Task 7: In the Click event of cmdAdd, call the method to add a new Titles record.

Task 8: In the Click event of cmdCancel, set current bookmark back to its previous value as stored in the Private variable strOldBookmark.

Task 9: In the click event of cmdDelete, call the Delete method of the recordset of datTitles and then move to the next record.

Task 10: In the click event of cmdFind, after we've got the desired search string from the user, make the RecordSource property of datTitles hold new SQL string and then call the Refresh method of datTitles.

Task 11: In the click event of cmdSave, if recordset of datTitles isn't currently in an edit mode, then call its Edit method.

Task 12: In the click event of cmdCancel, call the recordset's CancelUpdate method.

    Form frmPublishers in File PUBS.FRM

This Form (see fig. I.21) is called from the frmTitles Form to provide inFormation on publishers. In its Activate event, the Form checks the intCurrentPublisher property of the frmTitles Form to determine which publisher to display initially.

This Form uses a combination of Data Access Objects and a Data Control to display read-only inFormation about publishers. The Data Access Object provides the connection to the Publishers table. Whenever the record pointer is moved in this table, we refresh the datTitles data control pointing to Titles. A DBGrid is bound to the datTitles data control and thus shows the current publisher's titles.

FIG. I.21⇒

This Form allows the user to view Publisher information.

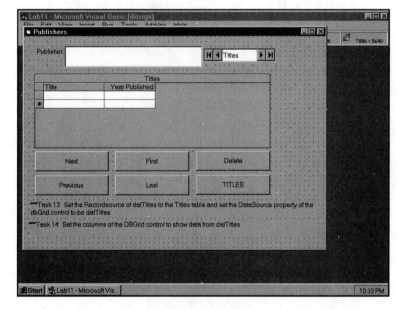

Task 13: In the Properties window, set the Recordsource of datTitles to the Titles table and set the DataSource property of the dbGrid control to be datTitles.

Task 14: At design time, set the columns of the DBGrid control to show data from datTitles.

Task 15: In the Form_Load event procedure, initialize the recordset object rsPublishers by setting it to the result of the OpenRecordset method of the db object (table name is "Publishers"). Second argument to OpenRecordset should specify that we want to open the recordset as a table. Because it's a table, we can set the index property.

Task 16: In the Form_Activate evcent procedure, call the Seek method of the rsPublishers recordset. Look for an exact match with the contents of frmTitles.intCurrentPublisher (a Public variable of that Form which was set just before activating this Form).

Task 17: In the ReadFromBuffer Sub Procedure, update the txtName control with the contents of the Name field from the rsPublishers Recordset. Append a blank string to make sure we don't try to assign null data to txtName.

Task 18: In the cmdDelete button's click event procedure, begin a transaction, so both publisher and publisher's titles get deleted together.

Task 19: Assuming all went well, end the transaction by committing the changes.

Task 20: In the Click event procedure of cmdFirst, call the MoveFirst method of the rsPublishers recordset.

Task 21: At the end of the Click event procedure of cmdFirst, call the ReadFromBuffer procedure to update the controls on this Form.

Task 22: In the Click event procedure of cmdPrevious, call the MovePrevious method of the rsPublishers recordset.

Task 23: After calling MovePrevious, check to see whether the record pointer is at the beginning-of-file buffer area. If it is, call the Recordset's MoveFirst method.

Task 24: At the end of the Click event procedure, call the ReadFromBuffer procedure to update controls on this Form.

Lab 12: DLLs and 16/32-Bit Issues

Note The material in this lab corresponds most closely to the topics of Chapter 14, "Creating 16-Bit and 32-Bit Applications" and Chapter 15, "Dynamic-Link Libraries (API)." To begin the lab, you should open the file lab12\exercise\lab12.vbp under the directory where you installed the lab exercises on your PC. ■

This small applet has a single Form with a single command button. When the user clicks the command button, a message box displays the path name of the system's Windows directory. The application can be compiled by both the 16-bit and 32-bit versions of VB 4.0.

In addition to this application, we provide in the same directory a test VB 3.0 Project file with a VB 3.0 custom control.

Standard Module Module1 in File 1632DLL.BAS

Task 1: Use conditional compiler directives to declare the GetWindowsDirectory API function for both 16- and 32-bit environments. If you have the API Text viewer installed for either or both the 16- and 32-bit environments, you can copy and paste the declarations from the API Text viewer. Otherwise, the declaration for the 32-bit environment is:

Public Declare Function GetWindowsDirectory _

Lib "kernel32" Alias _

"GetWindowsDirectoryA" _

(ByVal lpBuffer As String, ByVal nSize As Long) _

As Long

The declaration for the 16-bit environment is:

Public Declare Function GetWindowsDirectory _

Lib "kernel" _

(ByVal lpBuffer As String, ByVal nSize As Long) _

As Long

Task 2: Notice that:

◆ The Alias clause in the 32-bit declaration. What is the purpose of this clause?

◆ The function return type and the type of nSize are Long in the 32-bit declaration and Integer in the 16-bit declaration. What is the reason for this difference?

Task 3: Experiment with changing the capitalization of the name of the function and then attempt to run the application. Notice that capitalization doesn't matter in the 16-bit environment but DOES matter in the 32-bit environment.

Form Frm1632DLL in File 1632DLL.FRM

Both tasks for this Form are in the Click event procedure of the Command Button (see fig. I.22).

Part

VI

App

I

FIG. I.22⇒

This Form contains API declarations and calls the GetWindows Directory API from the Click event procedure of the Command-Button.

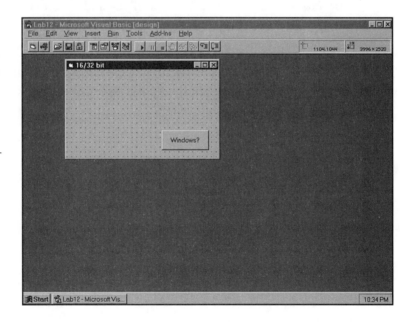

Task 4: Initialize strWinDir with 255 characters of ASCII character 0 (null string).

Task 5: Display a message box showing the current Windows directory. Apply the Left function to the value of strWinDir to strip off the null terminator at the end of the string. *Tip: The return value of GetWindowsDirectory will tell you how many characters are in the string.*

Visual Basic 3.0 Project Lab12.MAK

Task 6: In the Advanced tab of the Tools Options References dialog, make sure the that the Upgrade Custom Controls option is checked in the Project Load frame.

Task 7: Retrieve this file and respond to the prompt to upgrade the custom control.

Answers to Tasks with Questions

Task 2: The Alias clause in the 32-bit declaration allows the API function to have the same name in both 16- and 32-bit compilations of your code. The means you won't have to change the name anywhere else in your code just because you compile on both platForms.

The function return type and the type of nSize are Long in the 32-bit declaration and Integer in the 16-bit declaration because Integers in 16-bit API calls written in the C language become Longs in the 32-bit environment.

Lab 13: SetupWizard

Note The material in this lab corresponds most closely to the topics of Chapter 16, "Distributing an Application with SetupWizard." You should **not** open the VB project under this lab's directory on your PC, as we'll access that project only after SetupWizard is running. ■

This lab contains no project to modify. Instead, the Exercise directory contains the source code and other necessary files for the project used in Lab 10. This lab requires you to run SetupWizard against the project in Lab13\exercise.

Task 1: Follow the screens in Chapter 16 as you run SetupWizard against the Sport project in Lab13\exercise. Bear in mind the following points:

◆ The DAO 3.0 Object library is referenced by the project, so you'll see Screen 2 (Data Access).

Your setup target can be either floppy disks (have several ready!) in a disk drive, or the directory Lab13\answer.

◆ This project implements an OLE server, so you'll want to answer the prompt on Screen 6 appropriately.

Task 2: Examine the file Setup1.LST created by SetupWizard. You should find it on your distribution target.

Task 3: From Windows Explorer, run the SetUp.exe routine on your distribution target to see how your application will appear when it's distributed to users.

Sample Tests

Using the Self-Tests

The tests in this appendix are performance-based questions designed to test your problem-solving capabilities. The questions are divided into three main test structures:

- ◆ *Self-Assessment Test.* This would typically be the test you take first. This test is meant to give you a sense of where your strengths and weaknesses are on Visual Basic 4.0.

- ◆ *Chapter-End Test.* After reading a chapter from the study guide you will have the option to take a mini-test consisting of questions relevant only to the given chapter. These questions are listed in order of the chapters in this book.

- ◆ *Mastery Test.* This test simulates the exam situation, so you will give answers to all questions and then get your overall score.

All test questions are of multiple choice type offering four possible answers. The answers are all labeled A, B, C, and D. There will always be either one or two alternatives representing the right answer; thus, a right answer might be "A & D" or any other combination.

Note These questions are also included on the CD-ROM that accompanies this book. See Appendix H, "Using the CD-ROM," for information on how to access these questions and run the software included with the CD. ■

Self-Assessment Test

Note The answers to these questions can be found in order at the end of this section. Each answer also includes a section reference where you can find information about that question. ■

1. What will the user see in the Message Box when this code runs?

```
Dim NewNum As Integer
    Dim MyNum As Integer
    Do While NewNum < 30
        For MyNum = 20 To 11 Step -1
            NewNum = NewNum + 2
            If NewNum >= 20 Then
                Exit Do
            End If
        Next MyNum
    Loop
    MsgBox NewNum
```

Part VI App J

A. 20.

B. 11.

C. 30.

D. User will never see a message box.

2. A true fact about the relationship between the Public and Instancing built-in class properties is (pick two)

A. when Public is False, Instancing can only be Single Use or None.

B. when Public is True and Instancing is None, the class can't be instantiated by a controller but is visible to the controller.

C. when Public is False, the Instancing property's setting is ignored.

D. when Instancing is Creatable Single- or Multi-Use, the setting of Public is ignored.

3. If a TextBox's Enabled property is False, then

A. the text in the box will be grayed, and the user won't be able to set focus to the TextBox.

B. the text in the box will be grayed, the user can still set focus to the TextBox, but the user won't be able to make changes to the text.

C. the text in the box will be grayed, and the user can still make changes to the text.

D. the text in the box will appear as normal, but the user won't be able to set focus to the TextBox.

4. The following lines occur in a Standard Module's General Declarations section (there is no Option Base statement):

```
Type Star
        Name as String
        Type as String * 3
        Parsecs as Single
        Magnitude As Integer
    End Type
    Public Dim Stars(10) as Star
```

Which of the following lines will run without an error? (pick two)

A. Stars(10).Type = "A3"

B. Stars(9).Name = "Sirius"

C. Star(9).Parsecs = 3

D. Stars(0).Magnitude = -0.5

5. You can invoke the Menu Editor (pick two)

A. from the View menu.

B. with Ctrl+M.

C. from the Tools menu.

D. with Ctrl+E.

6. If you have the following code

```
Private Sub cmdOK_Click()
    MyVar = 17
    Process MyVar    'call to the Process procedure
    MsgBox MyVar
    MyVar = MyVar * 2
    MsgBox "MyVar = " & MyVar
End Sub
```

```
Private Sub Process(ThisVar as Integer)
    ThisVar = ThisVar + 20
End Sub
```

and you begin using the Step Over command on all lines starting with the line MyVar = 17

    A. VB will not execute the next line (Process MyVar) by stepping over it.

    B. VB will step through all of the code line by line, including the code lines in the Process procedure before returning to the cmdOK_Click event.

    C. VB will execute the next line (Process MyVar), but will not execute the code in the Process procedures.

    D. VB will step through all of the code line by line, except for the code in the Process procedure, which will run completely before returning to the cmdOK_Click event.

7. To maintain the same code in 16- and 32-bit VB

    A. There are no special considerations.

    B. You will have to make editing changes every time you switch between 16- and 32-bit compilers.

    C. If you have API calls, you will need to use conditional compilation to use different versions of the API.

    D. If you use custom controls, you will need to use conditional compilation to use different versions of the controls.

8. On the line immediately before the error handler in a routine

    A. you should put the line likely to cause an error.

    B. you must put On Error GoTo 0.

    C. you should put On Error GoTo *label*, where *label* is the name of the error handler.

    D. you should put an Exit Sub or Exit Function statement.

9. Two advantages of having more than one Workspace in a project are (pick two)

A. you can have more than one database object in the project.

B. you can define different user permission levels.

C. you can have non-nested transactions.

D. you make more efficient use of memory.

10. The relationship between a RecordSet and a RecordSource is that

A. RecordSet is an SQL string, and RecordSource is a record collection of type Dynaset, Snapshot, or Table.

B. RecordSource is an SQL string, and RecordSet is a record collection of type Dynaset only.

C. RecordSource is an SQL string, and RecordSet is a record collection of type Dynaset, Snapshot, or Table.

D. RecordSet is an SQL string, and RecordSource is a record collection of type Dynaset only.

11. If your application includes the following code:

```
Private Sub cmdOK_Click()
     MyVar = 17
     Process MyVar
     MsgBox MyVar
     MyVar = MyVar * 2
     MsgBox "MyVar = " & MyVar
End Sub

Private Sub Process(ThisVar as Integer)
     ThisVar = ThisVar + 20
End Sub
```

and the application is currently paused on the line *MsgBox MyVar.*

A. Use Set Next Statement to immediately execute *MyVar = 17*

B. If you use Set Next Statement on *MsgBox "MyVar = " & MyVar,* all lines up to that statement will execute.

C. Use Set Next Statement to immediately execute *ThisVar = ThisVar + 20*

D. You cannot re-run the line *MyVar=17* with Set Next Statement if VB has previously run this line.

12. You do the following things: 1) write a general procedure in a form and call it MySub_Click( ). 2) Later, place a command button on the form whose default name is Command1. 3) Write code in Command1's click event procedure. 4) Rename Command1 to MySub. What will happen when the user clicks the command button?

    A. Nothing.

    B. The original code in MySub_Click will run.

    C. The code in Command1_Click will run.

    D. The code in Command1_Click will run, but under the name MySub_Click.

13. The minimized icon of an MDI Child

    A. is unavailable to the user.

    B. appears on the MDI Form.

    C. appears on the Windows desktop.

    D. appears in the MDI Child that currently has focus.

14. An example of the correct syntax to begin a For Each loop would be

    A. For Each Control

    B. For Each ctrlCurr in Controls

    C. For Each ctrlCurr From 1 To Controls.Count

    D. For Each ctrlCurr in Controls From 1 To Controls.Count

15. The Move method

    A. has four required arguments.

    B. requires both a Left and a Top argument.

    C. requires only a Left argument.

    D. requires only a Top argument.

16. At run-time, my code can delete

    A. all items in a menu control array that had been created at run time.

B. only enabled items.

C. only disabled items.

D. all items in a menu control array.

17. The following is true of forms in an OLE server (pick two)

A. may be modal or modeless if the server is out-of-process.

B. may be modal or modeless if the server is in-process.

C. Startup Form of the project must be Sub Main( ) if the server is in-process.

D. must be modeless if the server is in-process.

18. To create a linked or embedded object on the OLE container control at run time

A. use CreateLink and CreateEmbed with a data file name.

B. use CreateLink with a data file name and CreateEmbed with no arguments.

C. use CreateLink with a data file name and a server name, and CreateEmbed with a server name only.

D. use both CreateLink and CreateEmbed with a data file name and a server name.

19. If a running VB application has various instances of Child Forms and encounters the statement Cancel = False in the MDI Form's Unload event

A. no Child Forms will unload.

B. all Child Forms will unload, but not the MDI Form.

C. the Child Forms will unload as well as the MDI Form.

D. a run-time error will occur.

20. When the user changes focus to another application, the currently active Form in your application

A. receives a DeActivate event.

B. receives a LostFocus event.

C. receives both DeActivate and LostFocus.

D. receives neither DeActivate nor LostFocus events.

21. Setup.Exe

   A. is the default name of the setup routine created by Setup Wizard for your application.

   B. is the name of the executable file that runs Setup Wizard.

   C. is the name of the generic, unmodifiable startup routine for a Setup.

   D. is the name of the default Setup Wizard template file.

22. If you have a ListBox named List1 and you want to refer to the contents of the last row in ListBox, you would use the expression:

   A. List1.ListCount

   B. List1.List(ListCount)

   C. List1.List(ListCount - 1)

   D. List1.(ListCount - 1)

23. A VB Form with its MDIChild property set to False

   A. can exist in an MDI application as a normal form.

   B. can't exist in an MDI application.

   C. can exist in an MDI application only as a modal form.

   D. can exist in an MDI application only as a modaless form.

24. Unused custom controls in your project that are on the project's Toolbox

   A. will appear on a list in Setup Wizard and should be removed.

   B. will not be listed by Setup Wizard.

   C. will appear on a list in Setup Wizard and cannot be removed.

   D. will not be distributed with your application even if they remain checked in the list in Setup Wizard.

25. Core API library names are

    A. User16, Kernel16, GDI16 for 16-bit Windows and User32, Kernel32, and GDI32 for 32-bit Windows.

    B. User, Kernel, GDI for 16-bit Windows and User32, Kernel32, and GDI32 for 32-bit Windows.

    C. User16, Kernel16, GDI16 for 16-bit Windows and User, Kernel, and GDI for 32-bit Windows.

    D. User, Kernel, and GDI for both 16- and 32-bit Windows.

26. You may call GetObject

    A. with a missing first parameter to create a new instance of a server class.

    B. with a blank string ("") as first parameter to create a new instance of a server class.

    C. with a file name as first parameter to create a reference to an existing instance of a server class.

    D. with no parameters to create an uninitialized object.

27. The DataBaseName property of the Data Control

    A. is always a file name.

    B. is always a directory name.

    C. is a logical name, so not necessarily a directory or file.

    D. is always a file name for Microsoft Access databases.

28. The 2nd parameter of the GetWindowsDir API function represents

    A. the length of the modified string parameter.

    B. the original length of the string parameter.

    C. a pointer to the string parameter.

    D. a mode indicator. If 0, GetWindowsDir will find the name of the Windows directory. If 1, it will find the name of the Windows\System directory.

29. You can use Err.Raise (pick two)

    A. to cause an error to occur.

    B. without the *number* argument, which will pass the default value of 0.

    C. with Err.Number to regenerate the current error inside an error handler.

    D. to increase the value of Err.Number stipulated by the *number* argument.

30. The following statement is syntactically correct:

    A. DBGrid1.("QueId").Width = 3000

    B. DBGrid1("QueId").Width = 3000

    C. DBGrid1.Columns("QueId").Width = 3000

    D. DBGrid1[QueId].Width = 3000

31. A menu item's Visible property

    A. will leave a blank space in the menu list when set to false.

    B. will cause a menu control to appear grayed out when set to false.

    C. will cause a control's surrounding menu items to close in together when set to 1.

    D. will cause a control's surrounding menu items to close in together when set to False.

32. A Form's or PictureBox control's AutoRedraw property

    A. is a bitmap representing the full-screen image of the object.

    B. is a Boolean that enables the Paint event when set to True.

    C. can be set to Automatic to enable automatic refresh.

    D. is a Boolean that enables automatic refresh when set to True.

33. Code in the Error event procedure of the Data Control

    A. will override any error handlers written elsewhere.

    B. is overridden by any error handlers written elsewhere.

C. happens when the user uses the Data Control without invoking any code written by you.

D. happens whenever there is an error related to the Data Control, either caused by your code or by a user action on the Data Control.

34. Visual Basic will warn you about incompatibility

A. when you change class properties already existing in the Compatible OLE Server and recompile.

B. whenever you recompile your server.

C. whenever you recompile your server with the Compatible OLE Server property set.

D. whenever you have made any changes not in the Compatible OLE Server and recompile.

35. The NegotiateMenus property

A. belongs to a Form and is True by default.

B. belongs to an OLE automation object and is True by default.

C. belongs to a Form and is False by default.

D. belongs to an OLE automation object and is False by default.

36 The Debug.Print method (pick two)

A. must be removed from your application before you compile the application.

B. will be ignored in the compiled version of the application.

C. can be typed in the Immediate Pane of the Debug Window to get the current value of the stipulated expression.

D. is used to write to the Immediate Pane of the Debug Window.

37. A Breakpoint that marks a code line (pick two)

A. can be toggled On and Off with F9.

B. displays the code line in a different color.

C. indicates that the code line will be skipped when the code runs.

D. will be saved when the code file is saved.

38. If a module with Option Base 0 has a one-dimensional array strNames( ) of string with 20 elements containing employee names, how would you add another employee to the array?

   A. Redim strNames(21)

   B. Redim Preserve strNames(20)

   C. strNameAdd(20)

   D. Redim Preserve strNames(21)

39. Pick two that are true of the On Error statement

   A. On Error Go To *label*—directs the application to a designated error handler.

   B. On Error Go To 0—disables the current error handler.

   C. On Error Go To—disables the error handler.

   D. On Error Resume Next—saves the property settings of the err object.

40. The Class' Terminate event will always run when

   A. OLE shuts down the server.

   B. an END statement executes in the server's code.

   C. once all forms have been unloaded.

   D. once all forms have become invisible.

41. Case sensitivity is an issue

   A. only in the 32-bit API.

   B. only in the 16-bit API.

   C. in both 32- and 16-bit APIs.

   D. in the UniCode version of the 16-bit API.

42. The value of the Name property

    A. is visible to the user at run time.

    B. provides a default value for the Caption property.

    C. takes its default value from the Caption property.

    D. can't be changed at run time.

43. OLE Servers used by this application

    A. are specified in the same Setup Wizard step as data sources are specified.

    B. are specified on a separate screen of the Setup Wizard.

    C. are specified when you specify the target distribution media for the application.

    D. are specified when you specify custom control files.

44. When declaring an API routine in a Form Module

    A. you must use the Static keyword.

    B. you must use the Public keyword.

    C. you must use the Private keyword.

    D. you need use no special keyword in front of the Declare keyword.

45. The ScaleTop and ScaleHeight properties

    A. indicate the internal dimensions of a form or PictureBox— always in twips.

    B. indicate the internal dimensions of a form or PictureBox— always in the units given by ScaleMode.

    C. indicate a control's size in the units given by the containing form's or PictureBox control's ScaleMode.

    D. indicate a control's position in the units given by the ScaleMode of its container.

46. The NoMatch property of the Recordset

    A. becomes True after a successful Find or Seek.

    B. becomes False after a successful Find or Seek.

    C. becomes True after a successful Find, only.

    D. becomes False after a successful Seek, only.

47. You might be able to reference a specific MDI Child instance in code

    A. with the name property you assigned at run time.

    B. with the name you gave it at design time.

    C. by checking its Tag property.

    D. by checking its position in the Forms collection.

48. You can use the up and down arrow buttons in the Menu Editor to

    A. change a menu control's level in the menu hierarchy.

    B. change a menu control's position in the menu list.

    C. move the selection highlight through different controls in the list.

    D. add or delete menu controls.

49. A form named frmMyForm contains the following statements in its General Declarations section:

```
Public IsOK as Boolean
Private IsTrue as Boolean
```

Which of the following lines will run from another module of the application? (pick one)

    A. MsgBox frmMyForm.IsOK

    B. MsgBox frmMyForm.IsTrue

    C. MsgBox IsOK

    D. MsgBox IsTrue

Part

VI

App

J

50. To enable keystroke validation at both the Form and control levels, you must

   A. set the KeyPreview property of controls to True.

   B. set the KeyPreview property of controls to False.

   C. set the KeyPreview property of the Form to True.

   D. set the KeyPreview property of the Form to False.

51. GetWindowsDirectoryA and GetWindowsDirectoryW represent

   A. 16- and 32-bit versions of the GetWindowsDirectory API, respectively.

   B. 32- and 16-bit versions of GetWindowsDirectory, respectively.

   C. ANSI and UniCode versions of the 32-bit API, respectively.

   D. UniCode and ANSI versions of the 16-bit API, respectively.

52. Static variables (pick two)

   A. are not implemented on the stack.

   B. have application-wide scope.

   C. have module-wide lifetime.

   D. have local scope.

53. An access key for a TextBox control

   A. can be provided in the TextBox's Caption property.

   B. can be provided in the TextBox's Text property.

   C. can be provided in an accompanying Label control.

   D. can be provided in the TextBox's Label property.

54. We initialize an object with the declaration

   Public objExcel as Excel.Application

and later we wish to set the Visible property of the object. We can use the following line of code:

   A. Excel.Visible = True

   B. objExcel.Application.Visible = True

   C. Excel.Application.Visible = True

   D. objExcel.Visible = True

55. An OLE server project's Name option as found on the Project tab of the Options dialog

   A. must be the same as the project's file name.

   B. will be the objecttype component when a controller instantiates appname.objecttype in the server.

   C. will be the appname component when a controller instantiates appname.objecttype in the server.

   D. must be the same as the main class name in the server.

56. You may lock a page in a Recordset with (pick two)

   A. the Edit method.

   B. the Lock statement.

   C. the LockEdits property.

   D. the AddNew method.

57. The OLE container's DoVerb method

   A. pops up the server's Verb menu.

   B. executes an available server verb.

   C. enables the user to run a verb from the Verb menu.

   D. places the server's Verb menu on the Form's menu, if the Form's NegotiatMenus property is True.

58. The DragDrop event

   A. triggers for a control when another control is dropped over it.

   B. triggers for a control when it is dropped.

   C. triggers for a control as it is being dragged.

   D. triggers for a control as another control is dragged over it.

59. For 16- and 32-bit versions of VB

   A. you can run 16-bit VB only on 16-bit platforms and 32-bit VB only on 32-bit platforms.

B. you can run 16-bit VB on either platform and 32-bit VB on only 32-bit platforms.

C. you can run both 16- and 32-bit VB on either 16- or 32-bit platforms.

D. you can run 32-bit VB on either platform and 16-bit VB on only 16-bit platforms.

60. To clear the graphics image in a PictureBox control named picFile, you could use the code

A. picFile.Image = ""

B. picFile.Picture = LoadPicture( )

C. picFile.Picture = Nothing

D. picFile.Picture = ""

61. If you call BeginTrans and then exit the application without calling CommitTrans or Rollback

A. VB will generate run-time error 3956.

B. VB will automatically write the transaction to the database.

C. the changes in the transaction will be lost.

D. VB will prompt the user to commit or roll back the transaction.

62. A line of code that checks to see if Ctrl+F3 was keyed in the KeyUp or KeyDown event might read

A. If (Shift = vbCtrlMask) AND (KeyCode = vbKeyF3) Then

B. If KeyCode = vbKeyControl + vbKeyF3 Then

C. If (Shift AND vbCtrlMask) AND _ (KeyCode = vbKeyF3) Then

D. If (Shift AND vbCtrlMask) AND _ (KeyCode AND vbKeyF3) Then

63. To prevent the user from being able to give focus to a control (activate a control)

A. set the control's TabIndex property to 0.

B. set the control's TabStop property to True.

C. set the control's TabStop property to False.

D. do none of the above.

64. To make an unloaded Form visible to the user

A. you only need to call the Load statement.

B. you only need to call the Show method.

C. you must call both Load and Show.

D. the only way is to set the Form's Visible property.

65. The relationship between ANSI and UniCode standards for strings
in VB is that

A. VB uses ANSI internally but converts to UniCode for use by
the programmer and in API calls.

B. VB uses UniCode internally but converts to ANSI for use by
the programmer and in API calls.

C. VB uses ANSI both internally and for use by the programmer
in API calls.

D. VB uses UniCode both internally and for use by the programmer in API calls.

66. Locking in ODBC databases

A. is implemented with the same procedures as for Jet databases.

B. is implemented by the underlying DBMS.

C. is not possible.

D. is implemented with the same procedures as for installable
ISAM databases.

67. Given the following code,

```
Dim intMyNum As Integer
Dim blnMyBool As Boolean
Dim lngMyLong as Long
Dim bytMyByte as Byte
Dim sngMySingle as Single
intMyNum = 2000
sngMySingle = 6000
lngMyLong = 30
```

Which of the following will not generate a run-time error (pick two)

    A. intMyNum = cInt(sngMySingle)

    B. bytMyByte = cByte(intMyNum)

    C. bytMyByte = lngMyLong

    D. blnMyBool = cBool(sngMySingle)

68. The Delete method (pick two)

    A. requires a pending Edit to run without an error.

    B. does not move the record pointer.

    C. requires a call to the Update method to become final.

    D. updates the recordset's data immediately.

69. You can use the Arrange method to (pick two)

    A. arrange Child icons on the MDI Form.

    B. tile open Child forms on the MDI Form.

    C. cascade the MDI Form along with other Windows applications running in the current Windows session.

    D. arrange icons on the Windows desktop.

70. What will a variant-type variable contain when set to nothing?

    A. Null.

    B. Empty.

    C. 0.

    D. "".

71. You can use Err.Raise

    A. to cancel the current error.

    B. to determine the current error number.

    C. to test whether the current Err.Number is a VB standard error or if it is a programmer-defined error.

    D. to test how your application reacts to a particular error.

72. A menu control's Name property

    A. is not supplied automatically when you initialize a menu control.

    B. provides the default value for the Caption property.

    C. can contain an ampersand indicating the shortcut key.

    D. is required to begin with "mnu."

73. The line of code

    ```
    ListBox.ListIndex = -1
    ```

    A. will cause a run-time error.

    B. will select the first item in the list.

    C. will select the last item in the list.

    D. will deselect any item in the list.

74. The CreateObject function

    A. always begins a new copy of the server.

    B. always references an existing copy of the server.

    C. references an existing copy of the server if one exists; otherwise, begins a new copy.

    D. generates a run-time error if there is no existing copy of the server.

75. A Dynaset-type Recordset cannot be updated when

    A. the Recordset is formed from any SQL query (as opposed to using a simple table name).

    B. the Recordset is formed from any SQL query using the Order By clause.

    C. the Recordset is formed from any SQL query using a Where clause.

    D. the Recordset is formed from any SQL query using a Where clause to join two or more tables.

76. A Recordset object contains

    A. a Fields collection.

    B. a Databases collection.

    C. a Workspaces collection.

    D. a Groups collection.

77. Menu title items

    A. have no event procedures.

    B. have a Click event procedure that you can access at design time by clicking the item.

    C. have a double-click event procedure that you can access at design time only from a code window.

78. You can create Object Browser help for your server (pick two)

    A. for methods.

    B. only for properties.

    C. for all methods and properties.

    D. for properties implemented with Property Let/Get.

79. If you check the Upgrade Custom Controls option in the Advanced Options dialog, VB 4.0

    A. will convert any and all 16-bit controls to 32-bit when you load a project.

    B. will convert only those 16-bit controls for which there are 32-bit replacements when you load a project.

    C. will convert any and all 16-bit controls to 32-bit when you save a project.

    D. will convert only those 16-bit controls for which there are 32-bit replacements when you save a project.

Answer Key

1-A. See "Getting Out of a Loop in a Hurry with Exit" (Chapter 3)

2-B,C. See "Instancing" and "Public" under "Class Module Properties for an OLE server" (Chapter 11)

3-A. See "Enabled" (Chapter 6)

4-B,C. See "Visual Basic's Standard Simple Data Types" and "Arrays" (Chapter 2)

5-C,D. See "Menu Editor" (Chapter 8)

6-D. See "Step-Over Mode" (Chapter 4)

7-C. See "Using Conditional Compilation with API Declarations" (Chapter 14)

8-D. See "Creating a Detour Around the Error Handler" (Chapter 5)

9-B,C. See "The Default Workspace and the Workspaces Collection" (Chapter 13)

10-C. See "The Recordset" (Chapter 12)

11-A. See "Set Next Statement" (Chapter 4)

12-B. See "Control Names and Event Procedure Code" (Chapter 3)

13-B. See "Understanding MDI Applications" (Chapter 9)

14-B. See "The For Each…Next statement" (Chapter 3)

15-C. See "Top, Left, Width, and Height and the Move Method" (Chapter 6)

16-A. See "Menu Control Arrays" (Chapter 8)

17-A,C. See "Managing Dialogs (Forms) in Your OLE Server" (Chapter 11)

18-A. See "Linking and Embedding at Run Time" (Chapter 10)

19-C. See "Using Unload and QueryUnload" (Chapter 9)

20-D. See "Activate/ DeActivate" (Chapter 7)

21-C. See "A Customized Setup Program" (Chapter 16)

22-C. See "ComboBox" (Chapter 3)

23-A. See "Setting Up MDI Child Classes" (Chapter 9)

Part
VI

App

J

24-A. See "Screen for Step 6: OLE Automation" (Chapter 16)

25-B. See "Declaring and Calling a DLL Routine" (Chapter 15)

26-B. See "CreateObject Function versus GetObject Function" (Chapter 10)

27-D. See "DataBaseName Property" (Chapter 12)

28-B. See "GetWindowsDirectory in 16- and 32-bit Versions" (Chapter 15)

29-A,C. See "Generating an Error with the Err Object's Raise Method" (Chapter 5)

30-C. See "Data-Bound Grid" (Chapter 12)

31-D. See "Visible Property" (Chapter 8)

32-D. See "AutoRedraw" (Chapter 7)

33-C. See "Error Event" (Chapter 12)

34-A. See "Managing Compatibility of Versions of Your Server" and "Compatible OLE Server" (Chapter 11)

35-A. See "Using the OLE 2.0 Container Control" (Chapter 10)

36-B,D. See "Debug.Print" (Chapter 4)

37-A,B. See "Toggling the Breakpoint" (Chapter 4)

38-B. See "Dynamically Resizing an Array" (Chapter 2)

39-A,B. See "Enabling/Disabling the Error Handler with On Error" (Chapter 5)

40-C. See "Class Terminate Event Procedure" and "Closing Your OLE Server" (Chapter 11)

41-A. See "Name of API" (Chapter 15)

42-D. See "MouseIcon" (Chapter 6)

43-B. See "Screen for Step 4: OLE Servers" (Chapter 16)

44-C. See "The Declare Keyword" (Chapter 15)

45-B. See "MousePointer" (Chapter 6)

46-B. See "Find Methods" and "Seek Method" (Chapter 12)

47-C. See "Referencing MDI Children" (Chapter 9)

48-B. See "Navigating Menu Items in the Menu Editor" (Chapter 8)

49-A. See "Variable Scope" (Chapter 2)

50-C. See "KeyPreview" (Chapter 7)

51-C. See "GetWindowsDirectory in 16- and 32-bit Versions" (Chapter 15)

52-A,D. See "Static Variables" (Chapter 2)

53-C. See "Providing Access Keys for Text Boxes" (Chapter 6)

54-D. See "Declaring a Variable to Hold an Instance of an OLE Server Class" (Chapter 10)

55-C. See "Name" under "Setting Project Options for an OLE Server" (Chapter 11)

56-A,D. See "Page Locking" (Chapter 13)

57-B. See "An OLE Server's Verbs" (Chapter 10)

58-A. See "DragDrop" (Chapter 7)

59-B. See "Understanding 16- and 32-bit Application Differences" (Chapter 14)

60-B. See "PictureBox" (Chapter 3)

61-C. See "Using Transactions" (Chapter 13)

62-C. See "KeyUp and KeyDown" (Chapter 7)

63-B,D. See "Name" (Chapter 6)

64-B. See "Show and Hide" (Chapter 7)

65-B. See "Using the Same Name for Unicode and ANSI Versions" (Chapter 15)

66-B. See "Page Locking" (Chapter 13)

67-C,D. See "Data Type Conversion" (Chapter 2)

68-B,D. See "Deleting Records" (Chapter 12)

69-A,B. See "Arrange Method" (Chapter 9)

70-A. See "Variant: The Lonely Default" (Chapter 2)

71-D. See "Using Err.Raise as a Debugging Technique" (Chapter 5)

72-A. See "Name Property" (Chapter 8)

73-D. See "ListBox" (Chapter 3)

74-A. See "CreateObject Function versus GetObject Function" (Chapter 10)

75-D. See "Using the Where Clause to Connect Tables" (Chapter 13)

Part

VI

App

J

76-A. See "Recordset Objects and the Recordsets Collection" and "Using Transactions" (Chapter 13)

77-D. See "Attaching Code to a Menu Item's Click Event Procedure" (Chapter 8)

78-A,D. See "Your OLE Server and the Object Browser" (Chapter 11)

79-B. See "Converting VBX to OLE Controls" (Chapter 14)

Chapter Tests

Note The answers to these questions can be found in order at the end of this section. Each answer also includes a section reference where you can find information about that question. ■

Chapter 2

1. The Option Explicit statement

   A. should appear at the beginning of each routine.

   B. allows you to specify arrays' default lower bounds.

   C. should appear at the beginning of each program.

   D. should appear in the Declarations section of each module.

2. If a program contains an array declaration

   ```
   Dim strNames(10, 5 to 10, 5) as String
   ```

   and the module contains no Option Base statement, then the total number of elements in the array will be

   A. 500.

   B. 250.

   C. 396.

   D. 330.

3. The possible arguments to the Option Base statement are

   A. 0 and 1.

   B. any positive number.

   C. any number between 0 and 32K.

   D. Option Base takes no arguments.

4. What value will a variant contain before it's initialized?

   A. Null.

   B. Empty.

C. 0.

D. "".

5. If a module with Option Base 0 has a one-dimensional array strNames( ) of string with 20 elements containing employee names, how would you add another employee to the array?

A. Redim strNames(21)

B. Redim Preserve strNames(20)

C. strNameAdd(20)

D. Redim Preserve strNames(21)

6. A form named frmMyForm contains the following statements in its General Declarations section:

```
Public IsOK as Boolean
Private IsTrue as Boolean
```

Which of the following lines will run from another module of the application? (pick one)

A. MsgBox frmMyForm.IsOK

B. MsgBox frmMyForm.IsTrue

C. MsgBox IsOK

D. MsgBox IsTrue

7. Static variables (pick two)

A. are not implemented on the stack.

B. have application-wide scope.

C. have module-wide lifetime.

D. have local scope.

8. Assume a form contains only the following code:

```
[General declarations]
Public NumTimes as Integer
Private Sub cmdOK_Click()
    Dim intNumTimes as integer
    intNumTimes = intNumTimes + 1
    SetOK intNumTimes
    MsgBox NumTimes
```

```
      End Sub
Public Sub SetOK(NumTimes as Integer)
        NumTimes = NumTimes + 1
      End Sub
```

After the code runs for the first time, the user will see a

   A. message box displaying 0.

   B. message box displaying 1.

   C. message box displaying 2.

   D. run-time error "Variable not defined."

9. Assume that the following is the only code in a form

```
[General declarations]
      Public NumTimes as Integer
      Private Sub cmdImOK_Click()
          Static intNumTimes as integer
          intNumTimes = intNumTimes + 1
          SetOK intNumTimes
          MsgBox NumTimes
      End Sub
      Private Sub cmdYourOK_Click()
          SetOK(NumTimes)
      End Sub
      Public Sub SetOK(NumTimes as Integer)
          NumTimes = NumTimes + 1
      End Sub
```

If the user clicks first on the cmdYourOK button and then on the cmdImOK button, the user will see

   A. a run-time error "Variable not defined."

   B. 1.

   C. 2.

   D. 0.

10. If a control array has the name txtName and the variable intNumElems keeps track of the number of elements in the array, what code will add another element to the control array at run time, correctly maintaining the intNumElems counter?

   A. You can't add another element at run time in code

   B. intNumElems = intNumElems + 1

      txtName.Add intNumElems

    C. intNumElems = intNumeElems + 1

       Load txtName(intNumElems)

    D. AddItem intNumElems + 1

11. The following code

```
For each Myctrl in Controls
      MyCtrl.Text = Ucase(MyCtrl.Text)
Next MyCtrl
```

    A. will give a run-time error if there is a label on the current form.

    B. will change text properties of all controls on all forms.

    C. will always be able to change text property of all controls on current form.

    D. will give a run-time error if there is a label anywhere in the project.

12. Which String concatenation statement will give a run-time error?

    A. "" & Str("")

    B. "" + 0

    C. "" & 0

    D. "" + Str(0)

13. A field designating that `Customer Wants More Information` is best implemented with

    A. Boolean

    B. String

    C. Integer

    D. Variant

14. `Social Security Number` is best implemented with

    A. Integer

    B. String

    C. Long

    D. Double

15. A variable for population of a city is best implemented with

    A. String

    B. Long

    C. Double

    D. Date

16. A variable for Number of Dependents is best implemented with

    A. Long

    B. Integer

    C. Double

    D. Single

17. The following lines occur in a Standard Module's General Declarations section (there is no Option Base statement):

```
Type Star
        Name as String
        Type as String * 3
        Parsecs as Single
        Magnitude As Integer
     End Type
     Public Dim Stars(10) as Star
```

Which of the following lines will run without an error? (pick two)

    A. Stars(10).Type = "A3"

    B. Stars(9).Name = "Sirius"

    C. Star(9).Parsecs = 3

    D. Stars(0).Magnitude = -0.5

18. What will a variant-type variable contain when set to nothing?

    A. Null.

    B. Empty.

    C. 0.

    D. "".

19. Given the following code,

```
Dim intMyNum As Integer
Dim blnMyBool As Boolean
Dim lngMyLong as Long
Dim bytMyByte as Byte
Dim sngMySingle as Single
intMyNum = 2000
sngMySingle = 60000
lngMyLong = 30
```

which of the following will not generate a run-time error (pick two)?

A. intMyNum = cInt(sngMySingle)

B. bytMyByte = cByte(intMyNum)

C. bytMyByte = lngMyLong

D. blnMyBool = cBool(sngMySingle)

20. In your code you make the declaration

```
Dim MyNames(20) as String
```

then you insert some data in all the existing elements. There is no Option Base statement in the module.

After the line

```
REDIM MyNames(21)
```

executes, the array contains

A. 21 blank elements.

B. 21 elements with 20 previous elements' original contents intact.

C. 22 elements with 21 previous elements' original contents intact.

D. 22 blank elements.

Chapter 3

1. You create a function procedure. You do not specify the data type of the return value. This will

A. cause an error.

B. make the function's return type Void.

C. mean the function will have no return value.

D. make the function's return type Variant.

2. While a procedure is running the Stack holds (pick two)

   A. the procedure's local variables.

   B. the procedure's static variables.

   C. the address of the calling line of code.

   D. the procedure's return value.

3. You have the following code in a form:

```
[General Declarations]
Public strName as String
Private Sub cmdOK_Click()
     strName = "Jones"
     ViewName(strName)
     MsgBox strName
End Sub

Private Sub ViewName(strName as String)
     strName = UCase(strName)
     MsgBox "Name is " & strName
End Sub
```

When the message box in the cmdOK_Click event procedure displays, the user will see:

   A. jones

   B. JONES

   C. Jones

   D. Name is JONES

4. You can check to see whether an Optional parameter named strName was passed to the current procedure with the following code:

   A. If strName = Nothing

   B. If IsMissing(strName)

   C. If strName = ""

   D. If IsEmpty(strName)

5. What will the user see when the following code runs? (pick two)

```
Select Case MyVal
      Case 13,15,17
            MsgBox "A"
      Case Is < 20
            MsgBox "B"
      Case Is > 10
            MsgBox "C"
      Case Else
            MsgBox "D"
End Select
```

   A. "B" and "C" if MyVal is 18.

   B. "C" if MyVal is 20.

   C. "A," "B," and "C" if MyVal is 17.

   D. "D" will never appear.

6. If a program contains two String variables with their contents assigned as follows,

```
strFirst = "Bill Smith"
strSecond = "Paul Jones"
```

what expression will yield the string "Bill Jones?"

   A. Mid(strFirst,1) & Mid(strSecond,6)

   B. Mid(strFirst,1,5) & Mid(strSecond,6)

   C. Left(strFirst,4) + Right(strSecond,5)

   D. Left(strFirst,5) + Right(strSecond,5)

7. The return value of Instr("Bobby Young," "Y") would be

   A. "Y"

   B. 0

   C. 5

   D. 7

8. What will the user see in the Message Box when this code runs?

```
Dim NewNum As Integer
   Dim MyNum As Integer
```

```
Do While NewNum < 30
    For MyNum = 20 To 11 Step -1
        NewNum = NewNum + 2
        If NewNum >= 20 Then
            Exit Do
        End If
    Next MyNum
Loop
MsgBox NewNum
```

A. 20.

B. 11.

C. 30.

D. User will never see a message box.

9. The ParamArray argument

   A. must be of type Variant.

   B. must be of type Array.

   C. can be any valid data type.

   D. has no data type.

10. If a form has the following code:

```
[General Declarations]
Private intCounter as Integer
Private Sub cmdBegin_Click()
    Timer1.Enabled = true
End Sub
Private Sub Timer1_Timer()
    intCounter = intCounter + 1
End Sub
Private Sub cmdOK_Click()
    MsgBox intCounter
End Sub
```

What will be the effect of the user clicking the Begin button and later clicking the OK button?

   A. User won't see anything either time.

   B. User will always see a message box with 1.

   C. User will always see a message box with 0.

   D. User will see a message box whose exact value depends on timer's Interval and how long it's been running.

11. The line of code

```
ListBox.ListIndex = -1
```

    A. will cause a run–time error.

    B. will select the first item in the list.

    C. will select the last item in the list.

    D. will deselect any item in the list.

12. The purpose of the DoEvents functions in the following code

```
Command1.Value = true
DoEvents
Call MySub
```

    A. is to ensure that MySub will run only after Command1's value property has changed.

    B. is to put Command1's click event on the event queue.

    C. is to ensure that Command1's click event procedure will run before MySub runs.

    D. is to ensure that Command1's click event procedure and MySub will run simultaneously.

13. Which of the following lines of code will cause an event to happen? (pick two)

    A. Command1_Click

    B. Command1.Value = True

    C. Command1.SetFocus

    D. Command1_GotFocus

14. You do the following things: 1) write a general procedure in a form and call it MySub_Click(). 2) Later place a command button on the form whose default name is Command1. 3) Write code in Command1's click event procedure. 4) Rename Command1 to MySub. What will happen when the user clicks the command button?

    A. Nothing.

    B. The original code in MySub_Click will run.

C. The code in Command1_Click will run.

D. The code in Command1_Click will run, but under the name MySub_Click.

15. To implement a read-only custom property for a form

A. declare a Private variable with the property name.

B. write a Property Let procedure without a Property Get.

C. write a Property Get procedure without a Property Let.

D. write a Property Get and Property Let procedure that use an underlying Private variable with a different name.

16. To clear the graphics image in a PictureBox control named picFile, you could use the code:

A. picFile.Image = ""

B. picFile.Picture = LoadPicture()

C. picFile.Picture = Nothing

D. picFile.Picture = ""

17. When the following line of code runs (pick two)

```
Text1.Seltext = "Hello"
```

A. the text "Hello" replaces the previously selected text.

B. the text "Hello" inserts into the text box in front of the previously selected text.

C. Text1.SelLength becomes 5.

D. everything visible in Text1 disappears and is replaced by "Hello."

18. If you have a ListBox named List1 and you want to refer to the contents of the last row in ListBox, you would use the expression:

A. List1.ListCount

B. List1.List(ListCount)

C. List1.List(ListCount - 1)

D. List1.(ListCount - 1)

19. Consider the code:

```
Dim MyCounter As Integer
MyCounter = 4
Do
MyCounter = MyCounter + 1
MsgBox MyCounter
Loop Until MyCounter > 3
MsgBox MyCounter
```

When this code runs, the user will see

A. one MessageBox displaying 4.

B. one MessageBox displaying 5.

C. one MessageBox displaying 4 followed by another displaying 5.

D. one MessageBox displaying 5 followed by another displaying 5.

20. An example of the correct syntax to begin a For Each loop would be

A. For Each Control

B. For Each ctrlCurr in Controls

C. For Each ctrlCurr From 1 To Controls.Count

D. For Each ctrlCurr in Controls From 1 To Controls.Count

Chapter 4

1. To determine and observe the code that runs initially in your application, you should

A. start your application from the design environment with F5.

B. start your application from the design environment with Ctrl+Break.

C. start your application from the design environment with F8.

D. place the Debug.Print method in your code.

2. If you have the following code

```
Private Sub cmdOK_Click()
    MyVar = 17
    Process MyVar     'call to the Process procedure
    MsgBox MyVar
```

```
        MyVar = MyVar * 2
        MsgBox "MyVar = " & MyVar
    End Sub

    Private Sub Process(ThisVar as Integer)
        ThisVar = ThisVar + 20
    End Sub
```

and you begin using the Step Over command on all lines starting with the line MyVar = 17

    A. VB will not execute the next line (Process MyVar) by stepping over it.

    B. VB will step through all of the code line by line, including the code lines in the Process procedure before returning to the cmdOK_Click event.

    C. VB will execute the next line (Process MyVar), but will not execute the code in the Process procedures.

    D. VB will step through all of the code line by line, except for the code in the Process procedure, which will run completely before returning to the cmdOK_Click event.

3. When you press Ctrl+Break while the application is running in the VB design environment

    A. you will break on the next line of code to be executed.

    B. you will always go to a Debug window.

    C. you will only go to a paused line of VB code if VB was running your code at the moment you pressed Ctrl+Break.

    D. you will end the application.

4. If your application includes the following code:

```
    Private Sub cmdOK_Click()
        MyVar = 17
        Process MyVar
        MsgBox MyVar
        MyVar = MyVar * 2
        MsgBox "MyVar = " & MyVar
    End Sub

    Private Sub Process(ThisVar as Integer)
        ThisVar = ThisVar + 20
    End Sub
```

Part

VI

App

J

and the application is currently paused on the line *MsgBox MyVar:*

    A. Use Set Next Statement to immediately execute *MyVar = 17.*

    B. If you use Set Next Statement on *MsgBox "MyVar = " & MyVar*, all lines up to that statement will execute.

    C. Use Set Next Statement to immediately execute *ThisVar = ThisVar + 20.*

    D. You cannot re-run the line *MyVar=17* with Set Next Statement if VB has previously run this line.

5. If your application contains the following code:

```
Private Sub cmdOK_Click()
    MyVar = 17
    Process MyVar
    MsgBox MyVar
    MyVar = MyVar * 2
    MsgBox "MyVar = " & MyVar
End Sub

Private Sub Process(ThisVar as Integer)
    ThisVar = ThisVar + 20
End Sub
```

and the application is currently paused on the line *MsgBox MyVar*

    A. you can use Step To Cursor to execute the line *MyVar = 17.*

    B. you cannot use Step to Cursor on the line *End Sub.*

    C. if you use Step to Cursor on the line *End Sub*, all lines up to End Sub will execute immediately and VB will pause at End Sub.

    D. if you use Step to Cursor on the line *End Sub*, VB will pause briefly on each line up to *End Sub*, where it will stop.

6. A Breakpoint that marks a code line (pick two)

    A. can be toggled On and Off with F9.

    B. displays the code line in a different color.

    C. indicates that the code line will be skipped when the code runs.

    D. will be saved when the code file is saved.

7. If you have many breakpoints in your code and want to clear them all, the fastest way would be to

    A. perform an Edit Search to find each one and toggle it Off using F9.

    B. exit the project and then reopen it.

    C. choose Run, Clear All Breakpoints from the menu.

    D. select the Clear All Breakpoint button on the toolbar.

8. If a Watch Expression's type is "Watch Expression"

    A. VB will automatically break when the value changes.

    B. VB will automatically break when it reaches a designated range of values.

    C. you will need to pause the application to see it.

    D. you will always see it whenever VB encounters a breakpoint.

9. If a Watch Expression's type is "Break when value changes"

    A. you will automatically see its value whenever the value changes.

    B. you will automatically see its value only when it reaches a designated value or range of values.

    C. you will need to explicitly pause the application and bring up the Debug Window to see it.

    D. you will automatically see it whenever VB encounters a breakpoint.

10. If the Watch Type of a Watch is "Break when expression is true"

    A. you will automatically see its value whenever the value changes.

    B. you will automatically see its value whenever it reaches a designated value or range of values.

    C. you will need to explicitly pause the application and bring up the Debug Window to see it.

    D. you will automatically see it whenever VB encounters a breakpoint.

Part
VI

App
J

11. The Calls Dialog box (pick two)

    A. can be invoked with Ctrl+L.

    B. will show you the history of all sub and function procedures called during this run of your application.

    C. must be turned off before distributing your executed application to the user.

    D. will show the chain of procedure calls leading to and including the currently executing procedure.

12. The Debug.Print method (pick two)

    A. must be removed from your application before you compile the application.

    B. will be ignored in the compiled version of the application.

    C. can be typed in the Immediate Pane of the Debug Window to get the current value of the stipulated expression.

    D. is used to write to the Immediate Pane of the Debug Window.

Chapter 5

1. You begin an error-handling routine in your code by

    A. placing a labeled line in the General Declarations section of a standard module that references the error-handling routine.

    B. placing a labeled line in a special error-handling function.

    C. placing a labeled line above the error-handling routine.

    D. placing a labeled line just below the error-handling routine.

2. On the line immediately before the error handler in a routine

    A. you should put the line likely to cause an error.

    B. you must put On Error GoTo 0.

    C. you should put On Error GoTo *label*, where *label* is the name of the error handler.

    D. you should put an Exit Sub or Exit Function statement.

3. The code in an error handler (pick two)

   A. must always give some visual cue to the user.

   B. must do something to rectify or react to the error.

   C. must provide instructions for where to restart once the error has been handled.

   D. must always be in a separate procedure.

4. If there is no Resume statement in your error handler

   A. the error handler processes through to the End Function or End Sub statement of the current procedure.

   B. the app receives a run-time error invoked within the error handler.

   C. the app receives a compiler error.

   D. VB defaults to a Resume Next strategy.

5. Pick two that are true of the On Error statement

   A. On Error Go To *label*—directs the application to a designated error handler.

   B. On Error Go To 0—disables the current error handler.

   C. On Error Go To—disables the error handler.

   D. On Error Resume Next—saves the property settings of the err object.

6. You can use On error Resume Next (pick two)

   A. to direct VB where to resume execution from within an error handler.

   B. to handle an error immediately after the line where the error occurred.

   C. to ignore the problem that caused the error.

   D. to resume to the next labeled error handler.

7. If you wish to use the Inline style of error handling in a procedure, you must remember to

  A. use the Resume statement.

  B. use the Resume Next statement.

  C. disable error trapping at the beginning of the routine with On Error GoTo 0.

  D. explicitly clear the error condition when you are done handling it.

8. You can write wrapper functions for error-prone statements that (pick two)

  A. do not need to contain error handlers.

  B. return a value indicating success or failure.

  C. pass any error code back to the calling routine to be handled there.

  D. do their error handling internally to the wrapper function.

9. A centralized error-handling routine (pick two)

  A. entirely eliminates the need for error handlers in routines that call it.

  B. allows you to paste a simple standardized error handler into routines that call it.

  C. can return a flag telling the calling routine how to resume execution after the error.

  D. can contain a label that all other routines' On Error GoTo statements can point to.

10. You can use Err.Raise (pick two)

  A. to cause an error to occur.

  B. without the *number* argument, which will pass the default value of 0.

C. with Err.Number to regenerate the current error inside an error handler.

D. to increase the value of Err.Number stipulated by the *number* argument.

11. You can use Err.Raise

    A. to cancel the current error.

    B. to determine the current error number.

    C. to test whether the current Err.Number is a VB standard error or if it is a programmer-defined error.

    D. to test how your application reacts to a particular error.

12. The Err.Raise can cause an error to be handled further up in the call stack (pick two)

    A. whenever it is used.

    B. when you use it from within an error handler.

    C. when you set the *number* argument to 0.

    D. when you use it in a routine that has no error handler of its own.

Chapter 6

1. Which of these statements will assign the value of the CommandButton's Caption property to the TextBox's Text property?

    A. Text1 = Command1

    B. Text1 = Command1.Caption

    C. Text1.Text = Command1

    D. All three of the above statements will work.

2. To display a newly created Label control with a 3-D appearance,

    A. you have to include the custom THREED.OCX file in your project.

    B. you must change the Appearance property to 3-D from its default of Flat.

C. you must change the BorderStyle property.

D. Labels do not have an Appearance property.

3. The statement

```
Form1.BackColor = RGB(0,0,0)
```

A. will cause a run-time error.

B. will cause a compiler error.

C. will change the form's background color to black.

D. will change the form's background color to white.

4. To provide a title for an Option Button, you should

A. put the text in the control's Caption property.

B. put the text in the control's Text property.

C. put the text in an accompanying Label control.

D. put the text in the control's Label property.

5. To define Alt+X as the access key for a Command Button

A. set the Caption property to E_xit.

B. set the Caption property to &E_xit.

C. set the Caption property to E&xit.

D. choose Alt-X from the dropdown list of available access keys.

6. A control's DragIcon property (pick two)

A. provides the image the user will see while dragging the control with the mouse.

B. must be set to True to allow the user to drag the control.

C. if set to False, will cause an outline of the control to display when the user drags it.

D. if left blank, will cause an outline of the control to display when the user drags it.

7. If you change the DragMode property,

    A. you will determine whether the control can use a custom DragIcon or not.

    B. you can set the name of the file containing the drag icon's image.

    C. you can control whether the user is able to drag the control without any code.

    D. you can determine whether the user is able to drag with the mouse versus the Shift+arrow keys.

8. If a TextBox's Enabled property is False, then

    A. the text in the box will be grayed, and the user won't be able to set focus to the TextBox.

    B. the text in the box will be grayed, the user can still set focus to the TextBox, but the user won't be able to make changes to the text.

    C. the text in the box will be grayed, and the user can still make changes to the text.

    D. the text in the box will appear as normal, but the user won't be able to set focus to the TextBox.

9. The color listed in a Shape's BackColor property

    A. always displays the color designated in the BackColor property.

    B. only displays when the Shape's FillStyle is Transparent.

    C. only displays when the Shape's FillStyle is Solid.

    D. the Shape control is a lightweight control and therefore, it has no BackColor property.

10. A CommandButton control

    A. doesn't have a BackColor property.

    B. displays its BackColor only when the CommandButton has focus.

    C. displays its BackColor value when Appearance is 3-D.

    D. displays its BackColor behind the button's Caption text.

Part

VI

App

J

11. A control's Tag property

    A. represents the brief pop-up tip a user sees when the mouse pauses over the control.

    B. represents an internal read-only name the application uses to identify the control.

    C. defaults to the control's Caption property.

    D. is described by none of the above.

12. Changing a control's hWnd property at run time in your code

    A. will change the Width property of the control.

    B. will allow another Windows application to manipulate the control's properties directly.

    C. will assign the control to a different form.

    D. is something you should never attempt.

13. The Move method

    A. has four required arguments.

    B. requires both a Left and a Top argument.

    C. requires only a Left argument.

    D. requires only a Top argument.

14. An access key for a TextBox control

    A. can be provided in the TextBox's Caption property.

    B. can be provided in the TextBox's Text property.

    C. can be provided in an accompanying Label control.

    D. can be provided in the TextBox's Label property.

15. The Index property

    A. uniquely identifies an MDI child form.

    B. identifies a control's position in the tab order.

    C. identifies the control as an element of a control array.

    D. associates a help file topic with the current control.

16. The value of the Name property

    A. is visible to the user at run time.

    B. provides a default value for the Caption property.

    C. takes its default value from the Caption property.

    D. can't be changed at run time.

17. The ScaleTop and ScaleHeight properties

    A. indicate the internal dimensions of a form or PictureBox—always in twips.

    B. indicate the internal dimensions of a form or PictureBox—always in the units given by ScaleMode.

    C. indicate a control's size in the units given by the containing form's or PictureBox control's ScaleMode.

    D. indicate a control's position in the units given by the ScaleMode of its container.

18. To prevent the user from being able to give focus to a control (activate a control)

    A. set the control's TabIndex property to 0.

    B. set the control's TabStop property to True.

    C. set the control's TabStop property to False.

    D. do none of the above.

Chapter 7

1. A Click event can be triggered (pick two)

    A. when the user tabs to a control.

    B. when the user changes the selected item in a ListBox.

    C. when the program calls a Click event procedure in code.

    D. when the program sets an OptionButton's Value property to True.

Part
VI
App
J

2. The timing of the KeyPress event is

   A. before KeyDown but after KeyUp.

   B. before KeyUp but after KeyDown.

   C. after KeyDown and KeyUp.

   D. independent of the timing of KeyDown and KeyUp.

3. KeyPress receives a parameter that is

   A. Integer and provides the number of keys pending.

   B. Long and gives the code for the physical key pressed on the keyboard.

   C. Integer and gives the ASCII value of the character corresponding to the key just pressed.

   D. String and gives the character corresponding to the key just pressed.

4. A CommandButton's DblClick event

   A. can be triggered by the ENTER key or the mouse.

   B. can be triggered by the button's access key or the mouse.

   C. can only be triggered by the mouse.

   D. doesn't exist.

5. A line of code that checks to see if Ctrl+F3 was keyed in the KeyUp or KeyDown event might read:

   A. If (Shift = vbCtrlMask) AND (KeyCode = vbKeyF3) Then

   B. If KeyCode = vbKeyControl + vbKeyF3 Then

   C. If (Shift AND vbCtrlMask) AND _ (KeyCode = vbKeyF3) Then

   D. If (Shift AND vbCtrlMask) AND _ (KeyCode AND vbKeyF3) Then

6. To enable keystroke validation at both the Form and control levels, you must

    A. set the KeyPreview property of controls to True.

    B. set the KeyPreview property of controls to False.

    C. set the KeyPreview property of the Form to True.

    D. set the KeyPreview property of the Form to False.

7. A Form's MouseMove event is triggered

    A. when the mousepointer moves anywhere over the Form.

    B. only when the mousepointer moves over the Form's empty surface or a non–PictureBox control.

    C. only when the mousepointer moves over the Form's empty surface.

    D. only when the mousepointer moves over the Form's empty surface or over a disabled or invisible control.

8. A MouseUp event can happen (pick two)

    A. before a DblClick event.

    B. before a Click event.

    C. after a DblClick event.

    D. after a Click event.

9. A Form's or PictureBox control's AutoRedraw property

    A. is a bitmap representing the full-screen image of the object.

    B. is a Boolean that enables the Paint event when set to True.

    C. can be set to Automatic to enable automatic refresh.

    D. is a Boolean that enables automatic refresh when set to True.

10. If Form1 is your project's startup Form and you put the line

    Form2.Show

    in Form1's Load event procedure

    A. you'll receive a compiler error.

    B. you'll receive a run-time error.

Part

VI

App

J

C. Form1 will end up as the active Form after all initial code has run.

D. Form2 will end up as the active Form after all initial code has run.

11. The difference between QueryUnload and Unload events is that

A. QueryUnload happens first and Unload receives the UnloadMode parameter.

B. QueryUnload happens first and QueryUnload receives the UnloadMode parameter.

C. Unload happens first and Unload receives the UnloadMode parameter.

D. Unload happens first and QueryUnload receives the UnloadMode parameter.

12. The Paint event is triggered

A. at the moment you reset the AutoRedraw property in code.

B. when you call a Graphics method in code and AutoRedraw is False.

C. when a Form is resized and AutoRedraw is False.

D. when a Form is resized and AutoRedraw is True.

13. To clear the Debugger's Immediate Pane in your code

A. you can call Debug.Clear.

B. you can call Debug.Cls.

C. there is nothing you can do.

D. you can call Debug.Print "".

14. To send the printer to a new page, you may call

A. Printer.NewPage

B. Printer.PageDef = vblf + vbcr

C. Printer.CurrentY = 0

D. Printer.PageBreak

15. When the user changes focus to another application, the currently active Form in your application

    A. receives a DeActivate event.

    B. receives a LostFocus event.

    C. receives both DeActivate and LostFocus.

    D. receives neither DeActivate nor LostFocus events.

16. To make an unloaded Form visible to the user

    A. you only need to call the Load statement.

    B. you only need to call the Show method.

    C. you must call both Load and Show.

    D. the only way is to set the Form's Visible property.

17. The Form's Terminate event

    A. always happens before Unload.

    B. always happens after Unload.

    C. happens only when you set the Form to Nothing after an Unload.

    D. happens whenever you set the Form to Nothing.

18. The DragDrop event

    A. triggers for a control when another control is dropped over it.

    B. triggers for a control when it is dropped.

    C. triggers for a control as it is being dragged.

    D. triggers for a control as another control is dragged over it.

19. The DragMode property

    A. determines whether or not the user will see an icon as a control is dragged.

    B. determines whether or not you must use the Drag method in code to allow the user to drag a control.

    C. determines whether a control can be dragged by the mouse or by Shift+arrow keys.

    D. indicates whether a control is currently being dragged.

Part

VI

App

J

20. The Screen object's dimensions

    A. aren't available at run time.

    B. are always given in twips.

    C. are always given in the units specified in the Screen's ScaleMode property.

    D. are always given in the units specified in the current Form's ScaleMode property.

Chapter 8

1. A menu control's access key (pick two)

    A. is specified from a list in the Menu Editor.

    B. is specified with an ampersand in the Name property.

    C. is specified with an ampersand in the Caption.

    D. is limited to an Alt- key combination for main menu items.

2. A menu control's shortcut key (pick one)

    A. is specified from a list in the Menu Editor.

    B. is specified with an ampersand in the Name property.

    C. is specified with an ampersand in the Caption.

    D. is limited to an Alt- key combination.

3. The maximum value for a menu control's level in Visual Basic is

    A. determined by available memory.

    B. 4.

    C. 5.

    D. 256.

4. You can invoke the Menu Editor (pick two)

    A. from the View menu.

    B. with Ctrl+M.

    C. from the Tools menu.

    D. with Ctrl+E.

5. A menu control's Name property

    A. is not supplied automatically when you initialize a menu control.

    B. provides the default value for the Caption property.

    C. can contain an ampersand indicating the shortcut key.

    D. is required to begin with "mnu."

6. A menu control's Caption property

    A. is used to refer to the menu control in code.

    B. has an initial default value equal to the Name property.

    C. can contain an ampersand indicating the access key.

    D. is automatically initialized to a sequential name by VB.

7. You can specify that a menu control will be a separator bar by

    A. supplying a space (" ") as the Name.

    B. supplying a dash ("-") as the Caption.

    C. supplying a dash ("-") as the Name.

    D. supplying an underscore ("_") as the Caption.

8. A menu item's Checked property (pick two)

    A. will show a checkmark if set to true.

    B. has a default value of 1.

    C. has a default value of False.

    D. will hide a checkmark if set to true.

9. A menu item's Visible property

    A. will leave a blank space in the menu list when set to false.

    B. will cause a menu control to appear grayed out when set to false.

    C. will cause a control's surrounding menu items to close in together when set to 1.

    D. will cause a control's surrounding menu items to close in together when set to False.

Part

VI

App

J

10. A menu control's Enabled property

   A. will cause a menu control to disappear when set to False.

   B. will cause a menu control to appear grayed out when set to False.

   C. is not available at design time.

   D. must always be used in conjunction with the Visible property.

11. The NegotiatePosition property

   A. is only useful with embedded OLE applications that have menus.

   B. must be set to true on a form to allow embedded OLE menus to coexist with the form's menu.

   C. must always be set for any form that wants to display menus.

   D. will block the embedded OLE object's menus from appearing if set to None.

12. The WindowList property (pick two)

   A. displays a standard interface for handling MDI children.

   B. causes a menu item to list all open forms in any current application.

   C. implements a list of all open Windows processes, similar to Task Manager.

   D. is used on menu systems of MDI parent forms.

13. The Index property of a menu control

   A. is case-sensitive.

   B. can be used to store string information about a menu control.

   C. will implement a menu control array if set to a value of 0 or more.

   D. can only be set at run time.

14. A menu control's menu level (pick two)

   A. can be set at design or run time.

   B. can only be set at run time.

C. can only be set at design time.

D. must be equal to or one greater than the preceding menu control's.

15. To initialize and use a run-time element of a menu control array

A. you must use Dim … As New ….

B. you must set the Enabled property to True.

C. you must use the Load statement.

D. you must programmatically specify its position.

16. You can use the up and down arrow buttons in the Menu Editor to

A. change a menu control's level in the menu hierarchy.

B. change a menu control's position in the menu list.

C. move the selection highlight through different controls in the list.

D. add or delete menu controls.

17. You can destroy a menu control array item

A. by setting the Index to 0.

B. by decreasing incrementally the array's upper bound.

C. with Redim Preserve.

D. with the Unload statement.

18. At run time, my code can delete

A. all items in a menu control array that had been created at run time.

B. only enabled items.

C. only disabled items.

D. all items in a menu control array.

19. A Pop-up menu

A. must be invoked with the mouse.

B. can't be visible on the main menu bar.

Part
VI
App
J

C. is invoked with the Form's PopupMenu method.

D. must be invoked on another form.

20. Menu title items

A. have no event procedures.

B. have a Click event procedure that you can access at design time by clicking the item.

C. have a double-click event procedure that you can access at design time only from a code window.

D. have a Click event procedure that you can access at design time only from a code window.

Chapter 9

1. You can create a Parent MDI Form at design time by

A. setting a Form's MDIChild property to False.

B. setting a Form's MDIParent property to True.

C. using the Insert menu.

D. writing code such as

Load MDIForm1 vbMDI

2. The correct syntax for instantiating a copy of a Child Form whose design-time name property is the value frmMDIChild would be

A. Load frmNew as New frmMDIChild.

B. Dim frmNew as New frmMDIChild.

C. Dim frmMDIChild as New frmNew.

D. Load frmMDIChild as New frmChild.

3. The maximum number MDI Forms in an application is

A. 256.

B. determined by available system resources.

C. 512.

D. 1.

4. The minimized icon of an MDI Child

    A. is unavailable to the user.

    B. appears on the MDI Form.

    C. appears on the Windows desktop.

    D. appears in the MDI Child that currently has focus.

5. The maximum number of run-time instances of an MDI child is

    A. 256.

    B. determined by available system resources.

    C. 512.

    D. 1.

6. The maximum number of MDI Child Forms allowable in a project at design time is

    A. 256.

    B. determined by available system resources.

    C. 2.

    D. 1.

7. A VB Form with its MDIChild property set to False

    A. can exist in an MDI application as a normal form.

    B. can't exist in an MDI application.

    C. can exist in an MDI application only as a modal form.

    D. can exist in an MDI application only as a modaless form.

8. Examples of MDI applications are (pick two)

    A. Excel.

    B. Write.

    C. NotePad.

    D. Word.

9. You might be able to reference a specific MDI Child instance in code

   A. with the name property you assigned at run time.

   B. with the name you gave it at design time.

   C. by checking its Tag property.

   D. by checking its position in the Forms collection.

10. The menu on an MDI form (pick two)

    A. will override a Child Form's menu when the Child's AutoMenu property is set to False.

    B. will appear when there are no active instances of Child Forms.

    C. will appear above the Child menu when there is an active instance of a Child Form.

    D. will appear when active Child Form instances have no menus.

11. You can place the following directly on an MDI Form's surface (pick two)

    A. any control with an Align property.

    B. Image controls.

    C. PictureBox controls.

    D. controls with the MDIChild property set to True.

12. For a menu to implement a drop-down list of all open Child forms in an application

    A. the menu must be named Window (only requirement).

    B. the menu's WindowList property must be True (only requirement).

    C. the menu's WindowList property must be True and the menu must be named Window.

    D. the menu's WindowList property must be True and your application must programmatically add each newly instantiated Child's name to a menu control array.

13. You can use the Arrange method to (pick two)

    A. arrange Child icons on the MDI Form.

    B. tile open Child forms on the MDI Form.

    C. cascade the MDI Form along with other windows applications running in the current Windows session.

    D. arrange icons on the Windows desktop.

14. If a running VB application has various instances of Child Forms and encounters the statement Cancel = False in the MDI Form's Unload event:

    A. no Child Forms will unload.

    B. all Child Forms will unload, but not the MDI Form.

    C. the Child Forms will unload as well as the MDI Form.

    D. a run-time error will occur.

15. If a running VB application has various instances of Child Forms and encounters the statement Cancel = True in the Unload event of one of the Child Forms, then

    A. all Child Forms whose Unload events occurred before this one are unloaded, and the unloading process halts.

    B. all Child Forms in the app will unload, except for the Child with Cancel = True in its Unload event.

    C. the MDI Form and all Child Forms with Cancel = True in their Unload events will stay loaded. All other Child Forms will unload.

    D. run-time error 453 "Invalid Operation" occurs.

Chapter 10

1. To include the appropriate library for an OLE server in your application, you must

    A. use the Tools, References menu option.

    B. use the Tools, Options menu option.

Part

VI

App

J

C. edit the Windows Registry.

D. use the Tools, Custom Controls menu option.

2. You can get information about methods and properties of the classes of a server whose library you've included in your application by

A. selecting the property or method in your code and pressing F1.

B. selecting the property or method in your code and pressing Shift-F2.

C. invoking the Object Browser and locating the server in the Classes/Libraries list.

D. locating the server name under VB's Help, Search menu option.

3. In order for a server's objects to be exposed

A. they must be registered in the Windows Registry.

B. the server must be currently running in the background.

C. you must register them with VB's Tools, References menu option.

D. you must register them with VB's Tools, Options menu option.

4. The following line will cause early binding:

A. Dim objExcel As Excel.Application

B. Dim objExcel As Object

C. Set objExcel = Excel.Application

D. Set objExcel = Object

5. We initialize an object with the declaration

Public objExcel as Excel.Application

and later we wish to set the Visible property of the object. We can use the following line of code:

A. Excel.Visible = True

B. objExcel.Application.Visible = True

C. Excel.Application.Visible = True

D. objExcel.Visible = True

6. The OLE container's Object property

    A. makes the methods and properties of the contained server class available programmatically.

    B. is a string containing the name of the contained server class.

    C. is True if the container holds an object and False if it's empty.

    D. represents the contained server object's visual interface.

7. The user can pop up the available verbs for an object in an OLE container by

    A. right-clicking the mouse over the container.

    B. double-clicking over the container.

    C. left-clicking over the container.

    D. triggering some event (such as a CommandButton's click event), which calls the ShowVerb method.

8. The NegotiateMenus property

    A. belongs to a Form and is True by default.

    B. belongs to an OLE automation object and is True by default.

    C. belongs to a Form and is False by default.

    D. belongs to an OLE automation object and is False by default.

9. The CreateObject function

    A. always begins a new copy of the server.

    B. always references an existing copy of the server.

    C. references an existing copy of the server if one exists, otherwise begins a new copy.

    D. generates a run-time error if there is no existing copy of the server.

10. You may call GetObject

    A. with a missing first parameter to create a new instance of a server class.

    B. with a blank string ("") as first parameter to create a new instance of a server class.

Part

VI

App

J

    C. with a file name as first parameter to create a reference to an existing instance of a server class.

    D. with no parameters to create an uninitialized object.

11. If there is no existing instance of Excel.Application in your application, the following line of code will generate a run-time error:

    A. Set objExcel = CreateObject("Excel.Application")

    B. Set objExcel = GetObject(,"Excel.Application")

    C. Set objExcel = GetObject("C:\MyFile.Xls")

    D. Set objExcel = GetObject("","Excel.Application")

12. To assign an OLE container's server instance to an OLE object variable named objExcel, you would write this code:

    A. objExcel = OLE1

    B. Set objExcel = OLE1.Application

    C. Set objExcel = OLE1.Object

    D. Set objExcel = OLE1

13. To programmatically refresh the list of OLE verbs available at any given time in an OLE container control, you should

    A. call the FetchVerbs method.

    B. call the OleVerbs method.

    C. reset the OleVerbsCount property.

    D. reset the OleVerbs collection.

14. The OLE container's DoVerb method

    A. pops up the server's Verb menu.

    B. executes an available server verb.

    C. enables the user to run a verb from the Verb menu.

    D. places the server's Verb menu on the Form's menu, if the Form's NegotiateMenus property is True.

15. Setting the OLE container's AutoVerbmenu property to True

    A. immediately causes the contained server's Verb menu to pop up.

    B. allows the user to pop up the server's Verb menu.

    C. allows the VB application to display the server's Verb menu by calling the Form's PopupMenu method.

    D. adds the server's Verb menu to the Form's menu.

16. To create a linked or embedded object on the OLE container control at run time

    A. use CreateLink and CreateEmbed with a data file name.

    B. use CreateLink with a data file name and CreateEmbed with no arguments.

    C. use CreateLink with a data file name and a server name, and CreateEmbed with a server name only.

    D. use both CreateLink and CreateEmbed with a data file name and a server name.

17. The OLE container's displaytype property

    A. determines whether server menus are visible or not.

    B. determines whether the server appears iconized or normal.

    C. determines whether the server appears within or outside of the container.

    D. determines the screen resolution of the server.

18. Setting the OLE container's SizeMode property to vbOLESizeClip means that

    A. the OLE data resizes to fit the container exactly.

    B. the OLE data resizes to fit the container as closely as possible while still maintaining its original proportions.

    C. the OLE data maintains its original size and may or may not fit within the container.

    D. the OLE Container control resizes to fit the data.

Chapter 11

1. An OLE server

    A. can be either in-process or out-of-process if it is an EXE.

    B. can be either in-process or out-of-process if it is a DLL.

    C. can have its class Instancing properties be Creatable SingleUse if it is a DLL.

    D. can have its class Instancing properties be Creatable MultiUse if it is an EXE.

2. An OLE server project's Name option as found on the Project tab of the Options dialog

    A. must be the same as the project's file name.

    B. will be the objecttype component when a controller instantiates appname.objecttype in the server.

    C. will be the appname component when a controller instantiates appname.objecttype in the server.

    D. must be the same as the main class name in the server.

3. An OLE server project's startup form option on the Project tab of the Options dialog

    A. must be Sub Main( ) in an out-of-process server.

    B. must be a form in an out-of-process server.

    C. may be a form in an in-process server.

    D. must be Sub Main( ) in an in-process server.

4. The purpose of an OLE server project's Start Mode option on the Project tab of the Options dialog is

    A. to determine whether the server will be in-process or out-of-process.

    B. to determine whether the server will be single- or multi-use.

    C. to cause the project to compile as an OLE server.

    D. to allow Visual Basic to temporarily register the server and keep it running in design mode.

5. A true fact about the relationship between the Public and Instancing built-in class properties is (pick two)

    A. when Public is False, Instancing can only be Single Use or None.

    B. when Public is True and Instancing is None, the class can't be instantiated by a controller but is visible to the controller.

    C. when Public is False, the Instancing property's setting is ignored.

    D. when Instancing is Creatable Single- or Multi-Use, the setting of Public is ignored.

6. You would put the statement

```
Private colStars as Collection
```

    A. in the Parent Class.

    B. in the Dependent Collection Class.

    C. in the Dependent Class.

    D. in the Controller Application.

7. The following code will implement a read-only property

    A. `Public Status as Boolean`

    B. `Private Status as Boolean`

    C.
```
Private gblnStatus as Boolean
Public Property Get Status() as Boolean
Status = gblnStatus
End Property
```

    D.
```
Private gblnStatus as Boolean
Public Property Let Status() as Boolean
Status = gblnStatus
End Property
```

Part
VI

App

J

8. The Class'Terminate event will always run when

   A. OLE shuts down the server.

   B. an END statement executes in the server's code.

   C. once all forms have been unloaded.

   D. once all forms have become invisible.

9. A collection's built-in Item method

   A. has an integer parameter that indexes the item's position in the collection.

   B. has a string parameter that looks up the item's key in the collection.

   C. has a variant parameter.

   D. has no parameter.

10. If Stars is the name of a dependent collection class in a server and Star is the name of the dependent class, what code must I put in the server's parent class (Universe) to implement the collection?

   A. Public Stars as New Stars

   B. Private Stars as New Collection

   C. Public Stars as Universe.Stars 'in General Declarations

   ... 'Somewhere else in the parent's code

   Set Stars = CreateObject("Universe.Stars")

   D. No new code is necessary in the parent class.

11. The following is true of forms in an OLE server (pick two)

   A. may be modal or modaless if the server is out-of-process.

   B. may be modal or modaless if the server is in-process.

   C. Startup Form of the project must be Sub Main( ) if the server is in-process.

   D. must be modaless if the server is in-process.

12. The End statement

    A. is the recommended way to close any OLE server.

    B. should never be used in an in-process server.

    C. is not recommended, but can be used in an in-process server.

    D. is the recommended way to close an out-of-process server.

13. Your server will close if it is not currently running any code and

    A. it's out-of-process, no controller is requesting it, and all forms are invisible.

    B. no controller is requesting it and all forms have been unloaded.

    C. no controller is requesting it, regardless of whether forms are present.

    D. the server's startup form unloads.

14. What code would pass an error whose error number is stored in the variable ErrNum to the controller from the server?

    A. Err.Raise ErrNum

    B. Err.Raise ErrNum + vbObjError

    C. The current method must be a function and you must provide a result code.

    D. Err.Raise vbObjError

15. You can create Object Browser help for your server (pick two)

    A. for methods.

    B. only for properties.

    C. for all methods and properties.

    D. for properties implemented with Property Let/Get.

16. Before running a test copy of your server at design time you should

A. temporarily set its creatable classes' Instancing properties to Creatable MultiUse.

B. temporarily set its creatable classes' Instancing properties to Creatable SingleUse.

C. compile it.

D. temporarily set its project's Startup Mode property to Standalone.

17. To make a temporary Windows Registry entry for your server while it runs in design mode

A. make its project's Startup Mode property be Standalone and then run the project.

B. make its project's Startup Mode property be Compatible OLE server and then run the project.

C. make its project's Startup Mode property be OLE Server and then run the project.

D. compile the project and then run it.

18. In order to fix a MISSING reference to your server at design time you must

A. restart the design-time copy of your controller application.

B. uncheck the reference to the server in the controller's Tools References, then recheck it.

C. recompile your server application.

D. make sure the server's Startup Mode property is OLE Server.

19. In order to register an out-of-process OLE server, you can (pick

A. run the regsvr32 utility against it.   two)

B. run it standalone.

C. compile it with File Make OLE DLL.

D. run it with the /REGSERVER option.

20. Visual Basic will warn you about incompatibility

A. when you change class properties already existing in the Compatible OLE Server and recompile.

B. whenever you recompile your server.

C. whenever you recompile your server with the Compatible OLE Server property set.

D. whenever you have made any changes not in the Compatible OLE Server and recompile.

Chapter 12

1. When viewing a recordset of type Dynaset, the user can

   A. view other users' adds and deletes, but not their edits.

   B. view other users' edits, but not their adds or deletes.

   C. view other users' edits, adds, and deletes.

   D. not view other users' edits, adds, or deletes.

2. The default Recordset type is

   A. Snapshot

   B. Table

   C. Dynaset

   D. DataBase

3. The Data Control's Connect property

   A. is always a directory name.

   B. must always be manually entered by the programmer.

   C. may be picked off a list if it's an installable ISAM.

   D. may be picked off a list if it's an ODBC data source.

4. To bind a textbox to a Data Control, you should

    A. set the RowSource and DataField properties.

    B. set the RowSource and BoundField properties.

    C. set the DataSource and DataField properties.

    D. set the DataBaseName and DataField properties.

5. The DataBaseName property of the Data Control

    A. is always a file name.

    B. is always a directory name.

    C. is a logical name, so not necessarily a directory or file.

    D. is always a file name for Microsoft Access databases.

6. The relationship between a RecordSet and a RecordSource is that

    A. RecordSet is an SQL string, and RecordSource is a record collection of type Dynaset, Snapshot, or Table.

    B. RecordSource is an SQL string, and RecordSet is a record collection of type Dynaset only.

    C. RecordSource is an SQL string, and RecordSet is a record collection of type Dynaset, Snapshot, or Table.

    D. RecordSet is an SQL string, and RecordSource is a record collection of type Dynaset only.

7. A SnapShot

    A. is implemented entirely on the local workstation.

    B. implements a copy buffer and a set of record pointers on the local workstation, and retrieves data from the server.

    C. is implemented entirely on the server.

    D. implements a copy buffer on the local workstation and retrieves data from the server. It does not use a set of record pointers.

8. The AddNew method of the Data Control's Recordset

    A. increments a record counter if the underlying DBMS supports this feature.

    B. adds a permanent record to the data.

C. initializes a temporary editing buffer.

D. requires the programmer to explicitly clear fields so the user can edit the new record's data.

9. You could use a statement such as "Select ★ from Customers where State = 'CA'"

A. to create a Dynaset-type recordset only.

B. to create a Dynaset or a Snapshot-type recordset.

C. to create a Dynaset, Snapshot, or Table-type recordset.

D. nowhere—can't use a WHERE clause to create a recordset.

10. In the Validate event procedure, the programmer

A. must set Save to True to force changes to be saved.

B. must set Action to True to allow the pending action to complete.

C. must set Action to 0 to cancel the pending action.

D. must set Action to false to cancel the pending action.

11. The NoMatch property of the Recordset

A. becomes True after a successful Find or Seek.

B. becomes False after a successful Find or Seek.

C. becomes True after a successful Find, only.

D. becomes False after a successful Seek, only.

12. Code in the Error event procedure of the Data Control

A. will override any error handlers written elsewhere.

B. is overridden by any error handlers written elsewhere.

C. happens when the user uses the Data Control without invoking any code written by you.

D. happens whenever there is an error related to the Data Control, either caused by your code or by a user action on the Data Control.

13. The relationship between the Seek method and the Find- methods is that

   A. both can be used on any type of recordset.

   B. Find- methods can be used on any type of recordset; Seek only on tables with the Index property set to a valid index.

   C. Seek can be used on any type of recordset; Find- methods only on tables with the Index property set to a valid index.

   D. Find- methods can be used only on Dynasets and Snapshots; Seek only on tables with the Index property set to a valid index. .

14. The record pointer will move

   A. when you call the Data Control's UpdateRecord method.

   B. when you call the Recordset's Update method.

   C. when you call either UpdateRecord or Update.

   D. neither when you call UpdateRecord nor Update.

15. CancelUpdate (pick two)

   A. could be called with the syntax Data1.CancelUpdate.

   B. could be called with the syntax

   Data1.RecordSet.CancelUpdate.

   C. changes the position of the record pointer.

   D. cancels all changes to bound controls only after an AddNew.

16. The following statement is syntactically correct:

   A. DBGrid1.("QueId").Width = 3000

   B. DBGrid1("QueId").Width = 3000

   C. DBGrid1.Columns("QueId").Width = 3000

   D. DBGrid1[QueId].Width = 3000

17. The BoundText property of the DB List or Combo Box contains

   A. name of the key field in the parent (controlling) recordset.

   B. current record's contents for the field specified in the BoundColumn property.

C. current record's contents for the field specified in the ListField property.

D. name of the key field in the lookup recordset.

18. The Delete method (pick two)

A. requires a pending Edit to run without an error.

B. does not move the record pointer.

C. requires a call to the Update method to become final.

D. updates the recordset's data immediately.

19. Assuming we have an ODBC datasource named MyData that uses the Oracle ODBC driver, the following is valid syntax in the Data Control's Connect property

A. ODBC;MyData

B. ODBC=Oracle;DSN=MyData;

C. ODBC;MyData;

D. ODBC;DSN=MyData;

20. You can use installable ISAM drivers for (pick two)

A. Oracle.

B. Paradox.

C. Excel.

D. Sybase.

Chapter 13

1. The SQL statement

Select F1, F2, F3 From T1 INNER JOIN T2 ON F1 = F2

will return

A. all rows from both tables, with matching rows together.

B. all rows from T1, and only matching rows from T2.

C. all rows from T2, and only matching rows from T1.

D. only rows where both tables match.

2. The following query will generate a read-only Dynaset-type Recordset when used in a database object's OpenRecordset method:

A. Select EmpName, DeptName From Emps, Depts
   Where Emps.Dept_ID = Depts.Dept_ID

B. Select EmpName, DeptName From Emps
   INNER JOIN Depts ON Emps.Dept_ID = Depts.Dept_ID

C. Select EmpName From Emps Order By EmpName

D. Select EmpName From Emps Where EmpName LIKE 'S★'

3. If you call BeginTrans and then exit the application without calling CommitTrans or Rollback

A. VB will generate run-time error 3956.

B. VB will automatically write the transaction to the database.

C. the changes in the transaction will be lost.

D. VB will prompt the user to commit or roll back the transaction.

4. One advantage of using transactions is that

A. more activity takes place on the server when you use transactions.

B. you can use SQL Passthrough only if a transaction is defined.

C. transactions can be more efficient.

D. transactions allow you to lock multiple pages in the same Recordset.

5. Two advantages of having more than one Workspace in a project are (pick two)

A. you can have more than one database object in the project.

B. you can define different user permission levels.

C. you can have non-nested transactions.

D. you make more efficient use of memory.

6. A Recordset object contains

    A. a Fields collection.

    B. a Databases collection.

    C. a Workspaces collection.

    D. a Groups collection.

7. When setting references to DAO object libraries, remember that (pick two)

    A. DAO 2.5 can be used by both 16- and 32-bit VB.

    B. DAO 3.0 can be used by both 16- and 32-bit VB.

    C. DAO 2.5/3.0 is preferred for 16-bit projects.

    D. DAO 3.0 is preferred for 32-bit VB.

8. The native data access engine for VB is

    A. ODBC.

    B. Installable ISAM.

    C. Jet.

    D. Microsoft SQL Server.

9. You can enable pessimistic locking on a Recordset by

    A. setting the Edit property to True.

    B. setting the LockEdits property.

    C. calling the AddNew method.

    D. calling either AddNew or Edit.

10. You can have multiple transactions pending on the same workspace

    A. never.

    B. as long as the transactions are nested within each other.

    C. as long as there is a possible Rollback paired with each CommitTrans.

    D. under all conditions.

Part

VI

App

J

11. The best choice for the first line of a loop to process all records on a recordset named rs would read

    A. Do While rs.Eof
    B. Do Until rs.Eof
    C. Do Until rs.Bookmark = rs.RecordCount
    D. Do While rs.AbsolutePosition <= rs.RecordCount

12. A Dynaset-type Recordset cannot be updated when

    A. the Recordset is formed from any SQL query (as opposed to using a simple table name).
    B. the Recordset is formed from any SQL query using the Order By clause.
    C. the Recordset is formed from any SQL query using a Where clause.
    D. the Recordset is formed from any SQL query using a Where clause to join two or more tables.

13. Generally, more workstation resources are used by

    A. Snapshot-type Recordset.
    B. Dynaset-type Recordset.
    C. Table-type Recordset.
    D. Snapshot- or Table-type Recordset, depending on the size and number of records.

14. Generally, fewer workstation resources are used by

    A. Snapshot-type Recordset.
    B. Dynaset-type Recordset.
    C. Table-type Recordset.
    D. Snapshot- or Table-type Recordset, depending on the size and number of records.

15. You may lock a page in a Recordset with (pick two)

    A. the Edit method.
    B. the Lock statement.

C. the LockEdits property.

D. the AddNew method.

16. You may unlock a Recordset's page with (pick two)

A. the LockEdits property.

B. the Unlock statement.

C. the Update method.

D. a movement of the record pointer.

17. Before calling a Recordset's Update you must have (pick two)

A. called the Edit method.

B. called the LockEdits method.

C. called the AddNew method.

D. moved the record pointer.

18. Locking in ODBC databases

A. is implemented with the same procedures as for Jet databases.

B. is implemented by the underlying DBMS.

C. is not possible.

D. is implemented with the same procedures as for installable ISAM databases.

Part
VI
App
J

Chapter 14

1. VB 3.0 Controls

A. are implemented in VBX files and can't be carried over when you convert a VB 3.0 app to VB 4.0.

B. are implemented in VBX files and may be carried over when you convert a VB 3.0 app to VB 4.0.

C. are implemented in OCX files and can't be carried over when you convert a VB 3.0 app to VB 4.0.

D. are implemented in OCX files and may be carried over when you convert a VB 3.0 app to VB 4.0.

2. For 16- and 32-bit versions of the same application

   A. you can run the 16-bit version on both 16- and 32-bit platforms, but the 32-bit version can only run on 32-bit platforms.

   B. you can run the 32-bit version on both 16- and 32-bit platforms, but the 16-bit version can only run on 16-bit platforms.

   C. you can run the 16-bit and 32-bit versions on both 16- and
32-bit platforms.

   D. the 16-bit version can only run on 16-bit platforms and the
32-bit version can only run on 32-bit platforms.

3. To maintain the same code in 16- and 32-bit VB

   A. There are no special considerations.

   B. You will have to make editing changes every time you switch
between 16- and 32-bit compilers.

   C. If you have API calls, you will need to use conditional compilation to use different versions of the API.

   D. If you use custom controls, you will need to use conditional
compilation to use different versions of the controls.

4. For 16- and 32-bit versions of VB

   A. you can run 16-bit VB only on 16-bit platforms and 32-bit VB
only on 32-bit platforms.

   B. you can run 16-bit VB on either platform and 32-bit VB on
only 32-bit platforms.

   C. you can run both 16- and 32-bit VB on either 16- or 32-bit
platforms.

   D. you can run 32-bit VB on either platform and 16-bit VB on
only 16-bit platforms.

5. The conditional compiler constants, Win16 and Win32 indicate

   A. whether the application is running in a 16- or 32-bit operating
system.

   B. whether the application was compiled by 16- or 32-bit VB.

C. whether the running copy of VB is 16- or 32-bit.

D. whether the design-time environment is a 16- or 32-bit operating system.

6. If you wish to conditionally use 16- or 32-bit API calls in the same application, you must

A. use different standard code modules containing alternate sets of API calls.

B. use conditional compiler directives with the Win32 and Win16 constants.

C. use If…Else…EndIf constructs in your code with the Win32 and Win16 constants.

D. maintain two different copies of the application.

7. If you check the Upgrade Custom Controls option in the Advanced Options dialog, VB 4.0

A. will convert any and all 16-bit controls to 32-bit when you load a project.

B. will convert only those 16-bit controls for which there are 32-bit replacements when you load a project.

C. will convert any and all 16-bit controls to 32-bit when you save a project.

D. will convert only those 16-bit controls for which there are 32-bit replacements when you save a project.

8. You convert VB 3.0 controls to VB 4.0 controls by

A. editing the 3.0 project file (MAK file) before conversion to VB 4.0.

B. editing the 4.0 project file (VBP file) after conversion to VB 4.0.

C. recompiling your application.

D. answering Yes when prompted to convert.

9. When converting a VB application that uses API calls from VB 3 to 32-bit VB 4

    A. You must convert all API calls manually to 32-bit API.

    B. You have the option of leaving the API calls as 16-bit.

    C. VB will automatically convert the API calls to 32-bit the first time you load the project in VB 4.

    D. Some calls may be left as is, others (string-handling routines) must be converted manually to 32-bit API.

Chapter 15

1. When passing a string argument from a VB application to a routine in a DLL

    A. the string should always be passed By Reference.

    B. the string should always be passed By Value.

    C. the string should be passed By Reference when you expect it to be modified, otherwise it should be passed By Value.

    D. it makes no difference whether you pass the string By Reference or By Value.

2. If a DLL routine's documentation calls for an argument of type char, VB should pass

    A. a fixed-length string of length 1.

    B. a single quote-delimited character.

    C. a variable of type byte.

    D. a variable of type integer.

3. Before you pass a String variable from VB as an argument to a DLL routine

    A. pad the string with extra characters.

    B. set the string to "".

    C. set the string to vbNullString.

    D. the string to vbNullPointer.

4. In order to use a String variable after it has been passed from VB as an argument to a DLL routine

    A. you should OR the String with a string of 255 ASCII null characters.

    B. you may use the String as is.

    C. you should strip off an ASCII null character from the end of the string.

    D. you should add an ASCII null character to the end of the string.

5. The format for string implementation in VB and DLL routines is

    A. LPSTR for VB and BSTR for DLL routines.

    B. LPSTR for DLL routines and BSTR for VB.

    C. BSTR for both.

    D. LPSTR for both.

6. You might use the ALIAS clause in an API declaration (pick two)

    A. to resolve naming convention conflicts between VB and DLL routines.

    B. to determine whether or not you are compiling a 16- or a 32-bit application.

    C. to give 16- and 32-bit versions of an API call the same name.

    D. to give 16- and 32-bit version of an API call different names.

7. In the API declaration

   Declare Sub MyAPI Lib "YourAPI" Alias ThisAPI (x As Long)

    A. MyAPI is the original name of the routine inside the YourAPI library file.

    B. ThisAPI is the original name of the routine inside the YourAPI library file.

    C. YourAPI is the original name of the routine inside the MyAPI library file.

    D. ThisAPI is the original name of the routine inside the MyAPI library file.

8. When declaring an API routine in a Form Module

    A. you must use the Static keyword.

    B. you must use the Public keyword.

    C. you must use the Private keyword.

    D. you need use no special keyword in front of the Declare keyword.

9. The Lib keyword in an API declaration (pick two)

    A. precedes the name of the API library file.

    B. follows the name of the API library file.

    C. requires a quote-delimited string.

    D. requires a single-quote-delimited string.

10. If a DLL routine's documentation calls for an argument of type Int, VB should pass

    A. an Integer in 16- and 32-bit environments.

    B. a Long in 16- and 32-bit environments.

    C. an Integer in 16-bit environment, Long in 32-bit environment.

    D. Long in a 16-bit environment, Integer in 32-bit environment.

11. The return value of the GetWindowsDirectory API function represents

    A. a result code indicating success (>0) or failure (=0).

    B. the modified string.

    C. a pointer to the modified string.

    D. the length of the modified string parameter.

12. The 2nd parameter of the GetWindowsDir API function represents

    A. the length of the modified string parameter.

    B. the original length of the string parameter.

    C. a pointer to the string parameter.

    D. a mode indicator. If 0, GetWindowsDir will find the name of the Windows directory. If 1, it will find the name of the Windows\System directory.

13. GetWindowsDirectoryA and GetWindowsDirectoryW represent

    A. 16- and 32-bit versions of the GetWindowsDirectory API, respectively.

    B. 32- and 16-bit versions of GetWindowsDirectory, respectively.

    C. ANSI and UniCode versions of the 32-bit API, respectively.

    D. UniCode and ANSI versions of the 16-bit API, respectively.

14. Case sensitivity is an issue

    A. only in the 32-bit API.

    B. only in the 16-bit API.

    C. in both 32- and 16-bit APIs.

    D. in the UniCode version of the 16-bit API.

15. Core API library names are

    A. User16, Kernel16, GDI16 for 16-bit Windows and User32, Kernel32, and GDI32 for 32-bit Windows.

    B. User, Kernel, GDI for 16-bit Windows and User32, Kernel32, and GDI32 for 32-bit Windows.

    C. User16, Kernel16, GDI16 for 16-bit Windows and User, Kernel, and GDI for 32-bit Windows.

    D. User, Kernel, and GDI for both 16- and 32-bit Windows.

Part
VI
App
J

16. When API documentation requires you to pass a null pointer as an argument, the value you should pass is

    A. vbNull.

    B. "".

    C. vbNullString.

    D. 0.

17. If you need to pass a Form or Control as an argument to an API routine

    A. pass the object itself by value.

    B. pass the object itself by reference.

    C. pass a Form's hWnd property by value, pass the control itself by reference.

    D. pass the object's hWnd property by reference.

18. The following lines appear in a standard module's Declarations section:

```
#If Win32 Then
Declare Sub MySub Lib "MyLib32" Alias "MySubA"
#End If
#If Win16 Then
Declare Sub MySub Lib "MyLib" Alias "MySub"
#End If
```

The effect of these lines is that

    A. the same copy of the application's executable file can run in 16- or 32-bit Windows.

    B. the same source code can be compiled by 16-bit or 32-bit VB.

    C. both 16- and 32-bit versions of the application can use 16-bit API.

    D. both 16- and 32-bit versions of the application can use the 32-bit API.

19. The compatibility of 16- and 32-bit applications with the API is that

    A. 32-bit applications can use both 16- and 32-bit APIs, and 16-bit applications can only use the 16-bit API.

    B. 16-bit applications can use both 16- and 32-bit APIs, and 32-bit applications can only use the 32-bit API.

    C. 32-bit applications can only use the 32-bit APIs, and 16-bit applications can only use the 16-bit API.

    D. both 32- and 16-bit applications can use both sets of APIs.

20. The relationship between ANSI and UniCode standards for strings in VB is that

    A. VB uses ANSI internally but converts to UniCode for use by the programmer and in API calls.

    B. VB uses UniCode internally but converts to ANSI for use by the programmer and in API calls.

    C. VB uses ANSI both internally and for use by the programmer in API calls.

    D. VB uses UniCode both internally and for use by the programmer in API calls.

Chapter 16

1. To install your application with ODBC capability

    A. select ODBC on the list of data drivers on Screen 2 of the Setup Wizard.

    B. distribute ODBC diskettes to the user.

    C. select the ODBC Data Source on the list on Screen 2 of the Setup Wizard.

    D. select ODBC and then the ODBC Data Source on Screen 2 of the Setup Wizard.

2. To install your application as an OLE Server

   A. choose the Install In Application Directory option on Screen 6 of the Setup Wizard.

   B. choose the Install as OLE Automation Shared Component option on Screen 6 of the Setup Wizard.

   C. compile the application as an OLE DLL at design time.

   D. let Setup Wizard read the project's properties when it recompiles your application.

3. To decide whether to create your application's installation files on diskettes or in a directory

   A. specify the Installation Target option in your project's Options dialog under the Advanced Tab.

   B. let Setup install to diskettes and copy the installation files to a directory if necessary.

   C. let Setup install to a directory and copy the installation files to diskettes if necessary.

   D. choose the Disk Drive or Directory option on Setup Wizard's Screen 3.

4. A Setup Wizard template (pick two)

   A. can be used as a starting point for future setups of this application.

   B. can be used as a default setup for all future applications.

   C. can be used to quickly create new VB projects modeled after the current project.

   D. can be saved at the end of the current Setup Wizard session.

5. OLE Servers used by this application

   A. are specified in the same Setup Wizard step as data sources are specified.

   B. are specified on a separate screen of the Setup Wizard.

   C. are specified when you specify the target distribution media for the application.

   D. are specified when you specify custom control files.

6. Unused custom controls in your project that are on the project's Toolbox

   A. will appear on a list in Setup Wizard and should be removed.

   B. will not be listed by Setup Wizard.

   C. will appear on a list in Setup Wizard and cannot be removed.

   D. will not be distributed with your application even if they remain checked in the list in Setup Wizard.

7. The file Setup1.VBP (pick two)

   A. contains VB code for the Setup132 or Setup1 routine.

   B. contains VB code for the Setup routine.

   C. is read-only (for information only).

   D. is customizable.

8. Setup.Exe

   A. is the default name of the setup routine created by Setup Wizard for your application.

   B. is the name of the executable file that runs Setup Wizard.

   C. is the name of the generic, unmodifiable startup routine for a Setup.

   D. is the name of the default Setup Wizard template file.

8. When you specify to Setup Wizard that you want to install a file as an OLE Server

   A. the file is installed directly under the system's WINDOWS directory.

   B. the file is installed directly under the system's WINDOWS\SYSTEM directory.

   C. the file is installed in its own directory.

   D. the file is installed in the OLESVR directory.

Part

VI

App

J

Answer Key

Chapter 2

1-D. See "Implicit versus Explicit Variable Declaration"

2-C. See "See Figuring Out How Many Elements Are in an Array"

3-A. See "Default Base for an Array's Lower Bound and Option Base Statement"

4-B. See "Variant: The Lonely Default"

5-B. See "Dynamically Resizing an Array"

6-A. See "Variable Scope"

7-A,D. See "Static Variables"

8-A. See "Variable Scope"

9-B. See "Variable Scope"

10-C. See "Adding and Deleting Control Array Elements at Run Time"

11-A. See "Accessing a Form's Controls with the Controls Collection"

12-B. See "Conversion of non-String Arguments in String Concatenation"

13-A. See "Visual Basic's Standard Simple Data Types"

14-B. See "Visual Basic's Standard Simple Data Types"

15-B. See "Visual Basic's Standard Simple Data Types"

16-B. See "Visual Basic's Standard Simple Data Types"

17-B,C. See "Visual Basic's Standard Simple Data Types" and "Arrays"

18-A. See "Variant: The Lonely Default"

19-C,D. See "Data Type Conversion"

20-D. See "Arrays"

Chapter 3

1-D. See "Declaring the Return Type"

2-A,C. See "Procedure and Function Calls and the VB Stack"

3-C. See "Extra Parentheses around Each Argument to be Sent By Value"

4-B. See "Optional Arguments and the IsMissing(. Function"

Chapter 4

5-B,D. See "Enumerating Values in a Case"

6-D. See "Common String Manipulation Functions"

7-D. See "Instr"

8-A. See "Getting Out of a Loop in a Hurry with Exit"

9-A. See "Array Arguments and the ParamArray Argument"

10-D. See "Calling Conventions for Procedures and Functions"

11-D. See "ListBox"

12-C. See "Synchronizing Events with DoEvents"

13-B,C. See "Calling an Event Procedure versus Causing an Event to Happen"

14-B. See "Control Names and Event Procedure Code"

15-C. See "Public and Property Procedures"

16-B. See "PictureBox"

17-A,C. See "TextBox"

18-C. See "ComboBox"

19-D. See "Looping"

20-B. See "The For Each…Next Statement"

1-C. See "Single-Step Mode"

2-D. See "Step-Over Mode"

3-C. See "Going into Break Mode"

4-A. See "Set Next Statement"

5-C. See "Step to Cursor"

6-A,B. See "Toggling the Breakpoint"

7-C. See "Clear All Breakpoints"

8-C. See "Watch Expression"

9-A. See "Break When Value Changes"

10-B. See "Break when Expression Is True"

11-A,D. See "Viewing the Call Stack"

12-B,D. See "Debug.Print"

Chapter 5

1-C. See "Defining the Error Handler with a Label"

2-D. See "Creating a Detour around the Error Handler"

3-B,C. See "Writing Code to Handle the Error"

4-A. See "Using the Resume Statement to Recover"

5-A,B. See "Enabling/Disabling the Error Handler with On Error"

6-B,C. See "On Error Resume Next"

7-D. See "Trapping an Error Immediately after it Occurs"

8-B,D. See "Write Generic Code for Frequently-Used Functionality"

9-B,C. See "Pass Error Codes to a Centralized Error-Handling Function"

10-A,C. See "Generating an Error with the Err Object's Raise Method"

11-D. See "Using Err.Raise as a Debugging Technique"

12-B,D. See "Using Err.Raise to Pass an Error up the Call Stack"

Chapter 6

1-D. See "Default Property or Value of a Control and Performance"

2-C. See "Appearance"

3-C. See "BackColor, the RGB Function, and Color Constants"

4-A. See "Caption"

5-C. See "Providing Access Keys for Controls with a Caption Property"

6-A,D. See "DragIcon"

7-C. See "DragMode"

8-A. See "Enabled"

9-D. See "BackColor"

10-B. See "BackColor"

11-D. See "Tag"

12-D. See "hWnd Property"

13-C. See "Top, Left, Width, and Height and the Move Method"

14-C. See "Providing Access Keys for Text Boxes"

15-C. See "Index"

16-D. See "MouseIcon"

17-B. See "MousePointer"

18-B,D. See "Name"

19-B. See "ScaleMode, ScaleTop, ScaleLeft, ScaleHeight, ScaleWidth Properties of a Form or PictureBox"

20-D. See "Setting the Tab Order of Controls on a Form with the TabIndex and TabStop Properties"

Chapter 7

1-B,D. See "Click"

2-B. See "KeyPress"

3-C. See "KeyPress"

4-D. See "DblClick"

5-C. See "KeyUp and KeyDown"

6-C. See "KeyPreview"

7-D. See "MouseMove"

8-B,C. See "MouseUp"

9-D. See "AutoRedraw"

10-C. See "Load, Unload, and QueryUnload"

11-B. See "Load, Unload, and QueryUnload"

12-C. See "Paint"

13-C. See "Debug"

14-A. See "Printer"

15-D. See "Activate/ DeActivate"

16-B. See "Show and Hide"

17-C. See "Initialize/ Terminate"

18-A. See "DragDrop"

19-B. See "DragMode"

20-B. See "Screen"

Chapter 8

1-C,D. See "Hot Keys"

2-A. See "Shortcut Keys"

3-C. See "Menu Level"

4-C,D. See "Menu Editor"

5-A. See "Name Property"

6-C. See "Caption Property"

7-B. See "Separator Bars"

8-A,C. See "Checked Property"

9-D. See "Visible Property"

10-B. See "Enabled Property"

11-A. See "NegotiatePosition Property"

12-A,B. See "WindowList Property"

13-C. See "Index Property"

14-C,D. See "Menu Level"

15-C. See "Menu Control Arrays"

16-B. See "Navigating Menu Items in the Menu Editor"

17-D. See "Menu Control Arrays"

18-A. See "Menu Control Arrays"

19-C. See "Add a Pop-Up Menu to an Application with

the Form's PopupMenu Method"

20-D. See "Attaching Code to a Menu Item's Click Event Procedure"

Chapter 9

1-C. See "Setting Up MDI Child Classes"

2-B. See "Initializing MDI Children with As New"

3-D. See "Setting Up an MDI Form"

4-B. See "Understanding MDI Applications"

5-B. See "Understanding MDI Applications"

6-B. See "Setting Up MDI Child Classes"

7-A. See "Setting Up MDI Child Classes"

8-A,D. See "Understanding MDI Applications"

9-C. See "Referencing MDI Children"

10-B,D. See "Determining Parent or Child Menu Validity"

11-A,C. See "Creating Toolbars"

12-B. See "WindowList Property"

13-A,D. See "Arrange Method"

14-C. See "Using Unload and QueryUnload"

15-A. See "Using Unload and QueryUnload"

Chapter 10

1-A. See "Setting a Reference to an OLE Server"

2-C. See "Using the Object Browser to Find Out about an OLE Server"

3-A. See "Understanding OLE Automation"

4-A. See "Declaring a Variable to Hold an Instance of an OLE Server Class"

5-D. See "Declaring a Variable to Hold an Instance of an OLE Server Class"

6-A. See "OLE Automation with the Object Property"

7-A. See "An OLE Server's Verbs"

8-A. See "Using the OLE 2.0 Container Control"

9-A. See "CreateObject Function versus GetObject Function"

10-B. See "CreateObject Function versus GetObject Function"

11-B. See "CreateObject Function versus GetObject Function"

12-C. See "OLE Automation with the Object Property"

13-A. See "An OLE Server's Verbs"

14-B. See "An OLE Server's Verbs"

15-B. See "An OLE Server's Verbs"

16-A. See "Linking and Embedding at Run Time"

17-B. See "Controlling the Object's Appearance"

18-C. See "Controlling the Object's Appearance"

Chapter 11

1-D. See "Out-of-Process versus In-Process Servers"

2-C. See "Name" under "Setting Project Options for an OLE Server"

3-D. See "Startup Form"

4-D. See "Start Mode" under "Setting Project Options for an OLE Server"

5-B,C. See "Instancing" and "Public" under "Class Module Properties for an OLE server"

6-B. See "Storing Multiple Instances of an Object in a Collection"

7-C. See "Implementing a Read-Only Property"

8-C. See "Class Terminate Event Procedure" and "Closing Your OLE Server"

9-C. See "Implementing the Dependent Collection Class' Built-In Methods and Properties"

10-A. See "Initializing the Collection in the Parent Class"

11-A,C. See "Managing Dialogs (Forms) in Your OLE Server"

12-B. See "Closing Your OLE Server"

13-B. See "Closing Your OLE Server"

14-B. See "Error Handling in the Server and the Controller"

15-A,D. See "Your OLE Server and the Object Browser"

16-A, See "Testing and Debugging an OLE Server at Design Time"

Part
VI

App
J

17-C. See "Temporarily Registering Your Server at Design Time"

18-B. See "What to Do about a MISSING Reference to Your Server"

19-B,D. See "Registering Your Compiled OLE Server"

20-A. See "Managing Compatibility of Versions of Your Server" and "Compatible OLE Server"

Chapter 12

1-B. See "The Recordset"

2-C. See "The Recordset"

3-C. See "Connect Property"

4-C. See "Binding Other Controls to the Data Control"

5-D. See "DataBaseName Property"

6-C. See "The Recordset"

7-A. See "Snapshots"

8-C. See "Adding Records"

9-B. See "The Recordset"

10-C. See "Validate Event"

11-B. See "Find Methods" and "Seek Method"

12-C. See "Error Event"

13-D. See "Find Methods" and "Seek Method"

14-B. See "Saving Editing Changes with the Update Method"

15-B,C. See "Canceling an Update"

16-C. See "Data-Bound Grid"

17-B. See "Data-Bound List Box and Data-Bound Combo Box"

18-B,D. See "Deleting Records"

19-D. See "ODBC"

20-B,C. See "Installable ISAM Drivers"

Chapter 13

1-D. See "Using JOIN Clauses to Connect Tables"

2-A. See "Using the Where Clause to Connect Tables"

3-C. See "Using Transactions"

4-C. See "Using Transactions"

5-B,C. See "The Default Workspace and the Workspaces Collection"

6-A. See "Recordset Objects and the Recordsets Collection" and "Using Transactions"

7-A,D. See "Setting a Reference to a Type Library"

8-C. See "Visual Basic, the Jet Engine, and the Data Access Libraries"

9-B. See "LockEdits Property and Pessimistic versus Optimistic Locking"

10-B. See "Using Transactions"

11-B. See "Navigating through a Recordset"

12-D. See "Using the Where Clause to Connect Tables"

13-A. See "The Recordset" of Chapter 12 "Using the Data Control"

14-C. See "The Recordset" of Chapter 12 "Using the Data Control"

15-A,D. See "Page Locking"

16-C,D. See "Page Locking"

17-A,C. See "Updating a Record"

18-B. See "Page Locking"

Chapter 14

1-B. See "Converting VBX to OLE Controls"

2-A. See "Understanding 16- and 32-bit Application Differences"

3-C. See "Using Conditional Compilation with API Declarations"

4-B. See "Understanding 16- and 32-bit Application Differences"

5-C. See "Using Conditional Compilation with API Declarations"

6-B. See "Using Conditional Compilation with the API"

7-B. See "Converting VBX to OLE Controls"

8-D. See "Converting VBX to OLE Controls"

9-B. See "Using Conditional Compilation with the API"

Part

VI

App

J

Chapter 15

1-B. See "Pass String Arguments to API Calls by Value"

2-C. See "C 'char' Data Type as a DLL Argument"

3-A. See "Stuff String Arguments with Extra Character"

4-C. See "Strip String Argument's Null Terminator After API Call"

5-B. See "Visual Basic Strings and C DLL Routines"

6-A,C. See "Alias Clause"

7-B. See "Alias Clause"

8-C. See "The Declare Keyword"

9-A,C. See "Library Name"

10-C. See "C 'int' Data Type as a DLL Argument"

11-D. See "GetWindowsDirectory in 16- and 32-bit Versions"

12-B. See "GetWindowsDirectory in 16- and 32-bit Versions"

13-C. See "GetWindowsDirectory in 16- and 32-bit Versions"

14-A. See "Name of API"

15-B. See "Declaring and Calling a DLL Routine"

16-C. See "Passing a Null Pointer to a DLL Routine"

17-D. See "Passing Control Properties"

18-B. See "16- versus 32-bit Compilation of the Same Code"

19-C. See "16- versus 32-bit Compilation of the Same Code"

20-B. See "Using the Same Name for Unicode and ANSI Versions"

Chapter 16

1-B. See "Screen for Step 2: Data Access Engine"

2-B. See "Screen for Step 6: OLE Automation"

3-D. See "Screen for Step 3: Target for Setup Files"

4-A,D. See "Screen for Step 7: Additional Files"

5-B. See "Screen for Step 4: OLE Servers"

6-A. See "Screen for Step 6: OLE Automation"

7-A,D. See "Setup.exe and SetupWizard's Custom Setup"

8-C. See "A Customized Setup Program"

Mastery Test

Note The answers to these questions can be found in order at the end of this section. Each answer also includes a section reference where you can find information about that question. ■

1. A menu item's Checked property (pick two)

    A. will show a checkmark if set to true.

    B. has a default value of 1.

    C. has a default value of False.

    D. will hide a checkmark if set to true.

2. The OLE container's Object property

    A. makes the methods and properties of the contained server class available programmatically.

    B. is a string containing the name of the contained server class.

    C. is True if the container holds an object and False if it's empty.

    D. represents the contained server object's visual interface.

3. The following is true of forms in an OLE server (pick two)

    A. may be modal or modaless if the server is out-of-process.

    B. may be modal or modaless if the server is in-process.

    C. Startup Form of the project must be Sub Main( ) if the server is in-process.

    D. must be modaless if the server is in-process.

4. To clear the graphics image in a PictureBox control named picFile, you could use the code:

    A. picFile.Image = ""

    B. picFile.Picture = LoadPicture( )

    C. picFile.Picture = Nothing

    D. picFile.Picture = ""

Part
VI

App
J

5. The following lines occur in a Standard Module's General Declarations section (there is no Option Base statement):

```
Type Star
        Name as String
        Type as String * 3
        Parsecs as Single
        Magnitude As Integer
    End Type
    Public Dim Stars(10) as Star
```

Which of the following lines will run without an error? (pick two)

    A. Stars(10).Type = "A3"

    B. Stars(9).Name = "Sirius"

    C. Star(9).Parsecs = 3

    D. Stars(0).Magnitude = -0.5

6. Consider the code:

```
Dim MyCounter As Integer
   MyCounter = 4
Do
   MyCounter = MyCounter + 1
   MsgBox MyCounter
Loop Until MyCounter > 3
MsgBox MyCounter
```

When this code runs, the user will see

    A. one MessageBox displaying 4.

    B. one MessageBox displaying 5.

    C. one MessageBox displaying 4 followed by another displaying 5.

    D. one MessageBox displaying 5 followed by another displaying 5.

7. What value will a variant contain before it's initialized?

    A. Null.

    B. Empty.

    C. 0.

    D. "".

8. The return value of Instr("Bobby Young","Y") would be

    A. "Y"

    B. 0

C. 5

D. 7

9. A variable for Number of Dependents is best implemented with

A. Long

B. Integer

C. Double

D. Single

10. To determine and observe the code that runs initially in your application, you should

A. start your application from the design environment with F5.

B. start your application from the design environment with Ctrl+Break.

C. start your application from the design environment with F8.

D. place the Debug.Print method in your code.

11. The Paint event is triggered

A. at the moment you reset the AutoRedraw property in code.

B. when you call a Graphics method in code and AutoRedraw is False.

C. when a Form is resized and AutoRedraw is False.

D. when a Form is resized and AutoRedraw is True.

12. Unused custom controls in your project that are on the project's Toolbox

A. will appear on a list in Setup Wizard and should be removed.

B. will not be listed by Setup Wizard.

C. will appear on a list in Setup Wizard and cannot be removed.

D. will not be distributed with your application even if they remain checked in the list in Setup Wizard.

13. You can use installable ISAM drivers for (pick two)

A. Oracle.

B. Paradox.

Part

VI

App

J

C. Excel.

D. Sybase.

14. The Calls Dialog box (pick two)

   A. can be invoked with Ctrl+L.

   B. will show you the history of all sub and function procedures called during this run of your application.

   C. must be turned off before distributing your executed application to the user.

   D. will show the chain of procedure calls leading to and including the currently executing procedure.

15. The following code

```
For each Myctrl in Controls
      MyCtrl.Text = Ucase(MyCtrl.Text)
Next MyCtrl
```

   A. will give a run-time error if there is a label on the current form.

   B. will change text properties of all controls on all forms.

   C. will always be able to change text property of all controls on current form.

   D. will give a run-time error if there is a label anywhere in the project.

16. The Form's Terminate event

   A. always happens before Unload.

   B. always happens after Unload.

   C. happens only when you set the Form to Nothing after an Unload.

   D. happens whenever you set the Form to Nothing.

17. The menu on an MDI form (pick two)

   A. will override a Child Form's menu when the Child's AutoMenu property is set to False.

   B. will appear when there are no active instances of Child Forms.

C. will appear above the Child menu when there is an active instance of a Child Form.

D. will appear when active Child Form instances have no menus.

18. The purpose of an OLE server project's Start Mode option on the Project tab of the Options dialog is

    A. to determine whether the server will be in-process or out-of-process.

    B. to determine whether the server will be single- or multi-use.

    C. to cause the project to compile as an OLE server.

    D. to allow Visual Basic to temporarily register the server and keep it running in design mode.

19. Before running a test copy of your server at design time you should

    A. temporarily set its creatable classes' Instancing properties to Creatable MultiUse.

    B. temporarily set its creatable classes' Instancing properties to Creatable SingleUse.

    C. compile it.

    D. temporarily set its project's Startup Mode property to Standalone.

20. To decide whether to create your application's installation files on diskettes or in a directory

    A. specify the Installation Target option in your project's Options dialog under the Advanced Tab.

    B. let Setup install to diskettes and copy the installation files to a directory if necessary.

    C. let Setup install to a directory and copy the installation files to diskettes if necessary.

    D. choose the Disk Drive or Directory option on Setup Wizard's Screen 3.

21. The Option Explicit statement

    A. should appear at the beginning of each routine.

    B. allows you to specify arrays' default lower bounds.

    C. should appear at the beginning of each program.

    D. should appear in the Declarations section of each module.

22. A SnapShot

    A. is implemented entirely on the local workstation.

    B. implements a copy buffer and a set of record pointers on the local workstation, and retrieves data from the server.

    C. is implemented entirely on the server.

    D. implements a copy buffer on the local workstation and retrieves data from the server. It does not use a set of record pointers.

23. Core API library names are

    A. User16, Kernel16, GDI16 for 16-bit Windows and User32, Kernel32, and GDI32 for 32-bit Windows.

    B. User, Kernel, GDI for 16-bit Windows and User32, Kernel32, and GDI32 for 32-bit Windows.

    C. User16, Kernel16, GDI16 for 16-bit Windows and User, Kernel, and GDI for 32-bit Windows.

    D. User, Kernel, and GDI for both 16- and 32-bit Windows.

24. When setting references to DAO object libraries, remember that (pick two)

    A. DAO 2.5 can be used by both 16- and 32-bit VB.

    B. DAO 3.0 can be used by both 16- and 32-bit VB.

    C. DAO 2.5/3.0 is preferred for 16-bit projects.

    D. DAO 3.0 is preferred for 32-bit VB.

25. The ScaleTop and ScaleHeight properties

    A. indicate the internal dimensions of a form or PictureBox—always in twips.

    B. indicate the internal dimensions of a form or PictureBox—always in the units given by ScaleMode.

C. indicate a control's size in the units given by the containing form's or PictureBox control's ScaleMode.

D. indicate a control's position in the units given by the ScaleMode of its container.

26. What will the user see when the following code runs? (pick two)

```
Select Case MyVal
     Case 13,15,17
          MsgBox "A"
     Case Is < 20
          MsgBox "B"
     Case Is > 10
          MsgBox "C"
     Case Else
          MsgBox "D"
End Select
```

A. "B" and "C" if MyVal is 18.

B. "C" if MyVal is 20.

C. "A," "B," and "C" if MyVal is 17.

D. "D" will never appear.

27. A Dynaset–type Recordset cannot be updated when

A. the Recordset is formed from any SQL query (as opposed to using a simple table name).

B. the Recordset is formed from any SQL query using the Order By clause.

C. the Recordset is formed from any SQL query using a Where clause.

D. the Recordset is formed from any SQL query using a Where clause to join two or more tables.

28. Assume that the following is the only code in a form

```
[General declarations]
     Public NumTimes as Integer
     Private Sub cmdImOK_Click()
          Static intNumTimes as integer
          intNumTimes = intNumTimes + 1
          SetOK intNumTimes
          MsgBox NumTimes
```

```
        End Sub
        Private Sub cmdYourOK_Click()
            SetOK(NumTimes)
        End Sub
        Public Sub SetOK(NumTimes as Integer)
            NumTimes = NumTimes + 1
        End Sub
```

If the user clicks first on the cmdYourOK button and then on the cmdImOK button, the user will see

A. a run-time error "Variable not defined."

B. 1.

C. 2.

D. 0.

29. A menu control's Name property

A. is not supplied automatically when you initialize a menu control.

B. provides the default value for the Caption property.

C. can contain an ampersand indicating the shortcut key.

D. is required to begin with "mnu"

30. Case sensitivity is an issue

A. only in the 32-bit API.

B. only in the 16-bit API.

C. in both 32- and 16-bit APIs.

D. in the UniCode version of the 16-bit API.

31. The Data Control's Connect property

A. is always a directory name.

B. must always be manually entered by the programmer.

C. may be picked off a list if it's an installable ISAM.

D. may be picked off a list if it's an ODBC data source.

32. We initialize an object with the declaration

Public objExcel as Excel.Application

and later we wish to set the Visible property of the object. We can use the following line of code:

A. Excel.Visible = True

B. objExcel.Application.Visible = True

C. Excel.Application.Visible = True

D. objExcel.Visible = True

33. You can create Object Browser help for your server (pick two)

   A. for methods.

   B. only for properties.

   C. for all methods and properties.

   D. for properties implemented with Property Let/Get.

34. For a menu to implement a drop-down list of all open Child forms in an application

   A. the menu must be named Window (only requirement).

   B. the menu's WindowList property must be True (only requirement).

   C. the menu's WindowList property must be True and the menu must be named Window.

   D. the menu's WindowList property must be True and your application must programmatically add each newly instantiated Child's name to a menu control array.

35. The Index property of a menu control

   A. is case–sensitive.

   B. can be used to store string information about a menu control.

   C. will implement a menu control array if set to a value of 0 or more.

   D. can only be set at run time.

36. The code in an error handler (pick two)

   A. must always give some visual cue to the user.

   B. must do something to rectify or react to the error.

   C. must provide instructions for where to restart once the error has been handled.

   D. must always be in a separate procedure.

Part
VI

App
J

37. The color listed in a Shape's BackColor property

    A. always displays the color designated in the BackColor property.
    B. only displays when the Shape's FillStyle is Transparent.
    C. only displays when the Shape's FillStyle is Solid.
    D. the Shape control is a lightweight control and therefore, it has no BackColor property.

38. The difference between QueryUnload and Unload events is that

    A. QueryUnload happens first and Unload receives the UnloadMode parameter.
    B. QueryUnload happens first and QueryUnload receives the UnloadMode parameter.
    C. Unload happens first and Unload receives the UnloadMode parameter.
    D. Unload happens first and QueryUnload receives the UnloadMode parameter.

39. The SQL statement

    Select F1, F2, F3 From T1 INNER JOIN T2 ON F1 = F2

will return

    A. all rows from both tables, with matching rows together.
    B. all rows from T1, and only matching rows from T2.
    C. all rows from T2, and only matching rows from T1.
    D. only rows where both tables match.

40. The NoMatch property of the Recordset

    A. becomes True after a successful Find or Seek.
    B. becomes False after a successful Find or Seek.
    C. becomes True after a successful Find, only.
    D. becomes False after a successful Seek, only.

41. To programmatically refresh the list of OLE verbs available at any given time in an OLE container control, you should

A. call the FetchVerbs method.

B. call the OleVerbs method.

C. reset the OleVerbsCount property.

D. reset the OleVerbs collection.

42. When API documentation requires you to pass a null pointer as an argument, the value you should pass is

A. vbNull.

B. "".

C. vbNullString.

D. 0.

43. Which of these statements will assign the value of the CommandButton's Caption property to the TextBox's Text property?

A. Text1 = Command1

B. Text1 = Command1.Caption

C. Text1.Text = Command1

D. All three of the above statements will work.

44. The NegotiatePosition property

A. is only useful with embedded OLE applications that have menus.

B. must be set to true on a form to allow embedded OLE menus to coexist with the form's menu.

C. must always be set for any form that wants to display menus.

D. will block the embedded OLE object's menus from appearing if set to None.

45. In order to use a String variable after it has been passed from VB as an argument to a DLL routine

A. you should OR the String with a string of 255 ASCII null characters.

B. you may use the String as is.

C. you should strip off an ASCII null character from the end of the string.

D. you should add an ASCII null character to the end of the string.

46. If you wish to use the Inline style of error handling in a procedure, you must remember to

A. use the Resume statement.

B. use the Resume Next statement.

C. disable error trapping at the beginning of the routine with On Error GoTo 0.

D. explicitly clear the error condition when you are done handling it.

47. The Windowlist property (pick two)

A. displays a standard interface for handling MDI children.

B. causes a menu item to list all open forms in any current application.

C. implements a list of all open Windows processes, similar to Task Manager.

D. is used on menu systems of MDI parent forms.

48. A centralized error-handling routine (pick two)

A. entirely eliminates the need for error handlers in routines that call it.

B. allows you to paste a simple standardized error handler into routines that call it.

C. can return a flag telling the calling routine how to resume execution after the error.

D. can contain a label that all other routines' On Error GoTo statements can point to.

49. OLE Servers used by this application

A. are specified in the same Setup Wizard step as data sources are specified.

B. are specified on a separate screen of the Setup Wizard.

C. are specified when you specify the target distribution media for the application.

D. are specified when you specify custom control files.

50. A VB Form with its MDIChild property set to False

A. can exist in an MDI application as a normal form.

B. can't exist in an MDI application.

C. can exist in an MDI application only as a modal form.

D. can exist in an MDI application only as a modaless form.

51. If a program contains an array declaration

```
Dim strNames(10, 5 to 10, 5) as String
```

and the module contains no Option Base statement, then the total number of elements in the array will be

A. 500.

B. 250.

C. 396.

D. 330.

52. If you wish to conditionally use 16- or 32-bit API calls in the same application, you must

A. use different standard code modules containing alternate sets of API calls.

B. use conditional compiler directives with the Win32 and Win16 constants.

C. use If...Else...EndIf constructs in your code with the Win32 and Win16 constants.

D. maintain two different copies of the application.

53. In the API declaration

Declare Sub MyAPI Lib "YourAPI" Alias ThisAPI (x As Long)

A. MyAPI is the original name of the routine inside the YourAPI library file.

B. ThisAPI is the original name of the routine inside the YourAPI library file.

C. YourAPI is the original name of the routine inside the MyAPI library file.

D. ThisAPI is the original name of the routine inside the MyAPI library file.

54. Changing a control's hWnd property at run time in your code

A. will change the Width property of the control.

B. will allow another Windows application to manipulate the control's properties directly.

C. will assign the control to a different form.

D. is something you should never attempt.

55. A Breakpoint that marks a code line (pick two)

A. can be toggled On and Off with F9.

B. displays the code line in a different color.

C. indicates that the code line will be skipped when the code runs.

D. will be saved when the code file is saved.

56. You can use Err.Raise

A. to cancel the current error.

B. to determine the current error number.

C. to test whether the current Err.Number is a VB standard error or if it is a programmer-defined error.

D. to test how your application reacts to a particular error.

57. When you press Ctrl+Break while the application is running in the VB design environment

A. you will break on the next line of code to be executed.

B. you will always go to a Debug window.

C. you will only go to a paused line of VB code if VB was running your code at the moment you pressed Ctrl+Break.

D. you will end the application.

58. You can get information about methods and properties of the classes of a server whose library you've included in your application by

    A. selecting the property or method in your code and pressing F1.

    B. selecting the property or method in your code and pressing Shift–F2.

    C. invoking the Object Browser and locating the server in the Classes/Libraries list.

    D. locating the server name under VB's Help, Search menu option.

59. When converting a VB application that uses API calls from VB 3 to 32-bit VB 4

    A. you must convert all API calls manually to 32-bit API.

    B. you have the option of leaving the API calls as 16-bit.

    C. VB will automatically convert the API calls to 32-bit the first time you load the project in VB 4.

    D. some calls may be left as is, others (string-handling routines) must be converted manually to 32-bit API.

60. A Form's MouseMove event is triggered

    A. when the mousepointer moves anywhere over the Form.

    B. only when the mousepointer moves over the Form's empty surface or a non-PictureBox control.

    C. only when the mousepointer moves over the Form's empty surface.

    D. only when the mousepointer moves over the Form's empty surface or over a disabled or invisible control.

61. The Delete method (pick two)

    A. requires a pending Edit to run without an error.

    B. does not move the record pointer.

    C. requires a call to the Update method to become final.

    D. updates the recordset's data immediately.

Part

VI

App

J

62. The relationship between ANSI and UniCode standards for strings in VB is that

  A. VB uses ANSI internally but converts to UniCode for use by the programmer and in API calls.

  B. VB uses UniCode internally but converts to ANSI for use by the programmer and in API calls.

  C. VB uses ANSI both internally and for use by the programmer in API calls.

  D. VB uses UniCode both internally and for use by the programmer in API calls.

63. A menu control's menu level (pick two)

  A. can be set at design or run time.

  B. can only be set at run time.

  C. can only be set at design time.

  D. must be equal to or one greater than the preceding menu control's.

64. The timing of the KeyPress event is

  A. before KeyDown but after KeyUp.

  B. before KeyUp but after KeyDown.

  C. after KeyDown and KeyUp.

  D. independent of the timing of KeyDown and KeyUp.

65. You can write wrapper functions for error-prone statements that (pick two)

  A. do not need to contain error handlers.

  B. return a value indicating success or failure.

  C. pass any error code back to the calling routine to be handled there.

  D. do their error handling internally to the wrapper function.

66. To initialize and use a run-time element of a menu control array

  A. you must use Dim … As New ….

  B. you must set the Enabled property to True.

C. you must use the Load statement.

D. you must programmatically specify its position.

67. The maximum number of run-time instances of an MDI child is

    A. 256.

    B. determined by available system resources.

    C. 512.

    D. 1.

68. The Class' Terminate event will always run when

    A. OLE shuts down the server.

    B. an END statement executes in the server's code.

    C. once all forms have been unloaded.

    D. once all forms have become invisible.

69. You can check to see whether an Optional parameter named strName was passed to the current procedure with the following code:

    A. If strName = Nothing

    B. If IsMissing(strName)

    C. If strName = ""

    D. If IsEmpty(strName)

70. The OLE container's DoVerb method

    A. pops up the server's Verb menu.

    B. executes an available server verb.

    C. enables the user to run a verb from the Verb menu.

    D. places the server's Verb menu on the Form's menu if the Form's NegotiatMenus property is True.

71. Before calling a Recordset's Update you must have (pick two)

    A. called the Edit method.

    B. called the LockEdits method.

    C. called the AddNew method.

    D. moved the record pointer.

72. The Lib keyword in an API declaration (pick two)

    A. precedes the name of the API library file.

    B. follows the name of the API library file.

    C. requires a quote-delimited string.

    D. requires a single-quote-delimited string.

73. If a running VB application has various instances of Child Forms and encounters the statement Cancel = True in the Unload event of one of the Child Forms, then

    A. all Child Forms whose Unload events occurred before this one are unloaded, and the unloading process halts.

    B. all Child Forms in the app will unload, except for the Child with Cancel = True in its Unload event.

    C. the MDI Form and all Child Forms with Cancel = True in their Unload events will stay loaded. All other Child Forms will unload.

    D. run-time error 453 "Invalid Operation" occurs.

74. Visual Basic will warn you about incompatibility

    A. when you change class properties already existing in the Compatible OLE Server and recompile.

    B. whenever you recompile your server.

    C. whenever you recompile your server with the Compatible OLE Server property set.

    D. whenever you have made any changes not in the Compatible OLE Server and recompile.

75. Static variables (pick two)

    A. are not implemented on the stack.

    B. have application-wide scope.

    C. have module-wide lifetime.

    D. have local scope.

76. VB 3.0 Controls

    A. are implemented in VBX files and can't be carried over when you convert a VB 3.0 app to VB 4.0.

    B. are implemented in VBX files and may be carried over when you convert a VB 3.0 app to VB 4.0.

    C. are implemented in OCX files and can't be carried over when you convert a VB 3.0 app to VB 4.0.

    D. are implemented in OCX files and may be carried over when you convert a VB 3.0 app to VB 4.0.

77. An access key for a TextBox control

    A. can be provided in the TextBox's Caption property.

    B. can be provided in the TextBox's Text property.

    C. can be provided in an accompanying Label control.

    D. can be provided in the TextBox's Label property.

78. The DragMode property

    A. determines whether or not the user will see an icon as a control is dragged.

    B. determines whether or not you must use the Drag method in code to allow the user to drag a control.

    C. determines whether a control can be dragged by the mouse or by Shift+arrow keys.

    D. indicates whether a control is currently being dragged.

79. The DataBaseName property of the Data Control

    A. is always a file name.

    B. is always a directory name.

    C. is a logical name, so not necessarily a directory or file.

    D. is always a file name for Microsoft Access databases.

Part

VI

App

J

80. The maximum number of MDI Child Forms allowable in a project at design time is

    A. 256.
    B. determined by available system resources.
    C. 2.
    D. 1.

81. You can specify that a menu control will be a separator bar by

    A. supplying a space (" ") as the Name.
    B. supplying a dash ("-") as the Caption.
    C. supplying a dash ("-") as the Name.
    D. supplying an underscore ("_") as the Caption.

82. If a module with Option Base 0 has a one-dimensional array strNames() of string with 20 elements containing employee names, how would you add another employee to the array?

    A. Redim strNames(21)
    B. Redim Preserve strNames(20)
    C. strNameAdd(20)
    D. Redim Preserve strNames(21)

83. To make a temporary Windows Registry entry for your server while it runs in design mode

    A. make its project's Startup Mode property be Standalone and then run the project.
    B. make its project's Startup Mode property be Compatible OLE Server and then run the project.
    C. make its project's Startup Mode property be OLE Server and then run the project.
    D. compile the project and then run it.

84. Setup.Exe

    A. is the default name of the setup routine created by Setup Wizard for your application.
    B. is the name of the executable file that runs Setup Wizard.

C. is the name of the generic, unmodifiable startup routine for a Setup.

D. is the name of the default Setup Wizard template file.

85. You can destroy a menu control array item

   A. by setting the Index to 0.

   B. by decrementing the array's upper bound.

   C. with Redim Preserve.

   D. with the Unload statement.

86. An OLE server project's Name option as found on the Project tab of the Options dialog

   A. must be the same as the project's file name.

   B. will be the objecttype component when a controller instantiates appname.objecttype in the server.

   C. will be the appname component when a controller instantiates appname.objecttype in the server.

   D. must be the same as the main class name in the server.

87. The BoundText property of the DB List or Combo Box contains

   A. name of the key field in the parent (controlling) recordset.

   B. current record's contents for the field specified in the BoundColumn property.

   C. current record's contents for the field specified in the ListField property.

   D. name of the key field in the lookup recordset.

88. If you have a ListBox named List1 and you want to refer to the contents of the last row in ListBox, you would use the expression:

   A. List1.ListCount

   B. List1.List(ListCount)

   C. List1.List(ListCount - 1)

   D. List1.(ListCount - 1)

89. You can have multiple transactions pending on the same workspace

    A. never.

    B. as long as the transactions are nested within each other.

    C. as long as there is a possible Rollback paired with each CommitTrans.

    D. under all conditions.

90. Your server will close if it is not currently running any code and

    A. it's out-of-process, no controller is requesting it, and all forms are invisible.

    B. it's in-process, no controller is requesting it, and all forms are invisible.

    C. no controller is requesting it, regardless of whether forms are present.

    D. the server's startup form unloads.

91. To create a linked or embedded object on the OLE container control at run time

    A. use CreateLink and CreateEmbed with a data file name.

    B. use CreateLink with a data file name and CreateEmbed with no arguments.

    C. use CreateLink with a data file name and a server name, and CreateEmbed with a server name only.

    D. use both CreateLink and CreateEmbed with a data file name and a server name.

92. Before you pass a String variable from VB as an argument to a DLL routine

    A. pad the string with extra characters.

    B. set the string to "".

    C. set the string to vbNullString.

    D. set the string to vbNullPointer.

93. The OLE container's displaytype property

    A. determines whether server menus are visible or not.

    B. determines whether the server appears iconized or normal.

    C. determines whether the server appears within or outside of the container.

    D. determines the screen resolution of the server.

94. The following lines appear in a standard module's Declarations section:

```
#If Win32 Then

  Declare Sub MySub Lib "MyLib32" Alias "MySubA"

#End If

#If Win16 Then

  Declare Sub MySub Lib "MyLib" Alias "MySub"

#End If
```

The effect of these lines is that

Part
VI

App
J

    A. the same copy of the application's executable file can run in 16- or 32-bit Windows.

    B. the same source code can be compiled by 16-bit or 32-bit VB.

    C. both 16- and 32-bit versions of the application can use 16-bit API.

    D. both 16- and 32-bit versions of the application can use the 32-bit API.

95. The record pointer will move

    A. when you call the Data Control's UpdateRecord method.

    B. when you call the Recordset's Update method.

    C. when you call either UpdateRecord or Update.

    D. neither when you call UpdateRecord nor Update.

96. What will the user see in the Message Box when this code runs?

```
Dim NewNum As Integer
    Dim MyNum As Integer
    Do While NewNum < 30
        For MyNum = 20 To 11 Step -1
            NewNum = NewNum + 2
            If NewNum >= 20 Then
                Exit Do
            End If
        Next MyNum
    Loop
    MsgBox NewNum
```

A. 20.

B. 11.

C. 30.

D. User will never see a message box.

97. If the Watch Type of a Watch is "Break when expression is true"

A. you will automatically see its value whenever the value changes.

B. you will automatically see its value whenever it reaches a designated value or range of values.

C. you will need to explicitly pause the application and bring up the Debug Window to see it.

D. you will automatically see it whenever VB encounters a breakpoint.

98. On the line immediately before the error handler in a routine

A. you should put the line likely to cause an error.

B. you must put On Error GoTo 0.

C. you should put On Error GoTo *label*, where *label* is the name of the error handler.

D. you should put an Exit Sub or Exit Function statement.

99. The following line will cause early binding:

A. Dim objExcel As Excel.Application

B. Dim objExcel As Object

    C. Set objExcel = Excel.Application

    D. Set objExcel = Object

100. A Recordset object contains

    A. a Fields collection.

    B. a Databases collection.

    C. a Workspaces collection.

    D. a Groups collection.

101. You do the following things: 1) write a general procedure in a form and call it MySub_Click(). 2) Later place a command button on the form whose default name is Command1. 3) Write code in Command1's click event procedure. 4) Rename Command1 to MySub. What will happen when the user clicks the command button?

    A. Nothing.

    B. The original code in MySub_Click will run.

    C. The code in Command1_Click will run.

    D. The code in Command1_Click will run, but under the name MySub_Click.

102. An example of the correct syntax to begin a For Each loop would be

    A. For Each Control.

    B. For Each ctrlCurr in Controls.

    C. For Each ctrlCurr From 1 To Controls.Count.

    D. For Each ctrlCurr in Controls From 1 To Controls.Count.

103. To bind a textbox to a Data Control, you should

    A. set the RowSource and DataField properties.

    B. set the RowSource and BoundField properties.

    C. set the DataSource and DataField properties.

    D. set the DataBaseName and DataField properties.

104. A true fact about the relationship between the Public and Instancing built-in class properties is (pick two)

  A. when Public is False, Instancing can only be Single Use or None.

  B. when Public is True and Instancing is None, the class can't be instantiated by a controller but is visible to the controller.

  C. when Public is False, the Instancing property's setting is ignored.

  D. when Instancing is Creatable Single- or Multi-Use, the setting of Public is ignored.

105. You might be able to reference a specific MDI Child instance in code

  A. with the name property you assigned at run time.

  B with the name you gave it at design time.

  C. by checking its Tag property.

  D. by checking its position in the Forms collection.

106. To clear the Debugger's Immediate Pane in your code

  A. you can call Debug.Clear.

  B. you can call Debug.Cls.

  C. there is nothing you can do.

  D. you can call Debug.Print "".

107. You may lock a page in a Recordset with (pick two)

  A. the Edit method.

  B. the Lock statement.

  C. the LockEdits property.

  D. the AddNew method.

108. Which String concatenation statement will give a run-time error?

  A. "" & Str("")

  B. "" + 0

C. "" & 0

D. "" + Str(0)

109. A Form's or PictureBox control's AutoRedraw property

A. is a bitmap representing the full-screen image of the object.

B. is a Boolean that enables the Paint event when set to True.

C. can be set to Automatic to enable automatic refresh.

D. is a Boolean that enables automatic refresh when set to True.

110. For 16- and 32-bit versions of the same application

A. you can run the 16-bit version on both 16- and 32-bit platforms, but the 32-bit version can only run on 32-bit platforms.

B. you can run the 32-bit version on both 16- and 32-bit platforms, but the 16-bit version can only run on 16-bit platforms.

C. you can run the 16-bit and 32-bit versions on both 16- and 32-bit platforms.

D. the 16-bit version can only run on 16-bit platforms and the 32-bit version can only run on 32-bit platforms.

111. To provide a title for an Option Button, you should

A. put the text in the control's Caption property.

B. put the text in the control's Text property.

C. put the text in an accompanying Label control.

D. put the text in the control's Label property.

112. You have the following code in a form:

```
[General Declarations]

Public strName as String
Private Sub cmdOK_Click()
    strName = "Jones"
    ViewName(strName)
    MsgBox strName
End Sub

Private Sub ViewName(strName as String)
    strName = UCase(strName)
    MsgBox "Name is " & strName
End Sub
```

Part

VI

App

J

When the message box in the cmdOK_Click event procedure displays, the user will see:

A. jones

B. JONES

C. Jones

D. Name is JONES

113. If Form1 is your project's startup Form and you put the line

Form2.Show

in Form1's Load event procedure

A. you'll receive a compiler error.

B. you'll receive a run-time error.

C. Form1 will end up as the active Form after all initial code has run.

D. Form2 will end up as the active Form after all initial code has run.

114. A line of code that checks to see if Ctrl+F3 was keyed in the KeyUp or KeyDown event might read:

A. If (Shift = vbCtrlMask) AND (KeyCode = vbKeyF3) Then

B. If KeyCode = vbKeyControl + vbKeyF3 Then

C. If (Shift AND vbCtrlMask) AND _
   (KeyCode = vbKeyF3) Then

D. If (Shift AND vbCtrlMask) AND _
   (KeyCode AND vbKeyF3) Then

115. Generally, more workstation resources are used by

A. Snapshot-type Recordset.

B. Dynaset-type Recordset.

C. Table-type Recordset.

D. Snapshot- or Table-type Recordset, depending on the size and number of records.

116. Code in the Error event procedure of the Data Control

    A. will override any error handlers written elsewhere.

    B. is overridden by any error handlers written elsewhere.

    C. happens when the user uses the Data Control without invoking any code written by you.

    D. happens whenever there is an error related to the Data Control, either caused by your code or by a user action on the Data Control.

117. To define Alt+X as the access key for a Command Button

    A. set the Caption property to E_xit.

    B. set the Caption property to &E_xit.

    C. set the Caption property to E&xit.

    D. choose Alt-X from the drop-down list of available access keys.

118. If a Watch Expression's type is "Watch Expression"

    A. VB will automatically break when the value changes.

    B. VB will automatically break when it reaches a designated range of values.

    C. you will need to pause the application to see it.

    D. you will always see it whenever VB encounters a breakpoint.

119. A control's Tag property

    A. represents the brief pop-up tip a user sees when the mouse pauses over the control.

    B. represents an internal read-only name the application uses to identify the control.

    C. defaults to the control's Caption property.

    D. is described by none of the above.

120. Two advantages of having more than one Workspace in a project are (pick two):

    A. you can have more than one database object in the project.

    B. you can define different user permission levels.

Part

VI

App

J

    C. you can have non–nested transactions.

    D. you make more efficient use of memory.

121. The CreateObject function

    A. always begins a new copy of the server.

    B. always references an existing copy of the server.

    C. references an existing copy of the server if one exists, otherwise begins a new copy.

    D. generates a run-time error if there is no existing copy of the server.

122. If a DLL routine's documentation calls for an argument of type char, VB should pass

    A. a fixed-length string of length 1.

    B. a single quote-delimited character.

    C. a variable of type byte.

    D. a variable of type integer.

123. A menu control's shortcut key (pick one)

    A. is specified from a list in the Menu Editor.

    B. is specified with an ampersand in the Name property.

    C. is specified with an ampersand in the Caption.

    D. is limited to an Alt- key combination.

Answer Key

1-A,C. See "Checked Property" (Chapter 8)

2-A. See "OLE Automation with the Object Property" (Chapter 10)

3-A,C. See "Managing Dialogs (Forms) in Your OLE Server" (Chapter 11)

4-B. See "PictureBox" (Chapter 3)

5-B,C. See "Visual Basic's Standard Simple Data Types" and "Arrays" (Chapter 2)

6-D. See "Looping" (Chapter 3)

7-B. See "Variant: The Lonely Default" (Chapter 2)

8-D. See "Instr" (Chapter 3)

9-B. See "Visual Basic's Standard Simple Data Types" (Chapter 2)

10-C. See "Single-Step Mode" (Chapter 4)

11-C. See "Paint" (Chapter 7)

12-A. See "Screen for Step 6: OLE Automation" (Chapter 16)

13-B,C. See "Installable ISAM Drivers" (Chapter 12)

14-A,D. See "Viewing the Call Stack" (Chapter 4)

15-A. See "Accessing a Form's Controls with the Controls Collection" (Chapter 2)

16-C. See "Initialize/Terminate" (Chapter 7)

17-B,D. See "Determining Parent or Child Menu Validity" (Chapter 9)

18-D. See "Start Mode" under "Setting Project Options for an OLE Server" (Chapter 11)

19-A. See "Testing and Debugging an OLE Server at Design-Time" (Chapter 11)

20-D. See "Screen for Step 3: Target for Setup Files" (Chapter 16)

21-D. See "Implicit versus Explicit Variable Declaration" (Chapter 2)

22-A. See "Snapshots" (Chapter 12)

23-B. See "Declaring and Calling a DLL Routine" (Chapter 15)

24-A,D. See "Setting a Reference to a Type Library" (Chapter 13)

25-B. See "MousePointer" (Chapter 6)

Part
VI

App
J

26-C,D. See "Enumerating Values in a Case" (Chapter 3)

27-D. See "Using the Where Clause to Connect Tables" (Chapter 13)

28-B. See "Variable Scope" (Chapter 2)

29-A. See "Name Property" (Chapter 8)

30-A. See "Name of API" (Chapter 15)

31-C. See "Connect Property" (Chapter 12)

32-D. See "Declaring a Variable to Hold an Instance of an OLE Server Class" (Chapter 10)

33-A,D. See "Your OLE Server and the Object Browser" (Chapter 11)

34-B. See "WindowList Property" (Chapter 9)

35-C. See "Index Property" (Chapter 8)

36-B,C. See "Writing Code to Handle the Error" (Chapter 5)

37-D. See "BackColor" (Chapter 6)

38-D. See "Load, Unload, and QueryUnload" (Chapter 7)

39-D. See "Using JOIN Clauses to Connect Tables" (Chapter 13)

40-B. See "Find Methods" and "Seek Method" (Chapter 12)

41-A. See "An OLE Server's Verbs" (Chapter 10)

42-C. See "Passing a Null Pointer to a DLL Routine" (Chapter 15)

43-B. See "Default Property or Value of a Control and Performance" (Chapter 6)

44-A. See "NegotiatePosition Property" (Chapter 8)

45-C. See "Strip String Argument's Null Terminator after API Call" (Chapter 15)

46-D. See "Trapping an Error Immediately after it Occurs" (Chapter 5)

47-A,D. See "WindowList Property" (Chapter 8)

48-B,C. See "Pass Error Codes to a Centralized Error-Handling Function" (Chapter 5)

49-B. See "Screen for Step 4: OLE Servers" (Chapter 16)

50-A. See "Setting up MDI Child Classes" (Chapter 9)

51-C. See "See Figuring Out How Many Elements are in an Array" (Chapter 2)

52-B. See "Using Conditional Compilation with the API" (Chapter 14)

53-B. See "Alias Clause" (Chapter 15)

54-D. See "hWnd Property" (Chapter 6)

55-A,D. See "Toggling the Breakpoint" (Chapter 4)

56-D. See "Using Err.Raise as a Debugging Technique" (Chapter 5)

57-C. See "Going into Break Mode" (Chapter 4)

58-C. See "Using the Object Browser to Find out about an OLE Server" (Chapter 10)

59-A. See "Using Conditional Compilation with the API" (Chapter 14)

60-D. See "MouseMove" (Chapter 7)

61-B,D. See "Deleting Records"(Chapter 12)

62-B. See "Using the Same Name for Unicode and ANSI Versions" (Chapter 15)

63-C,D. See "Menu Level" (Chapter 8)

64-B. See "KeyPress" (Chapter 7)

65-B,D. See "Write Generic Code for Frequently Used Functionality" (Chapter 5)

66-C. See "Menu Control Arrays" (Chapter 8)

67-B. See "Understanding MDI Applications" (Chapter 9)

68-C. See "Class Terminate Event Procedure" and "Closing Your OLE Server" (Chapter 11)

69-B. See "Optional Arguments and the IsMissing(. Function" (Chapter 3)

70-B. See "An OLE Server's Verbs" (Chapter 10)

71-A,C. See "Updating a Record" (Chapter 13)

72-A,C. See "Library Name" (Chapter 15)

73-A. See "Using Unload and QueryUnload" (Chapter 9)

74-A. See "Managing Compatibility of Versions of Your Server" and "Compatible OLE Server" (Chapter 11)

75-A,D. See "Static Variables" (Chapter 2)

76-B. See "Converting VBX to OLE Controls" (Chapter 14)

77-C. See "Providing Access Keys for Text Boxes" (Chapter 6)

78-B. See "DragMode" (Chapter 7)

79-D. See "DataBaseName Property" (Chapter 12)

80-B. See "Setting up MDI Child Classes" (Chapter 9)

81-B. See "Separator Bars" (Chapter 8)

82-B. See "Dynamically Resizing an Array" (Chapter 2)

83-C. See "Temporarily Registering Your Server at Design Time" (Chapter 11)

84-D. See "A Customized Setup Program" (Chapter 16)

85-D. See "Menu Control Arrays" (Chapter 8)

86-C. See "Name" under "Setting Project Options for an OLE Server" (Chapter 11)

87-B. See "Data-Bound List Box and Data-Bound Combo Box" (Chapter 12)

88-C. See "ComboBox" (Chapter 3)

89-B. See "Using Transactions" (Chapter 13)

90-B. See "Closing Your OLE Server" (Chapter 11)

91-A. See "Linking and Embedding at Run Time" (Chapter 10)

92-A. See "Stuff String Arguments with Extra Character" (Chapter 15)

93-B. See "Controlling the Object's Appearance" (Chapter 10)

94-B. See "16- versus 32-bit Compilation of the Same Code" (Chapter 15)

95-B. See "Saving Editing Changes with the Update Method" (Chapter 12)

96-A. See "Getting Out of a Loop in a Hurry with Exit" (Chapter 3)

97-B. See "Break When Expression Is True" (Chapter 4)

98-D. See "Creating a Detour around the Error Handler" (Chapter 5)

99-A. See "Declaring a Variable to Hold an Instance of an OLE Server Class" (Chapter 10)

100-A. See "Recordset Objects and the Recordsets Collection" and "Using Transactions" (Chapter 13)

101-B. See "Control Names and Event Procedure Code" (Chapter 3)

102-B. See "The For Each…Next Statement" (Chapter 3)

103-C. See "Binding Other Controls to the Data Control" (Chapter 12)

104-B,C. See "Instancing" and "Public" under "Class Module Properties for an OLE Server" (Chapter 11)

105-C. See "Referencing MDI Children" (Chapter 9)

106-C. See "Debug" (Chapter 7)

107-A,D. See "Page Locking" (Chapter 13)

108-B. See "Conversion of Non-String Arguments in String Concatenation" (Chapter 2)

109-D. See "AutoRedraw" (Chapter 7)

110-A. See "Understanding 16- and 32-bit Application Differences" (Chapter 14)

111-A. See "Caption" (Chapter 6)

112-C. See "Extra Parentheses around each Argument to be Sent By Value" (Chapter 3)

113-C. See "Load, Unload, and QueryUnload" (Chapter 7)

114-C. See "KeyUp and KeyDown" (Chapter 7)

115-A. See "The Recordset" of Chapter 12 "Using the Data Control" (Chapter 13)

116-C. See "Error Event" (Chapter 12)

117-C. See "Providing Access Keys for Controls with a Caption Property" (Chapter 6)

118-C. See "Watch Expression" (Chapter 4)

119-D. See "Tag" (Chapter 6)

120-B,C. See "The Default Workspace and the Workspaces Collection" (Chapter 13)

121-A. See "CreateObject Function versus GetObject Function" (Chapter 10)

122-C. See "C 'char' Data Type as a DLL Argument" (Chapter 15)

123-A. See "Shortcut Keys" (Chapter 8)

Part
VI

App
J

Index

Symbols

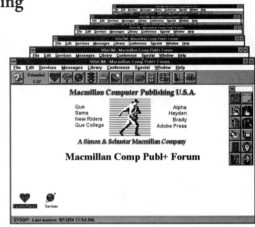

Complete and Return this Card
for a *FREE* Computer Book Catalog

Thank you for purchasing this book! You have purchased a superior computer book written expressly for your needs. To continue to provide the kind of up-to-date, pertinent coverage you've come to expect from us, we need to hear from you. Please take a minute to complete and return this self-addressed, postage-paid form. In return, we'll send you a free catalog of all our computer books on topics ranging from word processing to programming and the internet.

☐   Mrs. ☐   Ms. ☐   Dr. ☐

...me (first) ☐☐☐☐☐☐☐☐☐☐   (M.I.) ☐   (last) ☐☐☐☐☐☐☐☐☐☐☐☐☐☐☐☐☐

...dress ☐☐☐☐☐☐☐☐☐☐☐☐☐☐☐☐☐☐☐☐☐☐☐☐☐☐☐☐☐☐☐☐☐☐☐

☐☐☐☐☐☐☐☐☐☐☐☐☐☐☐☐☐☐☐☐☐☐☐☐☐☐☐☐☐☐☐☐☐☐☐

...y ☐☐☐☐☐☐☐☐☐☐☐☐☐☐☐☐☐   State ☐☐   Zip ☐☐☐☐☐   ☐☐☐☐

...ne ☐☐☐ ☐☐☐☐   Fax ☐☐☐ ☐☐☐☐

...mpany Name ☐☐☐☐☐☐☐☐☐☐☐☐☐☐☐☐☐☐☐☐☐☐☐☐☐☐☐☐☐☐☐☐☐

...mail address ☐☐☐☐☐☐☐☐☐☐☐☐☐☐☐☐☐☐☐☐☐☐☐☐☐☐☐☐☐☐☐☐☐

...lease check at least (3) influencing factors for ...purchasing this book.

...nt or back cover information on book .... ☐
...ecial approach to the content .... ☐
...mpleteness of content .... ☐
...thor's reputation .... ☐
...blisher's reputation .... ☐
...ok cover design or layout .... ☐
...dex or table of contents of book .... ☐
...ce of book .... ☐
...ecial effects, graphics, illustrations .... ☐
...her (Please specify): _____ ☐

...How did you first learn about this book?

...w in Macmillan Computer Publishing catalog .... ☐
...commended by store personnel .... ☐
...w the book on bookshelf at store .... ☐
...commended by a friend .... ☐
...ceived advertisement in the mail .... ☐
...w an advertisement in: _____ ☐
...ad book review in: _____ ☐
...her (Please specify): _____ ☐

...How many computer books have you purchased in the last six months?

...is book only .... ☐   3 to 5 books .... ☐
...books .... ☐   More than 5 .... ☐

4. Where did you purchase this book?

Bookstore .... ☐
Computer Store .... ☐
Consumer Electronics Store .... ☐
Department Store .... ☐
Office Club .... ☐
Warehouse Club .... ☐
Mail Order .... ☐
Direct from Publisher .... ☐
Internet site .... ☐
Other (Please specify): _____ ☐

5. How long have you been using a computer?

☐ Less than 6 months   ☐ 6 months to a year
☐ 1 to 3 years   ☐ More than 3 years

6. What is your level of experience with personal computers and with the subject of this book?

	With PCs	With subject of book
New	☐	☐
Casual	☐	☐
Accomplished	☐	☐
Expert	☐	☐

Source Code ISBN: 0-7897-0864-7

7. Which of the following best describes your job title?

Administrative Assistant .... ☐
Coordinator .... ☐
Manager/Supervisor .... ☐
Director .... ☐
Vice President .... ☐
President/CEO/COO .... ☐
Lawyer/Doctor/Medical Professional .... ☐
Teacher/Educator/Trainer .... ☐
Engineer/Technician .... ☐
Consultant .... ☐
Not employed/Student/Retired .... ☐
Other (Please specify): _____ ☐

8. Which of the following best describes the area of the company your job title falls under?

Accounting .... ☐
Engineering .... ☐
Manufacturing .... ☐
Operations .... ☐
Marketing .... ☐
Sales .... ☐
Other (Please specify): _____ ☐

9. What is your age?

Under 20 ....
21-29 ....
30-39 ....
40-49 ....
50-59 ....
60-over ....

10. Are you:

Male ....
Female ....

11. Which computer publications do you read regularly? (Please list)

_____
_____
_____
_____
_____
_____
_____
_____
_____

Comments: _____

_____

_____

Fold here and scotch-tape to m

Check out Que® Books on the World Wide Web
http://www.mcp.com/que

As the biggest software release in computer history, Windows 95 continues to redefine the computer industry. Click here for the latest info on our Windows 95 books

Make computing quick and easy with these products designed exclusively for new and casual users

Examine the latest releases in word processing, spreadsheets, operating systems, and suites

The Internet, The World Wide Web, CompuServe®, America Online®, Prodigy® —it's a world of ever-changing information. Don't get left behind!

Find out about new additions to our site, new bestsellers and hot topics

In-depth information on high-end topics: find the best reference books for databases, programming, networking, and client/server technologies

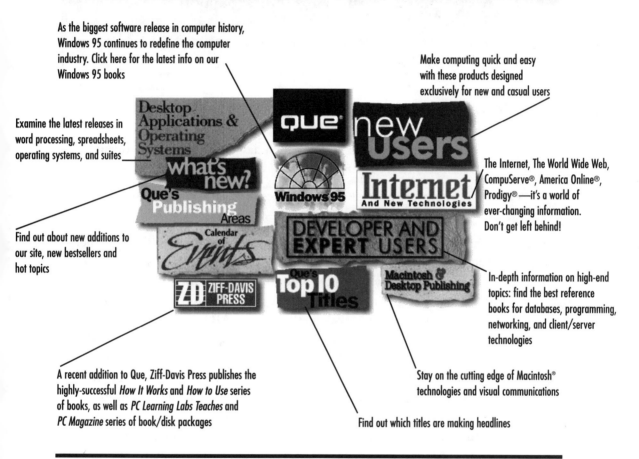

A recent addition to Que, Ziff-Davis Press publishes the highly-successful *How It Works* and *How to Use* series of books, as well as *PC Learning Labs Teaches* and *PC Magazine* series of book/disk packages

Stay on the cutting edge of Macintosh® technologies and visual communications

Find out which titles are making headlines

With 6 separate publishing groups, Que develops products for many specific market segments and areas of computer technology. Explore our Web Site and you'll find information on best-selling titles, newly published titles, upcoming products, authors, and much more.

- Stay informed on the latest industry trends and products available
- Visit our online bookstore for the latest information and editions
- Download software from Que's library of the best shareware and freeware

Before using any of the software on these discs, you need to install the software you plan to use. See Appendix H "Using the CD-ROM," for information on installing this software correctly. If you have problems with this disk, please contact Macmillan Technical Support at (317) 581-3833. We can be reached by e-mail at **support@mcp.com** or on CompuServe at **GO QUEBOOKS**.

License Agreement

This package contains a CD-ROM that includes software described in this book. See applicable chapters for a description of these programs and instructions for their use.

By opening this package you are agreeing to be bound by the following:

This software is copyrighted and all rights are reserved by the publisher and its licensers. You are licensed to use this software on a single computer. You may copy the software for backup or archival purposes only. Making copies of the software for any other purpose is a violation of United States copyright laws. THIS SOFTWARE IS SOLD AS IS, WITHOUT WARRANTY OF ANY KIND, EITHER EXPRESSED OR IMPLIED, INCLUDING BUT NOT LIMITED TO THE IMPLIED WARRANTIES OF MERCHANTABILITY AND FITNESS FOR A PARTICULAR PURPOSE. Neither the publisher nor its licensers, dealers, or distributors assumes any liability for any alleged or actual damages arising from the use of this software. (Some states do not allow exclusion of implied warranties, so the exclusion may not apply to you.)

The entire contents of this disc and the compilation of the software are copyrighted and protected by United States copyright laws. The individual programs on these discs are copyrighted by the authors or owners of each program. Each program has its own use permissions and limitations. To use each program, you must follow the individual requirements and restrictions detailed for each. Do not use a program if you do not agree to follow its licensing agreement.